ANNOTATED BIBLIOGRAPHY OF AFGHANISTAN

by

M. JAMIL HANIFI

Fourth Edition, Revised

This volume is a revision of the earlier bibliography by
DONALD N. WILBER,
which has appeared in three editions.

HRAF PRESS
New Haven
1982

DS
351.5
H36
1982

INTERNATIONAL STANDARD BOOK NUMBER: 0-87536-230-3
LIBRARY OF CONGRESS NUMBER: 82-82467
©1982
HUMAN RELATIONS AREA FILES, INC.
NEW HAVEN, CONNECTICUT
ALL RIGHTS RESERVED
MANUFACTURED IN THE UNITED STATES OF AMERICA

NOTE FROM THE PUBLISHER

To save costs in a time of economic difficulty for scholarly publishing, we publish some books that we do not edit ourselves. This is one such book, in which the responsibility for editing and proofreading lies solely with the author.

CONTENTS

	Page
Preface to the Fourth Edition	vii
Preface to the Third Edition	ix
Preface to the Second Edition	ix
Preface to the First Edition	x

I. GENERAL SOURCES OF INFORMATION AND REFERENCE WORKS — 1
   Bibliographies; encyclopedias; catalogues; histories and surveys; periodicals

II. GEOGRAPHY — 31
   Geology; topography; exploration; travel and description; natural history; atlases and maps

III. HISTORY — 107
   Pre-Achaemenid; Achaemenid; Parthian; Sassanian; Buddhistic; Islamic; Anglo-Afghan and Anglo-Russian relations; foreign relations

IV. SOCIAL ORGANIZATIONS — 182
   Character of society; size and geographical distribution of population; ethnic groups; culture; social structure

V. SOCIAL EVOLUTION AND INSTITUTIONS — 230
   Cultural development and expression; applied sciences; education; religion; public information; press and publications; health and public welfare; social attitudes

VI. POLITICAL STRUCTURE — 283
   Structure of government; political dynamics; public order; foreign policies; official propaganda; international problems; political issues and prospects

VII. ECONOMIC STRUCTURE — 331
   Agriculture; industry; trade; finance; taxation; handicrafts; labor force

VIII. LANGUAGES AND LITERATURE — 377
   Languages and dialects; lexicons; grammars; dictionaries; literature in prose and poetry; manuscripts and editions of manuscripts; folklore; songs and ballads; inscriptions

IX. ART AND ARCHAEOLOGY   439
    Archaeology; historical monuments and sites;
    excavation reports and publications; art;
    history of art; material culture; architecture;
    numismatics

    INDEX   497

PREFACE TO THE FOURTH EDITION

Although our knowledge of Afghanistan is still limited and there undoubtedly still exists an important need for further research, the changes of government in 1973 and 1978 have stimulated much journalistic commentary as well as scholarly interest in the country, leading writers and scholars, both Afghan and non-Afghan, to ask important new questions. They are looking at the constitution of Afghan society, its ethnolinguistic composition and diversity, its history, culture and geography as well as at a host of other topics. Concomitantly, the results of research begun in the 1960s are being published. Thus, the serious gaps which existed in research and scholarship about Afghanistan have begun to be addressed, leaving us at this time in a better position than we were in previously to assess the scope of our knowledge about the country.

The sheer volume of material published on Afghanistan since the appearance of the third edition of the Annotated Bibliography of Afghanistan, as well as the need for technical and substantive adjustments in it, led to the decision to publish an extensively revised and enlarged fourth edition rather than a supplement to the third one. The number of entries for the fourth edition has more than doubled. The titles which are included in this edition appeared before January 1982.

This revised edition of the bibliography has maintained the general classification arrived at by the author of the previous editions. Only sub-categories are slightly modified and made more specific. Like its antecedents, the fourth edition is meant to be comprehensive rather than exhaustive. Not all entries are annotated. Some previous and new titles well describe their content. Others which have not been annotated were not accessible to this writer. Nevertheless, the bulk of the entries have been examined and annotations have been provided for them. In addition, some entries do not carry full bibliographic information or are not (when in a non-English language) fully translated. But every entry includes some basic bibliographic information which will readily assist the researcher in locating and/or assessing a specific title. The sources of a few periodical titles are noted by abbreviation. These abbreviations are according to the World List of Scientific Periodicals.

The technical style of the fourth edition is different from that of the previous editions and is designed to render more clarity and uniformity, and to reflect current conventions regarding bibliographic citations. Asterisks have been eliminated. Previous editions had included asterisks for those entries considered most valuable under each subject heading. Researchers can decide on their own what is essential since in most cases the titles and annotations speak for themselves. A series of changes in the entries of the previous editions has been introduced regarding the translation of works, particularly those in Dari and Pushtu. Also, "Muslim" is used, as in the third edition, for "Moslem" and "Dari" for "Persian."

The previous editions included material on populations straddling the eastern boundary of Afghanistan. This edition also includes, to the extent feasible, entries which deal with societies, cultures, and ethnolinguistic groupings which have significant affinities and relationships to the people of northern, western, and southern Afghanistan and who are within the boundaries of the USSR, Iran and Pakistan.

The prefaces of the previous editions by Donald N. Wilber have been kept intact. It was considered appropriate to reprint the former prefaces so that the history of the development of this bibliography would be maintained. When necessary, however, the identification numbers of bibliographic entries referred to in the prefaces have been changed to coincide with the appropriate numbers in the present edition.

A number of persons and institutions provided valuable assistance during the preparation of the fourth edition. Northern Illinois University presented a research grant from its Graduate School Fund that provided partial support for my research while its Department of Anthropology rendered needed technical assistance, for both of which I am thankful. My graduate student assistants Angelica Auer, Yuphaphann Hoonchamlong, and Lori Ann Stanley gave valuable help during the initial organizational phase of this work. For this I wish to thank them. My appreciation is extended to the Center for Afghanistan Studies, University of Nebraska-Omaha which shared with me a list of their library holdings. I am thankful also to Jon W. Anderson for his helpful advice on recent German language material on Afghanistan. Ms. Karen Hipps and Ms. Cheryl Fuller of the office of the Dean of Liberal Arts and Sciences, Northern Illinois University, typed the final manuscript. Their expertise, patience, and generous dispensation of technical and editorial advice is gratefully acknowledged. The responsibility for the structure and contents of this bibliography is, however, exclusively mine.

This work is dedicated to the people of Afghanistan and their friends.

Dekalb, IllinoisM. Jamil Hanifi
April 1982

PREFACE TO THE THIRD EDITION

This third edition has been extensively revised and re-edited. Rather than presenting new material in a Supplement, as was the case for the second edition, all the titles have been integrated into a consecutive numerical sequence.

The last several years have witnessed a rising tide of books and articles on Afghanistan. As a result, it has not been possible to annotate all the more recent items, especially those in Russian and in the languages of Afghanistan.

Attention is directed to two very important recent bibliographies of Afghanistan. One is item No. 82, the first bibliography of its kind to be published in Afghanistan. It is indexed under the name of its compiler, Ghulam Riza Mayel Heravi, with the title translated as "List of Books Printed in Afghanistan from the year 1951 to 1965 (15 years)." The second (No. 39) is indexed under Bibliografiya Afganistana, with the full title translated as "A Bibliography of Afghanistan: Literature in Russian." It lists some 5,680 items.

In 1964, Afghanistan adopted a new constitution, one of the articles of which names the national languages of the country as Dari and Pushtu. Dari is the name now officially given to the form of the Persian (farsi) language used in Afghanistan, sometimes known as farsi-Kabuli. Recent works in Persian have, therefore, been described as published in Dari.

Very valuable assistance in the transliteration and translation of Pushtu and Dari titles was given by Peter B. Edmonds, while Mary E. Armstrong undertook the transliteration and translation of titles in Russian. Arthur Paul generously placed his uniquely extensive library of books on Afghanistan at the disposal of the writer.

1967   Donald N. Wilber

PREFACE TO THE SECOND EDITION

This second edition includes a Supplement covering articles and books which have appeared between 1956 and June 1962. It also includes a number of items published prior to 1956 which were not noted in the first edition.

As in the first edition, the aim has been to produce a bibliography which is comprehensive, but selective rather than exhaustive. A serious effort was made to record the growing volume of material printed in Persian and Pushtu at Kabul. Although no single source keeps track of new publications, the writer acknowledges the assistance of the Press Department of the government of Afghanistan in assembling the necessary information. Since the quarterly <u>Afghanistan</u> appears to reach a very limited audience, the listing of all its articles, begun in the first edition, was not continued. Many of the titles of items in Russian have been selected from the publications of the Central Asian Research Centre in London. For a more exhaustive coverage of works in Russian, the reader should consult these publications and the extensive bibliographies of recent Soviet works on Afghanistan.

Scholarly users of the first edition found that the systems used for transliterating Persian and Pushtu were not identical with their favorite systems, and--to cite a single illustration--Pashto is preferred to Pushtu by this community. However, scholars able to read Persian and Pushtu can certainly recreate the original titles of the works they wish to consult. Valuable help in the translation of Pushtu titles and in their annotation was given by M. H. Maiwandwal, Ambassador of Afghanistan in Washington; while Professor Martin B. Dickson of Princeton University undertook the transliteration and translation of titles in Russian.

July 1962   Donald N. Wilber

PREFACE TO THE FIRST EDITION

<u>Principal features</u>: Just as Afghanistan has long remained isolated and outside the realm of international interest and concern, so too has it failed to attract scholarly research until recent years. Now, however, the Afghans themselves are opening up subjects and areas which will be pursued by scholars of other countries. In the field of bibliography, the Russians made an impressive beginning for the general area in the nineteenth century, but up until this time only one important work devoted to Afghanistan has been published. This is the Bibliographie Analytique de l'Afghanistan (No. 19) by Mohammed Akram, which was published in 1947. Only the first volume, dealing with works published outside of Afghanistan, was issued and the present writer has been informed that no other volumes are forthcoming. The present publication augments and extends the work of Akram, since it takes in a wider range of material in respect to time, places, and tongues, including-- in addition to material in the usual European languages--works in Russian, Arabic, Persian, and Pushtu, published both within and outside of Afghanistan.

The bibliography is annotated and indexed, with the items numbered consecutively and arranged alphabetically under subject headings. Within each subject heading the most valuable items are marked by asterisks.

Afghanistan defined: For the purpose of this bibliography, Afghanistan is defined as the country within its existing frontiers. The delimitation of the country may be said to date from the middle of the eighteenth century and the conquests of Ahmad Shah Durrani, since in earlier times no extensive, cohesive country known as Afghanistan existed. Instead, at many different times rulers of Iran controlled regions north and south of the Amu Darya River, while less frequently local rulers in the area south of the Hindu kush widened their control or moved on to take over parts of the Indian subcontinent.

With this limitation to present-day Afghanistan, it is necessary to exclude material on the once-vast areas of Transoxiana and Khorasan, areas which took in regions north and south of the Amu Darya. In the same way, such key centers for the old history and culture of Afghanistan as Bokhara and Samarqand, both now within the U.S.S.R., fall beyond this scope. However, in these particular examples and in other cases where the area under Afghan rulers once covered a larger amount of territory than today, a limited number of primary sources and general surveys have been included.

The former North West Frontier Province, just to the east of the Afghan frontier, also falls outside of the geographical limits of this bibliography, although in cases where the residents of this area have blood relatives within Afghanistan or have mutually inclusive codes of behavior, some items have been included. The skeletal material presented on this region--now within Pakistan--may be greatly augmented from Pakistan: A Select Bibliography (No. 77), by A. R. Ghani, published in 1951.

Coverage described: This bibliography is designed to be comprehensive but not exhaustive. It is selective inasmuch as an effort has been made to leave out repetitious, diffusive, inapplicable, and uncritical material. A few examples of the type of coverage given to various subjects may be of interest.

Much of the published material on Afghanistan was the direct result of the conflict of the Russian and the British empires in the nineteenth century. The efforts of the British to anticipate and to meet the threatening Russian advance toward India resulted in their occupation of the eastern border regions of the Afghans and led to the First and Second Anglo-Afghan Wars. Scores of military men wrote of their years of duty, exploration, and warfare, and since Afghanistan was otherwise sealed off from the outer world, the country was known primarily through the eyes of these somewhat biased participants. About a fourth of all the titles in Akram's Bibliographie Analytique de l'Afghanistan are by these officers or by their contemporaries in India and England. These titles have been reviewed and a great many eliminated.

Some bibliographies dealing with Moslem countries contain a chapter or heading on Islam, under which may be found a great many titles dealing with the religion itself, and its various sects, manifestations, customs, and practices. Such items appear here under the most appropriate heading, but all material not directly applicable to the country has been eliminated. Afghanistan is avowedly and ardently Moslem, but there has been very little written by local writers in the way of applicable commentaries on Islam or descriptions of the sects, shrines, practices, and present status of the faith within the country.

Only in a few technical or specialized subjects has the coverage been so extensive that a process of selection was possible. In the field of geology, however, a considerable number of rather ephemeral and dated articles have been left out, as well as some sketchy notes on flora and fauna.

In view of the fact that contemporary coverage in European languages is limited, consideration was given to the inclusion of all known books and articles. However, examination of the material itself led to the exclusion of articles which reworked secondary sources and made no original contribution. In the same way, numerous topographical notes with attractive and provocative titles proved to be valueless and were discarded.

While the coverage in European languages is less exhaustive in the publication than in the research stage, the coverage in the local languages of Afghanistan is adequate only within the limits of material available in this country. Comments will be made on the subject of items in Persian and Pushtu in other paragraphs; here it is necessary to say only a few words on the availability of such material. No organ nor institution within Afghanistan publishes lists of books published within the country, nor is there an index of articles in local periodicals. Such periodicals may notice new books, but these descriptions do not conform to bibliographical standards. While the Afghan government promised assistance in the compilation of published material presented in a standardized format, such aid did not materialize in time for inclusion in this text. An effort was made, however, to examine every item in these languages available in major collections, and to this end the author had direct access to the Afghan material at the Library of Congress, at Harvard University, and at Princeton University.

Annotation: The majority of the items in the bibliography are annotated, the intention being to describe the contents of the item, to identify the author if possible, to evaluate the items, and to point out any special features. Certain items in European languages are not annotated, either because the books are not to be found in this country or because they are not in collections available to the researchers of this bibliography. Certain articles are not annotated because of the fact that they were published in inaccessible periodicals. In the case of books printed in Persian or in Pushtu, all items were inspected and recorded, but since it was not possible to read and summarize every book, not every such item is annotated. Manuscripts are not annotated in any detail, since adequate descriptions are included in the catalogues of the collections in which the manuscripts are to be found.

Asterisks: The items marked with asterisks represent those sources considered to be essential in gaining an over-all understanding of the topic represented.

Transliteration and translation: Although the bibliographical cards from which this text was made up supply the full paraphernalia of macrons, overlines, underlines, and other signs and symbols used to indicate characters of the Cyrillic and Arabic alphabets, as well as those Persian and Pushtu characters supplementary to the Arabic alphabet, requirements of reproduction necessitated the omission of such markings. The Arabic characters ayn and hamzah are indicated, without distinction, as apostrophes.

The transliteration of the Arabic characters and of the languages other than Arabic which employ these characters is certain to draw the critical comments of linguists, each scholar favoring his personal modification of one of the more usual systems. In this case, the source has been the publication entitled: The Transliteration of Arabic and Persian. Special Publication No. 78. Department of the Interior. U.S. Board on Geographical Names. Washington, D.C. November, 1946. Unfortunately lacunae become apparent when this system is applied. For this bibliography, the author was fortunate in securing the services of Dr. Rudolph Mach, Arabic and Persian cataloguer for the Princeton University Library, to handle the material in these languages. Dr. Mach was able to extend the system referred to above and to achieve internal consistency.

The translation and transliteration of titles in Pushtu presented a special problem. For such translation, the author secured the assistance of Muhammad Bashir Ludin of Washington, D.C. The transliteration was complicated by the fact that Pushtu includes the Arabic characters employed in both Arabic and Persian and, in addition, some eight special Arabic symbols that are not found in any other orthography. It may be that grammarians have underdeveloped aesthetic sensibilities; at any rate they must enjoy producing words which look as if they would not be pleasant to pronounce. Applied to Pushtu, the tendency has been to indicate the special Arabic symbols as doubled consonants and the long vowels as doubled vowels, producing such results as zzbaarre, raddioo (radio) and even afghaanistaan. Since pedagogical exactitude with respect to phonology is not the primary objective of this bibliography, in most cases the special Arabic characters in Pushtu have been transliterated in terms of their closest normal Arabic or Persian symbols. In this way the users of the bibliography should have all the information required to identify each work.

Another problem stems from the way in which the names of authors writing in Persian, Arabic, and Pushtu should be presented. An approach which has been used in catalogues of manuscripts has been to list the name of each author in the order in which the name is spoken, with the first word of the name supplying the index letter for the entire name. This manner of dealing with Arab-type names is no longer satisfactory, however, since the Moslem world is actively adopting family names of the type common in Europe. Family names were brought into being by law in both Turkey and Iran more than a score of years ago. Within Afghanistan, the swing to family names is just gathering momentum. Some government officials have taken such names and some have not, but in order to be listed in the Kabul telephone directory a family name is mandatory. All individuals who are engaged in historical writing, research into linguistics and cultural background, journalism, and the editing of Persian and Pushtu manuscripts have taken such names and would object to being listed under the additive form. Given the fact that the names of the present-day Afghan writers are to be indexed exactly as those of European authors, the current problem concerns the manner of indexing earlier Eastern authors. A decision was made to extract the core of the additive name wherever possible, and in cases where this method was impractical, to employ the form as found in catalogues of manuscripts. While this approach has not resulted in complete consistency, it is hoped that it has made the bibliography convenient and easy to use.

Acknowledgments: It is a pleasure to record the invaluable support and assistance received from a number of scholars and researchers. At the Library of Congress, Dr. Robert F. Ogden, Head, Near East Section of Orientalia, and Dr. Benjamin Schwartz of the same section gave the author every facility for inspecting nearly 2,000 volumes in Persian and Pushtu and contributed freely of their time. At Harvard, D. W. Lockard, Executive Secretary, Center for Middle Eastern Studies, and Professor Richard N. Frye arranged for the author to enjoy access to the collections of the Harvard University Library. Professor Frye also checked the titles of Russian items and made additions, while Dr. Charles A. Ferguson of Harvard reviewed the linguistic items of the bibliography and made valuable comments. Dr. Peter G. Franck, of Washington, D.C., undertook the task of investigating and reporting on unpublished studies and documents relating to the economic structure and situation of Afghanistan.

At Princeton, Dr. Rudolph Mach of the Princeton University Library staff translated and transliterated the items in Arabic and Persian. Anne Lucie McCabe worked as a researcher for the author for a period of months and with that background took over the responsibility for typing the manuscript.

February 1956   Donald N. Wilber

I. GENERAL SOURCES OF INFORMATION AND REFERENCE WORKS

Bibliographies; encyclopedias;
catalogues; histories and
surveys; periodicals

The titles listed within this chapter are somewhat adequate for the presentation of a comprehensive and currently accurate account of the country. Within the category of bibliographies, particular care was devoted to publications covering the languages common to Afghanistan. However, there are so many catalogues covering so many collections of manuscripts in Pushtu, Dari, English, German, Arabic, Urdu, etc., that it was necessary to restrict the number of manuscripts which have not been edited in printed or lithographed versions. Also, since this work is concerned with the present area of Afghanistan and not with this region as part of a much greater area, many comprehensive histories have been eliminated.

Few periodical are included, again with the aim of avoiding unwieldy diversity. Given the existence of specialized guides to periodical literature, the reader may go directly from these sources to the article rather than to the file of periodicals.

1. Academy of Sciences, USSR
   1959 Afghan Shinasi Shorawi dar 'Arsae Chehl Sol [Afghan Studies in the Soviet Union During the Past Forty Years]. Moscow: Institute of Oriental Studies. Pp. 96. (In Dari).

   Includes discussion of Russian works on Afghanistan in the fields of history, economics, languages and literature by leading Soviet authorities on Afghanistan.

2. Afghan Studies
   1978 A journal Published by the Society for Afghan Studies, London.

   It publishes articles in English, and other European languages on topics in archaeology, ethnography, ecology, and reports on current research. The society was initially organized in 1972 publishing a newsletter.

3. Afghanistan. Quarterly publication first appearing in 1946 at Kabul.

   Early years offered separate editions in French and English; later on a single edition, each issue with some articles in French and some in English. Articles by local scholars, public officials and informed foreigners on

I. GENERAL SOURCES

history, archaeology, social institutions, foreign relations, topography, etc.

4   Afghanistan Council, Asia Society
    Recent Books About Afghanistan: A Selected Annotated
        Bibliography, 1968-1973. New York: Afghanistan Council,
        Asia Society, 1973, pp. 19.

5   Afghanistan: Development in Brief
        1958 London: Information Bureau, Royal Afghan Embassy,
        pp. 120.

    A well-illustrated review of recent developments, followed
    by a brief of the geography, history, culture, and people
    of the country.

6   Afghanistan Dar Hal-i Pishraft va Taraqi [Afghanistan in a
        State of Advance and Progress].
        n.d. [Kabul]: no publisher. Not paged.

    An illustrated brochure sponsored by the United States
    A.I.D. mission.

7   Afghanistan at a Glance.
        1957 Kabul: Government Printing House. Pp. 170 and 28.

8   Afghanistan Journal
        1974 The first Western Journal devoted exclusively to
            scholarly publications on Afghanistan.

    The Journal is published in Austria and most of its content are in German. Some material in French and English has also appeared. It has appeared on a regular quarterly basis since 1974. In addition to articles, the journal carries reviews, brief notes, and information about new publications about Afghanistan.

    A general description of the country.

9   Afghanistan News
        1959-1964 A Journal published by the Afghanistan Embassy
            in London.

    A variety of topics are covered in abbreviated and summary form. Mostly covers politics, economic development, history, archaeology, literature, current news.

10 Afghanistan Studies
        1973 A series published in Germany.

I. GENERAL SOURCES

       Contains articles, research reports, and news. An important source for German language works on Afghanistan.

11   Afgánistán: Zeměpisný, hospodářský, politický a kulturní přhled 1952 [Afghanistan: Geographical, Economic, Political and Cultural Survey]. Prague: Orbis.

12   Afghanistan Present and Past
      1958 Kabul: Government Printing House. Pp. 86.

      A general survey published by the Board of Afghan Publicity, Cultural Relations Office, Department of Press and Information.

13   Ahang, Mohammed Kazem
      1968-1970 "The background and beginning of the Afghan press system," Afghanistan 21(1):70-76, (2):41-48, (3):43-47, (4):37-47, 22(1):28-31, (2):73-80, (3-4):52-73.

14   Ahang, Mohammed Kazem
      1970 A Short History of Journalism in Afghanistan. (In Dari). Kabul: Government Publishing.

15   Ahlan bikum fi Afghanistan [Welcome to Afghanistan].
      1965 Cairo: al-Maktab al-thaqafi wa-al-sihafi. Pp. 132.

16   Ahmad, Fazl
      1948 Rahnuma-yi Afghanistan [Guide to Afghanistan]. Kabul: Matba'eh-yi 'umumi. Pp. 382; map. (1327 A.H.)

      Material collected by the Department of Press presented in Persian by a member of that department. Chapters deal with subjects such as agriculture, trade, finances, government, education, etc., and a long section describes the routes through the countries and the important towns along these routes.

17   Ahmad, Jamal-ud-din and Muhammad Abdul Aziz
      1936 Afghanistan: A Brief Survey. London and New York: Longmans, Green and Co. Pp. xx, 160; bibliography; appendices.

      A concise summary of information on Afghanistan, divided into sections on geography, history, and government. The section on history gives a brief account of the successive conquerors and their dynasties, with a note on the cultural influence of each. That on government gives

I. GENERAL SOURCES

biographies of the Kings Nadir Shah and Zahir Shah, and of the leading members of the royal family; an outline of national, local and tribal administration, and short paragraphs on many such subjects as prisons, finance, roads, industry, etc.

18 Akhramovich, R. T. and L. A. Erovchenkov (trans)
    1957 Afganistan [Afghanistan]. Moscow: Gosudarstvennoe izdatel'stvo geographicheskoy literaturi. Pp. 141; map.

An abridged translation of the New Guide to Afghanistan of Mohammad Ali, see item 15.

19 Akram, Mohammad
    1947 Bibliographie Analytique de l'Afghanistan. I. Ouvrages parus hors de l'Afghanistan [Analytical Bibliography of Afghanistan. I. Works Issued outside of Afghanistan]. Paris: Centre de Documentation Universitaire. Pp. 504.

Annotated list of nearly 2,000 titles, grouped under subject headings. Comprehensive but not exhaustive, and not as strong in Arabic, Persian, and Pushtu references as for European languages.

20 Aleksandrov, I. and R. Akhramovich
    1956 Gosudarstvenníy stroy Afganistana [The Governing Class of Afghanistan]. Moscow: Gosudarstvennoe izdatel'stvo yuridicheskoy literaturí. Pp. 62.

A pamphlet in the semi-popular series, The Governing Class of the Countries of the World. Includes chapters on the constitution, the powers of the ruler, government administration, history, and the economic situation.

21 Ali, Mohammad
    1933 Progressive Afghanistan. Lahore: Punjab Educational Electric Press. Pp. xiv, 232.

By the rather prolific Professor of History at Habibiya College, Kabul. The title may be somewhat misleading in that the book deals with the overthrow of Amanullah, the short domination of Bacha Saqqao, and the restoration of authority by Nadir Khan. The closing pages deal with the inauguration of Nadir Shah and with his plans for the future.

I. GENERAL SOURCES

22   Ali, Mohammad
1938 Guide to Afghanistan. Kabul: Government Printing House. Pp. 181; appendices.

Part I includes a general survey of the geography, the people and their mode of life, while Part II is on government. Part III presents a tourists' guide to Afghanistan. With bibliographies of books in Russian on Afghanistan, books in oriental languages and a list of periodicals.

23   Ali, Mohammad
1959 A New Guide to Afghanistan. Lahore: Northern Pakistan Printing and Publishing Co. Pp. 131; appendices; bibliography; map.

A revised third edition of no. 22.

24   Ali, Mohammad
1965 The Afghans. Lahore: Punjab Educational Press. Pp. 161.

A popular work which repeats material published elsewhere by the same author, notably that on Afghan manners and customs.

25   Allan, N. J. R.
1973 Recent sources of data on Afghanistan. Geographical Review 63(3):397-399.

26   Apercu Général sur l'Afghanistan [General Survey of Afghanistan]
1958 Paris: Mazarine. Pp. 31.

Includes brief description of areas attractive to tourists.

27   Arberry, A. J.
1937 Catalogue of the Library of the India Office. Vol. 2, Part IV: Persian Books. London. Pp. 571.

The books are listed by title and by author, with annotations under the title entries.

28   Arunova, Marianna R. (ed)
1964 Afganistan: spravochnik [Afghanistan: A Handbook]. Moscow: Nauka. Pp. 276; index.

I. GENERAL SOURCES

29   Aryana [Aryana]
        1942- A monthly periodical which began publication in Kabul.

        Printed in Persian, it is the organ of the Anjuman-i Tarikh [Historical Society] of the Afghan Academy.

30   Aryana da'iratu'l-ma'arif [Aryana Encyclopedia]
        1949 Shu'a', mir 'Ali Asghar, ed. Kabul: Matba'eh-yi 'umumi. (1328 A.H.)

        This comprehensive work began to come off the press in a Persian edition in 1949, with separate fascicules appearing in rapid order. Most of the articles are by Afghan scholars and officials, although some were taken from a comparable work put out at Tehran by Dehkhoda. In 1951 a Pushtu edition of the work began to come off the press.

31   Aryana Dayratulmuaref [Aryana Encyclopedia]
        1955 Afghanistan. Kabul: Aryana Dayratulamuaref. (In Dari). Pp. 398.

        Written by Afghan professionals and scholars, the work covers a variety of topics dealing with Afghanistan. Major topics covered are history, literature, fine arts, museums, education, geology, agriculture, geography, zoology, botany, commerce and industry.

32   Atlantic Report
        1962 Atlantic 210(4):26, 28, 34, 36. October.

        A useful, well-written general survey.

33   Bartholomew, John George
        n.d. A Literary and Historical Atlas of Asia. New York: E. P. Dutton and Co. (Everyman's Library). Pp. xi, 226; maps; plates.

        Maps showing the great empires, the routes of the explorers, temperature, rainfall, vegetation, etc., many of which include Afghanistan. There is a brief chapter on the coinages of Asia and a "Gazetteer of Towns and Places in Asia," with short historical notes on each.

34   Basic Facts on Afghanistan
        1961 Washington, D.C.: Department of Research, American Friends of the Middle East, Inc. Pp. 20.

I. GENERAL SOURCES

> A brief, useful, and generally reliable summary of the topography, history, and modern developments.

35 Becka, Jiri
1965 Afghanistan. Prague: Nakladatelstvi politicke literatury. Pp. 143; bibliography.

> A pocket-size, reliable general survey with emphasis on the present. Includes a chapter on Czech-Afghan relations.

36 Beeston, Alfred F. L.
1954 Catalogue of the Persian, Turkish, Hindustani and Pushtu Manuscripts in the Bodleian Library. Part III: Additional Persian Manuscripts. Oxford: Clarendon Press. Pp. viii, 177.

37 Berger, Nina, Ursulla Schillinger, Rolf Sator
1969 Bibliographie der Sozialwissenschaftlichen Literatur ueber Tuerkei--Iran--Afghanistan [Bibliography of Social Science Literature on Turkey--Iran--Afghanistan]. Koelner Zeitschrift für Soziologie und Sozialpsychologie 1969, Supplement 13:788-795.

38 Bibliografiiâ Afganistana [Bibliography of Afghanistan]
1908 S. D. Maslovskii, ed. Obshchestre vostokovedeniiâ. Sbornik sredne-aziatskogo otdela. Part 2. St. Petersburg.

39 Bibliografiiâ Afganistana: literatura na russkom yazyka [A bibliography of Afghanistan: Literature in Russian].
1965 Tatiyana I. Kukhtina, comp.; Yuriy V. Gankovskiy, ed. Moscow: Nauka. Pp. 271. Lists 2680 items.

40 Bibliographical Survey of the Soviet Literature on Afghanistan 1918-1967
1979 Central Asian Institute of the University of Peshawar, Pakistan.

41 Bibliographie Géographique Internationale [International Geographic Bibliography]. Paris: Libraire Armand Colin.

> An annual publication first issued about 1890 under the title of Bibliographie géographique and taking its present title in 1931.

42 Bibliography of Asian Studies. Journal of Asian Studies.

> Annual publication.

I. GENERAL SOURCES

43   Bibliography of Recent Soviet Source Material on Soviet Central Asia and the Borderlands. London: Central Asian Research Center.

A biannual which began publication in 1957, listing books and articles in some 51 periodicals and newspapers. Russian elites are given in transliteration, but are not translated into English although each item is annotated.

44   Bibliography of Russian Works on Afghanistan
1956 London: Central Asian Research Centre. Pp. 12.

Some 160 titles of books and articles, most listed with transliteration and translation of the Russian.

45   Bibliography on Afghanistan Available in Kabul Libraries
1975 Kabul: UNICEF. Pp. vii, 341.

A partial list of publications of works on Afghanistan in several languages. Emphasis on works in Dari and Pushtu.

46   Bibliotheca Afghanica
n.d. Based in Liestal, Switzerland, Bibliotheca Afghanica contains a bank of approximately 4,000 bibliographic entries on Afghanistan. Particularly strong in material in German on the country. An important source and tool for researchers, the Bibliotheca Afghanica is catalogues and directed by Mr. Bucherer-Dietschi. Address: Redaktion, Bibliotheca Afghanica, CH 4410 Liestal, Switzerland.

47   Bisnek, A. G. and K. I. Shafrovskii
1935 Bibliografiiâ bibliografii Srednei Azii [Bibliography of the Bibliographies of Central Asia]. Bibliografiiâ Vostoka. Parts 8 and 9. Leningrad.

Not as valuable a work as is suggested by the impressive title: it does list rare items not noticed elsewhere.

48   Blumhardt, James Fuller
1893 Catalogues of the Hindu, Penjabi, and Pushtu Printed Books. London: British Museum.

49   Bolshaia Sovetskaia Entsiklopedia [The Great Soviet Encyclopedia]
1949-1950 5 vols. Moscow.

Afghanistan is covered on page 492 f. of Volume Three.

I. GENERAL SOURCES

50 Bonine, Michael E.
    1975 Urbanization and City Structure in Contemporary Iran and Afghanistan: A Selected Annotated Bibliography. Monticello, Illinois: Council of Planning Librarians. Pp. 31.

51 Burke, J.
    1963 Fight for the Land of Hindu Kush. Life 55, August 9. Pp. 18-27.

52 Caspani, E. and E. Cagnacci
    1951 Afghanistan Crocevia dell'Asia [Afghanistan, Crossroads of Asia]. 2n ed. Milan: Antonio Vallardi. Pp. xv, 282.

    An informed, up-to-date compendium on history, customs and habits, and modern life by two Italians who resided in Afghanistan for more than a decade. Includes itineraries for the main motor routes and descriptions of monuments and points of interest.

53 Catalogue of the Marathi, Gujarati, Bengali, Assamese, Oriya, Pushtu, and Sindhi Manuscripts in the Library of the British Museum
    1905 London: British Museum.

54 Central Asian Review
    London: Central Asian Research Centre.

    A quarterly which began publication in 1953. Issues since 1956 contain reviews of Soviet writing on Afghanistan under the heading. Borderlands of Soviet Central Asia.

55 Current Problems in Afghanistan
    1961 Princeton: Princeton University Conference. Pp. 150.

    Articles presented at the thirteenth Near East Conference at Princeton University by twelve authors concerned with history, contemporary politics, natural resources, foreign relations, education, foreign private enterprise, the Durand Line of 1893, Soviet aid, American aid, and problems of social development.

56 Dagher, Joseph A.
    1937 L'Orient dans la litterature francaise d'après guerre 1919-1933 [The Orient in Post-War French Literature, 1919-1933]. Beirut: Edouard Angelil.

I. GENERAL SOURCES

Of interest primarily for references to articles in French periodicals on specialized subjects.

57   Deutsche im Hindukusch; Bericht der Deutschen Hindukusch-expedition 1935 der Deutschen Forschungsgemeinschaft [Germans in the Hindu Kush. Report of the German Hindu Kush Expedition of 1935 of the German Exploration Society]
1937 Berlin: Karl Siegismund. Pp. viii, 351; maps.

58   Dollot, René
1937 L'Afghanistan [Afghanistan]. Paris: Payot. Pp. 318.

A traveler's survey--not burdened by profundity--of the history, physical features, folklore, customs, and archaeology of the country, by a former French Ambassador at Kabul. Special emphasis is placed upon the impact of French culture on Afghanistan and French sponsored activities within the country.

59   Dupree, Ann, Louis Dupree, A. A. Motamedi
1964 A Guide to the Kabul Museum. The National Museum of Afghanistan. Kabul: Education Press. Pp. 157; illus.

60   Dupree, Louis
1973 Afghanistan. Princeton: Princeton University Press. (Revised and reissued in paperback 1980, 1981). Pp. xxiv, 760.

This is the most comprehensive work written by a western scholar on Afghanistan. Although the focus is anthropological, the book contains comprehensive description and analysis of Afghan culture, society, history, economics, geography, archaeology, and contemporary politics. A significant reference item, which reflects almost twenty years of first-hand research and study in Afghanistan.

61   Dupree, Louis
1959-1980 American Universities Field Staff Reports. South Asia Series (Afghanistan). Hanover, New Hampshire: American Universities Field Staff.

Occasional reports, on a variety of subjects, by an anthropologist and a well informed observer. The following titles by Louis Dupree, related to Afghanistan, have appeared during 1959-1980:

The Burqa Comes Off, 1959. Pp. 4.

I. GENERAL SOURCES

An Informal Talk With Prime Minister Daud, 1959. Pp. 4

Afghanistan's Big Gamble: Part I. Historical Background of Afghan-Russian Relations, 1960. Pp. 20.

Afghanistan's Big Gamble: Part II. The Economic and Strategic Aspects of Soviet Aid, 1960. Pp. 20.

Afghanistan's Big Gamble: Part III. Economic Competition in Afghanistan, 1960. Pp. 10.

The Mountains Go to Mohammad Zahir: Observations on Afghanistan's Reaction to Visits From Nixon, Bulganin-Krushchev, Eisenhower and Krushchev, 1960. Pp. 40.

The Bamboo Curtain in Kabul, 1960. Pp. 7.

A Note on Afghanistan, 1960. Pp. 32.

American Private Enterprise in Afghanistan, 1960. Pp. 12.

"Pushtunistan": The Problem and its Larger Implications. Part I. The Complex Interrelationships of Regional Disputes, 1961. Pp. 11.

"Pushtunistan": The Problem and its Larger Implications. Part II. The Effects of the Afghan-Pakistan Border Closure, 1961. Pp. 16.

"Pushtunistan": The Problem and its Larger Implications. Part III. The Big Gamble Continues, 1961. Pp. 7.

India's Stake in Afghan-Pakistan Relations, 1962. Pp. 5.

The Indian Merchants in Kabul, 1962. Pp. 9.

Landlocked Images, 1962. Pp. 23.

The Afghans Honor a Muslim Saint, 1963. Pp. 26.

A Suggested Pakistan-Afghanistan-Iran Federation. Part I. The Empty Triangle, 1963. Pp. 18.

A Suggested Pakistan-Afghanistan-Iran Federation. Part II. Political and Economic Consideration, 1963. Pp. 14.

The Green and the Black, 1963. Pp. 30.

The Decade of Daud Ends, 1963. Pp. 29.

I. GENERAL SOURCES

An Informal Talk with King Mohammad Zahir of Afghanistan, 1963. Pp. 8.

Mahmud Tarzi: Forgotten Nationalist, 1964. Pp. 22.

The Peace Corps in Afghanistan, 1964. Pp. 18.

Constitutional Development and Cultural Change. Part I. Social Implications of Constitution Making, 1965. Pp. 5.

Constitutional Development and Cultural Change. Part II. Afghan Constitutional Development, 1965. Pp. 18.

Constitutional Development and Cultural Change. Part III. The 1964 Afghan Constitution (Articles 1-56), 1965. Pp. 29.

Constitutional Development and Cultural Change. Part IV. The 1964 Afghan Constitution (Articles 57-128), 1965. Pp. 34.

Constitutional Development and Cultural Change. Part V. The Background of Constitutional Development on the Subcontinent, 1965. Pp. 15.

Constitutional Development and Cultural Change. Part VI. The Future of Constitutional Law in Afghanistan and Pakistan, 1965. Pp. 24.

Aq Kupruk: A Town in Northern Afghanistan. Part I. The People and Their Cultural Patterns, 1966. Pp. 29.

Aq Kupruk: A Town in Northern Afghanistan. Part II. The Political Structure and Commercial Patterns, 1966. Pp. 24.

An Ethnographic "Puzzle", 1966. Pp. 11.

Kabul Gets a Supermarket, 1966. Pp. 14.

Afghanistan: 1966, 1966. Pp. 32.

The Chinese Touch Base and Strike Out, 1966. Pp. 30.

A Kabul Supermarket Revisited, 1968. Pp. 7.

Afghanistan: 1968. Part I. Government and Bureaucracy, 1968. Pp. 8.

I. GENERAL SOURCES

Afghanistan: 1968. Part II. Economy and Development, 1968. Pp. 19.

Afghanistan: 1968. Part III. Problems of a Free Press, 1968. Pp. 14.

Afghanistan: 1968. Part IV. Strikes and Demonstrations, 1968. Pp. 6.

Sports and Games in Afghanistan, 1970. Pp. 20.

Free Enterprise in Afghanistan. Part I. The Private Sector and the New Investment Law, 1970. Pp. 20.

Free Enterprise in Afghanistan. Part II. Peter Baldwin and Indamer Afghan Industries, Inc., 1970. Pp. 12.

Free Enterprise in Afghanistan. Part III. Programs, Problems, and Prospects, 1970. Pp. 19.

The 1969 Student Demonstrations in Kabul, 1970. Pp. 13.

Population Dynamics in Afghanistan, 1970. Pp. 11.

Population Review 1970: Afghanistan, 1971. Pp. 20.

A Note on Afghanistan: 1971, 1971. Pp. 35.

Afghanistan Continues its Experiment in Democracy: The Thirteenth Parliament is Elected, 1971. Pp. 15.

Comparative Profiles of Recent Parliaments in Afghanistan, 1971. Pp. 18.

Parliament Versus the Executive in Afghanistan: 1969-1971, 1971. Pp. 17.

Nuristan: "The Land of Light" Seen Darkly, 1971. Pp. 24.

A New Decade of Daoud?, 1973. Pp. 9.

The Afghan American Educational Commission, 1973. Pp. 17.

A New Look in American Aid to Afghanistan, 1974. Pp. 9.

A Note on Afghanistan, 1974, 1974. Pp. 23.
The Emergence of Technocrats in Afghanistan, 1974. Pp. 17.

I. GENERAL SOURCES

Saint Cults in Afghanistan, 1976. Pp. 26.

It Wasn't Woodstock, But--The First International Rock Festival in Kabul, 1976. Pp. 11.

Imperialism in South Asia, 1976. Pp. 8.

Afghan Studies, 1976. Pp. 32.

Anthropology in Afghanistan, 1976. Pp.

Kessel's "The Horsemen", 1976. Pp. 16.

The Afghans Honor a Muslim Saint: Reprise, 1976. Pp. 12.

Serge de Beaurcueil, 1976. Pp. 9.

Ajmal Khattack: Revolutionary Pushtun Poet, 1976. Pp. 12.

Afghanistan: Landlocked Images Fifteen Years Later, 1976. Pp. 27.

The Saints Come Marching In: A Review of A. S. Ahmed's Millenium and Charisma Among Pathans, 1977. Pp. 4.

USAID and Social Scientists Discuss Afghanistan's Development Prospects, 1977. Pp. 19.

Afghanistan 1977: Does Trade Plus Aid Guarantee Development?, 1977. Pp. 13.

Toward Representative Government in Afghanistan. Part I. The First Five Steps, 1978. Pp. 12.

Toward Representative Government in Afghanistan. Part II. Steps Six Through Nine--and Beyond, 1978. Pp. 10.

The Role of Folklore in Modern Afghanistan, 1978. Pp. 7.

The Democratic Republic of Afghanistan, 1979. Pp. 11.

Red Flag Over the Hindu Kush. Part I. Leftist Movements in Afghanistan, 1979. Pp. 17.

Red Flag Over the Hindu Kush. Part II. The Accidental Coup, or Taraki in Blunderland, 1979. Pp. 16.

I. GENERAL SOURCES

> Militant Islam and Traditional Warfare in Islamic South Asia, 1980. Pp. 12.
>
> Red Flag Over the Hindu Kush. Part III. Rhetoric and Reforms, or Promises! Promises!, 1980. Pp. 14.
>
> Red Flag Over Afghanistan. Part IV. Foreign Policy and the Economy, 1980. Pp. 10.
>
> Red Flag Over the Hindu Kush. Part V. Repressions or Security Through Terror Purges I-IV, 1980. Pp. 14.
>
> Red Flag Over the Hindu Kush. Part VI. Repressions or Security Through Terror, 1980. Pp. 10.
>
> Afghanistan: 1980, 1980. Pp. 13.

62 Dupree, Louis and Linette Albert (eds)
1964 Afghanistan in the 1970s. New York: Praeger Publishers. Pp. 266.

Following chapters by fourteen authors are included: Afghanistan: Problems of A Peasant Society; Trends in Modern Afghan History; The Search for National Identity; Foreign Relations; Recent Economic Development; The Modernization of Rural Afghanistan; Nomadism in Modern Afghanistan; Afghan Women; Kabul University; Education; Archaeology and the Arts; Music.

63 Dvoryankov, N. A. (ed)
1960 Sovremenniy Afganistan [Contemporary Afghanistan]. Moscow: Izdatel'stvo vostochnoy literaturi. Pp. 502; maps; charts; tables; bibliography; indices.

Some 26 writers contributed to this handbook which covers several aspects of modern Afghanistan. Statistical and other detailed material takes up the final 115 pages. The fifteen-page bibliography lists sources in the language of origin, each in its own script. Many of the Russian titles have not been included in this publication and the specialist should consult the Soviet handbook.

64 Edwards, Edward
1922 A Catalogue of the Persian Printed Books in the British Museum. London. Pp. viii, 484.

The books are listed and annotated under the author's name, with an index of titles and a subject index.

I. GENERAL SOURCES

65   Elphinstone, Mountstuart
        1815 An Account of the Kingdom of Caubul, and its Dependencies in Persia, Tartary and India: Comprising a View of the Afghaun Nation, and a History of the Dooraunee Monarchy. London: Longman, Hurst, and John Murray. Pp. xxi, 675; map; appendices.

The first detailed account of Afghanistan from a British observer, compiled by an envoy from the East India Company to the court at Kabul in 1809. A number of members of the envoy's mission collected information on such subjects as geography, government, languages, manners and customs, education, religion, and tribes. Its popularity resulted in French editions in 1817 and 1842 and an expanded English edition in 1842. Reprinted 1972 in two volumes.

66   Engert, Cornelius van H.
        1924 A Report on Afghanistan. U. S. Department of State, Division of Publications. Series C. No. 53. Afghanistan No. 1. Washington. Pp. iv, 225; extensive bibliography; appendices; map.

In response to Afghan overtures towards formalizing relations with the United States, a young diplomatic officer was sent to Kabul to study the situation. His report covers the history and background, as well as contemporary events.

67   Ethe, Hermann
        1903 Catalogue of the Persian Manuscripts in the Library of the India Office. Vol. 1. Oxford: Horace Hart. Pp. xxiii, columns 1631.

Histories of the Afghans, columns 230-238.

68   Ethe, Hermann
        1930 Catalogue of the Persian, Turkish, Hindustani and Pushtu Manuscripts in the Bodleian Library. Part II: Turkish, Hindustani, Pushtu and Additional Persian Manuscripts. Oxford: Clarendon Press. Columns 1159-1766.

69   Ethe, Hermann and Edward Edwards
        1937 Catalogue of the Persian Manuscripts in the Library of the India Office. Vol. 2: Containing Additional Descriptions and Indices. Oxford: Clarendon Press. Pp. vi, columns 1374.

I. GENERAL SOURCES

70 Evans, Hubert
    Recent Soviet Writing on South and Central Asia. Royal
       Central Asian Journal 51, no. 2 (1964): 149-158; 51,
       no. 3/4 (1964): 306-314; 52, no. 2 (1965): 146-154; 53
       (1966): 50-58.

71 Farid, Ahmad
    1965 Bibliyugrafi [Bibliography]. Kabul: Puhani
       matba'eh. Pp. 27. (1344 A.H.)

    Two hundred and fifty-six titles of books published in
    Afghanistan in Dari, Pushtu, and English are grouped under
    the headings of sponsoring organizations such as
    ministries, faculties of Kabul University, and learned
    societies. Within these headings, the arrangement is not
    alphabetical, and there is no index. The majority of the
    books listed were published within the last decade.

72 Farrukh, Mahdi
    1937 Tarikh-i Mukhtasar-i Afghanistan [A Brief History of
       Afghanistan]. Tabriz: no publisher. Pp. 78. (1316
       A.H.)

73 Field, Henry
    1953-1962 Bibliographies on Southwestern Asia: I-VII.
       Coral Gables: University of Miami Press. Pp. 1, 834;
       subject indexes (1959-64) 429 pp.

    Includes some 50,000 titles from 6,000 journals in 43
    languages and covers the subjects of anthropology, natural
    history, zoology, and botany. More than 90 titles dealing
    with Afghanistan, mostly from elusive periodicals, are
    included.

74 Fraser-Tytler, Sir W. Kerr
    1958 Afghanistan. A Study of Political Developments in
       Central Asia. London: Oxford University Press. (1st
       issued 1950; reissued 1953.) Pp. xiii, 330; maps;
       selected bibliography; genealogical table.

    Decades of service in India, the North West Frontier
    Province, and Afghanistan where he held diplomatic posts
    at Kabul including that of British Minister created a
    knowledgeable background for the author's study of the
    "Great Game" in Central Asia--the rivalry of the Russian
    and British empires for control of Afghanistan. Rounded
    out with historical material and descriptions of the

I. GENERAL SOURCES

various ethnic groups. The second edition contains an added chapter of 18 pages on events in Afghanistan from 1947 through 1951.

75 Frembgen, Juergen
    1980 Neues Schrifttum Ueber die Indoarischen Bergvoelker des Afghanischen Hindukush (1975-1980). Anthropos 75:937-941.

New literature about the Indo-Arian mountain peoples of the Afghan Hindukush.

76 Furon, Raymond
    1951 L'Iran: Perse et Afghanistan [Iran: Persia and Afghanistan]. Paris: Payot. Pp. 336; bibliography; maps.

Represents the reworking of two books published in 1926 and in 1938. The author, a French geologist with years of residence and travel in Iran and Afghanistan, has much of value to convey but many of the pages are sketchy and impressionist rather than factual.

77 Ghani, A. R.
    1951 Pakistan: A Select Bibliography. Lahore: Ripon Printing Press, 1951. Pp. xxii, 339.

Titles relating to ethnic groups within Afghanistan may be found on pages 41-45 dealing with the North West Frontier Province and on pages 86-91 dealing with the peoples of Pakistan.

78 Grassmuck, George and Ludwig W. Adamec with Frances H. Irwin (eds)
    1969 Afghanistan: Some New Approaches. Ann Arbor: Center for Near Eastern and North African Studies, The University of Michigan. Pp. vii, 405.

Includes very useful chapters on Afghan ethnography, literature, politics. A chronology of major political events is provided. The book contains a bibliography of recent works related to the topics covered. Reprinted 1980.

79 Hall, Lesley
    1980 A Brief Guide to Sources for the Study of Afghanistan in the India Office Records. London: India Office Library and Records. Pp. 65.

I. GENERAL SOURCES

Part I provides a chronological survey of sources. Part II deals with the files of the British Legation in Kabul from 1923 to 1948.

80 Hanifi, M. Jamil
    1976 Historical and Cultural Dictionary of Afghanistan. Metuchen, N.J.: Scarecrow Press. Pp. viii, 141.

    Includes condensed material on historical, social, and cultural aspects of Afghanistan arranged in an encyclopedic style.

81 Henning, W. B.
    1950 Bibliography of Important Studies on Old Iranian Subjects. Tehran: Ketab-Khaneh Danesh. Pp. 53.

    This work, by the then professor at the School of Oriental and African Studies, London, contains a short introduction in Persian by a faculty member of the Tehran University. Items relating to Afghan languages and dialects are found on pages 38-44.

82 Heravi, Ghulam Riza Mayel
    1965 Fehrest-i kotob matbu' Afghanistan az sal 1330 ila 1344. 15 sal [List of Books Printed in Afghanistan from the Year 1951 to 1965. (15 years)]. Kabul: Doulati matba'eh. Pp. 77. (1344 A.H.)

    Lists 450 titles in Dari and Pushtu alphabetically under the first letter of the titles. An index identifies authors and translators. Regrettably, the quality of the printing is poor.

83 Heravi, Ghulam Riza Mayel
    1962 Mo'arefi ruznameh-ha, jaraid, majallat Afghanistan [Introduction to the Newspapers, Journals, and Magazines of Afghanistan]. Kabul: Parwan doulati matba'eh. Pp. 144. (1341 A.H.)

84 Houtsma, Martyn Theodor
    1913-1916 The Encyclopedia of Islam: A Dictionary of the Geography, Ethnography, and Biography of the Muhammadan Peoples, Prepared by a Number of Leading Orientalists. Leyden and London.

    Excellent articles may be found under such subject headings as Afghanistan, Durrani, Ghaznavids, Ghor, Hazara, etc. A new edition, which began to appear in 1955, included a revised article on Afghanistan.

I. GENERAL SOURCES

85 Imperial Gazetteer of India
    1907-1908 New Edition Published under the Authority of His Majesty's Secretary of State for India in Council. Oxford: Clarendon Press. Afghanistan, vol. 5, 26-65; map. Afghan-Turkistan, vol. 5, 65-69.

    This is the third edition of an extremely valuable work of reference. The article on Afghanistan represents a condensed survey of topography, climate, history, population, resources, administration, etc. The heading Afghan-Turkistan is typical of many other entries relating to places, peoples, etc. of Afghanistan.

86 Indiya i Afganistana: Ocherki Istorii i Ekonomiki [India and Afghanistan: Essays on History and Economics].
    1958 Moscow: Izdatel'stvo Vostochnoy Literatury. Pp. 290.

87 James, Eloise
    1975 Far Middle East: An Annotated Bibliography of Materials at Elementary School Level for Afghanistan, Iran, Pakistan. Unpublished M.A. thesis. University of Rhode Island.

88 Jawhar, Hasan Muhammad and 'Abd al-Hamid Baywami
    1961 Afghanistan. Cairo: Dar al-ma'ref. Pp. 117.

89 Jettmar, Karl (editor and in collaboration with Lennart Edelberg)
    1974 Cultures of the Hindukush: Selected Papers From the Hindu-Kush Cultural Conference Held at Moesgard 1970. Wiesbaden: Franz Steiner Verlag. Pp. 146.

    Collection of important anthropological, sociological, and linguistic articles dealing with the society and culture of the people of Nuristan.

90 Jones, Schuyler
    1966 An Annotated Bibliography of Nuristan (Kafiristan) and the Kalash Kafirs of Chitral I. Kobenhavn: Munksgaard. Pp. 110.

91 Jones, Schuyler
    1969 A Bibliography of Nuristan (Kafiristan) and the Kalash Kafirs of Chitral II: Selected Documents From the Secret and Political Record, 1885-1900. Kobenhavn: Munksgaard. Pp. 274.

I. GENERAL SOURCES

92　　Kabul [Kabul]
　　　　Founded in 1931 at Kabul.

　　　　An illustrated monthly in Pushtu, published by the Pushtu
　　　　Tulaneh section of the Afghan Academy. The intervals of
　　　　publication have varied from year to year.

93　　Da Kabul Kalani [The Annual of Kabul]
　　　　Kabul: Matba'eh-yi 'umumi.

　　　　Publication of this annual, sponsored by the Afghan
　　　　government, began in 1311 [1933] under the title of Sal-
　　　　nameh-yi Kabul [The Kabul Annual]. Each issue of several
　　　　hundred pages contained articles in Persian and Pushtu,
　　　　and some issues contained a few pages in French. In 1319
　　　　[1940] the name of the publication was changed to Da Kabul
　　　　Kalani and more articles in Pushtu feature the succeeding
　　　　issues. Some contained short summaries in English. In
　　　　1331 [1952] the publication appeared under the name of Da
　　　　Afghanistan Kalani. Each issue has been extensively
　　　　illustrated and over the years the editors have included
　　　　such scholarly writers as Na'imi, Binava, Rishtiya, and
　　　　Taraki.

94　　Kamrany, Nake M., Lois H. Godiksen, Eden Naby, Richard N. Fry
　　　　1977　An Inventory of Afghanistan Research Materials.
　　　　　　Afghanistan Journal 2:79-82.

95　　Kessel, Joseph
　　　　1959　Afghanistan. London: Thames and Hudson. Pp. 45;
　　　　　　201 plates.

　　　　Striking illustrations in black and white and in color,
　　　　accompanied by a description of the plates, a record of
　　　　the author's travels, and a very brief account of the
　　　　country and the people.

96　　Kraus, Willy
　　　　1975　Afghanistan. (Third Revised Edition.) Hamburg:
　　　　　　Erdmann. Pp. 428.

97　　Kukhtina, T. I.
　　　　1965　Bibliografia Afghanistana: Literatura na Russkom
　　　　　　Iazyka. Moscow.

　　　　Includes 5,680 entries of Russian language works on
　　　　Afghanistan published before 1965.

I. GENERAL SOURCES

98 Kukhtina, Tat'yana and A. K. Sverchevskaya (comps)
    1964 Kratkaya Bibliografiya knig i statey po Afganistanu, Iranu i Turtsii, vyshedshikh v 1963 g. (Na Russk. yaz) [A Short Bibliography of Books and Articles About Afghanistan, Iran and Turkey Which Have Appeared in Russian During the Year 1963 (in Russian)]. Moscow: Institut Narodov Azii, Kratkiye Soobshcheniya 77:130-137.

99 Lentz, Wolfgang
    1937 Sammlungen zur afghanischen Literatur-und Zeitgeschichte [Collections in Afghan Literature and Contemporary History]. Zeitschrift der deutschen morgenlandischen Gesellschaft 91:711-732.

    Cursive treatise on a number of headings illustrative of Afghan bibliography. Includes material published in Afghanistan, such as newspapers, government publications and Pushtu literature, with titles transliterated.

100 Lival, Rahmatullah
    1947 Rahnuma-yi tajer [Merchant's Guide]. Kabul: Matba 'eh-yi 'umumi. Pp. 150. (1326 A.H.)

101 Lytle, Elizabeth Edith
    1976 A Bibliography of the Geography of Afghanistan: Background for Planning. Monticello, Illinois: Council of Planning Libraries. Pp. 40.

102 Massignon, Louis (ed)
    1955 Annuaire du Monde Musulman. Statistique, historique, social et économique [Yearbook of the Muslim World. Statistical, Historic, Social and Economic]. Paris: Presses Universitaires de France. Pp. xvi, 428.

    Afghanistan is dealt with on pages 157-162 under such headings as population, government, administration, labor, and production.

103 Messerschmidt, Ernst A. and Willy Kraus
    1968 Bibliographie der Afghanistan-Literatur, 1945-1967. Hamburg Deutsches Orient-Institut.

    A comprehensive two volume bibliographic compendium of works on Afghanistan.

104 The Middle East (yearly); A Survey and Directory of the Countries of the Middle East, Compiled by the Publishers

I. GENERAL SOURCES

> in Collaboration with the Intelligence Unit of The Economist. London: Europa Publications, Ltd.
>
> This volume has appeared annually since 1950, with each issue giving the year as part of the title. Encyclopedic type of information on each country, including Afghanistan.

105 The Middle East and North Africa, 1980-81
> 1981 Afghanistan. The Middle East and North Africa, 1980-81. London: Europa Publications. Pp. 187-217.
>
> The MENA is source book published annually. It usually contains updated and critical information about the Middle East including Afghanistan. In the above (most recent) issue, the chapter on Afghanistan includes sections on physical and social geography, history, economy, current affairs, constitutional development, government, political parties, religion, press, trade and industry, finance, radio and television, transportation, defense, education, tourism, and atomic energy. It is one of the most important reference sources for almost all shades of interest.

106 Middle East Journal
> Washington, D.C.: The Middle East Institute.
>
> A valuable quarterly, which began publication in 1947. Each issue contains a Bibliography of Periodical Literature, in which some 150 periodicals are reviewed, including all those which would carry material on Afghanistan except for those published within the country.

107 Military Report, Afghanistan
> 1925 History, Geography, Resources, Armed Forces, Forts and Fortified Posts, Administration and Communications. Calcutta: General Staff, India.

108 Newsletter, Afghanistan Council
> 1973 A newsletter published by the Afghanistan Council, Asia Society, New York. In English.
>
> The newsletter appeared in 1973 with volume 1, number 1 and continues to appear regularly on a one volume per year basis. Each volume usually has four issues which appear in January, March, June, and September. A representative newsletter carries a chronology of current events, reprints and/or summaries of important news about Afghanistan, book reviews, announcement of recent

I. GENERAL SOURCES

>publications, and documents. Very useful for both casual and serious interests.

109 Nustraty, Mohammad Yonus (ed)
    1963 Afghanistan, Land of Culture. Washington: International Student Press. Pp. 53.

Contains 28 short articles written by Afghan students on various aspects of Afghan life.

110 Pazhwak, Abdur Rahman
    n.d.(1954?) Aryana [Ancient Afghanistan]. Hove, England: Key Press, Ltd. Pp. 144.

An expanded reissue of an earlier undated and anonymous booklet of the same title and from the same press. A popular, well-written, general account of the ancient and modern history of the country and of many aspects of local life. The author has been attached to the Afghan Information Bureau in London.

111 Pearson, J. D. (comp)
    Index Islamicus. Cambridge: W. Heffer & Sons, Ltd.

A catalogue of articles on Islam in periodicals and other collective publications. The volume covering the years 1906-1955 appeared in 1958, that for 1956-1960 in 1962.

112 Pikulin, M. G.
    1956 Afghanistan: Ekonomicheskiy ocherk [Afghanistan: An Economic Survey]. Tashkent: Akademiya Nauk Uzbek SSR. Pp. 301; bibliography.

A general account of the country with emphasis upon economic data through 1953.

113 Pocket Guide to Afghanistan
    n.d.(1946) Washington: U.S. Department of State, U. S. Government Printing Office. Pp. 51; map.

Small format and too brief to be of real value. Provided with a small-scale, useful, folding map.

114 Point Four: Near East and Africa
    1951 A Selected Bibliography of Studies on Economically Underdeveloped Countries. Washington: U. S. Department of State, Division of Library and Reference Services.

I. GENERAL SOURCES

115   Poullada, Leila
1979 Bibliography of American Periodical Literature on Afghanistan, 1890 to 1946. New York: Afghanistan Council, the Asia Society. Occasional paper No. 18. Pp. 21.
A useful compendium of periodical literature about Afghanistan in the United States illustrating the fragmentary and impressionistic interest in Afghanistan in U.S. scholarship. An annotated version is contemplated.

116   Pourhadi, Ibrahim V.
1976 Afghanistan's Newspapers, Magazines and Journals. Afghanistan Journal 3(2)75-77.

117   Pourhadi, Ibrahim V.
1979 Persian and Afghan Newspapers in the Library of Congress, 1871-1978. Washington: Library of Congress Publications (U. S. Government Printing Office). Pp. 102.

118   Rasmi Jarideh [Official Journal]

A bimonthly publication of the Ministry of Justice. First issue, March 1964. Contains Pushtu and Persian (Dari) texts of new laws, royal decrees, cabinet decisions, treaty documents, and all information having legal status.

119   Rathjens, Carl
1981 Neue Forschungen in Afghanistan [New Research Projects in Afghanistan]. Opladen: Lesk and Budrich. Pp. 245.

Collection of partly revised lectures given at the fifth work session of the Arbeitsgmeinschaft Afghanistan in Mannheim, February 1-3, 1979. Includes contributions to topics of politics and current history, economy, the natural sciences, geography and ethnology, culture history, and art history. An excellent source on German works on Afghanistan. Most sections include comprehensive bibliographies of recent works, particularly in German.

120   Redard, Georges (ed)
1964 Indo-Iranica, mélanges présenté à Georg Morgenstierne à l'occasion de son soixante-dixième anniversaire [Indo-Iranica, miscellanea offered to Georg Morgenstierne on the occasion of his seventieth anniversary]. Wiesbaden: Otto Harrassowitz. Pp. viii, 195.

Articles relating to the interest of this preeminent scholar of Iranian languages.

I. GENERAL SOURCES

121　　Reisner, Igor Mikhailovich and R. T. Akhramovich
　　　　　1956　Nash sosed Afganistan [Our Neighbor Afghanistan].
　　　　　Moscow: Znaniye. Pp. 48.

122　　Rieu, Charles
　　　　　1879, 1881, 1883　Catalogue of the Persian Manuscripts in
　　　　　　the British Museum. 3 vols. London. Pp. (1) 1-432;
　　　　　　(2) vii, 433-877; (3) xxviii, 881-1229.

　　　　　The manuscripts are catalogued under subject headings,
　　　　　with a note under each on the writer, the manuscript and
　　　　　its contents. In the Classed Index (vol. 3, page 1192)
　　　　　are listed the eleven manuscripts which concern the
　　　　　Afghans.

123　　Rieu, Charles
　　　　　1895　Supplement to the Catalogue of the Persian Manu-
　　　　　　scripts in the British Museum. London: Gilbert and
　　　　　　Rivington, Ltd. Pp. ix, 308.

124　　Romodin, V. A.
　　　　　1967　Fifty Years of Soviet Oriental Studies (Brief
　　　　　　Reviews), 1917-1967: Afghan Studies. Moscow: USSR
　　　　　　Academy of Sciences. Pp. 42.

　　　　　Includes a brief summary of Soviet works on Afghanistan
　　　　　along with a bibliography of these contributions during
　　　　　this fifty year period. Emphasis on major works and
　　　　　highlights.

125　　Sachau, Edward and Hermann Ethe
　　　　　1889　Catalogue of the Persian, Turkish, Hindustani, and
　　　　　　Pushtu Manuscripts in the Bodleian Library. Part I.
　　　　　　The Persian Manuscripts. Oxford: Clarendon Press. Pp.
　　　　　　xii, columns 1150.

126　　Sal-nameh-yi Kabul [The Kabul Annual]

　　　　　See Da Kabul Kalani.

127　　Schlag nach über Iran, Afghanistan, Arabien and Indien; wissen-
　　　　　werte Tatsachen, Übersichten und Tabellen nebt einer
　　　　　mehrfarbigen Übersichtskarte [Research on Iran,
　　　　　Afghanistan, Arabia and India; Valuable Facts, Surveys and
　　　　　Tables with a Colored Survey Map]. Leipzig: Fachschrift-
　　　　　leitungen des Bibliographischen Instituts.
　　　　　1942　Pp. 32; maps.

I. GENERAL SOURCES

128 A Select Bibliography: Asia, Africa, Eastern Europe and Latin America
1960 New York: American Universities Field Staff. Pp. 534.

Contains some 6,000 titles, more than a third of which are annotated. Supplements were issued in 1961, 1963, and 1965.

129 Selected Bibliography of Published Material on the Area Where Pushtu Is Spoken: Afghanistan, Baluchistan and the North-West Frontier Province.
1951 U. S. Department of State, Division of Library and Reference Service, Bibliography No. 60, October 30. Pp. 11.

Neither exhaustive nor selective, with emphasis upon articles in periodicals of recent date.

130 Shalizi, Abdul Satar
n.d. (1961) Ancient Land with Modern Ways. No place (Washington, D.C.): no publisher. Pp. 199; 247 un-numbered illustrations.

Excellent illustrations in black and white and in color, accompanied by pages of matching text in English and in Pushtu.

131 Shalizi, Prita K.
1966 Here and There in Afghanistan. Kabul: Education Press.

A collection of articles originally printed in Afghan newspapers and periodicals. Subjects include travel sketches, women in society, and the Afghan cuisine.

132 Sharqawi, Muhammad 'Abd al-Mun'im al-, et al.
1961 Afghanistan. Cairo: Matbu 'at ma 'had al-darasat al-Islamiyah. Pp. 135.

A survey, in Arabic, by several authors.

133 Smith, Harvey Henry and others
1973 Area Handbook for Afghanistan (4th edition). Washington: U. S. Government Printing Office. Pp. lvi, 452.

I. GENERAL SOURCES

A summary and descriptive work on various facets and conditions of Afghanistan. Superficially written. Includes a useful bibliography.

134 Snesarev, A. E.
     1921 Afganistan. (Afghanistan). Moscow.

135 Sovetskoye Afganovedeniye za 40 let.
     1961 Tekst na yaz. pushtu [Forty Years of Afghan Studies in the USSR. Text in Pushtu]. Moscow: Izdatel'stvo Vostochnoy Literatury. Pp. 128.

136 Sovetskoye Afganovedeniye za 40 let.
     1960 Tekst na yaz. farsi-kabul [Soviet Afghan studies over 40 years. Text in Farsi-Kabuli]. Moscow: Izdatel'stvo Vostochnoy Literatury. Pp. 95.

137 Stanishevskii, A. V.
     1940 Afganistan. [Afghanistan]. Moscow: USSR Academy of Sciences.

138 Storey, Charles A.
     1927, 1935, 1936, 1939, 1953 Persian Literature. A Bio-Bibliographical Survey. Vol. 1. London: Luzac and Co. Pp. 1443.

     The sections of Volume 1, Qur'anic Literature; History and Biography, were published at intervals and paged consecutively. An index of titles and an index of authors, subjects, etc. closes the volume.

139 Sykes, Sir Percy M.
     1940 A History of Afghanistan. 2 vols. London: Macmillan and Co. Pp. (1) xiii, 411; (2) ix, 414; maps; appendices; list of authorities.

     A painstakingly constructed compilation of material on the region and on the country of Afghanistan. Invaluable as a reference book. The closing chapters contain reliable material on trends of the 1930s. Reprinted 1975.

140 Taillardat, C. F.
     1928 Études sur l'Afghanistan [Studies on Afghanistan]. L'Asie Francaise. Pp. 266-278.

141 Trudy Sessii po voprosam istorii i ekonomiki Afganistana, Irana, Turtsii [Reports of the Session on the History and the Economy of Afghanistan, Iran and Turkey].

I. GENERAL SOURCES

        1963 Moscow, Institut Narodov Azii, Kratkiye Soobscheniya 73:252.

142 Valiyan, 'Abd al-'Azim
        1961 Kolliyat az awza'-i siyasi u iqtisadi u ijtima'i-yi Afghanistan [Collection concerning the Political, Economic and Social Situations of Afghanistan]. Tehran: Zavvar. Pp. 170; maps. (1340 A.H.)

A work in Persian.

143 Vanecek, Petr.
        1952 Afghanistan. Prague: Mladá fronta.

144 Voelkerkundliche Bibliographie
        1937 Asien. Allgemeine Voelkerkunde ab 1928 [Ethnological Bibliography. Asia. General Ethnology from the Year 1928]. Stuttgart: E. Schweizerbart.

145 Von Hentig, Werner Otto
        1962 Mein Leben, eine Dienstreise [My Life, A Journey of Service]. Göttingen: Vandenhoeck & Ruprecht. Pp. 497.

The story of a German diplomat whose posts included Kabul in 1915.

146 Waleh, Abdul H.
        1963 Afghanistan Today. Washington: Royal Afghan Embassy. Not paged.

An attractive, illustrated survey for the general reader.

147 Watkins, Mary Bradley
        1963 Afghanistan. Land in Transition. Princeton: D. Van Nostrand. Pp. 262; bibliography; index.

A general survey, with emphasis on contemporary society and cultural conditions.

148 Weeks, Richard V. (ed)
        1978 Muslim Peoples: A World Ethnographic Survey. Westport, Connecticut: Greenwood Press. Pp. 546.

A comprehensive ethnographic coverage of various Muslim ethnic groups throughout the world. Each entry includes a brief ethnographic description and a useful bibliography and usually has a different author. Muslim ethnic groups in Afghanistan covered here are: Baluch (Pp. 64-69) by Stephen L. Pastner; Hazara (Pp. 163-167) by Robert L.

I. GENERAL SOURCES

>   Canfield; Kirgis (Pp. 215-219) by Victor L. Mote; Pushtun
>   (Pp. 323-330) by Louis Dupree; Tajik (Pp. 389-395) by
>   Louis Dupree; Turkmen (Pp. 427-433) by William G. Irons;
>   Uzbek (Pp. 464-469) by Louis Dupree; Nuristani (Pp. 292-
>   297) by Louis Dupree.

149 Wilber, Donald N. (ed)
     1956 Afghanistan. New Haven: Human Relations Area Files.
           Pp. 501; charts; tables; maps; bibliography; index.

     A volume in the publisher's Country Survey Series. A
     comprehensive study of the history, ethnology, sociology,
     government, politics, and economic structure by five
     contributors.

150 Wilber, Donald N. (ed)
     1962 Afghanistan its people its society its culture. New
           Haven: Human Relations Area Files Press. Pp. 320; maps;
           charts; tables; illustrations; bibliography; index.

     An extensively revised and rewritten edition of item 149,
     with contributions by six specialists.

151 Yusufi, Muhammad Akbar
     1963 Tatbiq-i sanavat [Comparative Years]. Kabul:
           Doulati matba'eh. Pp. 86. (1342 A.H.)

     Tables for conversion of the dates of the Muslim lunar
     calendar to Christian solar years.

152 Zambaur, Eduard Karl Marx von
     1927 Manuel de généalogie et de chronologie pour
           l'histoire de l'Islam, avec 20 tableaux généalogiques
           hors texte et 5 cartes [Manual of Geneaology and
           Chronology for the History of Islam, with 20 Genealogi-
           cal Tables Separate from the Text and 5 Maps].
           Hanover: H. Lafaire. Pp. xii, 388; a supplementary
           volume includes the tables and maps.

II. GEOGRAPHY

Geology, topography, exploration; travel and description; natural history; atlases and maps

Much of the earlier work on the topography of the country was concentrated on descriptions of the country between India and Kabul and Qandahar. This period was followed by one in which the General Staff, India, made detailed studies of the routes within the country and compiled military reports, which included exhaustive accounts of the topography and resources of the country: these publications, although unclassified, remain very hard to obtain.

Recent material in this general category fails to reflect present opportunities for travel and exploration. Such writings are largely concerned with those towns, sites and developments along the so-called "great circle route"--the roads which encircle the country, beginning at Kabul and running north to Mazare Sharif, then west to Herat, then south to Qandahar and, finally, northeast through Ghazni to Kabul. Articles in periodicals bear titles of promise with reference to the more remote regions, but most of them add relatively little information. The vast central area of Afghanistan remains comparatively unknown, as does the southeastern region--a major area of Pushtu speaking groups. Afghan writers have begun to take cognizance of the gaps in knowledge and to publish accounts of their researches in local periodicals, but until some systematic survey is undertaken these various contributions will be scattered and sketchy.

Afghanistan is adequately mapped. It has not been considered necessary to include older, superseded maps in the bibliography, and those of recent data are available from the various cartographic centers (which initiated and participated in the mapping process) or from libraries which have large specialized holdings on Afghanistan.

153   Abbas, Agha (of Shiraz)
        1843 Journal of a Tour through parts of the Punjab and Afghanistan in the year 1837 (translated by R. Leech). Journal of the Asiatic Society of Bengal 12:564-621.

154   Afghan Geological Survey Department, Ministry of Mines and Industries.

        1969 Geological Map of Afghanistan. Kabul: Afghan Cartographic Institute, 1:2,500,00.

155   Afghanistan: Official Standard Names
        1971 Approved by the United States Board of Geographic Names. Washington, D.C.: U. S. Geographic Names Division, Pp. xvi, 170.

II. GEOGRAPHY

156   Aitchison, James Edward T.
On the Flora of the Kuram Valley in Afghanistan. Botany, Journal of the Linnean Society (London) 18(1881):113; 19(1882):139-200; folding map; plates.

An account of the summer of 1879, spent with the British forces in the Kuram Valley. A description of the country, plants and agriculture gives an intimate picture of the rural life of the inhabitants. There are lists of specimens, plates, and a folding map.

157   Aitchison, James Edward T.
1888 The Botany of the Afghan Delimitation Commission. The Transactions of the Linnean Society. Botany, 2d ser., 3:1-139; maps; plates. London.

A readable description of the plants found in Northern Baluchisan, Afghanistan and Iran. There are lists of the specimens and incidental notes on the country and the people. The author was Secretary to the Surgeon-General of Her Majesty's Forces in Bengal, and attached as naturalist to the Afghan Delimitation Commission.

158   Akram, Mohammad
1948 La géomorphogénie de l'Ouest [The Geomorphogeny of the West]. Afghanistan 3(2):67-71; (3):5-12.

A fairly detailed description of the valley of the Nari Rud River and an account of the lower Helmand case; short bibliography.

159   Akram, Mohammad
1949 Les grandes voies do passage à travers de l'Afghanistan [The Great Travel Routes across Afghanistan]. Afghanistan 4(4):27-35; map.

Of only moderate interest, this sketch emphasizes the antiquity of certain of the routes.

160   Akram, Mohammad
1951 L'Ouest Afghan (étude physique) [The Afghan West (A Physical Study)]. Afghanistan 6(2):57-62.

161   Akram, Mohammad
1951 Ouvrage nouveau sur l'Afghanistan [A New Work on Afghanistan]. Afghanistan 6(3):56-57.

II. GEOGRAPHY

A review of revised edition of Raymond Futon's Iran: Perse et Afghanistan (see no. 76).

162   Alee, Shekh Khash.
        1845 Account of the Eusafzai-Afghans inhabiting Sama (the Plains), Swat, Bunher and the Chamla Valley, being a detail of their clans, villages, chiefs and force, and the tribute they pay to the Sikhs. Journal of the Asiatic Society of Bengal 54:736-46.

163   Alexander, Michael
        1960 Offbeat in Asia. London: Weidenfeld and Nicholson. Pp. 180.

        Inconsequential travel, livened by the companionship of a "beautiful model girl."

164   Alexandrescu-Dersca, M. M.
        1977 La Campagne de Timur en Anatolie. E. J. Brill, maps; illustrations. Pp. 228. (1402 A.H.)

165   Ali, Mohammad
        1953 Afghanistan's Mountains Afghanistan 3(1):40-53.

        The location of Afghanistan's mountains, their appearance, vegetation, and the routes of the mountain passes.

166   Allan, Nigel John Roger
        1978 Men and Crops in the Central Hindukush. Unpublished Ph.D. Dissertation. Syracuse University. Pp. 335.

        A human-ecological perspective on agricultural activity in Kuh Daman, Afghanistan.

167   Amin, Hamidullah and Gordon B. Schilz
        1978 A Geography of Afghanistan. Omaha: Center for Afghanistan Studies. Pp. 204.

        A detailed description and analysis of the topic with a useful bibliographic appendix.

168   Anderson, Steven C.
        1967 A New Species of Eremias (Reptilia: Lacertidae) from Afghanistan. San Francisco: Occasional Papers of the California Academy of Sciences (64):4.

169   Anderson, Steven C. and Alan E. Leviton
        1969 Amphibians and Reptiles Collected by the Street Expedition to Afghanistan, 1965. San Francisco:

II. GEOGRAPHY

        Proceedings of the California Academy of Sciences, 4th Series 37(2):25-56.

170 Anderson, Steven C. and Alan E. Leviton
      1967 A New Species of Phrynocephalus (Sauria: Agamidae) from Afghanistan With Remarks on Phrynocephalus Ornatus Boulenger. San Francisco: Proceedings of the California Academy of Sciences, 4th Series 35(11):227-233.

171 Anderson, W.
      1849 Notes on the Geography of Western Afghanistan. Journal of the Asiatic Society of Bengal 58:553-87 (with further notes by J. Avdall, pp. 588-94).

172 Arefi, Abdul Ghafoor.
      1976 Urban Policies, Planning and Implementation in Kabul, Afghanistan. Unpublished Ph.D. Dissertation. Indiana University.

173 Arens, H. J.; G. Braach, S. Gurtler, E. Nast, und W. Paszkowski.
      1974 Landerstudie Afghanistan. Spektrum der dritten Welt Nr. 12, Wentorf/Hamburg.

174 Arez, G.
      1969 Eqlime Afghanistan [The Climate of Afghanistan]. Kabul: Government Printing.

175 Arez, G.
      1970 Geography of Afghanistan, Kabul Times Annual. Pp. 19-93.

176 Aristov, N. A.
      1896 Ob Avganistane i ego naselenii [About Afghanistan and its Population]. Xhiraia Starina, 8. St. Petersburg.

      Characteristic work by a leading Tsarist authority on Afghanistan; an ethnologist by training. This article, and others listed under other headings are now outmoded as well as containing speculative material which has not stood the test of time.

177 Arrowsmith, J.
      Map of Central Asia. Journal of the Royal Geographical Society. 45:420.

II. GEOGRAPHY

178   Aurembou, Renee
      1977 Vermißt in Afghanistan. Stuttgart: Solothurn, Schweizer Jugend-Verlag. Pp. 180.

179   Balsan, Francois
      1949 Inquisitions de Kaboul au Golfe Persique [Research from Kabul to the Persian Gulf]. Paris: J. Peyronnet et Cie. Pp. 285; maps.

      Somewhat limited observations of a French business man who traveled through Southern Afghanistan in 1937.

180   Balsan, Francois
      1972 Exploring the Registan Desert. Asian Affairs 59(2):153-156.

181   Baluch, M. S. K.
      1977 History of Baluch Race and Baluchistan. 2nd ed. London: E. J. Brill. Pp. 298.

182   Barrat, J.
      1972 Some characteristic outlines of Afghanistan. Annales de Geographie 81(444):206-219.

183   Bayderin, Viktor A.
      1961 Za Gindukushem; putevyye zametki [Across the Hindu Kush; Notes of a Journey]. Stalinabad: Tadzhikgosizdat. Pp. 128.

184   Bearth, P.
      1967 Die Ophiolithe der Zone von Zermatt. Bern: Saas Fee.

185   Bellew, Henry Walter
      1874 From the Indus to the Tigris: A Narrative of a Journey through the Countries of Balochistan, Afghanistan, Korassan and Iran, in 1872. London: Trubner and Co., 1874. Pp. vii, 496.

186   Bellew, Henry Walter
      1978 Afghanistan, a Political Mission in 1857, with an Account of the Country and People. London: E.J. Brill, (repr. of 1920 ed.). Pp. xvi, 480; illustrations; appendix.

187   Benava, Abdul Raouf
      1953 Punjwai. Afghanistan 8(3):23-26.

II. GEOGRAPHY

A rambling account of Punjwai's caves, the moat surrounding the ruind city, and the graves of three local poets.

188 Benava, Abdul Raouf
1954 Dawar ou Zamine Dawar [Dawar and Samine Dawar]. Afghanistan 9(4):26-30.

On the region along the Helmand River called Zamine Dawar--its ancient cities, its agriculture, and its people.

189 Bernhardt, P.
1975 Koh-e-Urgun im Afghanischen Hindukusch. Afghanistan Journal 2(4):152.

190 Biddulph, M. A.
1881 The March from the Indus to the Helmand and Back, 1878, 1879. Journal of the Royal United Service Institution 24:613-64.

191 Binkowski, Andraej
1962 Von Taschkent nach Kabul [From Tashkent to Kabul]. Leipzig, Pp. 238.

A translation into German from a travel account in Polish.

192 Blake, Stephen
1979 The Patrimonial-Bureaucratic Empire of the Mughals. Journal of Asian Studies 39(1):77-94.

193 Blanford, H. F.
1881 On the Voles (Arvicolae) of the Himalayas, Tibet and Afghanistan. Journal of the Asiatic Society of Bengal 50(2):88-117.

194 Bochkarev, P.
1953 Afganistan [Afghanistan]. Moscow: Gosudarstvennö izdatel'stvio geograficheskoi literature. Pp. 66; map.

A brief, descriptive survey by a student of Reisner.

195 Boernstein-Bosta, F. and Mandana Baschi
1925 Reisen und Erlebnisse eines deutschen Arztes in Afghanistan. Travels and Experiences of a German Doctor in Afghanistan]. Berlin: Reimar Hobbin. Pp. 176; map.

II. GEOGRAPHY

> The travels of the German doctor took him from Europe into Afghanistan by way of Herat, thence to Kabul--to which town he devoted most of his observations--and then on to India.

196 Bordet, P.
    1972 Le volcanisme recent du Dacht-e-Nawar meridional-Afghanistan central. Revue de Geographie Physique et de Geologie Dynamique 14(4):427-432.

197 Bouillance de Lacoste, Emile Antoine
    J. G. Anderson). London: Sir I. Pitman and Sons. Pp. xxxi, 217.

198 Boutiere, A. and R. Clocchiatti
    1971 Sur les roches pyroclastiques au Nord du Dachte-Nawar-Afghanistan: les quartz et leurs inclusions vitreuses. Bull. Soc. geol. de France (7), 13(3-4):430-438.

199 Bouvat, Lucien
    1912 Un voyage en Afghanistan [A Voyage in Afghanistan]. Revue du Monde Musulman 9:289-291.

> An abridged version of the account of the travels of Muhammad Reza Shirazi in Afghanistan.

200 Breckle, S. W.
    1971 Vegetation in Alpine Regions of Afghanistan. *In* Plant Life of South-West Asia. Edited by P. H. Davis, D. C. Harper and I. C. Hedge. Edinburgh. Pp. 107-116.

201 Breckle, S. W.
    1973 Mikroklimatische Messungen und okologische Beobachtungen in der alpinen Stufe des afghanischen Hindukusch. Botanische Jahrbucher 93:25-55.

202 Breckle, S. W.
    1974 Notes on Alpine and Nival Flora of the Hindu Kush, East Afghanistan. Bot. Notisder 127:278-284.

203 Breckle, S. W.
    1975 Okologische Beobachtungen oberhalb der Waldgrenze des Safed Koh (Ost-Afghanistan). Vegetatio 30:89-97.

204 Breckle, S. W.
    1979 Afghanische Drogen und ihre Stammpflanzen (II). Süßholz. Afghanistan Journal 6(3):87-91. Illustrations.

II. GEOGRAPHY

205 Breckle, S. W. and W. Frey
1974 Die Vegetationsstufen im Zentralen Hindukusch. Afghanistan Journal 1(3):75-80. Photos; maps, figures.

206 Breckle, S. W. and W. Frey
1976 Die hochsten Berge im Zentralen Hindukusch. Afghanistan Journal 3(3):91-100. Photos; maps.

207 Breckle, S. W. and U. Breckle
1977 Erganzende Bemerkungen zu "Honigienen in Afghanistan." Afghanistan Journal 4(1):37-38.

208 Breckle, S. W. and W. Unger
1977 Afghanische Drogen und ihre Stammpflanzen (I). Gummiharze von Umbelliferen. Afghanistan Journal 4(3):86-95. Map; photos; illustrations.

209 Breitenbach, Markus
1981 Im Land der Wilden Reiter: Abenteür bei den Kirghisen. Frankfurt: Fischeer Taschbenbuch Verlag. Pp. 158.

Description of travels among the Kirghiz of Afghanistan. General information based upon passing observations.

210 Broadfoot, J. S. (ed)
1885 Reports on Parts of the Ghilzi, and on some of the Tribes in the Neighbourhood of Ghazni; and on the Route from Ghazni to Dera Ismail Khan by the Ghwalari Pass (written in 1839). Royal Geographical Society Supplementary Papers I(3).

211 Brown, Douglas
1971 Overland to India: A Practical Guide to Getting There Through Istanbul, Turkey, Iran, Afghanistan and West Pakistan, Cheaply and Unhassled. Toronto: New Press. Pp. 149, maps.

Includes a travel guide for motorists in Afghanistan.

212 Bruckl, Karl
1935 Über die Geologie von Badakhschan und Kataghan [The Geology of Badakhshan and Qataghan]. Neüs Jahrbuch für Mineralogie, Abt. B, 74:360-401.

213 Bruggey, J.
1973 Mesozoikum und Alttertiar in Nord-Paktia (SE-Afghanistan). Geologie Jb. 3:3-61.

II. GEOGRAPHY

214   Bucherer, Paul A.
        1975 Die Qala-e-Shah im Munjan-Tal (Afghanistan). Ethnologische Zeitschrift Zurich, 2:113-128.

215   Bucherer, Paul A.
        1975 Trekking uber den Anjuman Pass. Afghanistan Journal 2(2):74-75. Map; photos.

216   Buchroithner, Manfred F.
        1978 Zur Geologie des Afghanischen Pamir. <u>In</u> Groß Pamir. Edited by R. Senarclens de Grancy and R. Kostka Graz, Austria: Akademishe Druckiu Verlag. Pp. 85-118.

217   Buchroithner, Manfred F.
        1979 Literaturbericht regionale Geologie: Progress in the geology of Afghanistan 1972-1978. In Zbl. Geol. Palaont. 1(5/6):328-376.

218   Buchroithner, M. F. and H. Kolmer
        1979 Notes on the Wakhan Formation of the Great Afghan Pamir and the Eastern Hindu Kush. Afghanistan Journal 6(2):54-62. Tables; plates; maps.

219   Buchroithner, M. F. and S. M. Scharbert
        1979 Geochronological Data From the Great Afghan Pamir and the Eastern Hindu Kush. N. Jb. Geol. Palaont. Mh. 8:449-456.

220   Burkner, F. C.
        1976 Afghanistan. Reisefuhrer mit Landeskunde, Mai's Weltfuhrer Nr. 13,(5). Buchenhain vor Munchen.

221   Butcher, George.
        1955 Unbelievable Valley--Bamiyan. Middle East Forum, 2:12-16.

        Impressionistic account of a visit to the site in 1954.

222   Buttiker, W.
        1959 Notizen uber die Vogeljagd in Afghanistan. Z. Jagdwiss. 5:95-105.

223   Caldwell, John Cope
        1968 Let's Visit Afghanistan. New York: John Day Company. Pp. 96.

        A brief description of Afghanistan designed for travellers and elementary schools.

II. GEOGRAPHY

224   Caspani, P. E.
       1947 Picnic Grounds and Archaeology. Afghanistan
          2(2):42-46.

       Lists excursions and walks in the vicinity of Paghman,
       west of Kabul, each featured by the presence of Moslem
       shrines or modern royal villas.

225   Cizancourt, H. de
       1938 Remarque sur la structure de l'Hindou-Kouch [Note on
          the Structure of the Hindu Kush]. Bulletin de la
          Société Géologique de France, sér. 5,7:377-400; biblio-
          graphy.

       Reliable technical description from personal observations
       by the author and his associates. Not, however, a
       definitive statement on this subject.

226   Clark, Richard J.
       1969 Report on a Collection of Amphibians and Reptiles
          From Afghanistan. San Francisco: Proceedings of the
          California Academy of Sciences 36(10):279-315.

227   Clerk, C.
       1861 Notes in Persia, Khorassan, and Afghanistan.
          Journal of the Royal Geographical Society 31:37-64.

228   Codrington, K. de B.
       1944 A Geographical Introduction to the History of
          Central Asia. Geographical Journal 104(1/2):27-40;
          (3/4):73-91; map.

       Part I is a verbose paper on the influence of geography on
       history--through trade, art and nomadic movements. There
       is more of history than geography. Part II is again more
       historical than geographical--particularly there is an
       account of the Greek Kings of Bactria and their
       successors.

229   Conolly, Arthur
       1838 Journey to the North of India, Overland from England
          through Russia, Persia, and Afghanistan. London. Pp.
          834.

       This is the second edition of a useful work which contains
       itineraries and descriptions of the routes followed over
       hundreds of miles.

II. GEOGRAPHY

230 Conolly, Arthur
1841 Journal Kept While Travelling in Seistan. Journal of Asiatic Society of Bengal, 10:319-40.

231 Conolly, E.
1840 Sketch of the Physical Geography of Seistan. Journal of the Asiatic Society of Bengal, 9:924-37.

232 Cressey, George B.
1960 Crossroads: Land and Life in Southwest Asia. Chicago: J. B. Lippincott Company. Pp. 593; bibliographies; glossary; index; many unnumbered illustrations; tables; charts.

Chapter 17, pages 545 through 582 deal with the transport system, water resources, and human environment of Afghanistan, and pages 136 through 139 with the Helmand River.

233 Curzon, George Nathaniel
1895 A Recent Journey in Afghanistan. London: W. Clowes and Sons, Ltd. Pp. 12.

Permanent record of a lecture by the British scholar and diplomat.

234 Curzon, George Nathaniel
1978 The Pamirs and the Source of the Oxus. Revised and reprinted from "The Geographical Journal" for July, August, and September, 1896. Nachdruck durch Kraus Reprint, Nendeln/Liechtenstein. Pp. 84.

235 De Baer, Oliver R.
1956 The Cambridge Expedition to Afghanistan, 1955. Royal Central Asian Journal 43:121-125.

Summary account of the travels of a group of students in the province of Badakhshan. See item 236.

236 De Baer, Oliver R.
1957 Afghan Interlude. London: Chatto & Windus. Pp. 223.

The light-hearted account of a tour by automobile from England to Afghanistan, including the "great circle" route, by four Cambridge undergraduates.

237 De Croze, J. Berjane
1946 Images de route vers Mazar-i-Sharif [Pictures of the Road to Mazar-i Sharif]. Afghanistan 1(4):22-29.

II. GEOGRAPHY

>Transitory and precious impression of landscapes by night and day.

238 De Croze, J. Berjane
>1947 Dreaming of Kabul. Afghanistan 2(3):12-16.

>Fugitive memories of Kabul as it is and as the author would like to see it.

239 Delapraz, Alan and Micheline Delapraz.
>1964 Afghanistan. Neuchâtel: Avanti Club. Pp. 127.

>An historical sketch, followed by an account of travels, beautifully illustrated with color photographs and drawings. Also, separate editions in French and German.

240 Department of Mineral Exploration
>1971 Lapis lazuli of Afghanistan. Kabul: Royal Afghan Ministry of Mines and Industries. Pp. 6.

241 Desio, A.
>1964 Tectonic position of central Badakhshan 1:2000,000 auf: DESIO et al. (1964): Geological map of central Badakhshan (Afghanistan). Institute of Geology, University of Milan, Italy.

242 Desio, A., E. Martina, and G. Pasquare
>1964 On the geology of central Badakhshan. Quart. Journ. Geol. Soc. London: Pp. 120, 127-151.

243 Desio, A., E. Tangiorgi, and G. Ferrara.
>1964 On the geological age of some granites of the Karakorum, Hindu Kush and Badakhshan (central Asia). XXII Int. Congr. India, 1964, Part XI, proc. sect. 11.

244 Desio, A.
>1975 Geology of Central Badakhshan (North-East Afghanistan) and Surrounding Countries. Italian Expeditions to the Karakorum (K2) and Hindu Kush, scientific reports 3(3). Leiden: E.J. Brill. Pp. 645.

245 Dietrich, Brandenburg
>1978 Herat: Eine Timuridische Hauptstadt [Herat: A Timurid Capital]. Graz, Austria: Akademische Druck. Verlag. Pp. 135.

II. GEOGRAPHY

An interesting description with illustrations of Herati architecture, ornamental architecture, and culture history. Based on data gathered during 1970-75.

246   Diver, Katherine Helen Maud
         1935 Kabul to Kandahar. London: P. Davies. Pp. 191.

247   Doerrer, I., W. Gaebe, G. Hoehl, and C. Jentsch
         1980 Zur Geographie der länelichen siedlungen in afghanistan [On the Geography of Land Settlements in Afghanistan]. Mannheim: Geographisches Institute der Universität Mannheim.

248   Dor, Remy
         1977 Orature du Nord-Est Afghan II. Les Ozbek du Badakhchan. In Turcica, Revue d'etudes Turques 9(1):30-97. (Paris, Strasbourg).

249   Douglas, William O.
         1952 Beyond the High Himalayas. New York: Doubleday & Co. Pp. 352.

Includes accounts of two visits to Afghanistan, the longer one across the country by automobile.

250   Drummond (Captain)
         1841 On the Mines and Mineral Resources of Northern Afghanistan. Journal of the Asiatic Society of Bengal 10:74-93.

251   Dunin, M. S.
         1952 Iz Kabula v Szhelalabad [From Kabul to Jalalabad]. Vokrug Sveta (12):39-43. Moscow.

252   Dunin, M. S.
         1952 Po Afganistanu, Pakistanu, Inddi [To Afghanistan, Pakistan, and India]. Moscow: Gosudarstvennoe izdatel'stvo geograficheskoi literatury. Pp. 382; maps.

A second edition was published in 1954.

253   Dunsheath, J. and E. Baoillie
         1961 Afghan Quest. London: George G. Harrup & Co. Ltd. Pp. 236.

Two intrepid British women climb mountains and collect botanical specimens to the astonishment of the rural Afghans.

II. GEOGRAPHY

254   Durrieu, M. G.
        1973 Les champignons phytopathogenes du centre de l'Afghanistan. Aspects biogeographiques. Comptes rendues Academie des Sciences naturale Paris 276, Series D: 541-544.

255   Efa, Francois
        1972 Untersuchungen an Echinococcus granulosus (Batsch, 1786) aus Afghanistan. Unpublished Ph.D. Dissertation. University of Bonn.

256   Eiselin, Max
        1963 Wilder Hindukusch, Erlebnisse in Afghanistan [The Wild Hindu Kush, Experiences in Afghanistan]. Zurich: Orell Füssii. Pp. 185; 2 maps; illus. and plates.

257   Eisner, Curt and Clas M. Naumann
        1980 Beitrag zur Okologie and Taxonomie der afghanischen Parnassiidä (Lepidoptera). In Zoologische Verhandelingen uitgegeven door het Rijksmuseum von Natuurlijke Historie te Leiden. Leiden: Brill, 178:35

258   Emmanuel, W. F.
        1939 Some Impressions of Swat and Afghanistan. Journal of the Royal Central Asian Society 26, pt. II, 195-213; maps.

        Descriptive mainly of Northern India and Afghanistan, with some references to the people and the political and economic situation. The material on Afghanistan begins on page 202.

259   English, Paul
        1973 The Traditional City of Herat, Afghanistan. In From Medina to Metropolis Heritage and Change in the Near Eastern City. Edited by Carl L. Brown. Princeton, N.J.: The Darwin Press. Pp. 73-90.

260   Falconer, H.
        1851 Description of the Asa-foetida Plant of Central Asia. Trans. Linn. Soc. Bot. 20:285-291.

261   Farsan, Nur Mohammed
        1972 Stratigraphische und Palägeographische Stellung der Khenjan-serie und Deren Pelecypoden (Trias, Afghanistan). Unpublished Ph.D. Dissertation. University of Bonn.

II. GEOGRAPHY

262   Fedorova, T. I.
       1971 Shahrhoi Tajikiston. [Cities of Tajikiston].
           Dushanbe: Irfon. Pp. 48.

       A brief historical sketch of the major towns and cities of
       Tajikistan along with a brief geographical and historical
       account. In Tajiki.

263   Ferrier, J. P.
       1857 Caravan Journeys and Wanderings in Persia,
           Afghanistan, Turkistan, and Beloochistan; With
           Historical Notices of the Countries Lying Between Russia
           and India. Translated by Captain William Jesse.
           London: John Murray. Pp. xxii, 534; map.

       The French officer, General Ferrier, came out to this part
       of the world to be Adjutant-General to the Persian Army.
       Traveling extensively from Iran across Afghanistan and
       Central Asia into India he developed a masterly knowledge
       of the history, geography, and languages of the area. The
       present work is valuable for its description of remote
       regions of Afghanistan, such as the Hazara and Ghur areas
       and the Helmand Valley.

264   Fischer, D.
       1970 Waldverbreitung im ostlichen Afghanistan. Afghan-
           ische Studien 2. Meisenheim am Glan.

265   Flohn, H.
       1969 Zum Klima und Wasserhaushalt des Hindukuschs und der
           benachbarten Hochgebirge. Erdkunde 23:205-215.

266   Flohn, H.
       1970 Beitrage zur Meteorologie des Himalaya. Khumbu
           Himal 7(2):25-47.

267   Fly, C. L.
       1950-1956 Reports and Soil Maps of Kandahar and other
           parts of Afghanistan. Boise, Idaho: Land Development
           Division, Morrison-Knudsen Afghanistan, Inc.

268   Forbes, F.
       1844 Route from Turbat Haidari in Khorasan to the river
           Heri Rud, on the borders of Sistan. Journal of the
           Royal Geographical Society 14:145-92.

269   Forbes, Rosita
       1937 Forbidden Journey. Kabul to Samarqand. London:
           Cornell and Co. Pp. xii, 290; map.

II. GEOGRAPHY

270 Forster, George
    1970 A Journey from Bengal to England; through the northern parts of India, Kashmire, Afghanistan, and Persia, and into Russia by the Caspain Sea. Lahore: Patialal Languages Department, (2 volumes).

A travel account by the author during mid-nineteenth century. Compiled from previously unpublished material.

271 Forrest, George W. (ed)
    1906 Selections from the Travels and Journals Preserved in the Bombay Secretariat. Bombay: Government Central Press. Pp. xxviii, 304.

Of the thirteen documents printed in this volume, eight are directly concerned with Afghanistan and with the period between 1830 and 1850.

272 Fostner, Ulrich
    1971 Geochemische und Sedimentpetrographische Untersuchungen and den Endseen und an Deren Zuflussen in Afghanistan. Unpublished Ph.D. Dissertation. University of Heidelberg.

273 Fox, Ernest F.
    1937-1938 Travels in Afghanistan. New York: The Macmillan Company. Pp. xxiv, 285; map.

Travels of an American geologist, searching for mineral deposits, into remote northeastern and south central Afghanistan.

274 Fox, John, as told to Roland Goodchild
    1958 Afghan Adventure. London: Robert Hale Ltd. Pp. 190.

A tale of high adventure in the year 1945. A special force, traveling by caravan, tracks down smugglers of war material in western Pakistan and at Kabul.

275 Fraser-Tytler, Sir W. Kerr
    1942 Afghanistan: A Brief Description. Journal of the Royal Central Asian Society 29:165-175.

By a former British officer and diplomat who spent thirty years in the general area and left Kabul in 1941, vacating his post as British Minister. The article is a succinct account of the topography, principal routes and population elements of Afghanistan--with the people grouped into

II. GEOGRAPHY

dwellers in Afghan Turkistan, within the Hindu Kush, and in Southern and Eastern Afghanistan.

276 Fraser-Tytler, Sir W. Kerr
  1942 A Great North Road. Journal of the Royal Central Asian Society 29, Pt. II:129-135; sketch map.

Details the historical routes across the Hindu Kush, lists efforts to create roads in modern times and describes the building of the motor road across the Shibar Pass.

277 Freitag, H.
  1971 Die naturliche Vegetation Afghanistans. Beitrage zur Flora und Vegetation Afghanistans I. Vegetatio 22:285-344.

278 Frey, W.
  1967 Zur Vegetation des Zentralen Afghanischen Hindukusch. In Zwischen Munjan und Bashgal I. Edited by W. Frey. Pp. 17-46, 51-56. Goppingen.

279 Frey, W.
  1974 Die Lebermoose des Iran und Afghanistans. The Bryologist 77:48-56.

280 Frey, W., W. Probst and A. Shaw
  1976 Die Vegetation des Jokham-Tals im Zentralen Afghanischen Hindukusch. Afghanistan Journal 3(1):16-21. Maps; color photos.

281 Frey, W. and W. Probst
  1978 Vegetation und Flora des Zentralen Hindukus (Afghanistan). Beihefte zum Tubinger Atlas des Vorderen Orients. Reihe A, Nr. 3. Weisbaden: Dr. Ludwig Reichert-Verlag. Pp. 126.

282 Furon, Raymond
  1927 L'Hindou-Kouch et la Kaboulistan. Contribution a l'étude géologique et géomorphogénique de l'Afghanistan [The Hindu Kush and Kabulistan. A Contribution to the Geological and Geomorphogenical Study of Afghanistan]. Paris: Albert Blanchard. Pp. 169; maps.

The reflection of research in the field, made in the vicinity of Kabul--here called Kabulistan--and in one section of the Hindu Kush.

II. GEOGRAPHY

283 Furon, Raymond
1941 Géologie du Plateau Iranien (Perse-Afghanistan-Baloutchistan) [Geology of the Iranian Plateu (Persia-Afghanistan-Baluchistan)]. Mémoires du Muséum National d'Histoire Naturelle, n.s. 7, p. 2, 177-414; geological map; bibliography. (Paris).

This lengthy article is based upon nearly a score of years of field work and study on the subject. Certainly the most important work in the field and accompanied by a list of over 400 titles in the field as well as the first geological map in the country. Unfortunately in a publication difficult to find.

284 Furon, Raymond and Louis-Felicien Rosset
1952 Contribution a l'étude de trias en Afghanistan [Contribution to the Study of the Triassic in Afghanistan]. Afghanistan 7(2):19-28.

Descriptions of triassic specimens.

285 Furon, Raymond and Louis-Felicien Rosset
1954 L'Afghanistan et les milieux paléontologiques mondizus [Afghanisan and the World Paleontoligcal Contexts]. Afghanistan 9(4):48-50.

A summary of the completed stratigraphic series in Northern Afghanistan.

286 Gabert, G.
1962 Bericht zur Ubersichtskartierung des Registan-E und N-Randes. Kabul (unveroff. Bericht).

287 Gabriel, Alfons
1939 Aus den Einsamkeiten Irans; Dritte Forschungsfahrt durch die Wüste Lut und Persisch-Balocistan mit einer Reise durch üd-Afghanistan [From the Solitudes of Iran; Third Expedition Through the Lut Desert and Persian Baluchistan, with a Journey through Southern Afghanistan]. Stuttgart: Strecker und Schroder. Pp. xv, 186.

The author's journey through southern Afghanistan. with observations of the land, the people and the climate (pages 153-168). Information is rather heavily interlarded with poetic flights.

II. GEOGRAPHY

288   Gaisler, J.
    1975 Comparative ecological notes on Afghan Rodents. Monographiä Biologicä 28:59-73.

289   Galkin, M.
    1954 Po dorogam Afganistana [Along the Roads of Afghanistan]. Vokrug Sveta (5):24-28 (6):34-37. Moscow.

290   Ganns, O.
    1964 Zur geologischen Geschicte der Belutschistan - Indus - Geosynklinale. Geology Jb. 82.

291   Geerken, Hartmut
    1978 Zur Mykologie Afghanistans. Afghanistan Journal 5(1):6-8.

292   General Atlas of Afghanistan
    n.d. Atlas general de l'Afghanistan. Tehran: Geographic and Drafting Institute. Pp. 201.

293   Gerber, Alfred
    1942 Afghanische Mosaike, Erlebnisse im verschlossenen Land [Afghan Mosaics, Experiences in a Locked Land]. Braunschweig: G. Wenzel. Pp. 150; map.

294   Gevemeyer, Jan-Heeren, Wolfgang Holzwarth, and Hans G. Kippenberg
    1975 Jurm: Berich aus einer Afghanischen Stadt [Jurm: A Report from an Afghan Town]. Mardom Nameh 1:14-25.

295   Gilbert, O., D. Jamieson, H. Lister, and A. Pendlington
    1969 Regime of an Afghan Glacier. Journal of Glaciology 8:51-65.

296   Gilli, A.
    1969 Afghanische Pflanzengesellschaften, I. Vegetatio 16:307-375. (Part II. Vegetatio 23:199-234, 1976).

297   Gobl, Robert
    1976 Die Tonbullen vom Tacht-e Suleiman. Ein Neitrag zur spatsasani-dischen Sphragistik (Deutsches Archaologisches Institut. Abteilung Tehran. Tacht-e Suleiman, Ergebnisse der Ausgrabungen. Herasugegeben von Rudolf Maumann). Berlin: Deitrich Reimer Verlag. Pp. 176; plates.

II. GEOGRAPHY

298 Goldsmid, F. J.
 1873 Journey from Bandar Abbas to Mash-had by Sistan, with some account of the last named province. Journal of the Royal Geographical Society 43:65-83.

299 Goldsmid, F. J.
 1875 On Journeys between Herat and Khiva. Journal of the United Services Institution 19:1-21.

300 Gonsior, Bernhard
 1979 Untersuchung von Spektralchemogrammen im Bereich der Mykologie Afghanistans. Afghanistan Journal 6(3):92-94.

301 Gordon, T. E.
 1876 The Watershed of Central Asia, East and West. Journal of the Royal Society 46:381-96.

 Discusses the Amu basin as the main agricultural area of Central Asia.

302 Gratzl, K. (ed)
 1972 Hindukusch--Oesterreichische Forschungsepedition in den Wakhan 1970 [Austrian Research Expedition in the Wakhan, 1970]. Graz, Austria: Akademische Druck. Verlag. Pp. 148.

303 Gratzl, K. (ed)
 1977 Grosser Pamir--Österreichische Forschungsunternehmen 1975 in den Wakhan-Pamir, Afghanistan [Greater Pamir--Austrian Research Expedition in Wakhan-Pamir, Afghanistan, 1975]. Graz, Austria: Akademische Druck. Verlag. Pp. 412.

304 Grey-Wilson, C.
 1974 Some Notes on the Flora of Iran and Afghanistan. Kew Bulletin 29:19-81.

305 Griffith, Dr.
 1841 Extracts from a Report on Subjects Connected with Afghanistan. Journal of the Asiatic Society of Bengal 10:977-1007.

306 Griffith, Dr.
 1842 Tables of Barometrical and Thermometrical Observations, made in Afghanistan, Upper Scinde, and Kutch Gundava, during the years 1839-40. Journal of the Asiatic Society of Bengal 11:49-90.

II. GEOGRAPHY

307   Grodekov, N. I. (Grodekoff, N.)
       1880 Itinéraire dans le Turkestan Afghan [Itinerary in Afghan Turkistan]. Bulletin de la Société de Géographie, sér. 6(20):1240-141. Paris.

       A version, freely rendered into French from a Russian account of the difficulties of this Russian General Staff Offier in attempting to overcome local resistance to travel in the area in question. Includes an account of strategic considerations of the region. See also no. 465.

308   Grötzbach, Erwin
       Kulturgeographische Wandel in Norodost-Afghanistan seit dem 19. Jahrhundert. Afghanische Studien nr. 4. Meisenheim am Glan: Anton Hain Verlag.

309   Grötzbach, Erwin
       1964 Vorlaufiger Bericht uber die "Munchner Hindukusch-Kundfahrt 1963". Erde 95:291-298.

310   Grötzbach, E., and C. Rathjens
       19696 Die heutige und die jungpleistozane Vergletscherung des Afghanischen Hindukusch. Zeitschrift für Geomorphologie, sppl. 8:58-75.

311   Grötzbach, Erwin
       1972 Kulturgeographischer Wandel in Nordost-Afghanistan seit dem 19. Jahrhundert. Meisenheim: Verlag. pp. 302.

312   Grötzbach, Erwin
       1974 Anardarrah-das verborgen "Tal der Granatapfel." Afghanistan Journal 1(4):114-117. Maps; photos.

313   Grötzbach, E. (ed)
       1975 Aktuelle Probleme der Regionalentwicklung und Stadtegeogrphie Afghanistans. Afghanische Studien 14:250.

314   Grötzbach, Erwin
       1975 Die gesamtwirtschaftlichen Funktionen von Gebirgen am Beispiel Afghanistans. In Entwicklungsproblem in Gergregionen 1(3):37-39.

315   Grötzbach, Erwin
       1975 Probleme der Stadtentwicklung and Stadtplanung in Afghanistan. Zeitschrift der Technisch Universitat Hannover 2(1):1-14.

II. GEOGRAPHY

316   Grötzbach, Erwin
       1975 Zur jungen Entwicklung Afghanischer Provinzstadte. Ghazni und Mazar-i-Sharif als Beispiele. Geographische Rundschaue 10:416-424.

317   Grötzbach, Erwin (ed)
       1976 Aktuelle Probleme der Regionalentwicklung und Stadtgeographie Afghanistans [Current Problems of Regional Development and Urban Geography of Afghanistan]. Afghanische Studien. Meisenheim am Glan: Verlag Anton Hain.

318   Grötzbach, W.
       1965 Landschaft und Mensch im Afghanischen Hindukusch. Der Bergsteiger 32:529-539.

319   Gubanov, I. A., V. N. Pavlov, and M. C. Younos
       1975 Notes on rare species of Afghanistan. (Russian) Bjull. Mosk. Obsch. Ispit. Prirod., Otd. Biol. 80(6):82-91.

320   Gurevich, Aleksandr Mikhailovich
       1929 Afganistan [Afghanistan]. Moscow: Izdatel'stvo TSK MOPR SSSR. Pp. 60; map; bibliography.

321   Gzerski, G.
       1944 Lapis-lasuli in Badakhshan; unveroff. Rapport No. 10 des afghan. Minenministeriums, Kabul.

322   Hackin, Joseph
       1934 In Persia and Afghanistan with the Citroen Trans-Asiatic Expedition. Geographical Journal 83:353-363; map.

323   Haekel, Ingeborg (ed)
       1938 Botanische Ergebnisse der deutschen Hindukuschexpedition 1935 [Botanical Results of the German Expeditions of 1935 to the Hindu Kush]. Berlin: Verlag des Repertoriums. Pp. v; plates; bibliographies.

324   Hafisi, A. S. and N. Osmani
       1976 Geologische Entwicklung des Gebietes von Panjwai bei Kanadahar. Afghanistan Journal 3(2):70-74.

II. GEOGRAPHY

325   Hahn, Helmut
    1964 Die stadt Kabul (Afghanistan) und ihr Umland. I. Gestaltwandel einer orientalischen Stadt [The City of Kabul (Afghanistan) and its Vicinity]. I. The Changing Form of an Oriental City]. Bonn: Fer. Dümmlers Verlag. Pp. 88; bibliogaphy: 3 city plans.

326   Hahn, Helmut
    1972 Wachstumsablaufe in einer Orientalischen Stadt am Beispiel von Kabul/Afghanistan. Erdkund 26:16-32.

327   Hamilton, Angus
    1906 Afghanistan. London: William Heinemann. Pp. xxi, 562; map; appendices.

Much of the material within the volume falls outside the scope of the title for several chapters deal with Russian Turkistan and another with Sistan, which the author saw while a member of the survey mission of Sir Henry MacMahon. However, the work contains descriptions of the Murghab Valley, Herat, Qandahar and Kabul, and reflects a tremendous energy in the avid collection of material on the government, army, trade, and foreign relations--much of it presented in appendices.

328   Hanstein, Otfried von
    1928 Im Wilden Afghanistan, ein Land der Zukunst, Reisen, Abenteur und Forschungen [In Wild Afghanistan, a Land of the Future, Travel, Adventure and Research]. Leipzig: Deutsche Buchwerkstatten. Pp. 176; map.

329   Hashmat, A.
    1948 Notes of a Journey. Afghanistan 3(4):30-43.

An account, in diary form, by the Afghan who accompanied a Danish expedition into Nuristan and north to Fayzabad. Scattered material on the Nuri tribes.

330   Hasse, D.
    1961 Vorlaufiger Bericht uber eine Hindukuschkundfaht
    1960. Erde 92:59-70.

331   Hassinger, Jerry D.
    1968 Introduction to the Mammal Survey of the 1965 Street Expedition to Afghanistan. Chicago: Field Museum of Natural History, Fieldiana: Zoology 55(1):81.

II. GEOGRAPHY

- 332 Hassinger, Jerry D.
    1973 A Survey of the Mammals of Afghanistan, Resulting From the 1965 Street Expedition (excluding bats). Chicago Field Museum of Natural History, Fieldiana: Zoology, 60:xi, 195.

- 333 Hautsluoma, J. E. and V. Kasman
    1975 Description of Peace Corps Volunteer's Experience in Afghanistan. Topics in Culture Learning 3:79-96. Honolulu: East-West Center.

- 334 Havelka, Jan
    1961 Afghanistan tajuplnosti zbaveny [Mysterious, Entertaining Afghanistan]. Prague: Lidova demokracie.

- 335 Hay, William R.
    1933 Demarcation of the Indo-Afghan Boundary in the Vicinity of Aramdu. Geographical Journal 82:351-354; maps.

    The paper describes briefly the work of a Commission to settle the Afghan-Indian dispute over the boundary to Dokalim. Major Hay was the British member of the Commission. A technical note by Captain D. R. Crone, of the Royal Engineers, folows the article proper.

- 336 Hay, William R.
    1936 Band-i-Amir. Geographical Journal 87:348-350.

    Popular description of the five, sparkling blue lakes, together with local legends regarding their formation. The lakes are precisely located by latitude and longitude.

- 337 Hay, William R.
    1840 Notes on the Wild Sheep of the Hindoo Koosh, and a species of Cicada. Journal of the Asiatic Society of Bengal 9:440-44.

- 338 Hayden, H. H.
    1911 The Geology of Northern Afghanistan. Memoirs of the Geological Survey of India 39:1-96. Calcutta.

    Deals with the region in which the Hindu Kush and the Kuh-i Baba ranges come together. Drawings, photographs and a colored geological map at the scale of 1:2,027,520.

II. GEOGRAPHY

339 Hayward, G. S. W.
1868-69 Route from Jellalabad to Yarkand through Chitral, Badakhshan, and Pamir Steppe, given by Mahamed Amin of Yarkand. Proceedings of the Royal Geographical Society 13:122-30.

340 Hedge, I. C. and P. Wendelbo
1970 Some Remarks on Endemism in Afghanistan. Israel Journal of Botany 19:401-417.

341 Hekmat, Alim
1976 Mit schwarzem Zelen durch Afghanistan. Göttingen: W. Fischer-Verlag. Pp. 144; photos.

342 Herberg, Werner
1976 Topographische Feldarbeiten in Ghor. Bericht uber Forschung-sarbeiten zum Problem Jam Ferozkoh. Afghanistan Journal 3(2):57-69.

343 Herbordt, O.
1926 Die Erzlagerstatten Afghanitan [Afghanistan as a Mining Country]. Internationale Bergwirschaft 2. Leipzig, August-September.

344 Herbst, Dean Finley
1969 Flight to Afghanistan. Austin: Steck-Vaugh. Pp. 260.

A travel description and experiences in Afghanistan.

345 Herrmann, G.
1968 Lapis lazuli: The Early Phases of its Trade. Iraq 30:1, 21-57.

346 Hess, A.
1966 Geologie des Begietes Kalat-Ghilzai und seine Stellung im sudostafghanischen Gebirgsbau.

347 Holdich, Thomas Hungerford
1881 Geographical Results of the Afghan Campaign. Proceedings of the Royal Geographical Society, New Series, 3:65-84.

348 Holdich, Thomas Hungerford
1884 Notes on Recent Surveys on the Afghan Border. Journal of the Royal United Service Institution 28:553-66.

II. GEOGRAPHY

349   Holdich, Thomas Hungerford
        1885 Afghan Boundary Commission; Geograhical Notes. Proceedings of the Royal Geographical Society, n.s. 7:39-44, 160-166, 273-292, map.

        Parts I and II are a description of the country from Quetta to Herat, with special attention to the water supply. Part III is preceded by some historical remarks on the Commission by General J. T. Walker, and contains a description of a Sarik Turkoman camp. A discussion of the paper, giving some information on the politico-geographical situation, begins on page 284.

350   Holdich, Thomas Hungerford
        1900 An Orographic Map of Afghanistan and Baluchistan. Geographical Journal 16:527-531; folding map, scale 1" - 96 miles, opposite p. 596.

        The brief article is a technical description of the principal physical features of the area.

351   Holdich, Thomas Hungerford
        1910 The Gates of India, Being an Historical Narrative. With Maps. London: Macmillan and Co. Pp. xvi, 555; maps.

        Chapters 3 through 17 contain an extended history of the explorations of Afghanistan.

352   Howland, Felix
        1940 Afghanistan Has no Frontiers. Asia 40:633-635.

353   Howland, Felix
        1940 Crossing the Hindu Kush. Geographical Review 30:272-278; 2 small maps.

        Describes the roads and trails which traverse the Hindu Kush, with particular attention to the motor road, ordered by King Mohammed Nadir and completed in 1933. The pass on this road is variously referred to as Shibar or Ghilan and is at 9,800 feet.

354   Humlum, Johannes
        1950 Pirsada; Rejser i Indien og Afghanistan [Pirzada; Journey to India and Afghanistan]. Copenhagen: Gyldendalske boghandel. Nordisk forlag. Pp. 211; maps.

II. GEOGRAPHY

355   Humlum, Johannes
      1959 La géographie de l'Afghanistan [The Geography of
      Afghanistan]. Copenhagen: Gyldenal. Pp. 421; 349
      illustrations; tables; maps; bibliography; index.

      An extremely valuable and reliable work which ranges far
      beyond its title, including material on farming practices,
      ethnic groups, political structure, and numerous other
      subjects.

356   Hunter, Edward
      1959 The Past Present. London: Hodder and Stoughton.
      Pp. 352.

      The record of a year in Afghanistan with travel notes and
      personal judgments on "an inflammable area." Crudely
      biased and impressionistic.

357   Huntington, Ellsworth
      1909 The Afghan Borderland: Part I, The Russian
      Frontier. Part II, The Persian Frontier. National Geo-
      graphical Magazine 20:788-799; 866-876.

      Relation of a journey by the author in 1903 and 1904 along
      the northwestern and western frontiers of Afghanistan.
      The first section deals with the Russian boundary and the
      second part with the frontier with Persia. Fairly
      specific material on geographical and strategic aspects.

358   Hussein, Mia
      1954 Merve Rud. Afghanistan 9(3):8-17; (4):19-25.

      Description of the city and its ruins, and of the cities
      which once surrounded it, with a list of their famous
      scholars and poets.

359   Hutton, T.
      1840 Wool and Woollen Manufacturers of Khorassan. Jour-
      nal of the Asiatic Society of Bengal 9:327-34.

360   Hutton, T.
      1842 On the Wool of the Bactrian, or Two-Humped Camel
      (Camelus Bactrian). Journal of the Asiatic Society of
      Bengal 11:1182-87.

361   Hutton, T.
      1845 Rough Notes on the Zoology of Candahar and the
      Neighbouring Districts. Journal of the Asiatic Society
      of Bengal 14:340-56.

II. GEOGRAPHY

362 Hutton, T.
    1847 Rough Notes on the Ornithography of Candahar and its Neighbourhood. Journal of the Asiatic Society of Bengal 16:775-94.

363 Huwyler, Edwin
    1977 Der Steinbock in der Vorstellungswelt des Mungan-Tals (Nordost-Afghanistan). Lizentiatsarbeit am Ethnolog. Seminar der Universität Basel. Pp. 86.

364 Huwyler, E. and I. V. Moos
    1975 Bemerkungen zum Steinbockmotiv im oberen Kokcha- und im Munjantal (Afghanistan). Ethnologische Zeitschrift Zurich 2:129-135.

365 Iavorskii, I. L.
    1882-1883 Puteshestvie russkogo posol'stva po Avganistanau i Bukharskomu Khanstvo v 1878-1879 [Travels of a Russian Embassy in Afghanistan and the Khanate of the Bokhara People in 1878-1879]. 2 vols. St. Petersburg.

    An interesting document which, in spite of its comprehensive title is primarily concerned with Afghanistan.

366 Iran, Afganistan i Sin'tszian (Zap-Kitai): Politiko-ekonomiches kie ocherki
    1936 Pod redaktsiei V. Petrina (Iran) Prof. I. M. Reisnera (Afganistan) i Prof. P. M. Fesenko (Sin'tszian) S prilozheniem dvukh kart [Tran. Afghanistan and Sinkiang (Western China) (Politico-Economic Outlines) Edited by V. Petrin (Iran) Prof. I. M. Reisner (Afghanistan) and Prof. P.M. Fesenko (Sinkiang). With Two Maps]. Moscow: Gosundarstvennoe Sotsial'no-ekonomicheskoe izdatel'stvo. Pp. 400; two folding maps; bibliographies.

367 Irwin, Lieutenant
    1840 Memoir of the Climate, Soil, Produce, and Husbandry of Afghanistan and the Neighbouring Countries. Journal of the Asiatic Society of Bengal 9:33-65; 189-97.

368 Iven, H. E.
    1933 Das Klima von Kabul [The Climate of Kabul]. Breslau: F. Hirt. Pp. 74.

II. GEOGRAPHY

>Invaluable study based on precise observations taken at Kabul from 1924 until 1932 and dealing with rainfall, humidity, temperatures, winds, overcasts, etc. Seventeen tables and comparison with climatic conditions in neighboring areas.

369 Iven, Walther
1935 Vom Pandshir zum Pandsch. Bericht über eine Forschungreise im Hindukusch und in Nordost-Afghanistan [From Pandshir to Pandsh. Report of a Voyage of Discovery in the Hindu Kush and in Northeastern Afghanistan]. Petermanns Geographische Mitteilunger 81:113-117, 157-161; map.

>In 1932 the German author and two companions set out from Kabul to follow up the valley of the Panjshir River. Crossing the Hindu Kush they went into Badakhshan and then returned to Kabul by a different pass across the Hindu Kush. Acute observations on geography, geology and social life and the 1:500,000 map contains corrections of earlier ones.

370 James, Ben
1934 The Secret Kingdom: An Afghan Journey. New York: Reynal and Hitchcock. Pp. 295.

>A young American writer and adventurer penetrated a remote land and emerges with general observations, primarily relating to the political scene and atmosphere. A London edition of a year later is entitled Afghan Journey.

371 Jakel, K.
1972 Funftausend Jahre Gaschichte auf dem Boden des Landes. In Afghanistan; Natur, Geschichte und Kultur, Staat, Gesellschaft und Wirtschaft. Edited by W. Kraus. Tübengen: Erdman. Pp. 95-125.

372 Jentsch, Christoph
1971 Das Namadentum in Afghanistan: Eine Geographische Untersuchung zu Lebens- und Wirtschaftsformen im Asiatischen Trockengebiet. Unpublished Ph.D. Dissertation. Saarbrucken University.

373 Jentsch, C.
1977 Die afghanische Zentralroute. Afghanistan Journal 4(1):9-19; maps; photos.

II. GEOGRAPHY

374 Jones, Paul S.
1956 Afghanistan Venture. San Antonio: The Naylor Company. Pp. 454; index.

Sub-titled, "Discovering the Afghan people-the life, contacts and adventures of an American Civil Engineer during his two year sojourn in the Kingdom of Afghanistan." The author was engaged in the construction of dams on the Helmand river.

375 Jung, Chris L.
1972 Some Observations on the Patterns and Processes of Rural-Urban Migration to Kabul. New York: Afghanistan Council, the Asia Society. Occasional paper no. 2. Pp. 13.

Examines the effect of a significant influx of peasants who are moving to Kabul with aspirations of economic gain.

376 Kaever, M.
1970 Die alttertiaren Großforaminiferen Sudost-Afghanistan. Forsch. Geol. Paleont., 16/17.

377 Karutz, R.
1911 Unter Kirgisen und Turkmenen.

378 Kasim, Jan Mohd.
1935 Aryans in the East. Boston: Meador Publishing Co. Pp. 91; map.

Discusses the historical, geographical, social and political events of the past and present Aryan land of Asia--Afghanistan.

379 Katrak, Sorab K. H.
1929 Through Amanullah's Afghanistan. A Book of Travel. Karachi: D.N. Patel. Pp. xxxiv, 145; bibliography.

An Indian commercial traveler puts together an account of progress under King Amanullah and of the inconveniences and trials of travel. Includes a limited bibliography and the full text of the Afghan-British Treaty of November 22, 1921.

380 Kaye, E.
1879 The Mountain Passes leading to the Valley of Bamian. Proceedings of the Royal Geographical Society (New Series I:244-59).

II. GEOGRAPHY

381   Kessel, Joseph, Karl Flinker, and Max Klimburg
      1959 Legende Afghanistan [Legendary Afghanistan]. Köln:
      M. Dumont Schauberg. Pp. 55; 163 ilus.; map.

Another edition of Kessel 1959.

382   Khalil, Muhammad Ibrahim
      1960 Mazarat-i shahr Kabul [Tombs of the City of Kabul].
      Kabul: Doulati matba'eh. Pp. 268. (1339 A.H.)

383   Khalil, Afghan
      1930-1931 Asar-i Harat [Monuments of Herat]. 3 vols.
      Herat: Matbe'eh-yi fakhriyeh-yi saljuqi, (1309-1310
      A.H.). Pp. (1):196; (2):197-510; (3):281. (1309-1310
      A.H.)

An exhaustive account in Persian of the major mosques and shrines of Herat, of its minor tombs, and of the pious and learned men resident in the ancient town.

384   Khan, Rajah (of Cabool)
      1845 Account of the Panjkora Valley, and of Lower and
      Upper Kashkar. Journal of the Asiatic Society of Bengal
      14:812-17.

385   Khanikoff, Nicolas de
      1861 Mémoire sur la partie méridionale de l'Asie centrale. (Khorassan, Afghanistan, Seistan, midi de la Perse) [Memoir on the Southern Part of Central Asia. (Khorasan, Afghanistan, Sistan and Central Persia)].
      Recueil de voyages et de mémoires publiés par la Société de Géographie 7:239-451. Paris.

386   Khoroshkhin, A.
      1876 Sbornik statei, Kasaiushchikhsia do turkestanskogo
      Kraia [Collected Articles Dealing with the Turkistan
      Region]. St. Petersburg.

387   Kieffer, C.
      1975 Wardak, toponyme et ethnique d'Afghanistan.
      Hommages Et Opera Minora Monumentum, H.S. Nyberg, Acta
      Iranica, Teherian-Liege. Pp. 475-483.

388   King, Peter
      1966 Afgahnistan: Cockpit in High Asia. London:
      Geoffrey Bles.

Experiences while searching for medicinal plants.

II. GEOGRAPHY

389   Kingsbury, Patricia and Robert
1960 Afghanistan and the Himalayan States. Garden City, New Jersey: Nelson Doubleday, Inc. Pp. 64.

A brief sketch of Afghanistan, Northwest Pakistan, Nepal and Sikkim. Some excellent original photographs are enclosed.

390   Kitamuro, S.
1960 Flora of Afghanistan. Kyoto.

391   Klass, Rosanne
1964 Afghanistan: Land of the High Flags. New York: Random House. Pp. 319

A travel memoir of an American who taught in Kabul from 1951 to 1954.

392   Klockenhoff, H.
1969 Uber die Kropfgazellen, Gazella subgutturosa (Guldenstädt), 1780 Afghanistans und ihre Haltung im Zoologischen Garten Kabul. Freunde des Kolner Zoo 12:91-96.

393   Klockenhoff, H. and G. Madel
1970 Uber die Flamingos (Phoenicopterus ruber roseus) der Dascht-e-Newar in Afghanistan. Journal of Ornithology 111:78-84.

394   Kloft, W. and E. Kloft
1971 Bienenfunde in Nuristan und im sudkaspischen Tieflandwald. All. dtsch. Imkerz. 4.

395   Kloft, W. and P. Schneider
1969 Gruppenverteidigungsverhalten bei wildlebenden Bienen (apis cerana Fabr.) in Afghanistan. Naturwissenschaften 56:219.

396   Knust, T. A. (ed)
1973 Marco Polo: Von Venedig nach China. 2 Aufl. Tubingen: Erdmann. Pp. 339.

397   Kohzad, Ahmad Ali
1948 The Panjsher. Afghanistan 3(4):17-29.

A topographical description of this attractive valley, some 80 kilometers north of Kabul, is followed by a list of villages and some comments on community life.

II. GEOGRAPHY

398   Kohzad, Ahmad Ali
        1950   Afghanistan Coeur de l'Asie [Afghanistan, Heart of Asia]. Afghanistan 5(1):25-28.

General description and praise of Afghanistan.

399   Kohzad, Ahmad Ali
        1951-1954   Along the Koh-i-Baba and the Hari-Rud. Afghanistan 6(1):1-16; (2):1-21; 7(1):50-55; 8(4):54-65; 9(1):20-43; (2):1-21.

Lengthy description of a journey in Central and North-Western Afghanistan.

400   Kohzad, Ahmad Ali
        1954   Les sommets des montagnes du monde [The Summits of the Mountains of the World]. Afghanistan 9(3):22-35.

The identification of the five mountains of Ghur, described by a medieval historian, Qazi Menhadje Seradje, as the mountain tops of the world, with five not-so-high mountains of modern Ghur, which are now known by other names.

401   Kohzad, Mohammad Nabi
        1948   Notes de voyage [Travel Notes]. Afghanistan 3(3):47-53; (4):8-13.

An account, in diary form, of two trips on which the Afghan author accompanied a foreign scholar.

402   Kohzad, Mohammad Nabi
        1954   Un coup d'oeil sur la Vallée de Nedjrau [A Glance at the Valley of Nejrao]. Afghanistan 9(2):60-62.

A description of the fertile valley and of its crops, with a note on the four languages, especially Parachi, spoken there.

403   Kohzad, Mohammad Nabi
        n.d.   Les Sites Touristiques de l'Afghanistan [Tourist Sites in Afghanistan]. Kabul: Government Printing House. Pp. 20.

404   Koie, M. and K. H. Reichinger
        1955   Symbolae Afghanicae [Afghan Contributions]. Konglige Danske Videnskabernes Selskab. Biologiske Skrifter 8(1):1-80. Copenhagen.

II. GEOGRAPHY

    405   Koie, M. and K. H. Reichinger
           1956 Symbolae Afghanicae. Copenhagen: Ejnar Munksgaard. Pp. 215.

           These works in Danish, enumerate and describe the plants collected by the Third Danish Expedition to Central Asia. A third volume was by Reichinger and was published in Copenhagen in 1959. It was entitled Leguminosae, and dealt with the subject in 208 pages.

    406   Konishi, Masatoshi
           1969 Afghanistan. Tokyo: Kodansha International Ltd. Pp. 146.

           A brief discussion along with numerous excellent color photographs.

    407   Krause, Walter W.
           1957 Wenn es zwolf schlagt in Kabul [When it Strikes Twelve in Kabul]. Munich. Pp. 291.

           An account of travel.

    408   Kraus, Willy (ed)
           1975 Afganistan: Natur, Geschichte, Geselschaft, Staat, Wirtschaft und Kultur. Tubingen: Erdman. Pp. 427.

           An important work on the geography, history, society, cities, economy, and culture of Afghanistan. Useful bibliographic information is included.

    409   Kreyberg, Leiv
           1951 Afghanistan; en norsk leges reise i Hindu-Kusj-landet [Afghanistan: A Norwegian Pysician's Journey into the Hindu Kus Country]. Oslo: J.W. Cappelen. Pp. 164.

    410   Kuhi, Muhammad Nasir
           1949 Armaghan-i Maymaneh [Souvenir of Maymaneh]. Maymaneh: Matbaeh-yi storai. Pp. (unnumbered) 266. (1328 A.H.)

           A compilation of material about this town of Northern Afghanistan, its shrines and monuments, its residents, and about the surrounding area.

    411   Kuhn, Delia and Ferdinand Kuhn
           1962 Borderlands. New York: Alfred Knopf. Pp. 335.

II. GEOGRAPHY

A perceptive account of travels, which includes a section on Afghan Turkestan.

412 Kuhnert, Gerd
1971 Vogelhaltung in Afghanistan. Gef. Welt 9:173-176.

413 Kuhnert, Gerd
1980 Falknerei in Afghanistan. Homo Ventor: Schriften zur Geschichte und Sociologie der Jagd III. Bonn: Rudolf Halbet Verlag. Pp. 102.

Discusses the sport of falconry in Afghanistan, chiefly in Logar and Paktia provinces.

414 Kulke, Holger
1976 Die Lapislazuli-Lagerstatte Sare Sang (Badakhshan). Geologies, Entstehung, Kulturgeschichte und Bergbau. Afghanistan Journal 3(2):43-56. Color photos; maps.

415 Kulke, H. and W. Schreyer
1973 Kyanite - talc schist from Sar e Sang, Afghanistan. Earth and planet. sci. letters 18:324-328.

416 Kull, U. and S. W. Breckle
1975 Verhalten der Fettsauren wahrend der Entwicklung einiger Therophyten der Steppe von Kabul (Afghanistan). Zeitschrift fur Pflanzenphysiologie 75:332-338.

417 Kullmann, E.
1966 Der Tiergarten in Kabul - ein Zoo in statu nascendi. Freunde des Kolner Zoo 9:130-134.

418 Kullmann, E.
1967 Wozu bauen wir einen Zoo in Kabul. Freunde des Kolner Zoo 10:43-49.

419 Kushkaki, Burhan al-Din
1924 Rohnoma-i Qataghan va Badakhsah. [Guide to Qataghan and Badakhshan]. Kabul: Ministry of War. Pp. 456. In Dari. (1302 A.H.)

An important survey work of northeastern Afghanistan by an Afghan writer. It includes notes on geography, commerce communication, population, climate, and other conditions in the various parts of Qataghan and Badakhsahn. The work was commissioned by Mohammed Nadir, Minister of War in Amir Amanullah's Government. Nadir became King of Afghanistan from 1929-1933 and is the father of the ex-king Mohammed Zahir. The book includes a preface co-

II. GEOGRAPHY

>authored by Mohammed Nadir who in addition to his ministry of war portfolio at that time held the position of head of the security commission for the province of Qataghan and Badakhshan. Maps for sub-provinces are included for Qataghan and Badakhshan.

420 Kushkaki, Burkhan al-Din Khan
1926 Kattagan i Badakhshan. Dannye po geografii strany, estestvenno-istoricheskim usloviiam naseleniiu, ekonomike i putiam soobshcheniia. S 34 Kartami. Perevod s persidskogo P. P. Vvedenskogo, B. I. Dolgopolova i E. V. Levkievskogo pod redaktsiei, s predisloviem i primechaniiami prof. A. A. Semenova [Qataghan and Badakhshan. Information about the Geography of the Country, the Natural-Historical Conditions, the Economy, and the Means of Communication. With 34 Maps. Translated from the Persian by P. P. Vvedenskii, B. I. Dolgopolov, and E. V. Levkievskii, under the Editorship and with a Preface and Remarks by Professor A. A. Semenov]. Tashkent. Pp. xiii, 248; maps

A translation from the Persian. The notes of Semenov, a retired professor of Arabic at the Central Asia University, are especially valuable. The book is very complete, but has many inaccuracies. Translation of no. 419.

421 Lal, Mohan
1834 Journal of a Tour through the Panjab, Afghanistan, Turkistan, Khorasan, and a Part of Persia, in Company with Lieut. Burnes and Dr. Gerard. Calcutta: Baptist Mission Press. Pp. xx, 340.

First edition of a work published in London in 1835 and again in somewhat different form at London in 1846. The author was an Indian clerk thoroughly familiar with Persian and avid at collecting information.

422 Land, D.
1971 Uber das Jungtertiar und Quartar in Sud-Afghanistan. Beih. geol. Jb., 96.

423 Lang, J.
1975 Les Bassins intramontagneux cenozoiques de l'Afghanistancentral; un modele de sedimentation molassique continentale en climat semi-aride. Sci. de la Terre 20(1):115.

II. GEOGRAPHY

424 Lang, J. and H. Meon-Vilain
1976 Contribution a l'analyse pollinique des Bassins intramontagneux cenozoiques de Bamian, de Yakawlang et du Ghorband en Afghaistan Central. Geobios. 9(4):425-480.

425 Lansdell, Henry
1887 Through Central Asia (with a map and appendix on the diplomacy and delimitation of the Russo-Afghan Frontier). London: S. Low, Marston, Searle, and Rivington. Pp. xix, 668.

426 Lapparent, A. F. de
1972 L'Afghanistan et la derive du continent indien. Rev. geogr. phys et geol. dynam., 14(4):449-456.

427 Lapparent, A. F. de
1974 Tres hautes terrasses et catures dans les monts de Turkman (Afghanistan). Revue de Gemorphologie Dynamique 23(4):159-162.

428 Lapparent, A. F. de and J. Blaise
1966 Un Itineraire Geologique en Afghanistan Central, de Tirin a Panjao, par Ghizao. Revue de Geographyie Physique et de Geologie Dynamique 8.

429 Leech, R. (trans)
1843 Journal of a Tour through Parts of the Panjab and Afghanistan in the Year 1837, by Agha Abbas of Shiraz. Arranged and Translated by Major R. Leech. Journal of the Asiatic Society of Bengal 12:564-621.

Disguised as a fakir, Agha Abbas, a soldier of fortune, traveled in India and Afghanistan, making notes on the villages, population and fighting strength for Major Leech. To preserve his disguise, he unblushingly distributed charms, discovered thieves and cured the sick, usually with the aid of detonating powder.

430 Leech, R.
1844 A Description of the Country of Seistan. Journal of the Asiatic Society of Bengal 13:115-20.

431 Leech, R.
1844 Route from Dera Ghazee Khan to Candahar, through the Sakhi Sarwar Pass and Buzdur, with other Routes. Journal of the Asiatic Society of Bengal 13:527-50.

II. GEOGRAPHY

432   Leech, R.
        1845 An Account of the Early Ghiljaees. Journal of the Asiatic Society of Bengal 14:306-28.

433   Leech, R.
        1845 Accounts (Part II) of parts of the Cabool and Peshawar Territories, and of Sama, Sudoon, Bunher, Swat, Deer and Bajour, visited by Mulla Aleem-ullah of Peshawar, in the latter part of the year 1837. Journal of the Asiatic Society of Bengal 14:660-701.

434   Leech, R.
        1845 A Supplementary Account of the Hazarahs. Journal of the Asiatic Society of Bengal 14:445-70.

435   Le Fevre, Georges
        1933 Expédition Citroen Centre-Asie. La Croisière Jaune. Troisième mission Haardt-Audouin-Dubreuil [The Citroen Expedition to Central Asia. The Yellow Cruiser. Third Haardt-Audouin-Dubreuil Mission]. Paris: Plon. Pp. xivi, 368; maps.

        Chapter III, pages 33-53, deals with the arduous motor crossing of Afghanistan in 1931. Well illustrated. An English translation appeared in 1935 under the title of An Eastern Odyssey.

436   Le Fort, P.
        1975 Himalayas: the Collided Range. Present Knowledge of the Continental Arc. American Journal of Science, 275-A:1-44.

437   Le Roy, Marie
        1953 Étude préliminaire sur le facies lagunaire: Bajocien-Bathonien de Karkar [Preliminary Study of the Lagoon Facies: Bajocian-Bathonian of Karkar]. Afghanistan 8(2):33-39.

        A discussion of some fossils found at Karkar and of the indications that a great lagoon, part of the Jurassic Sea, covered that part, at least, of Afghanistan.

438   Le Roy, Marie
        1953 La mer triasique à Douab [The Triassic Sea at Douab]. Afghanistan 8(3):18-22.

        A description of fossils which indicate the existence of a triassic sea in Northern Afghanistan.

II. GEOGRAPHY

439 Le Strange, Guy
1930 The Lands of the Eastern Caliphate. Mesopotamis, Persia and Central Asia, from the Muslim Conquest to the Time of Timur. Cambridge University Press. Pp. xx, 536; maps.

Reprint of a work of great value for indicating reliable source material which first appeared in 1905. Several chapters are directly concerned with the area covered by present-day Afghanistan.

440 Lewis, Robert E.
1973 Siphonaptera Collected During the 1965 Street Expedition to Afghanistan. Chicago: Field Museum of Natural History, Fieldiana: Zoology 64:xi, 161.

441 Linchevskii, I. A. and A. V. Prozorovskii
1944 K pozhaniiu rasitel'nosti Afganistana [On the knowledge of the vegetation of Afghanistan]. Botanicheskii Zhurnal 29(4):114-23.

442 Linchevskii, I. A. and A. V. Prozorovskii
1946 Osnovnye zakonomernosti raspredeleniia rastitel'nosti Afganistana [THe Principal regularities in Vegetation Distribution in Afghanistan]. Sbornik Nauchnykh Rabot Botanicheskii Instituta imena V. L. Komarova, 183-218. Leningrad.

443 Linchevsky, I. A. and A. V. Prozorovsky
1949 Basic Principles of the Distribution of the Vegetation of Afghanistan. Kew Bulletin 2:179-21; map. London.

444 Lindberg, K.
1949 Observations au sujet de quelques grottes asiatiques: Afghanistan [Observations on Some Asiatic Caves: Afghanistan]. Afghanistan 4(3):39-44.

Notes by a Swedish doctor and speleologist on how to hunt caves in Afghanistan and what he found.

445 Lister, H.
1968 Mass balance of Mir Samir West Glacier. In Environmental research in the Samir Valley of the Hindu Kusch, Afghanistan. Final Technical Report 1.1-1.7, Newcastle upon Tyne.

II. GEOGRAPHY

446 Lumsden, P.
  1885 Countries and Tribes Bordering on the Koh-i-Baba Range. Proceedings of the Royal Geographical Society (New Series 7:561-83).

447 Lys, M.
  1977 Biostratigraphie du Carbonifere et du Permien d'Afghanistan (Micro-paleontologie). Mem. h. ser. Soc. geol. 8:291-308. (France).

448 MacGregor, G. H.
  1844 Geographical Notice of the Valley of Jullalabad. Journal of the Asiatic Society of Bengal 13:117-30; 867-81.

449 Mackenzie, Franklin
  1949 Brief Glimpses of Afghanistan. Afghanistan 4(3):49-59.

Impressions of a trip by motor bus from Peshawar to Kabul, another bus trip north to Mazar-i Sharif, a third to Ghazni, and a fourth to Bamiyan. By an American teacher employed in a Kabul high school.

450 MacMahon, A. H.
  1897 The Southern Borderlands of Afghanistan. Geographical Journal 9:392-415.

Following the agreement on the Durand Line in 1893 Captain MacMahon was charged to establish the precise boundary between Afghanistan and Baluchistan: work carried on in 1894 through 1896 is described.

451 Madadi, M. Akbar
  1968 Was'-i Ijtima'i-yi Ghaznaviyan. [Social Conditions of the Ghaznavids]. Kabul. In Dari. Pp. xii, 608; illustrations; map. (1356 A.H.)

452 Mahran, G. H., T. S. M. A. El Alfy, and S. M. A. Ansary
  1975 A phytochemical study of the gum and resin of Afghanian Asa foetida. Bull. Fac. Pharm. Univ. Cairo 12:119.

453 Maillart, Ella K.
  1947 The Cruel Way. London: William Heinemann Ltd. Pp. 217.

II. GEOGRAPHY

>One of several books about travel in Asia by this Swiss journalist. The second hundred pages deal with Afghanistan, describing the wearing journey in the author's tortured car from Herat along the northern route through Mazar-i Sharif and back across the Hindu Kush to Kabul. Burdened by exaggerated sensibilities and problems of personal relationships. An edition in French was published at Geneva in 1952.

454 Manuchariants, Maiorov, Suderkin and Krekov
   1965 Report of the results of prospecting exploratory works for lapis lazuli in Afghanistan; unveroff. Rapport des afgh. Minenministeriums, Kabul.

455 Map, Afghanistan
   1954 Scale, 1:2,000,000. New York, United Nations Map. No 279, rev. 2, provisional edition January.

>Topographic sheet with approximate contours, figures indicating height of passes and peaks, routes of motorable roads, outline of provincial boundaries, etc. The circulation of this map was restricted by the United Nations.

456 Map, Persia and Afghanistan
   1950 Scale, 1:4,550,050, or one inch equals 64 miles. Directorate of the Military Survey, Geographic Section, General Staff, Great Britain 2149, 1912, 3d edition revised for railroads and boundaries in 1950.

>Physical features map with reliable material and the local transportation systems.

457 Map of Kabul
   n.d. Kabul: Matba'eh-yi doulati. Single folding sheet.

>Useful map of the capital with English text issued by the Afghan Tourist Organization.

458 Maps, Afghanistan
   1941-- Quarter-inch Series. Scale 1:253,440. Survey of India, Dehra-Dun; numerous sheets revised or reprinted by the Directorate of Military Survey as Geographic Section, General Staff, Great Britain 3919.

>Covers the country in large 1 degree x 1 degree topographical sheets. On a number of sheets contouring is missing in parts and unreliable in others. Many place-names are incorrect or garbled and the entire seris would benefit by a reworking on the ground.

II. GEOGRAPHY

459   Maps of Afghanistan
        n.d. International Series, Scale 1:1,000,000. Early edition. Sheets NG41, NH41, Nh42, NI41, NI42, NI43, NJ41, NJ42.

        Latest and updated edition available in varying scales from U. S. Government and Institute of Cartography, Ministry of Mines and Industries, Kabul, Afghanistan. The country was extensively mapped with the assistance of the governments of the USSR and USA during 1960s and 1970s.

460   Markham, C. R.
        1875-76 Afghan Geography. Proceedings of the Royal Geographical Society 20:241-52.

461   Markham, C. R.
        1879 The Basin of the Helmand. Proceedings of the Royal Geographical Society (New Series) 1:191-201.

462   Markham, C. R.
        1879 The Mountain Passes on the Afghan Frontier of British India. Proceedings of the Royal Geographical Society (New Series) 1:38-62.

463   Markham, C. R.
        1879 The Upper Basin of the Kabul River. Proceedings of the Royal Geographical Society (New Series) 1:110-21.

464   Markoroski, Bruno
        1932 Die materielle Kultur des Kabulgebietes [The Material Culture of the Kabul Region]. Leipzig: Asia Major. Pp. vii, 154; bibliography.

        Reflections of a residence of three years at Kabul expressed in a systematic study of the environment and patterns of living of the Afghans.

465   Marvin, Charles (trans)
        1880 Colonel Grodekoff's Ride from Samarqand to Herat, through Afghan Turkestan. London. Pp. 244.

        Translated into English and published the same year that the original Russian edition appeared in St. Petersburg. Covers areas not included in his account of Turkestan. See no. 307.

II. GEOGRAPHY

466 Marvin, Charles
    1884 Reconnoitering Central Asia: Pioneering Adventures in the Region Lying Between Russia and India. London: S. Swan Sonneinschein and Co., 1884. Pp. xviii, 418.

    A British journalist, specialist on the subject of Russia in Asia and author of several books on that subject, collects a number of contemporary accounts of travel and exploration in the region of Russia and Afghan Turkistan.

467 Masal'skii, F. I.
    1913 Turkestanskii Krai [The Turkistan Region]. Rossiia . . . vol. 19. St. Petersburg.

468 Masson, Charles
    1842 Narrative of Various Journeys in Belochistan, Afghanistan, and the Panjab; Including a Residence in those Countries from 1826 to 1836. 3 vols. London: Richard Bentley. Pp. (1) xxvii, 471; (2) xvi, 464; (3) xvi, 496.

    In spite of the rather general title of the work these volumes by British traveler are devoted almost entirely to Afghanistan. Displaying a keen observation and a devotion to detail they were long consulted as a major work of reference. Volume 3 includes an account of the commercial mission of Burnes to Kabul in 1836-37. Reprinted 1974.

469 Mazhar, 'Ali
    1950 Afghanistan [Afghanistan]. Cairo: Matba'ah al'sanah al'muhammadiah. Pp. 141; list of sources. (1369 A.H.)

470 McNair, W. W.
    1884 A Visit to Kafiristan. Proceedings of the Royal Geographical Society (New Series) 6:1-18.

471 Meher-Homji, V. M., R. K. Gupta and H. Freitag
    1973 Bibliography on "Plant Ecology" in Afghanistan. Excerpta Botanica Sectio B Sociologica 12:310-315.

472 Mele, Pietro F.
    1965 Afghanistan. Milan: Amilcare Pizzi. n.p.

    Some 56 photographs, with a sketchy introduction and unsatisfactory captions.

473 Mennessier, G.
    1973 Geological Maps 1:100,000. Mission geologie Francaises en Afghanistan, 15 Blatter, Paris.

II. GEOGRAPHY

474   Mennessier, G.
1973 Geological Maps of the Kabul-Gardez Region 1:250 000. Mission Geologie Francaises en Afghanistan, 8 Blatter, Paris.

475   Michaud, Roland and Sabrina
1978 Caravans to Tartary. New York: Viking Press. Pp. 76, richly illustrated.

Includes superb pictures of the Afghan landscape and people with ample descriptive text.

476   Michaud, Roland and Sabrina
1980 Memmoire de l'Afghanistan. Paris: Ste Nlle des Editions du chene. Pp. 132.

Narrative of travels and experiences in Afghanistan accompanied by excellent photographs of the country.

477   Michel, Aloys A.
1960 On Writing the Geography of Strange Lands and Faraway Places--Afghanistan, for example. Economic Geography 36(4):355-368.

A review article inspired by the publication of La Géographie de l'Afghanistan by J. Humlum.

478   Michel, Janine (trans)
1958 Intermede Afghan [Afghan Interlude]. Paris: Julliard. Pp. 287.

A translation of De Baer 1957.

479   Michener, James A.
1955 Afghanistan, Domain of the Fierce and the Free. Reader's Digest 67(403):161-172.

A rather romanticized description, emphasizing the beauty and contrast of the country; ending with the reassurance that Afghanistan is turning to the United States rather than to Russia.

480   Miller, Constance O. and Edward M. Gilbert, Jr.
1976 The Complete Afghan Hound. New Revised third edition. New York: Howel Book House, Pp. 303; illustrations.

II. GEOGRAPHY

481   Minaev, I.
         1879 Svedenia o stranch po verkhov'iam Amu-Dar'i
         [Information about the Countries on the Upper Amu
         Darya]. St. Petersburg.

482   Mirazai, N. A. and S. W. Breckle
         1978 Untersuchungen an Afghanischen Halophyten. I
         Salzverhaltnisse in Chenopodiaceen Nord-Afghanistans.
         Bot. Jahrb. Syst. 99/4:565-578.

483   Mirepois, Camille
         1971 Afghanistan in Pictures. New York: Sterling Publishing Company. Pp. 64.

484   Mitchell, R.
         1884 The Regions of the Upper Oxus. Proceedings of the
         Royal Geographical Society (New Series) 6:489-512.

485   Mochtar, Said Gholam and Hartmut Geerken
         1979 Die Halluzinogene Muscarin und Ibotensaure im
         Mittleren Hindukusch. Afghanistan Journal 6(2):63-64.

486   Mohn, Paul
         1930 Resa till Afghanistan [Travel in Afghanistan].
         Stockholm: F. A. Norstedt, Soners Forlag,. Pp. 364;
         map.

         Several principal subjects are treated in this Swedish
         account: a general historical survey; an account of the
         provinces of Kabul and Badakhshan; and the period of
         transition between Amanullah and Nadir Shah.

487   Monakhov, F. I.
         1952 Kharakteristika afganskikh glubokofokusnykh zemletriasneii [Characteristics of Afghan Deep-Focus
         Earthquakes]. Akademiia Nauk S.S.S.R., Geofizicheskii
         Institut, Trudy, (14):3-12. Moscow.

488   Montgomerie, T. G.
         1871 Report of the Mirza's Exploration from Caubul to
         Kahsgar. Journal of the Royal Geographical Society
         41:132-93.

489   Montgomerie, T. G.
         1872 A Havilar's Journey to Faizabad. . . . Proceeding of
         the Royal Geographical Society 253-61. See below.

II. GEOGRAPHY

490   Montgomerie, T. G.
       1872 A Havildar's Journey through Chitral to Faizabad in
             1870. Journal of the Royal Geographical Society 42:180-
             201.

491   Moorcroft, William and George Trebeck
       1838 Travels in the Himalayan Provinces of Hindustan and
             the Panjab; in Ladakh and Kashmir; in Peshawar, Kabul,
             Kunduz, and Bokhara; from 1819 to 1825. 2 vols.
             London: John Murray. Pp. (1) lvi, 459; (2) viii, 508.

       In the second volume the authors, British army officers,
       recount a ride from Peshawar to Bokhara by way of Kabul,
       Bamiyan, Qunduz and Mazar-i Sharif. The emphasis is upon
       description of the route and the delays and difficulties
       caused by local authorities.

492   Morgan, Delmar E.
       1892 The Pamir: A Geographical and Political Sketch. The
             Scottish Geographical Magazine 8:15-23.

       Informative description of some of the six divisions that
       make up the valleys of the Pamir.

493   Mouchet, J.
       1972 La Vallee du Wakhan. Afghanistan 25(2):57-70.

494   Muhammad 'Ali Khan
       1927 Afghanistan. Lahore: Mufid-i 'amm, Pp. 163; map.
             (1306 A.H.)

       An account in Persian of the geography and topography of
       Afghanistan.

495   Muhammad Husayn Khan
       1927 Jughrafiya-yi Afghanistan [Geography of
             Afghanistan]. Lahore: Mufid-i 'amm, Pp. 71. (1306
             A.H.)

       A summary account of the subject in Persian.

496   Munneke, R. J.
       1980 The Bazaar in Market-Towns in Northern Afghanistan:
             Methods of Presentation. In From Field-Case to Show-
             Case. Edited by W. R. Gulik. Amsterdam: Gieben. Pp.
             85-86.

II. GEOGRAPHY

497   n. a.
  1887 Captain Maitland's and Captain Talbot's Journeys in Afghanistan. Proceedings of the Royal Geographical Society (New Series) 9:102-07.

498   n.a.
  1844 From Herat to Cabool, via Candahar. Journal of the Asiatic Scoiety of Bengal 13:838-52.

499   n.a.
  1881 Geographical Notes. Proceedings of the Royal Geographical Society (New Series) 3:311-12.

500   n.a.
  1884 Geographical Notes. Proceedings of the Royal Geographical Society (New Series) 6:662-63.

501   n.a.
  1885 Geographical Notes. Proceedings of the Royal Geographical Society (New Series) 7:607-08.

502   n.a.
  1886 Geographical Notes. Proceedings of the Royal Geographical Society (New Series) 8:331-32; 644; 783.

503   n.a.
  1889 Geographical Notes. Proceedings of the Royal Geographical Society (New Series) 9:103-104; 171-75.

504   n.a.
  1844 Itinerary from Yazd to Herate. Journal of the Asiatic Society of Bengal 13:827-38.

505   n.a.
  1883 Lessar's Second Journey in the Turkoman Country-- Askabad to Ghurian near Herat. Proceedings of the Royal Geographical Society (New Series) 5:1-23.

506   n.a.
  1844 Route From Candahar to Herat. Journal of the Asiatic Society of Bengal 13:121-34.

507   n.a.
  1881 Transport Service for Asiatic Warfare, with a brief account of the Transport Operations from Sukkur to Quetta in 1879. Journal of the Royal United Service Institution 24:489-521.

II. GEOGRAPHY

508 Nalivkin, I. D.
1932 Obzor geologii Pamira i Badakchana [The Geological Survey of the Pamirs and Badakhshan]. Moscow-Leningrad: Transactions of the United Geological and Prospecting Service of the U.S.S.R. Pp. 104; geological map.

The essential conclusions of this Soviet study are summarized in English on pages 73-101.

509 Nariman, G. K.
1927 Afghanistan Today. Islamic Culture 1:252-258. Hyderabad, India.

Account of a visit to Afghanistan by an Indian subject in response to an invitation from Amir Amanullah. A stay of two months is reflected in a multitude of scattered observations on the people and the rapid surge of modernization: the author did regret that his modest supply of whiskey was confiscated when he entered the country.

510 Naseri, A.
1963 The history of Lapis Lazuli in Afghanistan (part III). Afghanistan, revue trimestr. Soc. etudes d'Afghan. 18:23-28.

511 Naumann, Clas M.
1973 Ein ehemaliges Wildyak-Vorkommen im Afghanischen Pamir. Bonn. zool. Beitr. 24:249-253.

512 Naumann, Clas M.
1974 Pamir und Wakhan - Kurzbericht zqeier Expeditionen (1971 und 1972) nebst einigen allgemeinen Bemerkungen. Afghanistan Journal 1(4):91-104. Photos; maps.

513 Naumann, C. and J. Niethammer
1973 Zur Saugetirfauna des Afghanischen Pamir und des Wakhan. Bonn. zool. 24:327-248.

514 Naumann, C. and G. Nogge
1973 Die Großauger Afghanistans. Zeitschrift des Kolner Zoo, Jg. 16(3):79-93.

515 Nauroz, K. M. and C. M. Naumann
1975 Bemerkungen zur Verbreitung des Markhors, Capra falconeri (Wagner, 1839) in Afghanistan. Saugetierkundliche Mitteilungen 23(2):81-85.

II. GEOGRAPHY

516   Nesterovich, S.
1958   Russkiye puteshestvenniki v Afganistane [Russian Travelers in Afghanistan]. Zvezda Vostoka (3):158-160.

An account of the favorable reception accorded to Soviet visitors to Afghanistan.

517   Neubauer, H. F.
1954   Die Walder Afghanistans. Angew. Pflanzensoz. E. Aichinger Festschrift I:494-503.

518   Neubauer, H. F.
1954   Versuch einer Kennzeichnung der Vegetationsverhaltnisse Afghanistans. Ann. Naturhist. Mus, Wien 60:77-113.

519   Neubauer, H. F.
1977   Zur Bienenzucht in Afghanistan. Afghanistan Journal 4(1):36-37.

520   Neubauer, H. F.
1954   Bemerkungenuber das Vorkommen wilder Obstsorten in Nuristan. Angew. Bot. 28:81-88.

521   Neuhauser, Hans N. and Anthony F. DeBlase
1974   Notes on Bats (Chiroptera: Vesperitliondae), new to the Faunal Lists of Afghanistan and Iran. Chicago: Field Museum of Natural History, Fieldiana: Zoology 62(5):85-96.

522   Newby, Eric
1959   A Short Walk. New York: Doubleday and Co. Pp. 240.

A literate, informative, and entertaining account of travel in the Hindu Kush and in Nuristan.

523   Niedermayer, Oskar von
1924   Afghanistan [Afghanistan]. Leipzig: K. W. Hiersemann. Pp. xv, 70; 24 illustrations.

The head of the secret German expedition to Afghanistan in 1914-1917 put together a short but interesting text dealing with economic and social conditions and the problems of the tribes as a framework for an abundance of marvelous photographs of landscape, people, and ancient and modern sites.

II. GEOGRAPHY

524   Niedermayer, Oskar von
       1937 Persien und Afghanistan (Handbuch der geographischen
            Wissenschaft: Vorder- und Südasien) [Persia and
            Afghanistan (Handbook of Geographical Science: Near and
            South Asia)]. Potsdam.

       Listed for its potential value, considering the background
       and experience of the author. Includes important informa-
       tion on the geography of the country.

525   Niethammer, G.
       1971 Vogelleben am Ab-e-Istada (Afghanistan). Vogelwarte
            26:221-27.

526   Niethammer, G.
       1972 Storche uber Afghanistan. Z. Kolner Zoo 15:47-54.

527   Niethammer, G.
       1973 Zur Vogelwelt des Afghanischen Pamir und des Darwaz.
            Bonn. zool. Beitr 24, 3:270-284.

528   Niethammer, G. and J.
       1967 Hochgebirgsvogelzug in Afghanistan. Zool. Beitr.
            N.F. 13:501-507.

529   Niethammer, J.
       1967 Storche in Afghanistan. Vogelwarte 24:42-44.

530   Niethammer, J.
       1967 Zwei Jahre Vogelbeobachtungen an stehenden Gewassern
            bei Kabul in Afghanistan. Journal of Ornithology 108:
            118-164.

531   Niethammer, J.
       1970 Die Flamingos am Ab-i-Istada in Afghanistan. Natur
            und Museum 100:201-210.

532   Niethammer, J.
       1973 Das Mauswiesel (Mustela nivalis) in Afghanistan.
            Bonn. Zool. Beitr. 24:1-6.

533   Niethammer, J.
       1973 Zur Kenntnis der Igel (Erinaceidea) Afghanistans.
            Zeitschr. f. Saugetierkunde 38:271-76.

534   Niethammer, J. and J. Martens
       1975 Die Gattungen Rattus und Maxomys in Afghanistan und
            Nepal. Z. Saugetierk. 40:325-355.

II. GEOGRAPHY

535   Nitecki, Mathew H. and Albert F. de Lapparent
        1976 Upper devonian Receptaculites Chardini n. sp. from Central Afghanistan. Fieldiana Geology 35, 5:41-82. Field Museum of Natural History, Chicago.

536   Nogge, Gunther
        1972 Kabul-Zoo, the Show-window of Afghan Fauna. The Outdoorman 3:32-35.

537   Nogge, Gunther
        1973 Erfahrungen beim Aufbau eines Zoologischen Gartens in Kabul/Afghanistan. Zool. Garten N.F. 43:166-178.

538   Nogge, Gunther
        1973 Vogeljagd am Hindukusch. Natur und Museum 103:276-279.

539   Nogge, Gunther
        1973 Ornithologische Beobachtungen im Afghanischen Pamir. Bonn. zool. Beitr. 24, 3:254-269.

540   Nogge, Gunther
        1974 Beobachtungen an den Flamingobrutplatzen Afghanistans. Journal of Ornithology 115:142-151.

541   Nogge, Gunther
        1974 Sieben Jahre Kabul-Zoo Afghanistan. Zeitschrift des Kolner Zoo 17:105-109.

542   Nogge, Gunther
        1976 Ventilationsbewegungen bei Solifugen (Arachnida, Solifugae). Zool. Anz. 196:145-149.

543   Nogge, Gunther
        1977 Die Bedeutung des Kabul-Zoos fur Afghanistan. Afghanistan Journal 4(1):31-35.

544   Nogge, Gunther
        1978 Storchenjagd am Hindukusch - wie lange noch? Das Tier 18, (11):16-19.

545   Nogge, Gunther and K. Nogge
        1974 Der Tiergarten des Hadji Sayed Abdul Rahman. Tierschutz in Wurzburg, 4:42-44.

546   Obruchev, Vladimir A.
        1927 Iskopayemyye bogatstva Afganistana [Mineral Wealth of Afghanistan]. Novyy Vostok (16-17):226-231. Moscow.

II. GEOGRAPHY

547   Olufsen, Ole
        1904 Through the Unknown Pamirs: The Second Danish Pamir Expedition 1898-99. London: W. Heinemann. Pp. xxii, 229.

548   On Tabular Returns
        1841 On Tabular Returns of the N. W. Frontier Trade with Afghanistan. Journal of the Asiatic Society of Bengal 10:251-65.

549   Pelt, M. M., J. C. Hayon and C. Younos
        1965 Plantes medicinales et drogues de l'Afghanistan. Bull. de la Societe de Pharmacie de Nancy 66:16-61.

550   Pernot, Maurice
        1927 L'inquiétude de l'Orient. En Asie Musulmane [The Uneasiness of the Orient. In Moslem Asia]. Paris: Hachette. Pp. viii, 244.

        Some 40 of the opening pages are devoted to personal impressions of Afghanistan by a writer commissioned to travel from the Mediterranean to India.

551   Peter of Greece (and Denmark), Prince
        1947 A Trip to the Oxus. Journal of the Royal Central Asian Society 34:51-55.

        An account of what the author claimed to be the first motor trip from Mazar-i Sharif to the Oxus (Amu Darya) River.

552   Planhol, Xavier de
        1973 Forest exploitation and Deforestation in Afghanistan. Annales de Geographie 82(451):365-366.

553   Planhol, Xavier de
        1973 Sur la Frontiere Turkmene de l' Afghanistan. Revue Geographique de l'Est 13(1-2):1-16.

554   Planhol, Xavier de
        1976 Le Repeuplement de la Basse Valle Afghan du Mourghab. Studia Iranica 5(2).

555   Planhol, Xavier de and Francois Denizot
        1977 La Neige Qui Vient du Salang. Afghanistan Journal 4(2):74-75. Photos.

II. GEOGRAPHY

556 Podlech, D.
    1973 Neue und bemerkenswerte Astragalus-Arten aus Afghanistan (Beitrage zur Flora von Afghanistan VI). Mitt. Bot. Munchen 11:259-321.

557 Podlech, D.
    1975 Zur Kenntnis der Chenopodiaceen-Flora Afghanistan (Beitrage zur Flora von Afghanistan VII). Mitt. Bot. Munchen 12:51-90.

558 Podlech, D.
    1975 Revision der Sektion Caraganella BGE. der Gattung Astragalus L. Mitt. Bot. Munchen 12:153-166.

559 Podlech, D. and O. Anders
    1977 Florula des Wakhan (Nordost-Afghanistan). Mitt. Bot. Munchen 13:361-502.

560 Podlech, D. and O. Bader
    1974 Chromosomenstudien and Afghanischen Pflanzen II. Mitt. Bot. Munchen 11:457-488.

561 Postans, J.
    1841 Memorandum on the Trade Between the Towns of Shikarpore and Candahar. Journal of the Asiatic Society of Bengal 10:12-16.

562 Proundlock, R. V.
    1949 The Miranzai Valley. Journal of the Royal Central Asian Society 36:307-308.

    Brief note on this valley astride the Afghan-Pakistan frontier by a military observer of raids and tribal migrations through the valley.

563 Puget, A.
    1969 Contribution a l'etude des oiseaux de nord-est de l'Afghanistan. Ph.D. Dissertation. University of Toulouse. Pp. 487.

564 Pulyarkin, Valery A.
    1964 Afganistan; ekonomicheskaya geografiya [Afghanistan; Economic Geography]. Moscow: Mysl'. Pp. 253; maps.

565 Qamus-i a'lam-i jughrafiya'i-yi Afghanistan
    1948 [Dictionary of Geographical Names of Afghanistan]. Kabul: Matba'eh-yi 'umumi. Pp. 168. (1327 A.H.)

II. GEOGRAPHY

A valuable work in Persian, issued by the Da'iratu'l-ma'arif [Encyclopedia] board of Afghanistan.

566 Rahmati, Mohebullah
1972 Geography of Afghanistan. Kabul: Ministry of Education, (in Dari). Pp. 287.

567 Rahnuma-yi Qattaghan va Badakhshan ya'ni mulakhkhas-i safarnameh-yi 1301 sipahsalar-i sardar-i Muhammad Nadir Khan vzir-i harbiyeh murattabeh-yi janab Mawlawi Burhan al-Din Khan Kushkaki
1925 [Guide to Qattaghan and Badakhshan, that is, Selections from the Travel Diary of 1301 of General Muhammad Nadir Khan, Minister of War, Arranged by His Excellency Mawlawi Burhan al-Din Khan Kushkaki]. Kabul. (1304 A.H.)

A valuable account of a trip made through two northern provinces in 1923 and containing material on geography, resources, history and population groups.

568 Ramstedt, Gustav John
1978 Seven Journeys Eastward 1898-1912, Among the Cheremis, Kalmyks, Mogols; and in Turkestan to Afghanistan. Publications of the Mongolia Society, Occasional Paper #9. Translated from the Swedish and edited by John R. Krueger. Bloomington, Indiana: The Mongolia Society.

569 Rathjens, Carl
1957 Kabul, Die Hauptstadt Afganistans [Kabul, The Capital of Afghanistan]. Leben und Umwelt 13:73-82.

570 Rathjens, Carl
1972 Fragen der horizontalen und vertikalen Landschaftsgliederung im Hochgebirgssystem des Hindukusch. Erdwissenschaftliche Forschung 4:205-220.

571 Rathjens, Carl
1974 Forests of Nuristan and Paktia - ecological conditions and utilization of woodlands of eastern Afghanistan. Geographische Zeitschrift 62(4):295-311.

572 Rathjens, Carl
1974 Klimatische Jahreszeiten in Afghanistan. Afghanistan Journal 1(1):13-18. Color photos.

II. GEOGRAPHY

573   Rathjens, Carl
      1975 Witterungsbedingte Schwankungen der Ernahrungsbasis in Afghanistan. Erdkunde, 29.

574   Rathjens, Carl
      1978 Hohe Tagessummen des Niederschlags in Afghanistan. Afghanistan Journal 5(1):22-25. Photos.

575   Rathjens, Carl
      1978 Klimatische Bedingungen der Solifluktionsstufe im sommertrockenen Hochgebirge, am Beispiel des Afghanischen Hindukusch. Z. Geomorph. N.F., Suppl. 30:132-142.

576   Rattray, James
      1848 The Costumes of the Various Tribes, Portraits of Ladies of Rank. Celebrated Princes and Chiefs. Views of the Principal Fortresses and Cities, and Interior of the Cities and Temples of Afghaunistaun. London: Hering and Remington. Pp. 34; plates.

577   Raufi, F. and O. Sickenberg
      1973 Zur Geologie und Palaontologie der Becken von Lagman und Jelalabad. Geol. Jg. 3:63-99.

578   Raunig, W.
      1975 Vorlaufiger Kurzbericht uber die ethnographischen Arbeiten im Rahmen von Exploration Pamir 75. Ethnologische Zeitschrift Zurich 2:105-111.

579   Raverty, Henry George
      1854 Some Remarks on the Origin of the Afghan People and Dialect and on the Connexion of the Pashto Language with the Zend and Pehlavi and the Hebrew. Journal of the Asiatic Society of Bengal 34:550-88.

580   Raverty, Henry George
      1857 Notes on Kafiristan. Journal of the Asiatic Society of Bengal 28:317-68.

581   Raverty, Henry George
      1864 An Account of Upper Kash-Kar and Chitral or Lower Kash-Kar, together with the Independent Afghan State of Panj-Korah, including Talash. Journal of the Asiatic Society of Bengal 33:125-151.

582   Rawlinson, H. C.
      1842 Comparative Geography of Afghanistan. Journal of the Royal Geographical Society 12:112-14.

II. GEOGRAPHY

583 Rawlinson, H. C.
  1872 Monograph on the Oxus. Journal of the Royal Geographical Society 42:482-513.

584 Rawlinson, H. C.
  1872-73 Notes on Seistan. Proceedings of the Royal Geographical Society 17:92-95.

585 Rawlinson, H. C.
  1872-73 On Badakhshan and Wakhan. Proceedings of the Royal Geographical Society 17:108-16.

586 Rawlinson, H. C.
  1873 Notes on Seistan. Journal of the Royal Geographical Society 43:272-94.

587 Rechinger, K. H.
  1981 Dei Sqergpalme Nannorhops Ritchiaa (Griff.) Aitch. Afghanistan Journal 8(1):21-23.

588 Regteren, C. O. van
  1970 Notes on Land Slugs, 16: Deroceras From Afghanistan, Including Description of D. Kandaharensis. Chicago: Field Museum of Natural History, Fieldiana: Zoology, Volume 51(15):175-178.

589 Reinaud, M.
  1849 Mémoire géographique, historique et scientifique sur l'Inde antérieurement au milieu du XIème siècle de l'ère christieene, d'après les écrivans arabes persans et chinois [Geographica, Historical and Scientific Memoirs on India prior to the Middle of the Eleventh Christian Century, Taken from Arab, Persian and Chinese Writers]. Paris: Imprimerie nationale. Pp. ii, 400; map.

  Includes very useful material on the area now covered by Eastern Afghanistan.

590 Reisner, Igor Mikhailovich
  1929 Nesavisimy Afganistan [Independent Afghanistan]. Moscow: Trudy Moskovskogo Instituta Vostokoredenia N. N. Narimanova. Pp. 221.

  Reisner has long been known as the leading professor of Colonial History at Moscow and the greatest Soviet specialist on Afghanistan. This useful text faithfully reflects Marxist doctrines.

II. GEOGRAPHY

591 Reisner, Igor Mikhailovich
1939 Afghanistan: S Kartami i skhemami [Afghanisan. With Maps and Charts]. 2d ed. Moscow: Kommunisticheskaia Akademiia. Institute Mirovogo Khoziaistva i Mirovoi Politiki. Kolonial'naia Serila. Pp. viii, 267.

A later and more comprehensive reworking of the same author's Independent Afghanistan, including certain ideological revisions.

592 Riedle, H. and H. Freitag
1972 Drei neue Boraginaceen-Species der Flora von Afghanistan. Osterr. Bot. Z. 120:137-142.

593 Ringer, Karlernst
1974 Die Entwicklung Afghanistans. Indo-Asia 16(3):248-257.

594 Rishtin, Sadiquallah
1955 Da Hind Safar [The Hind Voyage]. Kabul. Pp. 172. (1334 A.H.)

An account in Pushtu of a visit to India.

595 Rishtya, Sayed Qasim
1947 L'Afghanistan au point de vue géographique [Afghanistan from the Geographical Point of View]. Afghanistan 2(1):16-22.

A general sketch, with emphasis on the mountain systems.

596 Rishtiya, Sayed Qasim
1947 The Rivers of Afghanistan. Afghanistan 2(2):8-14.

A general introduction is followed by accounts of the courses of the Kabul and the Amu Darya Rivers.

597 Ross, Frank E. (ed)
1939 Central Asia. Personal Narrative of General Josiah Harlan, 1823-1841. London: Luzac and Co. Pp. 155; folding map.

In 1826 Harlan attached himself to an ex-king of Kabul in exile in India and soon went into Afghanistan in disguise and as a secret agent: probably the first American to visit the ocuntry. Later he took service under Amir Dos Muhammad. His story stresses two subjects, an account of the province of Balkh and its inhabitants and a military topography of Northern Afghanistan.

II. GEOGRAPHY

598   Rosset, Louis-Felicien
1947   Les pierres précieuses en Afghanistan [Precious Stones in Afghanistan]. Afgahnistan 2(1):23-44; (2):21-41.

Deals with the incidence and types of diamonds in Afghanistan and their current local prices. A number of pages describe Kabul River Valley sties where garnets are found.

599   Rosset, Louis-Felicien
1947   Vers le nord Afghan [To the Afghan North]. Afghanistan 2(4):24-53.

Technical and dull account of abserved geology along the route from Kabul north to Bactria.

600   Rosset, Louis-Felicien
1949   Les cuvettes d'effondrement du Kaboulistan: Lataband hills et terrasses fluviales de Sarobi [The Trench Basins of Kabulistan: Lataband Hills and Fluvial Terraces of Sarobi]. Afghanistan 4(2):1-13.

Highly technical account of geological observations in the Lataband Pass.

601   Rosset, Louis-Felicien
1949   Prospection paléontologique dans les plissements secondaires du Nord Hindu-Koush [Paleontological Exploratin in the Secondary Foldings of the North Hindu Kush]. Afghanistan 4(4):36-47.

The results of geological observations made at Doab.

602   Rosset, Louis-Felicien
1951   Afghanistan "à la gloire de la Route du Nord" [Afghanistan: "The Glory of the Northern Route"]. Afghanistan 6(2):32-39; (3):11-19.

A geological tour of the northern Kabul-Doab Route on the Hindu Kush; with explanations and identifications of the rocks and formations.

603   Rosset, Louis-Felicien
1952   Participation à l'étude tectnique de l'Hindou-Kouch. Sur "l'anomalie" du déversement des plis en directi nordsu [Participation in the Tectonic Study of the Hindu

II. GEOGRAPHY

        Kush. On the Anomaly of the Turn of the Ridges in the North-South Direction]. Afghanistan 7(2):60-64; (3):56-64; (4):1-20; maps; bibliography.

        Research on the tectonic structure of the Hindu Kush.

604   Rosset, Louis-Felicien
        1953 Phénomènes volcaniques anciens dans le nord Afghan [Ancient Volcanic Phenomena in the Afghan North]. Afghanistan 8(4):27-41.

        Research on various geological aspects of the Hindu Kush region.

605   Rosset, Louis Felicien
        1953 Voyages d'étude en Afghanistan [Study-Trips in Afghanistan]. Afghanistan 8(1):20-33.

        Report of a geological tour in the Maiden and Angarand valleys and the Hindu Kush, with notes on the formations found in these regions.

606   Rosset, Louis-Felicien
        1954 Nouvell prospection à Karkar (près Poul-i-khomry) [New Exploration at Karkar (near Pol-i Khumri)]. Afghanistan 9(1):11-19.

        Stratigraphic and paleontologica description of the region around Karkar.

607   Rosset, Louis-Felicien
        1954 Afghanistan "board de mer" [Afghanistan's "Sea Coast"]. Afghanistan 9(2):27-35.

        On the fossil evidence that proves the existence of the triassic Gulf of Doab.

608   Rosset, Louis-Felicien
        1954 Parallèle entre la flore rhétienne du Gondwana (partie péinsulaire) et celle de même époque (ferghana-angara) du continent sino-sibérien. (Douab-Eshpochta-Saighan) [A Parallel between the Rhaetian Flora of Gondwana (Peninsular Part) and that of the Same Epoch of the Sino-Siberian Continent. (Doab-Eshpochta-Saighan)]. Afghanistan 9(3):56-62; (4):30-47.

        A comparison between fossils of North Afghanistan, India, and South Africa.

II. GEOGRAPHY

609   Rybitschka, Emil
    1927 Im gottgebenen Afghanistan als Gaste des Emirs [In God-given Afghanistan as the Guest of the Amir]. Leipzig: F. A. Brockhaus. Pp. xi, 295; map.

610   Salem, M. Zarif
    1969 Characteristics, Genesis and Classification of Some Soils of Afghanistan and a Study of Ant Pedoturbation in a Wisconsin Forest Soil. Unpublished Ph.D. Dissertation. University of Wisconsin - Madison. Pp. 170.

    Field and laboratory study of the genesis and classification of eight soil sample repreentative of Agricultural potential in Afghanistan.

611   Samin, Abdul Quhar
    1971 Phosphorus Fractionation of some Calcereous Soils of Afghanistan and Oklahoma. Unpublished Ph.D. Dissertation. Oklahoma State University. Pp. 154.

    A study of calcarious soil, and mineralogical composition of the soil in Afghanistan and Oklahoma.

612   Sareen, Anuradha
    1975 India and Afghanistan, 1907-21. Unpublished Ph.D. Dissertation. Jawaharlal Nehru University. Pp. iii, 272.

613   Sarif, Gul Janan
    1972 Das Afghanische Schulwesen: zu Seiner Geschichtlichen Bedingung und Gegenwartigen Problemage. Unpublished Ph. D. Dissertation. Frankfurt University.

614   Sawitzki, Hans-Henning
    1972 Die Elitegruppe der Akademiker in einem Entwicklungsland. dargestellt am Beispiel Afghanistan. Meisenheim: Verlag, 1972. Pp. 160.

615   Schapka, U. and O. H. Volk
    1979 Ein Verzeichnis von in Afghanistan gebrauchlichen Pfanzennamen. Afghanistan Journal 6(1):3-14.

616   Schefer, Charles H. A.
    1878 Itinéraires (de Pichaver à Kaboul, de Kaboul à Qandahar, de Qandahar a` Herat) (Extraits du Tarikh-i-Ahmad de Muhammad Abdul Karim Monshi), trad. du persan [Itineraries (from Peshawar to Kabul, from Kabul to Qandahar, from Qandahar to Herat) (Extracts from the

II. GEOGRAPHY

    Tarikh-i-Ahmad of Muhammad Abdul Karim Monshi), translated from Persian]. Paris: École Nationale des Langues Orientales Vivantes. Pp. iii, 380; map.

    The material is found in pages 361-375 of a volume in the series, Receuil d'Itineraires.

617 Scheibe, A.
    1937 Deutsche im Hindukusch. Bericht der Deutschen Hindukusch-Expedition 1935 der Deutschen Forschungsgemeinschat. Berlin: Deutsche Forschung, N.F., 1.

618 Schinasi, May
    1975 L'Afghanistan à l'époque Serâdjiya (1901-1919). Etude de Sarâdj ul-Akhbâr (1911-1918) (Afghanistan during the Sirajiya Period (1901-1919): Study of the Siraj-ul-Akhbar (1911-1918). Unpublished Ph.D. Dissertation. Sorbonne-Nouvelle (Paris III). Pp. 360.

619 Schinasi, May
    1979 Afghanistan at the Beginning of the Twentieth Century. Nationalism and Journalism in Afghanistan: A Study of Seraj ul-akhbar (1911-1918). Naples: Istituto Universitario Orientale, Seminario di studi Asiatici. Pp. 302.

620 Schlimm, Wolfgang
    1976 Zur Geologie des Palazoikums von Malestan (Zentralafghanistan). [On the Geology of the Paleozoic of Malestan Central Afghanistan.] Unpublished Ph.D. Dissertation. Bonn University. Pp. 168.

621 Schneider, Peter
    1976 Honigbienen und ihre Zucht in Afghanistan. Afghanistan Journal 3(3):101-104.

622 Schneider, P. and A. S. Djalal
    1970 Vorkommen und Haltung der Ostlichen Hanoigbiene (Apis cerana Fabr.) in Afghanistan. Apidologie 1:329-341.

623 Schneider, P. and W. Kloft
    1971 Beobachtungen zum Gruppenverteidigungsverhalten der Ostlichen Honigbiene (Apis cerana Fabr.). Z. Tierpsychol. 29:337-342.

624 Schramm, Ryszard W.
    1977 Polnische Bergsteiger in Darwax. Afghanistan Journal 4(3):96-99. Maps; photos.

II. GEOGRAPHY

625 Schwarz, Fred
1949 Bakschisch und Feidah. Erinnerungen an Afghanistan [Bakhshish and Faydeh. Recollections of Afghanistan]. Munich: F. Bassermann. Pp. 120.

626 Scully, J.
1887 On the Mammals and Birds collected by Captain C. E. Yate, C. S. I., of the Afghan Boundary Commission. Journal of the Asiatic Society of Bengal 56(2:68-89).

627 Sedqi, Mohammad Osman
1952 Qandahar [Qandahar]. Afghanistan 7(4):21-34.

The situation and history of Afghanistan's second-largest city.

628 Sedqi, Mohammad Osman
1952 La plaine de Herat [The Plain of Herat]. Afghanistan 7(4):54-55.

A description of the plain, its appearance, climate, and winds.

629 Sedqi, Mohammad Osman
1952 Les villes d'Ariana [The Cities of Aryana]. Afghanistan Journal 7(1):5-21; (2):29-41; (3):31-44.

A list of 140 cities of ancient Bactria, with an explanatory note on the location and history of each.

630 See Afghanistan
1959 Kabul: Defense Ministry Printing Press. Pp. 70; map.

631 Sellman, Roger R.
1954 An Outline Atlas of Eastern History. London: E. Arnold Ltd. Pp. 63.

Fifty-three maps, chronologically arranged and with historical explanations of each, showing the spread of empires, and of religions, etc. Some ten of them are concerned with Afghanistan.

632 Serfaty, A.
1948 Au sujet d'un cas tératologique chex un scorpion afghan [On a Teratological Case in an Afghan Scorpion]. Afghanistan 3(3):18-19.

II. GEOGRAPHY

The author lists seven authenticated cases of scorpions with two tails, and gives a bibliography.

633 Shah, S. I. A.
    1977 Afghanistan of the Afghans. London: E. J. Brill, (repr. of 1928 ed.). Pp. 272; illustrations; frontispiece.

634 Sheptunov, I.
    1958 Budni Kabula [Work Days in Kabul]. Sovremenny Vostok 7:33-36.

    Impressions of a visitor, with emphasis on projects built with Soviet aid.

635 Shor, Jean Bowie
    1955 After You, Marco Polo. New York: McGraw Hill Book Company, Inc. Pp. 294.

    Following the route of Marco Polo, the Shors journeyed across Asia, through untraveled parts of Afghanistan and the Wakhan Corridor, to Hunza. The description tends largely to the personal discomfort of the Shors. Their experiences in the huts of the Afghans are interesting, though unreliable as to general information.

636 Shor, Jean Bowie and Franc Shor
    1950 We Took the Highroad in Afghanistan. National Geographic Magazine 98:673-706.

    Lightly written, but very informative, account of a trip into the seldom visited Wakhan Corridor. Splendid color photographs.

637 Shroder, John F. Jr., Cathleen M. DiMarzio, Dennis E. Bussom, and David Braslau
    1978 Remote Sensing of Afghanistan. Afghanistan Journal 5(4):123-128.

638 Siddiqi, I. H.
    n.d. Some Aspects of Afghan Despotism in India. London: E.J. Brill. Pp. xxiv, 184; bibliography; index.

639 Siiger, Halfdan
    1948 Henning Haslunc-Christensen: In Memoriam. Afghanistan 3(3):33-35.

    A tribute to the head of the Danish Scientific Mission who died at Kabul.

II. GEOGRAPHY

640   Sinclair, Gordon
            1936   Khyber Caravan. Through Kashmire, Waziristan,
                Afghanistan, Baluchistan and Northern India. London:
                Hurst and Blackett, Ltd. Pp. 278; maps.

            An American edition published in 1936 under the same title
            runs to 316 pages.

641   Singh, Narenderpal
            1963   Furrows in the Snow. New Delhi: Vidya Prakashan
                Bhavan. Pp. 147.

            A record of travel in Afghanistan in 1958. Originally
            published in Punjabi under the title of Aryana.

642   Sircar, Joydeep
            1974   The Himalayan Handbook: An Annotated Index of the
                Named Peaks Over 6095 Meters (19998 feet) of Afghanistan
                and the Indian Subcontinent. Calcutta: Sircar.

643   Sivall, T. R.
            1977   Synoptic-Climatological Study of Asian Summer
                Monsoon in Afghanistan. Geografiska Annaler Series A -
                Physical Geography 59(1-2):67-87.

644   Smith, R. B.
            1842   Notes on the Recent earthquakes on the Northwestern
                Frontier. Journal of the Asiatic Society of Bengal
                11:242-55.

645   Snead, Rodman E.
            1978   Geomorphic History of the Mundigak Valley. Afghani-
                stan Journal 5(2):59-69. Maps; photos; diagram.

646   Snesarev, A. E.
            1921   Afganistan [Afghanistan]. Moscow.

647   Snoy, Peter
            1975   Bagrot - Eine Dardische Talschaft im Karakorum.
                Graz, Austria: Akademische Druck u. Verlagsanstalt.

648   Sokolov-Strakhov, K.
            1930   V gornykh dolinakh Afganistana [In the Mountain
                Valleys of Afghanistan]. Moscow: Moskovskoe T-vo
                Pisatelei. Pp. 78.

649   Sonin, I. I.
            1977   Geologo-strukturnyi analiz Tsentral'nogo Afganistana
                po dannym nazemnykh i aerokosmicheskikh issledovanii.

II. GEOGRAPHY

>Geologic-Structural Analysis of Central Afghanistan Based on Data from Surface and Aerospace Research.) Unpublished Ph.D. Dissertation. Moskovskii gosudarstvennyi universitet.

650 Spivack, M. R.
>1964 The Figured Mountains of Afghanistan. Bayonne, NJ: Y. Seldon. n.p.

651 Stanislaw, Miarkowski
>1976 On the Roads of Afghanistan. Moscow: Nauka Publishers.

652 Starmuhlner, Ferdinand
>1957 Salzseen und Steppen. Eine hindernisreiche Autoreise durch Persien und Afghanistn [Salt Seas and Steppes. An obstacle-filled Auto Tour through Persia and Afghanistan]. Vienna: Büchergilde Gutenberg. Pp. 208.

653 Stemuller, Camille Mirepois
>1971 Afghanistan in Pictures. New York: Sterling Publishing Company. Pp. 64.

654 Stentz, Edward
>1946 The Climate of Afghanistan: Its Aridity, Dryness and Divisions. New York: Polish Institute of Arts and Sciences in America. Pp. 16; maps.

655 Stentz, Edward
>1947 The Climate of Afghanistan: Its Aridity, Dryness and Divisions. Geographical Review 37:672.

>A note on Dr. Stentz' climatic-regions map of Afghanistan and his "dryness index."

656 Stentz, Edward
>1946 Earthquakes in Afghanistan. Afghanistan 1(1):41-50.

>Afghanistan considered as part of the Hindu Kush seismic area.

657 Stenz, Edward
>1957 Precipitation, Evaporation and Aridity in Afghanistan. Acta Geophysica Polnica 5:245-255.

658 Steponov, I.
>1952 [From Mazar-i-Sharif to Kabul.] Vokrug Sveta 6:43-48. Moscow.

II. GEOGRAPHY

659 Stewart, C. E.
   1886 The Herat Valley and the Persian Border, from the Hari-Rud to Sistan. Proceedings of the Royal Geographical Society, New Monthly Series, 8:137-156.

   Discursive, disorganized account of wanderings and incidents, mostly on the Iranian side of the fronties. In 1885 he visited Herat and gives an interesting description of the town. The author was Assistant Commissioner of the Afghan Boundary Commission.

660 Stratil-Sauer, G.
   1929 From Leipzig to Kabul. An Account of my Motor-Cycle Ride to Afghanistan and my Nine Months' Imprisonment in that Country. London: Hutchinson. Pp. 284; map.

   A mad idea and a crazy journey. English version of the German original which had been published a year earlier at Berlin.

661 Sykes, Christopher
   1934 Some Notes on a Recent Journey in Afghanistan Geographical Journal 84:327-336; map.

   A young English writer tells of a trip by private car from Iran to Herat, and thence via the northern route to Kabul. Well written, keen observations on such subjects as city life at Herat and country life among the Turkoman along the northern road.

662 Tanner, H. C.
   1881 Notes on the Chugani and Neighbouring Tribes of Kafiristan. Proceedings of the Royal Geographical Society 3.

663 Tanzi, Gastone
   1929 Viaggo in Afghanistan [Travel in Afghanistan]. Milan: Maia. Pp. 267.

   The second part of this work by an Italian traveler concerns Afghanistan: Nell'inquiete Afghanistan [In Restless Afghanistan], Pp. 135-267. Rather general travel description, augmented by observations on the government of King Amanullah.

664 Tarzi, Mahmud
   1915 Siyahet-mamah yi sih qit'eh yi ruyi zamin [Travel Account of Three Continents]. Kabul: 'Inayet, (1333 A.H.)

II. GEOGRAPHY

Account in Persian of a journey through Asia, Africa and Europe by the author in the year 1890 A.D. Tarzi, one of the first Afghan journalists, broadened the local horizon between 1912 and 1916 by publishing a number of works, including translations from French and Turkish. He won favor under Amir Amanullah who became his son-in-law and made Tarzi the principal journalistic editor and then Foreign Minister of Afghanistan.

665 Tate, George Passman
1909 The Frontier of Baluchistan. Travels on the Borders of Persia and Afghanistan. London: Witherby and Co. Pp. vi, 261; maps.

Professional study by a member of the Survey of India, attached to the two MacMahon missions of 1884-85 and 1903-04, dealing with the geography, water supply and population of a part of the Afghan-Indian frontier. Reprinted 1976 with an introduction by Henry McMahon.

666 Tate, George Passman
1910-1912 Seistan. A Memoir on the History, Topography, Ruins and People of the Country. 2 vols. Calcutta: Superintendent, Government Printing, India. Pp. (1):1-272; (2):272-378.

A uniquely detailed and valuable source, although the bulk of the descriptive material concerns territory within Iran rather than in Afghanistan.

667 Tate, George Passman
1973 The Kingdom of Afghanistan. A Historical Sketch. With an introduction note by H. M. Durand. London: E. J. Brill, 1973 (reprint of 1911 ed.). Pp. x, 224; map; index; appendix.

668 Temple, R. C.
1880 Remarks on the Afghans Found Along the Route of the Tal Choitiali Field Force, in the Spring of 1879. Journal of the Asiatic Society of Bengal 49(1):91-106; 143-80).

669 Thomas, Lowell J.
1925 Beyond Khyber Pass into Forbidden Afghanistan. Revised Edition, Illustrated with Many Photographs Taken by Harry A. Chase and the Author. New York: Grosset and Dunlap. Pp. xvii, 255; maps.

II. GEOGRAPHY

>An account of a journey through Afghanistan where, in 1925, few Europeans were admitted. There are vivid characterizations of the Afghans and much informative (and highly-colored) background material.

670 Tichy, Herbert
1937 Zum Heiligstenberg der Welt. Auf Landstrassen und Pilgerfahrten in Afghanistan, Indien und Tibet. Geleitwort von Sven Hedin [To the Holiest Mountain in the World. On Highways and Pilgrimmages in Afghanistan, India and Tibet. Foreword by Sven Hedin]. Vienna: W. L Seidel und Sohn. Pp. 192; 2 maps.

A young Austrian geologist set out by motorcycle to complement the explorations of Sven Hedin. Afghanistan was the first country visited and the tales from this country set the atmosphere for the balance of the book.

671 Tichy, Herbert
1938 Tibetan Aventure. Travels through Afghanistan, India and Tibet. With a Preface by Sven Hedin. London: Faber and Faber. Pp. 261; 2 maps.

672 Tichy, Herbert
1940 Afghanistan, das Tor nach Indien [Afghanistan, the Gateway to India]. Leipzig: W. Goldmann. Pp. 237; bibliography; 4 maps.

Part I is a political and military history of Afghanistan. Part II, more briefly, deals with the people, the present position and the future. Good background material.

673 Tilman, H. W.
1948 Wakkan: Or How to Vary a Route. Journal of the Royal Central Asian Society. 35:249-254.

Detailed record, with attention concentrated upon topographical features of a trip on horseback from Kashghar through the Afghan corridor to Fayzabad in Afghanistan and thence to Chitral. Date of trip not given, but apparently a number of years prior to this publication.

674 Todd (Major)
1844 Report of a Journey from Herat to Simla, via Candahar, Cabool and the Punjab, undertaken in the year 1838. Journal of the Asiatic Society of Bengal 13:339-60.

II. GEOGRAPHY

675 Tosi, M.
   1974 The lapis lazuli trade across the Iranian plateau in the 3rd millenium B. C. Istituto universitario orientale: Gururamanjarika, Studi in onore di G. Tucc, 1:3-22, Napoli.

676 Toynbee, Arnold J.
   1961 Between Oxus and Jumna. London: Oxford University Press. Pp. 211.

677 Toynbee, Arnold
   1962 A Journey in Afghanistan and in the North-West Frontier. Royal Central Asian Journal 49(3-4):277-88.

   The author prophetically reports that enmity between Afghanistan and Pakistan will inevitably lead to Soviet penetration of both countries unless they compose their differences (which he considered unlikely).

678 Trautman, Kathleen
   1972 Spies Behind the Pillars, Bandits at the Pass. New York: David McKay.

679 Trench, F.
   1873 The Central Asian Question. Journal of the Royal United Service Institution 18:184-211.

680 Trinkler, Emil
   1925 Quer durch Afghanistan nach Indien [Through Afghanistan to India]. Berlin: Kurt Vowinckel. Pp. 234; sketch map. (See no. 682.)

681 Trinkler, Emil
   1928 Afghanistan. Eine landskundliche Stuie auf Grund der vorhandenen Materiel und einiger Beogachtung [Afghanistan: An Informed Study Based on Existing Material and Personal Observation]. Petermanns Mitteilunger, Ergänzungsheft Nr. 196. Gotha: Justur Perthes. Pp. 80; maps; plates; bibliography.

682 Trinkler, Emil
   1928 Through the Heart of Afghanistan; Edited and Translated by B. K. Featherstone. Boston: Houghton, Mifflin Co. Pp. 246; map.

   The original work in German was published in 1925 (see no. 680). The author was a geologist accompanying members of a German trading company from Russia through Afghanistan to India in 1923. Knowing Persian he acquired and

II. GEOGRAPHY

recorded information on a large range of subjects: crossing the heart of the country from Herat to Kabul, he prospected for coal and iron.

683 Trussell, James and Eleanor Brown
1979 A Close look at the Demography of Afghanistan. Demography (Population Association of America) 16:137-156.

684 Turri, E.
1961 Mulini a vento nell'oasi di Herat. Rivista Geografica Italiana 68:71-75.

685 Uddin, Islam
1972 Agrargeographische Untersuchung in Guldara und Ghori als Beispiele fur alt-und Jungsiedelland im Afghanischen Hindukush: Gegenuberstellung und Vegleich. Unpublished Ph.D. DDissertation. University of Koln.

686 Uhlig, Helmut
1978 Am Thron der Gotter: Abenteurerliche Reisen im Hindukusch und Himalaya. Munchen. Pp. 253.

687 Vakili, 'Aziz-al-Din
1968 Ghaznah dar du Qarni-i Akhir. [History of Ghaznah in the Last Two Centuries]. Kabul. Pp. 234 (Dari text); plates. (1346 A.H.)

688 Vambery, Arminius
1864 Travels in Central Asia, Being an Account of a Journey from Teheran across the Turkoman Desert on the Eastern Shore of the Caspian to Khiva, Bokhara and Samargand Performed in the Year 1863. London: John Murray. Pp. xxvi, 443; map.

A member of the Hungarian Academy who undertook a linguistic mission for that Academy in Central Asia. Calls special attention to the advance of Russia in Asia. Chapters XII, XIII, XIV, and XXIV are especially concerned with Afghanistan.

689 Vambery, Arminius
1885 The Geographical Nomenclature of the Disputed Country between Merv and Herat. Proceedings of the Royal Geographical Society 7:591-596.

II. GEOGRAPHY

A serious attempt, which falls short of a real contribution due to lack of support from reliable, earlier sources. In this same volume, F. Goldsmid made additions and corrections to the article on pages 823-824.

690 Vambery, Arminius (trans)
1899 The Travels and Adventures of the Turkish Admiral Sidi Ali Reis in India. Afghanistan, Central Asia, and Persia, during the Years 1553-56. London: Luzac and Co. Pp. xviii, 123.

The original manuscript of these travels had been published in its native Turkish, in German and in French prior to the English edition. This English edition contains notes and a more scholarly appreciation of the original text. Two chapters deal with Afghanistan: one with the general area of Badahkshan and the other with the region of Kabul.

691 Verchere, A. M.
1866-1867 Kashmir, the Western Himalaya and the Afghan Mountains with a note on the fossils by M. Edouard de Verneuil. Journal of the Asiatic Society of Bengal 25 (part I:89-133; 159-202). Part II of the work appears in the Journal of the Asiatic Society of Bengal 26:9-50; 83-115.

692 Vertunni, Renato
1949 Afghanistan. Afghanistan 4:(2)18-24.

Impressions of landscape, literature, legend and modern Kabul, with imagined sound effects of music, airplanes and national songs.

693 Vigne, Godfrey T.
1840 A Personal Narrative of a Visit to Ghuzni, Kabul, and Afghanistan, and of a Residence at the Court of Dost Mohamed; with Notices of Runjit Sing, Khiva, and the Russian Expedition. London: Whittaker and Co. Pp. xii, 479; map.

From Peshawar the British author crossed into Afghanistan in the Gomal area, south of the Khyber Pass, and made his way to Ghazni and thence to Kabul before returning to Peshawar. Useful observations made in tribal territory (Sulayman Khel) and a good account of the court of Amir Dost Muhammad.

II. GEOGRAPHY

694　Visit Afghanistan
　　　1958　London: Information Bureau, Royal Afghan Embassy. Pp. 39.

　　　Well-illustrated, clearly written presentation of the tourist attractions of the country. No longer published.

695　Volk, O. H.
　　　1954　Klima und Pflanzen-Verbreitung in Afghanistan. Vegetatio 6:422-433.

696　Volk, O. H.
　　　1955　afghanische Drogen. Planta Medica 3:129-146.

697　Volk, O. H.
　　　1964　Klima und Pflanzenverbreitung in Afghanistan. Vegetatio 5-6:422-423.

698　Wagner, W.
　　　1962　Afghanistan. Medizin Heute 11:84.

699　Wahab Khan, Abdul
　　　1950　Observations concerning Andkhoy Water. Afghanistan 5(2):36-46; (3):18-24.

　　　The rivers and springs that irrigate the agricultural land, including a detailed description of the country.

700　Waley, Arthur (trans)
　　　1931　The Travels of an Alchemist. The Journey of the Taoist Ch'and-Ch'un from China to the Hindukush at the Summons of Chingiz Khan. London: George Routledge and Sons, Ltd. Pp. xi, 166; map.

　　　At the end of the long journey from east of Peking the monk and his companion, who recorded the trip, crossed the Oxus River and passed through Balkh and then over the Hindu Kush to near the site of Kabul. Extremely summary account of the route and things observed.

701　Wallbrecher, Echard
　　　1974　Zur Geologie der Sudflanke der Afghanischen Hindukush zwischen den Flussen Salang und Parandeh. On the Geology of the Southern Slope of the Afghan Hindukush Between the Salang and Parandeh Rivers.) Unpublished Ph.D. Dissertation. Freie Universität Berlin. Pp. 150.

II. GEOGRAPHY

702 Weippert, D.
1970 Zur geologischen Entwicklung von Zentral- und Sud-Afghanistan. Beih. Geol. Jb. 92.

703 Whistler, Hugh
1945 Materials for the Ornithology of Afghanistan. Journal of the Bombay Natural History Society, 45:61-72; 106-122; 462-485.

704 Whitemore, Richard
1980 An American in Afghanistan. Social Education 44(3):202-6.

705 Wiebe, Dietrich
1975 Zum Problem stadtplanerischer Entscheidungsprozesse in Afghanistan. Afghanistan Journal 2(4):135-147. Photos, map.

706 Wiebe, Dietrich
1978 Stadtstruktur und kulturgeographischer Wandel in Kandahar und Sudafghanistan. Kiel: Selbstverlag des Geografish Institut der Universität. Pp. 400.

707 Willcocks, Sir James
1904 From Kabul to Kumassi: Twenty-four Years of Soldiering and Sport. London: John Murray. Pp. xvi, 440.

708 Williams, Maynard Owen
1931 The Citroen-Haardt Trans-Asiatic Expedition Reaches Kashmir. National Geographic Magazine 60:387-444.

In this account of a trip across Asia several pages and a number of excellent photographs are devoted to the crossing of Afghanistan following the long route from Herat through Qandahar, Ghazni, and Kabul to Peshawar.

709 Williams, Maynard Owen
1933 Afghanistan Makes Haste Slowly. National Geographic Magazine 64:731-769.

Ancient manners and modes of life are contrasted, through illustrations, with the efforts of the Afghan government to modernize the land.

710 Williams, Maynard Owen
1946 Back to Afghanistan. National Geographic Magazine, 90:517-544.

II. GEOGRAPHY

> After thirteen years the writer returns to Afghanistan and comments on the far-reaching changes effected during that time. Illustrated with remarkable color photographs.

711 Wilson, Andrew
   1961 North from Kabul. London: George Allen & Unwin Ltd. Pp. 180.

> According to the dust jacket, "This is Afghanistan as few people have seen it and come back to tell the story," ... "a country ... filled with rumor and intrigue, and made precarious by the dangerous political liaison of an autocratic government ..." The text is somewhat less lurid.

712 Wittekind, H.
   1973 Geologische Karte Zentral-und Sud-Afghanistan 1:500 000. 4 Blatter mit Erlauterunger. Hannover. Pp. 109.

713 Wolfart, Reinhard and Hanspeter Wittekindt
   1980 Geologie von Afghanistan. Stuttgart: Gebrueder Borntraeger. Pp. 513.

714 Wolfart, R. and M. Kursten
   1974 Stratigraphie und Palageographie des Kambriums im mittleren Sud-Asien (Iran bis Nord-Indien). Geology Journal Bulletin 8:185-234.

715 Wood, John
   1841 A Personal Narrative of a Journey to the Source of the River Oxus by the Route of the Indus, Kabul, and Badakhshan. Performed under the Sanction of the Supreme Government of India in the Years 1836, 1837, 1838. London: John Murray. Pp. xv, 424.

716 Wyart, J., P. Bariand, and J. Filippi
   1972 Le lapis-lazuli de Sar-e-Sang (Badakhshan, Afghanistan) Rev. geogr. phys. et geol. dynam. 14(4):443-448.

717 Yate, Arthur Campbell
   1887 England and Russia Face to Face in Asia; Travels with the Afghan Boundary Commission. London: W. Blackwood and Sons. Pp. vi, 481; folding map.

> Covers much the same ground as the account of the work of the Boundary Commission by his brother Charles (see no. 719), but is not as complete, since the author left before the survey work was finished.

II. GEOGRAPHY

718 Yate, Charles Edward
1887 Notes on the City of Herat. Journal of the Asiatic Society of Bengal 56:84-106.

An article of scholarly value for its description of Moslem monuments of Herat and the translation into English of a number of Persian inscriptions on these structures.

719 Yate, Charles Edward
1888 Northern Afghanistan, or Letters from the Afghan Boundary Commission. With Route Maps. Edinburgh and London: W. Blackwood and Sons. Pp. viii, 430; maps.

Describes the activity of the commission--by a British officer member--in 1885 in northwestern Afghanistan and then their long trip back to Lahore through Afghanistan. The closing chapters deal with the return of the mission in 1887 for the actual demarcation of the frontier. Includes a plan of Balkh, a map of the northwestern frontier of Afghanistan and sketch map.

720 Yule, H.
1872 Papers Connected with the Upper Oxus Regions. Journal of the Royal Geographical Society 42:438-481; map.

Contains Pandit Manphul's report on Badakhshan, an account of a journey by Munshi Paiz Baksh from Peshawar through Kabul and Badakhsah to Kashghar, and corrections of the editor to erroneous notions on the topography of the Upper Oxus regions.

721 Zachova, Eliska
1960 Tajamny Afghanistan [Mysterious Afghanistan]. Prague: Stami nakladztelstvi detske literatury.

722 Zalmay, M. Wali
1972 Kandahar. Kabul: Zuri's Publishing House. 2 volumes. Pp. 427

723 Zaman, Mohammad
1951 The Regions of Drybelts in Afghanistan. Afghanistan 6(2):63-68.

The location of the dry-belts, their vegatation, and its uses.

II. GEOGRAPHY

724 Zeigler, J. M.
1958 Geological Study of Shamshir Ghar Cave, S. Afghanistan, and Report of Terraces along Panshir Valley near Kabul. Journal of Geology 66:16-27.

725 Ziemke, Kurt
1939 Als deutscher Gesandter in Afghanistan [As the German Envoy in Afghanistan]. Stuttgart and Berlin: Deutsche Berlagsanstalt. Pp. 393; map.

Accounts of travel in Afghanistan in 1933. First from Lahore through the Khyber Pass to Kabul, and then a "circular tour" of the country. The closing section deals with life at Kabul and with an estimation of the character of the Afghans.

726 Zurmati, Fazl Ahmad
1951 Khosh Amadid bah Kabul [Welcome to Kabul]. Kabul: Matba'eh-yi 'umumi. Pp. 1-36; 1-24; plan of Kabul. (1330 A.H.)

The left-hand cover reads "Welcome to Kabul," followed by 36 pages in English; the right cover has the Dari title, followed by the Dari text.

III. HISTORY

Pre-Achaemenid; Achaemenid; Parthian;
Sassanian; Buddhistic; Islamic
Anglo-Afghan and Anglo-Russian
relations; foreign relations

The very names of the historical periods of Afghanistan reflect its focal position in Asia as an area which attracted various ethnic groups, as a corridor for migratory movements and conquering armies, and as a region which in turn was subject and then overlord. Certain of those periods of the thousand or so years prior to the influx of the Moslems into the region have been studied by scholars--the intensive concentration on the Buddhistic by French linguists and archaeologists is an example--but major problems related to chronology, the extent and duration of local kingdoms, the direction and force of artistic and cultural influences, and the origin of ethnic groups remain unresolved. Most welcome for everyone interested in this part of the world would be a fresh, new history of the area prior to Islam. The Afghan scholars are themselves producing such a work in Persian, but it may be too detailed and too unemphatic to fill the gap.

For the Islamic centuries, the source material in Arabic, Persian, and Pushtu is moderately adequate. It should be noted that Afghan scholars are engaged in editing and publishing these manuscripts, a number of which are quite unknown to foreign linguists and historians. In addition, some of these same local scholars are writing accounts of the reigns of noted rulers, based upon this newly available material.

As concerns the history of Afghanistan in the nineteenth and early twentieth centuries, it has been pointed out that British writers publishing in India and England dominated this field, although Russian scholars did produce some important works which failed to have any impact abroad. The contemporary history of the country is not receiving adequate attention: too many current works, with few exceptions, are based upon speculation and personal attitudes rather than on documentation. Soviet writers appear to be very active, and some of their material is published in foreign languages when it is regarded advisable to stress certain policy or propaganda lines. What are needed, however, are serious studies based on official documents and reports and on first-hand contact with the officials and individuals now engaged in making the history of the Afghans.

727   Abaeva, T. G.
          1964 Ocherki istorii Badakhshana [Sketches from the
          History of Badakhshan]. Tashkent: Izdatel'stvo "Nauka"
          Uzbekskoy SSR. Pp. 164; bibliography.

III. HISTORY

The first comprehensive study of a comparatively little-known area of Afghanistan. Its three chapters concern its geography and resources, trade routes, and an historical and political outline from ancient times. Based on original and secondary sources.

728 Abd al-Karim 'Alavi
     1848 Muharabeh-i Kabul va Qandahar [The War of Kabul and Qandahar]. Lucknow. Pp. 87.

Lithographed account in Persian of the first British invasion of Afghanistan in 1838-42, based in part on a heroic poem, Akbar nameh, on the deeds of Akbar Khan, by Qasim Jan. Another edition was put out at Lucknow in 1850 and one at Cawnpore in 1851.

729 Abd al-Karim 'Alavi
     1266 Tarikh-i Ahmad [History of Ahmad]. Lucknow: ultan al-matabi, [1850]. Pp. 56

A lithographed work in Persian dealing with the Durrani dynasty from the reign of Ahmad Shah to the flight of Muhammad Shah in 1797. Based upon the Husayn Shahi of Imam al-Din Husayn Chishti.

730 'Abdul Rahman, Amir
     1904 Taj al-tavarikh, ya'ni savarat-i 'umri [The Crown of Histories, or an Account of a Life]. 2 vols., lithographed. Kabul.

Apparently a revised Persian edition of Mir Munshi 1900.

731 Ademec, Ludwig W. (ed)
     1972 Historical and Political Gazetteer of Afghanistan I: Badakhshan Province and Northeastern Afghanistan. Graz, Austria: Akademische Druck Verlag. Pp. 272.

Revised edition of the formerly secret gazetteer of Afghanistan. Originally compiled in 1914. Includes original text and adds new information, a glossary, a persian index and a large map section is added. An important reference source for historical and social science research. Subsequent volumes cover different areas of the country and are arranged in the same style.

III. HISTORY

732 Adamec, Ludwig W. (ed)
1973 Historical and Political Gazetteer of Afghanistan II: Farah and Southwestern Afghanistan. Graz, Austria: Akademische Druck Verlag. Pp. 385.

733 Adamec, Ludwig W. (ed)
1974 Notes on the Afghanistan Gazetteer Project. Afghanistan Journal 1(4):118.

734 Adamec, Ludwig W. (ed)
1975 Historical and Political Gazetteer of Afghanistan III: Herat and Northwestern Afghanistan. Graz, Austria: Akademische Druck Verlag. Pp. 521.

735 Adamec, Ludwig W.
1979 First Supplement to the Who's Who of Afghanistan. Graz, Austria: Akademische Druck Verlag. Pp. 53.

Includes brief sketches of major figures in Afghan politics since 1978. Names of cabinet members as well as other officials of post April 1978 Afghan bureaucracy are provided.

736 Adamec, Ludwig W. (ed)
1979 Historical and Political Gazetteer of Afghanistan IV: Mazar-i Sharif and North-central Afghanistan. Graz, Austria: Akademische Druck Verlag. Pp. 693.

737 Adamec, Ludwig W. (ed)
1980 Historical and Political Gazetteer of Afghanistan V: Kandahar and South-central Afghanistan. Graz, Austria: Akademische Druck Verlag. Pp. 667.

738 Adamec, Ludwig W. (ed)
1980 Historical and Political Gazetteer of Afghanistan VI: Kabul and Eastern Afghanistan. Graz, Austria: Akademische Druck Verlag.

739 Adye, Sir John Miller
1897 Indian Frontier Policy; an Historical Sketch. London: Smith, Elder and Company. Pp. 61.

740 Adye, John
1867 Sitana: A Mountain Campaign on the Borders of Afghanistan in 1863. London: Richard Bentley. Pp. iv, 101; sketch maps.

III. HISTORY

741   al-Afghani, Jamal al-Din
        1901 Tatimmat al-bayan fi tarikh al-Afghan [Completion of the Exposition of the History of the Afghans]. 'Ali Yusuf al-Kurdili, ed. Cairo. Pp. 192.

        A little-known work, edited in Arabic by 'Ali Yusuf al-Kurdili, by the renowned reformer of Islam.

742   Afghanistan
        1909 Revue du Monde Musulman 8:491-498.

        Contains informative material on the Amir Habibullah, including the results of his voyage to India in 1907.

743   Ahmad, A.
        1969 Afghani's Indian contacts. Journal of the American Oriental Society 89(3):476-504.

744   Ahmad, Jan
        1893 Tarikh-i Afghanistan [History of Afghanistan]. Peshawar.

        One of several well-known works by an Afghan scholar who lived at Peshawar and taught Afghan languages to British personnel.

745   Ahmad, N. D.
        1973 The Survival of Afghanistan: The Two Imperial Giants Held at bay in the Nineteenth Century. Lahore: People's Publishing House. Pp. x, 92.

746   Aitchison, C. U.
        1933 A Collection of Treaties, Engagements and Sanads Relating to India and Neighbouring Countries 13:203-305; appendices clxxi-ccix. Calcutta: Superintendent of Government Printing, India.

        As indicated, this thirteenth volume of the long series contains treaties and state papers relating to Afghanistan.

747   Akhramovich, Roman T.
        1958 Nezavisimyy Afganistan. 40 let nezavisimosti [Independent Afghanistan. 40 years of Independence]. Moscow: Izdatel'stvo Vostochnoy Literatury. Pp. 269.

748   Akhramovich, Roman T.
        1960 K kharakteristike vneshney politiki Afganistana v nachal'nyy period Vtoroy Mirovoy Voyny, 1939-1941gg [On

III. HISTORY

        the characteristics of Afghanistan's foreign policy at the beginning of the Second World War, 1939-1941]. Kratkiye Soobshcheniya Instituta Vostokovedeniya 37:1-8. Moscow.

749   Akhramovich, Roman T.
        1961 Afganistan posle vtoroy mirovoy voyny - ocherk istorii [Afghanistan after World War Two - An Historical Outline]. Moscow: Izdatel'stvo Vostochnoy Literatury. Pp. 175.

        Based primarily on the Afghan press, the work describes the political and economic situation during World War II, discusses international relations from 1946 to 1953, characterizes the period of Prime Minister Daud, and closes with a study of developments through 1960.

750   Akhramovich, Roman T.
        1962 Mirolyubivaya politika Afganistana [Peaceful policy of Afghanistan], in Bor'ba Narodov Azii za Mir, 1945-1961. Moscow: Izdatel'stvo Vostochnoy Literatury. Pp. 41-61.

751   Akhramovich, Roman T.
        1966 Outline History of Afghanistan After the Second World War. Moscow: Nauka Publishing House. Pp. 190.

        A marxist analysis of Afghan politics after World War II. Based on personal observations and journalistic sources.

752   Akhramovich, Roman T.
        1967 Concerning the Recent Stages in Afghanistan's Social History. Moscow: USSR Academy of Sciences.

753   Alder, Garry J.
        1974 The ropped Stitch. Afghanistan Journal 1(4):105-113.

754   Alder, Garry J.
        1974 The Key to India?: Britain and the Herat problem 1830-1863. Middle Eastern Studies 10(2):186-209.

755   Alder, Garry J.
        1975 The Dropped Stitch: The Course of Anglo-Afghan Relations. Afghanistan Journal 2(1):20-27.

756   Ali, Mirza Fazl
        1905 Tarikhi Badakhshan. [History of Badakhshan]. In Persian. Published in 1325 A.H. Probably in Bukhara.

III. HISTORY

        Originally a handwritten manuscript later reprinted. A very useful work on the late nineteenth-early twentieth century history of Badakhshan.

757   Ali, Mohammad
        1957 Aryana or Ancient Afghanistan. Kabul: Government Printing House. Pp. 117.

    An account of the ancient history of the region up to the coming of Islam.

758   Ali, Mohammad
        1958 Afghanistan. The National Awakening. Lahore: Punjab Educational Press. Pp.142.

    Concerns the reigns of the Hotaki and Durrani rulers.

759   Ali, Mohammad
        1959 Afghanistan (The Mohammedzai Period). Lahore: Punjab Educational Press. Pp. 211.

    A political history of Afghanistan from the beginning of the thirteenth century, with emphasis on the foreign relations of the country.

760   Ali, Mohammad
        1960 Afghanistan, the War of Independence, 1919. Lahore: Pubjab Educational Press. Pp. 62; map.

761   Ali, Mohammad
        n.d. Afghanistan. An Historical Sketch. Kabul: Government Printing House. Pp. 27.

762   Ali, Mohammad
        1965 The Afghans. Lahore: Punjab Educational Press.

763   Ali Khan, Mohammad
        1936 Progress in Afghanistan. Asiatic Review n.s. 32:863-866. London.

    Praise of the advances made in government and education since the accession of Nadir Shah in 1930.

764   Ali Quili Mirza
        1856-57 I'tizad al-Saltaneh. Tarikh-i Vaqa'i' va Savanih-i Afghanistan [History of Accidents and Events of Afghanistan]. Tehran: Muhammad Husayn Mirza. Pp. 216; map. (1273 A.H.)

III. HISTORY

A lithographed work of moderate value in Persian.

765 Allen, R. A. and R. K. Ramazani
1957 Afghanistan: Wooed But Not Won. Swiss Review of World Affairs 7(7):16-19.

A review of Afghanistan's position with respect to Soviet aid and to relations with the U.S.S.R.

766 Amoss, Harold L.
1965 The Story of Afghanistan. Wichita: McCormick-Mathers. Pp. 164; index.

One of the Global Culture Series of the publisher. A story line conveys an excellent account of the country for young readers.

767 Andrew, Sir William Patrick
1880 Our Scientific Frontier. London: W. H. Allen and Company. Pp. 103; appendices.

Covers a number of broad topics such as a description of Afghanistan, the independent tribes of the Afghan frontier and their relations with the British, probable routes of attack toward India through Afghanistan, and a consideration of the powindeh, or soldier-merchants of Afghanistan.

768 Anonymous (G. R. Elmslie?)
1863 Epitome of Correspondence Regarding our relations with Afghanistan and Herat. Lahore.

769 Anonymous
1935 Tarikh-i sistan. Edited by Malik al Shuara. Tehran (In Dari).

770 Antoine, Giles
1973 Aux sources de l'Afghanistan modern: l'oeuvre interieure de l'Emir Abdur Rahman Khan (1880-1901) [Sources of Modern Afghanistan: The Reign of the Emir Abd-er-Rahman Khan, 1880-1901]. Afghanistan 26(1):90-105.

771 Arbadzhyan, A. Z.
1960 Vneshnyaya politika i economicheskoye raxvitiye Irana i Afganistana [The Foreign Policy and Economic Development of Iran and Afghanistan]. Problemy Vostokovedeniya 3:42-54. Moscow.

III. HISTORY

772   Arefi, Abdul Ghafoor
            1975 Urban Policies, Planning and Implementation in
                Kabul, Afghanistan. Unpublished Ph.D. Dissertation.
                University of Indiana. Pp. 481.

773   Arends, A. K. (editor and trans)
            1962 Istoriya Mas'uda (1030-1041) [The History of
                Mas'ud]. Tashkent: Akad. Nauk Uzbekskoy S.S.R. Pp. 748

        First translation into a European language of the remark-
        able history by Abul Fazl Bayhaqi.

774   Argyll, George Douglas Campbell
            1879 The Afghan Question From 1841 to 1878. London:
                Strahan and Company, Ltd. Pp. 288.

        First-hand knowledge of the area sparingly reflected in a
        rather ponderous and detailed survey of the British posi-
        tion and actions toward Afghanistan.

775   Aristov, N. A.
            1896 Anglo-indiiskii "kavkaz." Stolknoveniia Anglii s
                avganskimi pogranichnymi plenenami [The Anglo-Indian
                "Caucasus," English Clashes with Afghan Border Tribes].
                Zhivaia Starina 10. St. Petersburg.

776   Artamonov, E.
            1949 American Penetration into Afghanistan. New Times
                (14):11-14. Moscow.

        An indignant Soviet protest against "mercenary, military
        and political imperialist" activities of American interest
        in Afghanistan; pointing to the damage already done there
        and to the rivalry between the British and Americans for
        control.

777   Ashe, Waller (ed)
            1881 Personal Records of the Kandahar Campaign, by
                Officers Engaged Therein. Edited and Annotated, with an
                Introduction by Major Ashe. London: David Bogue. Pp.
                lxxvi, 252.

778   Ataullah, Qazi Khan Sahib
            1947-1948 Da Pushtanu tarikh [The Pushtun History]. 2
                vols. Peshawar: Manzor Am Press.

        Volume 1 covers the history of Afghanistan from 1622 to
        1838 and vol. 2 from 1838 to 1842. The work is in Pushtu.

III. HISTORY

779 Atkinson, James
1842 The Expedition into Afghanistan. Notes and Sketches Descriptive of the Country, Contained in a Personal Narrative during the Campaign of 1839 and 1840 up to the Surrender of Dost Mohamed Khan. London: W. H. Allen and Co. Pp. xx, 428; map.

Of less interest as concerns the account of part of the First Anglo-Afghan War, by a participant, than for chapters devoted to the Durrani family and the person of Shah Shoja'.

780 Babakhodzhayev, A. Kh.
1960 Iz istorii bukharo-afganskikh otnosheniy, 1920-1924gg [From the history of Bukhara-Afghan relations, 1920-1924]. Izvestiya Akademii Nauk Uzbekskoy SSR, Seriya Obshchestvennykh Nauk 4:8-13. Tashkent.

781 Babakhodzhayev, Marat A.
1960 Bor'ba Afganistana za nezavisimost', 1838-1842 [Afghanistan in its Struggle for Independence, 1838-1842]. Moscow: Izdatel'stvo Vostochnoy Literatury. Pp. 160; bibliography.

782 Bacon, Elizabeth E. and Alfred E. Hudson
1941 Afghanistan Waits. Asia 41:31-36. New York.

783 Badakhshi, Shah Abdullah
1952 Yamgan. Afghanistan 7(4):56-58.

A short description of the district and its people.

784 Bahar, Malik al-Shu'ara' (ed)
1935 Tarikh-i Sistan, ta'lif dar hudud-i 445-725 [History of Sistan, Composed between 445-725 A.H.]. Tehran: Fardin va-bivadar. (1314 A.H.)

785 Baker, Anne and Air Chief Marshal Sir Ronald Ivelaw-Chapman
1975 Wings Over Kabul, the First Airlift. London: William Kimber. Pp. 190; map; illustrations.

786 al-Balkhi, Abu Bekr ibn 'Abdullah 'Umar ibn Da'ud al-Vayz Safi al-Din
n.d. Faza'il-i Balkh [The Virtues of Balkh].

Translation into Persian of an Arabic manuscript written at the end of the fifteenth century. The work contains a history of the province, a description of the town, traditions relating to the superiority of the town, and the

III. HISTORY

> lives of some 70 of the revered inhabitants. Copies of the manuscript are in the Bibliothèque Nationale and other collections.

787 Ballis, William B.
1966 Recent Soviet Relations with Afghanistan. Bulletin of the Institute for the Study of the U.S.S.R. 13(6):3-13.

Traces the nature of these relations from the nineteenth century to the present.

788 Banerjee, J. M.
1976 History of Firuz Shah Tughluq. London: E. J. Brill. Pp. xii, 228.

789 Barthold, Wilhelm
1928 Turkestan down to the Mongol Invasion. London: Luzac and Co., 2d ed. Pp. 513; folding map.

A reference work of great value, displaying vast erudition by the late Russian scholar. Includes the details of the history of Central Asia in the Moslem centuries prior to the Mongol invasions, a discussion of the source material--assembled in a comprehensive bibliography--and a geographical survey of Transoxiana. The work is in the E. J. W. Gibb Memorial Series. n.s. 5.

790 Barthold, Wilhelm
1965 Tarikh-i siyasi va ijtima'i Asiya markazi ta qarne davazdeh [Political and Social History of Central Asia to the Twelfth Century]. Kabul: Matba'eh Pohantun. Pp. 270. (1344 A.H.)

A Dari translation by Ali Muhammad Rahnuma of no. 789.

791 Bayhaqi, Abu al-Fazl Mohammad ibn Hasayn
1945 The Tarikhe Baihaqi Containing the Life of Massaud, son of Sultan Mahmud of Ghaznayn. Tehran: National Iranian Bank. Pp. 706. (In Dari).

792 Beaurecueil, S. de Laugier de
1962-1963 Les Publications de la Société d'Histoire d'Afghanistan [The Publications of the Historical Society of Afghanistan]. Mélanges, Institut Dominicain d'Etudes Orientales du Cairo 7:236-240.

Lists 12 items in European languages and 52 works in Dari or in Pushtu.

III. HISTORY

793 Bell, M. S.
1890 The Defence of India, and its Imperial Aspect. Journal of the Royal United Service Institution 34:939-68.

794 Bellew, Henry Walter
1862 Journal of a Political Mission to Afghanistan in 1857, under Major (now Colonel) Lumsden; With an Account of the Country and People. London: Smith, Elder and Co. Pp. xv, 480.

The first part of the book is the author's maiden effort to describe the history, country and people of Afghanistan--an effort repeated and expanded in his later works. The second part describes the route of the mission and tells of its purpose and results.

795 Bellew, Henry Walter
1879 Afghanistan and the Afghans. Being a Brief Review of the History of the Country and an Account of its People, with a Special Reference to the Present Crisis and War with the Amir Shir Ali Khan. London: Sampson Low, Marston, Searle and Rivington. Pp. 230.

A sketch of the history of the country precedes a rather lengthy summary of Anglo-Afghan relations. The author favors the so-called "Forward Policy" of bold British action to counter the threat of Russian advance in Asia.

796 Bellew, Henry Walter
1977 A General Report on the Yusufzais. London: E.J. Brill. (repr. of 1864 ed.). Pp. vii, 265; appendix.

797 Benava, Abdul Raouf
1946 Mir Wais Nikeh [Mir Wais the Ancestor]. Kabul: Matba'eh-yi 'umumi. Pp. 114; bibliography. (1325 A.H.)

An historical study in Pushtu.

798 Benava, Abdul Raouf
1956 Hotakiha [The Hotakis]. Kabul: Matba'eh-yi Doulati. Pp. 177. (1335 A.H.)

799 Bennet, Lieutenant
1839 Biographical Sketch of Shah Soojah, Ex-King of Cabul, Written by Himself, at Loodianah, in 1826-27. Translated by . . . Lieutenant Bennet of Artilery. Asiatic Journal (New Series) 39(2)2:6-15.

III. HISTORY

800   Bernard, P.
       1967 Deuxième campagne de fouilles d'Ai Khanoum en Bactriane, Comptes rendus d'Académie des Inscriptions et Belles-Lettres:360-24.

       Deals with the reigns of Shah Muhammad, Shah Ashraf, and Shah Husayn of the Hotaki dynasty in Persian.

801   Bernard, P.
       1968 Ai Khanoum, Troisième campagne de fouilles à Ai Khanoum, Comptes rendus d' Académie des Inscriptions et Belles-Lettres:263-79.

802   Bernard, P.
       1968 Ai Khanoum, Proccedings of the British Academy 53:71-95.

803   Besant, Annie Wood
       1931 England, India and Afghanistan and the Story of Afghanistan; Or, Why the Tory Government Gags the India Press. Madras: Theosophical Publishing House. Pp. 123.

       First print in London in 1879.

804   Biryukor, A.
       1950 The Soviet Union and Afghanistan. New Times 22:16-17.

       Emphasizes the friendly, selfless attitude of the U.S.S.R. toward Afghanistan, in contrast to the alleged rapacious attitude of the United States.

805   Boldyrev, A. N. (ed)
       1959 Ta'rikh-i Badakhshan ("Istoriya Badakhshana") [History of Badakhshan]. Leningrad: Izdatel'stvo Leningradskoqo universiteta. Pp. 68 and 253; index.

       The second part of the work gives the Persian text of the history.

806   Bosworth, Clifford Edmund
       1962 The Imperial Policy of the early Ghaznavids. Islamic Studies 1(3):49-82.

807   Bosworth, Clifford Edmund
       1962 The Titulature of the Early Ghaznavids. Oriens 15:210-233.

III. HISTORY

808 Bosworth, Clifford Edmund
1963 Early Sources for the History of the First Four Ghaznavid Sutans (977-1041). Islamic Quarterly 7(1/2):3-22.

809 Bosworth, Clifford Edmund
1963 The Ghaznavids. Their Empire in Afghanistan and Eastern Iran 994-1040. Edinburgh: Edinburgh University Press. Pp. xi, 331; maps; bibliography; index.

Thorough research in original sources, resulting in work of outstanding merit and interest.

810 Bosworth, Clifford Edmund
1977 The Later Ghaznavids: Splendor and Decay. New York: Columbia University Press. Pp. iv, 196.

A brief sketch of the Ghaznavid dynasty in Afghanistan and northern India by one of the best scholars of the Ghaznavid dynastic tradition in Central and South Asia.

811 Bosworth, Clifford Edmund
1977 The Medieval History of Iran, Afghanistan and Central Asia. 23 Studies in English and French. London: Variorum Reprints. Pp. 374.

812 Boukhary, Mir Abdoul Kerim
1876 Histoire de l'Asie centrale (Afghanistan, Boukhara, Khiva, Khoqand) depuis les dernières années du règne de Nadir Chah (1153), jusqu'en 122 de l'Hégire (1740-1818). Publiée, traduite et annotée par Charles Schefer [History of Central Asia (Afghanistan, Bokhara, Khiva, Khoqand) from the Last Years of the Reign of Nadir Shah (1153) to the Year 1233 of the Hegira (1740-1818). Edited, Translated and Annotated by Charles Schefer]. Paris: Leroux. Pp. vii, 306; map.

Pages 9-92 tell the stories of Ahmad Shah and those of his descendants who ruled in Afghanistan.

813 Boulonger, Robert
1974 Iran, Afghanistan. Paris: Hachette. Pp. 383; maps.

814 Bouvat, Lucien
1926 Essai sur la Civilisation Timouride [Essay on the Timurid Civilization]. Journal Asiatique 208:193-299.

A minutely detailed examination of almost every aspect of life under Timur and his successors.

III. HISTORY

815   Brereton, J. M.
            1978 Superior Person and Absolute Amir. Blackwood's
                Magazine 324(1954):141-151.

816   Bruce, George
            1967 Retreat from Kabul. London: Mayflower-Dell. Pp.
                205.

            An examination of the British attempt to control events in
            Afghanistan leading to the First Anglo-Afghan War.

817   Bushev, P. P.
            1959 Herat i anglo-iranskaya voyna 1856-1857 g.g. [Herat
                and the Anglo-Iranian War of 1856-1857]. Moscow:
                Izdatel'stvo vostochnoy literaturI. Pp. 251; biblio-
                graphy; index.

            The extensive bibliography includes many titles in
            Russian.

818   Caroe, Olaf
            1958 The Pathans 550 B.C.-A.D. 1957. London: Macmillan &
                Co. Ltd. Pp. xxii, 521; appendice; glossary; maps.

            An important work by a former British official who was
            governor of the Northwest Frontier Province from 1945
            through 1947. Concerns the origins of the Pushtuns their
            history in the Muslim Middle Ages, the period of the
            Durrani and Sikh rulers, and the British period.
            Reprinted 1976.

819   Caspani, P. E.
            1947 The First American in Afghanistan. Afghanistan
                2(3):37-42.

            The story of John Harlan. See no. 932.

820   Castagne, Joseph A.
            1935 Les relations nippo-afghanes [Japanese-Afghan Rela-
                tions]. France-Japan Journal 7:88-89. Paris.

            A very brief sketch of the subject, with some details on
            the first representatives from each country to the other.

821   Castagne, Joseph A.
            1935 Soviet Imperialism in Afghanistan. Foreign Affairs
                13:698-703.

III. HISTORY

An exceedingly well-informed article by a French specialist on Soviet activities among Moslems within and without the U.S.S.R. Traces the Soviet attitude toward Afghansitan from 1919 up through their active support of the last days of the reign of Amir Amanullah.

822 Causes of the Afghan War, Being a Selection of the Papers Laid Before Parliament, with a Connecting Narrative and Comment.
1879 London: Chatto and Windus. Pp. xii, 325.

823 Chakravarty, Suhash
1976 From Khyber to Oxus: A Study in Imperial Expansion. New Delhi: Orient Longman. Pp. vii, 280.

A historical discourse about the colonial activities of Britain and Russia in Afghanistan during the nineteenth century.

824 Chapman, E. F.
1882 The March from Kabul to Kandahar in August, and the Battle of 1st September, 1880. Journal of the Royal United Service Institution 25:282-315.

825 Chatelier, A. le
1907 L'Emir d'Afghanistan aux Indes [The Amir of Afghanistan in India]. Revue du Monde Musulman 2:35-49.

Describes the visit paid to India by the Amir Habibullah in 1906.

826 Chishti, Imam al-Din Husayn
n.d. Husayn Shahi [(The Book of) Husayn Shahi].

An important manuscript, copies of which are found in leading collections. Completed in 1798 A.D., the author writes in Persian of the times of the first Durrani rulers--Ahmad Shah, Timur Shah, and Shah Zamn--and of events in which he took part. The work is named in honor of the author's spiritual guide and literary master.

827 Chokaiev, Mustafa
1939 The Situation in Afghanistan. Asiatic Review 26:324-339.

Contains a detailed analysis of the fall of King Amanullah and of the Soviet attitude toward this event and toward Habibullah (Bacha-i Saqao).

III. HISTORY

828   Churchill, Rogers Platt
            1939 The Anglo-Russian Convention of 1907. Cedar Rapids,
               Iowa: The Torch Press. Pp. 365.

        Of particular interest is Chapter VI: The Convention
        Respecting Afghanistan, on pages 269-308.

829   La Civilisation Iranienne (Perse, Afghanistan, Iran Extérieur)
            Iranian Civilization [Persia, Afghanistan, Outer Iran)].
            1952 Paris: Payot. Pp. 346.

        This general work, produced by some 21 French scholars, is
        not identified by the name of an editor. Two chapters,
        comprising some 80 pages, deal specifically with Afghanistan in the sketchy, impressionist manner that characterizes the volume.

830   Clifford, Mary Louise
            1962 The Land and People of Afghanistan. New York: J. B.
               Lippincott. Pp. 160; index.

        A well-written account for younger readers. Reprinted
        1973.

831   Connlly, E.
            1940 Notes on the Eusofzye tribes of Afghanistan. Journal of the Asiatic Society of Bengal 9:924-37.

832   Constable, A. G.
            1879 Afghanistan: The Present Seat of War, and the Relations of That Country to England and Russia. Bulletin
               of the American Geographical Society 11:41-58.

        A British officer's perceptions of political affairs in
        Afghanistan during the last three quarters of the 19th
        century and the British interference in that country.

833   Constable, A. G.
            1978 An 1879 Lecture on Afghanistan. New York: Afghanistan Council, The Asia Society. Occasional paper No.
               16. Pp. 30. (Introduction and notes by Christopher J.
               Brunner.)

        A 1879 lecture reviewing Afghan political affairs for the
        American public. The introduction provides a list of some
        other works on Afghanistan during the period of 1840-1890.

III. HISTORY

The paper was originally published in the Bulletin of the American Geographical Society, 11, 1879, pp. 41-58 and later appeared as no. 97 in Harper's Half-Hour Series.

834 Correspondence Relating to Persia and Afghanistan
1839 London: J. Harrison and Son. Pp. xi, 524.

Official correspondence of the British Foreign Office with its representatives in India and elsewhere.

835 Courcy, Kenneth de (ed)
n.d. Report on India and Afghanistan. Intelligence Digest: Review of World Affairs 9(107):9-12.

A "special observer's" report on the Northwest Frontier Province: on the political situation there, recommending immediate settlement. Includes a very brief historical sketch of modern Afghanistan.

836 Curzon, George Nathaniel
1889 Russia in Central Asia in 1889, and the Anglo-Russian Question. London: Longmans, Green and Co., 2d ed. Pp. xii, 477; folding maps; bibliography.

The second edition of an exhaustive and soundly informative account of the spread of the Russian empire.

837 Dai, Shen-yu
1966 China and Afghanistan. China Quarterly 25:213-221. London.

Traces the history of relations between the two countries from the earliest times to the present.

838 Davidov, A. and N. Chernakhovskaia
1973 Afghanistan. Moscow: Novotsi Publishing Agency.

839 Davies, C. Collin
1942 The Problem of the North-West Frontier, 1890-1908, with a Survey of the Policy since 1849. Cambridge University Press. Pp. xii, 220; 3 maps.

Authoritative study by a former British officer in India who then taught the history of India at the University of London. The political and human geography of the area is described as is the establishment and maintenane of the frontier in question. Pages 153-173 discuss the "Afghan Problem," and the bibliography lists Parliamentary Papers on Afghanistan.

III. HISTORY

840 De Croze, Joel
1947 Afghanistan Today. Journal of the Indian Institute of International Affairs 3:29-49. New Delhi.

A well-informed, rather broad survey of efforts to bring the country abreast of the modern world, with emphasis upon political relations.

841 Defremery, M. C. (trans)
1844 Histoire des Sultans Ghouides extraite du Rouzet Essefa . . . de Mirkhond; traduite en francais par M. C. Defremery [History of the Sultans of Ghor taken from the Ruzeh es-Safa of Mirkhond, Translated into French by M. C. Defremery]. Journal Asiatique 4(2):167-200; 3:258-291.

For the complete edition of this work see no. 985.

842 Dickson, W. E. R.
1924 East Persia. A Backwater of the Great War. London: E. Arnold and Co. Pp. vii, 279; folding map.

A first-hand account of experiences during World War I. Chapter XII, "The Afghan War of 1919," describes the measures taken by the author along the Persian-Afghan frontier in anticipation of possible fighting.

843 Dieterle, Alfred
1973 Vegetationskundliche Untersuchungen im Gebeit von Band-i-Amir (Zentralafghanistan) [Phytosociological Investigations in the District of Band-i-Amir (Central Afghanistan)]. Unpublished Ph.D. Dissertation. Munchen.

844 Dietmar, Rudolf Georg
1976 Zur Geologie des Kabul-Beckens, Afghanistan [On the Geology of the Kabul Basin, Afghanistan]. Unpublished Ph.D. Dissertation. Universiät Köln. Pp. 113.

845 Djouzdjani
1963 Tabakat-i Nasiri. Persian translation by Abdul Hai Habibi. Kabul.

846 Dodwell, H. H. (ed)
1929 The Cambridge History of the British Empire, vol. 4. British India, 1497-1858. Cambridge University Press. Pp. xxii, 683.

III. HISTORY

>Chapter XXVII, Afghanistan, Russia and Persia, by W. A. J. Archbold, including pages 483-520, deals with the situation in Afghanistan from the end of the eighteenth century until 1842. The detailed acount of political maneuvering and of British military triumphs and disaster is documented from official sources. (This same work is Volume 5 of the Cambridge History of India.)

847 Dodwell, H. H. (ed)
1934 The Cambridge Shorter History of India. Cambridge University Press. Pp. xix, 970; sketch maps.

Extraordinarily condensed and crowded account, featuring thousands of names of people and places. Regarding Afghanistan, the most pertinent material is in Pt. I, Chapter V: Foreign Invaders of North-West India and in several chapters within Pt. II: Muslim India.

848 Dollot, Rene
1958 Situation de l'Afghanistan [The Situation of Afghanistan]. Politique Étrangère 23:353-364.

A summary of recent events, with emphasis upon foreign relations.

849 Dor, Remy
1975 Introduction a l'etude des Kirghiz du Pamir Afghan. [Introduction to the Study of the Kirghiz of the Afghan Pamir]. Unpublished Ph.D. Dissertation. Paris-Sorbonne (Paris IV). Pp. 353.

850 Dor, R. and C. M. Naumann
1978 Die Kirghisen des Afghanischen Pamir. Akademische Druck. Verlag. Pp. 124; plates.

851 Dorn, Bernhard (trans)
1829 History of the Afghans: Translated from the Persian of Nimatullah, by Bernhard Dorn. London: Oriental Translation Committee. Pt. I, xv, 184; Pt. II, viii, 131.

The translation of a manuscript in the library of the Royal Asiatic Society was carried out by the Professor of Oriental Literature of the Imperial University at Kharkov. The original work was composed in 1609-1611 and as given here--not in its entirety--comprises the history of the Afghans up until the sixteenth century and the biographies of 68 Moslem saints of Afghan origin. See no. 942.

III. HISTORY

852   Duke, Joshua
            1883 Recollections of the Kabul Campaign, 1879 and 1880.
                London: Allen. Pp. xvi, 424.

853   Dupree, Louis
            1956 Afghanistan Between East and West. Royal Central
                Asian Journal 43(1):52-60; 2 maps.

            Summary of six series of invasions of Afghanistan between
            the second century B.C. and 1222 A.D.

854   Dupree, Louis
            1964 Afghanistan: The Canny Neutral. The Nation 199(7):
                134-137.

855   Dupree, Louis
            1965 Afghanistan in the Twentieth Century. Royal Central
                Asian Journal 52(1):20-30.

856   Dupree, Louis
            1967 The Retreat of the British Army From Kabul to
                Jalalabad in 1842: History and Folklore. Journal of
                the Folklore Institute 4(1):50-74.

857   Dupree, Louis
            1974 The First Anglo-Afghan War: Folklore and History.
                Afghanistan 26(4):1-28.

858   Dupree, Louis
            1977 Afghan and British Military Tactics in the First
                Anglo-Afghan War (1838-1842). The Army Quarterly and
                Defense Journal 107(2):214-221.

859   Dupree, Louis
            1977 Afghanistan, 1880-1973. In Commoners, Climbers and
                Notables. Edited by C. A. O. van Nieumwenhuijze.
                Leiden: Brill. Pp. 152-174.

860   Dupree, Louis and Nancy Hatch
            1967 Dr. Brydon's Report of the British Retreat From
                Kabul in January, 1852: An Important Historical Docu-
                ment. Afghanistan 20(3):55-65.

861   Dupree, Nancy Hatch
            1970 Nineteenth Century Uzbak Khanates of Northern
                Afghanistan. United Nations Mirror 4(37):3-7.

III. HISTORY

862 Dupree, Nancy Hatch
1975 The Question of Jalalabad During the First Anglo-Afghan War. Asian Affairs 62:45-59, 177-188.

863 Dupree, Nancy Hatch
1975 Will the Sikhs take Jalalabad? A Footnote to the First Anglo-Afghan War. Afghanistan Journal 2(2):53-59. Map; illustrations.

864 Durand, Sir Henry Marion
1879 The First Afghan War and its Causes. London: Longmans, Green and Co. Pp. xxxvii, 445.

A heavy, detailed account of British-Afghan relations preceding the war and the war itself up to March of 1842. The author spent many years in India as an army officer and administrator.

865 East India (Afghanistan)
1919 Papers Regarding Hostilities with Afghanistan. London: H. M. Stationery Office. Pp. vi, 36.

Letters from the Amir of Afghanistan to the Viceroy of India, etc. Text of the Peace Treaty.

866 East India (Military)
1929 Report on the Air Operations in Afghanistan Between December 12, 1928 and February 25th, 1929. Presented by the Secretary of State for India to Parliament by Command of His Majesty. September, 1929. London: H. M. Stationery Office. Pp. 44.

A report of the Royal Air Force officer commanding India on the evacution of British civilians from Kabul.

867 Elias, N. (ed)
1895 The Tarikh-i-Rashidi of Mirza Muhammad Haidar Doughlat, translated by E. Denison Ross. London: Sampson Low. Pp. xxiv, 535; map.

868 Elias, R.
1881 A Streak of the Afghan War--Lieutenant-General Sir Donald Stewart's March from Kandahar to Ghazni, with Actions of Ahmed Khel and Urzu. Journal of the Royal United Service Institution 24:666-75.

III. HISTORY

869 Enayat-Seraj, Khalilullah and Nancy Hatch Dupree
1979 The KES Collection of Vintage Photographs: Summary Catalogue. New York: Afghanistan Council, The Asia Society. Occasional paper No. 17. Pp. 101.

An abbreviated preliminary summary catalogue of pictures covering the political history of Afghanistan from the period of Amir Dost Mohammed to the reign of Habibullah (Bacha-i Saqao). The catalogue is indexed by personalities including brief biographies and subject. They are all from the collection of Khalilullah Enayat-Seraj (KES). Nancy Dupree has done an excellent job in organizing Khalilullah's collection and has made it available to public use.

870 Essad Bey, Mohammed
1937 Allah est grand. Décadence et résurrection du monde islamique. Préface et traduction de G. Montandon [Allah Is Great! The Decadence and Resurrection of the Islamic World. Preface and Translation by G. Montandon]. Paris: Payot. Pp. 355; maps.

The author's basic concern is with the political renaissance of the Moslem lands: pages 246-260 deal with Afghanistan.

871 Exchange of Notes Between His Majesty's Government in the United Kingdom and the Government of Afghanistan Regarding Treaty Relations with Afghanistan
1930 London, May 6, 1930. London: H. M. Stationery Office. Pp. 2.

872 Exchange of Notes Between His Majesty's Government in the United Kingdom and the Government of India and the Government of Afghanistan in Regard to the Boundary between India and Afghanistan in the Neighbourhood of Arnawai and Dokalim
1934 Kabul, February 3, 1934. London: H. M. Stationery Office. Pp. 6; folding map.

With a facsimile in Persian of a note from the Minister for Foreign Affairs of Afghanistan.

873 Exchange of Official Publications
1944 Agreement between the United States of America and Afghanistan. Effected by Exchange of Notes, Signed at Kabul, February 29, 1944, Effective February 29, 1944. Washington: U.S. Government Printing Office. Pp. 15.

III. HISTORY

874   Eyre, Vincent
          1843 The Military Operations at Cabul, which Ended in the
             Retreat and Destruction of the British Army, January
             1842. With A Journal of Imprisonement in Afghanistan.
             London: John Murray. Pp. xxvii, 436; map of Kabul.

        A personal narrative of British operations against Kabul,
        the revolt of the Afghans, and their destruction of the
        retreating British forces. Those pages describing life in
        Afghan prisons are of interest and less harrowing than
        might be expected. Reprinted 1976.

875   Fairservis, W. A. Jr.
          1971 The Roots of Ancient India. New York: Macmillan.
             Pp. 482; maps; illustrations.

876   Farhang, Mir Muhammad Sadiq (trans)
          1959 Masaleh-i Afghan az 1841 ta 1878 [The Afghan Ques-
             tion from 1841 to 1878]. Kabul: Matba'eh-yi 'umumi.
             Pp. 210. (1338 A.H.)

        A translation into Dari of no. 774.

877   Ferrier, J. P.
          1858 History of Afghans. Translated from the Orignal
             Unpublished Manuscript by Captain William Jesse.
             London: John Murray. Pp. xxi, 491; 2 maps.

        General Ferrier came to this part of the world to be
        Adjutant-General to the Persian Army. Traveling exten-
        sively from Iran across Afghanistan and Central Asia into
        India, he developed a masterly knowledge of the history,
        geography, and languages of the area. The present work
        concentrates attention on the period from about 1700 until
        1850 and includes valid criticl coments on British policy.

878   Fletcher, Arnold
          1950 Afghanistan: Highway of Conquest; The Position of
             Afghanistan in Relation to East and West. Current
             History 18:337-341. Philadelphia.

        Emphasizes the role of the Pushtu-speaking Afghans in
        determining the course of Afghanistan's foreign relations,
        as well as Afghanistan's positon in relation to East and
        West. By a former American teacher at Kabul.

879   Fletcher, Arnold
          1965 Afghanistan, Highway of Conquest. Ithaca: Cornell
             University Press. Pp. vii, 325; bibliography, index.

III. HISTORY

The history of the country, with emphasis on the Islamic period, and particularly the twentieth century.

880 Fleury, Antoine
1977 La Penetration Allemande au Moyen-Orient 1919-1939: Le cas de la Turquie, de l'Iran et l'Afghanistan. Leiden, Sijthof: Institut Universite de Haute Etudes Intenationales, Collection de Relation Internationales, band 5. Pp. 447.

881 Forbes, Archibald
1892 The Afghan Wars 1839-42 and 1878-1880. New York: Charles Scribner's Sons. Pp. 337.

882 Franz, Heinrich Gerhard
1980 Kunst im Reich der Kushana. Afghanistan Journal 7(2):43-49.

883 Friendship and Diplomatic and Consular Representation
1936 Provisional Agreement between the United States of America and the Kingdom of Afghanistan. Signed March 26, 1936. Effective March 26, 1936. Washington: U.S. Government Printing Office. Pp. 2.

884 Fulfalza'i (Popalzai), 'Aziz al-Din
1953 Timur Shah Durrani [Timur Shah the Durrani]. Kabul: Matbe'eh-yi 'umumi. Pp. 257; genealogical table. (1332 A.H.)

885 Fulfalza'i (Popalzai), Aziz al-Din Vakili
1958 Dorrat al-Zaman-Tarikh-i Shah Zaman [The Pearl of the Age. The History of Shah Zaman]. Kabul: Matba'eh-yi doulati. Pp. 470. (1337 A.H.)

886 Gafurov, Bobodzan Gafurovich
1972 Tajiki: Drevneishaya, Drevnyaya i Srednevekovaya Istoria. [Tajiks: Prehistoric, and Medieval History]. Moscow: USSR Academy of Sciences. Pp. 664.

Tajik history from a Soviet scholarly perspective written by a leading contemporary Tajik historian.

887 Gankovskii, Y. V.
1958 Imperiya Durrani: ocherki administrativnoy i voyennoy sistemy [The Durrani Empire: Essays on the Administrative and Military Systems]. Moscow: Izdatel'stvo Vostochnoy Literatury. Pp. 170; bibliographial notes; genealogical chart.

III. HISTORY

>Based on the accounts of travelers and on primary sources for the second half of the eighteenth century.

888 Gankovskiĭ, Y. V.
>1958 Missiya Bogdana Aslanova v Afganistan v 1764 g. [The Mission of Bogdan Aslanov to Afghanistan in 1764]. Sovetskoye Vostokovedeniye 2:82-87.

>Tells of the effort by a representative of the government of Catherine II to establish diplomatic relations with Afghanistan.

889 Gardner, Alexander (with an introduction by S. Jones)
>1977 A Sketch on Kaffiristan and the Kaffirs. Afghanistan Journal 4(2):47-53.

890 Gardner, Alexander
>1853 Abstract of a Journal Kept by Mr. Gardiner During his travels in Central Asia - with a Note & Introduction by M. P. Edgeworth. Journal of the Asiatic Society of Bengal, vol. 22, pp. 283-305, 383-386, 431-442.

891 Gaulier, Simone, et al
>1976 Buddhism in Afghanistan and Central Asia. Leiden: Brill. Two volumes.

>Essays on the history and impact of Buddhism on the cultures of Afghanistan and Central Asia.

892 Gavrilin, V.
>1961 Na stroĭkakh Afganistana. [Soviet-Afghan Cooperation]. New Times 10:13-14. Moscow.

>A letter from Kabul describes the value of the Soviet aid programs and contrasts the projects with such undertakings as the American built Helmand Canal, adding that "it is not water but unadulterated whiskey that flows in it."

893 Ghirshman, Roman
>1948 Les Chionites-Hephthalites [The Chionite-Hephthalites]. Cairo: Imprimerie de l'Institute Français d'Arthéologie Orientale. Pp. xiii, 156; plates.

>Based mainly on numismatics and ancient manusripts, a history of the two branches of the Chionites--the Hephthalites in Bactria and the Zabulites in the South. The volume constitutes Volume LXXX of the Mémoires de

III. HISTORY

l'Institut Français d' Archéologie Orientale du Caire and Volume XIII of the Mémoires de la Délégation Archéologique Française en Afghanistan.

894 Ghose, Dilip K.
1960 England and Afghanistan: A Phase in Their Relations. Calcutta: The World Private Press. Pp. 230; bibliography.

A study of relations in the second half of the nineteenth century.

895 Ghosh, Biswanath
1966 British Policy Towards the Pathans and the Pindaris in Central India, 1805-1818. Calcutta: Punthi Pustak. Pp. 364.

896 Ghubar, Mir Ghulam Muhammed
1943 Ahmad Shah baba-yi Afghan [Ahmad Shah, Father of the Afghan]. Kabul: Matba'eh-yi 'umumi. Pp. 352. (1322 A.H.)

A work in Persian, with a list on pages 342-346 of sources used. A translation into Russian was published at Moscow in 1959.

897 Ghubar, Mir Ghulam Muhammed
1947 Afghanistan bi-yak nazar [Afghanistan in One Glance]. Kabul: Matba'eh-yi 'umumi. Pp. 101. (1326 A.H.)

A general survey of the country in Persian.

898 Ghubar, Mir Ghulam Mohammed
1967 Afghanistan dar Masire Tarikh [Afghanistan in the Course of History]. Kabul: Daulati M'atba'. Pp. 852, references, eratra. In Dari. (1346 A.H.)

Includes a general introduction to Afghan geography, society and other conditions. Devoted mostly to the period of 600 B. C. to the end of Amir Amanulah's reign. This is the first comprehensive work by an Afghan historian on the political history of Afghanistan. A most important source for the students of Afghan history. The second half of the book is more sketchy and condensed. The initial printing was very limited. In 1978 a widely circulated second printing became available.

III. HISTORY

899   Gobl, Robert
       1963 Geschichte Afghanistans zwischen Alexander und
           Mohammed [History of Afghanistan between Alexander and
           Mohammed]. Bustan (Vienna)3:26-31.

900   Goldsmid, F. J.
       1881 From Bamian to Sonmiani. Journal of the Royal
           United Service Institution 24:479-97.

901   Government of India
       1910 Gazetteer of Afghanistan. Part IV. Fourth Edition,
           Kabul. Calcutta: The Division of the Chief of Staff.

902   Great Britain, Foreign Office
       n.d. Correspondence Relating to the Affairs of Persia and
           Afghanistan, Covering Period of February 1837-December
           1911; January 3, 1834-May 19, 1838; January 1922-
           September 1930. London: Microfilmed by the Public
           Record Office. Available in the US at Library of
           Congress and Center for Afghanistan Studies, University
           of Nebraska-Omaha (and possibly in other libraries).

903   Gregorian, Vartan
       1967 Mahmud Tarzi and the Araj-al-Akhbar, Middle East
           Journal 21(3):345-68.

904   Gregorian, Vartan
       1969 The Emergence of Afghanistan: Politics of Reform
           and Modernization, 1880-1946. Stanford: Stanford
           University Press. Pp. 586.

       Beginning with the ascent of Abdul Rahman and through
       1946, the author covers the political processes which
       intended to modernize Afghanistan. One of the best
       historical works based upon exhaustive library research.
       A very useful bibliography.

905   Grenard, Fernand
       1931 Baber. First of the Moguls. London: Thornton
           Butterworth, 1931. Pp. 253; bibliography.

906   Griesinger, W.
       1918 German Intrigues in Persia. The Niedermayer Expedi-
           tion through Persia to Afghanistan and India. London:
           Hodder and Stoughton, 1918. Pp. 39.

       This brief work consists of translations of extracts from
       the diary of the German agent Griesinger.

III. HISTORY

907 Griffiths, John C.
    1967 Afghanistan. New York: Praeger. Pp. xi, 179.

    Brief sketches of Afghan history, society, economics, politics.

908 Grötzbach, Erwin
    1970 Kulturgeographischer Wandel in Nordost-Afghanistan seit dem. Jahrhunert [Changes in Cultural Geography in Northeastern Afghanistan Since the 19th Century]. Unpublished Ph.D. Dissertation. University of Saarland. Pp. 302

909 Gul, Muhammad
    1900 Ayineh-yi jihan-numa [Mirror of the Image of the World]. Kabul: Dar al-saltaneh. Pp. 316. (1318 A.H.)

910 Gupta, Harl Ram
    1944 Studies in the Later Mughal History of the Panjab 1707-1793. Lahore. Pp. 348.

    Contains considerable material on the activities of Afghan warriors and rulers in the Punjab, as seen from the point of view of a contemporary Hindu historian.

911 Gurdon, B. E. M.
    1936 Early Explorers of Kafiristan. The Himalayan Journal 8:25-43. Oxford.

912 Habberton, William
    1934 Anglo-Russian Relations Concerning Afghanistan, 1837-1907. Unpublished Ph.D. Dissertation. University of Illinois at Urbana-Champaign.

913 Habberton, William
    1937 Anglo-Russian Relations concerning Afghanistan, 1837-1907. Urbana: University of Illinois Press, 1937. Pp. 102; bibliography; maps; appendices containing pacts and conventions made between Russia and England concerning Afghanistan.

    A sound research study starting from the larger view of over-all relations and conflicts between the rival empires and intended to extract the single thread from an elaborate pattern of diplomacy. Ends with the agreement of 1907, which brought all Afghanistan under British influence.

III. HISTORY

914   Habib, Mohammad
       1951 Sultan Mahmud of Ghaznin. A Study. Bombay: D. B.
       Taraporevala and Co. Pp. 108; 2nd ed.

       A study from original sources by a professor of History
       and Politics at Muslim University, Aligarh. The interest
       of the text is enhanced by the author's familiarity with
       the local geography covered by the campaigns of Mahmud.

915   Habibi, Abdul Hai
       n.d. Loyi Ahmad Shah [Great Ahmad Shah]. Kabul: An his-
       torical study in Pushtu.

916   Habibi, Abdul Hai
       1962 Tarikh-i Afghanistan dar 'asr-i Gurgani-yi Hind
       [History of Afghanistan in the Time of the Ghurids of
       India]. Kabul: Marba'eh-yi Pohani. Pp. 400. (1341
       A.H.)

       An important work in Persian, with genealogies, illustra-
       tions, and indices.

917   Habibi, Abdul Hai
       1967 The History of Afghanistan after Islam. Kabul:
       Government Printing 1967.

918   Habibi, Abdul Hai
       1968 A glance at historiography and the beginning of the
       Historical Society of Afghanistan. Afghanistan 21(2):1-
       19.

919   Habibi, Abdul Hai
       1969 Afghan and Afghanistan, Afghanistan 22(2):1-6.

920   Habibi, Abdul Hai
       1977 Lineage and Birthplace of Sayyed Jamaluddi al-
       afghani. Kabul: Baihaqi Publishing House. Pp. 100;
       illustrations. (1355 A.H.)

921   Habibi (Tabibi), Abdul Hakim
       1977 Al-Afghani's Political Struggles. Kabul: Baihaqi
       Publishing House. Pp. 171. (1355 A.H.)

922   Habibullah, Amir
       n.d. My Life: From Brigand to King. Autobiography of
       Amir Habibullah. London: Sampson Low, Marston and
       Company, Ltd. Pp. xii, 276.

III. HISTORY

923 Habibullah, Sardar
1929 Tarikh-i Afghanistan [History of Afghanistan]. Lahore Matba'eh-yi mufid-i 'amm. Pp. 80. (1306 A.H.)

A teacher at the Habibiyah school at Kabul composed in Persian a history, with emphasis upon rulers and events of the eighteenth and nineteenth centuries.

924 Halim, A.
1974 History of the Lodi Sultans of Delhi and Agra. London: E. J. Brill. Pp. 298.

925 Hambly, E. B.
1876 The Strategical Conditions of our Indian Northwest Frontier. Journal of the Royal United Service Institution 23:1027-46.

The importance of the Pushtun borderland area between Pakistan and Afghanistan is discussed.

926 Hambly, Gavin (ed)
1966 Central Asia. New York: Delacorte Press. Pp. 388.

Discusses the history of the area from the Achaemenid period to the Russian Revolution. A Number of well-known authors have contributed to the volume. Of interest to Afghanists who are interested in the history of the country in a Central Asian context.

927 Hameed-ud Din
1962 Les Afghans à la conquête du pouvoir en Indie [The Afghans toward the conquest of power in India]. Journal Asiatique 250(2):191-213.

928 Hamid-Kashmiri, Hamid Allah
1951 Akbar-nameh [The Book of Akbar]. Kabul: Matba'eh-yi 'umumi. Pp. 246. (1330 A.H.)

This work, in Persian verse, is in the form of a mathnavi on the exploits of Akbar Khan, a son of Dost Muhammad. It was completed in 1844. This edition was annotated by 'Ali Akbar Na'imi, with the collaboration of Muhammad Ibrahim Khalil and Muhammad Shafi' Wangazar.

929 Hamley, E.
1884 Russia's Approaches to India. Journal of the Royal United Service Institution 28:395-425.

III. HISTORY

>An example of the early and perpetual concern of the British about the creation of Afghanistan as a buffer between Russia and British India.

930 Hanna, Henry B.
1899, 1904, 1910 The Second Afghan War, 1878-79-80. Its Causes, its Conduct, and its Consequences. 3 vols. Westminster and London: Constable and Co. Pp. (1) x, 386; (2) vii, 372; (3) vii, 583; maps; plans.

>An exhaustive and elaborately documented study by a witness who also collected material from many others. The first volume sets the background of the so-called Afghan problem, the second carries the war through 1879, and the third finishes it off--at enormous expense.

931 al-Haravi, Sayf ibn Muhammad ibn Ya'qub
1944 Tarikh-nameh-yi- Harat [History of Herat]. Calcutta: Baptist Mission Press. Pp. xxvi-i, 821.

>Edited and with an introduction by Muhammad Zubayr al-Siddiqi. Using contemporary and earlier sources, the author covered the years from 1221 until the completion of the work in 1320 A.D. Many later historians have relied upon this source.

932 Harlan, Josiah
1842 A Memoir of India and Avghanistaun, with Observations on the Present Exciting and Critical State and Future Prospets of those Countries. Philadelphia, J. Dobson. Pp. vi,, 208; map.

>The author's own account of adventures that are presented in relation to their background in a considerably later work (see no. 597). Includes remarks on the massacre of the British army at Kabul and a reply to Count Bjornstjerna's work on British India. See no. 819.

933 Harmatta, J. (ed)
1979 Prolegomena to the Sources on the History of Pre-Islamic Central Asia. Budapest: Akademiai Kiado. Pp. 339.

934 Hasan, K.
1962 Pakistan-Afghanistan Relations. Asian Survey 2(14-19).

III. HISTORY

935   Hashim Khan, Mir
            n.d. Tarikhcheh-yi Afghanistan [Short History of Afghanistan]. Kabul.

        A work in Persian by an Afghan writer now deceased.

936   Hasrat, Aman Allah
            1963 Afghanistan va milal-i mottahid [Afghanistan and the United Nations]. Kabul: Doulati matba'eh. Pp. 162. (1342 A.H.)

937   Haughton, John C.
            1879 Char-ee-kar and Service There with the 4th Regiment (Shah Shooja's Force) in 1841: An Episode of the First Afghan War (2nd ed). London: Provost. Pp. 62.

938   Hauser, Ernest O.
            1944 Afghan Listening Post. Saturday Evening Post 216(39):19.

        The uneasy position of Afghanistan during World War II, when both sides in the conflict tried to sway the chosen course of neutrality.

939   Havelock, Henry
            1840 Narrative of the War in Afghanistan, 1838-1839. 2 vols. London: Henry Colburn (2nd ed.). Pp. (1) xix, 336; (2) 324; appendix.

        Still another personal narrative of the First Anglo-Afghan War. Of moderate interest.

940   Hensman, Howard
            1882 The Afghan War of 1879-80. London: W. H. Allen. Pp. xiii, 567.

941   Henze, Dietmar
            1979 Entdecker und Erforscher Afghanistans (I). Afghanistan Journal 6(3):73-83.

942   Herati, Muhammad Husayn
            1954 Vaqi'at-i Shah Shoja' [The Events of Shah Shoja']. Kabul: Matba'eh-yi 'umumi. Pp. 162. (1333 A.H.)

        The first section of the work contains the memoirs of Shah Shoja', the second is material supplied by the author on the events of his reign.

III. HISTORY

943 Heravi, Ghulam Riza Mayel
1965 Montakhab-i ash'ar Sayyid Mir Heravi [Selections from the Poems of Sayyid Mir Heravi]. Kabul: Vizarat-i etala'at va Kultur. Pp. 63. (1344 A.H.)

Selections, with commentaries, of the work of a nineteenth-century Afghan poet, in Dari.

944 Heravi, Saifi
n.d. Tarikh Nama-i Herat. [History of Herat]. Publisher, place and specific date of publication unknown. (1320 A.H.)

945 Herawi, Nayer
1973 An historical edict from Amir Shair Ali Khan. Afghanistan 25(4):69-72.

946 Hobberton, W.
1937 Anglo-Russian Relations Concerning Afghanistan: 1837-1907.

947 Holden, E. S.
1975 The Mughal Emperors of Hindustan 1398-1707. London: E. J. Brill. Pp. 365.

948 Holdich, Thomas Hungerford
1881 Between Russia and India. Journal of the Royal United Service Institution 24:522-34.

949 Holdich, Thomas Hungerford
1901 The Indian Borderland, 1880-1900. London: Methuen and Co. Pp. xii, 402; folding map; appendix.

The appendix gives a chapter on the history of Afghanistan.

950 Hough, W.
1841 Narrative of the March and Operations of the Army of the Indus, in the Expedition to Afghanistan in the Years 1838-1839. Comprising Also the History of the Dooranee Empire from Its Foundation to the Present Time, and an Appendix. London: W. H. Allen, 1841. Pp. xl, 443; 95 pages of appendices; map.

A member of the British force describes the route followed to Qandahar, Ghazni and Kabul. Noteworthy is Chapter XVII, which deals with the history of the Durranis from the founding of the dynasty in 1747.

III. HISTORY

951   Hughes, Thomas P. (ed)
        1872 Tarikh-e-Morassa' [The Gem-Studded History]. Peshawar.

        This edition presents a translation, with additions, into Pushtu of the Makhzan-i Afghani (see no. 851). The version is by Afzal Khan Khatak, grandson of the Pushtu poet Khushhal Khatak.

952   al-Husaini, Mahmud (Al-Munshi ibn Ibrahim al-Djami)
        1974 Tarikhi Ahmad Shahi. Volume I. Moscow: USSR Academy of Sciences. Translated by D. Saidmuradova. Pp. 648.

        An important historical work on Ahmad Shah Durrani written probably in 1186 A.H. (1773-74 A.D.). A facsimile of the original handwritten text along with Russian and English commentary is provided by the translator-editor.

953   al-Husaini, Mahmud (Al-Munshi ibn Ibrahim al-Djami)
        1974 Tarikhi Ahmad Shahi. Volume II. Moscow: USSR Academy of Sciences. Translated by D. Saidmuradova. Pp. 649-1295. See above.

954   Imamuddin, S. M.
        1948 The Tarikhe Khan-i-Jahani wa-Makhzan-i-Afghani. Islamic Culture 22:128-142. Hyderabad: Islamic Culture Board.

        Discusses this important history of the Afghans (see no. 851), in its two editions, and gives and account of the historian's life. See also no. 951.

955   Imperial Gazeteer of India
        1907-09 Published under the authority of His Majesty's Secretary of State for India, 26 Volumes. Oxford: Clarendon Press.

        Official publication of the British Government dealing with the colonization of India and other such activities in Central and South Asia. Useful for history students of British activities in Afghanistan.

956   India Army, General Staff Branch
        1926 The Third Afghan War, 1919: Official Account. Calcutta: Government of India, Central Publication Branch. Pp. ii, 174.

III. HISTORY

957   In Whose Benefit?
         1955 New Times 28:17. Moscow.

      An editorial claiming that American militarists are obstructing efforts to settle the Afghanistan-Pakistan conflict, hoping to "bludgeon Afghanistan into abandoning its policy of non-participation in aggressive blocs."

958   Istoriy Tadzhikskogo Naroda
         1963 Tom 1: s drevneyshikh vremen do U.v.n.e. [The History of the Tadzhik people. Vol. 1: From Ancient Times to the 5th Century]. Moscow: Izdatel'stvo Vostochnoy Literatury. Pp. 595.

959   Jalabert, Louis
         1937 Du roman en plein histoire: L'aventure de quelques allemands en Afghanistan et en Perse pendant la guerre [Historical Romance: The Adventures of Some Germans in Afghanistan and Persia during the War]. Études, 20 mars, pp. 744-755; 5 avril, pp. 57-70. Paris.

      A summary account of the German mission of Niedermayer, Schunemann, and Zugmayer, which failed to arouse the Afghans in World War I. These articles also mention the activity of Wassmuss in Iran.

960   Jalalabadi, Shir Ahmad
         1896 Fath-nameh-yi Kafiristan [Account of Victory in Kafiristan]. Lahore. Pp. 16.

      A poem in Persian on the conquest of this region by the Afghans in 1896.

961   Jawzjani, Minhaj al-Din ibn Seraj al-Din Tabaqat-i Nasiri
         1963-1964 [Compendium of Nasiri]. Kabul: Matbe'eh-yi doulati. Vol. 1, pp. 501; vol 2, pp. 507. (1342, 1343 A.H.)

      Important history, in Dari, of the Ghurid period. Edited by Abdul Hai Habibi.

962   Jones, Sarah
         1978 The Hazaras and the British in the Nineteenth Century. Afghanistan Journal 5(1):3-5.

III. HISTORY

963 Kakar, M. Hasan
1968 The Consolidation of Central Authority in Afghanistan Under Amir Abd al-Rahman, 1880-1896. M. A. thesis, School of Orienal an African Studies, University of London.

964 Kakar, M. Hasan
1971 Afgahnistan: A Study in International Political Development, 1880-1896. Lahore: Punjab Educational Press. Pp. 318.

One of the first attemps by an Afghan at a systematic history of the first phase of Abdul Rahman's reign and the beginnings of the consolidation of a nation state in Afghanistan.

965 Kakar, M. Hasan
1973 The Pacification of the Hazaras of Afghanistan. New York: Afghanistan Council, the Asia Society. Occasional paper no. 4. pp. 15.

A historical sketch of the pacification of the Hazaras of Central Afghanistan during the reign of Amir Abdul Rahman.

966 Kakar, M. Hasan
1975 Afghanistan in the Reign of Amir 'Abd al-Rahman Khan, 1880-1901. Ph.D. Dissertation. University of London. Pp. 507.

967 Kakar, M. Hasan
1978 The Fall of the Afghan Monarchy in 1973. International Journal of Middle Eastern Studies 9:195-214.

968 Kakar, Hasan Kawun
1979 Government and Society in Afghanistan: The Reign of Amir Abdal-Rahman Khan. Austin: University of Texas Press. Pp. 328.

A systematic and comprehensive study of the reign of Abdul Rahman undertaken by a keen and professional Afghan historian. Probably the best history for this period.

969 Kamel, Dost Muhammad Khan (ed)
1920 Kolliyat-i Khushhal Khan Khattak [The Collected Works of Kushhal Khan Khattak]. Peshawar. 2nd ed.

III. HISTORY

970   Kapur, Harish
      1966   Soviet Russia and Asia 1917-1927. A study of Soviet
      Policy toward Turkey, Iran and Afghanistan. Geneva: M.
      Joseph. Pp. 266; map.

      Based primarily on Russian source material.

971   Keddie, Nikki R.
      1968   An Islamic Response to Imperialism: Political and
      Religious Writings of Sayyid Jamal ad-Din'al-Afghnai.
      Berkeley.

972   Keddie, Nikki R.
      1972   Sayyid Jamal ad-Din al-Afghani: A Political
      Biography. Los Angeles: University of California Press.
      Pp. xvii, 479.

973   Kedourie, E.
      1972   Afghani in Paris - note. Middle Eastern Studies
      8(1):103-105.

974   Khafi, Mirza Yaqub 'Ali
      1955, 1957   Padshahan Mot'akher [Recent Rulers]. 2 vols.
      Kabul: Matba'eh-yi doulati. Pp. (1) 246; (2) 196.
      (1334, 1336 A.H.)

      An important work in Persian, dealing primarily with
      rulers of the nineteenth century.

975   Khalfin, N. A.
      1959   Proval britanskoy agresii v Afganistane, 19v.-
      nachalo 20v. [Downfall of British agression in Afghani-
      stan, 19th century to the beginning of the 20th
      Century]. Moscow: Izdatel'stvo Sotsial'no-
      ekonomicheskoy Literatury. Pp. 208; maps; index.

976   Khalfin, N. S.
      1964   Russia's Policy in Central Asia, 1857-68. (H.
      Evans, trans.) London.

977   Khalil, Muhammad Ibrahim
      1961   Amir Khosro. Kabul: Doulati matba'eh. Pp. 91.
      (1340 A.H.)

978   Khalili, Khalilullah
      1954   Saltanat-i Ghaznaviyan [The Empire of the Ghazna-
      vides]. Kabul: Matba'eh-yi 'umumi. Pp. 371; biblio-
      graphy. (1333 A.H.)

III. HISTORY

>A work in Persian by a contemporary scholar; compiled from Persian and Arabic sources.

979 Khan, Ghulam Mustafa
>1955 A History of Bahram Shah of Ghaznin. Lahore: Caravan Press. Pp. 99.

>Includes an account of the Shah's career, his literary interests, and a record of his sons and courtiers in the early twelfth century.

980 Khan, Mohammed Said
>1972 The Voice of the Pukhtoons. Lahore: Ferozsons Limited Press. Pp. 307.

>A collection of short essays dealing with Pushtun identity, their struggle for independence, their general social and cultural features, and their contribuiton to the emergence of Pakistan. Intended to apply to Pushtuns in Pakistan.

981 Khan, M. M. S. M. (ed)
>1981 The Life of Abdul Rahman, Amir of Afghanistan. Karachi: Oxford University Press.

982 Khan, Said Alim, S. H.
>1929 l'Emir de Boukharie. La Voix de la Boukharie Opprimeé [The Voice of Oppressed Bokhara]. Paris: Maisonneuve Frères. Pp. 71; map.

>Describes the unsucessful resistance to the Bolshevik advance into Bokhara, details military aid given by Afghanistan, and concludes with the amir fleeing to Afghaistan in 1921.

983 Khan, Subedar Muhammad Hussain
>1886 Report on the Hazarajat. Afghan Boundary Commission. London: India Office Library and Record.

984 Khaturvatana (Torwayana), Najibullah
>n.d. Aryana [Aryana]. Kabul.

>An historical study in Persian.

985 Khwand-Amir, Ghiyas al-Din ibn Humam al-Din
>1938 Dastur al-vuzara'; shamil ahval-i vauzara-yi islam ta inqiraz-i Timuriyan [Instruction of the Viziers;

III. HISTORY

>Containing the Conditions of the Viziers of Islam til the Extinction of the Timurids]. Tehran: Kitab-furushi va chapkhaneh-yi Iqbal. Pp. 514. (1317 A.H.)

>An edition of this important work by Sa'id Nafisi. See no. 841.

986 Kieffer, Charles M.
>1962 Les Ghorides Une Grande Dynastie Nationale [The Ghurides. A Great National Dynasty]. Kabul: Historical Society of Afghanistan. No. 71. Pp. 50.

987 Kieffer, Charles M.
>1967 A propos de la circoncision à Caboul et dans le Logar. Wiesbaden: Festschrift für Wilhelm Eilers. Pp. 191-201.

988 King, David
>1929 Living East: Photographs by Lowell Thomas. New York: Duffield and Co. Pp. 265.

>A record of the author's adventures in India and Afghanistan.

989 Klein, I.
>1974 Who Made Second Afghan war. Journal of Asian History 8(2):97-121.

990 Klimburg, Max
>1966 Afghanistan. Das Land im Historischen Spannungsfeld Mittelasians [Afghanistan. Land in the Historical Area of Discord of Middle Asia]. Vienna: Österreichischer Bundesverlag. Pp. 313; plates; index; bibliography.

>A comprehensive study of history, social structure, and modern development.

991 Kohzad, Ahmad Ali
>n.d. In the Highlights of Modern Afghanistan. Kabul: Government Printing house. Pp. 144.

>Articles drawn from documentary sources on the history of Afghanitan in the nineteenth century, translated from Persian.

992 Kohzad, Ahmad Ali
>n.d. Men and Events through 18th and 19th Century Afghanistan. Kabul: Government Printing House. Pp. 179.

III. HISTORY

>Translations of 49 short articles originally written in Persian and embodying documentary research.

993 Kohzad, Ahmad Ali
n.d. Rijal va-ruydadha-yi tarikhi [Historical Personalities and Events]. Kabul: Matba'eh-yi 'umumi. Pp. 146.

>A number of short sketches in Persian on individuals such as Ahmad Shah, Timur Shah, and Sardar Muhammad Azim Khan and on important historical incidents.

994 Kohzad, Ahmad Ali
1946 Cultural Relations between Afghanistan and India. Afghanistan 1(2):12-30.

>The emphasis is on place names found in the Vedas and the Avesta, on the development of Buddhism, and on the influence of Islam in India.

995 Kohzad, Ahmad Ali
1950 Les Ratbils Shahs de Kaboul [The Ratbil Shahs of Kabul]. Afghanistan 5(2):1-18.

>About the Kings of Kabul, who governed a large territory in Central Asia in the first two centuries of the Hijra.

996 Kohzad, Ahmad Ali
1950 Two Coronations. Afghanistan 5(3):38-40.

>The story of the coronation of Ahmad Shah with an ear of wheat, and of Dost Mohammed with an ear of barley.

997 Kohzad, Ahmad Ali
1950 Two of the Last Buddhist Rulers of Ghazni and Bamian. Afghanistan 5(4):37-39.

>The fall of the Ruler of Bamian (nameless) and of the Ruler of Ghazni (variously named) to Eleptagin in the fourth century of the Hijra.

998 Kohzad, Ahmad Ali
1951 Huit légendes concernant la fondation de la ville de Herat [Eight Legends about the Foudning of the City of Herat]. Afghanistan 6(4):11-21.

>A recounting of the legends, followed by a comment on their possible historical foundations.

III. HISTORY

999 Kohzad, Ahmad Ali
1952 Afghanistan, A Great Mountainous Mesopotamia. Afghanistan 7(4):49-53.

A short sketch of Afghan history.

1000 Kohzad, Ahmad Ali
1952 Émir Cher Ali Khan en face de la diplomatie anglaise, la fidélit des tribus [Amir Sher Ali Khan, in the Face of English Diplomacy, the Fidelity of the Tribes]. Afghanistan 7(4):59-66.

1001 Kohzad, Ahmad Ali
1952 Sher Shah Souri: A Representative of the Afghan Spirit in India. Afghanistan 7(4):35-40.

The life of Sher Shah, Showing him as the embodiment of the finest Afghan traits.

1002 Kohzad, Ahmad Ali
1952 Dar zavaya-yi tarikh-i mu'asir-i Afghanistan [On Aspects of the Contemporary History of Afghanistan]. Kabul: Matba-eh-yi 'umumi. Pp. 148. (1331 A.H.)

A compilation of articles written in Persian dealing with history.

1003 Kohzad, Ahmad Ali
1953 Les capitales de l'empire afghan koushanide au temps de Kanischka [The Capitals of the Afghan Kushanid Empire at the Time of Kanishka]. Afghanistan 8(2):22-30.

On Kanishka's summer capital, Capici, excavated at Begram near Alexander's Nicea, and on Poura-Shapoura (Peshawar), a prosperous city and a center of Buddhism.

1004 Kohzad, Ahmad Ali
1953 Zaman Shah et l'activité des puissances coloniales [Zaman Shah and the Activity of Colonial Powers]. Afghanistan 8(4):5-26.

A history of the embattled reign of Zaman Shah. The author accuses the British, paticularly the Directors of the East India Company, of fomenting strife and insurrection in Afghanistan in order to keep Zaman Shah out of India.

III. HISTORY

1005 Kohzad, Ahmad Ali
1957 Bala Hesare Kabul va pish amadhayi tarikhi [The Bala Hesar of Kabul and the Related Events of History]. Kabul: Matba'eh-yi doulati. Pp. 316. (1336 A.H.)

A history of the renowned fortification at Kabul.

1006 Kohzad, Mohammad Nabi
1954 Le événements de Shah Shodjaa [The Events of Shah Shoja']. Afghanistan 9(3):45-48.

On the appearance of a book edited by the Society of Historical Studies of Afghanistan, and written by Shah Shoja' and Mohammad Husayn Herati. The review gives a brief sketch of the Shah's life and an uncomplimentary note on the collaborator, Mohammad Husayn.

1007 Konow, Sten
1933 A Note on the Sakas and Zoroastrianism. In Oriental Studies in Honor of Cursetji Erachji Parry. Edited by Jal Dastur Cursetji Parry. London: Oxford University Press. Pp. 220-222.

The author considers a few facts which indicate that the Sakas made not attempts to propagate Zoroastrianism outside Sistan.

1008 Koshkaki, Mawlawi Borhan al-din Khan (Kushkaki)
1979 Qataghan et Badakhshan. Translated by Marguerite Reut. Paris: CNRS, Centre de recherches archeologiques. (Publications de l'URA, no. 10, Memoire no. 2). Three Volumes.

1009 Kumar, B.
1973 The Early Kushans. London: E. J. Brill. Pp. 329.

1010 Kundu, N.
1959 The Afghan Policy of Lord Lawrene, 1864-9. Unpublished M.A. Thesis. London.

1011 Kureischie, Azizullah
1977 Zur Geologie des Arghandab-Plutons und angrenzender Sediment-Serien bei Almaytu in Zentral-Afghanistan. [On the Geology of the Arghandab River Pluton and Adjacent Sediment Series in Almaytu in Central Afghanistan.] Unpublished Ph.D. Dissertation. Bonn University. Pp. 189.

III. HISTORY

1012 Kushan, G. Hazrat (trans)
1954 Khaterah-yi Salferinu. Kabul: Matba'eh-yi dafa' melli. Pp. 160. (1343 A.H.)

Bears the English subtitle: "A Memory of Solferino, J. Henry Dunant, translated into Durri by G. Hazrat Koshan."

1013 Kushkaki, Burhan Al-Din
1925 Rahnama-ye Qattaghan wa Badakshan. Kabul. (1303 A.H.)

1014 Kushkaki, Burhan al-Din
1931 Nadir-i Afghan [Nadir the Afghan]. Kabul: Matba'eh-yi 'umumi. Pp. 611; maps. (1310 A.H.)

The life of Nadir Shah, from his birth until his ascent to the throne in 1929, written in Persian by an Afghan scholar. Well documented and with a score of fascinating contemporary photographs. The work is labeled Volume 1, but others have not appeared.

1015 Lal, Mohan
1846 Life of the Ameer Dost Mohammed Khan of Kabul, with his Political Proceedings towards the English, Russian and Persian Governments, Including the Victories and Disasters of the British Army in Afghanistan. 2 vols. London: Longman, Brown, Green and Longman. Pp. (1) 399; (2) 497.

A work of importance, written by the Indian clerk of Sir Alexander Burnes, who accompanied the latter to Kabul and gathered material directly from the courtiers and relatives of Dost Mohammed. Includes a comprehensive account of relations between Afghanistan and the rival Russian and British empires. Reprinted 1978 with an introduction by Nancy Hatch Dupree.

1016 Lal, Mohan
1979 Travels in the Punjab, Afghanistan, Turkistan, to Balkh, Bokhara and Herat, and a visit to Great Britain and Germany. London: E. J. Brill. (first edition 1846). Pp. 528.

1017 Lamb, Harold
1961 Babur the Tiger. New York: Doubleday & Co. Pp. 336.

Historical novel, drawn from the autobiography of the conqueror of India who was fondest of his years at Kabul.

III. HISTORY

1018   Lane-Poole, Stanley
        1899 Babar. Oxford: Clarendon Press. Pp. 206.

1019   Lee, Vladimir
        1961 Storm Clouds over the Khyber Pass. New Times 51:27-28. Moscow.

        A defence of the Afghan position on the Pushtunisan issue. Includes some exaggerations about the size of the Pushton population in Afghanistan and Pakistan.

1020   Leech, Major R.
        n.d. A Supplementary Account of the Hazaras. Journal of the Asiatic Society of Bengal 14:1.

1021   Leshnik, Lorenz S.
        1968 Ghor, Firozkoh and the Minar-i-Jam. Central Asiatic Journal, 14(1):36-49. Wiesbaden.

1022   Levine, J. O.
        1931 L'Angleterre, la Russie et l'Afgjanistan [England, Russia and Afghanistan]. Monde Slave 1:336-363. Paris.

        Traces the relationships between Afghanistan and its powerful neighbors in the nineteenth century, concluding with a brief resumé of contemporary relations.

1023   Levine, J. O.
        1936 L'U.R.S.S. et l'Afghanistan [The U.S.S.R. and Afghanistan]. Affaires Étrangères, de année, pp. 283-289.

        An article giving the history of the amicable political and economic relations between Russia and Afghanistan and pointing out the advantage to the Soviets of a Communist Afghanistan and Russia's hopes for a "social revolution" there.

1024   Liberman, A. A.
        1974 Seismichnost Afganistana [The Seismicity of Afghanistan]. Unpublished Ph.D. Dissertation. Moskovskii gosudarstvennyi universitet imeni M. V. Lomonosova.

1025   Lobanov-Rostovsky, A.
        1951 Russia and Asia. Ann Arbor: Wahr. Pp. 342.

III. HISTORY

1026 Lockhart, Laurence
1938 Nadir Shah. A Critical Study Based Mainly upon Contemporary Sources. London: Luzac and Co. Pp. xv, 344; bibliography; maps.

The story of the life of this eighteenth-century ruler of Iran includes his campaigns which drove the Afghans from Iran, and his passage through Afghanistan as he marched into India. For some years a resident of Iran, the British author knows the topography of much of this story.

1027 Lochkhart, Laurence
1958 The Fall of the Safavi Dynasty and the Afghan Occupation. Cambridge: Cambridge University Press. Pp. xiii; 584; map; appendices; bibliography; index.

1028 Lushington, Henry
1844 A Great Country's Little Wars, Or England, Afghanistan, and Sinde; being a Sketch, with reference to their morality and policy, of recent transactions on the northwestern frontier of India. London: J. W. Parker. Pp. 303.

1029 MacGregor, C. M. (ed)
1871 Central Asia. Part II: A Contribution Towards the Better Knowledge of the Topography, Ethnology, Resources and History of Afghanistan. Calcutta.

1030 Mackenzie, C. F. and Sir H. M. Elliot (trans)
1955 Tarikh-i Salatin-i Afghana by Ahmad Yadgar and Makhzan-i Afghani and Tarikh-i Khane Jahan Lodi by Ni'amatullah. Calcutta. Pp. 152.

A reprint of the well-known history of India by Elliot and Dowson.

1031 MacMunn, George Fletcher
1929 Afghanistan, from Darius to Amanullah. London: G. Bell and Sons. Pp. xii, 359; 9 maps.

A British Lieutenant-General conducts a fairly detailed survey of the history of the area throughout the ages. Emphasis is on the earliest Afghan-British relations and on contacts with India at all periods. Includes genealogical tables of the Durrani.

III. HISTORY

1032 Macrory, Patrick A.
1966 Signal Catastrophe. The Story of the Disastrous Retreat from Kabul 1842. London: Hodder and Stoughton. Pp. 288; maps; bibliography.

Also published under the title, "The Fierce Pawns." New York: J. B. Lippincott. An extremely detailed, well-written, and interesting account of the First Anglo-Afghan War.

1033 Malhotra, R. I.
1974 Afghan Frontier Settlements 1872-93 and the Press. Journal of Indian History 52(2/3):421-432.

1034 Malleston, George Bruce
1879 History of Afghanistan. From the Earliest Period to the Outbreak of the War of 1878. London: Allen. Pp. xxvii, 453; map.

A popular, narrative history of Afghanistan from the Ghaznavid period, comprising a series of brief chapters on various dynasties and rulers.

1035 Malleston, George Bruce
1880 Herat: The Granary and Garden of Central Asia. London: Allen and Co. Pp. vi, 196.

A valuable work of observation and compilation. The history of Herat is traced by interesting excerpts from earlier historians. Routes leading from Herat are described.

1036 Mann, Oskar
1898 Quellenstudien zur Geschicte des Ahmed Shah Durrani (1747-1773) [Source Studies on the History of Ahmed Shah Durrani (1747-1773)]. Zeitschrift der deutschen morgenlandischen Geseelschaft 52:97-188; 161-186; 323-358.

1037 Marshall, D. N.
1976 The Afghans in India Under the Delhi Sultanate and the Mughul Empire: A Survey of Relevant Manuscripts. New York: Afghanistan Council, The Asia Society. Occasional paper no. 10. Pp. 27.

1038 Martin, G.
1879 Survey Operations of the Afghanistan Expedition: the Kurram Valley. Proceedings of the Royal Geographical Society (New Series I):333-34; 712-13.

III. HISTORY

> Preliminary report of a survey for Afghan Boundary Commission.

1039 Masson, Vadim M. and Vadim A. Romodin
1964-1965 Istoriya Afganistana [History of Afghanistan]. 2 vols. Moscow: Nauka. (1):464; (2):551.

1040 Masson, V., and V. Sarianidy
1969 Afghanistan in the Ancient East. Afghanistan 22(2):7-19.

1041 McChesney, Robert D.
1973 Waqf at Balkh: A Study of the Endowments of the Shrine of Ali ibn Abi Talib. Unpublished Ph. D. Dissertation. Princeton University. Pp. 403.

The Wagf (Islamic institution of endowments) for the shrine of Ali in northern Afghanistan is examined over four hundred years. The effects of political, economic, and social environments on Waqf for this shrine are described.

1042 McGovern, William M.
1939 The Early Empires of Central Asia: A Study of Scythians and the Huns and the Part They Played in World History (with special reference to the Chinese sources). Chapel Hill: University of North Carolina Press. Pp. 529.

A comprehensive historical account of the development of early empires in Central Asia including Afghanistan. Included is a very good account of the Koshan Empire and the place of Afghanistan in the context of the Scythian and Hun Empires.

1043 Melia, J.
1930 Visages royaux d'Orient [Rulers of the East]. Paris: Bibliothèque Charpentier. Pp. 228.

The pages dealing with Amanullah, 5-72, represent a definite contribution to the study of his successes and impending failure.

1044 Memoirs of Zehir-ed-din Muhammed Babur, Emperor of Hindustan
1921 Written by himself, in the Chagatai Turki and Translated by J. Leyden and W. Erskine Annotated and Revised by Sir Lucas King. 2 vols. Oxford. (1):cxi, 324; (2):471; map.

III. HISTORY

>Excellent edition of one of the most fascinating and revealing of autobiographies.

1045 Miles, C. V.
>1909 The Zakka Khel and Mohamand Expeditions. Rawalphindi. Pp. 66.

1046 Miller, Charles
>1977 Khyber: British India's North West Frontier: A Story of an Imperial Migraine. London: Macdonald and Jane's. Pp. xix, 393.

>An interesting political history of Afghanistan beginning with the British involvement in the affairs of that country.

1047 Mir-Khwand (Muhammad ibn Khwand-Shah ibn Mahmud)
>1853-56 Rawzat al-safe [Garden of Purity]. Tehran.

>A general history in seven parts, composed in Persian by a writer long resident at Herat. Parts Four through Six include material on the rulers and dynasties of this area, while the Seventh--by another hand--deals with the patrons of the author, the Sultan Husayn and his sons.

1048 Mir Munshi, Sultan Mohammed Khan (ed)
>1900 The Life of Abdur Rahman, Amir of Afghanistan. 2 vols. London: John Murray. 1:295; 2:319; map in pocket to scale 1:1,520,640.

>The first volume contains the ruler's own narrative of his early life and final accession to the throne. The second volume details his efforts as a ruler, taken down in his own words on various occasions by the editor, his former State Secretary. Fascinating account of a resolute determined, cruel, and superstitious man.

1049 Mizuno, S. (ed)
>1971 Basawal and Jelalabad-Kabul. Kyoto: Kyotot University, 2 volumes. Volume I: pp. 127. Volume II: plates, maps, drawings.

1050 Mohammad-Zoda, Kurbon, and Muhabbat Shoh-Zoda
>1973 Istoriya Badakhshanda. [History of Badakhshan]. Moscow: USSR Academy of Sciences. Pp. 248.

III. HISTORY

>The manuscript was probably written in early twentieth century in Persian. The original handwritten text is included along with a type-set transcription. A Russian introduction and index is provided by B. I. Iskandarov.

1051 Mohebi, Ahmad Ali
1955 Samanian [The Samanids]. Kabul: Matba'eh-yi 'Umumi. (1334 A.H.)

>A history of the Samanid dynasty in Central Asia.

1052 Molesworth, Lieutenant-General George N.
1962 Afghanistan 1919. An Account of Operations in the Third Afghan War. Bombay: Asia Publishing House. Pp. 183; maps; index.

1053 Moorish, C.
1930 Afghanistan in the Melting Pot. Lahore: Civil and Military Gazette Press. Pp. 61.

>From the vantage point of Peshawar, the author kept track of the overthrow of Amanullah and the campaign for the re-establishment of Mohammedzai rule in Afghanistan by Mohammed Nadir.

1054 Morley, William Hood (ed)
1862 Tarikh-i-Baihaqi. Containing the Life of Massaud, Son of Sultan Mahmud of Ghaznin; Edited by W. H. Morley and Prited under the Supervision of Capt. W. N. Lees. Calcutta: College Press. Pp. 868.

>The title comes from the birthplace of that author Abu Fazl Baihaqi, the village of Baihaq, near Nishapur in Iran. The work is a history of the Ghaznavid dynasty up to the lifetime of the author. Other editions have been published at Delhi, Cairo, and Bombay.

1055 Morrison, Ronald M. S. H. M.
1934 King Mohammad Nadir Shah-i-Ghazi of Afghanistan. Naji-i-Millat [Savior of the Nation]. Journal of the Royal Central Asian Society 21:170-175.

>A tribute to Nadir Shah, written after the assassination of the ruler. Includes material covering an Afghan law on citizenship.

1056 Muhammad Abu'l-Fayz
1902 Mukhammas-i Saghar-i bazm-ashub. (The title is not translatable.) Gujranwala. Pp. 16.

III. HISTORY

>A lithographed work in Persian dealing with the warfare between Dost Muhammad Khan and Sardar Hari Singh.

1057 Muhammad Hayat Khan
    1867 Hayat-i Afghan [Afghan Life]. Lahore. Pp. 714; folding maps.

>On the history of the country, with special emphasis on accounts of the principal tribes. Includes a table of contents in English, a key to each chapter, and a page of the Persian text.

1058 Muhammad Kabir ibn Shaykh Isma'il
    n.d. Afsaneh-yi Shahan [Tale of the Kings].

>An undated manuscript in Persian composed of anecdotes collected by the author about the Afghan rulers of India. Copies exist in the British Museum and elsewhere.

1059 Muhyi al-Din
    1931 Buhran va najat [Crisis and Salvation]. Kabul: Matba'eh-yi anis. Pp. 288; map. (1310 A.H.)

>A work in Persian describing the overthrow of Amir Amanullah and the assent of Mohammed Nadir to the kingship of Afghanistan, his and his brother's rule of the country.

1060 Myrdal, Jan
    1980 The Silk Road. A journey from the High Pamirs and Ili through Sinkiang and Kansu. Translated from the Swedish by Ann Henning. London: Victor Gollancz Ltd. Pp. 293.

1061 n. a.
    1882 Indian Surveys for the Year 1880-81. Proceedings of the Royal Geographical Society (New Series) 4:344-355.

1062 Nafisi, Sa'id
    1936 Asar-i gum shudeh-yi Abu Fazl-i Bayhaqi [Lost Works of Abu Fazl Bayhaqi]. Tehran: Mihr. Pp. 108. (1315 A.H.)

>An Iranian scholar and editor writes in Persian of little-known works by one of the most reliable historians of Islam.

1063 Naimi, Ali Ahmad
    1949 Un regard sur Ghor. Préambule: la géographie, l'histoire, et les sites historiques [A Look at Ghor.

III. HISTORY

>Preamble: Geography, History and Historic Sites]. Afghanistan 4(4):1-23.

>Useful and important article, with some documentation. Follows the history of the various rulers and includes brief descriptions of some thirteen historical sites.

1064 Naimi, Ali Ahmad
  1952 Gauhar Shad, une reine afghane du neuvième siècle de l'hégire [Gowhar Shad, an Afghan Queen of the Ninth Century of the Hijra]. Afghanistan 7(1):22-34.

  Gowhar Shad--of whom little is known--was the wife of Shah Rokh, son of Tamerlane. The article deals with her father-in-law, her husband, and the probable events of her own life, with notes on her sons, her mausoleum, and her mosque at Mashhad.

1065 Naimi, Ali Ahmad (ed)
  1958 Akbar nameh [The History of Akbar]. Kabul: Matba'eh-yi doulati. Pp. 246. (1337 A.H.)

  An edition of a work by Hamid Kashmiri, apparently a translation from Persian into Pushtu, describing the struggles of a member of the family of Dost Muhammed against the British in Afghanistan. The exact date of publication is open to question.

1066 Naimi, M. Omar
  1971 Decision-making in the Disraeli Government in Regard to Armed Intervention in Afghanistan: An Analytical Approach. Unpublished Ph. D. Dissertation. University of Okalahoma. Pp. 355.

  Discussion of the British decision to declare war on Afghanistan in 1878 and examination of the development of Anglo-Afghan relations focusing on policies from 1869 to 1875.

1067 Najibadadi, Akbar Shah Khan
  1947 Khan Jahn Ludi. Kabul: Matba'eh-yi 'umumi. Pp. 94. (1326 A.H.)

  A translation of a Persian text into Pushtu by Aziz al-Rahman Sayfi.

III. HISTORY

1068 Narimanov, L.
1929 Afganistan v ogne grazhdanskoi voiny [Afghanistan in the Flame of the Civil War]. Leningrad: Priboi. Pp. 98.

1069 al-Narshakhi, Abu Bakr Mohammed ibn Ja'far
n.d. Tarikh-i Bukhara [History of Bokhara]. Translated into Persian by Abu Nasr Ahmad ibn Mohammed al-Qubavi, abridged by Mohammed ibn Zufar ibn 'Umar. Tehran: Sana'i. Pp. 128.

The manuscript was complete prior to 959 A.H. by a scholar at the Samanid court; translated into Persian in 1128 and abridged in 1178 A.D.

1070 Nash, Charles (ed)
1843 History of the War in Afghanistan Form its Commencement to its Close. London: T. Brooks. Pp. viii, 412.

1071 Nazarov, X.
1968 K Karakteriske Narodi Dvexheni Kontha 19 Veka V Afganistane [Characteristics of the Rural People of Afghanistan During the 19th Century]. Dushanbe, Tajikistan, USSR: Irfon. Pp. 48.

1072 Nazarov, X.
1969 Iz Istorii Dvizheniia Narodnykh Mass Afghanistan V Nachale XX Veka [History of the Rural Masses of Afghanistan During the Twentieth Century]. Dushanbe, Tajikistan, USSR: V. I. Lenin State University. Pp. 87.

1073 Nazarrov, Haqnazar
1963 Ravobiti Bukhoro va Afgonistan az Barpo Shudani Davlati Durromiho to Ghaltidani Amorati Bukhoro. [The Relations of Bukhara and Afghanistan from the Rise of the Durrani State to the Fall of the Rule of Bukhara]. Dushanbe: Tajikistan SSR Academy of Sciences. Pp. 179.

Discusses the relationship of the Bukhara Amirate with the Afghan Governments from the rise of the Durani Empire until the decline of the Bukhara Amirate.

1074 Nazim, Muhammad
1931 The Life and Times of Sultan Mahmud of Ghazna. Cambridge University Press. Pp. xv, 271; map.

Emphasis is placed on the military campaigns and conquests of Mahmud. References are to primary sources.

III. HISTORY

1075   Nazim, Muhammad
       1939 Hayat va-awqat-i Sultan Mahmud-i Ghaznavi [Life and
           Times of Sultan Mahmud of Ghazni]. Kabult: Matba'eh-yi
           'umumi. Pp. 209; bibliography. (1318 A.H.)

       A translation into Persian, by 'Abd al-Ghafur Amini, of a
       work written in English and published in 1931 (see no.
       1074). The bibliography lists works in European
       languages, both in the Latin alphabet and in Persian
       translation.

1076   Niedermayer, Oskar von
       1925 Unter der Glutsonne Irans. Kriegerlebnisse der
           deutschen Expedition nach Persien und Afghanistan [Under
           Iran's Scorching Sun. War Experiences of the German
           Expedition to Persia and Afghanistan]. Dachau/
           Munich: Einbornverlag. Pp. 331; sketch map.

       Narrative of a "political and military" mission through
       India, Afghanistan, and Persia in 1915-1916. Pages 126-
       182 deal with the journey through Afghanistan--observa-
       tions on the country and meetings with Afghan officials.

1077   Niedermayer, Oskar von
       1936 Im Weltkrieg vor Indiens Toren. Der Wüstenzug der
           deutschen Expedition nach Persien und Afghanistan [At
           the Gates of India in the World War. The Desert Passage
           of the German Expedition to Persia and Afghanistan].
           Hamburg: Hanseatische Verlagsanstalt. Pp. 228; map.

       A later edition of the same author's Unter der Glutsome
       Irans (see above).

1078   Nollau, Günther and Hans J. Wiehe
       1963 Russia's South Flank; Soviet Operations in Iran,
           Turkey, and Afghanistan. New York: Praeger. Pp. 171.

1079   Norris, J. A.
       1967 The First Afghan War: 1838-42. London: Cambridge
           University Press. Pp. xvi, 500.

1080   Notes on the Discovery of Hebrew Inscriptions in the Vicinity
           of the Minaret of Jam.
       1963 East and West 14(3-4):206-208. Rome.

1081   Nukhovich, Eduard S.
       1962 Vneshnyaya politika Afganistana [The Foreign Policy
           of Afghanistan]. Moscow: Izdatel'stvo Instituta
           mezhdunatodnikh otnosheniy. Pp. 108.

III. HISTORY

>Stress is placed upon Afghanistan's relations with the U.S.S.R. and the United States, and on the country's policy of definite neutrality.

1082 Nur-Muhammad, Hafez
>1946 Tarikh-i Mazar-i Sharif vaqe'Balkh [The History of Mazar-i Sharif, Balkh Locality]. Kabul: Matba'eh-yi 'umumi. (1325 A.H.)

1083 Ocherki po novoi istorii stran Srednego Vostoka
>1951 Pod red. I. M. Reisnera i N. M. Goldberga [Sketches on Modern History of the Middle Eastern Countries. Edited by I. M. Reisner and N. M. Goldberg]. Moscow: Izdatel'stvo Moskovskogo Universiteta.

>The section dealing with Afghanistan (pp. 53-81) is by Reisner and is useful, recognition being given by the foreign reader to the Marxist perspective.

1084 Official History of Operations on the N. W. Frontier of India, 1936-37.
>1943 Delhi: Government of India Press. Pp. xviii, 256.

1085 Operations in Waziristan 1919-1920.
>1924 London: His Majesty's Stationery Office. Pp. viii, 194.

>A detailed account of one section of the operations incidental to the Third Anglo-Afghan War.

1086 Osetrov, N.
>1957 Za dal'neysheye razvitiye sovetsko-afganskogo sotrudnich-estva [On the further Development of Soviet-Afghan Cooperation]. Sovremenniy Vostok 2:17-18.

>A soviet account of Soviet-Afghan diplomatic relations since 1919.

1087 Osipov, A. M. (ed)
>1958 Indiya i Afganistan [India and Afghanistan]. Moscow: Izdatel'stvo vostochnoy literaturï. Pp. 290.

>This work is subtitled, "Sketches of History and Economics." On pages 57-87, Yu. V. Gankovskiĭ discusses "The Army and Military System of the Durrani Shahs," and on pages 284-290 he reviews recent Afghan writings on the history of the Durrani Shahs.

III. HISTORY

1088 Osman, Shir Muhammad
    1948 Yaftaliyan [The Yaftalites]. Kabul: Matba'eh-yi 'umumi. Pp. 40. (1326 A.H.)

1089 Palwal, Abdul Raziq
    1968 History of Former Kafiristan. Afghanistan 21(3):61-68.

1090 Palwal, Abdul Raziq
    1969 History of Former Kafiristan. Afghanistsn 22(1):6-27.

1091 Palwal, Abdul Raziq
    1969 History of Former Kafiristan. Afghanistan 22(2):20-46.

1092 Palwal, Abdul Raziq
    1970 History of Former Kafiristan. Afghanistan 22(3-4):130-146.

1093 Palwal, Abdul Raziq
    1970 History of Former Kafiristan. Afghanistan 23(2):21-52.

1094 Palwal, Abdul Raziq
    1970 History of Former Kafiristan. Afghanistan 23(4):24-36.

1095 Palwal, Abdul Raziq
    1971 History of Former Kafiristan. Afghanistan 24(2-3):10-17.

1096 Pandey, Awadh B.
    1956 The First Afghan Empire in India (1451-1526). Calcutta: Bookland Ltd. Pp. 320.

    An account of the Lodi Afghans, based on sources in Persian and Sanskrit.

1097 Pandey, D. P.
    1973 The Shahis of Afghanistan and the Punjab (Indo-Afghan Studies III). Daryaganj, Delhi: Historical Research Institute. Pp. xiv, 268, xx; plates, map.

1098 Panjshiri, Safdar
    1963 Mobarezeh-yi Sayyid Jamal al-Din Afghan [The Struggle of of Sayyid Jamal Al-Din Afghan]. Kabul: Matba'eh-yi ma'aref. Pp. not numbered. (1342 A.H.)

III. HISTORY

1099   Papers Relating to Military Operations in Afghanistan
            1863 Presented to both Houses of Parliament, by Command
                of Her Majesty. Calcutta: William Rushton. Pp. xiii,
                526.

1100   Peers, Ellis Edward
            1954 'Uruj-i Barakza'i [Barakzai Ascendency]. Kabul:
                Matba'eh-yi 'umumi. Pp. 187; bibliography. (1333
                A.H.)

            A translation into Persian by 'Abd al-Rahman Pazhwak and
            Muhammad 'Usman Sidqi of a work in English entitled
            "Afghanistan in the Nineteenth Century." The bibliography
            is taken from the original work and is reproduced in the
            Latin alphabet.

1101   Peter of Greece and Denmark, Prince
            1947 Post-War Developments in Afghanistan. Journal of
                the Royal Central Asian Society 34:275-286.

            A brief history of Afghanistan since 1838, and general
            remarks on, and an explanation of, economic and political
            conditions and foreign relations. Prince Peter was at the
            time a correspondent of The Times, and was intimate with
            members of the Afghan Royal Family.

1102   Philips, Cyril Henry
            1951 Handbook of Oriental History. London: Royal
                Historical Society. Pp. vii, 239.

            Section II: India and Pakistan, includes on pp. 87-88,
            under the heading Muslim Dynasties, a list of the
            Ghaznavids and the Rulers of Ghur; and on pages 93-94, a
            list of the Amirs of Afghanistan.

1103   Planhol, X. de
            1973 Sur la frontiere turkmene de l'Afghanistan. Revue
                Geographique de l'Est 13:1-16.

1104   Popowski, Jozeph
            1893 The Rival Powers in Central Asia; or the Struggle
                Between England and Russia in the East (translated from
                German). Westminister: A. Constable and Company. Pp.
                xxii, 235.

1105   Priestly, H. (trans)
            1874 Afghanistan and Its Inhabitants, by Sirdar Muhammad
                Hayat Khan. Lahore.

III. HISTORY

A translation of the Hayat-i Afghan. See no. 1057.

1106 The Problem of Afghanistan
1926 Journal of the Central Asian Society 13:187-204.

This article contains the account of a meeting held at London and attended by many British authorities on Afghanistan and India. The subject for discussion was the threatened annexation of Afghan Turkestan by the U.S.S.R. and the possibility of a Russian move as far as Herat. Some urged that the British government take urgent measures if the Russians intervened directly in Afghan affairs.

1107 Qandahari, Ghulam Morteza Khan
1901 Halat-i valahazrat Amir 'Abd al-Rahman Khan [The Times of His Royal Highness Amir 'Abd al-Rahman Khan], Mashhad. Lithographed. (1319 A.H.)

1108 Qanungo, K. R.
1965 Sher Shah and His Times. Calcutta: Orient Longmans. Pp. 459.

1109 Qasim, 'Ali Khan
1856 Muharabeh-yi abul [The Battle of Kabul]. Agra: Sulaymani. Pp. 535. (1272 A.H.)

An epic poem in Persian, dealing with the exploits of Shah Shoja'. The work is lithographed.

1110 Rahim, M. A.
1961 History of the Afghans in India A.D. 1545-1631, with Especial Reference to their Relations with the Mughals. Karachi: Pakistan Publishing House. Pp. 326.

1111 Rahmany, Magdalina
1948 La reine Razia: Impératrice afghane aux Index [Queen Razia: Afghan Empress of India]. Afghanistan 3(3):13-17.

Account of the reign of a Ghorid queen who reigned at Delhi from 1210-1235 A.D.

1112 Rahmany, Magdaline
1949 Le reine Gawarchade [Queen Gowhar Shad]. Afghanistan 4(2):14-17.

Sketch of the contributions of this queen, wife of Shah Rokh, son of Timur.

III. HISTORY

1113 Ramazani, R. K.
1958 Afghanistan and the U.S.S.R. Middle East Journal 12(2):144-152

An account of Soviet aid to Afghanistan and the attitudes of both nations to this aid and to each other.

1114 Rao, J. Sambashiva
1929 King Amanullah. Madras.

1115 Rapp, Eugen Ludwig
1973 Mainzer Afghanica. In Jahrbuch der Vereinigung Freunde der Univesität Mainz. Pp. 51-90.

1116 Rapp, Eugen Ludwig
1971 Die persischheraischen Inschriften Afghanistans aus dem 11. bix 13. Jahrhundert. In Jahrbuch der Vereinigung Freunde der Universität Mainz. Pp. 74-118.

1117 Rastogi, Ram S.
1965 Indo-Afghan Relations 1880-1900. Lucknow: Nav-Jyoti Press. Pp. 256; bibliography.

A descriptive account of Indian (British)-Afghan relations, including a full treatment of the delimitation of Afghanistan's frontiers with Russia and India.

1118 Raverty, H. G.
1888 Notes on Afghanistan and Baluchistan. London.

1119 Rebuff
1954 New Times 25:20-21. Moscow.

An editorial commenting on an editorial in the New York Times, and including an answer to the Times by an Afghan attaché in Washington.

1120 Reindke, Gisela
1976 Genesis, Form und Funktion Afghanischer Stadte, dargestellt am Beispiel von Kandahar, Herat, Mazar-i-Sharif und Jalalabad [Genesis, Form and Function of Cities in Afghanistan, Shown in the Examples of Kandahar, Herat, Mazar-i-Sharif, and Jalalabad]. Unpublished Ph.D. Dissertation. Freie Universität Berlin, Pp. 378.

1121 Reisner, Igor Mikhailovich
1954 Razvitie feodalizma i obrazovanie gosudarstva u Afgantsev [Development of Feudalism and Formation of the

III. HISTORY

        Afghan State]. Moscow: Izdatel'stvo Akademii Nauk S.S.S.R. Pp. 415

        A careful and thorough study of the formation of the Afghan state under Mir Wais and his successors. Completely Marxist in approach and deductions.

1122 Reissner, Larissa
        1930 Afghanistan. *In* Ausgewahlte Schriften, Berlin. Edited by Karl Radek. Berlin: Neuer Deutscher Verlag. Pp. 294; 309-437.

        Sections entitled Vanderlip in Afghanistan (page 294) and Afghanistan (pages 309-437).

1123 Reynolds, James (trans)
        1858 The Kitab-i-Yamini, Historical Memoirs of the Amir Sabaktagin, and the Sultan Mahmud of Ghazna Translated from the Persian Version of the Contemporary Arabic Chronicle of Al Utbi, by the Rev. J. Reynolds. London: Oriental Translation Fund. (For the original Arabic text see no. 1163.)

1124 Rishtin, Sadiqullah
        1952 Da pushtanu mojahedi [The Pushtu Pioneers]. Kabul: Matba'ehy-yi 'umumi. Pp. 93. (1331 A.H.)

        Parallel columns of Persian and Pushtu give accounts of Afghans who fought for independence in the period following the arrival of the British in India.

1125 Rishtiya, Sayed Qasim
        1950, 1957 Afghanistan dar garn-i nuzdahum [Afghanistan in the Nineteenth Century]. Kabul: Matba'eh-yi 'umumi. Pp. 256. Second edition 1957. (1329, 1336 A.H.)

1126 Rishtiya, Sayed Qasim
        1958 Afganistan v XIX v. [Afghanistan in the Nineteenth Century]. Gankovskiy, Yuriy V., ed., L. N. Dorofeyevnaya, M. K. Kurkin, and Muhammad Rahim Khan, trans. Moscow: III. Pp 487; bibliography.

1127 Roberts, Frederick Sleigh, 1st Earl of
        1897 Forty-One Years in India. 2 vols. New York: Longmans, Green and Co. London: Richard Bentley and Son. Pp. (1)xx, 511; (2) xii, 522; appendices, numerous maps.

        A Field-Marshal reports on his long career in India and adjacent countries. The second volume is nearly entirely

III. HISTORY

>   devoted to Anglo-Afghan relations and conflicts of these years. In the 1898 one-volume edition, the material on Afghanistan, corresponding to Volume 2 of the first edition, begins on page 280.

1128 Robson, Brian
    1973 Maiwand, 27th July 1880. Journal of the Society for Army History Research 51(208):194-229.

1129 Roos-Keppel, George Olof
    1901 Translation of the Tarikh-i Sultan Mahmud-i-Ghaznavi. Allahabad: Pioneer Press. Pp. 65.

1130 Roskoschny, Hermann
    1885 Afghanistan und sein Nachbaränder [Afghanistan and her Neighbors]. 2 vols. Leipzig: Gresner und Schramm. Pp. (1) 1-176; (2) 177-336.

> Discusses Afghanistan as the scene of the presumed final conflict between Russia and England in Central Asia.

1131 Rosset, Louis-Felicien
    1946 Le Padishah Baber--1483-1530. Son passage à Kaboul [The Padishah Babur--1483-1530. His Visits to Kabul]. Afghanistan 1(3):36-46.

> Tells of the ruler's trips from India back to his beloved Kabul.

1132 Rosset, Louis-Felicien
    1951 Afghanistan, carrefour de l'Asie, terre de contrastes d'histoire [Afghanistan, Crossroads of Asia, Land of Historic Contrasts]. Afghanistan 6(4):27-51.

> Highlights of Afghan history, with emphasis on the invaders: Alexander in Bactria, Chengiz Khan in Bamian and Babur.

1133 Roy, Nirodbhusan
    1958 Niamatuallah's History of the Afghans. Makhzan-i-Afghani. Part I: Lodi Period. Santinketam (West Bengal): Bidyut Ranjan Basu. Pp. 211.

1134 Rubinstein, Alvin Z.
    1957 Afghanistan and the Great Powers. United States Naval Institute Proceedings 83:62-68.

> The background and present status of Afghanistan's major foreign relations.

III. HISTORY

1135   Rubio-Garcia, Leandro
        1975 Components of contemporary Afghanistan: an historical perspective (Los componentes del Afganistan contemporaneo: una perspectiva historica). Rev. de Pol. Int. (137):99-131, (138):73-98, (139):93-124, (140):81-118.

1136   Sale, Lady Florentia
        1843 A Journal of the Disasters in Afghanistan, 1841-2. London: John Murray. Pp. xvi, 451; map.

        The wife of the British commander at Kabul, General Sale, describes the revolt of the Afghans at Kabul in 1841, the British retreat, and her own captivity of eight months in Afghan hands. Her frankness gives the work a value beyond its account of personal experiences.

1137   Salimi, Muhammad Arslan and Muhammad Shah Arshad
        1960 Zama Yadana mu'alef valahazrat Marshal Shah Wali Khan Ghazi Fateh Kabul [My Recollections by His Highness Marshal Shah Wali Khan Ghazi, Victor of Kabul]. Kabul: Matba'eh-yi doulati. Pp. 97.

        Reminiscences of Marshal Shah Wali, in Pushtu.

1138   Salisbury, Harrison E.
        1962 Peaceful Competition Along Russia's Border. New York Times Magazine. April 8. Pp. 294.

        Includes a discussion of Afghan-Soviet relations.

1139   Saljuqi, Fekri
        1962 Gazargah, Qesmat-i az Tarikh-i Herat-i Bastan [Gazargah, a Part of the History of Ancient Herat]. Kabul: Matba'eh-yi doulati. Pp. 91. (1341 A.H.)

        An account, in Dari, of the history of the shrine of Khwaja Abdullah Ansari at Gazargah, adjacent to Herat.

1140   Savad-i mu'ahadeh-yi dawlatayn-i 'aliyatayn-i Afghanistan va-Iran
        1921 [Transcript of the Agreement between the Sublime Governments of Iran and Afghanistan]. Kabul. Pp. 11.

        Text of the agreement in Persian.

III. HISTORY

1141 Schinasi, May
1980 The Afghans in Australia. New York: Afghanistan Council, The Asia Society. Occasional paper No. 22. Pp. 24.

A brief sketch of the life of immigrant Pushtuns in Australia.

1142 Schwarzenhach, Annemarie Clark
1940 Military Importance of Afghanistan. Living Age 358; 577-581.

Afghanistan's uneasy Tribal Territory and the difficulty of maintaining its uncertain loyalty against Russia.

1143 The Second Afghan War (1878-80)
1908 Official Account. Produced in the Intelligence Branch, Army Head-Quarters, India. London: John Murray. Pp. x, 734; 40 appendices; maps; plans.

An exhaustive, descriptive account of the British military operations against the Afghan forces. Originally treated as a secret work, its publication was held up for years until time had dulled the spirit of controversy.

1144 Seifi, Aziz al-Rahman (trans)
1959 Dehli da Pushtun Wazhe Wakhatki [Delhi in the Time of the Pushtuns]. Kabul: Matba'eh-yi doulati. Pp. 79. (1338 A.H.)

A translation from the Persian text of Khan Ghazi.

1145 Seraj, Minhajuddin
1963-64 Tabaqati Nasiri. (In Dari, edited by A. H. Habibi). Kabul: Historical Society of Afghanistan. 2 Volumes.

1146 Shah Shoja' al-Molk Saduza'i
n. d. Swanihe Shah Shoja' [The Biography of Shah Shoja']. Kabul.

An important work in Pushtu by a ruler of Afghanistan.

1147 Shah Sirdar Ikbal Ali
1921 Bolshevism in Central Asia. Edinburgh Review 234:136-146.

168

III. HISTORY

> A succinct account of Russian expansion in Central Asia is followed by a summary of the unsuccessful efforts of Russian agents to involve Afghanistan in World War I.

1148 Shah Sirdar Ikbal Ali
n.d. Afghanistan. London: Sampson Low and Co. Pp. x, 342. (1939?)

> The first part of this work repeats background material familiar from other works by this Afghan writer. Then attention is concentrated upon the person and the government of Nadir Shah. Useful pages describe the political and social structure of Afghanistan at this period.

1149 Shamir, Haim
1975 Der Deutsche Einfluss in Afghanistan 1940. -ein Beitrag zur Geschichte des Eindringens Deutschland in den Mittleren Osten [The German Influence in Afghanistan 1940: A Monograph on the History of German Penetration in the Middle East]. Jahrbuch des Instituts fur Deutsche Geschichte 4:479-483.

1150 Shcherbinovsky, N.
1953 Soviet Scientists in Afghanistan. New Times 25:29-31. Moscow.

> A review of M. S. Dunin's Afghanistan, Pakistan and India According to the reviewer, Professor Dunin recalls with pride Russia's efforts toward friendship with Afghanistan, and regrets the backwardness and misery brought about there by British and American imperialists. See no. 252.

1151 Shir Muhammad Khan
1894 Tavarikh-i Khorshid-i Jahan [Histories of the Sun of the World]. Lahore: Islamieh. Pp. ix, 320. (1311 A.H.)

> A genealogical history of the Afghans, written in Persian and lithographed.

1152 Siddiqi, Iqtidar Husain
1964 Advent of the Afghans to Power. Studies in Islam 1(4):213-37.

1153 Siddiqi, Iqtidar Husain
1965 The Army of the Afghan Kings in North India. Islamic Culture 39(3):223-43.

III. HISTORY

1154   Siddons, Joachim H.
            1843 Memorials of Afghanistan: Being State Papers, Official Documents, Dispatches, Authentic Narratives, etc. Calcutta: J. H. Stocqueler. Pp. viii, 304, clxii.

1155   Sidqi, Mohammed 'Usman
            1948 Yaftaliyan [Ephthalites]. Kabul: Matba'eh-yi 'umumi. Pp. 40. (1326 A.H.)

        A treatment in Persian of the arrival of the Ephthatlite Huns, of their activity, and of their disappearance from the region.

1156   Sidqi, Mohammed 'Usman
            1977 Al-Afghani the Forerunner of Revolution in the East. Kabul: Baihaqi Publishing House. Pp. 160. (1355 A.H.)

1157   Singh, Ganda
            1953 Ahmad Shah: The Man and His Achievements. Afghanistan 8(1):1-19.

        A glowing portrait, with much personal detail about the Shah's appearance, his dress, his taste in literature and art, and his government policy.

1158   Singh, Ganda
            1959 Ahmad Shah Durrani. Father of Modern Afghanistan. Bombay: Asia Publishing House. Pp. 475; appendices; chronology; bibliography; index.

        A comprehensive, documented study based on manuscript sources in Persian, on material in Indian languages, and on works by European writers. The extensive bibliography is uniquely valuable.

1159   Singhal, D. P.
            1963 India and Afghanistan 1876-1907. A Study in Diplomatic Relations. St. Lucia, Queensland: University of Queensland. Pp. 216; appendices; index.

        A documented study, drawing on British source material.

1160   Smith, Major C. B. E.
            1879-80. Official Journals of the South Afghanistan Field Force 1879-80. India Office Library and Records, L/P & S/20/B310.

III. HISTORY

1161 Sokolov-Strakhov, K. I.
    1931 Grazhdanskaya voyna v Afganistane, 1928-1929gg. [Civil War in Afghanistan, 1928-1929]. Moscow: Voyenizdat. Pp. 79.

1162 Sperling, O.
    1934 Mein Traum Indien [My Indian Dream]. Berlin. Pp. 430.

Deals with plans to incite India to revolt against the British Empire during World War I.

1163 Sprenger, A. and Maulawi Mamluk al' Ali (eds)
    1847 Tarikh Yamimi. Delhi.

An edition of the history in Arabic of the Amir Subuktigin and Sultan Mahmud of Ghazni by Abu Nasr Mohammed b. 'Abd al-Jabar al-'Utbi, one of the secretaries of Sultan Mahmud.

1164 Squire, Sir Giles
    1950 Recent Progress in Afghanistan. Journal of the Royal Central Asian Society 37:6-18.

An Englishman who was first British Minister, then Ambassador, at Kabul from 1943 to 1949, summarizes his impressions of the varied progress and change achieved during his residence.

1165 Stack, Shannon Caroline
    1975 Herat: A Political and Social History. Unpublished. Ph. D. Dissertation. University of California, Los Angeles. Pp. 592.

A history of Herat from the neolithic to the present. Major emphasis is on the Ghurid-Timurid period and the nineteenth century.

1166 Stawiski, Boris
    1979 Mittelasien - Kunst der Kuschan. Leipzig: Veb E. A. Seemann Verlag.

1167 Stewart, Rhea Talley
    1973 Fire in Afghanistan, 1914-1929: Faith, Hope, and the British Empire. Garden City: Doubleday. Pp. vii; 614.

A passionate yet systematic work dealing with the reign of Amanullah and the events preceeding it.

III. HISTORY

1168 Stoda, M. Ibrahim and Abdurrahman Palwal
1977 Description of Transfer of Coffin of al-Afghani. Kabul: Kabul University Press. Pp. 63. (1355 A.H.)

1169 Sultan Muhammad ibn Musa Khan
1881 Tarikh-i Sultani [The Sultani History]. Bombay: Muhammadi. Pp. 291. (1298 A.H.)

A lithographed work in Persian, written about 1865 A. D. and dealing with the history of Afghanistan up to 1862.

1170 Sykes, Sir Percy M.
1926 Sir Mortimer Durand, A Biography. London: Cassel. Pp. xi; 356.

The life of the delineator of the Durand Line, who served several times in Kabul.

1171 Sykes, Sir Percy M.
1940 Afghanistan: The Present Position. Asiatic Review. 36:279-310.

A recapitulation of Afghan political history and relations with Russia, Britain, and Germany from the middle of the nineteenth century to the present--with a strong British bias. Sir Percy spent almost 50 years in the British Consulate in Persia. Discussion follows the paper.

1172 Tabibi, A. Hakim
1958 Hoquq al-doval va monasabat-i an ba mamalek-i mohafez ba Khoskka [International Law and its Relation to Landlocked Countries]. Kabul: Matba'eh-yi doulati. Pp. 59. (1337 A.H.)

A study of this subject in Persian by a member of the delegation of Afghanistan to the United Nations, who has specialized in this field.

1173 Tabibi, A. Hakim
1973 Afghanistan and Indian Historical Ties. Afghanistan 26(1):86-89.

1174 Taillardat, C. F.
1929 Révolte Afghane [The Afghan Revolt]. l'Asie Française. Pp. 15-20; 50-55.

1175 Tarikh-i Afghan
1861 [Afghan History]. Constantinople: Jaideh Khaneh. Pp. 174. (1277 A. H.).

III. HISTORY

A reprint in Persian of a basic work by a Jesuit, Father J. T. Krusinski, resident at Isfahan in the early eighteenth century.

1176   Tarikh-i Afghanistan
            1946 [History of Afghanistan]. 3 vols. Kabul: Matba'eh yi 'umumi. Pp. (1) 495; (2) 600; (3) 150. (1325 A.H.)

An important work in Persian, for which aditional volumes are contemplated. The first volume, from earliest times to the period of Alexander, is by A. A. Kohzad and M. U. Sidqi; the second continues to the rise of Islam and is by A. A. Kohzad. The third volume, through the Taharid dynasty, is by M. Ghubar and A. A. Na'imi. Only the first volume has an index.

1177   Tarikh-i Afghanistan
            1957 Jeld-i sevum [History of Afghanistan. Volume Three]. Kabul: Matba'eh-yi doulati. Pp. 669. (1336 A.H.)

This work, part of a semi-official history of the country in Persian, appears to overlap sections of no. 1176. M. Ghubar deals with the influence of Islam, A. A. Nai'imi with the Taharid dynasty. M. G. S. Farhang with the Safarid dynasty, A. Mohebit with the Samanid dynasty, and K. Khalili with the Ghaznavid period. There is no index.

1178   Tarikh-i Khayran
            1953 Shamilke Avakhiri Safaviyeh Fitney-yi Afghan, Saltanet-i Nadir Shah va Ahval-i jam'i az Buzurgan [History of Khayran (?); Comprising the End of the Safavids, the Afghan Revolt, the Reign of Nair Shah and Biographies of a Number of Important People]. Isfahan: Ta'yid. Pp. 140. In Dari. (1332 A.H.)

The second printed edition of an apparently obscure work in Dari.

1179   Tarikhe Sistan
            1935 Tarikhe Sistan, revised by Malik-al Shuara Behar. Tehran: Eastern Institute. Pp. 415. (In Dari).

1180   Tarn, W. W.
            1938 The Greeks in Bactria and India. Cambridge University Press. Pp. 539; bibliography; maps.

An account of the Greek kingdoms set up in Afghaninstan, Central Asia, and India following the death of Alexander.

III. HISTORY

>All pertinent sources are clearly presented: Bactria is given a prominent place, and the nomadic conquest of this region is discussed.

1181 Tarzi, Mahmud
    n.d. Siraj al-Tavarikh [The Luminary of Histories]. Kabul.

1182 Tarzi, Mahmud (trans)
    1916-17 Tarikh-i Muharabeh-yi Rus va-Zhapan [History of the Russo-Japanese War]. 3 vols. Kabul: 'Inayet. Pp. (1) 296; (2) 260; (3) 304. (1334-5 A.H.)

>Translation from Turkish into Persian of a history compiled by officers of the Turkish General Staff.

1183 Tate, George Passman
    1911 The Kingdom of Afghanistan. A Historical Sketch. Bombay and Calcutta: The Times of India Offices. Pp. 224.

>Attention is concentrated on the modern history of the country, beginning with the period of Mir Wais. Includes an account of the Pushtu language and a map of the "three cities" of Qandahar.

1184 Tavaquli, Ahmad
    1948 Ravabat-i Siassi yi Iran va Afghanistan [Political Relations of Iran and Afghanistan]. Tehran: Mehr. Pp. 135. (1327 A.H.)

1185 Tavaquli, Ahmad
    1949 Afghanistan [Afghanistan]. Tehran. Pp. 135. (1328 A.H.)

>A general survey in Persian, with the emphasis on Irano-Afghan relations.

1186 Temirkhanov, L.
    1972 Hazareitsie: Ocherki Novoi Istorii. [The Hazaras: New History Works]. Moscow: USSR Academy of Sciences. Pp. 140.

>A useful Soviet work on the history of the Hazaras with particular reference to more recent works on these people both by Soviet and non-Soviet authors.

III. HISTORY

1187　Temple, R. C.
　　　　1879　An Account of the Country Traversed by the Second Column of the Tal-Cho'tia'li Field Froce in the Spring of 1879. Journal of the Royal Geographical Society 49:190-319.

　　　　Includes field reports on the geographic and social conditions on the Afghan border. Conducted for the Afghan Boundary Commission.

1188　Teplinskiy, Leonid B.
　　　　1961　Sovetsko-Afganskiye Otnosheniya 1919-1960; Kratkiy ocherk [Soviet-Afghan Relations 1919-1960; a short Essay]. Moscow: Izdatel'stvo sotsial'no-ekonomicheskoy literaturey. Pp. 214; bibliography; indices.

1189　Terenzio, Pio-Carlo
　　　　1947　La rivalité anglo-russe en Perse et an Afghanistan jusqu'aus accords do 1907. [The Anglo-Russian Rivalry in Persia and Afghanistan prior to the Agreements of 1907]. Paris: Rousseau. Pp. 178.

1190　Thabet, Mohammed Ibrahim
　　　　1965　Sultan Shahab al-Din Ghuri. Kabul: Matba'eh-yi doulati. Pp. 162. (1344 A.H.)

　　　　A work in Pushtu on the kingdom of this ruler.

1191　Thesiger, Wilfred
　　　　1980　The Last Nomad. One Man's Forty Year Adventure in the World's Most Remote Desserts, Mountains and Marshes. New York: E. P. Dutton. Pp. 304.

　　　　An autobiography of travels through Abyssinia, Kurdistan, Arabia, Afghanistan and Yemen.

1192　The Third Afghan War (1919)
　　　　1926　Official Account. Compiled in the General Staff Branch, Army Headquarters, India. Calcutta: Government of India, Central Publication Branch. Pp. ii, 174; maps; plans.

　　　　The detailed accounts of military operations which lasted from May 6th until June 2nd, 1919, are preceded by a number of pages describing the composition of the Afghan forces at that period; their advantages and their disabilities.

III. HISTORY

1193 Thornton, Ernest
1910 Leaves From an Afghan Scrapbook; the Experience of An English Official and his Wife in Kabul. London: J. Murray. Pp. xvi, 225.

1194 Tissot, Louis
1948 Un grain de blé entre deux meules, l'Afghanistan [A Grain of Wheat between Two Mill-Stones--Afghanistan]. Revue de défense nationale (New Series) 6:597-606.

An examination of Afghanistan's history in foreign relations, her present economic situation, and her position between Iran, India, Baluchistan, and Soviet Russia.

1195 Toynbee, Arnold J.
1925 Survey of International Affairs 1920-1923. Oxford and London. Pp. xv, 526; appendices; maps.

Pages 376-378--"Relations between British India, Soviet Russia and Afghanistan, 1912-1923"--give a history of the brief Afghan War of 1919 and a text of the Treaty of August 8, 1919. There is an explanation of the ensuing agreements with the British and of the Russo-Afghan and Turko-Afghan treaties of 1921.

1196 Toynbee, Arnold J.
1927 The Islamic World since the Peace Settlement. Survey of International Affairs (1925) 1:xv, 587; appendices; folding map. London.

Pages 546-569--"India, Afghanistan and the Frontier Tribes"--give a history of the troubles with the rebellious tribes on either side of the Durand Line and of the attempts of the British in India and of the Afghan government's less enthusiastic attempts to subdue them.

1197 Toynbee, Arnold J.
1961 Impressions of Afghanistan and Pakistan's North-West Frontier: In Relation to the Communist World. International Affairs 37(2):161-69. London.

1198 Trever, K. V.
1954 Kushany, khionity i eftality po armianskim istochnikam IV-VII vv; K istorii narodov Srednei Axii [The Kushans, Chionites and Ephthalites according to Armenian Sources of the Fourth to the Seventh Centuries; History of the Peoples of Central Asia]. Sovetskaia Arkheologiaa 21:131-147. Moscow.

III. HISTORY

1199 Tripathi, G. P.
 1973 Indo-Afghan Relations, 1882-1907. New Delhi: Kumar Brothers. Pp. xi, 203.

1200 Tucci, Guiseppe
 1954 Une lettre [A Letter]. Afghanistan 9(2):59.

A letter from the president of the Italian Institute for the Middle and Far East, thanking the Afghan Minister of Foreign Affairs for the offer of a visit from Ahmad Ali Kohzad.

1201 Uberoi, J. P. Singh
 1969 The History of Andarab District, Northern Afghanistan, 500 B.C.-1925 A.D. Afghanistan 24(1):57-69.

1202 Utbi, Muhammad
 1856 Tarikh-i Yamini [History of Yamin (al-Dawleh)]. Translated into Persian by Abu'l-Sharaf Nasih Jarfadaqani. Tehran. Pp. 460.

A lithographed translation into Persian from the Arabic by Abu'l-Sharif Nasih Jarfadaqani. The text is a history of Amir Sabuktagin and Mahmud of Ghazni.

1203 Vaughan, J. L.
 1879 On Afghanistan and Military Operations Therein. Journal of the Royal United Service institute 22:1003-26.

1204 Vali, Marshal Shah
 n.d. Yaddashthai Man [My Memoirs]. Kabul: Matba'eh-yi doulati. Pp. 108.

1205 Vaqi'at-i Durrani [The Events of the Durranis]
 1875 Cownpore. A translation into Urdu of the Tarikh-i Ahmad by 'Abd al-Karim 'Alavi. Translated by Mir Varis 'Ali Sayfi. See no. 729.

1206 Vaqi'at-i Shah Shuja' [The Events of Shah Shuja']
 1954 Kabul: Matba'eh-yi doulati. Pp. 162. (1333 A.H.)

1207 Varma, B.
 1968 English East India Company and the Afghans, 1757-1800. Calcutta: Punthi Pustak. Pp. 171.

III. HISTORY

> A study of the attitude of the English East India Company toward the Afghan invasion of India in the second half of the eighteenth century and an assessment of the fortunes of the English colonial enterprise in South Asia.

1208 Viollis, Andrée
> 1930 Tourmente sur l'Afghanistan [Storm over Afghanistan]. Paris: Librarie Valois. Pp. 240.

> A French woman writer arrives at Kabul by Soviet plane to find herself plunged into the fury of the hectic days following the capture of the capital by Mohammed Nadir. Other chapters concern the error of King Amanullah and the brief power of Habibullah (Bachai Saqao).

1209 Vogel, Renate
> 1973 Die Persien- und Afdghanistanexpedition. Oskar Ritter von Niedermayers 1915, 16 [Oskar Ritter von Niedermayer's Expedition to Persia and Afghanistan, 1915-1916]. Unpublished Ph.D. Dissertation. University of Münster. Pp. 330.

1210 Volsky, D.
> 1962 The Soviet Union and Afghan Progress. New Times 22:18-19. Moscow.

> A description of Soviet aid programs in the fields of highway construction and irrigation facilities, as contrasted with American aid which is concerned with "pumping money out of the Afghan treasury."

1211 Walker, Philip F.
> 1881 Afghanistan: A Short Account of Afghanistan, its History, and Our Dealings with it. New York: Dutton. Pp. 166.

1212 Walters, Royce Eugene
> 1974 Across the Khyber Pass: British Polciy Toward Afghanistan, 1852-1857. Unpublished Ph.D. Dissertation. University of Pennsylvania. Pp. 513.

> Traces the development of the British policy toward Afghanistan (1852-57). Details the British pressure on Persia to end its intervention in Herat, the restoration of relations in 1855 with the Amir of Kabul and the establishment of Afghanistan as a buffer for India.

III. HISTORY

1213 Warburton, Robert
1900 Eighteen Years in the Khyber, 1879-1898. London: John Murray. Pp. 351.

Good descriptions of borderland Pushtuns by a British officer who fought in the first Anglo-Afghan War and whose mother was an Afghan, a blood relative of Amir Dost Mohammad. Reprinted 1970.

1214 Weiers, M.
1969 Vorlaufiger Bericht über sprachwissenschaftliche Aufnamen bei den Moghol von Afghanistan 1969. Zentralasiatische Studien 3:417:30.

1215 Weston, Christine
1962 Afghanistan. New York: Charles Scribner's Sons. Pp. 162; map; glossary; index.

A personalized account of Afghan life and history.

1216 Wheeler, Stephen
1895 The Ameer Abdur Rahman. London: Bliss, Sands and Foster. Pp. xvi, 251.

A study of contemporary history is followed by a detailed acount of the reign of this Afghan ruler, based almost exclusively on the ruler's autobiography.

1217 Wiebe, Dietrich
1975 Stadtstruktur und kulturgeographischer Wandel in Kandahar und Sudafghanistan [Municipal Structure and Change in Human Geography in Kandahar and Southern Afghanistan]. Unpublished Ph. D. Dissertation. University of Kiel. Pp. xiv, 326.

1218 Wilber, Donald N.
1953 Afghanistan, Independent and Encircled. Foreign Affairs 31(3):486-494.

An examination of the modern political scene, with emphasis on Afghanistan's relations with the U.S.S.R., the U.S., and Pakistan.

1219 Wild, Roland
1932 Amanullah, Ex-King of Afghanistan. London: Hurst and Blackett. Pp. 228.

III. HISTORY

>Journalistic style and approach, with a certain amount of valuable material such as a description of the "great council" held in 1928.

1220 Wutt, K.
    1978 Uber Herkunft und kulturelle Merkmale einiger Pashai-Gruppen. Afghanistan Journal 5(2):43-58. Photos; map.

1221 Yapp, M. E.
    1959 British Policy in Central Asia, 1830-43. Ph. D. thesis. London: University of London.

1222 Yapp, M. E.
    1962 Disturbances in Eastern Afghanistan, 1839-42. Bulletin of the School of Oriental and African Studies 25:499-523.

1223 Yapp, M. E.
    1963 Disturbances in Western Afghanistan, 1839-41. Bulletin of the School of Oriental and African Studies 26(2):288-313.

1224 Yapp, M. E.
    1964 The Revolution of 1841-42 in Afghanistan. Bulletin of the School of Oriental and African Studies 27(2):333-381.

1225 Yate, Arthur Campbell
    1887 England and Russia Face to Face in Asia: Travels with the Afghan Boundary Commission. Edinburgh: W. Blackwood. Pp. 481.

1226 Yate, C. E.
    1887 Notes on the City of Hera. Journal of the Asiatic Society of Bengal 56(1):84-106.

1227 Yavorskii, I. L.
    1881 Russkaya Missya v Kabule v 1878-1879. [The Russian Mission in Kabul During 1878-1879]. Russkii Vestnik 155(9-10).

1228 Yuldashbayeva, Fatime K.
    1963 Iz istorii angliyskoy kolonial'noy politiki v Afganstane i Sredney Azii, 70-80 gody XIX v. [On the History of British Colonial Policy in Afghanistan and West Asia, during 70-80 years of the Nineteenth Century]. Tashkent: Gos. Izd-vo Uzbekskoy S.S.R. Pp. 189; bibliography.

III. HISTORY

1229 Wali, Shah
n.d. Yaddashtha-yi Man [My Memmoirs]. Kabul: Press Department. Pp. 96.

Shah Wali's (uncle of King Zahir) notes dealing with the recapture of Kabul and the installation of Mohammed Nadir as King of Afghanistan. English translation available, 1970.

1230 Zaidi, Manzur
1962 Afghanistan: Case Study in Competitive Peaceful Co-Existence. Pakistan Horizon 2:93-101.

Outlines the disputes between Afghanistan and Pakistan, and states that Afghanistan profits by dealing with both the United States and the U.S.S.R.

1231 Zulfiqar Ali Khan
1925 Sher Shah Suri, Emperor of India. Lahore: Civil and Military Gazette. Pp. 114.

1232 Zur-Mohammed, Hafiz
1946 Tarikh-i Mazar-i Sharif vaqi'ai Balkh [History of Mazar-i Sharif and the Situation of Balkh]. Kabul: Matba'eh-yi 'umumi. (1325 A.H.)

IV. SOCIAL ORGANIZATION

Character of society; size and
geographical distribution of
population; ethnic groups;
culture; social structure

The coverage of this basic subject is relatively adequate. The Afghan governments did not and do not possess reliable figures on the total size and geographical distribution of the population and do not have prospects of obtaining those figures in the near future. Existing material relating to the ethnic groups, although in many cases important initial steps, has serious gaps. Most of this work has been done by Western ethnographers and social scientists. The commonly accepted picture of these groups dates from the nineteenth century, and in certain cases the studies done at that time merely confound confusion. Obviously, some of this confusion has been reduced through recent systematic research. It does appear that careful examination of those early manuscripts recently edited by Afghan and non-Afghan authors could provide the springboard for clarifying the situation as regards ethnic elements, their culture and social structure. However, the long-established structure of nomadic and settled life is currently in a state of flux, with new patterns about to emerge.

Anthropologists (particularly ethnographers and ethnologists) and a few other social scientists have done some basic field research in the country, willingly assisted by the facilities of the Afghan government within the limitations of prevailing political conditions. However, far too little work of this nature has been undertaken by the Afghans themselves. There are only a few research-based scholarly works produced by the Afghans in the past two decades.

1233   Afghanistan Council, Asia Society
        1978 Ethnic Processes and Intergroup Relations in Contemporary Afghanistan. Occasional Paper No. 15. New York. Pp. 46.

        Includes the following papers: "Ethnic Competition and Traibal Schism in Eastern Nuristan", by Richard F. Strand; "Ethnic Relations and Access to Resources in Northeast Badakhshan", by M. Nazif Shahrani; "The Impact of Pushtun Immigration on Nomadic Pastoralism in Northeastern Afghanistan", by Thomas J. Barfield; "Religious Myth as Ethnic Boundary", by Robert L. Canfield; "Introduction and Overview", by Jon W. Anderson. A condensed but very useful bibliography accompanies the texts.

IV. SOCIAL ORGANIZATION

1234   Ahmed, Akbar S.
        1976 Millennium and Charisma Among Pathans: A Critical Essay in Social Anthropology. London: Routledge and Kegan Paul. Pp. 173.

        A critical re-examination of Fredrik Barth's study of the Pushtuns of Swat. The author challenges some of Barth's basic methodological and theoretical assumptions and offers an alternative model for the Understanding of Swat Pushtuns.

1235   Ahmed, Akbar S.
        1977 Social and Economic Change in the Tribal Areas, 1972-1976. Karachi: Oxford University Press. Pp. 81.

        Concerned with socioeconomic changes in the Pushtun tribal areas of Pakistan.

1236   Ahmed, Akbar S.
        1978 An Aspect of the Colonial Encounter in the North-West Frontier Province. Asian Affairs 9:319-327.

1237   Ahmed, Akbar S.
        1978 More on Views of the Swat Pathans. Current Anthropology 19(1):222.

        A sequel to Dupree's 1977 article on Pushtuns in this journal. See no. 1333.

1238   Ahmed, Akbar S.
        1978 The Economic and Social Organization of Selected Mohmand Pukhtun Settlements. Ph.D. Dissertation. University of London. Pp. 549.

1239   Ahmed, Akbar S.
        1980 Afghanistan and Pakistan: The Great Game of the Tribes. Journal of South Asian and Middle Eastern Studies 3(4):23-41.

1240   Ahmed, Akbar S.
        1980 Pushtun Economy and Society: Traditional Structure and Economic Development in a Tribal Society. London: Routledge and Kegan Paul. Pp. 406.

        A systematic social anthropological analysis of the Pushtun tribal society focused on the adaptational processes among the Tribal and Settled Area Mohmand tribal groups in Pakistan.

IV. SOCIAL ORGANIZATION

1241   Ahmed, Akbar S.
        1980 Resettlement of Afghan Refugees and the Social
            Scientists. Journal of South Asian and Middle Eastern
            Studies 4(1):77-89.

1242   Ahmed, Akbar S.
        1980 Tribes and States in Central and South Asia. Asian
            Affairs 11:152-168.

        Discussion of certain principles pertaining to the complex
        relationship between tribes and states in Central and
        Southwest Asia, particularly Afghanistan and Pakistan
        (before 1947).

1243   Ahmed, Akbar S.
        1981 The Arab Connection: Emergent Models of Social
            Structure Among Pakistani Tribesmen. Asian Affairs
            12:167-172.

        As a result of increasing numbers of Pushtun males working
        in Arab countries, there seems to be emerging a pattern of
        absent men resulting in possible compromise of Pushtun
        women's honor. Other consequences of this new pattern of
        work in Arab countries are leadership based on money and
        the exacerbation of ethnic divisiveness.

1244   Ali, Mohammad
        1958 Manners and Customs of the Afghans. Lahore: The
            Punjab Educational Press. Pp. 81.

        Short chapters on hospitality, tribal codes of conduct,
        nomadic life, ceremonies at the New Year, typical Afghan
        names, sports, and folklore.

1245   Amos, Harold L.
        1967 Dane Zul: Village in Transition. In American His-
            torical Anthropology: Essays in Honor of Leslie Spier.
            Edited by Carroll L. Riley and Walter W. Taylor.
            Carbondale: Southern Illinois University Press. Pp. 23-
            36.

        A brief ethnographic sketch of Dane Zul, A Hazara rural
        village in Central Afghanistan by an anthropologist.

IV. SOCIAL ORGANIZATION

1246   Anderson, Jon W.
        1975 Tribe and Community Among the Ghilzai Pushtun. Anthropos 70:575-601.

The author argues that the Pushtuns social organization is comprised of various schemes or strategies which tend to complement and uphold each other. The author has done extensive field work among the Ghilzai of Afghanistan and his contributions, as an American anthropologist, are both original and stimulating.

1247   Anderson, Jon W.
        1978 There are no Khans Anymore: Economic Development and Social Change in Tribal Afghanistan. Middle East Journal 32(2):167-183.

An anthropological analysis of the processes of disintegration of the tribal structure of the Pushtuns in Afghanistan caused by the introduction of technology and non-Afghan models of economic development.

1248   Anderson, Jon W.
        1979 Doing Pakhtu: Social Organization of the Ghilzai Pakhtun. Unpublished Ph.D. Dissertation. University of North Carolina-Chapel Hill. Pp. 256.

Based on anthropological field work during 1971-1974, the dissertation focuses on the terms in which Ghilzai Pushtun in Afghanistan interpret social action, finding social organization to be problematic or uncertain rather than determinative or determinable. One of the most original works on the society and culture of the Pushtuns, it is being prepared for publication.

1249   Anderson, Jon W. and Richard F. Strand (eds)
        1978 Ethnic Processes and Intergroup Relations in Contemporary Afghanistan. New York: Afghanistan Council, The Asia Society. Occasional paper no. 15. Pp. 46. See no. 1233.

A series of papers on ethnic relations in Afghanistan presented at the eleventh annual meeting of the Middle East Studies Association, New York, November 10, 1977.

1250   Andreev, M. S.
        1927 Po Etnologii Afganistan. Dolina Pandzshir. [On the Ethnology of the Valley of Panjshir]. Tashkent: Uzbekistan SSR Academy of Sciences.

IV. SOCIAL ORGANIZATION

>Ethnographic sketches in the Panjshir valley based on research during 1926 in Afghanistan.

1251 Andreev, M. S.
>1958 Tadziki Dolinie Khuf [Tajiks of the Khuf Valley]. Stalinabad: Tajikistan SSR Academy of Sciences. Volume II. Pp. 521.

>A detailed ethnography of Tajiks in the upper Amu river areas. Especially detailed on material culture.

1252 Arefi, Abdul Ghafoor
>1975 Urban Policies, Planning and Implementation in Kabul, Afghanistan. Unpublished Ph.D. Dissertation. Indiana University. Pp. 481.

>A study of the institutional, environmental, agricultural and socio-economic ramifications resulting from the dynamics of increased urbanization in Kabul, Afghanistan.

1253 Aristov, N. A.
>1896 Zametki ob etnicheskom sostave tiurkskikh plemen i narodnostei i svedeniia ob ikh chislennosti [Remarks about the Ethnic Composition of the Turkic Tribes and Nationalities and Information about their Number]. Zhivaia Starina 6. St. Petersburg.

1254 Azoy, Geoffrey Whitney
>1979 Buzkashi--So That His Name Shall Rise. Ph.D. Dissertation. University of Virginia. Pp. 501.

>An analysis and description of Buzkashi in Northern Afghanistan. Included are also glimpses about the transformation of the game in recent times and under current changing conditions. The reader is left with the impression that Buzkashi is common throughout Afghanistan and that Afghan political behavior is a macrocosm of a game which is only played in restricted local areas of Northern Afghanistan.

1255 Azoy, Whitney
>1982 Buzkashi: Game and Power in Afghanistan. Philadelphia: University of Pennsylvania Press. Pp. 170, plates; index.

IV. SOCIAL ORGANIZATION

An anthropological description of the game of Buzkashi in northern Afghanistan. The author's contention that through the understanding of Buzkashi (a predominantly non-Pushtun, non-Baluch, non-Hazara, etc. game) one can understand all Afghan political behavior needs an important qualification. The book was available in December 1981.

1256 Bacon, Elizabeth E.
    1946 A Preliminary Attempt to Determine the Culture Areas of Asia. Southwestern Journal of Anthropology 2:117-132.

Deals with sedentary and nomadic cultures of southwestern Asia, including Afghanistan.

1257 Bacon, Elizabeth E.
    1951 The Hazara Mongols of Afghanistan: A Study in Social Organization. Unpublished Ph.D. Thesis. University of California. Graduate Division, Northern Section. Pp. 144; bibliography.

1258 Bacon, Elizabeth E.
    1951 An Inquiry into the History of the Hazara Mongols of Afghanistan. Southwestern Journal of Anthropology 7:230-247.

The author examines the usually-held belief that the Hazaras are descended from military garrisons left in Afghanistan by Ghengis Khan in the early thirteenth century by consulting contemporary sources and concludes that the region was populated by Chagatai, moving in between 1229 and 1447 A.D.

1259 Bacon, Elizabeth E.
    1958 Obok. A Study of Social Structure in Eurasia. Viking Fund Publications in Anthropology 25. New York: Wenner-Gren Foundation for Anthropological Research, Inc. Pp. 235; bibliography; index.

Pages 1-65 deal with the social organization and the cultural make-up of the Hazara Mongols of Afghanistan.

1260 Balland, D.
    1974 Vieux Sedentaires Tajik et Immigrants Pashtoun dans le Sillon de Ghazni (Afghanistan Oriental). Bulletin Association des Geographes Francais 417-418:171-180.

IV. SOCIAL ORGANIZATION

1261 Baloch, Mir Khuda Baksh Bijarani Marri
   1974 Searchlights on Baloches and Balochistan. Karachi: Royal Book Co.

   Includes a chapter on the Pashtuns and some insights about official and unofficial Baluch attitudes toward Pashtuns.

1262 Barfield, Thomas Jefferson III
   1978 The Central Asian Arabs: Pastoral Nomadism in Transition. Ph.D. Dissertation. Harvard University. Pp. 305.

   Discussion of a small group in northern Afghanistan which calls itself Arab. An account of the changes that have taken place in their society over the past fifty years as they switched from subsistence pastoralism to a cash economy.

1263 Barfield, Thomas
   1979 The Impact of Colonial Disputes on Isolated Populations in the Upper Oxus: The Case of Central Asian Arabs. Journal of South Asian and Middle Eastern Studies 3(2):20-25.

1264 Barfield, Thomas
   1981 The Central Asian Arabs of Afghanistan: Pastoral Nomadism in Transition. Austin: University of Texas Press. Pp. 208. See no. 1261.

1265 Barrat, Jacques
   1971 Kabul, Capitale de l'Afghanistan. Unpublished Ph.D. Dissertation. University of Paris.

1266 Barth, Fredrik
   1956 Ecological Relationships of Ethnic Groups in Swat, North Pakistan. American Anthropologist 58:1079-1089.

1267 Barth, Fredrik
   1959 Segmentary Opposition and the Theory of Games: A Study of Pathan Organization. Journal of the Royal Anthropological Institute 89:5-21.

1268 Barth, Fredrik
   1964 Competition and Symbiosis in Northeast Baluchistan. Folk 6(1).

1269 Barth, Fredrik
   1965 Political Leadership Among Swat Pathans. New York: Humanities Press. Pp. 143.

IV. SOCIAL ORGANIZATION

Discusses political organization among Swat Pushtuns, based on field work in 1954, and argues that this organization is built around the constitution of authority and of corporate bodies out of sets of personal relations.

1270 Barth, Fredrik
1969 Pathan Identity and its Maintenance. In Ethnic Groups and Boundaries, edited by Fredrik Barth. Boston: Little, Brown and Company. Pp. 117-134.

1271 Barth, Fredrik
1971 Role Dilemmas and Father-Son Dominance in Middle Eastern Kinship Systems. In Kinship and Culture, edited by Francis L. K. Hsu. Chicago: Aldine Publishing Company. Pp. 87-95.

An attempt to show the way in which behavioral characteristics in one kinship relationship are in part constrained and determined by the existance of another, dominant kinship relationship. The author tests this assertion with Swat Pushtun and Cyrenaica Bedouin data.

1272 Barth, Fredrik
1972 Ethnic Processes on the Pathan-Baluch Boundary. In Directions in Sociolinguistics, edited by John J. Gumperz and Dell Hymes. New York: Holt, Rinehart and Winston. Pp. 454-464.

The author questions the identification of Pushtuns and Baluchs as two completely distinct social entities. He deals with these two societies as component groups operating within the same ecological systems and as members of a single linguistically diverse region.

1273 Barth, Fredrik
1977 Political Leadership Among Swat Pathans. In Friends, Followers, and Factions, edited by Steffen W. Schmidt, Laura Gausti, Carl H. Lande, and James C. Scott. Berkeley: University of California Press. Pp. 207-219. (Condensed version of Barth 1965). See no. 1268.

1274 Barth, Fredrik
1981 Features of Person and Society in Swat: Collected Essays on Pathans. (Selected Essays of Fredrik Barth, Volume II). Boston: Routledge and Kegan Paul. Pp. 190.

IV. SOCIAL ORGANIZATION

>Brings together Barth's various writings on the Pushtuns of Swat. The essays address some specific theoretical issues and tries to re-address some previously stated anthropological issues, especially those for which the author has been criticized in more recent anthropological works.

1275 Bellew, Henry Walter
>1864 A General Report on the Yusufzeis in Six Chapters. Lahore: Government Press. Pp. ix, 266.

1276 Bellew, Henry Walter
>1880 The Races of Afghanistan, Being a Brief Account of the Principal Nations Inhabiting that Country. Calcutta: Thacker, Spink and Co. Pp. 124.

>A preliminary study in preparation for the later work by this author: An Inquiry into the Ethnography of Afghanistan. Reprinted 1976.

1277 Bellew, Henry Walter
>1891 An Inquiry into the Ethnography of Afghanistan. Woking: The Oriental University Institute. Pp. iv, 208.

>Work of a retired Surgeon-General of the Bengal Army. Material drawn from sources of unestablished reliability, or doubtful reliability, in such a complex manner as to be without present-day value. Reprinted 1973.

1278 Benjamin, J. J., II
>1859 Eight Years in Asia and Africa from 1846 to 1855. Hanover. Pp. xv, 332; map.

>An ardent Jewish traveler visited his co-religionists in many parts of the world. In this work, first published in German in 1857, two chapters are devoted to the manners and customs of the Jewish community at Kabul.

1279 Biddulph, J.
>1880 Tribes of the Hindoo Koosh. Calcutta: Office of the Superintendent of Government Printing. Pp. 164 and appendices.

>A rare work which treats the subject in a most detailed and thoroughly confusing manner. Included are extensive wordlists and brief sketches of grammers. Reprinted 1971.

IV. SOCIAL ORGANIZATION

1280   Blanc, Jean Charles
         1976 L'Afghanistan et ses Populations. Bruxelles: Editions Complex. Pp. 168; maps; plates.

1281   Boesen, Inger W.
         1980 Women, Honour and Love. Some Aspects of the Pashtun Woman's Life in Eastern Afghanistan. Afghanistan Journal 7(2):50-59.

1282   Bourgeois, Jean and Danielle
         1972 Les Seigneurs d'Aryana: Nomades Contrabandiers d'Afghanistan. Paris: Flammarion. Pp. 250.

1283   Bravin, N. and I. Beliaev
         1903 Ukazatel' plemennykh imen k stat'e N. A. Aristova: "Zametki ob etnicheskom sostave tiurkskikh plemen i svendeniia o okh chislennosti." Izdano pod redaktsiei P. M. Melioranskogo [An Index of Tribal Names to the Article by N. A. Aristov: "Remarks about the Ethnic Composition of the Turkic Tribes and Nationalities and Information about their Number." Edited under the Supervision of P. M. Melioranskii]. Zapiski Imp. russk. geogr. obshchestva po otdel. etnografii 28, no. 2. St. Petersburg.

1284   Bray, Denys
         1913 Ethnographic Survey of Baluchistan, 2 Volumes. Bombay.

1285   Broadfoot, J. S.
         1885 Reports on Part of the Ghilzai Country, and on Some of the Tribes in the Neighborhood of Ghazni, and on the Route from Ghazni to Dera Ismail by the Ghwalari Pass. Journal of the Royal Geographical Society, Supplementary Papers 1:1-60.

         Notes taken by Lieutenant Broadfoot in 1839 were finally edited and published by Major W. Broadfoot. Most useful for the account of tribes found around Ghazni.

1286   Burnes, Alexander
         1838 On the Siah-Posh Kaffirs with Specimens of their Language and Costume. Journal of the Asiatic Society of Bengal 7:325-333.

IV. SOCIAL ORGANIZATION

>Captain Burnes interviewed several Kafirs, a Muslim and a Hindu--both of whom had traveled among the Kafirs--from whom he learned of their customs. There is a short vocabulary of the Kafir language, with sentences, and a shorter one of the Pashai dialect, with sentences.

1287 Çağatay, Babur and Andrée F. Sjoberg
1955 Notes on the Uzbek Culture of Central Asia. Texas Journal of Science 7(1):72-112.

Discusses characteristics of Uzbek culture and society in the city of Kabul. Based on the study of an Uzbek community in that city.

1288 Canfield, Robert LeRoy
1971 Faction and Conversion: A Study of Religious Alignment in a Plural Society. Ph.D. Dissertation. University of Michigan. Pp. 197.

An ethnographic analysis of the dynamics of ethnicity among the Hazara of Afghanistan and the problems raised by the geographic distribution of religious sects in Bamian, Afghanistan.

1289 Canfield, Robert L.
1973 The Ecology of Rural Ethnic Groups and the Spatial Dimensions of Power. American Anthropologist 75:1511-1528.

Discusses the mechanisms which influence the locations of Hazara ethnic groups in Central Afghanistan.

1290 Canfield, Robert LeRoy
1973 Faction and Conversion in a Plural Society: Religious Alignment in the Hindu Kush. Anthropological Paper No. 50. Ann Arbor: University of Michigan Museum of Anthropology. Pp. 142. See no. 1287.

1291 Canfield, Robert L.
1973 Hazara Integration into the Afghan Nation: Some Changing Relations Between Hazaras and Afghan Officials. New York: Afghanistan Council, the Asia Society. Occasional paper no. 3. Pp. 14.

Discusses some internal changes in the social structure of the Hazara society because of contact with neighboring ethnic groups.

IV. SOCIAL ORGANIZATION

1292   Canfield, Robert L.
        1975 Suffering as a Religious Imperative in Afghanistan.
        In Psychological Anthropology. Edited by Thomas R.
        Williams. The Hague: Mouton. Pp. 465-486.

        The chapter deals with religion, healing and how religion
        defines social relations among the Hazaras of Afghanistan.

1293   Canfield, Robert L.
        1979 Maximization, Charisma, and Pathan Personality.
        Current Anthropology 20(2):420-422.

1294   Carless, Hugh
        1956 The Tajiks of the Panjshir Valley of the Hindu Kush.
        Revue Iranienne d'Anthropologie 1(4/5):40-54.

1295   Centlivres-Demont, Micheline
        1976 Types d'occupation et Relations Interethniques dans
        le Nord-est de l'Afghanistan. Studia Iranica 5(2):269-277.

1296   Centlivres, Micheline and Pierre and Mark Slobin
        1971 A Muslim Shaman of Afghan Turkestan. Ethnology
        10(2):160-173.

        An account of a therapeutic Seance performed by a shaman
        with the aid of a qobuz or horsehair fiddle in a town in
        northern Afghanistan.

1297   Centlivres, Pierre
        1972 Noms, Surnoms et Termes d'address dans le nord
        Afghanistan. Studia Iranica 1(1):89-102.

1298   Centlivres, Pierre
        1972 Un Bazar d' Asie Central: Forme et Organisation du
        Bazar de Tashqueghan (Afghanistan). Wiesbaden: L.
        Reichert. Pp. 226.

        An ethnographic study of the bazaar of Tashqurghan.
        Emphasis on morphology, administration and social organization. Based on fieldwork during 1966-68.

1299   Centlivres, Pierre
        1972 Les Uzbeks du Qattaghan. Afghanistan Journal
        2(2):28-36.

IV. SOCIAL ORGANIZATION

1300   Centlivres, Pierre
        1976 L'historie Recente de l'Afghanistan et la Configuration Ethnique des Provinces du Nord-est. Studia Iranica 5(2):256-267.

1301   Centlivres, Pierre
        1976 Problems d'identite Ethnique dans le Nord de l'Afghanistan. Iran Moderne 1:8-13.

1302   Centlivres, Pierre
        1980 Identity and Image of Outsiders in the Folk Anthropology of Afghanistan. Cahiers Vilfredo Pareto 18(53):29-41.

1303   Central Asian Review
        1965 The Rural Commune in the Tadzhik Areas of Afghanistan. Central Asian Review 13(2):121-130.

A precis of an extensive article by A. D. Davidov on Rural Commune and its Economic Significance in Afghanistan, 1963. Originally appeared in Russian in Vaprosy Ekonomiki Afghanistana, Moscow, 1963.

1304   Central Asian Review
        1966 The Rural Community of the Hazaras of Central Afghanistan. Central Asian Review 14(1):32-54.

A precis of A. D. Davidov's work on this topic which appeared originally in Russian in 1964. See no. 1315.

1305   Charpentier, C. J.
        1972 Bazaar-e Tashqurghan: Ethnographical Studies in an Afghan Traditional Bazaar. Uppsala: Studia Ethnographica Upsaliensia 36. Pp. 193.

A useful ethnographic description of the Tashqurghan Bazaar. Illustrations, notes, sketches, and bibliography. Emphasis on technology and economics, crafts, and social structure. Based on research during 1970-72.

1306   Charpentier, C. J.
        1973 The Use of Haschish and opium in Afghanistan. Anthropos 68(3-4):482-490.

1307   Charpentier, C. J.
        1974 Water-Pipes, Tobacco and Snuff in Afghanistan. Anthropos 69(5-6):939-944.

IV. SOCIAL ORGANIZATION

Probably the first systematic, however brief, attempt at describing some of the attendant paraphernalia of tobacco and snuff use in Afghanistan.

1308 Charpentier, C. J.
1976 Social Interaction as a Major Force in Asian Economy: An Analysis of "Asian Pseudo-Capitalism". Anthropos 71(1):289-293.

The author argues we should not use Western formal typologies of markets in attempting to understand Central Asian settings of commercial exchange (Bazars). Instead, we should note that the bazar serves a larger social role and that we should avoid using only conceptions of monetary transactions in our comparison of Western and Central Asian economic models. The author utilizes his own research in Tashqurghan and those of others to briefly make this very important point.

1309 Christensen, Asger
1980 The Pashtuns of Kunar: Tribe, Class and Community Organization. Afghanistan Journal 7(3):79-92.

1310 Collin-Delavaud, M. C.
1958 Deux exemples de mise en valeur dans l'Afghanistan septentrional [Two Examples of (Land) Improvement in Northern Afghanistan]. Bulletin de l'Association de Géographes Francais.

Factual information on Hazara society collected in the field in 1956.

1311 Cunningham, George
1947 Tribes of the North-West Frontier of India. World Review 2:23-29. London.

The author, governor of the North-West Frontier Province from 1937 to 1946, writes informatively, indicating that the large tribes along the frontier would rather remain undeveloped and free than governed and developed.

1312 Dames, M. Longworth
1904 The Baloch Race. A Historical and Ethnological Sketch. In Asiatic Society Monographs 4. London: Royal Asiatic Society. Pp. 90; bibliography; appendices.

On the divisions and subdivisions of the Baloch tribes living in India, Baluchistan and Sistan, their probable origin and their history in poetry and legends.

IV. SOCIAL ORGANIZATION

1313   Darmesteter, James
       1888   Lettres sur l'Inde: A la frontière Afghane [Letters on India: On the Afghan Frontier]. Paris: Lemerre. Pp. xxix, 355.

       A noted French comparative philologist describes a stay of seven months in 1887 in the area of Northwestern India and Afghanistan.

1314   Datta, Bhupendra Nath
       1939-1940   An Enquiry into the Racial Elements in Beluchistan, Afghanistan, and the Neighbouring Areas of the Hindu Kush. Man in India 19:174-186, 218-273; 20:1-43.

       A careful compilation and analysis of historical data on the ethnic groups of the area and of available physical anthropological measurements. This study is an English translation and elaboration of a doctoral dissertation submitted to the University of Hamburg in 1923. Relevant works published after 1923 have been made use of in the revision.

1315   Davidov, Aleksandr D.
       1964   Sel'skaya obshchina u Khazareytsev tsentral'-nogo Afganistan [The Rural Community of the Hazaras of Central Afghanistan]. Kratkiye Soobshcheniya Instituta Narodov Azii 77:1-19.

       A resumé of field research by Western scholars. An English translation appears in the Central Asian Review 14, 1, pp. 32-44. 1966.

1316   Davidov, Aleksandr D.
       1976   Socialno-Economichiskaia Struktura Derevne Afghanistana [The Socio-Economic Structure of Villages in Afghanistan]. Moscow: Akadeniia Nauk SSSR.

       A description and analysis of the economic organization of rural life in Afghanistan with emphasis on the non-Pushtun population. A representative Soviet materialist approach to the study of rural society in Afghanistan.

1317   Dianous, Hugues Jean de
       1961   Hazars et Mongols en Afghanistan [Hazaras and Mongols in Afghanistan]. Orient 19:71-98; 20:91-113.

IV. SOCIAL ORGANIZATION

1318 Dictionary of the Pathan Tribes on the North-West Frontier of India, Compiled under the Orders of the Quarter-Master General in India
1899 Calcutta: Government Printing Office. Pp. viii, 239.

A complex study, produced by the Intelligence Branch at Simla, dealing with tribal groups, subgroups, habitat, intra-tribal relations, leadership, etc. A map in color illustrates the areas of important groups.

1319 Dor, Remy
1975 Contribution a l'etude des Kirghiz du Pamir Afghan. Paris.

1320 Dor, Remy
1978 Die Kirghisen des Afghanischen Pamir. Graz: Akademische Druck und Verlagsanstatt. Pp. 124, 81 illustrations.

1321 Dor, Remy and Clas M. Naumann
1979 Die Kirghisen des Afghanischen Pamir [The Kirghiz of the Afghan Pamir]. Graz, Austria: Akademische Druck. Pp. 148.

General information by German Turkologists on the Kirghiz of Afghanistan. Probably the first in German language.

1322 Dupree, Louis
1954 The Disintegration of the Clan Village in Badwan, a Pathan Farming Village in Southwestern Afghanistan. Journal of the Alabama Academy of Sciences 26:98.

1323 Dupree, Louis
1956 The Changing Character of South-Central Afghanistan Villages. Human Organization 14(4):26-29.

1324 Dupree, Louis
1963 Culture Change in the Iranian Plateau Sub-Culture Area. The Academy Quarterly (Journal of the Academy for Rural Development, Peshawar) 2(5):225-234.

1325 Dupree, Louis
1965 Involvement: A Key to Development. Economic Development and Cultural Change 13(4):490-504.

IV. SOCIAL ORGANIZATION

1326   Dupree, Louis
        1968 Aq Kupruk: A Town in Northern Afghanistan. In City
            and Nation in the Developing World. Edited by
            Associates of the American Universities Field Staff.
            New York: American Universities Field Staff. Pp. 9-61.

1327   Dupree, Louis
        1970 Aq Kupruk: A Town in Northern Afghanistan. In
            Peoples and Cultures of the Middle East, Volume II.
            Edited by Louise Sweet. New York: Natural History
            Press. Pp. 344-387.

        The record of the emergence of proto-urban culture at Aq
        Kupruk is provided along with a discussion of the process-
        es of animal and plant domestication, agriculture, spe-
        cialization in the bazaar, and the contemporary efforts at
        national integration in this town in northern Afghanistan.

1328   Dupree, Louis
        1975 Aq Kupruk: A Town in Northern Afghanistan. Common
            Ground 1(2):11-18.

1329   Dupree, Louis
        1975 Settlement and Migration Patterns in Afghanistan: A
            Tentative Statement. Modern Asian Studies 9(3):385-400.

1330   Dupree, Louis
        1976 Tajik: Afghanistan and Soviet Union. Family of Man
            7(88):2443-2445.

1331   Dupree, Louis
        1976 Uzbek: Afghanistan and Soviet Union. Family of Man
            7(93):2577-2580.

1332   Dupree, Louis
        1977 On Two Views of the Swat Pushtun. Current Anthro-
            pology 18(3):514-517.

        This is a criticism of Barth's views on Pushtun social
        organization and is inspired by S. A. Ahmed's work on the
        Pushtuns. Comments on this article by F. Barth, C. J.
        Charpentier, J. Pettigrew, M. Slobin, B. Tavakolian are
        included.

1333   Dupree, Louis
        1979 Further Notes on Taqiyya: Afghanistan. Journal of
            the American Oriental Society 99(4):680-682.

IV. SOCIAL ORGANIZATION

1334 Dzhafarova, A. A.
    1963 Iz istorii zhenskogo voprosa v Afganistane [From the History of the Position of Women in Afghanistan]. In Kratkiye Soobshcheniya Instituta Narodov Azii 73:23-28. Moscow.

1335 Edelberg, Lennart
    1965 Nuristanske Solvpokaler. KUML, pp. 153-201.

1336 Edelberg, Lennart and Schuyler Jones
    1979 Nuristan. Graz, Austria: Academische Druck. Pp. 185.
    A comprehensive work on the peoples and culture of Nuristan, Afghanistan. Although descriptive, the work covers a variety of subjects on Nuristan and attempts at summarizing the works of other researchers on the Nuristanis.

1337 Edwardes, Herbert Benjamin
    1851 A Year on the Punjab Frontier in 1848-49. 2 vols. London: Richard Bentley. Pp. (1) xiv, 608; (2) xiv, 734.

    Only a limited part of this work is related to tribal elements on the Afghan side of the frontier; pages 385-369 describe the people of Murwat and their life.

1338 Einzmann, Harald
    1977 Religioses Volksbrauchtum in Afghanistan: Islamische Heiligenverehrung und Wallfahrtswesen im Raum Kabul. [Religious Folk Customs in Afghanistan: Islamic Veneration of Saints and Pilgrimages in the Kabul Area.] Ph.D. Dissertation. University of Heidelbert. Pp. ix, 346.

1339 Enriquez, Colin M. D.
    1910 The Pathan Borderland: A consecutive Account of the Country and People on and Beyond the Indian Frontier from Chitral to Dera Ismail Khan. Calcutta: Thacker, Spink and Company (reprinted 1921). Pp. 194.

1340 Fazy, Robert
    1953 L'Exploration du Kafiristan par les Européens [The Exploration of Kafiristan by Europeans]. Asiatische Studien, pp. 1-25; appendices. Bern.

    Brief accounts of the Europeans who have traveled in Kafiristan (Nuristan) with notes on their publications, of which the appendices contain extracts.

IV. SOCIAL ORGANIZATION

1341   Ferdinand, Klaus
        1956 Afghanistans Nomader [Afghan Nomads]. Fra National-
              museets Arbejdsmark (Copenhagen). Pp. 61-70.

        Material similar to that contributed by this author to no.
        355.

1342   Ferdinand, Klaus
        1957 Nomadestudier i Afghanistan. In Menneskets Mang-
              foldighed (Copenhagen). Pp. 126-41.

1343   Ferdinand, Klaus
        1959 The Baluchistan Barrel-vaulted Tent and its Affini-
              ties. Folk 1:27-50.

1344   Ferdinand, Klaus
        1959 Preliminary Notes on Hazara Culture. Det Kongelige
              Danske Videnskabernes Selskab, Historisk-filosofiske
              Meddelelser, Bd. 37, Nr. 5. Copenhagen: Ejnar Munks-
              gaard. Pp. 51; bibliography.

        Material collected on the Mongol tribes of Afghanistan
        between 1953 and 1955 by the Danish Scientific Mission to
        Afghanistan.

1345   Ferdinand, Klaus
        1962 Nomad Expansion and Commerce in Central Afghanistan.
              A Sketch of Some Modern Trends. Folk 4:123-59.

1346   Ferdinand, Klaus
        1964 Ethnographical Notes on the Chahar Aimaq, Hazara and
              Moghol. Acta Orientalia 28(1-2):175-203.

        An extensive review article of F. Schurmann's The Mongols
        of Afghanistan, 1962. It is a critical and informative
        analysis of Schurmann's work.

1347   Ferdinand, Klaus
        1965 Ethnographical Notes on Chahar Aimaq, Hazara, and
              Moghol. Acta Orientalia 28(3-4):175-204.

1348   Ferdinand, Klaus
        1969 Nomadism in Afghanistan With an Appendix on Milk
              Products. In Viehwirtschaft und Hirtenkultur. Edited
              by Laszlo Foeldes. Budapest: Academiai Kiado. Pp. 127-
              160.

IV. SOCIAL ORGANIZATION

Discusses the variety of nomadism in various parts of Afghanistan. Appended is a sketch of milk processing and milk products found among the Eastern nomads of the country.

1349   Field, Claud H.
       1908   With the Afghans. London: Marshall Brothers. Pp. 221.

       An account of missionary work with Afghans at Peshawar, in the tribal areas, and with Afghans from across the frontier.

1350   Franz, E.
       1972   Ethnographische Skizzen zur dage der Turkmenen in Afghanistan. Orient 4:175-184.

1351   Franz, E.
       1972   Gegenwaerigen Verbreitung und Gruppierung de Turkmenen in Afghanistan. Baessler-Archiv 20:191-238.

1352   Fremberg, Juergen
       1980   Neues Schrifttum ueber die Indo-Arischen Bergvoelker des Afghanischen Hindukush (1975-1980). Anthropos 75:937-941.

1353   Gafferberg, E. G.
       1936   Formy braka i svadebnye obriady u dzhemshidov i khezare [Forms of Marriage and Wedding Rituals among the Jamshidis and Khazars]. Sovetskaia etnografiia. Leningrad.

1354   Gafferberg, E. G.
       1953   Khazareiskaia (Afganistan) iurta khanaikhyrga; k voprosu ob istorii kochevogo zhilishcha [Hazara (Afghanistan) Yurt "Khanai Khyrga"; History of Nomadic Dwellings]. Akademiia nauk S.S.S.R. Muzei antropologii i etnografii. Sbornik 14:72-92. Moscow.

1355   Ghani, Ashraf
       1978   Islam and State-Building in a Tribal Society, Afghanistan: 1880-1901. Modern Asia Studies 12(2):269-283

       A critical analysis of the relationship between State and Religion in Afghanistan by a trained and creative Afghan Anthropologist.

IV. SOCIAL ORGANIZATION

1356 Gharzi, General Muhammad Safar Vakil
   1960 Nuristan [Nuristan]. Kabul: Matba'eh-yi doulati.
   (1338 A.H.)

  An account in Persian of travels in Nuristan and observations of the so-called Baluris by an Afghan army general.

1357 Glatzer, Bernt
   1975 Nomaden von Gharjistan: Aspekte der wirtschaftlichen, sozialen und politischen Organisation nomadischer Durrani-Paschtunen in Nordwestafghanistan. [The Nomads of Gharjistan: Aspects of the Economic, Social and Political Organization of the Nomadic Durrani Pashtuns in Northwest Afghanistan]. Ph.D. Dissertation. University of Heidelberg. Pp. xii, 234.

1358 Glatzer, Bernt
   1977 Nomaden von Gharjistan, Aspekte der wirtshaftlichen, sozialen, und politischen organisation Nomadischer Durrani-Paschtunen in Nordwest Afghanistan [Nomades of Gharjistan, Aspects of Economic, Social and Political Organization of the Nomadic Durrani Pushtun, Northwest Afghanistan]. Wiesbaden: Franz Steiner Verlag. Pp. 246. Published version of no. 1357.

1359 Hackin, Joseph
   1926 Les idoles du Kafiristan [The Idols of Kafiristan]. Artibus Asiae 4:258-262.

  Five illustrations show as many idols in the Kabul Museum, while the text describes how the conventionalized figures were executed solely by knives and hatchets, and tells of their roles in Kafir beliefs.

1360 Hackin, Ria and Ahmad Ali Kohzad
   1953 Légendes et coutumes Afghanes [Afghan Legends and Customs]. Paris: Imprimerie nationale, presses universitaires de France. Pp. xxvi, 204.

  The bulk of the volume consists in material collected during a decade by Mme. Hackin and Kohzad. The popular stories were gathered in the neighborhood of famous archaeological sites and relate to these sites. Material of quite another type is found in the pages devoted to popular customs and beliefs.

IV. SOCIAL ORGANIZATION

1361   Hanifi, M. Jamil
1971 Child Rearing Patterns Among Pushtuns of Afghanistan. International Journal of the Sociology of the Family 1(1):53-57.

An anthropological analysis of the Pushtun family structure, particularly its role in child training and early life experience.

1362   Hanifi, M. Jamil
1974 The Central Asian City and its Role in Cultural Transformation. New York: Afghanistan Council, Asia Society. Occasional Paper No. 6. Pp. 10.

Discussion of the morphology of Kabul and its sociocultural dynamics with respect to changing its surrounding rural environment.

1363   Hanifi, M. Jamil
1976 Pre-Industrial Kabul: Its Structure and Function in Transformational Processes in Afghanistan. In The Mutual Interaction of People and Their Built Environment. Edited by Amos Rapaport. The Hague: Mouton. Pp. 441-451.

Discusses the impact of Kabul on its rural environment. The haphazard growth of Kabul and its long-range consequences are examined.

1364   Hanifi, M. Jamil
1978 Cultural Diversity, Conflicting Ideologies, and Transformational Processes in Afghanistan. In The Nomadic Alternative. Edited by W. Weissleder. The Hague: Mouton. Pp. 387-396.

The sociocultural and ethnic diversity of the country is discussed and a model for the integration of this diversity is offered for Afghanistan.

1365   Hanifi, M. Jamil
1978 The Family in Afghanistan. In The Family in Asia. Edited by P. D. Bardis and M. S. Das. London: George Allen and Unwen. Pp. 47-69.

A critical examination of the organization of Family in Afghanistan. Emphasis on the cultural context of the family and how its form and dynamics are constrained by its cultural environment.

IV. SOCIAL ORGANIZATION

1366 Hanifi, M. Jamil
    1981 Islam in Contemporary Afghanistan. In The Crescent in the East. Edited by R. Israeli. London: Curzon Press. Pp. 23-35.

1367 Herrlich, Albert
    1938 Land des Lichtes. Deutsche Kundfahrt zu unbekannten Völkern im Hindukusch [The Land of Light. German Research with the Unknown Peoples of the Hindu Kush]. Munich: Knorr und Hirth. Pp. 177; sketch maps.

A member of the German expedition of 1935 describes the trip from Kabul into Nuristan (Land of Light). Valuable account of little-known areas, with a route map of the expedition.

1368 Holdich, Thomas Hungerford
    1896 Origin of the Kafirs of the Hindu-Kush. Geographical Journal 7:42-49.

A discussion of the historical background of the region leads to the conclusion that this group is of Iranian stock and moved from Badakhshan into their present habitat.

1369 Hudson, Alfred E. and Elizabeth Bacon
    1941 Social Control and the Individual in Eastern Hazara Culture. In Language, Culture, and Personality. Edited by L. Spier, I. Hallowell, S. S. Newman. Menasha, Wisconsin: Sapir Memorial Publication Fund. Pp. 239-258.

1370 Hunte, Pamela A.
    1975 Familial Structure and Fertility in Afghanistan. Unpublished M.A. Thesis. Northern Illinois University. Pp. 136.

Utilizing data from the Afghanistan Demographic Survey the author refutes the popular theory that the extended familial household unit in Afghanistan encourages a higher fertility than that of the nuclear family unit. It argues that in Afghanistan the extended familial structure appears to exert a negative influence on fertility.

1371 Hunte, Pamela A.
    1980 The Sociocultural Context of Perinatality in Afghanistan. Unpublished Ph.D. Dissertation. University of Wisconsin-Madison. Pp. 450.

IV. SOCIAL ORGANIZATION

An ethnological discussion of significant sociocultural factors which are related to and affect fertility and the period of perinatality in selected aspects of Afghan society.

1372   Hunte, Pamela A.
   1981 The Role of the Dai (Traditional Birth Attendant) in Urban Afghanistan: Some Traditional and Adaptational Aspects. Medical Anthropology 5(1):17-26.

Some basic aspects of the birth attendant's role in urban areas of Afghanistan are summarized and compared with the role of the Qabila (government-trained and licensed nurse-midwife).

1373   Hunte, Pamela A.
   1981 Traditional Methods of Fertility Regulation in Afghanistan. In Traditional Methods of Fertility Regulation. Edited by Lucile F. Newman. New Brunswick, N.J.: Rutgers University Press. Pp. 51-63.

A summary of traditional methods to induce, inhibit, and abort a pregnancy in traditional Afghan society.

1374   India, Department of the Army
   1910 Dictionary of the Pathan Tribes on the Northwest Frontier of India. Calcutta: Department of the Army, India.

1375   Interview of Pierre Centlivres and Micheline Centlivres
   1980 Views on Afghanistan. Actes de la Recherche en Sciences Sociales 34:3-16.

1376   Irons, William
   1968 The Turkoman Nomads. Natural History 77:44-51.

Although the work deals with Turkmens in Iran, it should be of interest to students of Turkmen society in Afghanistan.

1377   Irons, William
   1974 Nomadism as a Political Adaptation: The Case of the Yomut Turkmen. American Ethnologist 1(4):635-658.

1378   Irons, William
   1975 The Yomut Turmen: A Study of Social Organization Among a Central Asian Turkic-Speaking Population. Ann Arbor: Museum of Anthropology, University of Michigan. Pp. 193; illustrations.

IV. SOCIAL ORGANIZATION

> A study of social organization and ecology of the Yomut Turkmen of Northern Iran. Descriptions and interpretations applicable to the Turkmen of Afghanistan.

1379 Ivanov, W.
 1926 Notes on the Ethnology of Khurasan. Geographical Journal 67:143-158.

> The author, who lived for several years in Iran, discusses the population of a region which includes parts of both Iran and Afghanistan. He describes Persian stock, Turks, Kurds, Baluchis, Timuris, Barbaris (Hazaras), with the Afghan elements either overlapping the border as emigrants from Afghanistan in recent years, or as nomads moving across frontiers. A most informative article.

1380 Janata, Alfred
 1971 On the Origins of Firozkohis in Western Afghanistan. Archiv fur Volkerkunde 25:57-65.

1381 Janata, Alfred
 1981 Notizen Zur Bevoelkerungskarte Afghanistans. Afghanistan Journal 8(3):94-95.

> A brief discussion about the ethnic composition of Afghanistan supplemented by an ethnic map.

1382 Janata, Alfred and Reihanodin Hassas
 1975 Chairatman - Der gute Pashtune. Exkurs uber die Grundlagen des Pashtunwali. Afghanistan Journal 2(3):83-97.

1383 Jarring, Gunnar
 1939 An Uzbek's View on his Native-Town and its Circumstances. Ethnos 4:73-80. Stockholm.

> Is concerned with the town of Andkhui and its immediate vicinity. Reflects a visit made by the author in 1935. At that time he asked his local Uzbek informant to describe this town, its people, manners and customs and the article is a translation of that account.

1384 Jarring, Gunnar
 1939 On the Distribution of Turkic Tribes in Afghanistan: An Attempt at a Preliminary Classification. In Lunds Universitets Arsskrift, N.F., Ard. 1, Bd. 35, Nr. 4. Lund (Sweden): C. W. K. Gleerup. Pp. 104; bibliography.

IV. SOCIAL ORGANIZATION

A preliminary attempt to classify these tribes in Afghanistan by a Scandinavian diplomat and scholar who has specialized on the Turks of Central Asia. Attention is centered on the tribes of the center and north of the country. Supported by a valuable bibliography, including works in Russian.

1385 Jeanneret, André
1964 Contribution a l'étude des boulangers de Kaboul (Afghanistan) [A Contribution towards the Study of the Bakers of Kabul (Afghanistan)]. Bulletin Annuel du Museé Institut d'Ethnographie de la Ville de Geneve 7:35-48.

A study of baking methods, including kinds of ovens and types of bread.

1386 Jean-Yves, Loude
1980 Kalash--Les Derniers "Infideles" de l'Hindu-Kush. Paris: Berger-Levrault. Pp. 179.

1387 Jenkins, Robin
1960 Some Kind of Grace. London: Macdonald.

A novel by an Englishman who was resident at Kabul for several years.

1388 Jenkins, Robin
1961 Dust on the Paw. New York: G. P. Putnam's Sons. Pp. 384.

A perceptive novel, with modern Kabul as its setting.

1389 Jentsch, Christoph
1972 Das Nomadentum in Afghanistan [The Nomads in Afghanistan]. Meisenheim am Glan: Verlag Anton Hain. Volume #9 in Afghanische Studien Series.

1390 Jentsch, Christoph
1973 Das Nomadentum in Afghanistan. Meisenheim: Verlag Anton Hain.

1391 Jettmar, K.
1961 Ethnological Research in Dardistan 1958: Preliminary Report. Proceedings of the American Philosophical Society 105(1):79-97.

IV. SOCIAL ORGANIZATION

1392   Jones, Schuyler
       1967 The Political Organization of the Kam Kafirs: A
             Preliminary Analysis. Kobenhavn: Munksgaard. Pp. 61.

1393   Jones, Schuyler
       1970 The Waigal "Horn Chair". Man 5(2):253-257.

1394   Karmiesheva, B. X.
       1976 Ocherki Etnichesckoi Istorii Iozniekh Raionov
             Tadzikistana i Uzbekistana. [Ethnohistoric Works on the
             Southern Region of Tajikistan and Uzbekistan]. Moscow:
             USSR Academy of Sciences. Pp. 323.

1395   Karpov, G.
       1929 Turkmeniia i turkmeny [Turkmeniya and the Turkmen].
             Turkmenovedenie, No. 10 and 11. Ashkhabad.

       Useful work by a trained ethnologist who worked in
       Turkmeniya.

1396   Karpov, G.
       1925 Plemennoi i rodnoi sostav turkmen [Tribal and Family
             Composition of the Turkmen]. Poltoratsk.

1397   Karpov, G. I. and P. V. Arbekov
       1930 Salyry (Salory) [Salyr (Salor) People]. Turkmen-
             ovedenie, No. 6 and 7. Ashkhabad.

1398   Keiser, R. Lincoln
       1971 Social Structure and Social Control in Two Afghan
             Mountain Societies. Unpublished Ph.D. Dissertation.
             University of Rochester. Pp. 207.

       A discussion of the social and cultural context of the Sum
       and Kum of Nuristan, Afghanistan. The emphasis is on a
       comparison of the political processes in these two
       mountain communities.

1399   Keiser, R. Lincoln
       1973 Genealogical Beliefs and Social Structure Among the
             Sum of Afghanistan: A Study of Custom in the Context of
             Social Relations. New York: Afghanistan Council, the
             Asia Society. Occasional paper no. 5. Pp. 36.

1400   Keiser, R. Lincoln
       1974 Social Structure in the Southeastern Hindu-Kush:
             Some Implications for Pashai Ethno-History. Anthropos
             69(3-4):445-456.

IV. SOCIAL ORGANIZATION

1401   Keiser, R. Lincoln
          1981 The Relevancy of Structural Principles in the Study
             of Political Organization. Anthropos 76:430-440.

        Using ethnographic data from Nuristan, the author argues
        that political behavior in terms of a choice-making model
        must take serious note of the social rules and cultural
        values which provide the context of politically focused
        strategic behavior.

1402   Khadem, Qiyam al-Din
          1952 Pushtunwali [Pushtun Code]. Kabul: Matba'eh-yi
             'umumi. Pp. 204. (1331 A.H.)

        A uniquely valuable account of the values and customs
        which regulate Pushtun behavior, written in Pushtu.

1403   Khan, Ghani
          1958 The Pathans. A Sketch. Peshawar: University Book
             Agency. Pp. 58.

        A light-hearted account by a Pushtun, with chapters on
        history, customs, folk songs and tales, and tribal
        patterns of behavior.

1404   Kieffer, Charles M.
          1972 Uber das Volk der Pastunen und seinen Pastunwali.
             Beitrag zur Afghanischen Ethnologie. Mitteilungen des
             Instituts für Orientforschung 17(4):614-624.

1405   Kisliakov, N. A. and A. I. Pershits (eds)
          1957 Narodï Sredeney Azii [The Peoples of the Middle
             Asia]. Moscow: Izdatel'stvo Akademii Hauk SSR. Pp.
             614; bibliography.

        Pages 53-72 deal with the ethnic groups of Afghanistan; a
        map of population density is included.

1406   Kisliakov, Nikolai Andreevich
          1970 Tadziki Karategina i Darvaza. Volume 2. [The
             Tajiks of Qarategin and Darwaz]. Dushanbe: Tajikistan
             SSR Academy of Sciences. Pp. 313.

1407   Kisliakov, Nikolai Andreevich
          1976 Tadziki Karategina i Darvaza. Volume 3. [The
             Tajiks of Qarategin and Darwaz]. Dushanbe: Tajikistan
             SSR Academy of Sciences. Pp. 239.

IV. SOCIAL ORGANIZATION

        Both (nos. 1405 and 1406) are in a series of ethnographies on the Darwaz and Qarategin Tajiks in the USSR. Interesting for the Soviet ethnographic style which is descriptive and exhaustive, especially with respect to material culture. Of significant interest to those interested in the traditional culture of Tajiks in Afghanistan and USSR.

1408   Knabe, Erika
        1977 Frauenemanzipation in Afghanistan: ein empirisches Beitrag zur Untersuchung von sozio-kulturellem Wandel und sozio-kultureller Bestandigkeit. [Emancipation of Women in Afghanistan: An Empirical Contribution to the Investigation of Socio-Cultural Change and Socio-Cultural Persistence]. Ph.D. Dissertation. Köln University. Pp. xviii, 471.

1409   Kohzad, Ahmad Ali
        1952 Recherches sur l'étymologie et les origines des Ephthalites [Research on the Etymology and Origins of the Hephthalites]. Afghanistan 7(3):1-5.

        The names by which the Hephthalites were known in Europe, their possible origin, and a few words on their empire and fall.

1410   Kohzad, Ahmad Ali
        1954 The Nuristanis Are Aryans and Not Greek Remnants. Afghanistan 9(2):36-40.

        A refutation of the theory that the Nuristanis are the descendants of Alexander's Greeks.

1411   Komarov, I.
        1887 Kratkiie statisticheskiie svedeniia o plemenakh ersari, obitaiushchikh levyi bereg Amu-Dar'i ot pogranichnogo s Afganistan om seleniia Bossagi do Chardzhuia. 1886 [Brief Statistical Data about the Tribes of the Ersar who Live on the Left Bank of the Amu Darya, from the Settlement Bossag on the Border of Afghanistan to Charjuia. 1886]. Sbornik geograficheskikh, topograficheskikh i statisticheskikh materialov po Azii, Pt. 25, 278-97. St. Petersburg.

1412   Krader, Lawrence
        1963 Social Organization of the Mongol-Turkic Pastoral Nomads. The Hague: Mouton. Pp. 412.

IV. SOCIAL ORGANIZATION

1413 Krader, Lawrence
1966 Peoples of Central Asia. Bloomington: Indiana University Press. Pp. 322.

Includes ethnographic and ethnological discussion of Tajiks, Uzbeks, Turkmens, and the Kirghiz.

1414 Kussmaul, Friedrich
1965 Badaxsan und seine Tagiken [Badakhshan and its Tajiks]. Tribus 14:11-99.

Account of a trip made in 1962/63 through the Panjshir valley to Badakhshan. Valuable material on the life and customs of remote peoples.

1415 Kussmaul, Friedrich
1965 Siedlung und Gehoeft bei den Tagiken in den Berglaedern Afghanistan. Anthropos 60:487-532.

1416 Lentz, Wolfgang von
1972 Zeitrechnung in Nuristan am Pamir. Graz, Austria: Akademische Druck. Pp. 212. (Reprint of the 1939 edition).

The author was a member of the 1928 Soviet-German and the 1938 German expedition to the Hindukush and the Pamirs. The book contains much calendaric, linguistic and ethnographic information on the area.

1417 Ligeti, L.
n.d. Le lexique moghol de R. Leech [The Moghal Vocabulary of R. Leech].

A study of a vocabulary of the language of the Moghal Aimaks published by R. Leech in 1838.

1418 Ligeti, L.
1954 Recherches sur les dialects mongol et turcs de l'Afghanistan [Researches on the Mongol and Turkish Dialects of Afghanistan]. Acta Orientalia 4:93-117.

Summary in French of an account in Russian of field work conducted prior to World War II.

IV. SOCIAL ORGANIZATION

1419   Lindholm, Charles
        1977 The Segmentary Lineage System: Its Applicability to Pakistan's Political Structure. In Pakistan's Western Borderlands: The Transformation of a Political Order. Edited by Ainslie T. Embree. Durham: Carolina Academic Press. Pp. 41-66.

1420   Lindholm, Charles
        1979 Contemporary Politics in a Tribal Society: Swat District, NWFP, Pakistan. Asian Survey 19(5):485-505.

Describes the transformation, through time, of the indigenous political organization of the Pushtuns.

1421   Lindholm, Charles
        1979 Generosity and Jealousy: Social and Emotional Structure of the Swat Pakhtun. Unpublished Ph.D. Dissertation. Columbia University.

The dissertation deals with an analysis of Swat Pushtuns from an ecological, historical, political viewpoints. Its focus is the social structure and exchange system, and the development of personality. The author argues that the Swat Pushtun emotional structure is separate from, but interacts with, the social structure. The work is being prepared for publication.

1422   Lindholm, Charles
        1980 Images of the Pathan: The Usefulness of Colonial Ethnograpy. Archiv Europeennes de Sociologie 21:350-361.

Discusses the various portrayals of Pushtun personality by the British and how this, to some extent, has influenced and helped contemporary ethnographers of Pushtun culture and society.

1423   Lindholm, Charles
        1981 Leatherworkers and Love Potions. American Ethnologist 8(3):512-525.

Discusses the role of the water with which the body of a dead leatherworker has been washed in love magic among the Pushtuns of Swat.

IV. SOCIAL ORGANIZATION

1424 Lindholm, Charles
    1981 The Structure of Violence Among the Swat Pukhtun. Ethnology 20(2):147-156.

    The author argues that among Swat Pushtuns violence is more structured than elsewhere in the Middle East and that violence is a significant expression of the structural basis of Pushtun society and culture.

1425 Lindholm, Charles and Cherry Lindholm
    1979 Marriage as Warfare (For a Pakhtun, Whose Home is a Battlefield, Friendship is only a Fantasy). Natural History 88:11-20.

1426 Logofet, D. N.
    1913 Bukharskoe Khanstvo pod russkim protektoratom [The Khanate of the People of Bukhara under a Russian Protectorate]. 2 vols. St. Petersburg.

1427 Lumsden, Sir Peter
    1885 Countries and Tribes Bordering on the Koh-i-Baba Range. Proceedings of the Royal Geographical Society 7:561-583; map.

    Lively, entertaining description of the country north of Herat, and particularly of the life, habits and customs of the Saryk Turkoman; with duller quotations from other travelers in the same country. The discussion of the paper included some remarks read by Sir Henry Rawlinson on the two ancient cities called Merv.

1428 Majrouh, Sayd B.
    1977 La Femme Contestataire, Un certain visage de la femme Pashtoune dans la poesie populaire de la langue Pashto. Pasto Quarterly 1.

1429 Malik, Hafeez
    1979 Implications of European Imperialism for the Contemporary Anthropological Encounter in Afghanistan and Pakistan. Journal of South Asian and Middle Eastern Studies 3(2):3-6.

1430 Meakin, Annette M. B.
    1927 Quelques races indigènes de l'Asie centrale [Some Native Races of Central Asia]. Revue Anthropologique 38:241-245.

IV. SOCIAL ORGANIZATION

Emphasis upon the position of women in a brief review of the Uzbek, Tajik, Kirghiz and Turkoman population elements.

1431 Michaelson, Karen L.
1980 Knowledge to Policy: Developing Information Linkage in Afghanistan. Human Organization 39(2):191-196.

Discusses the problem of the absence of structured relationships between information, information gatherers, and policy makers.

1432 Michener, James
1963 Caravans. New York: Random House. Pp. 341.

A novel, not highly regarded by the Afghans nor those familiar with the country, since "his highly stereotyped characterizations never remotely penetrate the psychology of the Kabuli, the villager, or the nomad."

1433 Mo'tamedi, Ahmad Ali
1956 Iqtisad-i rustayi Nuristan [The Rural Economics of Nuristan]. Kabul: Puhantun. Pp. 76. (1335 A.H.)

A first-hand study, illustrated with photographs and sketches, in Persian by a graduate of Kabul Univerity.

1434 Mumand, Mohammad Gol
1948 Landakay Pushtu aw Pushtunwaleh [Brief Account of Pushtu and Pushtunwali]. Kabul: Matba'eh-yi 'umumi. Pp. 53. (1327 A.H.)

A general treatment of the subject in Pushtu.

1435 Nemenova, R. L.
1966 Slozhenie Tadzhiskogo Naseleniya Varzoba [The Composition of the Tajik Population of Varzob]. Sovietskaya Etnografia 43(5):31-44.

1436 Niedermayer, O. von
1924 Afghanistan; bearbeitet von O. von Niedermayer und E. Diez. Leipzig.

1437 The Non-Pathan Tribes of the Valley of the Hindu-Kush
1934 Journal of the Royal Central Asian Society 21:305-308.

IV. SOCIAL ORGANIZATION

The tribes and their dialects, divided geographically by rivers.

1438 Nuristani, Mohammad Alam
1971 The Waigal "Horn chair". Man 6(3):486-487.

1439 Oliver, Edward Emmerson
1890 Across the Border; or, Pathan and Biloch. London: Chapman and Hall, Ltd. Pp. xi, 344; folding map.

The map shows the locations of all the tribes discussed.

1440 Palwal, Abdul Raziq
1972 The Mother Goddess in Kafiristan: The Place of the Mother Goddess in the Religious Dualism of the Kafir Aryans, Afghanistan. Unpublished M.A. Thesis. Louisiana State University. Pp. 84.

The thesis describes how a pervasive dualism organizes the activities of the Kafirs in Nuristan into two distinctive, but complementary aspects. Male activities are spatially higher up and considered sacred while female activities are spatially lower down and perceived as profane.

1441 Palwal, Abdul Raziq
1977 The Kafir Status and Hierarchy and Their Economic, Military, Political, and Ritual Foundations. Unpublished Ph.D. Dissertation. Pennsylvania State University. Pp. 338.

Description and analysis of the development of the social hierarchies of the Kafir (Nuristanis) of Afghanistan and Chitral and how they functioned immediately before their wholesale Islamization in 1880s by the Afghan Government.

1442 Pastner, Carroll McClure
1971 Sexual Dichotomization in Society and Culture: The Women of Panjgur, Baluchistan. Unpublished Ph.D. Dissertation. Brandeis University. Pp. 277.

Based upon an ethnographic study of the oasis of Panjgur in Baluchistan, West Pakistan, the dissertation is concerned with the structural and ideological variables of a cultural configuration founded on the dichotomization of the sexes.

IV. SOCIAL ORGANIZATION

1443   Pastner, Stephen L.
        1971 Camp and Territory Among the Nomads of Northern Makran District, Baluchistan: The Role of Sedentary Communities in Pastoral Organization. Unpublished Ph.D. Dissertation. Brandeis University. Pp. 247.

        Deals with various dimensions of the social organization of the Baluchi-speaking peoples of Makran District, S. W. Baluchistan, Pakistan.

1444   Pastner, Stephen L.
        1971 Ideological Aspects of Nomad Sedentary Contact: A Case From Southern Baluchistan. Anthropological Quarterly 44:173-184.

1445   Pastner, Stephen L.
        1978 Powers and Pirs Among the Pakistani Baluch. Journal of Asian and African Studies 13(3-4):231-243.

1446   Pastner, Stephen L.
        1979 The Man Who Would be Anthropologist: Dilemmas in Fieldwork on the Baluchistan Frontier of Pakistan. Journal of South Asian and Middle Eastern Studies 3(2):44-52.

1447   Pastner, Stephen L.
        1980 The Competitive Saints of the Baluch. Asian Affairs 11:37-42.

1448   Pastner, Stephen L. and Carroll M. Pastner
        1972 Agriculture, Kinship and Politics in Southern Baluchistan. Man 7:128-136.

1449   Pennell, Theodore L.
        1909 Among the Wild Tribes of the Afghan Frontier. A Record of Sixteen Years' Close Intercourse with the Natives of the Indian Marches. London: Seeley and Co., Ltd. Pp. xvi, 324; maps.

        A British medical missionary, conversant in Pushtu, reports on years of close association with the Afghans of the region between Peshawar and the Afghan frontier. While the story takes place outside of Afghanistan, there is a great deal of valuable material related to the Afghan character and modes of life. The book was well received and a fourth edition appeared in 1912.

IV. SOCIAL ORGANIZATION

1450   Peshereva, E. M.
        1976 Yagnobskie Etnograficheski Materialie. [Yagnob
           Ethnographic Material]. Dushanbe: Donish. Pp. 98.

        A collection of brief essays on the language, culture, and
        society of the Yagnob Tajiks.

1451   Peter of Greece and Denmark, Prince
        1954 Jars Built Without a Wheel in the Hazarajat of
           Central Afghanistan. Man: A Monthly Record of Anthro-
           pological Science 54(73):5.

        A brief letter describing the life of Dai Zangi people
        near Herat, especially their method of making clay jars.

1452   Peter of Greece and Denmark, Prince
        1954 The Abdul Camp in Central Afghanistan. Journal of
           the Royal Central Asian Society 41:44-53.

        An ethnographical mission, led by Prince Peter, followed
        up rumors of a huge nomadic camp which met to elect kings
        and to trade; found the camp and were entertained there.

1453   Petermann, August Heinrich
        1944 Völker- und Sprachenkarte des Vorderen Orient
           [Peoples Linguistic Map of the Near East]. Petermanns
           Geographische Mitteilungen 90, Tafel 2.

        A facsimile of a map which shows the racial distribution
        of tribes in Afghanistan; unfortunately so reduced that
        much of it is illegible.

1454   Pikulin, M. G.
        1959 Beludkhi [Baluchi]. Moscow: Izdatel'stvo Vostochnoy
           Literatury. Pp. 210; bibliography.

1455   Rand, Christopher
        1955 From the Sweet to the Bitter. New Yorker 31(1):100-
           115.

        A colorful account of a visit to the Fakir of Ipi in his
        canyon stronghold. With descriptions of the Pathans,
        their feasts and dances; the biography and thumb-nail
        sketch of the Fakir himself. Although the Fakir lived in
        Pakistan, he sided with Afghanistan on the Pushtunistan
        issue.

IV. SOCIAL ORGANIZATION

1456 Rao, Aparna
      1981 Qui Sant les Jat d'Afghanistan? Afghanistan Journal 8(2):55-64.

1457 Rellecke, Willy Clemens
      1978 Ethnologische Aspekte bei der Realisierung eines Entwicklungsprojektes in Herat (Westafghanistan): der Agrarkredit als entwicklungsfordernde Massnahme. [Ethnological Aspects in the Realization of a Development Project in Herat (Western Afghanistan): Agricultural Credit as a Stimulus for Development]. Unpublished Ph.D. Dissertation. University of Freiburg. Pp. 172.

1458 Robertson, George S.
      1896 The Kafirs of the Hindu-Kush. London: Lawrence and Bullen, Ltd. Pp. xx, 658; map.

      A British army officer, interested in linguistics and ethnography, tells in narrative form of his trip through Kafiristan in 1889 and 1890. Important treatment of the Siah Push branch of the Kafirs and valuable comments on three local languages. A second edition appeared in 1900. Reprinted in 1974 with an introduction by Louis Dupree.

1459 Robinson, Nehemiah
      1953 Persia and Afghanistan and their Jewish Communities. New York: Institute of Jewish Affairs. Pp. 31.

      The economic, social and political situation of these communities is analyzed.

1460 Romodin, Vadim A.
      1951 Sotsial'no-ekonomicheskiy stroy yusufzayskikh plemen v XIX veke (sravitel'no s drugimi afganskimi plemenami) [Social-economic system of the Yusufzai tribes in the 19th century (compared with the other Afghan tribes)]. In Ocherki po novoy istorii stran Srednego Vostoka. Moscow: Moscow State University. Pp. 99-124.

IV. SOCIAL ORGANIZATION

1461   Rosman, Abraham and Paula G. Rubel
1976   Nomad-Sedentary Interethnic Relations in Iran and Afghanistan. International Journal of Middle Eastern Studies 7:545-570.

A study of nomad-sedentary relations viewed in terms of exchange. Based on a pilot field research project during summer 1971 in Zagros Mountains of Iran and in the Central Hazarajat of Afghanistan.

1462   Sakai, T., H. Hajime, O. Norikazu, and Y. Ohba
1973   Occlusion and inclination of Pashtun and Tajik in Afghanistan. Journal of the Anthropological Society of Nippon 81(4):268-276.

1463   Salzman, Philip C.
1971   Adaptation and Political Organization in Iranian Baluchistan. Ethnology 10(4):433-444.

1464   Salzman, Philip Carl
1972   Adaptation and Change Among the Yarahmadzai Baluch. Unpublished Ph.D. Dissertation. University of Chicago.

1465   Schurmann, H. F.
1961   The Mongols of Afghanistan. Hague: Mouton & Co. Pp. 435; 14 figures; ethnographical map; glossary; bibliograhy; indices.

An extensive descriptive ethnography of the Moghols and related peoples of Afghanistan.

1466   Scott, George Batley
1929   Afghan and Pathan--A Sketch. London: The Mitre Press. Pp. 188; map.

The first half of this work is given over to a general account of Afghanistan and the North-West Frontier Province during the nineteenth century. The second part is devoted to the border tribes, with valuable material on geographical distribution, characteristics of various groups, and conflicts between tribes and authorities. A sketch map shows tribal locations.

1467   Scott, Richard B.
1980   Tribal and Ethnic Groups in the Helmand Valley. New York: Afghanistan Council, The Asia Society. Occasional paper No. 21. Pp. 35.

IV. SOCIAL ORGANIZATION

1468   Shah, Sirdar Ikbal Ali
        1928 Afghanistan of the Afghans. London: The Diamond Press. Pp. 272; map.

        A brief historical sketch is followed by a collection of moderately and effectively assembled material on folklore and customs, religious beliefs and cosmology, and on the life of various ethnic groups.

1469   Shahrani, M. Nazif
        n.d. Kirghiz Pastoralists of the Afghan Pamirs: An Ecological and Ethnographic Overview. Folk 18:129-143.

1470   Shahrani, M. Nazif
        1978 The Retention of Pastoralism Among the Kirghiz of the Afghan Pamirs. In Himalayan Anthropology: The Indo-Tibetan Interface. Edited by J. F. Fisher. The Hague: Mouton. Pp. 233-50.

1471   Shahrani, M. Nazif Mohib
        1976 Kirghiz Pastoral Nomads of the Afghan Pamirs: A Study in Ecological and Intracultural Adaptation. Ph.D. Dissertation. University of Washington. Pp. 331.

        An excellent analysis of the Kirghiz society and culture in Wakhan, Afghanistan. One of the best cultural-ecological study on pastoral nomadism in Central Asia.

1472   Shahrani, M. Nazif Mohib
        1979 The Kirghiz and Wakhi of Afghanistan: Adaptation to Closed Frontiers. Seattle: University of Washington Press. Pp. xxiii, 264, maps, figures, illustrations, bibliography.

        An excellent study of the culture and society of the Kirghiz of Afghanistan with special reference to the ecological processes in the Afghan Pamir and Wakhan. Among the best anthropological works produced on an Afghan group, and on pastoral nomadic cultural ecology in Afghanistan.

1473   Shakur, M. A.
        1946 The Red Kafirs. Peshawar: Imperial Press. Pp. v, 42; folding sketch map; bibliography.

IV. SOCIAL ORGANIZATION

A first-hand survey of part of the region by the Curator of the Peshawar Museum resulted in this description of the topography, history, and social life of these little-known people. There are several illustrations of the characteristic carved wooden statuary.

1474 Shalinsky, Audrey C.
1979 Central Asian Emigrees in Afghanistan: Problems of Religious and Ethnic Identity. New York: Afghanistan Council, The Asia Society. Occasional paper no. 19. Pp. 15.

1475 Shalinsky, Audrey C.
1979 Central Asian Emigres in Afghanistan: Social Dynamics of Identity Creation. Unpublished Ph.D. Dissertation. Harvard University. Pp. 322.

Examines the adaptation of Uzbek immigrants from Soviet Central Asia in Qunduz, Northern Afghanistan.

1476 Shalinsky, Audrey C.
1979 History and Self Image: The Case of Central Asian Emigres in Afghanistan. Journal of South Asian and Middle Eastern Studies 3(2):7-19.

1477 Shaniyazov, Karim Shaniazovich
1974 K Ethnicheskoi Istorii Uzbekskogo Naroda. [On the Ethnic History of the Uzbek People]. Tashkent: Uzbekistan SSR Academy of Sciences. Pp. 342.

An ethnohistorical account of the Uzbek people including social, cultural, and material cultural history of the Uzbek peoples of Central Asia. Of significant interest to those who are interested in the ethnography of Northern Afghanistan.

1478 Sheehy, Ann
1970 The Baluchis of the Turkmen SSR. Mizan 12(1):43-54.

Traces the origins of Baluchs in this area and their adaptation to the new social, cultural and physical environment.

1479 Shepperdson, M. J.
1977 Pathans in Focus. Eastern Anthropologist 30(4):449-453.

Reviews the anthropological and sociological controversies about Pushtuns in the literature.

IV. SOCIAL ORGANIZATION

1480   Sigrist, Christian
           1970 Pastunwali. Das Stammesrecht der Paschtunen. Arbeitsgemeinschaft fur Kulturanthropologie. Basel.

1481   Siiger, Halfdan
           1963 Shamanism Among the Kalash Kafirs of Chitral (From the third Danish Expedition to Central Asia). Folk 5:295-303.

1482   Singer, Andre
           1973 Tribal Migrations on the Irano-Afghan Border. Asian Affairs 60:160-165.

1483   Singer, Andre
           1976 Problems of Pastoralism in the Afghan Pamirs. Asian Affairs 63(2):156-160.

1484   Slousch, N.
           1908 Les Juifs en Afghanistan [The Jews in Afghanistan]. Revue du Monde Musulman 4:502-511.

1485   Snoy, Peter
           1965 Nuristan und Mungan [Nuristan and Munjan]. Tribus 14:101-148.

        Observations in Nuristan, especially interesting for its photographs and account of the songs and dances of this region.

1486   Snoy, Peter
           1969 Ethnologische Feldforschungen in Afghanistan. Jahrbuch des Sudasien-Institut 127-130.

1487   Sous la Direction de L'Equipe Ecologie et Anthropologie des Societes Pastorales (ed)
           1977 Pastoral Production and Society. New York: Cambridge University Press. Pp. 493.

        An important source-book on pastoral societies including a very useful chapter on the "Organization of Nomadic Communities in Pastoral Societies of the Middle East", by Richard L. Tapper. The Chapter includes a brief discussion on the Pushtun nomads of Afghanistan.

IV. SOCIAL ORGANIZATION

1488   Spain, James W.
        1962 The Way of the Pathans. London: Robert Hale. Pp. 190.

        There is also an American edition under the title of "The People of the Khyber: The Pathans of Pakistan." New York: Praeger. Describes the tribal affiliations of the Pushtuns to the east of the Durand Line.

1489   Spain, James W.
        1963 The Pathan Borderland. The Hague: Mouton and Co. Pp. 293; map; bibliography; index.

        A useful study of these tribes, their internal rivalries, and their opposition to outside interference.

1490   Spooner, Brian
        1965 Kinship and Marriage in Eastern Persia. Sociologus 15(1):22-31.

1491   Spooner, Brian
        1969 Politics, Kinship and Ecology in Southeast Persia. Ethnology 7:139-152.

1492   Spooner, Brian
        1973 The Cultural Ecology of Pastoral Nomads. Reading, Massachusetts: Addison-Wesley Module in Anthropology #45. Pp. 50.

        An ecological approach to nomadism. General statements are formulated and developed into a generative model to account for all the elements of social organization and culture that derive from the nomadic adaptation. Significantly useful for the study and understanding of Afghan Pastoral Nomads.

1493   Steul, Willi
        1973 Eigentumsprobleme innerhalb paschtunischer Gemeinschaften in Paktia/Afghanistan. Heidelberg.

1494   Steul, Willi
        1981 Paschtunwali: Ein Ehrehkodex und seine rechtliche Relevanz [Pushtunwali: A Code of Honor and its Legal Relevance]. Wiesbaden: Franz Steiner Verlag.

1495   Strand, Richard F.
        1974 A Note on Rank, Political Leadership, and Government Among the Pre-Islamic Kom. In Cultures of the Hindukush (see below). Pp. 57-63.

IV. SOCIAL ORGANIZATION

1496   Strand, Richard F.
    1974 Principles of Kinship Organization Among the Kom Nuristani. In Cultures of the Hindukush: Selected Papers from the Hindu-Kush Cultural Conference Held at Moesgard. Edited by Karl Jettmar in collaboration with Lenart Edelberg. Beitrage zur Sudasienforschung, Sudaien-Institut, Universitat Heidelberg. Weisbaden: Franz Steiner Verlag. Pp. 1:51-56.

1497   Strand, Richard F.
    1975 The Changing Herding Economy of the Kom Nuristani. Afghanistan Journal 2(4):123-134.

1498   Stucki, Anneliese
    1978 Horses and Women. Afghanistan Journal 5(4):140-149. Photos.

1499   Stucki, Anneliese
    1978 Unter Turkmenen. Tages Anzeiger Magazin. Zurich. 44(4):6-13.

1500   Swidler, Nina Bailey
    1969 The Political Structure of a Tribal Federation: The Brahui of Baluchistan. Unpublished Ph.D. Dissertation. Columbia University. Pp. 193.

1501   Swidler, Nina Bailey
    1973 The Political Context of Brahui Sedentarization. Ethnology 12:299-314.

1502   Swidler, Warren W.
    1968 Technology and Social Structure in Baluchistan, West Pakistan. Unpublished Ph.D. Dissertation. Columbia University.

1503   Swidler, Warren W.
    1972 Some Demographic Factors Regulating the Formation of Flocks and Camp Among the Brahui of Baluchistan. Journal of Asian and African Studies 7:69-75.

1504   Tanner, H. C.
    1881 Notes on the Chugani and Neighbouring Tribes of Kafiristan. Proceedings of the Royal Geographical Society 3.

1505   Tapper, Nancy
    1972 The Role of Nomads in a Region of Northern Afghanistan. Final Report to the Social Science Research Council on Project HR 1141/1. Pp. 39.

IV. SOCIAL ORGANIZATION

1506   Tapper, Nancy
        1973 The Advent of the Pashtun Maldars in Northwestern Afghanistan. Bulletin of the London School of Oriental and African Studies 36(1):55-79.

1507   Tapper, Nancy
        1977 Pashtun Nomad Women in Afghanistan. Asian Affairs 8(2):163-170.

1508   Tapper, Nancy
        1979 Marriage and Social Organization Among the Durrani Pashtuns of Northern Afghanistan. Unpublished Ph.D. Dissertation. University of London. Pp. 567.

1509   Tapper, Nancy
        1980 Matrons and Mistresses: Women and Boundaries in Two Midle Eastern Tribal Societies. Archiv Europeennes de Sociologie 21:59-78.

The article examines some variables which may explain differences in the position of women in two Middle Eastern Societies. The Durrani of north-central Afghanistan and the Shahsevan of northwestern Iran are compared.

1510   Tapper, Nancy
        1981 Aspects of Acculturation in Afghan Turkestan: Relations Between Pashtun and Uzbek Women. In L'Acculturation turque dans l'Europe et la Mediterranee. Edited by X. de Planhol. Paris: Proceedings of the 1975 Colloquium.

1511   Tapper, Nancy
        1981 Direct Exchange and Brideprice: Alternative Forms in a Complex Marriage System. Man 18(3):385-407.

Marriage prestations and the transfer of women between households are seen as part of the wider system of exchange and control of all productive and reproductive resources among the Durrani Pushtuns of northern Afghanistan. Two modes of marriage among these Pushtuns are analyzed: direct exchange in the symmetrical mode and indirect exchange in the asymmetrical style.

1512   Tapper, Richard
        1975 Pakhtun Nomads. In Western and Central Asia (Peoples of the Earth, Volume 15). Edited by A. Singer. London: Mondadori. Pp. 102-113.

IV. SOCIAL ORGANIZATION

1513   Tapper, Richard
       1976   Durrani. Family of Man. Pp. 733-737.

1514   Tapper, Richard
       1979   Tribal Society and its Enemies: The Latest Round in the 'Great Game' of Asia. Royal Anthropological Institute News 34:6-7.

1515   Tapper, Richard
       1980   Tribe and State in Iran and Afghanistan. Social Science Research Council Newsletter 42:13-15.

1516   Tapper, Richard
       1981   Hybrid Camels and Turkish Acculturation in Iran and Afghanistan. In L'Acculturation turques dans l'Europe et la Mediterranee. Edited by X. de Planhol. Paris: Proceedings of the 1975 Colloquium.

1517   Tavakolian, Bahram
       1979   An Anthropologist in the Kingdom of Afghanistan: Mountstuart Elphinstone and the Afghans. Journal of South Asian and Middle Eastern Studies 3(2):26-43.

1518   Temple, R. C.
       1879   Rough Notes on the Distribution of the Afghan Tribes about Kandahar. Journal of the Asiatic Society of Bengal 48(1):181-185; map.

       While Lieutenant Temple was on foraging and reconnaissance expeditions, he took brief notes on the tribes, their subdivisions and locations.

1519   Temple, R. C.
       1880   Remarks on the Afghans Found Along the Route of the Tal Chotaili Field Force, in the Spring of 1879. Journal of the Asiatic Society of Bengal 49:91-106; 141-180; maps.

       Notes on the habitat and divisions of Pushtun tribes within Afghanistan and languages spoken by these groups.

1520   Thesiger, W.
       1955   The Hazaras of Central Afghanistan. Geographical Journal 121(3):312-319.

       Report on a tour of the Hazarajat in 1954.

IV. SOCIAL ORGANIZATION

1521 Thorburn, S. S.
  1876 Bannu; or Our Afghan Frontier. London: Trubner and Co. Pp. x, 480; map; appendices.

  A British officer, resident in the area for several years prior to publication, writes of a Pushtun element in the area just west of Waziristan and hence outside of Afghanistan. The work contains valuable material on Pushtu proverbs, popular stories, ballads and riddles.

1522 Tolstov, C. P., T. A. Zdanko, C. M. Abramzona, N. A. Kisliakov (eds)
  1962 Tadziki. [Tajiks]. In Narodie Srednie Azii i Kazakhstana. [People of Central Asia and Kazakhstan]. Edited by C. P. Tolstov, et al. Moscow: USSR Academy of Sciences. Volume I. Pp. 528-682.

  An ethnographic-ethnohistoric sketch of the Tajiks. Includes description of the traditional Tajik culture and the changes this culture has undergone during the Russian and Soviet periods. A very useful bibliography of Russian works on the Tajiks in the USSR is included.

1523 Tolstov, C. P., T. A. Zdanko, C. M. Abramzona, N. A. Kisliakov (eds)
  1962 Uzbeki. [Uzbeks]. In Narodie Srednie Azii i Kazakhstana. [People of Central Asia and Kazakhastan]. Edited by C. P. Tolstov et al. Moscow: USSR Academy of Sciences. Volume I. Pp. 165-407.

  An ethnographic-ethnohistoric sketch of the Uzbeks. Includes description of the traditional Uzbek culture and the changes which have been brought about during the Russian and Soviet periods. A very useful bibliography of Russian works on the Uzbeks in the USSR is included.

1524 Tolstov, C. P., T. A. Zdanko, C. M. Abramzona, N. A. Kisliakov (eds)
  1963 Kirgizi [Kirghiz]. In Narodie Srednie Azii i Kazakhstana. [People of Central Asia and Kazakhstan]. Edited by C. P. Tolstov, et al. Moscow: USSR Academy of Sciences. Volume II. Pp. 154-320.

  An ethnographic-ethnohistoric sketch of the Kirghiz. Includes description of the traditional Kirghiz culture and the changes this culture has undergone during the Russian and Soviet periods. A very useful bibliography of Russian works on the Kirghiz in the USSR is provided.

IV. SOCIAL ORGANIZATION

1525 Tolstov, C. P., T. A. Zdanko, C. M. Abramzona, N. A. Kisliakov (eds)
    1963 Turkmeni [Turkmens]. In Narodie Srednie Azii i Kazakhstana. [Peoples of Central Asia and Kazakhstan]. Edited by C. P. Tolstov, et al. Moscow: USSR Academy of Sciences. Volume II. Pp. 7-153.

    An ethnographic-ethnohistoric sketch of the Turkmens. Includes description of the traditional Turkmen culture and the changes this culture has undergone during the Russian and Soviet periods. A very useful bibliography of Russian works on the Turkmens in the USSR is provided.

1526 Uberoi, J. P. Singh
    1961 An Anthropologist in Afghanistan. Afghanistan 16(1):1-8.

1527 Vakil, Safar
    1948 Le Nouristan [Nuristan]. Afghanistan 3(4):3-7.

    Sketchy survey of topography, ethnic divisions, possible ethnic origin, idol worship; diet and local sports.

1528 Vambery, Arminius
    1885 Das Türkenvolk in seinen ethnologischen und ethnographischen Beziehungen [The Turkish People in their Ethnological and Ethnogrpahical Relations]. Leipzig: F. A. Brockhaus. Pp. xii, 638; bibliography.

1529 Voigt, Martin
    1933 Kafiristan. Versuch einer Landes Kunde auf Grund einer Reise im jahre 1928 [Kafiristan. Attempt at a Geography of a Country from the Basis of a Journey in the year 1928]. Bresleau: F. Hirt. Pp. 119; maps.

1530 Waleh, A. H.
    1951 Nooristan. Afghanistan 6(3):20-29.

    A sketch of Nuristani life, describing houses, customs, agriculture, religion, language, etc.

1531 Wegner, D.
    1964 Nomaden-und-Bauernteppiche in Afghanistan. Baessler-Archiv 12(1):141-177.

1532 Wolski, K.
    1963 Powindah-Patascy Koczownicy Afghanistanu i Pakistanu. Etnografia Polska:363-396.

IV. SOCIAL ORGANIZATION

1533   Woodd-Walker, R., H. Smith, V. Clarke
        1967 The blood groups of the Timuri and related tribes in
           Afghanistan. American Journal of Physical Anthropology
           27(2):195-204.

1534   Zadran, Alef-Shah
        1974 Dispute Resolution Among the Pushtuns of the Suliman
           Foothills of Afghanistan. Unpublished M.A. Project.
           State University of New York at Buffalo. Pp. 73.

        Describes certain aspects of the lives of the Pushtuns of
        the southern Suliman foothills in general and their way of
        conflict resolution in particular.

1535   Zadran, Alef-Shah
        1977 Socioeconomic and Legal-Political Processes in a
           Pashtun Village, Southeastern Afghanistan. Unpublished
           Ph.D. Dissertation. State University of New York at
           Buffalo. Pp. 350.

        A focused ethnography of Almara, a Pushtun village,
        primarily dealing with conflict resolution through the
        traditional legal system.

1536   Zarubin, I. I.
        1925 Spisok narodnostei Turkestanskogo Kraia [A List of
           Nationalities of the Turkestan Region]. Leningrad:
           Rossiiskaia akademiia nauk. Trudy Komissii po izuheniiu
           plemennogo sostava naseleniia Rossii'i sopredel'nykh
           stran, 9.

        A Linguistic study of the peoples and nationalities
        occupying Russian Turkistan.

1537   Zuyev, U. A.
        1970 Kirgizy-Buruty [The Kirghizian Buruts]. Sovetskaya
           Etnografiya 45(4):74-86.

V. SOCIAL EVOLUTION AND INSTITUTIONS

Cultural development and expression; applied
sciences; education; religion; public
information; press and publications;
health and public welfare;
social attitudes

A considerable number of titles appear under this heading, but they are of uneven merit and importance, and some of the subjects listed have been almost entirely neglected. There is, for example, very little reliable and up-to-date material on religion in Afghanistan and just as little on the subjects of health and public welfare. Once again, it is necessary to distinguish between writings by foreigners and by Afghan authors. Foreign publications reflect a fairly clear picture of trends in contemporary education, as well as of current attitudes of various elements of the population toward change and "modernization," whereas the articles by Afghans are rather less precise and conclusive.

The listing of newspapers, periodicals, and serial publications given in this section may be considered to be comprehensive and should indicate what enormous strides have been taken in the field of public information within the last few decades. All Afghan periodicals since 1973 could not be included because of irregular and intermittent publication pattern and very limited accessibility and circulation.

1538 'Abd al-Qudoos
    1927 Taftish-i Amaniyeh [The Amani Investigation]. Dehra Dun: Bahariyeh. Pp. 20.

    A short treatise on education, written in Persian and compiled with special reference to the reforms of Amir Amanullah. The work is lithographed.

1539 'Abdul Rahman, Amir
    1887 Kalimat amir al-bilad fi'l-targhib ila'l-jihad [Words of the ruler of the Countries Concerning Instigation to Holy War]. Kabul: Humayun. Pp. 40. (1304 A.H.)

    A lithographed work in Arabic by a ruler of Afghanistan concerning the duties and merits of conducting holy wars.

V. SOCIAL EVOLUTION AND INSTITUTIONS

1540   'Abdul Rahman, Amir
            1887 Sar-rishteh-yi Islamiyeh-yi Rum [The Islamic
                Ability of Turkey]. Kabul. Pp. 8. (1304 A.H.)

        A lithographed proclamation in Persian from the Amir to
        his Muslem subjects, regarding the ability of Turkey in
        dealing with European powers.

1541   'Abdul Rahman, Amir
            1894 Mir'at al-'uqul va Kalimat-i Maw'izat-i Asas [The
                Mirror of Intellects and Words of Fundamental
                Admonition]. Kabul: Dar al-Saltaneh. Pp. 28. (1311
                A.H.)

        A lithographed work in Persian, in which an Afghan ruler
        discusses this subject and concludes with advice to his
        people concerning their religious duties.

1542   Afghan Student News
            1956- News Bulletin of the Associated Students of
                Afghanistan in the United States. First issued in 1956,
                it appears irregularly from different addresses.

1543   Afghanistan
            1960 Washington, D.C.: Division of International Health.
                Pp. 171; tables; bibliography.

        Reproduced by mimeograph, this work is one of a series
        known as the International Epidemiology Series, which
        describes the state of the people's health in various
        countries.

1544   Afghanistan Ariana
            1961- A bimonthly (Dari and Pushtu) which began
                publication at Kabul in June 1961. Described in the
                first issue as a pictorial representation of
                Afghanistan's developments in educational, technical,
                industrial, and social fields, the text is in English
                and the illustrations in black and white and color.
                Publisher: Publicity Section of the Department of Press
                and Information. Does not appear regularly.

1545   Da Afghanistan Bank Mojalah [The Afghanistan Bank Magazine]
            1957- Began publication as a quarterly in 1957. Text in
                Dari and Pushtu.

V. SOCIAL EVOLUTION AND INSTITUTIONS

1546 L'Afghanistan Nouveau [The New Afghanistan]
1924 Paris: Royal Legation of Afghanistan. Pp. 95.

A general survey of the country, covering such subjects as history, international relations, and recent political and economic moves, with emphasis on French participation in archaeological research and education within the country.

1547 Ahadyar, Niaz M.
1975 Orientation Toward Time Among Educated vs. Uneducated Afghans. Unpublished Ph.D. Dissertation. University of Pennsylvania. Pp. 128.

1548 Ahang, M. K.
1972 The Background and the Beginning of the Afghan Press System: Part 12. Afghanistan 25(3):53-55.

1549 Ahmadyar, M. Nabi
1977 A Survey and Analysis of Primary School Curriculum Development in Afghanistan From 1966 to 1976. Unpublished Ph.D. Dissertation. University of Ottawa (Canada).

1550 Akhtar, S. A.
1939 On Some Nematode Parasites from Afghanistan. Proceedings of the Indian Academy of Sciences, Section B, 10(5):287-291. Bangalore.

A list and description, with two illustrations, of several parasites.

1551 Algar, H.
1976 The Naqsbandi Order: A Preliminary Survey of its History and Significance. Studia Islamica 42:123-152.

1552 Ali, Mohammad
1964 A Cultural History of Afghanistan. Lahore: Punjab Educational Press. Pp. 255.

A general survey of the history of Afghanistan, including material on some contemporary writers.

1553 Ali, Mohammad
1969 Afghanistan, Land of Glorious Past and Bright Future. Kabul: Franklin Books. Pp. x, 199.

V. SOCIAL EVOLUTION AND INSTITUTIONS

1554   Aman-i Afghan [Afghan Peace]
1919- The official daily paper published in Persian at Kabul during the reign of Amir Amanullah and for a part of this time under the editorship of Mahmud Tarzi. It replaced Serajal-Akhbar.

1555   Amin, Aminullah
1978 An Analysis of Education Policy and Institutional Goals of Kabul University--The Republic of Afghanistan. Unpublished Ph.D. Dissertation. University of Nebraska - Lincoln. Pp. 303.

Analyzes the educational policy and institutional goals of Kabul University. Emphasis on the perceived/preferred policy as viewed by some administrators, faculty members, and members of the University of Nebraska team at Kabul.

1556   Amos, Harold L.
1965 The Story of Afghanistan. Wichita, Kansas: McCormick-Mathers Publishing Company. Pp. 164.

A well illustrated descriptive account of the people, land, and culture of Afghanistan. Suitable for elementary and/or high school levels.

1557   Angar [Imagination]
1951- Privately published biweekly newspaper, issued in Persian and Pushtu in 1951 at Kabul by Faiz Mohammed Angar. No longer published.

1558   Anis [Companion]
1927- Began publication (Dari and Pushtu) at Kabul as a fortnightly newspaper in 1927. In recent years it has become the "national" evening daily, largely in Persian, with an estimated circulation of 5,000. In 1981 Anis became the official organ of the National Committee of the National Fatherland Front.

1559   Ansari, Mir Amon al-Din
1939 Dar Justajuy-i Kimia [In Search of Alchemy]. Kabul: Matba'eh-yi 'umumi. Pp. 86. (1318 A.H.)

A work in Persian by an American-educated official of the Ministry of Education. Largely translated from English. Intended as a textbook.

V. SOCIAL EVOLUTION AND INSTITUTIONS

1560 Ansary, Mir Amon al-Din
   1958 Buzkashi: Sport of the Asian Khans. Viewpoints 5(10):28-32.

   A general account of a game played on horseback--in northern Afghanistan.

1561 Aqa, Mir
   1978 The Perceptions of High School Vocational Agriculture Teachers and Their Graduates as to Curricular Needs for Vocational Agriculture in Afghanistan. Unpublished Ed.D. Dissertation. Oklahoma State University. Pp. 103.

   An evaluation of the curriculum for Afghanistan's vocational agriculture high schools, through the perceptions of teachers and graduate students in the country.

1562 Arberry, A. J. and R. Landau (eds)
   1943 Islam Today. London: Faber and Faber, Ltd. Pp. 258.

   Chapter 14, by Sir Percy M. Sykes, is on Afghanistan and places emphasis on the resources of the country and the program of modernization.

1563 Arshad, Mohammed Shah
   1964 Dimukrasi Islam [Democratic of Islam]. Kabul: Matba'eh-yi doulati. Pp. 66. (1343 A.H.)

   In this work in Dari, the author defines some principles of Islam as brotherhood, cooperation, social solidarity, consultation, justice, and equality and relates these to basic human rights.

1564 Ashida, K. et al.
   1972 Nutritional Study of Village People in Northern Afghanistan, in Particular Relation to Ascorbic Acid Metabolism. Nutritional Reports International 6(6):297-306.

1565 Assadullah, Said
   1971 La condition de la femme musulmane en Afghanistan. Etude de droit compare: afghan, marocain, tunisien, syrien. [The Condition of the Muslim Woman in Afghanistan. A Study of Comparative Law: Afghan, Moroccan, Tunisian, Syrian]. Unpublished Ph.D. Dissertation. Pantheon-Sorbonne (Paris I). Pp. 215.

V. SOCIAL EVOLUTION AND INSTITUTIONS

1566   Azoy, G. Whitney
        1982 Buzkashi: Game and Power in Afghanistan. Philadelphia: University of Pennsylvania Press. Pp. 147. Slightly modified version of the author's dissertation. The book was published and available in December 1981. See no. 1254.

1567   Badakhshan [Badakhshan]
        1945- A Persian-language daily paper published at Faizabad. Covers local and national news in Dari and Pushtu.

1568   Bailleau Lajoinie, S.
        1980 Conditions de Femmes en Afghanistan. Paris: Editions Sociales. Pp. 229; maps.

1569   Bakhtiari, 'Abdullah
        1956 Pushtana da Iqbal pa Nazar Kshe [Afghans From Iqbal's Point of View]. Kabul: Doulati matba'eh. Pp. 68. (1335 A.H.)

1570   Balikci, Asen
        1978 Buzkashi. Natural History. February:54-63.

1571   Balikci, Asen
        1978 Village Buzkashi. Afghanistan Journal 5(1):11-21. Photos.

1572   Balkh [Balkh]
        1949- Founded in 1949, this periodical is printed in Dari and Pushtu and published at Mazar-i Sharif by the Matba'eh-yi Mazar-i Sharif. Hand-set and hand-printed, the periodical apears monthly--or less frequently--and features short articles on the history and monuments of the province of Mazar-i Sharif.

1573   Bandawal, Juma Gul
        1974 A Proposed Student-Teaching Program for Teacher Training Institutions in Afghanistan. Unpublished Ed.D. Dissertation. Ball State University. Pp. 222.

Proposes a student teaching program for the training of prospective teachers in the country. Data derived from a questionnaire sent to 83 teacher training colleges in 26 countries.

V. SOCIAL EVOLUTION AND INSTITUTIONS

1574   Barg-i sabz [Green Leaf]
1944- A monthly magazine, established at Kabul in 1944. Sponsored by the Marestun [Social Service Center], the periodical runs articles in Persian on child care, hygiene, and allied subjects, most of which are translations from European and American sources.

1575   Baudet, Roger
1950, 1951 La philatélie en Afghanistan [Philately in Afghanistan] Afghanistan 5(3):10-17; 6(1):41-47.

After some advice to young philatelists, a description of Afghan issues from the first in 1868 to the present is provided.

1576   Baudet, Roger
1952 Les journées philatéliques de Kaboul [The Philatelic Days of Kabul]. Afghanistan 7(2):54-59.

Report on a Philatelic Exhibition, describing several notable collections that were on display.

1577   Baudet, Roger
1953 Les émissions commémoratives afghanes [Commemorative Afghan Issues]. Afghanistan 8(4):51-53.

Some remarks on special commemorative issues and on Afghan stamps in general--their rarity and the difficulties involved in collecting them.

1578   Baudet, Roger
1954 Aérophilatélie [Air-Philately]. Afghanistan 9(1):58-61.

On the rare and valuable stamps of the Afghan airmail service.

1579   Baum, F. L.
1949 Trachoma in Afghanistan. South African Medical Journal 23:214-215. Capetown.

1580   Bechhoefer, Sondra Howell
1975 Education and the Advancement of Women in Afghanistan. Unpublished M.A. Thesis. University of Maryland. Pp. 263.

Description of the changing role of women in Afghanistan. Intended as an overview of the problem and as a summary of the general conditions of urban women.

V. SOCIAL EVOLUTION AND INSTITUTIONS

1581   Beck, Sebastian
        1928 Das Afghanische Strafgesetzbuch vom Jahre 1924 mit dem Zusatz vom Jahre 1925. Aus dem persischen übersetz und mit einer allgemeinen Einleitung in die afghanische Strafgesetzgebung-Versehen [The Afghan Penal Code for the Year 1924 with Supplement for 1925. Provided with a Translation from Persian and a General Introduction of Afghan Penal Legislation]. Berlin.

1582   Becka, Juri
        1978 Tajik-Afghan Relations and the Writings of Sadriddin Aini. Archiv Orientalni 46:97-111.

1583   Bell, Marjorie Jewett (ed)
        1948 An American Engineer in Afghanistan: From the Letters and Notes of A. C. Jewett. Minneapolis: Minnesota University Press. Pp. 335; map.

        Letters written home by an American engaged in the arduous and frustrating task of introducing and installing engineering and power equipment in Afghanistan. Complements Frank A. Martin's Under the Absolute Amir. See no. 1740.

1584   Berke, Zuhdi
        1946 Inoculation Experiments Against Typhus in Afghanistan. British Medical Journal 2(4485):944-945.

1585   Berke, Zuhdi
        1946 La santé publiue et l'hygiène en Afghanistan [Public Health and Hygiene in Afghanistan]. Afghanistan 1(3):1-9.

        An account of current problems, with emphasis on the most prevalent diseases, and attempted solutions.

1586   Bidar [Wakeful]
        1921- A newspaper founded in 1921 at Mazar-i Sharif and published weekly in Dari, with occasional material in Pushtu.

1587   Bigham, Mir 'Abdul Rashid
        1946 Atlitik baray-i Javan-i Afghan [Athletics for the Afghan Youth]. Kabul: Matba'eh-yi 'umumi. Pp. 134. (1325 A.H.)

        A history of sports and games by the Director of Sports in the Ministry of Education.

V. SOCIAL EVOLUTION AND INSTITUTIONS

1588 Bleiber, F.
  1953 Afghanistan und die Sovietunion [Afghanistan and the Soviet Union]. Osteuropa 10:322-331. Stuttgart.

  Political and economic relations viewed from West Germany.

1589 Bogdanov, L.
  1929 Notes on the Afghan Periodical Press. Islamic Culture 3:126-152. Hyderabad.

  A very informative article by a scholar resident at Kabul. Describes the twelve newspapers and periodicals of the years 1919-1928 in considerable detail. Titles are given in Arabic characters and in transliteration and translation. In addition, a variety of general information, such as sketches of editors is provided.

1590 Borhani, Mo'in al-Din (ed)
  1963 Ershadat-i Dini [Religious Instructions]. Kabul: Doulati matba'eh. Pp. 302. (1342 A.H.)

  Guidance on religion from six writers, some contemporary.

1591 Boulanger, P. M.
  1948 Allocution du doyen de la Faculté de Médecine a l'occasion de la commémoration de la création de la Faculté de Médecine de Kaboul [Address of the Dean of the Faculty of Medicine on the Anniversary of the Creation of the Faculty of Medicine at Kabul]. Afghanistan 3(3):54-62.

  A resumé of the status of the Faculty is followed by an account of the needs of the school--in equipment and for improvements in curriculum.

1592 Boulenger, P. M.
  1950 La Faculté de Médecine de Kaboul, Afghanistan [The Medical Faculty at Kabul, Afghanistan]. Semaine des Hopitaux de Paris 26:1627-1631.

1593 Buck, Alfred A., et al.
  1972 Health and Disease in Rural Afghanistan. Baltimore: York Press. Pp. 231.

  A comprehensive epidemiological report on Afghanistan including general information about the country, kinds of common disease and health conditions.

V. SOCIAL EVOLUTION AND INSTITUTIONS

1594   Burnes, Sir Alexander
        1842 Cabool: A Personal Narrative of a Journey to, and
              Residence in, that City, in the Years 1836, 7 and 8.
              London: John Murray. Pp. xii, 398.

        Casual and informal account of life at Kabul by a British
        officer with years of travel and experience in the region.
        Many other subjects are treated in some detail, such as
        the Siah Push Kafirs. Reprinted 1973 with a preface and a
        recent select bibliography by M. Klimberg.

1595   Carlsen, Bodil Hjerrild
        1977 Some Aspects of Family Life in an Afghan Village.
              Acta Orientalia 38:29-40.

        A brief description of family organization and values in
        the village of Sangona, Panjsher Valley, Afghanistan.
        Based on a one month research (July), 1976. Main focus on
        women's role in the household.

1596   Castagne, Joseph A.
        1929 Le mouvement d'émancipation de la femme musulmane en
              Orient. III. Afghanistan [The Movement for the Freedom
              of Muslim Women in the Orient. III. Afghanistan].
              Revue des Études Islamiques 2:163-226.

        The reference is to several pages in a long article on the
        general subject. Pertinent material includes an article
        by a Soviet feminist, the marriage regulations in effect
        in 1921, and a brief discussion of clothing reform and the
        veil.

1597   Castagne, Joseph A.
        1932 Notes sur l'Afghanistan. I. La revue afghane
              "Kabul" II. Poètes afghans III. Note sur une brochure
              afghane IV. Bibliographie V. L'Ouverture du Conseil
              des Nations (6-7-1931) VI. Le développement économique
              de l'Afghanistan [Notes on Afghanistan. I. The Afghan
              Periodical "Kabul" II. Afghan Poets. III. Note on an
              Afghan Pamphlet IV. Bibliography V. The Opening of the
              National Assembly (6-7-1931) VI. The Economic
              Development of Afghanistan]. Revue des Études
              Islamiques 6:545-561.

V. SOCIAL EVOLUTION AND INSTITUTIONS

Section I gives the contents of the periodical for two issues; II, the summary of an article in "Kabul," with brief sketches of eight poets; III is on a pamphlet issued on Independence Day; IV is a note of an Afghan book dealing with the overthrow of Amir Amanullah and the Ascent of Mohammed Nadir; V details opening ceremonies, and VI quotes local papers on this subject.

1598   Central Asian Review
       1964   The Position of Women in Afghanistan. Central Asian Review 12:236-241.

A summary translation of a larger Russian work by A. A. Dzhafarova which appeared in 1963.

1599   Cervin, Vladimir
       1952   Problems in the Integration of the Afghan Nation. Middle East Journal 6:400-416.

The author, a social scientist, was resident in Afghanistan between 1938 and 1944. His article deals with the problems incidental to bringing such diverse elements as the ethnic groups, tribes, village communities, and the wealthy group within the framework of a modernized Afghanistan.

1600   Champagne, David C.
       1980   Afghans. Harvard Encyclopedia of American Ethnic Groups. Edited by Stephan Thernstrom. Cambridge: Harvard University Press. Pp. 3-5.

This brief note deals with Afghans as an ethnic community in the USA. The serious limitations of this article and most of the encyclopedia lie in lack of systematic research and availability of reliable data.

1601   Chu, Solomon, Robert N. Hill, Saxon Graham (eds)
       1975   National Demographic and Family Guidance Survey of the Settled Population of Afghanistan. Volume I: Demography. Washington, D.C.: Agency for International Development. Pp. 180.

Outlines the general demographic characteristics of the settled population of the country and sets out the methods and techniques for data collection and evaluation.

V. SOCIAL EVOLUTION AND INSTITUTIONS

1602 Chu, Solomon, Robert N. Hill, Paul A. Martino (eds)
  1975 National Demographic and Family Guidance Survey of the Settled Population of Afghanistan. Volume II: Methodology. Washington, D.C.: Agency for International Development. Pp. 276.

  Contains six detailed reports on the organization and methodology of the Afghanistan Demographic Survey. Reports are written by various staff members of the Survey.

1603 Chu, Solomon (ed)
  1975 National Demographic and Family Survey of the Settled Population of Afghanistan. Volume IV: Folk Methods of Fertility and the Traditional Birth Attendant (the Dai). Washington, D.C.: Agency for International Development. Pp. 98 and Appendices.

  Contains two reports. One on the folk methods of fertility among Afghans, the other on the practices of the traditional birth attendant.

1604 Clarke, Juno-Ann
  1970 Nutritional Status in the Hazarajat. Wheaton, Illinois: Medical Assistance Programs, Inc. Pp. 123.

1605 Clinch, Minty
  1972 Afghan Story. New Society 20(508):612-613.

  A very brief sketch of Shaiwaki, a village of about 5,000 people, Southeast of Kabul.

1606 Cresson, Rebecca A.
  1953 American Family in Afghanistan. National Geographic Magazine 104:417-432.

  Informal account of an American housewife's efforts to run a household at Kabul.

1607 Curriculum and Textbook Project (USAID/PTCCU)
  1972 Some Characteristics and Attitudes of Ten Year Old School Boys and Girls of Kabul City, Afghanistan. Kabul: Ministry of Education. Pp. 245.

1608 Cutler, J. C.
  1950 Survey of Venereal Diseases in Afghanistan. Bulletin of the World Health Organization 2:689-703. Geneva.

V. SOCIAL EVOLUTION AND INSTITUTIONS

1609   Daiwa [Lamp]
       1951- A newspaper published at Shiberghan in Juzjan
           province. Began as a weekly in 1951, became a semi-
           weekly in 1963, and a daily in 1965.

1610   Daly, Kate
       1905 Eight Years Among the Afghans. London. Pp. 194.

       The trials and tribulations of a courageous British woman
       doctor, Mrs. Daly, at Kabul: complements other accounts
       of the reign of Amir Habibullah.

1611   Davidov, A. D.
       1969 Afghanskaya Derevnya [Afghan Village]. Moscow:
           Nauka. Pp. 171.

1612   Debeth, G. F.
       1965 Anthropologicheskie Issledovanya B Afganistane.
           Volume I. Moscow: USSR Academy of Sciences.

1613   Debeth, G. F.
       1966 Anthropologicheskie Issledovanya B Bosochikh i
           Tsentralnikh Provinthiyakh Afganistana. Volume II.
           Moscow: USSR Academy of Sciences.

1614   Debeth, G. F.
       1970 Physical Anthropology of Afghanistan. Illustrated
           with notes by Louis Dupree. Translated from Russian by
           Eugene V. Portov and edited by Henry Field. Cambridge:
           Peabody Museum, Harvard University. Two Volumes.

1615   De Croze, J. Berjane
       1947 Tourism in Afghanistan for the Student. Afghanistan
           2(2):15-20.

       An investigation of how to attract student-tourists to
       Afghanistan, together with a suggested itinerary.

1616   Delloye, Isabelle
       1980 Des Femmes d'Afghanistan. Paris: Editions des
           Femmes. Pp. 158.

1617   Delor, J.
       1946 Musique Afghan [Afghan Music]. Afghanistan 1(3):24-
           29.

       Illustrated description of local instruments and a brief
       account of the character of the music.

V. SOCIAL EVOLUTION AND INSTITUTIONS

1618 Dianous, Hugues Jean de
    1960 Note sur la presse Afghane [A Note on the Afghan Press]. Orient 15:177-184.

Traces the history of newspapers and periodicals and cites numerous titles. Very valuable for its references.

1619 Dupaigne, Bernard
    1979 Le dernier jour des hommes. Enterrements de premiere classe et enterrements de derniere classe en Afghanistan. In Les Hommes et la Mort. Rituels funeraires a travers le Monde. Paris: Musee de l'Homme. Pp. 208-219.

1620 Dupree, Louis
    1956 Afghan Profile. Natural History 65(10):537-541.

1621 Dupree, Louis
    1964 Tribal Traditions and Modern Nationhood: Afghanistan. Asia 1:1-12.

Identifies and examines the divisive and cohesive factors active in the process by which the country is reaching for nationhood.

1622 Dupree, Louis
    1966 Moving Mountains in Afghanistan. In Cultural Frontiers of the Peace Corps. Edited by Robert Textor. Cambridge: MIT Press. Pp. 107-124.

Discusses the history, scope, and various activities in which the Peace Corps is involved in Afghanistan.

1623 Dupree, Louis
    1972 Afghanistan. In Population Perspective 1971. Edited by H. Brown and A. Sweezy. San Francisco: Freeman, Cooper and Company. Pp. 28-53.

1624 Dupree, Louis and Nancy Hatch Dupree
    1976 Afghanistan. Common Ground 2(1):29-35.

An article dealing with the position of women in Afghanistan written by two scholars who have spent more than twenty-five years in that country. This particular issue of Common Ground is devoted to women and men in India, Afghanistan, Africa, Mexico, Taiwan, China, France and Belgium, Yugoslavia, Sweden, and North America.

V. SOCIAL EVOLUTION AND INSTITUTIONS

1625   Dupree, Nancy Hatch
        1965 An Historical Guide to Kabul. Kabul: Afghan Tourist
            Organization. Pp. 171.

1626   Dupree, Nancy Hatch
        1966 Herat: A Pictorial Guide. Kabul: Afghan Tourist
            Organization. Pp. 66.

1627   Dupree, Nancy Hatch
        1967 The Road to Balkh. Kabul: Afghan Tourist
            Organization. Pp. 123.

1628   Dupree, Nancy Hatch
        1967 The Valley of Bamiyan. Kabul: Afghan Tourist
            Organization. Pp. 87.

        A brief but very useful historical and geographical guide
        for visitors interested in Bamian.

1629   Dupree, Nancy Hatch
        1971 An Historical Guide to Afghanistan. Kabul: Afghan
            Tourist Organization. Pp. 334.

        An important historical and archaeological guide to
        Afghanistan profusely illustrated. The country is divided
        into six regions and each region is dealt with
        independently. Useful to both serious and casual students
        of the country.

1630   Dupree, Nancy Hatch
        1977 An Historical Guide to Afghanistan. Kabul: Afghan
            Tourist Organization. Pp. 492.

        Expanded and updated version of the 1971 Historical Guide
        to Afghanistan by the same author.

1631   Dupree, Nancy Hatch
        1978 Behind the Veil in Afghanistan. Asia 1(2):10-15.

1632   Dupree, Nancy Hatch
        1981 Revolutionary Rhetoric and Afghan Women. New York:
            Afghanistan Council, The Asia Society. Occasional Paper
            No. 23. Pp. 22.

        History and analysis of reforms of women's status in
        Afghanistan.

V. SOCIAL EVOLUTION AND INSTITUTIONS

1633 Easterly, Edwin Michael
    1974 Impact of the Afghanistan Ministry of Education Curriculum and Textbook Project on Primary School Student Learning. Unpublished Ed.D. Dissertation. Columbia University Teachers College. Pp. 292.

    A plan is proposed for the assessment of the educational impact of the primary school project of the Afghan Ministry of Education as assisted by the United States Agency for International Development.

1634 Ebadi, Samiia
    1975 Osnovopolozhnik afganskoi zhurnalistiki Makhmud Tarzi i gazeta "Siradz al-akhbar" (1911-1918) [Mahmud-i-Tarzi, Founder of Afghan Journalism, and the Newspaper Seraj-ul-Akhbar (1911-1918)]. Unpublished Ph.D. Dissertation. Leningradskii gosudarstvennyi universitet imeni A. A. Zhdanova. Leningrad State University. Leningrad.

1635 Eckensberger, Lutz H. and Gunter F. Schneider
    1972 Identification Processes Among Change Agents in Technical Schools of Afghanistan. Journal of Social Psychology 87(1):145-146.

1636 Education in Afghanistan During the Last Half-Century
    1956 Munich: Royal Afghan Ministry of Education. Pp. 96.

1637 Educational Mission
    1952 Report on Afghanistan. Paris: UNESCO. Pp. 87.

    Conclusions of a team of UN specialists who studied the educational system of Afghanistan with a view toward suggested forms, innovations, and changes required to relate this system to Western concepts. Some of these suggestions are ill-related to current attitudes and cultural values of the Afghans. Other pages contain general material descriptive of certain aspects of present-day life.

1638 Educational Statistics, Afghanistan, 1968/1347
    1969 Department of Planning, Directorate of Statistics, Ministry of Education. Kabul.

1639 Educational Statistics, Afghanistan, 1969
    1970 Department of Planning, Directorate of Statistics, Ministry of Education. Kabul.

V. SOCIAL EVOLUTION AND INSTITUTIONS

1640   Einzmann, Harald
        1977 Religiöses Volksbrauchtum in Afghanistan: Islamische Heiligenverenhrung und Wallfahrtswese im Raum Kabul [Religious Folk Customs in Afghanistan: Islamic Veneration of Saints and Pilgrimages in the Kabul Area]. Doctor of Theology Dissertation. University of Heidelberg. Heidelberg. Pp. 356.

1641   Einzmann, Harald
        1977 Religioeses Volksbraunchtun in Afghanistan: Islamische Heilgenvereherung und Wallfahrtswesen in Raum Kabul [Religious Folk Customs in Afghanistan: Islamic Veneration of Saints and Pilgrimage in the Area of Kabul]. Wiesbaden: Franz Steiner Verlag. Pp. 250. See no. 1640.

1642   El-Hashimi, Sayed
        1952 Afghanistan Revisited. Contemporary Review 1039:21-24. London.

Generalized travel impresions, ending with the conclusion that "Afghanistan is certainly the happiest, least divided country in Asia that I have seen."

1643   Fairchild, Frank Louis
        1978 A Catalog of Teaching Competencies for the Preservice and Inservice Training of Primary Teachers in Afghanistan. Unpublished Ed.D. Dissertation. Columbia University Teachers College. Pp. 222.

A description of the content validity for a catalog of teaching competencies based on Afghanistan's new primary school teachers' guide.

1644   Faryab [Faryab]
        1951- A daily newspaper in Dari and Pushtu, published at Maimana.

1645   Feroz, G. A.
        1948 Bakhter News Agency. Afghanistan 3(3):20-21.

An account of the official news agency since its creation at the end of 1939, written by its director.

1646   Finley, Mark
        1949 Afghanistan. Contemporary Review 1000:225-230.

A brief survey of the contemporary economic and political structure of the country.

V. SOCIAL EVOLUTION AND INSTITUTIONS

1647 Fischer, Ludolph
    1968 Afghanistan: Eeine Geographisch-Medizinische Landeskunde [Afghanistan: A Geomedical Monograph]. Translated into English by J. A. Hellen and I. F. Hellen. Heidelberg: Spring-Verlag Berlin. Pp. 150.

Based upon research in 1938-1941 and 1950-1952, the monograph deals with folk medicine and indigenous medical practices in Afghanistan. The monograph also provides brief sketches of Afghan society, culture and geography, common diseases, hospital facilities, educational facilities, etc.

1648 Fodor, Eugene and William Curtis
    1973 Fodor's Islamic Asia: Iran-Afghanistan-Pakistan. New York: David McKay Co.

1649 Franz, Heinrich Gerhard
    1980 Neue Publikationen zur Kunst des Islam in Afghanistan und Mittelasien. Afghanistan Journal 7(4):139-143.

1650 Fucik, Julius
    1953 Na Piandzhe, kogda stemneet [On the Panj When Darkness Falls]. V Zashchitu Mira 28:34-40. Moscow.

1651 Furnia, Arthur H.
    1978 Syncrisis: The Dynamics of Health XXIV: Afghanistan. Washington: U.S. Department of Health, Education, and Welfare. Pp. 167.

A description and interpretation of the interactions of health and socioeconomic development in Afghanistan.

1652 Furon, Raymond
    1926 L'Afghanistan [Afghanistan]. Paris: Albert Blanchard. Pp. 133; 3 maps.

A general account of the geogaphy, history, ethnography, and progress in modern times.

1653 Furon, Raymond
    1952 René Grousset et l'Afghanistan [René Grousset and Afghanistan]. Afghanistan 7(3):65-67.

A tribute to the late René Grousset and his work on Afghan history.

V. SOCIAL EVOLUTION AND INSTITUTIONS

1654 Gandy, Christopher and Andre Singer
1973 Afghanistan: The Society's 1972 Tour. Journal of the Royal Central Asian Society 60(1):27-35.

1655 Ghaussi, M. Aref
1968 Criteria for Appraising Educational Planning in Underdeveloped Countries (With Examples from the Experience of Afghanistan). IIEP Occasional Papers No. 1. Paris: UNESCO. Pp. 67.

1656 Ghaussi, M. Aref
1974 Educational Planning and its Problems in Afghanistan. Internationales Asienforum 5(2):168-178.

1657 Ghubar, M.
1946 The Role of Afghanistan in the Civilization of Islam. Afghanistan 1(1):26-32.

Lists and describes briefly numbers of Afghan theologians, scribes, translators, scientists, and historians who contributed to the rise of Islamic culture.

1658 Gobar, Asad H.
1970 Suicide in Afghanistan. British Journal of Psychiatry 116(534):493-496.

1659 Gobar, Asad H.
1974 An overview of Psychiatric Morbidity in Afghanistan. International Mental Health Research Newsletter 16(4):11-13.

1660 Gobar, Asad H.
1976 Drug-abuse in Afghanistan. Bulletin on Narcotics 28(2):1-11.

1661 Godiksen, Lois Hansen
1974 Modernizing Afghanistan: A Symbolic Interactionist Approach. Unpublished Ph.D. Dissertation. Northwestern University. Pp. 353.

Provides a perspective for studying modernization using the symbolic interactionist mode of analysis. Also generates an hypothesis about the nature and dynamics of the modernizing proces, using historical and case study analysis.

1662 Gosti iz Afganistan [Guests from Afghanistan]
1954 Ogonek 32(3):12. Moscow.

V. SOCIAL EVOLUTION AND INSTITUTIONS

1663   Gray, John Alfred
        1901 At the Court of the Amir. London: Macmillan and Co. Pp. xxi, 523.

        An Englishman who lived for several years at Kabul, close to Amir Abdul Rahman, tells of a time of political and economic change.

1664   Gurash [Struggle]
        1978- A Turkmani language weekly newspaper. Publishes material on a variety of topics.

1665   Habibiyeh 1282-1322 [Habibiyeh 1903-1943]
        n.d. Kabul: Matba'eh-yi 'umumi. Pp. 36.

        A commemorative volume in Persian, marking the first 40 years in the life of this school. Numerous articles and lists of former students comprise the work.

1666   Haddad, Nikulay
        1947 Da Zhwandaheh Lari [The Roads of Life]. Kabul: Matba'eh-yi 'umumi. Pp. 93. (1326 A.H.)

        A general discussion of contemporary civilization and its aspects by an Egyptian author: translated into Pushtu by 'Aziz al-Rahman Saifi.

1667   Hadiyah ba Dustan [A Gift to Friends]
        1945- A monthly in Persian, sponsored by the newspaper Anis, which began its publication at Kabul in 1945.

1668   Hakim, Abdul
        1949 L'Organisation de l'instruction publique et des écoles en Afghanistan [The Organization of Public Education and Schools in Afghanistan]. Afghanistan 4(1):4-18.

        Technical and detailed study of the organization of the Ministry of Educaton, an account of subjects of study at the primary level, and a description of all the higher institutions of learning.

1669   Hamada, M.
        1978 Islamic Saints and Their Mausoleums. Acta Asiatica, Bulletin of the Institute of Eastern Culture 34:79-98.

V. SOCIAL EVOLUTION AND INSTITUTIONS

1670 Hamid, Abdul Aziz
    1974 An Analysis of Decision-Making in the Elementary School: Curriculum and Textbook Development Project in Afghanistan. Unpublished Ed.D. Dissertation. Columbia University Teachers College. Pp. 240.

Description and analysis of the processes of decision making in the establishment and implementation of the curriculum and textbook project in Afghanistan from its inception to the end of 1973. Cooperation and collaboration between the Afghan Ministry of Education and Teacher's College, Columbia University is described.

1671 Hannah, Norman B.
    1964 Afghanistan--A Problem of Timing and Balance. Asia 2:18-37.

An American diplomat, who served in Afghanistan, discusses the concept of fixing the country in time and space and then of interpreting its role on the Asian stage.

1672 Haqiqate Inqelabe Saur [The Truth About the Saur Revolution]
    1981- Organ of the Central Committee of the Peoples Democratic Party of Afghanistan.

1673 Haqiqate Sarbaz [The Truth of a Soldier]
    1981- A twice-weekly publication of the Afghan Ministry of National Defense.

1674 Harat [Herat]
    1932- An independent monthly periodical, founded at Herat in 1932 and printed in Persian.

The name of the periodical has changed from time to time; it is also called Adabi, or Adabi Harat [Literary Herat], in reference to the fact that it is the organ of the Literary Society of Herat.

1675 Harris, Fred et al.
    n.d. Public School Education in Afghanistan. (Kabul): The Public School Survey and Planning Team, United States Operations Mission to Afghanistan. Pp. 173.

A mimeographed survey of needs in this field and proposals for developments.

1676 Hautaluo, J. E. and R. J. Loomis
    1972 Perception of Visual Illusions in a Sample of Afghan Boys. Journal of Social Psychology 87(1):143.

V. SOCIAL EVOLUTION AND INSTITUTIONS

1677   Hawa [Air]
        1957- Quarterly journal of the Afghan Air Authority, which began publication at Kabul in 1957; articles in Pushtu and Dari.

1678   Heras, Henri
        1935 Les Jésuites en Afghanistan [The Jesuits in Afghanistan]. New Review 1. Calcutta.

1679   Heravy, Mir G. R. Ma'il
        1972 Book-making in Afghanistan During the Last Century. Afghanistan 25(3):68-77.

1680   Herbordt, Oskar
        1926 Eine Reise nach "Dar-i Nur" im Nordosten Afghanistans. Petermanns Mitteilungen 72:206-208.

1681   Hudson, Alfred E. and Elizabeth E. Bacon
        1940 Inside Afghanistan Today. Asia 40:118-122.

1682   Huffman, Arthur V.
        1951 The Administrative and Social Structure of Afghan Life. Journal of the Royal Central Asian Society 38:41-48.

        An American who taught for six years in an Afghan secondary school at Kabul crowds these pages with facts on politics, ethnic elements, economic progress, and the changing system of education.

1683   Hufford, Donald
        1951 Afghan Hospitality. Geographical Magazine 24:128-137.

1684   Hunte, Pamela A.
        1978 Women and Development Process in Afghanistan. Washington, D.C.: United States Agency for International Development. Pp. 128.

        Discussion of women's participation in the socio-cultural dynamics of Afghanistan.

1685   Huquq [Justice]
        1945- A monthly of the Faculty of Law of Kabul Univerity, with articles in Dari and Pushtu.

V. SOCIAL EVOLUTION AND INSTITUTIONS

1686   Huwyler, E. and I. V. Moos
            1975 Bemerkungen zum Steinbockmotiv im oberen Kokchaund
                im Munjan-Tal (Afghanistan). Ethnologique Zeitschrift
                Zurich 11. Zurich.

1687   Huwyler, Edwin
            1979 Uber den Steinbock in der Vorstellungswelt der
                Bewohner des Munjan-Tales. Afghanistan Journal
                6(4):133-143. Map; photos.

1688   Ilyas, M., N. Ali, M. I. Marshood, and K. Aziz
            1977 Coronary Rehabilitation in Pathans - Social Aspects.
                Cardiology 62(2):132-133.

1689   International Educational
            1960 Cultural and Related Activities for Afghanistan.
                Washington, D.C.: Bureau of Cultural Relations,
                Department of State. Pp. 52.

        Lists and describes activities in Afghanistan under the
        auspices of agencies of the American government, of other
        governments, and of the specialized agencies of the United
        Nations.

1690   Irfan [Knowledge]
            1924- Began publication in 1924 at Kabul under the name
                of Ayineh-yi 'irfan [Mirror of Knowledge] and continued
                irregularly, taking its present name in 1936. As an
                organ of the Ministry of Education it publishes articles
                on teaching, literature, history, and science, many of
                which are translations from the foreign press.

1691   Islah [Reform]
            1929- Founded in 1929 at Kabul.

        Semiofficial morning daily, with an estimated 5,000 circu-
        lation. Published in Dari and Pushtu. In 1973 renamed
        Republic.

1692   Itifaqi-i Islam [Concord of Islam]
            1919- Founded at Herat in 1919.

        This newspaper has appeared daily at some periods and
        weekly at others. Most of its contents are in Dari.

V. SOCIAL EVOLUTION AND INSTITUTIONS

1693   Itihad [Union]
1921- A biweekly newspaper published at Baghlan.

In its earlier years, when it was printed at Khanabad, most of its articles were in Pushtu, while later on more Persian has been used. At times called Ittihade Baghlan or Illihade Khan Abad.

1694   Itihad-i Mashriqi [Eastern Union]
1920- Founded in 1920 at Jalalabad and published weekly in Pushtu.

1695   Janssens, B. Busson de
1951 Les wakfs dans l'Islam contemprain [Waqfs in Contemporary Islam]. Revue des Études Islamiques (no volume number):13-14.

Within this long article, the pages indicated supply a brief indication of the fact that the waqfs--religious endowments--of Afghanistan were taken over by the State under Amir Abdul Rahman. Mosques, shrines, and religious schools are now supported privately and by state and municipal donations.

1696   Jarring, Gunnar
1937 The New Afghanistan. Svenska Orientsallskapets arsbok 131-145. Stockholm.

1697   Jeffrey, Thomas E.
1965 Educational Testing in Afghanistan. Human Organization 24(1):83-88.

1698   Jettmar, Karl
1965 Fruchtbarkeitsrituale und Verdienstfeste im Umkreis der Kafiren. MAGW, XCV:109-116.

1699   Jettmar, Karl (mit Beitragen von Schuyler Jones und Max Klimburg)
1975 Die Religionen des Hindukusch. Stuttgart.

1700   Jettmar, Karl
1980 The Religions of the Hindukush. With contributions by Schuyler Jones and Max Klimburg. Translated from the German by Adam Nayyar. London: Aris & Phillips, Ltd. Pp. 525.

1701   Da Kabul Puhantun Khabarunah [The Kabul University News]
1960- A monthly which began publication in 1960, with articles in Dari and Pushtu.

V. SOCIAL EVOLUTION AND INSTITUTIONS

1702 Kabul New Times
    1980- English language daily newspaper. Replaced Kabul Times.

1703 Kabul Times
    1962- Began publication at Kabul in March 1962 as a four-page daily paper in English, with emphasis upon foreign news. Publisher: Bakhtar News Agency. Since 1980 it has been renamed Kabul New Times. See above.

1704 Kakar, M. Aziz
    1976 A Survey of UNESCO Recommendations Concerning Teacher Education in Afghanistan with a Judgment as to their Practical Effects, 1949-1975. Unpublished Ph.D. Dissertation. George Peabody College for Teachers. Pp. 252.

1705 Kamali, Mohammad Hashim
    1976 Matrimonial Problems of Islamic Law in Contemporary Afghanistan. Unpublished Ph.D. Dissertation. London University. London. Pp. 309.

1706 Kayeum, Abdul
    1948 Recommendations for the Improvement of Instruction in the Social Sciences for the Schools of Afghanistan, Based on a Cultural Study of the Afghans. Unpublished Ph.D. Dissertation. Cornell University. Pp. 235.

1707 Kennedy, T. F.
    1966 Afghanistan Village. Auckland, New Zealand. Pp. 24.

A brief illustrated descriptive sketch of Shaiwaki, a village about six miles southeast of Kabul.

1708 Kennedy, T. F.
    1967 Afghanistan Village. London: Longmans. Pp. i, 25.

1709 Kerr, Graham B.
    1977 Demographic Research in Afghanistan: A National Survey of the Settled Population. New York: Afghanistan Council, The Asia Society. Occasional paper no. 13. Pp. 100; bibliography; charts; map.

A summary of the demographic survey of Afghanistan conducted during the early 1970s. Includes a list of publications of the Afghan demographic studies.

V. SOCIAL EVOLUTION AND INSTITUTIONS

1710   Kerr, Graham B.
            1979 Strategies of Collecting Information for Development
            Programs and Social Research Design: A Case Study of
            Afghanistan. Journal of South Asian and Middle Eastern
            Studies 3(2):53-69.

1711   Khalil, Muhammad Ibrahim
            1957 'Arof va Nozul-i Islam [The Ascents and Descents of
            Islam]. Kabul: Doulati matba'eh. Pp. 58. (1336 A.H.)

        A treatise on Islam in Dari.

1712   Khalq [People]
            1978- A newspaper which, after publishing six issues in
            1966 and was banned, reappeared as a newspaper of
            information, news, and commentary.

1713   Khawgiani, Mohammed Amin
            1939 Hayat-i Sayyid-i Jamal al-Din-i Afghani [Life of
            Jamal al-Din Afghani]. Kabul: Matba'eh-yi 'umumi

1714   Khodzhayov, T. K.
            1970 Kraniologiya Uzbekov Yuzhnogo Priaralya (Mizdakhkan)
            [The Craniology of the Uzbeks of the Southern Aral
            Region (Mizdakhkan)]. Sovetskaya Etnografiya 45(4):122-
            125.

1715   Khorasan
            1981- A quarterly magazine, organ of the Dari Department
            of the Academic and Research Center of the Academy of
            Sciences of the Democratic Republic of Afghanistan.
            Publishes material on languages, arts and literature.

1716   Khoshbeen, A. M.
            1970 Consequences of the Absence of Sex Education in
            Afghanistan. Revue de Neuropsychiatrie infantile et
            d'Hygiene Mentale de l'Enfance 18(10):853-861.

1717   Kieffer, C. M.
            1975 Les formules de lamentation funebre des femmes a
            Caboul. awaz andaxtan-e-zana. Note de dialectologie et
            d'ethnographie afghanes. In Melanges linguistiques
            offerts a Emilie Benveniste. Collection Linguistique
            publiee par la Societe de Linguistique de Paris 70:313-
            323.

V. SOCIAL EVOLUTION AND INSTITUTIONS

1718   Knabe, Erika
1977 Frauenemanzipation in Afghanistan: Ein Empirische Beitrag Zur Untersuchung von Sozio-Kulturellem Wandel und Sozio-Kultureller Beständigkeit [Emancipation of Women in Afghanistan: An Empirical Contribution to the Investigation of Socio-Cultural Change and Socio-Cultural Persistence]. Ph.D. Dissertation. University of Köln. Köln. Pp. 489.

1719   Knabe, Erika
1977 Frauenemanzipation in Afghanistan. Ein Empirischer Beitrag zur Untersuchung von Sozio-Kulturellem Wandel und Sozio-kultueller Bestandigkeit. Meisenheim: Verlag Anton Hain. (Volume 16 in the Afghanische Studien Series). Pp. 471.

1720   Kohzad, Ahmad Ali
1949 L'Afghanistan Modern [Modern Afghanistan]. Afghanistan 4(4):54-55.

A brief review of a publication with the above title issued in April 1949 by La Documentation Francaise. Certain errors are pointed out.

1721   Kohzad, Ahmad Ali
1952 Allocution prononcée à l'occasion du millénaire de la naissance d'Avicenne [Address Delivered on the Thousandth Anniversary of the Birth of Avicenna]. Afghanistan 7(3):51-65.

The life and work of Avicenna, a major philosopher and scientist in Islami Central Asia.

1722   Kohzad, Ahmad Ali
1953 L'Afghanistan au point de vue de la religion [Afghanistan From the Point of View of Religion]. Afghanistan 8(3):1-17.

A history of religions in Afghanistan from prehistoric times to the present--from the pre-Aryan worship of the mother goddess, through the Vedic cult, Zoroastrianism, Buddhism, Greek mythology, the Brahman sunworship, and Nestorianism to Islam.

V. SOCIAL EVOLUTION AND INSTITUTIONS

1723 Kohzad, Ahmad Ali
1954 Indo-Afghan Cultural Relations. Afghanistan 9(1):1-10.

The exchange of cultural and religious influences between Afghanistan and India in the prehistoric, Vedic, Zoroastrian, Buddhist, and Muslem periods.

1724 Kohzad, Ahmad Ali
1954 Un mois en Italie [A Month in Italy]. Afghanistan 9(3):1-7.

A summary of Mr. Kohzad's articles on his Italian visit, giving various traditions of the founding of Rome, accounts of his conferences at the Italian Institute for the Middle and Far East, and accounts of visits to Ostia Antiqua and Pompeii. He discusses the similarity between the art of Pompeii and the Greco-Buddhistic art of Bactria, mentions the likeness between the statue of St. Peter in Rome and a statue found at Charsada, and finishes with a note on the Etruscans. He adds that the Italian Institute will be allowed to excavate at Ghazni and Laghman.

1725 Kukhtina, Tat'yana I.
1963 Prosveshcheniye v nezavisimoy Afganistane [Education in Independent Afghanistan]. Moscow: Izdatel'stvo Vostochnoy Literatury. Pp. 131.

1726 Lajoinie, Simone Bailleau
1980 Conditions de Femmes en Afghanistan. Paris: Editiones Sociales. Pp. 222.

A systematic work on the status and condition of women in Afghanistan.

1727 Latifi, 'Abdul Baqi
1947 Afghanistan va Yak Nigah-i Ijmali bah awza' va Shu'un-i Mukhtalifeh va Halat-i 'Umumiyet [Afghanistan: A Brief Look into Various Conditions and Public Affairs]. Kabul: Matba'eh-yi 'umumi. Pp. 136. (1326 A.H.)

A number of chapters on the subject by different authors.

1728 Leyden, J.
1812 On the Rosheniah Sect and its Founder Bayezid Ansari. Asiatic Researches: or, Transactions of the Society Instituted in Bengal 11:363-428. London.

V. SOCIAL EVOLUTION AND INSTITUTIONS

The story of a horse dealer turned prophet, whose heretical order had great power in Afghanistan in the sixteenth and seventeenth centuries A.D. The first part of the article is a history of the order, taken largely from Akhund Darvizeh's Makhzan al-Islam (see no. 1766)--which is highly unsympathetic. The second part is a translation from Mohsani Fani's Dabistan, on Bayezid's education, teachings, and successors; the third explains the Ismailia Shi'a sect, to which the Rosheniah order bears a close resemblance.

1729 Lindauer, G.
1977 Afghanistan's Press. Some Remarks on Pourhardi's Two Articles. Afghanistan Journal 4(2):82.

1730 Lindberg, K.
1949 Le paludisme in Afghanistan [Malaria in Afghanistan]. Rivista de Malariologia 28:1-54. Rome.

1731 MacFadyen, D. R.
1978 Medical-Education in Afghanistan. Canadian Medical Association Journal 118(1):10.

1732 Magnus, Julius
1929 Die Höchsten Gerichte der Welt [The Highest Courts of the World]. Leipzig: W. Moeser. Pp. xii, 634.

Within Part IV of this work, under the heading "Afghanistan," may be found a reliable description of the judicial system, jurisdiction of the courts and administration of the courts during the rule of Amanullah.

1733 Mahfouz, Imza
1937 En Asie. II. Afghanistan [In Asia. II. Afghanistan]. Revue des Études Islamiques 11:405-412.

A series of brief reviews and notes from local-language papers in Afghanistan, Iran, and India are grouped under such headings as Afghanistan Moves Towards Modernism, Afghan-Japanese Relations, Afghan Wage Scales, Governmental Appointments, Afghan Independence Day, etc.

1734 La Maison des Francais [The House of the French]
1949 Afghanistan 4(1):36.

Describes the activities of a cultural center newly opened at Kabul--a library, lectures, national dances, and plays.

V. SOCIAL EVOLUTION AND INSTITUTIONS

1735 Majmu'a-i Sihat [Anthology of Health]
n.d. A monthly revue of hygiene published in Dari at Kabul by the Ministry of Public Health.

1736 Malakhov, M.
1946 Afghanistan. Geographical Sketch. New Times 7:23-29. Moscow.

A Soviet reporter in Afghanistan views the situation with a critical eye: Socialism is completely lacking and everything seems disorganized and backward. There is an "unexampled confusion of tribes and peoples," while "agriculture cannot keep the mass of the population above the starvation level."

1737 Malik al-Shu'ara, Bitab
n.d. 'Elm-i Ma'ani [The Knowledge of Meaning]. Kabul. Pp. 92.

1738 Malik al-Shu'ara, Bitab
1955 Guftar-i ravan dar 'Elm [A Spiritual Discourse on Knowledge]. Kabul. Pp. 23. (1334 A.H.)

A study of rhetoric, meaning and knowledge, in Dari.

1739 Maranjian, G.
1958 The Distribution of ABO Blood Types in Afghanistan. American Journal of Physical Anthropology 10:263.

1740 Martin, Frank A.
1907 Under the Absolute Amir. London and New York: Harper and Brothers. Pp. xii, 330.

Observations on private and public life at Kabul by an Englishman who was for eight years chief engineer to the Amirs Abdul Rahman and Habibullah. Displays an intimate knowledge of manners and customs, prisons and punishments, soldiers and their arms, and of the daily conduct of government by Amir Abdul Rahman.

1741 Martin, Ross J. et al.
1959 Kabul University: An Evaluation of its Present Status and Recommendations for Future Growth and Development to Accomplish its Role in Education, Research and Public Service for Afghanistan. Washington, D.C.: International Cooperation Administration. Pp. 187.

V. SOCIAL EVOLUTION AND INSTITUTIONS

1742 Martino, Paul and Susan F. Schultz (eds)
    1975 National Demographic and Family Guidance Survey of the Settled Population of Afghanistan. Volume III: Tables. Pp. 118.

    Computer printouts of the Afghanistan Demographic Survey data.

1743 Matthews, Herbert L.
    1943 Beyond the Khyber Pass. New York Times Magazine, July 18. Pp. 17f.

    Ancient, secluded Afghanistan becoming modern Afghanistan, with a characterization of the Afghans and a little of their history and culture.

1744 McKeller, Doris
    1971 Afghan Cookery. (2nd edition). New York: International Publications Service. Pp. 90.

1745 Mehrabi, Shah Mohammad
    1978 An Analysis and Evaluation of Economic and Education Sectors in Afghanistan. Unpublished Ed.D. Dissertation. University of Cincinnati. Pp. 282.

    Traces and constructs the economic and educational history of Afghanistan from 1929-present. Discusses the agricultural, industrial, construction, transportation, communication and education sectors.

1746 Mele, Pietro F.
    1971 Afghanistan. Florence: La Nuova Italia. Pp. 56.

    A brief text and a collection of photos by the author about Afghanistan.

1747 Melikian, L., A. Ginsberg, D. Cuceloglu, and R. Lynn
    1971 Achievement Motivation in Afghanistan, Brazil, Saudi Arabia, and Turkey. Journal of Social Psychology 83(2):183-184.

1748 Melikian, Levon H. and A. Zaher Wehab
    1969 First-drawn Picture: A Cross-cultural Investigation of the DAP. Journal of Projective Techniques and Personality Assessment 33(6):539-541.

1749 Merman [Lady]
    1953- A quarterly designed for women readers, with articles in Dari and Pushtu.

V. SOCIAL EVOLUTION AND INSTITUTIONS

1750   Meyer, Richard J.
        1978 Afghanistan: Transition to Television. Public Telecommunications Review 6(1):44-47.

1751   Michaud, Roland and Sabrina
        1980 Afghanistan: A Record of Timeless Culture Now Threatened With Change. Smithsonian. November:48-59.

1752   Mirepois, Camille
        1971 Afghanistan in Pictures. New York: Sterling Publishing Company, Inc. Pp. 64.

Brief description of the country, its landscape, its material culture, and its people. Profusely illustrated. Adequate for elementary school level.

1753   Monier, M. Ibrahim
        1977 Some Effects of an Activity Approach to Teaching Geometry in the High Schools in Afghanistan. Unpublished Ph.D. Dissertation. Oregon State University. Pp. 145.

1754   Naim, Elizabeth
        1946 "Élan Féminin" ["Feminine Spirit"]. Afghanistan 1(3):47-48.

Concerns the establishment of a women's society for assisting the poorer girl students at Kabul.

1755   Najaf 'Ali Khan
        1932 Maw'izeh-yi Nadireh [Admonition of Nadir]. Lahore: Firuz. Pp. 48. (1311 A.H.)

A lithographed work in Persian, consisting of letters addressed to King Mohammed Nadir concerning the modernization of Afghanistan.

1756   Najib-ullah Khan
        1950 Speech Delivered by Dr. Najib-ullah Khan at Delhi Province Post Graduate Teachers' Club. Afghanistan 5(2):47-62.

On the progress of modern education in Afghanistan since 1905, and its present condition.

1757   Nangarhar
        1918- A daily newspaper published at Jalalabad in Pushtu.

V. SOCIAL EVOLUTION AND INSTITUTIONS

1758 Nazari, Rahmattullah
    1975 An Evaluative and Descriptive Research on Democratic Educational Administration. Unpublished Ph.D. Dissertation. University of St. Louis. Pp. 150.

1759 Nendari [Exhibition]
    1953- First appeared at Kabul in 1953.

A monthly in Persian published by the Kabul Cinema.

1760 Newman, R. E.
    1965 Pathan Tribal Patterns: An Interim Study of Family Process and Structure. Bridgewood, New Jersey: Foreign Studies Institute. Pp. 111.

Pushtun personality is perceived as originating from a certain well-known indigenous personality characteristics, originating from the process of inter- and intra-familial interaction. Dubious methodology and disjointed text.

1761 Newspapers, Magazines and Journals
    n.d. For a list and discussion of newspapers, magazines and journals published in Afghanistan from 1875-1973, refer to I. V. Pourhadi 1976 in this bibliography. Some periodicals and newspapers are listed in this bibliography. Some other periodicals which have appeared since 1978 in Afghanistan are listed in this section of the bibliography. See nos. 1782 and 2948.

1762 Nida'-i Khalq [The Voice of People]
    1951- A privately-sponsored, biweekly paper in Dari and Pushtu, which was published by a duplication process at Kabul in 1951 and then closed by official action.

1763 Nilab [Blue water]
    n.d. A privately-sponsored weekly, which began publication in Persian and Pushtu in 1952, and was printed by the Government Central Press.

1764 Ningarhari, 'Abd al-Karim ibn Makhdum, Akhund Darvizeh
    1877 Makhzan al-islam [Treasure of Islam]. Delhi. n.p.

A famous encyclopedia of observances, rites, and dogmas of the Sunni sect of Islam, compiled in Pushtu about 1615 A.D.

V. SOCIAL EVOLUTION AND INSTITUTIONS

1765   Nizam-nameh-yi Tashkilat-i Asasi-yi Afghanistan [Regulation of the Principal Organizations or Administrations of Afghanistan].
1921   Kabul: Government Print Press. n.p.

1766   O'Bannon, George W.
1973   Project Afghanistan: Undergraduates in Dynamic Cross-Cultural Experiment. International Educational and Cultural Exchange 8(4):14-20.

1767   O'Bannon, George W.
1976   Project Afghanistan: From Experiment to Certainty. International Educational and Cultural Exchange 11(3):13.

1768   O'Connor, Ronald W.
1980   Managing Health Systems in Developing Areas: Experiences from Afghanistan. Lexington, MA: Lexington Books. Pp. 295.

Afghanistan-based health study which draws management conclusions applicable to Afghanistan and other countries. Examines health problems and traditional health systems of the country.

1769   Open Doors, a Report on Three Surveys: Foreign Students in U.S. Institutions of Higher Education, Foreign Faculty Members at U.S. Colleges and Universities, Foreign Doctors Training at U.S. Hospitals, 1954-55.
1955   New York: Institute of International Education. Pp. 56.

Tables indicate the number of Afghan students in the U.S., their academic status, sources of financial support, and fields of major interest.

1770   Palwal, Abdul Raziq
1969   Polytheism of the Kafirs. Afghanistan 21(4):61-88.

1771   Pamir
1952- A biweekly paper which began publication at Kabul in late 1952.

Some issues were printed and some produced by a duplication process. Articles in Dari and Pushtu.

1772   Papiha, S. S., D. F. Roberts, and A. G. Rahimi
1977   Genetic Polymorphisms in Afghanistan. Annals of Human Biology 4(3):233-241.

V. SOCIAL EVOLUTION AND INSTITUTIONS

1773   Parwan [Command]
        1952- A daily newspaper published at Charikar in Parwan
            province. Dari and Pushtu.

1774   Payam-i Imruz [Today's Message]
        1966- A privately owned biweekly, which began publication
            at Kabul in 1966 with material in both Dari and Pushtu.

1775   Payam-i Tandrusti [Message of Health]
        n.d. A monthly issued at Kabul in Persian by the
            Publicity Section of the Ministry of Public Health.

        Irregularly issued in Dari and Pushtu. The title is
        occasionally Tandrust [Healthy].

1776   Payind, Mohammad Alam
        1979 Academic, Personal and Social Problems of Afghan and
            Iranian Students in the United States. Educational
            Research Quarterly 4(2):3-11.

1777   Penkala, Danuta
        1980 "Hot" and "Cold" in the Traditional Medicine of
            Afghanistan. Ethnomedizin 6(1-4):201-228.

        A brief sketch of the principles of hot and cold in the
        folk medicine of north and central Afghanistan by a Polish
        ethnology student.

1778   Penzl, Herbert
        1959 Higher Education in Afghanistan. School and Society
            87:445.

1779   Pillsbury, Barbara L. K.
        1978 Afghanistan. In Traditional Health Care in the Near
            East. By Barbara L. K. Pillsbury. Washington: Agency
            for International Development. Pp. 64-76.

        A brief chapter on health and population overview, Afghan
        indigenous health practices, indigenous etiology,
        indigenous practitioners. A brief bibliography is
        included.

1780   Polishchuk, A. I.
        1974 Uchenye Afganistana o Voennoi Istorii Svoei Strany
            [Scholars of Afghanistan on Their Country's Military
            History]. Narody Azii i Afriki 4:164-167.

V. SOCIAL EVOLUTION AND INSTITUTIONS

1781 Poullada, L. B.
    1962 Problems of Social Development in Afghanistan. Royal Central Asian Journal 49(1):33-39.

1782 Pourhadi, I. V.
    1976 Afghanistan's Newspapers, Magazines and Journals. Afghanistan Journal 3(2):75-77.

A detailed list and brief description of various newsapers and other periodicals published in Afghanistan from 1875-1973.

1783 Price, M. Philips
    1949 A Visit to Afghanistan. Journal of the Royal Central Asian Society 35:124-234.

Stresses the fascination and appeal of changeless aspects, while emphasizing progress toward national unity and economic improvements.

1784 Pushtun Zhagh [The Pushtun Voice]
    1940- A monthly magazine published at Kabul by Kabul Radio.

Each issue contains the program of the station for the coming month, as well as articles in Persian and Pushtu.

1785 Qawa'id-i Seraj al-Milleh dar Kharidari-yi Mal az Duval-i Kharijah [Regulations of the "Luminary of the Nation" Concerning Imports from Foreign Countries]
    1904 Kabul: Dar al-saltaneh. Pp. 2, 66. (1321 A.H.)

A lithographed work in Dari, which includes decrees of Amir Habibullah concerning foreign imports.

1786 Rahmani, Magdeline
    1954 La société féminine de Bien-Faisance [The Women's Society of Good Work]. Afghanistan 9(4):56-59.

Discusses an Afghan women's organization, which aims to educate poor women and to raise their standard of living by selling their embroideries and handiwork.

V. SOCIAL EVOLUTION AND INSTITUTIONS

1787 Rahmanzai, Abdul Moqim
  1978 A Study to Identify the National Policy and the Professional Training Needs that Should be Included in the Development of a Prescriptive Training Program for Educational Administrators in Afghanistan. Unpublished Ed.D. Dissertation. State University of New York at Albany. Pp. 224.

  Identifies the national policy and planning goals of Afghanistan regarding the educational development that have implications for the training of educational administrators. The thesis also attempts to identify perceptions of Afghan educational administrator's professional and social leadership roles.

1788 Rahnuma-yi Tadavi va-Viqayeh az Maraz-i Trakhom [Guide to the Treatment and Protection from Trachoma]
  1942 Kabul: Matba'eh-yi 'umumi. Pp. 18. (1321 A.H.)

  A pamphlet published in Dari by the Ministry of Health.

1789 Rashad, Shah Muhammad
  n.d. Irshadat-i Dini [Religious Guidances]. Kabul: Matba'eh-yi doulati. Pp. 196.

  The text in Dari of 59 talks delivered over Radio Kabul.

1790 Rashad, Shah Muhammad (trans)
  n.d. Siassat-i Shar'ieh [Islamic Politics]. No publisher. Pp. 191.

  A translation into Dari of a work written in Arabic.

1791 Razi, Mohammad Houssain
  1975 Internal Institutional Communication at Kabul University. Unpublished Ed.D. Dissertation. Indiana University. Pp. 352.

1792 Redard, Georges
  1974 Afghanistan. Zurich: Editions Silva. Pp. 138.

  Excellent photos by Roland and Sabrina Michaud with text by Georges Redard.

1793 Reidsmit, E. R.
  1974 Library Development in Afghanistan. UNESCO Bulletin for Libraries 28(1):17-21.

V. SOCIAL EVOLUTION AND INSTITUTIONS

1794   Reports of the Member States
         1950 Afghanistan. UNESCO Document 5C/4 Afghanistan. Florence. Pp. 7.

1795   Reshad, Ahmad
         1965 Namhaye Nabatate Tibi ba Alsanae Dari, Inglisi, Foransawi, Latini [Names of Medical Plants in Dari, English, French, Latin]. Kabul: Faculty of Medicine and Pharmacy, Kabul University. Pp. 20.

         A useful list of medical plants found and used in Afghanistan. Dari names are given in Arabic script and others in Latin script.

1796   Rishtya, Sayed Qasim
         1946 Education in Afghanistan. Afghanistan 1(1):20-25.

         A sketchy account of the history of modern education. Current statistics are lacking.

1797   Rishtya, Sayed Qasim
         1946 Kabul Calling. Afghanistan 1(2):1-3.

         Sketch of the history of radio broadcasting in Afghanistan and of the installation of Radio Kabul.

1798   Rishtya, Sayed Qasim
         1948 Journalism in Afghanistan: A Brief Historical Sketch. Afghanistan 3(2):72-77.

         A description and record of the various newspapers and periodicals published in the country, and an account of the establishment of the Department of Press and Publication in 1939. By a former director of that Department.

1799   Roghtia [Health]
         n.d. An illustrated monthly published at Kabul in Persian and Pushtu by the Ministry of Public Health.

1800   Rosenthal, Jerry E.
         1973 Afghanistan's Population: Planning to Avoid a Crisis. War on Hunger 7(7):1-4.

1801   Rothmemund, D. (ed)
         1975 Islam in Southern Asia: A Survey of Current Research. Wiesbaden: Beitrage Zur Suedasien-Forschung Suedasien Institut, Universitaet Heidelberg.

V. SOCIAL EVOLUTION AND INSTITUTIONS

A comprehensive survey of scholarly research in Islamic South Asia. Included are a number of articles dealing with Afghanistan.

1802   Sadoi Sharq [The Voice of East]
            n.d. A periodical published at Dushanbe, formerly Stalinabad, in Soviet Tajistan. Prior to 1964 it was called Sharqi Surkh. It presents material on Afghan poets and folklore.

1803   Safa, Muhammad Ibrahim
            1953 Mukhtasar-i Mantiq; Bahis az Ta'lil-i Istoriqra' va Mituduluzhi [Outline of Logic; Investigation of Deduction and Methodology]. Kabul: Matba'eh-yi 'umumi. Pp. 200. (1332 A.H.)

        An original work in Dari, based upon European sources.

1804   Safi, Abdul Qayum
            1978 A Plan for a National Standardized Achievement Testing Program in Afghanistan. Unpublished Ed.D. Dissertation. Columbia University Teachers College. Pp. 226.

        A proposal based on the new elementary curriculum and instructional materials developed in experimental schools by the curriculum and textbook project, taking into account the new curriculum and proposal for the new national reform (1975-1978).

1805   Sahar, Hafiz
            1967 A Comparative Study of Educational Television in Selected Developing Countries and its Relevance to the Similar Use of Television in Afghanistan. Unpublished Ph.D. Dissertation. New York University. Pp. 211.

        Historical review of variant uses and effectiveness of television in selected developing countries and a discussion of elements of similarity/dissimilarity among these nations. The potentialities of the use of television for Afghanistan are examined.

1806   Sahraie, Hashem and Janet Sahraie
            1975 Educational Development in Afghanistan: History of the Teachers College. Unpublished Ed.D. Dissertation. Columbia University Teachers College. Pp. 543.

V. SOCIAL EVOLUTION AND INSTITUTIONS

       Joint Ed.D. Dissertation. History of educational development activities, assisted by the Teacher's College, Columbia University in Afghanistan from initiation to 1971. The main focus is on selected aspects of the process of educational development assistance. Framework for analysis derived from the literature on international cooperation.

1807 Saint-Brice
      1928 Le voyage du roi d'Afghanistan [The Travels of the King of Afghanistan]. Correspondance d'Orient 20(361):1-9.

      Amir Amanullah in France.

1808 Saint-Brice
      1929 La nouvelle ère Afghane [The New Afghan Era]. Correspondance d'Orient 21(383):193-200.

      A short account of Nadir Khan and the revolution of 1928-29 which gave him the throne.

1809 Saljuqi, Salah al-Din (trans)
      n.d. 'Ilm-i Akhlaq-i "Nikumakusi" az Aristu [Aristotle's Nichomachean Ethics]. Kabul: Matba'eh-yi 'umumi. Pp. 330.

      A translation into Dari from the work in English, "Nichomachean Ethics," by D. P. Chase.

1810 Saljuqi, Salah al-Din
      1952 Muqaddimeh-yi 'Ilm-i Mantiq [Introduction to Logic]. 2 vols. Kabul: Matba'eh-yi 'umkumi. Pp. (1) 412; (2) 413-764. (1331 A.H.)

      A compilation into Dari from an extensive range of sources.

1811 Saljuqi, Salah al-Din
      1956 Jabireh [Compensation]. Kabul: Metba'eh-yi doulati. Pp. 324. (1335 A.H.)

      A study in Dari of psychological and sociological aspects of behavior.

V. SOCIAL EVOLUTION AND INSTITUTIONS

1812   Saljuqi, Salah al-Din
       1965 Tajalli dar Afaq va Anfas [The Manifestation in the
             Worlds and the Individuals]. Kabul. Pp. 443. (1344
             A.H.)

       A philosophical and religious treatise in Dari translated
       from various Western sources.

1813   Sami, Mahmud
       1909 Tarbiyeh-i 'Askariyeh [Military Training]. Kabul:
             Mashin Khaneh. Pp. 15. (1327 A.H.)

       A lithographed text in Dari, containing a manual of
       infantry drill for the Afghan army.

1814   Samuelson, J.
       1975 Islam i Afganistan - under kung Muhammed Zahir Shah.
             En studie av moderniseringsprocessens foljder for islams
             stallnin g i Afganistan. [The Consequences for Islam of
             the Process of Modernization in Afghanistan].
             Stockholm: Stockholm Dissertations in Comparative
             Religion 1. Pp. 110. (Swedish, with English summary.)

1815   Samylovskiy, I. V.
       1963 Nauchnyye i kulturnyye svyazi S.S.S.R. so stranami
             Azii i Afrikii [Scientific and cultural communications
             of the U.S.S.R. with the countries of Asia and Africa].
             Moscow: Izdatel'stvo Vostochnoy Literatury. Pp. 67.

       Text of cultural agreements between the U.S.S.R. and
       Afghanistan, pp. 25-29.

1816   Sana'i [Sana'i--pen name of a poet]
       1952- A daily newspaper at Ghazni, which began publica-
             tion in 1952.

1817   Saraf, S. N.
       1975 Human Resources Development Through Literacy in
             Afghanistan. Functional Literacy Project of Pacca.
             Indian Journal of Adult Education 36(6):13-14.

1818   Sarif, Brigitte
       1977 Zur Situation der Frauen in Afghanistan [On the
             Situation of Women in Afghanistan]. Unpublished Ph.D.
             Dissertation. University of Frankfurt. Pp. 173.

V. SOCIAL EVOLUTION AND INSTITUTIONS

1819 Sarif, Gul Janan
    1972 Das Afghanische Schulwesen: Zu seiner geschichtlichen Bedingung und gegenwartigen Problemlage. [The Afghan Educational System: Its Historical Condition and Present Problems]. Ph.D. Dissertation. University of Frankfurt. Pp. ii, 287.

1820 Sarwari, M. Sadiq
    1974 Afghanistan zwischen Tradition und Modernisierung. Europaische Hochschulschriften Reihe XXXI Politikwissenschaft Bd. 2. Frankfurt: Verlag Peter Lang. Pp. 312.

1821 Sassani, Abul K.
    1961 Education in Afghanistan. Washington, D.C.: U.S. Government Printing Office. Pp. 55; tables; bibliography.

    A study, reproduced by mimeograph, by the Division of International Education of the U.S. Department of Health, Education, and Welfare, on the subjects of preprimary, primary, secondary, higher, and teacher's training education. Numerous ephemeral items in the accompanying bibliography are not included in this bibliography.

1822 Sawitzki, Hans-Henning
    1969 Alte und Neue Eliten in Einem Entwicklungsland. Die Akademiker in der Afghanischen Gesellschaft [Old and New Elites in a Developing Country, The Academic Professionals in the Afghan Society]. Kölner Zeitschrift fuer Soziologie und Sozialpsychologie 1969, Supplement 13:237-256.

1823 Schimmel, A.
    1978 Rumi: Ich bin Wind und bu bist Feuer. Leben und Werk des Grossen Mystikers. Diederichs Gelbe Reihe; 20. Köln: Eugene Diederichs Verlag. Pp. 232; illustrations.

1824 Schneider, Peter
    1973 Uber die Geruchsrezeptoren der Afghanischen Wustenassel. Naturw. 60:106-107.

1825 Schneider, Peter
    1975 Soziallebende Asseln in Afghanistan. Afghanistan Journal 4:148-150. Photos.

V. SOCIAL EVOLUTION AND INSTITUTIONS

1826   Schlegelberger, Franz
        1927 Rechtsvergleichendes Handwörterbuch für das Zivil-
            und Handelsrecht des in-und auslandes [A Dictionary of
            Comparative Law for Civil and Commercial Law, Domestic
            and Foreign]. Berlin: F. Wahlen.

        Under the heading "Afghanistan," beginning on page 291,
        may be found a comprehensive account of the laws in force
        during the reign of Amanullah.

1827   Seraj-ul Akbar [Crown of the News]
        n.d. Began publication as a bimonthly in Dari, edited by
            a leading Afghan reformist and writer, Mahmud Tarzi. It
            ceased publication in 1918.

1828   Sera Miasht [Red Crescent]
        n.d. Illustrated quarterly published at Kabul by the
            Afghan Red Crescent Society.

        Publication began in 1955 and articles were in Dari,
        Pushtu, and English.

1829   Sérignan, Claude
        1960 La condition des femmes en Afghanistan et son
            évolution récente [The Status of Women in Afghanistan
            and its recent development]. Orient 4(2):33-56.

        Describes steps taken to improve the status of women, and
        states that their inferior position remains as the major
        problem of the country.

1830   Siddiq, M.
        1962 Science Education in Afghanistan. Unpublished Ed.D.
            Dissertation. Columbia University. Pp. 196.

        Analyzes the problems involved in developing and improving
        science education programs in Afghanistan. Emphasis on
        the programs which would help the social and economic
        problems that face Afghanistan.

1831   Siddiq, Mir Abdul Fatah
        1966 Quantifiable Input Factors for Planning Educational
            Growth in Afghanistan. Unpublished Ed.D. Dissertation.
            Indiana University. Pp. 100.

        An exploration of the list of input factors which are
        quantifiable and are necessary to be taken into account in
        the planning and growth of education in Afghanistan.

V. SOCIAL EVOLUTION AND INSTITUTIONS

1832 Siddiqui, Nafis Ahmad
    1975 Some Neighbouring Countries: A Short Account of Afghanistan, Bangladesh, Nepal, Burma, Sri Lanka and Malaysia. New Delhi: Mukul Prakashan. Pp. 120.

1833 Simmons, J. S., T. F. Whayne, et al. (eds)
    1954 Global Epidemiology: A Geography of Disease and Sanitation. Volume III. The Near and Middle East. Philadelphia: J. P. Lippincott Co.

This extensive survey includes some material concerned with public health in Afghanistan.

1834 Simpich, Frederich
    1921 Every-Day Life in Afghanistan. National Geographic Magazine 39:85-110.

Frederick Simpich, formerly American consul at Tehran, translated and published the notes made by an unnamed European diplomat to the court of the new ruler, Amanullah.

1835 Sinha, Sri Prakash
    1980 Afghanistan im Aufruhr. Zurich: Hecht-Verlag. Pp. 208.

1836 Sirat, Abdul Satar
    1969 Sharia and Islamic Education in Modern Afghanistan. Middle East Journal 23(2):217-232.

1837 Sistan
    n.d. A biweekly in Persian and Pushtu, poorly printed at Farah.

1838 Soub [Struggle]
    1978- A Baluchi language weekly newspaper. Publishes material on a variety of subjects.

1839 Spitler, J. F. and N. B. Frank
    1977 Afghanistan - demographic uncertainty. Population Index 43(3):428-429.

1840 Spitler, James F. and Nancy B. Frank
    1978 Afghanistan, a Demographic Uncertainty. Washington: U.S. Government Printing Office. Pp. 12.

V. SOCIAL EVOLUTION AND INSTITUTIONS

1841   Splett, Oskar
        1979 Arbeit des Goethe-Instituts in Afghanistan. Verbeindung von Kultur-und Sozialhilfe. Auslandskurier 20/8. Schwabisch Hall, Eppinger-Verlag. Pp. 23.

1842   Stolz, Karl
        1954 Le théâtre afghan [The Afghan Theater]. Afghanistan 9(3):36-44.

        The article describes the plays, the entr'actes, and the audiences of the Afghan theater and mentions favorite actors, with an account of the Afghans' efforts to develop a modern theater on European models.

1843   Stone, Russell A., Saxon Graham, and Graham B. Kerr
        1974 Commercial Distribution of Contraceptives in Afghanistan: Actual and Potential Use of the Pharmaceutical Marketing System. Studies in Family Planning 5(2):83-89.

1844   Stone, Russell A., Saxon Graham, and Graham B. Kerr
        1974 Distribucion comercial de anticonceptivos en Afghanistan: utilizacion actual y potencial del sistema de mercadeo de productos farmaceuticos. Estudios de Planificacion Familiar 5(3):28-41.

1845   Storai [Star]
        n.d. A biweekly published in Dari and Pushtu at Maymaneh.

1846   Sullivan, Michael Gellinck
        1973 Schooling and National Integration in Afghanistan: A Study of Students in the Faculty of Education, Kabul University. Unpublished Ph.D. Dissertation. University of Pittsburgh. Pp. 223.

        Describes the development of Kabul University and its role in the national integration of Afghanistan. Specifically, it explores how attendance in the Faculty of Education facilitates the integration of students in the Afghan national society.

1847   Surkhakan va-Suret-i Tadabir-i Sihhi-yi An [Measles and the Manner of its Prevention]
        1936 Kabul: Matba'eh-yi 'umumi. Pp. 6. (1315 A.H.)

        A pamphlet in Dari issued by the Ministry of Public Health.

V. SOCIAL EVOLUTION AND INSTITUTIONS

1848   Sweetser, Anne T.
        1976 Family Formation Attitudes Among High School Girls
            in Kabul, Afghanistan: A Study in Population and Social
            Change. New York: Afghanistan Council, the Asia
            Society. Occasional paper no. 9. Pp. 11.

1849   Tafsire Sharif [Commentary on the Holy Qur'an]
        1957- 3 vols. Kabul: Matba'eh-yi doulati, 1323 [1954],
            1326 [1957], 1327 [1958]. Pp. (1) 1196; (2) 2470; (3)
            3521

        A translation into Pushtu, prepared by a group of
        leading Afghan theologians.

1850   Taillardat, C. F.
        1928 Le voyage du roi Amanu-Ullah. Le roi Amanu-Ullah en
            Angleterre. La fin du voyage du roi Amanu-Ullah [The
            Journey of King Amanullah. King Amanullah in England.
            The End of King Amanullah's Journey]. L'Asie Francaise
            53-54; 67-69; 184-188; 320-323.

1851   Takharistan
        1979- A weekly newspaper published in Dari and Pushtu in
            Takhar Province. Deals with current events and
            historical and political information specific to that
            province.

1852   Taraki, Muhammad Qadir
        1947 Mafhum-i Dawlat az Nuqtah-yi Nazar-i Huquq-i
            Ijtima'yat va-Falsafah [The Purpose of the State from
            the Points of View of Social Justice and Philosophy].
            Kabul: Matba'eh-yi 'umumi. Pp. 68. (1326 A.H.)

        An original work in Dari by a writer on the subjects of
        philosophy and law.

1853   Taraki, M. Rasal
        1945 A Proposed Functional Training Program for
            Elementary School Teachers in Afghanistan. Unpublished
            Ph.D. Dissertation. Cornell University. Pp. 82.

1854   The Holy Qur'an
        1949 Published in three volumes. Matba'eh-yi Umumi.
            (1324-1328 A.H.). Edited in Arabic and with translation
            and commentary in Pushtu by Mahmud Hasan Diwabandi and
            Shabir Ahmad Diwabandi.

V. SOCIAL EVOLUTION AND INSTITUTIONS

1855   Thornton, Ernest
            1910 Leaves From an Afghan Scrapbook: The Experiences of an English Official and his Wife in Kabul. London: J. Murray. Pp. xvi, 225.

        Valuable chapters are devoted to descriptions of daily and family life at Kabul.

1856   Threlkeld, Robert M.
            1979 Attitudes Toward Disability in Two Cultures: Afghanistan and the United States. Unpublished Ph.D. Dissertation. Boston College. Pp. 126.

        An imbalanced pedestrian and superficial comparison of attitudes of non-disabled persons toward physically-disabled persons in the two countries. Data is derived from rural and urban schools in Maine (1975) and two locations in Northern Afghanistan (1976). A poor and failing exercise.

1857   Trosper, Joseph F.
            1972 The Status of Insurance in Afghanistan. Unpublished Ph.D. Dissertation. Indiana University. Pp. vi, 142.

1858   Trumbull, David
            1968 The Development of a Reading Text in English for College Students in Afghanistan. Unpublished Ph.D. Dissertation. Columbia University. Pp. 333.

        Details of the drafting, testing, revision and final form of the special text to improve the reading of English of students at Kabul University.

1859   Trussell, T. James and Eleanor Brown
            1979 A Close Look at the Demography of Afghanistan. Demography 16(1):137-156.

1860   Tulu'-i Afghan [Afghan Sunrise]
            1924- A newspaper founded at Qandahar in 1924 and published daily in Pushtu.

1861   Uberoi, J. P. Singh
            1971 Men, Women, and Property in Northern Afghanistan. In India and Contemporary Islam (Transactions of the Indian Institute of Advanced Studies, Volume 6). Edited by S. T. Lokhandwalla. Simla, India. Pp. 388-416.

V. SOCIAL EVOLUTION AND INSTITUTIONS

1862 Urdu-yi Afghan [The Afghan Army]
   1921- A monthly periodical issued in Dari and Pushtu at Kabul by the Ministry of War.

   First appeared in 1921. The name has changed several times: it has been Urdu [Army] and Da Urdu Majalleh [The Army Magazine].

1863 Urmanova, Rukiya K.
   1958 Reformy afganskogo pravitel'stva v 1919-1925 gg. [The reforms of the Afghan Government, 1919-1925]. Tashkent: Izvestiya Akademii Nauk Uzbekskoy SSR 2:65-75.

1864 Utas, Bo
   1980 Notes on Afghan Sufi Orders and Khanaqahs. Afghanistan Journal 2:60-67. Photos.

1865 Vatan [Homeland]
   1951- A privately-sponsored weekly paper, which began publication at Kabul in 1951.

   Produced by a duplication process. The paper was closed down by official action in 1952. Claimed a circulation of 1,500 copies.

1866 Velichkovsky, Y.
   1955 Kabul Impressions. New Times 5:28-30. Moscow.

   A glowing report by the Director of the Moscow Institute for Advanced Training of Teachers, who was a member of a Soviet delegation invited to visit the University of Kabul. He describes briefly Kabul City, its schools, the University, Afghan art and drama, and the hospitality of the Afghan intellectuals.

1867 Vizhdani, Abdul Vakil
   1973 Perepis naseleniya v SSSR i Afganistan [A Census of the Population in the USSR and Afghanistan]. Kandidat of Science diploma in Economic Sciences. Kievskii Institut Narodnogo Khoziaistva. Kiev, Ukrain SSR.

1868 Wahdat [Unity]
   1966- A privately-owned weekly, which began publication at Kabul in 1966 with material in both Dari and Pushtu.

V. SOCIAL EVOLUTION AND INSTITUTIONS

1869   Wala, A. K.
         1948 We Want Peace and Security. Afghanistan 3(3):22-23.

         The author advocates universal friendship and moral armament.

1870   Walus [Community]
         1941- A weekly in Pushtu which began publication at Kabul in 1951.

1871   Warangah [Beam of Light]
         1941- A weekly in Pushtu published at Gardiz: began publication in 1941.

1872   Ward, Francis Blackiston, III
         1978 Education for National Allegiance in Afghanistan: A Study of the Development of a New Elementary School Social Studies Curriculum as a Means of Encouraging National Unity in a Developing Country. Unpublished Ph.D. Dissertation. Columbia University. Pp. 692.

         Study of the results of the national unity policy as manifested in curriculum and textbook development for the elementary grades (1973-1975). Comparison of the old textbooks with the material compiled by the curriculum and textbook project.

1873   Wardak, Guljan Wror
         1978 Changing Language Arts Curriculum Processes in Afghanistan Elementary Schools. Unpublished Ed.D. Dissertation. State University of New York at Buffalo. Pp. 287.

         Historical and descriptive study of the implementation of curriculum planning stages in the language arts curriculum planning processes for Afghan elementary schools.

1874   Wattan [Homeland]
         1954- Monthly publication of the Ministry of Finances, which first appeared in 1954. Articles are in Dari and Pushtu.

1875   Wazhma [Fragrance]
         1966- A quarterly Pustu magazine issued by Faculty of Letters and Humanities, University of Kabul. Publishes scholarly works dealing with history and literature.

V. SOCIAL EVOLUTION AND INSTITUTIONS

1876   Waziri, Rafiq
1973 Symptomatology of Depressive Illness in Afghanistan. American Journal of Psychiatry 130(2):213-217.

It is argued that a cross-cultural study of depressive symptoms in Afghan patients, the incidence of such symptoms as depressed mood and loss of appetite, sleep, and labido were similar to the reported incidence of these symptoms in depressed patients from a Western culture. The author is an Afghan with M. D. training in psychiatry in the West.

1877   Weinbaum, M. G.
1976 Foreign Assistance to Afghan Higher Education. Afghanistan Journal 3(3):83-86.

1878   White, Bryan
1963 Kabul. Geographical Magazine 35(12):682-693.

1879   Whittemore, Richard
1980 An American-Teacher in Afghanistan. Social Education 44(3):202-206.

1880   Whitteridge, Gordon
1972 Afghanistan: Background for the Visitor. Asian Affairs 59(2):147-152.

1881   Wiebe, D.
1976 Freizeitverhalten und Tourismus in Afghanistan. Ein Beitrag zur Fremdenverkehrsgeographie drittweltlicher Lander. Orient 141-157.

1882   Wiebe, D.
1980 Die Heutigen Kultstatten in Afghanistan und ihre Inwertsetzung fur den Fremdenverkehr. Afghanistan Journal 7(3):97-108. Maps; photos.

1883   Wilber, Donald N.
1951 Matbu'at-i Afghanistan. [The Press of Afghanistan]. Danesh 3:485-487. Tehran. (1330 A.H.)

A general survey in Persian of contemporary Afghan publications: newspapers, periodicals and historical studies.

1884   Wilber, Donald N.
1952 The Structure of Islam in Afghanistan. The Middle East Journal 6(1):41-48. Washington.

V. SOCIAL EVOLUTION AND INSTITUTIONS

A description of contemporary Muslim institutions and practices and an examination of local statements regarding the future role of Islam in the country.

1885 Wilson, Michael
1970 Starting Educational Broadcasting in Afghanistan. Educational Television International 4(4):274-281.

1886 Wolanga [Ray]
n.d. A daily newspaper published at Pushtu in Gardez.

1887 Wright, John C.
1969 An Estimate of the Vocational Preferences of University Freshmen in Afghanistan. Pakistan Journal of Psychology 2(2):39-41.

1888 Wulbern, J. P.
1974 Educational Policy in Afghanistan - Interim Review. Internationales Asienforum 5(2):179-194.

1889 Yawar, Ali
1978 Science Teachers Guide for Afghan Elementary Schools. Unpublished Ph.D. Dissertation. University of Northern Colorado. Pp. 126.

1890 Yoder, Richard Allen
1978 Class, Security, and Fertility: A Social Organizational/Social Justice Perspective on Fertility Behavior in Afghanistan. Unpublished Ph.D. Dissertation. University of Pittsburgh.

Describes social organizational/social justice explanations of different fertility systems by analyzing the role of differential access to the basic social and economic benefits of development.

1891 Yulduz [Star]
1978- A weekly newspaper publised in Uzbeki contains articles on Uzbek literature, poetry, and other material of political and ideological nature.

1892 Yunus, Parween Etemadi
1963 An Analysis of Mathematics Instruction in Afghanistan with Recommendations for Improvement. Unpublished M.A. Thesis. The American University. Pp. 88.

V. SOCIAL EVOLUTION AND INSTITUTIONS

Describes and reviews the development of the present system of mathematics instruction in Afghanistan on primary, secondary and university levels in light of the history, culture, and geographical location of the country.

1893 Yusofzai, Aziz Ahmad
    1978 The Development and Direction of the Materials Testing Program of Afghanistan's Curriculum and Textbook Project 1973-1976. Unpublished Ed.D. Dissertation. Columbia University Teacher's College. Pp. 242.

1894 Yussuf-zai, Baqi
    1974 The Goals of Kabul University: An Historical Approach. Unpublished Ph.D. Dissertation. Indiana University.

1895 Yussufi, Nadjib
    1977 Publizistik der Entwicklungslander am Beispiel Afghanistan [Political Journalism of Developing Nations: The Example of Afghanistan]. Unpublished Ph.D. Dissertation. Freie Universität Berlin. Pp. v, 175.

1896 Zahir, Payendeh Muhammad and Sayyid Muhammad Yusuf 'Elmi
    1960 Da Afghanistan da Ma'raef Tarikh [History of Education in Afghanistan]. Kabul: Ministry of Education. Pp. 177 and 184. (1339 A.H.)

A work with the text in parallel columns of Dari and Pushtu.

1897 Zahir-Shah, Mohammed
    1951 Discours inaugural prononcé par S. M. le Roi a l'occasion du 33ème anniversaire des fêtes de l'indépendence [Inaugural Address Delivered by H. M. the King on the Thirty-Third Anniversary of Independence Day]. Afghanistan 6(3):36-37.

On the Afghan government's plans, domestic and foreign, with reference to Pakistan and the Pushtunistan issue.

1898 Zahma, 'Ali Mohammed
    1960 Maqalat-i Ijtima'i va Falsafi [Essays on Sociology and Philosophy]. Kabul. Pp. 196. (1339 A.H.)

1899 Zaki, M. H.
    1974 Health Programming for Peace Corps in Afghanistan - Family Planning. American Journal of Public Health and the Nation's Health 64(11):1098-1099.

V. SOCIAL EVOLUTION AND INSTITUTIONS

1900   Zhwandun [Life]
            1948-   Illustrated periodical published weekly at Kabul in
            Dari and Pushtu by the Department of Press.

1901   Zirai [Good News]
            n.d. A weekly paper published in Pushtu at Kabul and
            sponsored by the Pushtu Tolaneh of the Afghan Academy.

VI. POLITICAL STRUCTURE

Structure of government; political dynamics; public
order; foreign policies; official propaganda;
international problems; political
issues and prospects

Material on the constitutions, the structures of governments, and the organization of administrative bureaucracies is rather extensive, but the coverage of the legislative bodies and councils, of the laws passed by these entities, and of functions and operations of the various subcomponents of the national bureaucracy is inadequate. Items on the operation of the government on the level of the general public are also lacking. There is some material on political parties and speculative sketches on their activities.

Users of the bibliography may be struck by the amount of material in a number of languages which the Afghan governments have published on the issue of Pushtunistan and other internal or external political and ideological issues--enough material to require a separate chapter for these subjects alone. We have here attempted to provide significant highlights and representative works. The effort to distinguish between publications on foreign policies and on foreign relations present a problem: in case of doubt, the reader should refer back to Chapter III for additional items on the history of foreign affairs of Afghanistan.

Material dealing with conditions since 1978 is sketchy and largely speculative and based on limited factual-verifiable data. Therefore, almost all of this material is not annotated and left to the judgment of those who are either casually or seriously interested in the dynamics of Afghan polity, society and culture since 1978.

1902 Abawi, Ahmad Omer
        1977 Die Rolle der englischen Interventions- und Expansionspolitik in Afghanistan im 19. Jahrhundert und deren Auswirkungen bis zur Gegenwart [The Role of the British Policy of Intervention and Expansion in Afghanistan during the 19th Century and Its Consequences up to the Present Time]. Unpublished Ph.D. Dissertation. University of Tübingen. Pp. vii, 227.

1903 Abidi, A. H. H.
        1977 Irano-Afghan Dispute over the Hellmand Waters. International Studied 16(3):357-378.

VI. POLITICAL STRUCTURE

1904   Adamec, Ludwig W.
            1967 Afghanistan, 1900-1923: A Diplomatic History.
                Berkeley: University of California Press. Pp. vi, 245.

1905   Adamec, Ludwig W.
            1974 Afghanistan's Foreign Affairs to Mid-twentieth
                Century: Relations with the USSR, Germany, and Britain.
                Tucson: Univesity of Arizona Press. Pp. ix, 324.

            A well researched description and analysis of
            Afghanistan's foreign relations with the three countries
            noted along with notes and bibliography.

1906   Adamec, Ludwig W.
            1975 Historical and Political Who's Who of Afghanistan.
                Graz, Austria: Akademische Druck Verlag. Pp. 490.

1907   Adelman, Kenneth L.
            1980 Jimmy's Geography Lesson: for the Soviet's there
                were lots of good reasons to invade Afghanistan, not the
                least of which was that no one was going to stop them.
                American Spectator 13:12-14.

1908   Aerial Bombardment of the Tribal Area by Pakistan Government
                Causing the Death of Hundreds of our Afghan Brothers.
            1949 Afghanistan 4(1):41-42.

            Deplores this action and warns Pakistan of the danger of
            arousing tribal enmity.

1909   The Afghan-Pakistan Conflict
            1955 New Times 16:22-23. Moscow.

            An editorial charging that Pakistan's attacks on
            Afghanistan are American-sponsored attempts to coerce
            Afghanistan into a Middle East military alliance.

1910   Afghanistan Dar Dowreh-i Hekumat-i Entaqali, Hut-1341-Mizan
                1344. [Afghanistan in the Period of the Transitional
                Government, March 1963-October 1965]
            1965 Kabul: Imprimerie d'État. Pp. 340.

1911   Afghanistan, Laws, Statutes, Etc.
            1975 English Translation of some of the new laws
                promulgated by the Republic of Afghanisyan. New York:
                Afghanistan Council, Asia Society. Special paper. Pp.
                29.

VI. POLITICAL STRUCTURE

1912   Afghanistan, Laws, Statutes, etc.
        1923-29 Nezam Nama-e Tashkilate Asasyia [Gazetteer of Basic Administration]. Kabul: Government Printing Office.

        A collection of laws and regulations during the reign of King Amanullah.

1913   L'Afghanistan moderne [Modern Afghanistan]
        1949 Documentation Française 1112, 3-39.

        An authoritative survey of the political and social institutions of the country, including the text of the Afghan constitution.

1914   Afghanistan and Pakistan
        1949 Afghanistan 4(2):25-27.

        The Pushtunistan issue, with reference to a bombing of Waziristan in February 1949.

1915   Afghanistan, The Truth About
        1980 The Truth About Afghanistan: Documents, Facts, Eyewitness Reports. Moscow: Novotsi Press Agency Pp. 158.

1916   Ahmad, Mohammed B.
        1951 Constitutions of Eastern Countries. In Select Constitutions of the World, Vol. I. Karachi: Governor General's Press and Publications, 2nd ed. Pp. 403.

        Page 43 begins a few pages describing the Afghan government, followed, on pages 48-59, by an English translation of the constitution of 1931, with the addendum of 1933. On pages 379-385, the features of this constitution are summarized.

1917   Ahmad, N. D.
        1975 The Survival of Afghanistan: The Two Imperial Giants Held at Bay in the 19th Century. Lahore: People's Publishing House.

1918   Ahmad, Syed Barakat
        1974 Panjdeh Incident and the Occupation of Egypt. Journal of International Affairs (India) 30(2):148-152.

1919   Ahmed, Akbar S.
        1980 How to Aid Afghan Refugees. Royal Antrhopological Institute News 39:6-9.

VI. POLITICAL STRUCTURE

1920   Ahmed, Feroz
            1975 Focus on Baluchistan and Pushtoon Question. Lahore: People's Publishing House. Pp. 116.

1921   Akhramovich, Roman T.
            1958 Novyye yavleniya v razviti obshchestvennoy mysli v Afganistane v svyazi s problemoy Pushtunistana [New Statements in the Development of Popular Opinion in Afghanistan in Connection with the Problem of Pushtunistan]. Sovetskoye Vostokovedeniye 4:155-161.

        A presentation of articles in the Afghan press on Pushtunistan as illustrative of new trends of popular opinion.

1922   Akhramovich, Roman T.
            1967 Afganistan B 1961-66 gg. [Afghanistan During 1961-66]. Moscow: Nauka. Partial Translation of Akhramovich 1966. See no. 751.

1923   Alder-Karlsson, Gunnar
            1980 The U.S. Embargo: Inefficient and Counterproductive. Aussenwirtschaft 35:170-187.

1924   Ali, Majid A.
            1980 Afghans in Exodus. Worldview 23(11):5-6.

1925   Amnesty Internatonal
            1979 Violations of human rights and Fundamental Freedoms in the Democratic Republic of Afghanistan. An Amnesty International Report. London. Pp. 34.

1926   An Analysis of Several Recent Afghan Laws
            1977 Papers presented at the Afghanistan Studies Association panel of the Middle East Studies Association annual meeting, 1976. New York: Afghanistan Council, the Asia Society. Occasional paper no. 12. Pp. 67.

        Includes papers on laws dealing agriculture, statistical law for domestic development, and Afghan Foreign and domestic private investment law. Texts of the laws discussed are appended.

1927   Armstrong, H. F.
            1956 North of the Khyber. Foreign Affairs 34(4):603-619.

        A detailed discussion of Afghanistan's domestic and foreign policies, including one of the first efforts to undelrine Soviet economic penetration of the country.

VI. POLITICAL STRUCTURE

1928 Arnold, Anthony
　　　1981 Afghanistan: The Soviet Invasion in Perspective. Stanford: Hoover Institution Publiations. Pp. 144.

　　　A description and evaluation of political dynamics in Afghanistan since 1978 with some background material.

1929 Artner, Stephen J.
　　　1980 Entspannungspolitik vor und nach Afghanistan. Aussenpolitik 31(2):134-146.

1930 Asas-nameh [Fundamental Law]
　　　n.d. Kabul: Matba'eh-yi 'umumi.

　　　A series of leaflets of various dates, containing basic laws and regulations, presented in parallel columns of Dari and Pushtu.

1931 Aspaturian, Vernon V.
　　　1980 Moscow's Afghan Gamble. New Leader 63:7-13.

1932 Atayee, M. Ibrahim
　　　1978 Terminology of Pashtun Tribal Customary Law and Usages. Kabul: Ministry of Education. Pp. 112.

1933 Baloch, Inayatullah
　　　1980 Afghanistan--Pashtunistan--Balochistan. Assen Politik 31(3):283-301.

1934 Baltabeav, D.
　　　1973 Bor'ba afganskogo naroda za ukeplenie politicheskoe nezavisimosti (1925-1929 gg.) [The Struggle of the Afghan People for the Strengthening of Political Independence, 1925-1929]. Unpublished Doctoral Dissertation. Tashkent Institut vostokovedeniia Akademii nauk Uzbekskoi SSR.

1935 Baluchistan Through the Ages
　　　1979 Selection from the British Government Records. 2 vols. London: E. J. Brill (Reprint of 1906 ed.). Pp. (1) 595; (2) 590. Vol. I: Geography and History. Vol. II: Tribes.

1936 Barfield, Thomas
　　　1980 Afghans Fight Old Battles in a New War. Asia. March-April:12-15, 46.

VI. POLITICAL STRUCTURE

1937   Bechtel, Marilyn
    1981 Afghanistan: The Proud Revolution. New World Review 49(1):4-15.

1938   Bechtel, Marilyn
    1981 Afghanistan: The Proud Revolution. New World Review 49(1):6-17.

1939   Bechtel, Marilyn
    1981 Afghanistan Revisited: A New Society Takes Shape. New World Review 49(5):6-11.

1940   Beneva, Abdul Raouf
    1950 Pashtoonistan. Afghanistan 5(1):10-24.

A nationalistic view of the history of the Pushtunistan movement.

1941   Beneva, Abdul Raouf
    1951 Pushtunistan. Kabul: Department of Press. Pp. 480. (in Pushtu).

1942   Beneva, Abdul Raouf
    1951 Pushtunistan [Pushtunistan]. Kabul: Matba'eh yi 'umumi. Pp. 480; folding map; bibliography. (1330 A.H.)

A very lengthy work in Pushtu, tracing the history of the area of so-called Pushtunistan from early times to the present. A host of transliterated or transcribed references are given in the bibliography, and the folding map illustrates the maximum area claimed for Pushtunistan. The most pertinent interest lies in the account of individuals curently active in the movement.

1943   Beneva, Abdul Raouf
    1952 Les leaders actuels du Pashtounistan [The Real Leaders of Pushtunistan]. Afghanistan 7(3):6-32.

Brief biographies of the Fakir of Ipi, Khan Abdul Ghafar Khan, and several other leaders of the movement.

1944   Bernstein, Carl
    1981 Arms for Afghanistan. New Republic (July)18:8-10.

1945   Beugel, Ernst van der
    1980 After Afghanistan. Survival 22(6):242-247.

VI. POLITICAL STRUCTURE

1946   Bhaneja, Balwant
            1973 Afghanistan: Political Modernizatin of a Mountain
            Kingdom. New Delhi: Spectra Publications. Pp. 87.

1947   Bierman, John
            1981 Russia's Afghan Enemy. New Republic, June 6:10-11.

1948   Blechman, Barry M. and Douglas M. Hart
            1980 Afghanistan and the 1946 Iran Analogy. Survival
            22(6):248-253.

1949   Borcke, A. V.
            1980 Invasion of Afghanistan - End of the Soviet-Policy
            of Coexistence. Beitrage Zur Konfliktforschung 1:29-47.

1950   Braker, H.
            1980 Iran, Afghanistan and Soviet Middle-East Policy.
            Europa Archiv 35(7):227-236.

1951   Brides, Lord Saint
            1981 New Perspectives South of the Hindu Kush. International Security 5(3):164-170.

1952   Broenner, Wolfram
            1980 Afghanistan-Revolution und Konterrevolution.
            Frankfurt: Verlag Marxistische. Pp. 277.

1953   Bujtar, August von
            1949 Ob Mann Afghanistan Kritizieren Darf? [Dare One
            Criticize Afghanistan?] Afghanistan 4(2):32-33.

        Stresses the need to know the ocuntry and its people
        before passing judgments.

1954   Burrell, R. M. and Alvin J. Cottrell
            1974 Iran, Afghanistan, Pakistan: Tensions and Dilemmas.
            The Washington Papers, Center for Strategic and International Studies 2(20). Beverly Hills: Sage Publications.

1955   Buultjens, Ralph
            1980 India, Afghanistan and U.S. Foreign Policy. America
            142(6):114-117.

1956   Canfield, Robert L.
            1980 Afghanistan. Washington University Magazine:44-49.

        The author provides a brief summary of current conditions
        in Afghanistan.

VI. POLITICAL STRUCTURE

1957   Canfield, Robert L.
            1981   Soviet Gambit in Central Asia. Journal of South
                Asian and Middle Eastern Studies 5(1):10-30.

1958   Caroe, Olaf
            1961   The North-West Frontier, Old and New. Royal Central
                Asian Journal 48(3/4):289-298.

            A discussion of the Pathan character and the origins of
            the Pushtunistan dispute, related to the genealogy of the
            Afghans.

1959   Caroe, Olaf
            1980   Afghanistan: The Strategic After-Effects of India's
                Partition. Round Table 278:129-131.

1960   Castagne, Joseph
            1921   Notes sur la politique extérieure de l'Afghanistan.
                Missions et traites, étude accompagńe d'annexes
                importantes, constitutions, monnaies, ordres afghans
                [Notes on the Foreign Policy of Afghanistan. Missions
                and Treaties, a Study Accompanied by Important Annexes,
                Constitutions, Monetary System, Afghan Decorations].
                Revue du Monde Musulman 48:1-74.

1961   Chaffetz, D.
            1980   Afghanistan in Turmoil. International Affairs 1:15-
                36. New York

1962   Chang, Y. C.
            1980   The Afghanistan Crisis and Relations Between
                Communist-China and Pakistan. Issues and Studies
                16(6):51-66.

1963   Charpentier, C. J.
            1979   One Year After the Saur-Revolution. Afghanistan
                Journal 6(4):117-120.

1964   Charters, David
            1980   Resistance to the Soviet Occupation of Afghanistan:
                Problems and Prospects. Conflict Quarterly 1:8-15.

1965   Chinoy, Mike
            1980   Afghanistan: War and Resistance. Eastern Horizon
                19(8):24-31.

1966   Chretien, Jean-Pierre
            1980   Nous Sommes Tous Des Feodaux Afghans. Esprit 2
                (M1667):28-32.

VI. POLITICAL STRUCTURE

1967 Chubin, Shahram
    1980 The Northern Tier in Disarray. World Today 35:474-482.

1968 Cleveland, Harlan and Andrew J. Goodpaster with Joseph J. Wolf
    1980 After Afghanistan--The Long Haul: Safeguarding Security and Independence in the Third World (The Atlantic Council's Working Group on Security Affairs). Atlantic Quarterly 18(1):27-41.

1969 Cohen, R.
    1979 Human-Rights in Afghanistan. Worldview 22(11):27-29.

1970 Concerning a Statement Made by the Governor-General of Pakistan
    1949 Afghanistan 4(1):43-44.

Questions whether the speaker could have made the "astounding and deeply regrettable" statement that "the Government of Pakistan considers that the Tribal Area form a part of Pakistan.

1971 Constitution of Afghanistan
    1964 9 Mizan 1343-1 (October 1964). Kabul: Education Press. Pp. 62.

Also available, but not separately listed, are editions in Pushtu, in Dari, and in French.

1972 Cummins, Ian
    1980 Afghanistan: "The Great Game" or the Domino Theory. Australian Outlook 34(2):141-147.

1973 Current Afghan Observations on Pashtonistan
    n.d. Kabul: The Government Central Press. Pp. 14. (1955?).

Contains statements made to the press in 1954 by the Prime Minister and the Minister of Foreign Affairs of Afghanistan on the subject of Pushtunistan.

1974 Dallin, A.
    1980 Russia's Afghanistan Move. Center Magazine 1980(3):2-6.

1975 Demchenko, P.
    1980 Afghanistan Enters a New Era. International Affairs June:114-20. Moscow.

VI. POLITICAL STRUCTURE

1976   Democratic Republic of Afghanistan
        1980   Undeclared War: Armed Intervention and Other Forms of Interference in the Internal Affairs of the Democratic Republic of Afghanistan. Kabul: Information Department, DRA Ministry of Foreign Affairs. Pp. 63.

1977   Democratic Republic of Afghanistan
        1980   White Book of the Democratic Republic of Afghanistan. Kabul: Information Department, DRA Ministry of Foreign Affairs. Pp. 158.

1978   Denitch, B.
        1980   After Afghanistan - Round 2. Dissent 27(3):270-272.

1979   Deutsches Orient-Institut
        1981   Afghanistan Seit Dem Struz Der Monarchie: Dokumentation Zur Politik, Wirtschaft Und Bevölkerung [Afghanistan Since the Overthrow of the Monarchy: Documents on Politics, Economics and Demography]. Hamburg: Deutsches Orient-Institut. Pp. 298; index; maps; bibliography.

        A reference book by German experts dealing with Afghan economy, politics, and demography. Documents and bibliography cover the period after 1973.

1980   Dil, Shaheen F.
        1977   The Cabal in Kabul: Great-Power Interaction in Afghanistan. American Political Science Review 71(2):468-476.

1981   Djabarov, A.
        1981   Afghanistan: The Revolutionary Process is Irreversible. Soviet Military Review 3:6-10.

1982   Djan-Zirakyar, Rahmat Rabi
        1978   Stammesgesellschaft, Nationalstaat und Irredentismus am Beispiel der Pashtunistanfrage. Ph. D. Dissertation. Pp. 344.

1983   Djilas, Milovan
        1980   Confusions About Afghanistan: Analyzing the Soviet Strategy. New Leader 63:5-6.

1984   Dor, R.
        1979   Nouvel Exil pour les Kirghiz? Afghanistan Journal 6(1):24-27.

VI. POLITICAL STRUCTURE

1985   Dor, R.
          1981 Noevelle des Refugies. Afghanistan Journal 8(1):24-29.

1986   Dorbieu, Paul-Louis
          1977 Afghanistan: De la royaute a la republique [Afghanistan: From Royalty to Republic]. Defense National 33(12):83-106.

1987   Dupree, Louis
          1963 A Suggested Pakistan-Afghanistan-Iran Federation. Middle East Journal 17(4):383-399.

1988   Dupree, Louis
          1963 Tribalism, Regionalism, and National Oligarchy: Afghanistan. In Expectant Peoples: Nationalism and Development. Edited by K. H. Silvert. New York: Random House. Pp. 41-76.

1989   Dupree, Louis
          1965 Afghanistan in the Twentieth Century. Royal Central Asian Society Journal 52(1):20-30.

1990   Dupree, Louis
          1966 Afghanistan: A Monarchy in the Mountains. In The Nations of Asia. Edited by Donald N. Wilber. New York: Hart Publishing Company. Pp. 34-63.

1991   Dupree, Louis
          1966 Islam in Politics: Afghanistan. The Muslim World 56(4):269-276.

1992   Dupree, Louis
          1967 The Political Uses of Religion: Afghanistan. In Churches and States: The Religious Institution and Modernization. Edited by AUSF Staff. New York: American Universities Field Staff. Pp. 195-212.

1993   Dupree, Louis
          1968 Democracy and the Military Base of Power. Middle East Journal 22(1):29-44.

1994   Dupree, Louis
          1969 Afghanistan and the Unpaved Road to Democracy. Royal Central Asian Journal 56(3):272-278.

1995   Dupree, Louis
          1971 Political Processes in Afghanistan, 1963 to 1971. Asia 22:1-19.

VI. POLITICAL STRUCTURE

1996   Dupree, Louis
        1978 Language and Politics in Afghanistan. In Contributions to Asian Studies, XI (Languages and Civilization Change in South Asia). Edited by Clarence Maloney. Leiden: Brill. Pp. 131-141.

1997   Dupree, Louis
        1979 Afghanistan Under the Khalq. Problems of Communism 28:34-50.

1998   Dupree, Louis
        1979 Inside Afghanistan, Yesterday and Today: A Strategic Appraisal. Strategic Studies (Islamabad, Pakistan) 2(3):64-83.

1999   Dupree, Louis
        1981 Soviet Aid: The Afghan Lesson. Asiaweek, January 30:29-30.

2000   Durand, Algernon G. A.
        1974 The Making of a Frontier; Five Years' Experience and Adventures in Gilgit, Hunza, Nagar, Chitral, and the Eastern Hindukush. London: J. Murray, 1899. Pp. xvi, 298. Reprinted 1974.

2001   Dziegiel, Leszek
        1977 Afganistan--Wyspa Izolacji Czy Kraj Przemian Kulturowych. [Afghanistan--an Island of Isolation or a Country of Cultural Change?] Etnografia Polska 21(2):13-22.

2002   Eberhard, Wolfram
        1967 Afghanistan's Young Elite. In Settlement and Social Change in Asia. By Wolfram Eberhard. Hong Kong: Hong Kong University Press. Pp. 397-414.

2003   Eiva, Andrew
        1981 The Russian Invasion of Afghanistan: The Facts Behind the Takeover. Islamic Defense Review 6(1):7-12.

2004   Eliot, Theodore L., Jr.
        1979 Afghanistan After the 1978 Revolution. Strategic Review 7:57-62.

VI. POLITICAL STRUCTURE

2005 English Historian's Verdict on Durand Line
1949 Afghanistan 4(3):36-38.

A solicited statement from Dr. Codrington of London University, stressing the fact that the Durand Line divided the Pushtun tribes and adding that the present attitude of Pakistan is inexplicable.

2006 Far Eastern News Letter
1950 A New State--Pakhtunistan Emerges in Asia. Afghanistan 5(4):17-30.

Another view of the Afghan-Pakistan dispute.

2007 Farid, F.
1960 Afghanistan and the United States of America (A Study of their Relations). Unpublished M. A. Thesis. The American University.

2008 Fayz Muhammad Khan, Molla
1913 Siraj al-tavarikh [The Luminary of Histories]. Kabul. (1331 A.H.)

A history of Afghanistan down to the accession of Amir 'Abdul Rahman.

2009 Fenyvesi, C.
1980 Peace at Hand in Afghanistan - Soviet Maneuvers. New Republic 26:15-17.

2010 Firoz, M. M.
1949 Journey to Moghalgai of the Observer's Mission. Afghanistan 4(3):26-35.

An account of a trip made to escort representatives from ten countries to a site inside Afghanistan which had been attacked and bombed by a plane from Pakistan.

2011 Fleury, Antoine
1974 La Politique Allemande au Moyen-Orient, 1919-1939: Etude Comparative de la Pénétration de l'Allemagne en Turquie, en Iran et an Afghanistan [German Politics in the Middle East, 1919-1939: Comparative Study of Germany's Penetration into Turkey, Iran and Afghanistan.] Ph. D. Dissertation. Institut Universitaire de Haute Etudes Internationales. Geneve, Switzerland. Pp. 449.

VI. POLITICAL STRUCTURE

2012   Fleury, Antoine
        1977 La constitution d'un "bloc oriental": le pacte de Saadabad comme contributiona la secuite collective dans les annees trente [The Creation of an "Eastern Block": The Saadabad Pact as a Contribution to Collective Security in the 1930's]. Rev. d'Hist. de la Deuxieme Guere Mondiale 27(106):1-18.

2013   Foot, Rosemary
        1980 Afghanistan: Sino-Soviet Rivalry in Kabul. Round Table 280:434-442.

2014   Foot, Rosemary
        1980 The Changing Pattern of Afghanistan's Relations With its Neighbours. Asian Affairs 11:55-62.

2015   Fountain, R.
        1973 Afghanistan: Moving Slowly out of Obscurity. New Middle East 56: 22-24.

2016   Franck, Dorothea Seelye
        1952 Pakhtunistan--Disputed Disposition of a Tribal Land. Middle East Journal 6(1):49-68.

        A history of the territory separated from Afghanistan by the Durand Line and the cases for partition, independence, and federation. Includes a map.

2017   Franz, Erhard
        1973 Bevoelkerungsprobleme der Grenzgebiete zwischen Iran, Afghanistan und Pakistan. Orient 14:126-136.

2018   Fraser, Malcolm
        1980 Afghanistan--Australia's Assessment and Response. Australian Foreign Affairs Record 51:16-29.

2019   Fraser-Tytler, Sir W. Kerr
        1953 The Expulsion of Axis Nationals From Afghanistan. In The Middle East in the War (Survey of International Affairs 1939-1946). Second edition edited by George Kirk. Oxford University Press. Pp. 141-146.

        The most authoritative account of this action taken under pressure from the Western powers, as witnessed by the author, who was the British Minister at Kabul until October 1941.

VI. POLITICAL STRUCTURE

2020   Frohlich, Dieter
        1969 Nationalis und Nationalstaat in Entwicklungslandern: Probleme der Integration ethnischer Gruppen in Afghanistan [Nationalism and Nation State in Developing Countries: Problems of Integrating Ethnic Groups in Afghanistan]. Unpublished Ph. D. Dissertation. University of Köln. Pp. 250.

2021   Fromkin, David
        1980 The Great Game in Asia. Foreign Affairs 58(4):936-951. Spring.

2022   Fukuyama, Francis
        1980 The Future of the Soviet Role in Afghanistan: A Trip Report. Santa Monica, California: Rand Corporation. Pp. 31.

2023   Garrity, Patrick J.
        1980 The Soviet Military Stake in Afghanistan: 1956-79. Journal of the Royal United Services Institute for Defence Studies 125:31-36.

2024   Ghani, Ashraf
        1980 Afghanistan's Sorrow and Pity. Natural History 89(7):64-77.

2025   Da Gharbi Pakistan Yunitt [The Western Unit of Pakistan]
        1954 Kabul. Pp. 38. (1333 A.H.)

A pamphlet in Pushtu by the Afghan Government as a position paper.

2026   Ghosh, K. P.
        1955 Afghanistan in World Affairs. Contemporary Review 1073:325-327.

Touches on Afghan government and relations with the United States and the Soviet Union, ending wih a pro-Afghan resumé of the Pushtunistan issue.

2027   Ghosh, K. P.
        1954 Afghanistan in World Affairs. Afghanistan 9(4):51-55.

Afghanistan's efforts to become financially and culturally modernized and to maintain friendly relations with the larger powers, though remaining always independent.

VI. POLITICAL STRUCTURE

2028 Ghubar, M.
1947 The Eastern Provinces of Afghnistan. Afghanistan 2(3):22-36.

Discusses the separation of these regions from Afghanistan and the current situation in the area.

2029 Gillett, Sir Michael
1966 Afghanistan. Royal Central Asian Journal 53(3):238-244.

A review of political developments from September 1953 to October 1964.

2030 Glaesner, Heinz
1974 Das Dritte Reich und der Mittlere Osten: politische und wirtschaftliche Beziehungen Deutschlands zur Turkeir 1933-1939, zu Iran 1933-1941 und zu Afghanistan 1933-1941. [The Third Reich and the Middle East: Political and Economic Relations between Germany and Turkey, 1933-1939; Germany and Iran, 1933-1941; and Germany and Afghanistan, 1933-1941]. Unpublished Ph. D. Dissertation. University of Wurzburg. Pp. xxvi, 625.

2031 Gochenour, Theodore S.
1965 A New Try for Afghanistan. Middle East Journal 19(1):1-19.

Discussion of trends, particularly those relating to the adoption of a new constitution in 1964.

2032 Goldman, Marshall I.
1980 What is the Soviet Union up to in the Middle East? Middle East Review 12(3):5-8.

2033 Gortemaker, Manfred
1980 Afghanistan und die Entspannungspolitik. Osteuropa 30(6):469-480.

2034 Griffith, William E.
1980 Super-power Relations After Afghanistan. Survival 22(4):6-9.

2035 Griffiths, John C.
1981 Afghanistan: Key to a Continent. Boulder, Colorado: Westview Press. Pp. 225.

VI. POLITICAL STRUCTURE

Deals with history, society, polity and culture. Includes an analysis of possible motives for the Soviet invasion of Afghanistan and discusses alternatives for the future. Based in part, on speculations.

2036 Gupta, Bhabani Sen
1980 The USSR in Asia: an Interperceptional Study of Soviet-Asian Relations; with a Critique of Soviet Role in Afghanistan. New Delhi: Young Asia Publications. Pp. 514.

2037 Hacker, J.
1980 Afghanistan and the Consequences. Osteuropa 30(7):599-614.

2038 Haggerty, Jerome J.
1980 Afghanistan--the Great Game. Military Review 60:37-44.

2039 Hall, Gus
1980 What Really Happened in Afghanistan? Political Affairs 59:1-8.

2040 Halliday, Fred
1978 Revolution in Afghanistan. New Left Review 112:3-44.

2041 Halliday, Fred
1979 Afghanistan--A Revolution Consumes Itself. The Nation. November 17:492-495.

2042 Halliday, Fred
1979 The Arc of Revolutions: Iran, Afghanistan, South, Yemen, Ethiopia. Race and Class 20(4):373-390.

2043 Halliday, Fred
1980 The War and Revolution in Afghanistan. New Left Review 119:20-41.

2044 Halliday, Fred
1980 Wrong Moves on Afghanistan. The Nation. January 26:70-73.

2045 Halliday, Fred
1981 Afghanistan Now. The Nation. January 17:48-52.

2046 Hamid, Abdul Aziz
1974 An Analysis of Decision-Making in the Elementary School Curriculum and Textbook Development Project in

VI. POLITICAL STRUCTURE

Afghanistan. Unpublished Ph. D. Dissertation. Columbia Teachers College. Pp. 208.

2047 Hamaoui, Ernest
1973 La fonction publique en Afghanistan. International Review of Administrative Sciences 39(3):259-264.

2048 Hanifi, M. Jamil
1962 United States-Soviet Union Economic Aid to Afghanistan: A Comparative Study. Unpublished M. A. Thesis. Michigan State University. Pp. 124.

A description and comparison of U.S.-Soviet economic aid to Afghanistan in the context of political and economic conditions and processes in that country.

2049 Hannah, Norman B.
1979 Afghanistan: The Great Gamble. Asian Affairs: An American Review 6(3):187-195.

2050 Harrison, Selig S.
1978 Nightmare in Baluchistan. Foreign Policy 32:136-160.

2051 Harrison, Selig S.
1980 Dateline Afghanistan: Exit Through Finland. Foreign Affairs 4:163-167.

2052 Harrison, Selig S.
1981 Baluch Nationalism and Superpower Rivalry. International Security 5(3):152-163.

2053 Harrison, Selig S.
1981 In Afghanistan's Shadow: Baluch Nationalism and Soviet Temptation. Washington, D.C.: Carnegie Endowment for International Peace. Pp. 228.

2054 Hasan, Zubeida
1964 The Policy of Afghanistan. Pakistan Horizon 17(1)48-57.

A good, documented survey of the country's foreign policy goals.

2055 Hashimzai, Mohammed Qasem
1975 The Judiciary in Afghanistan. Kabul: Government Printing Press. Pp. 26.

VI. POLITICAL STRUCTURE

A brief description of the organization of the Judiciary system of Afghanistan.

2056 Hassas, Burhanoddin
1974 Afghanistan's Policies in the United Nations, 1947-1967. Unpublished Ph. D. Dissertation. The Pennsylvania State University. Pp. 314.

Examines Afghanistan's role in the United Nations including its entry, policies and voting record. Attention is given to Afghanistan's position on the question of decolonization, Palestine and the general crisis in the Middle East.

2057 Hauner, Milan
1980 The Significance of Afghanistan - Lessons From the Past. Round Table (279):240-244.

2058 Hauner, Milan
1981 The Soviet Threat to Afghanistan and Indai, 1938-1940. Modern Asian Studies 15(2):287-309.

2059 Heller, Mark
1980 The Soviet Invasion of Afghanistan: Motivations and Implications. Center for Strategic Studies, Tel-Aviv University, Ramat-Aviv, Israel.

2060 Heywad [Homeland]
1949- This weekly paper of the Pushtunistan movement began publication at Kabul about 1949. The contents are in Pushtu.

2061 Hough, Jerry F.
1980 Why the Russians Invaded. The Nation, March 1:225; 232-233.

2062 Hussain, Syed Shabir, et al
1980 Afghanistan Under Soviet Occupation. Islamabad: World Affairs Publications. Pp. 208.

2063 Hyman, Anthony
1979 Afghanistan: Unpopular Revolution. Round Table 275:222-226.

2064 Hyman, Anthony
1980 Afghan/Pakistan Border Disputes. Asian Affairs 11:264-275.

VI. POLITICAL STRUCTURE

2065 Ihlau, Olaf
1981 Inside Afghanistan. World Press Review 28(9):29-31.

2066 Imbeck, Klaus
1980 Mit Allah gegen die Schurawi. Ein Bericht mit Schwarzweißfotos aus dem Besitzde Mudschahedin. Geo-Das neue Bild der Erde 8:60-76.

2067 Indian News Chronicle
1950 Afghanistan's Desire for Friendly Relations with Pakistan: Najib-Ullah Khan Explains Cause of Pukhtoonistan. Afghanistan 5(1):40-45.

Afghanistan's peaceable interest in a free Pushtunistan is stated by Najib-Ullah.

2068 Ingram, Edward
1973 A Preview of the Great Game in Asia. Middle Eastern Studies 9(1):3-18, (2):157-174, (3):296-314.

2069 Ingram, Edward
1974 A Preview of the Great Game in Asia. Middle Eastern studies 10(1).

2070 I'timadi, Muhammad Akbar Khan
n.d. Tasvib-i Ruz-i Pushtunistan [Approval of Pushtunistan Day]. Kabul: Matba'eh-yi 'umumi. Pp. 101.

A work in Dari, probably printed between 1950 nd 1954, reflecting a speech delivered in the National Assembly.

2071 Jadeer, Habiburrahman (trans)
1977 Articles on al-Afghani by Egyptian Writers. Kabul: Baihaqi Publishing House. Pp. 335. (1355 A.H.)

2072 Jafri, Hasan Ali Shah
1976 Indo-Afghan Relations, 1947-67. New Delhi: Sterling Publishers. Pp. vi, 192.

A descriptive discussion of relations between post colonial India and Afghanistan with emphasis on economic and political matters.

2073 Jakel, Klaus
1978 Nur Muhammad Tarakai. Afghanistan Journal (3):105-108.

VI. POLITICAL STRUCTURE

2074 Jones, Schuyler
1974 Men of Influence in Nuristan: A Study of Social Control and Dispute Settlement in Waigal valley, Afghanistan. New York: Seminar Press. Pp. xii, 299.

An ethnographic study of political behavior among the Kalasha of Nuristan, Afghanistan. A first such study published about a society in Nuristan.

2075 Kabir, Mukhammed
1973 Nalogi i valogovaia sistema Afganistana [The Taxes and Tax System of Afghanistan]. Unpublished Ph. D. Dissertation. Kievskii institut narodnogo khoziaistva. Kiev, Ukraine SSR.

2076 Kamali, M. Hashim
1976 Matrimonial Problems of Islamic Law in Contemporary Afghanistan. Unpublished Ph. D. Dissertation. University of London. Pp. 309.

2077 Kamlin, M.
1980 Russia in Afghanistan - Piercing a Window, or Bursting the Floodgates. Asia Pacific Community 8:67-93.

2078 Kapur, Harish
1966 Soviet Russia and Asia, 1917-1927: A Study of Soviet Policy Towards Turkey, Iran, and Afghanistan. London: The Geneva Graduate Institute of International Studies. Pp. 266.

2079 Karimi, A. R.
1946 The Constitution of Afghanistan. Afghanistan 1(1):3-8.

An analysis of the provisions of the constitution adopted in 1931.

2080 Karmal, Babrak
1980 The New Stage of the Afghan Revolutin. New World Review 48(2):11-13.

2081 Kazemi, Shamsuzakir
1970 Aspects of the Afghan Tax System. Unpublished Ph. D. Dissertation. University of Glasgow. Pp.373.

2082 Kennan, George F.
1980 Imprudent Response to the Afghan Crisis? Bulletin of Atomic Scientists 36(4):7-9.

VI. POLITICAL STRUCTURE

2083   Khairzada, Faiz and Ralph H. Magnus
        1981 Afghanistan From Independence to Occupation. Boulder, Colorado: Westview Press. Pp. 300.

2084   Khalfin, Naftula
        1981 British Plots Against Afghanistan: Pages From History. Moscow: Novotsi Press Agency. Pp. 99.

2085   Khalid Khan
        1950 Afghan Minority in Pakistan. Afghanistan 5(1):48-49.

        Khalid Khan's protest to the United Nations over Pakistan's imprisonment of thousands of Pushtun Nationals.

2086   Khalil, Hakim Taj Mohamed
        n.d. March of Pakhtoonistan. Bombay: Art Litho and Printing Press. Pp. 38. (1950?).

        Short articles by Afghans resident in India and excerpts from the Afghan and Indian press on the subject in question.

2087   Khalilzad, Zalmay
        1979/80 The Superpowers and the Northern Tier. International Security 4:6-30.

2088   Khalilzad, Zalmay
        1980 Afghanistan and the Crisis in American Foreign Policy. Survival 22(4).

2089   Khalilzad, Zalmay
        1980 The Return of the Great Game: Superpower Rivalry and Domestic Turmoil in Afghanistan, Iran, Pakistan, and Turkey. Santa Monica, California: California Seminar on International Security and Foreign Policy. Pp. 84.

2090   Khalilzad, Zalmay
        1980 Soviet-Occupied Afghanistan. Problems of Communism, November-December:23-40.

2091   Khalilzad, Zalmay
        1980 The Struggle for Afghanistan. Survey, A Journal of East and West Studies 25(2):189-216.

2092   Khalilzad, Zalmay
        1980 The Superpowers and the Northern Tier. International Security 4(3):6-30.

VI. POLITICAL STRUCTURE

2093 Khouri, Fred J.
    1980 The U.S. and Iran, Afghanistan, and the Arab-Israeli Conflict. New Outlook, September/October:20-23.

2094 Kimche, Jon
    1981 An Islamic "Munich". Midstream 27(4):3-7.

    Discusses the Islamic summit held at Taif, Saudi Arabia, and points out how the Summit failed in responding effectively to the Afghan problem.

2095 Klass, R. T.
    1979 The Tragedy of Afghanistan. Asian Affairs 7:1-7.

2096 Kohzad, Ahmad Ali
    1951 Frontier Discord Between Afghanistan and Pakistan. Kabul: Government Press Department. Pp. 25.

    The Afghan government's views on Pushtunistan.

2097 Kohzad, Ahmad Ali
    1951 Frontier Discord between Afghanistan and Pakistan. Afghanistan 6(1):54-67.

    A comment on Sir George Cunningham's article in the Manchester Guardian. Mr. Kohzad objects to British support of Pakistan.

2098 Kohzad, Ahmad Ali
    1951 Le Différend afghano-pakistanais vu par Sir George Cunningham [The Afghan-Pakistan Discord Seen by Sir George Cunningham]. Afghanistan 6(2):44-56.

    An unfavorable--though temperate--comment on Sir George Cunningham's article in the Manchester Guardian.

2099 Kohzad, Ahmad Ali
    1951 La politique extérieure afghane [The Afghan Foreign Policy]. Afghanistan 6(3):1-10.

    In commenting on Sir Giles Frederick Squire's article in the Martin Review, Mr. Kohzad complains of a century of English intervention in Afghanistan, and of England's now considering Afghanistan as a "buffer-state."

2100 Kohzad, Ahmad Ali
    1953 L'Afghanistan au voisinage de l'Hindustan [Afghanistan as a Neighbor of Hindustan]. Afghanistan 8(3):60-66.

VI. POLITICAL STRUCTURE

The difficulties Afghanistan has suffered as a neighbor to Hindustan--from conquerors eager for the riches of Hindustan and, especially in the last century, from the colonizing English; ending inevitably with an argument for the independence of Pushtunistan.

2101 L'Abeille, Lucerne
1954 Regards vers l'Afghanistan. L'Afghanistan dans la presse mondiale [Glances toward Afghanistan. Afghanistan in the World Press]. Afghanistan 9(4):60-62.

A general description of the country and the people, recommending Afghanistan to those hardy enough to endure travel hardships.

2102 Le Jeune, E.
1980 Afghanistan - Complete Soviet Intervention. Socialisme 1980(157):87-102.

2103 Lerzezynski, G. L.
1929 Die Landeseinteilung Afghanistans [The Land-Divisions of Afghanistan]. Neue Orient 9(2/3):46-57.

Contains the translation into German of the 1922 ordinance concerning the administrative divisions of the country.

2104 Levin, I. D. (ed)
1956 Konstitutsii gosudarstvo blizhnego i strednego vostoka [Constitutions of the States of the Near and Middle East]. Moscow: Izdatel'stvo inostrannoy literaturï. Pp. 591.

Pages 9-28 contain the constitution of Afghanistan and notes on its history.

2105 Lewis, Henry James
1977 A Southwest Asian Region: Iran, Afghanistan, Pakistan and India. Unpublished M. A. Thesis. The American University. Pp. 201.

A study of cooperative interaction in Southwest Asia and an examination of the political, socio-cultural, strategic, and economic conditions in a regional context.

2106 Lorimer, J. G.
1934 Customary Law of the Main Tribes in the Peshawar District. Revised by J. G. Acheson. Peshawar.

VI. POLITICAL STRUCTURE

2107 Loy Pushtun [Great Pushtun]
1953 A monthly in Pushtu, which began publication at Kabul.

2108 Lunt, J. D.
1980 Afghanistan. Army Quarterly 110:5-8.

2109 Luttwak, Edward N.
1980 After Afghanistan What? Commentary 69:40-49.

2110 Magnus, Ralph Harry
1972 The Ideology and Organization of Royalist Revolutions: A Comparative Study of Iran's White Revolution and Afghanistan's New Democracy. Unpublished Ph. D. Dissertation. University of California, Berkeley.

2111 Magnus, Ralph Harry
1976 Biographical Review: Mohammad Zahir Khan, Former King of Afghanistan. Middle East Journal 30(1):77-80.

2112 Maidan, I. G.
1974 Vneshniaia politika Afganistana posle vtoroi mirovoi voiny 1945-1973 gg. [The Foreign Policy of Afghanistan after World War II, 1945-1973]. Unpublished Ph. D. Dissertation. Kiev, Ukrain SSR: Kievski universitet.

2113 Malhotra, Joginder K.
1980 Indiens Aussenpolitik und die Afghanistan-Krise. Dt. Studien 18(70):132-143.

2114 March of Pakhtoonistan
n.d. Bombay: Art Litho and Printing Press. Sketch map of "Pakhtoonistan." Pp. 38.

Short articles by various personalities and reprints of newspaper articles and radio broadcasts, all favoring Pushtunistan. Sponsor and principal writer is Hakim Taj Mohamed Khalil, President of the Pakhtoon Khudai Khidmatgar Jirga at Bombay.

2115 Masannat, George S.
1969 Development and Diplomacy in Afghanistan. Journal of Asian and African Studies 4(1):51-60.

VI. POLITICAL STRUCTURE

2116   Mayne, Peter
        1955 The Narrow Smile. London: John Murray. Pp. 264.

        A former R.A.F. officer, with a background of four years of service on the North-West Frontier and a knowledge of Pushtu, returned in 1953 to look up old friends. Part Two, pages 115-176, concerns his visit to Kabul and a discussion concerning Pushtunistan. The American edition of the sam year was entitled "Journey to the Pathans."

2117   McGeehan, Robert
        1980 Carter's Crises: Iran, Afghanistan and Presidential Politics. The World Today 36(5):163-171.

2118   Medvedev, Roy
        1980 The Afghan Crises. New Left Review 121:91-96.

2119   Mehnert, Klaus
        1979 Afghanistan und seine neuen Herren. Indo-Asia 21(1):23-30.

2120   Meissner, Boris
        1980 Position of the Soviet-Union on Intervention and the Case of Afghanistan. Beitrage Zur Konfliktforschung 10(2):31-64.

2121   Meissner, Boris
        1980 Soviet Foreign Policy and Afghanistan. Aussen Politik 31(3):260-282.

2122   Menon, Rajan
        1979 Soviet Policy in the Indian Ocean Region. Current History 176-92.

2123   Middle East Research and Information Project (89)
        1980 This issued of this monthly journal deals exclusively with Afghanistan. Two articles, two interviews, and four documents are included. MERIP Reports deal mostly with the Middle East comprising of the Arab Middle East and Iran. This is their first attempt at Afghanistan, perhaps stimulated by the recent events in that country.

2124   Mieczkowski, Seiko
        1980 Afghanistan: Massive Soviet Invasion. Asian Thought and Society 5(13):85-88.

VI. POLITICAL STRUCTURE

2125   Mikhailov, K.
1980 Provocatory Campaign Over Afghanistan. Foreign Affairs March:97-100. Moscow.

2126   Mir Munshi, Sultan Muhammed Kahn
1900 The Constitution and Laws of Afghanistan. London: John Murray. Pp. vii, 164.

A scholarly study by the former State Secretary of Amir Abdul Rahman. Gives the constitution as promulgated by that ruler, together with his reasons for that action. Other aspects of Afghan law are also presented, but the entire subject is too much based on European writings on Muslem law.

2127   Mirnov, L. and G. Polyakov
1979 Afganistan: the Beginning of a New Life. International Affairs March:46-54. Moscow.

2128   Misra, K. P. (ed)
1981 Afghanistan in Crisis. New Delhi: Vikas Publishing House.

A compilation of articles expressing the Indian view of current political dynamics in Afghanistan. One chapter is devoted to a bibliography of material dealing with the Afghanistan crisis between April 1978 and June 1980.

2129   Missen, Francois
1980 Le syndrome de Kaboul--un Afghan Reconte. Aix-en-Provence: Edisud. Pp. 185.

2130   Modenov, S.
1980 Afghanistan's Constructive Proposals. International Affairs. (August):98-101. (Moscow).

2131   Monks, Alfred L.
1981 The Soviet Intervention in Afghanistan. Washington: American Enterprise Institute for Public Policy Research. Pp. 60.

2132   Mu'ahadeh Fi-mobayne Rus va-Afghanistan [Treaty Between Russia and Afganistan]
1921 Kabul. Pp. 6.

The Persian text of the Afghan-Russian treaty of 1921.

VI. POLITICAL STRUCTURE

2133 Mukerjee, D.
1975 Afghanistan Under Daud - Relations with Neighboring States. Asian Survey 15(4):301-312.

2134 Mustafa, Zubeida
1975 Afghanistan and Asian Power Balance. Pacific Community 6(2):283-299.

2135 Mustafa, Zubeida
1978 Pakistan-Afghanistan Relations and Central Asian Politics (1973-1978). Pakistan Horizon 31(4):14-37.

2136 Naby, Eden
1980 The Ethnic Factor in Soviet-Afghan Relations. Asian Survey 20(3):237-256.

Discusses ethnolinguistic diversity in Afghanistan and analyses the implications of such in Afghanistan and the conditions of the same order in Soviet Central Asia. Speculates about the future configuration of the Afghan state and relevant potential problems and prospects.

2137 Najibullah Khan
1948 Speech Delivered over the Radio. Afghanistan 38(2):1-38.

An introductory notice of the situation among the Pushtun tribes is followed by an acocunt of a trip of the author--then Acting Minister of Education--to Pakistan, where he discussed the need for the autonomy of "Afghan" tribes within Pakistan and other subjects with the highest officials of the neighboring country.

2138 Najibullah Khan
1949 Speech Delivered by His Excellency Najibullah Khan, Afghanistan Representative to the Indonesian Conference Held in New Delhi. Afghanistan 4(1):37-40.

Supports the nationalistic aspirations of the Indonesian people and refers to Pushtunistan.

2139 Najibullah Khan
1950 Puktonnistan Question: A Survey. Afghanistan 5(3):52-57.

Another review of the Afghan-Pakistan dispute.

VI. POLITICAL STRUCTURE

2140   Najibullah Khan
        1950 Cultural Traditions of Afghanistan. Afghanistan 5(4):40-45.

A brief cultural history--which becomes in the end political--with empahsis on cultural relations with India and Iran.

2141   Najibullah Khan
        1951 Statement Given by His Excellency Dr. Najibullah, Ambassador for Afghanistan in India on the Eleventh of August, 1951. Afghanistan 6(3):38-42.

A defense of Afghanistan against Pakistan's accusations.

2142   Najibullah Khan
        1952 Dr. Najibullah's Press Conference on the 19th June, 1952. Afghanistan 7(3):45-50.

A denial of Pakistan's report that there is danger for foreigners flying between Afghanistan and India, and protesting a ban on Afghan-Indian air communication.

2143   Najibullah Khan
        1953 Dr. Najibullah's Statement in New Delhi. Afghanistan 8(2):31-32.

A reaffirmation of Afghanistan's position with regard to Pushtunistan.

2144   Najibullah Khan
        1953 Dr. Najibullah Khan's Statement on Pashtoonistan Day. Afghanistan 8(3):45.

Afghanistan's duty to support Pushtunistan, meanwhile keeping peaceful relations with India.

2145   National Assembly
        1947 Afghanistan 2(2):47-48.

Features an abstract of the speech from the throne delivered to the Sixth Session of the National Assembly on May 22, 1947.

2146   Nayar, Kuldip
        1981 Report on Afghanistan. New Delhi: Allied Publishers. Pp. 194.

VI. POLITICAL STRUCTURE

A journalist's attempt at covering the post April 1978 political events in Afghanistan.

2147 Neal, F. W.
1980 Afghanistan - A Created Crisis. Bulletin of the Atomic Scientists 36(8):10-11.

2148 Negaran, Hannah (Pseudonym)
1979 The Afghan Coup of April 1978: Revolution and International Security. Orbus 23(1):93-113.

2149 Negaran, Hannah (Pseudonym)
1979 Afghanistan: A Marxiat Regime in a Muslim Society. Current History 76(446):172-175.

2150 Neumann, Robert G.
1979 Afghanistan Under the Red Flag. In The Impact of the Iranian Events Upon Persian Gulf and U. S. Security. Washington: American Foreign Policy Institute. Pp. 128-148.

2151 Newell, Nancy Peabody and Richard S.
1981 The Struggle for Afghanistan. Ithaca: Cornell University Press. Pp. 236.

The book is among the first to tackle the complex reason for the Soviet invastion of Afghanistan in December 1979. A number of reasons, among them, the Soviet desire for security along its southern border, fear of the emergence of a Muslim regime in that country, are offered for the invastion of Afghanistan.

2152 Newell, Richard S.
1969 Afghanistan: The Dangers of Cold War Generostiy. Middle East Journal 23(2):168-178.

2153 Newell, Richard S.
1972 The Politics of Afghanistan. Ithaca: Cornell University Press. Pp. 236.

The book primarily deals with the changing objectives and features of local and provincial government and the rapidly expanding administrative requirements brought about by economic, political, and social change in Afghanistan.

2154 Newell, Richard S.
1979 Revolution und Rebellion in Afghanistan. Europa-Archiv 21:662-672.

VI. POLITICAL STRUCTURE

2155   Newell Richard S.
        1979 Revolution and Revolt in Afghanistan. World Today 35(11):432-442.

2156   Newell, Richard S.
        1980 Islam and the Struggle for Afghan National Liberation. In Islam in the Contemporary World. Edited by Cyriac K. Pullapilly. South Bend, Indiana: Cross Roads Books. Pp. 251-260.

2157   Newell, Richard S.
        1980 Soviet Intervention in Afghanistan. The World Today 36(7):250-258.

2158   Newell, Richard S.
        1981 International Response to the Afghanistan Crisis. The World Today 37(5):172-181.

2159   Nizamnameh-yi Tashkilat-i Asasiyeh Afghanistan [Compendium of the Fundamental Laws of the Organization of Afghanistan]
        1926 Kabul: Rafiq Zivar Printing House. Pp. 108 and 7. (1305 A.H.)

        The Persian text of the country's first constitution.

2160   Noller, J. F.
        1980 Soviet Intervention in Afghanistan Reflected in the East-German Press. Gegenwartskunde Gesellschaft Staat Erziehung 29(3):333-335.

2161   Noorani, A. G.
        1980 Afghanistan and the Rule of Law. International Commission of Jurists Review:37-52. June.

2162   O'Ballance, Edgar
        1980 Soviet Tactics in Afghanistan. Militiary Review 60:45-52.

2163   Odell, Ernest
        1948 Afghanistan. Contemporary Review 988:240-244. London.

        Discusses Afghanistan's concern for the future of tribal groups along the North-West Frontier and the probable reasons for this concern.

VI. POLITICAL STRUCTURE

2164　On Sir Zaferullah Khan's Statement
　　　　1949　Afghanistan 4(2):28-31.

　　　　The Afghan writer objects to the statement that there is no problem to be solved between Afghanistan and Pakistan: the issue is said to be the right of the frontier Afghans to self-determination.

2165　Oren, Stephen
　　　　1974　The Afghani Coup and the Peace of the Northern Tier. World Today 30(1):26-32.

2166　Oren, Stephen
　　　　1974　Threatening Polarization of Mid East - Foreign Policy of Afghanistan Revolution. Europa Archiv 29(2):55-62.

2167　Overholt, William
　　　　1980　The Geopolitics of the Afghan War. Asian Affairs 7(4):205-217.

2168　Ozaki, R.
　　　　1980　Poverty, Political Strife, Pave Way for Afghan Intervention. Business Japan (4):38-48.

2169　Pachter, H.
　　　　1980　After Afghanistan--Round 3. Dissent 27(4):393-396.

2170　The Pakhtun Question
　　　　n.d.　Hove (Sussex). Pp. 60.

　　　　A publication, presumed to come from the Afghan Information Bureau at London, which deals with the Pushtunistan question.

2171　Pakhtunistan
　　　　1950-　Delhi: Coronation Press. n.p.

　　　　Fortnightly magazine published at Delhi in 1950, 1951, etc.

2172　Pakhtunistan Day (9th of Sunbola 1328 A.H.)
　　　　n.d.　Hove (Sussex): Key Press. Pp. 31.

　　　　Celebrates the hoisting of the flag of "Independent Paktunistan" on September 2, 1949. A summary of the history and background of the movement.

VI. POLITICAL STRUCTURE

2173 Le Pakistan et la Ligue Musulmane [Pakistan and the Muslim League]
1952 Afghanistan 7(1):56-59.

On whether the Pakistan Prime Minister should also be the president of the Muslim League.

2174 Pazhwak, Abdur Rahman
n.d. Paktunistan. The Khyber Pass as the Focus of the New State of Pakhtunistan. Hove (Sussex): Key Press, Ltd. Pp. 153; bibliography; sketch map. (1954?).

This is a later version of a booklet issued in 1951 by the Afghan Information Bureau in London, entitled "The Pushtun Question," and is sponsored by the same organization. A number of chapters describe the area in question, the people and their language and literature, the more recent history of the area, and the origin and growth of the dispute over the future of the region. The sketch map depicts the boundaries of "Pakhtunistan."

2175 Philips, James
1979 Afghanistan: Islam Versus Marxism. Journal of Social and Political Studies 4:305-320.

2176 Pickard, Cyril
1980 Afghanistan: Difficult Decisions for the West. Round Table 278:132-137.

2177 Pomeroy, William
1979 The New People's Republic of Afghanistan. New World Review 47:12-15.

2178 Pomeroy, William
1980 Afghanistan: Why Soviet Troops Intervened. New World Review 48(2):6-11.

2179 Poullada, Leon B.
1969 Some International Legal Aspects of Pushtunistan Dispute. Afghanistan 21(4):10-36.

2180 Poullada, Leon B.
1970 The Pushtun Role in the Afghan Political System. New York: Afghanistan Council, Asia Society. Occasional Paper No. 1. Pp. 29.

VI. POLITICAL STRUCTURE

2181 Poullada, Leon B.
1970 Reform and Rebellion in Afghanistan, 1919-1929: King Amanullah's Failure to Modernize a Tribal Society. Ph. D. Dissertation. Princeton University. Pp. 548.

Analysis of Amanullah's modernization efforts with emphasis on the role of Pushtun tribes, including a discussion of the Pushtun social and political organization.

2182 Poullada, Leon B.
1973 Reform and Rebellion in Afghanistan, 1919-1929: King Amanullah's Failure to Modernize a Tribal Society. Ithaca: Cornell University Press. Pp. xvii, 318.

An in-depth description and comprehensive account of the political dynamics of Afghanistan during Amanullah's reign. Published version of Poullada. See no. 2181.

2183 Poullada, Leon B.
1981 Afghanistan and the United States: The Crucial Years. Middle East Journal 35(2):178-190.

2184 Poulos, John W.
1980 Democratic Republic of Afghanistan. In Constitutions of the Countries of the World. Dobbs Ferry, N.Y.: Oceana Publications.

Analysis of all the Afghan constitutions including documents issued by the present regime. A bibliography is included.

2185 Da Pushtunistan peh bab kay da Afghanistan Nazariyat [The Ideas of Afghanistan on Pushtunistan]
1954 Kabul. Pp. 35. (1333 A.H.)

A pamphlet with statements in Dari and Pushtu. Much of the material reflects the opinions of Prime Minister Mohammed Daoud.

2186 Qureshi, Saleem
1980 Marx or Mohammad: Communist Coups and Islamic Resistence in Afghanistan. Asian Thought and Society 5(13):32-46.

2187 Ramati, Yohanan
1980 The Gambit in Afghanistan. Midstream 26:3-7.

VI. POLITICAL STRUCTURE

2188   Ramazani, Rouhollah K.
      1966   The Northern Tier: Afghanistan, Iran and Turkey. Princeton: Van Nostrand. Pp. 142.

2189   Rand, Christopher
      1955   Crisis in Afghanistan. Commonweal 63(1):7-10.

      An American writer, recently in Afghanistan, discusses the elements of crisis: the Pushtunistan issue, the current Soviet efforts at economic penetration, and the general isolation of the country from international interest and concern.

2190   Ratebzad, Anahita
      1981   Afghanistan's Road to the Future. New World Review 49(4):8-11.

2191   Rathjens, Carl
      1956-57   Die Staats-und Wirtschaftstruktur Afghanistans [The Structures of State and of the Economy of Afghanistan]. Geographisches Taschenbuch. Pp. 382-392.

2192   Ratnam, Perala
      1981   Afghanistan:s Uncertain Future. New Delhi: Tulsi Publishing House. Pp. 87.

      A view providing justification for the Soviet invasion of Afghanistan. The author has extensive experience in the Indian foreign service.

2193   Rectanus, Earl Frank
      1966   Soviet-Afghanistan Relations, 1919-1965. Unpublished M.A. Thesis. The American University. Pp. 192.

      Presents the motivating factors behind Russian investments in Afghanistan and the extent to which they effect Afghan independence and United States' policy.

2194   Relations of Afghanistan and the Soviet Union, 1919-1969
      1970   (Dari and Russian volumes) Kabul: Royal Government Printing Press. Pp. 289.

      Published on the occasion of the 50th anniversary of Soviet-Afghan relations.

2195   Ridout, Christine F.
      1975   Authority Patterns and the Afghan Coup of 1973. Middle East Journal 29(2):165-178.

VI. POLITICAL STRUCTURE

2196 Rishtin, Sadiquallah
1952 Pushtun Yar [The Pushtun Friend]. Kabul: Matba'eh-yi 'umumi. Pp. 135. (1331 A.H.)

Articles and poems in Pushtu by leaders of the movement for Pushtunistan.

2197 Roucek, Joseph S.
1980 Afghanistan in Geopolitics. Ukrainian Quarterly 36:150-163.

2198 Roy, Olivier
1980 Afghanistan: La "Revolution" Par Le Vide Esprit 5(M1667):78-87.

2199 Roy, Olivier
1981 What is Afghanistan Really Like? Dissent (Winter):47-54.

2200 Royal Afghan Embassy, New Delhi
1950 Paktoons Determined to Achieve Independence. Afghanistan 5(1):46-47.

A protest against Pakistani propaganda in the Pushtunistan trouble.

2201 Rubinstein, Alvin Z.
1980 Soviet Imperialism in Afghanistan. Current History 79(459):80-83, 103-104.

2202 Rubiogarcia, L.
1975 Components of Modern Afghanistan 1. Historical perspective. Revista de Politica internacional 137:99-131.

2203 Rubiogarcia, L.
1975 Components of Modern Afghanistan 2. Revista de Politica Internacional 138:73-98.

2204 Rubiogarcia, L.
1975 Components of Modern Afghanistan 3. Revista de Politica Internacional 139:93-124.

2205 Rubiogarcia, L.
1975 Components of Modern Afghanistan 4. Revista de Politica Internacional 140:81-118.

VI. POLITICAL STRUCTURE

2206   Rubiogarcia, L.
1975 Components of Modern Afghanistan 5. Revista de Politica Internacional 141:149-176.

2207   Rudersdorf, Karl-Heinrich
1980 Afghanistan--Eine Sowjetrupublik? Hamburg: Rowohlt Taschenbuch. Pp. 173.

2208   Sablier, Edouard
1950 Au coeur de l'Asie un nouvel état est né: le Pouchtounistan [At the Heart of Asia a New State Is Born: Pushtunistan]. Afghanistan 5(4):13-16.

2209   Safari, Hamid
1974 Arduous Path of a New Republic. World Marxist Review 17(7):117-121.

2210   Samuelsson, Jan
1975 Islam i Afgahnistan--under kung Muhammed Zahir shah. En studie av moderniseringsprocessens foljder for islams stallning i Afghanistan [Islam in Afghanistan Under King Mohammed Zahir. A Study of the Consequences for Islam of the Process of Modernization in Afghanistan]. Unpublished Ph. D. Dissertation. University of Stockholm. Pp. vii, 122.

2211   Sareen, Anuradha
1975 India and Afghanistan, 1907-1921. Unpublished Ph. D. Disseration. Jawaharlal Nehru University. New Delhi. Pp. 275.

2212   Sayeed, Khalid B.
1969 Pathan Regionalism. South Atlantic Quarterly 63(4):478-506.

Analysis of political organization and political structure of the Pushtuns with emphasis on tribalism and multicentrism.

2213   Schinasi, May
1971 Siradj al Akhbar, L'opinion Afghane et la Russie [Siradj al Akhbar, Afghan opinion and Russia]. Cahiers du Monde Russe et Sovietique 12(4):467-479.

2214   Schinasi, May
1972 Siradj al-Akhbar: L'opinion Afghane et la Russie [Siradj al-akhbar: Afghan opinion and Russia]. Afghanistan 25(2):29-41.

VI. POLITICAL STRUCTURE

2215 Schinasi, May
        1979 Afghanistan at the Beginning of the Twentieth Century: Nationalism and journalism in Afghanistan. A study of Seraj ul-akhbar (1911-1918). Naples: Istituto Universario Orientale. Pp. 302.

2216 Schwager, Joseph
        1932 Die Entwicklung Afghanistans als Staat und seine zwischenstaatlichen Beziehungen [The Development of Afghanistan as a State and her International Relations]. Leipzig: Noske. Pp. 110.

   Uniquely valuable study of the formation of Afghanistan's constitution, of the international relations of the country at this same period, and of the position of Afghanistan in relation to international law. Gives the full text of the constitution promulgated by Amanullah in 1923.

2217 Segal, Gerald
        1981 China and Afghanistan. Asian Survey 21(11):1158-1174.

   Discusses the relationship of Afghanistan and China. Chinese perceptions of contemporary events in Afghanistan and how important is China to the Soviet-Afghan crises are analyzed.

2218 Shah, Aurang
        1950 Voice of the People of Pakhtunistan. Afghanistan 5(4):35.

   A reaffirmation, by the President of the Azad Pakhtunistan Associaton of America, of the right of Pushtuns to be free.

2219 Shah, Sayad Amir
        1950 Pakhtunistan. Afghanistan 5(4):36.

   The Pushtuns will "never become subjects of Pakistan."

2220 Shah, Sirdar Ikbal Ali
        1933 The Tragedy of Amanullah. London: Alexander-Ousley, Ltd. Pp. xiv, 272; appendices.

   The first third of this work by a very prolific Afghan writer, long resident abroad, is the rather familiar background material common to a number of his works. The balance, which deals with the reign and eventual downfall

VI. POLITICAL STRUCTURE

        of King Amanullah, is of real importance. Appendices gives the texts of an Agnlo-Afghan Treaty of November 22nd, 1921; of an Afghan-German Treaty of September 14th, 1926; and of an Afghan-Soviet Treaty of August 31st, 1926.

2221 Shchedrov, I.
     1981 The USSR and Afghanistan: The Firm Foundation of Friendship and Cooperation. International Affairs January:14-19. (Moscow).

2222 Shorish, M. Mobin
     1980 Islam and Soviets in Afghanistan. Islamic Horizon 9(4):1-4.

2223 Shorish, M. Mobin
     1980 The Afghan Refugee in Iran. In Afghanistan News and Views. Plainfield, Indiana: Muslim Students Association Publications. Pp. 17.

2224 Shorish, M. Mobin
     1981 Dissent of the Muslims: Soviet Central Asia in the 1980s. Nationalities Papers 9(2):50-60.

2225 Sidky, M. Habib
     1978 The Theory and Conduct of Chinese Foreign Policy in South Asia: Peking's Relations with Pakistan and Afghanistan, 1970-1976. Unpublished Ph. D. Dissertation. University of Miami. Pp. 258.

2226 Sikoyev, Ruslan
     1979 Afghanistan: Revolution in the Interests of the Working People. Political Affairs 58:10-16.

2227 Skinner, G. R.
     1980 Soviet Invasion of Afghanistan Calls for Strategic Reappraisal. International Perspectives (March):7-11.

2228 Solovyov, Vladimir and Elena Klepikova
     1981 Afghanistan and Russian History. Worldview 24(1):4-6.

2229 Sommer, Theo and Andreas Kohlschutter
     1980 Afghanistan: What Next? World Press Review 27:23-25.

2230 Sonnenfeldt, Helmut
     1980 Afghanistan: Hard Choices for the U.S. Worldview 23(6):5-7.

VI. POLITICAL STRUCTURE

2231 Sonnenfeldt, Helmut
    1980 The Crisis in Afghanistan and Soviet-American Relations. Europa Archiv 35(6):169-178.

2232 Sonnenfeldt, Helmut
    1980 Implications of the Soviet Invasion of Afghanistan for East-West Relations. Atlantic Community Quarterly 18(2):184-192.

2233 Sreedhar
    1976 Sino-Afghan Economic Relations. China Report 12(5-6):7-9.

2234 Srivastava, M. P.
    1980 Soviet Intervention in Afghanistan. New Delhi: Ess Ess Publications. Pp. 128.

2235 Stack, Shannon Caroline
    1975 Herat: A Political and Social Study. Unpublished Ph. D. Dissertation. University of California-Los Angles. Pp. 603.

2236 Steel, R.
    1980 Tempest in a Vodka Glass - Afghanistan Does not Matter. New Republic 1980(7):14-15.

2237 Stephen, O.
    1974 Bedrohliche Polarisierung im Mittleren Osten: Außenpolitische Auswirkungen des Afghanischen Umsturzes. Europa Archiv 29(1):55-62.

2238 Stephens, Ian
    1953 Horned Moon. London: Chatto and Windus. Pp. x, 288; maps.

The former editor of a leading British-owned newpaper in India, the Statesman, returned to familiar places in 1953 in his account of a journey through Pakistan, Kashmir, and Afghanistan. Chapters 25 and 26 describe his trip to Kabul from Peshawar and include discussions of the Pushtunistan issue.

2239 Steul, Willi
    1979 Afgahnistan--mit dem Islan zur Nation. In Im Namen Allahs. Der Islam Eine Religion im Aufbruch. Edited by A. Buchholz. Frankfurt: Ullstein. Pp. 114-128.

VI. POLITICAL STRUCTURE

2240   Strauss, Franz Josef
         1980 After Afghanistan. The Atlantic Quarterly 18(2):179-192.

2241   Strauss, Franz Josef
         1980 After Afghanistan. Policy Review 12:109-114.

2242   Summerscale, Peter
         1980 Eastern Europe in the Wake of Afghanistan. The World Today 36(5):172-179.

2243   Tabibi, Abdul Hakim
         1953 Aftermath Created by British Policy in Respect to Afghanistan-Pakistan Relations. Unpublished Ph. D. Dissertation. American University. Pp. 133.

         A nationalist's journalistic attempt at promoting the cause of Pushtunistan. A brief descriptive summary of Afghan history, geography, tribal divisions. Basically, a compilation of already published materials dealing with the official Afghan side of the Pushtunistan issue and reasons behind this issue.

2244   Tabibi, Abdul Hakim
         1978 The Right of Free Access to and From the Sea for Land-locked States. Afghanistan Journal 5(1):9-10.

2245   Tahir-Kheli, Shirin R.
         1972 Pakistani Elites and Foreign Policy Towards the Soviet Union, Iran and Afghanistan. Unpublished Ph. D. Dissertation. University of Pennsylvania. Pp. 390.

         The role of the Pakistani elite in the formulation of foreign policy towards the Soviet Union, Iran and Afghanistan between 1955-1965 is examined. Correlation between perceptions, motivations, role of the elite and changes in Pakistan's foreign policy are described.

2246   Tahir-Kheli, Shirin R.
         1975 Pakhtoonistan and its International Implications. World Affairs 173(3):233-245.

2247   Talboys, B. E.
         1980 Afghanistan, Indochina, and ANZUS (Pact; Australia, New Zealand and the United States): Implications for New Zealand's Foreign Policy. New Zealand Foreign Affairs Review 30:3-9.

VI. POLITICAL STRUCTURE

2248   Tang, Peter S. H.
        1980 Afghanistan's National Liberation War Against Soviet
           Subjugation. Asian Thought and Society 5(14):209-211.

2249   Taraki, Noor M.
        1978 Sarra: Sciences Academy of Afghanistan.

        Written in 1955, is a scientific work of Taraki and
        underlines the feudal economic system and life under the
        previous governments in Afghanistan.

2250   Taraki, Noor M.
        1979 Sangsar: Theory and Education Department of the
           Central Committee of the People's Democratic Party of
           Afghanistan.

        This is a book giving an account of the life and problems
        of the people of Afghanistan and the nature of feudal
        relations. The book was written in 1943.

2251   Taraki, Noor M.
        1979 Zindagi Naveen. Kabul: Publication of the Peoples
           Democratic Party of Afghanistan.

        This book is a scientific work divided into three parts.
        The first part deals with the philosophy of materialism,
        the second part with political economy, and the third part
        with historical materialism and socialism.

2252   Tarzi, Nangyalai
        1970 Les relations Afghano-russes [Relations Between
           Afghanistan and the U.S.S.R.]. Unpublished Ph. D. Dis-
           sertation. Paris. Pp. 371.

2253   Tchardi-Wal
        1950 Les difficultés intérieures du Pakistan [Pakistan's
           Domestic Difficulties]. Afghanistan 5(1):50-54.

        In reply to Pakistan's propaganda, an "exposé" of
        Pakistan's real internal situation--economic instability,
        undemocratic parliament, lack of a free press, etc.

2254   Tchardi-Wal
        1951 La Ligne Durand et les relations afghano-
           pakistanaises [The Durand Line and Afghan-Pakistan
           Relations]. Afghanistan 6(3):58-61.

VI. POLITICAL STRUCTURE

Tchardi-Wal cites Sir Thomas Holdich's statement that the legality of the Durand Line depends on the Treaty of Gandomak and declares that that Treaty is no longer valid.

2255 Tchardi-Wal
1951 Les relations afghano-pakistanaises et le Pathanistan [Afghan-Pakistan Relations and Pushtunistan]. Afghanistan 6(4):22-26.

A reply to propaganda circulated by the Pakistani Prime Minister.

2256 Tchardi-Wal
1952 Le Cachemire et le Pachtounistan [Kashmir and Pushtunistan]. Afghanistan 7(1):33-38.

The Pushtunistan issue is of major importance, while the Kashmir issue is merely a "local war."

2257 Teicher, Howard
1980 Soviet Union in Afghanistan: The political-military costs. Leviathan 3:28-32.

2258 Thakur, R.
1980 Afghanistan: The Reasons for India's Distinctive Approach. Round Table 1980(280):422-433.

2259 Thorburn, S. S.
1978 Bannu; or, our Afghan Frontier. London: E. J. Brill. Reprint of 1876 edition. Pp. xii, 480.

2260 Toynbee, Arnold
1961 Impressions of Afghanistan and Pakistan's North-West Frontier in Relation to the Communist World. International Affairs 37:161-169. (London).

Communism is making headway in Afghanistan, and in time its threat may lead Afghanistan, Pakistan, and India to settle their common differences, according to this article.

2261 Tursunov, R.
1974 Uchastie republik Srednei Azii v ekonomicheskikh i kul'turnykh sviaziakh SSSR s Afganistanom (1960-1970-e gg.) [The Participation of Central Asian Republics in the Economic and Cultural Relations of the USSR with Afghanistan, 1960-1970]. Unpublished Ph. D. Dissertation. Institut vostokovedeniia Akademii Nauk SSSR.

VI. POLITICAL STRUCTURE

2262 Uberoi, J. P. Singh
1968 District Administration in the Northern Highlands of Afghanistan. Sociological Bulletin 17(1):65-90.

2263 Usul-i Asasi-yi Dawlet-i 'Aliyeh-yi Afghanistan [Fundamental Principles of the Sublime Governemnt of Afghanistan]
n.d. Kabul: Matba'eh-yi 'umumi. Pp. 20.

Official text of the Constitution of Afghanistan, printed in Dari and Pushtu in parallel columns. Separate sheets contain amendments.

2264 Usul-i Vaza'if-i Dakhili-yi Riyaset-i Shura-yi Milli-yi Afghanistan [Fundamentals of the Internal Duties of the Presidium of the National Assembly of Afghanistan]
1950 Kabul: Matbe'eh-yi 'umumi. Pp. 10. (1329 A.H.)

Text printed in Dari.

2265 Usul-Nameh [Basic Regulations]
n.d. Kabul: Matba'eh-yi 'umumi.

A series of pamphlets, each of which contains the printed text of one law together with its date of passage. The text is printed in Dari and Pushtu in parallel columns.

2266 Usul-Nameh
1960 Da Mahbusinu da Mokafatu aw Mojazat peh Afghanistan Kshe [Laws Governing the Penalties and Punishments for Prisoners in Afghanistan]. Kabul: Matba'eh-yi doulati. Pp. 30. (1339 A.H.)

The title is in Pushtu: the laws are presented in Pushtu and Dari, in parallel columns.

2267 Utas, B.
1978 Statskuppen i Afghanistan och den vasterlanska nyhetsrapporteringen. Sydasienbulletinen 3-4.

2268 Utas, B.
1979 Recent Events inAfghanistan. Annual Newsletter of the Scandinavian Institute of Asian Studies 11. Copenhagen.

2269 Valenta, Jiri
1980 From Prague to Kabul--The Soviet Style of Invasion. International Security 630:114-141.

VI. POLITICAL STRUCTURE

2270 Valenta, Jiri
1980 The Soviet Invasion of Afghanistan: The Difficulty of Knowing Where to Stop. Orbus 24(2):201-218.

2271 Van Praagh, D.
1979 Greater Game - Implications of the Afghan Coup. International Perspectives (March):12-16.

2272 Vastel, M.
1980 Impotence of the Big 7 in the Wake of Afghanistan. International Perspectives 1980(July):238-239.

2273 Vayrynen, R.
1980 Focus on Afghanistan. Journal of Peace Research 17(2):93-102.

2274 Vercellin, Giorgio
1979 Afghanistan 1973-1978: dalla Repubblica Presidenziale alla Repubblica Democratica con una Appendice di Documenti e una Cronologia dal 17 luglio 1973 al 30 giugno 1979. Quaderni del Seminario di Iranistica, Uralo-Altaistica e Caucasologia dell'Universta degli Studi di Venezia, No. 4, Venezia: Selbstverlag. Pp. 157.

2275 Vinogradov, V. M. et al (eds)
1971 Sovetsko-Afganskii Otnosheniya 1919-69. (Soviet-Afghan Relations 1919-1969). Moscow: Politizdat.

An important work composed of various articles dealing with Soviet-Afghan relations during 1919-1969 from the Soviet prespective.

2276 Vivekanandan, B.
1980 Afghanistan Invasion Viewed From India. Asia Pacific Community 1980(9):63-82.

2277 Volkov, Y., K. Gevorkyan, I. Mikhailenki, A. Polonsky and V. Svetozarov
1980 The Truth About Afghanistan. Documents, Facts, Eyewitneess Reports. Moscow: Novosti Press Agency Publishing House. Pp. 102.

2278 Voronin, A.
1971 U Istokov Druzhby I Dobrososedstva [At the Source of Friendship and Good Neighborly Relations]. Mezhdunarodnaia Zhizn' 18(3):65-75.

VI. POLITICAL STRUCTURE

2279 Wafadar, K.
1981 Afghanistan in 1980: The Struggle Continues. Asian Survey 21(2):172-180.

2280 Wagner, Wolfgang.
1980 Das Ost-West-Verhltnis Nach der Sowjetischen Intervention in Afghanstan. Die Eskalation der Enttauschungen in der Periode der Detente. Europe-Archiv 35(5):135-146.

2281 Warhurst, Geoffrey
1980 Afghanistan--A Dissenting Appraisal. Journal of the Royal United Services Institute for Defence Studies 125:26-29.

2282 Warner, Denis
1962 Afghanistan: A House Without Doors. Reporter 26(2):28-30.

A visit to Kabul by an Australiain journalist, with emphasis on reflections of Afghan-Soviet relations and the Pushtunistan issue.

2283 Weinbaum, Marvin G.
1972 Afghanistan: Nonparty Parliamentary Democracy. Journal of Developing Areas 7(1):57-74.

Considers the precedents for a parliamentary system in Afghanistan and the emergent constitutional framework for competitive politics and discusses how, in the absense of legal parties, have Afghan parliamentary norms and practices operated.

2284 Weinbaum, Marvin G.
1977 The Legislator as Intermediary: Integration of the Center and Periphery in Afghanistan. In Legislature in Plural Societies: The Search for Cohesion in National Development. Edited by Albert F. Eldridge. Durham, North Carolina: Duke University Press. Pp. 95-121.

Describes the process through which Afghan parliaments have made contributions to national integration.

2285 Weinbaum, Marvin G.
1980 Legal Elites in Afghan Society. International Journal of Middle Eastern Studies 12(1):38-57.

VI. POLITICAL STRUCTURE

A political scientist with research experience in Afghanistan discusses legal-political elites in present day Afghanistan and places them in a larger cultural, societal and political context.

2286 Wiegandt, Winifred
1980 Afghanistan: Nicht aus Heiterem Himmel. Zurich: Orel Fússel. Pp. 353.

2287 Wilber, Donald N.
1965 Document. Constitution of Afghanistan. Middle East Journal 19(2):215-29.

A commentary on the Constitution of 1964, pp. 215-16, is followed by the text of the document.

2288 Wiles, P.
1980 Economic Consequences of Invasion of Afghanistan. Futuribles 33:73-83.

2289 Wilson, Andrew
1960 Inside Afghanistan--A Background to Recent Troubles. Royal Central Asian Journal 47:286-295.

According to this writer, current iternal difficulties and the trouble with Pakistan are not the result of Soviet influence or intervention, since Soviet goals do not require direct control of the country.

2290 Wolkow, J. (ed)
1980 Die Wahrheit Ueber Afghanistan: Dokumente, Tasachen, Zeugnisse. Moscau: Presseagentur Nowotsi. Pp. 223.

2291 Wrong, Dennis H. et al.
1980 After Afghanistan. Dissent 2:135-143.

2292 Wuelbern, Jan-Peter.
1974 Bildungspolitik in Afghanistan: eine Zwischenbilanz. Internationales Asienforum 5:179-194.

2293 Wulburn, J. P.
1974 Bildungspolitik in Afghanistan - eine Zwischenbilanz. Internationales Asienforum 5(2):179-194.

2294 Yoshitsu, Michael M.
1981 Iran and Afghanistan in Japanese Perspective. Asian Survey 21(5):501-514.

VI. POLITICAL STRUCTURE

2295 Yusufzai, Saidal
1951 Regarding the Views of Sir George Cunningham. Afghanistan 6(1):68-74.

An uncomplimentary account of the career of Sir George Cunningham, "giving the lie" to his article in the Manchester Guardian entitled "Frontier Discord Between Afghanistan and Pakistan."

2296 Zeray, Saleh M.
1979 Afghanistan: Anbruch einer neuen Ara. Uber die Aprilrevolution 1978 berichtet ein Mitglied des Politburos der Demokratischen Volkspartei Afghanistans. Probleme des Friedens und des Sozialismus 22/1:81-86. Berlin-Ost; u.a.

2297 Zeray, Saleh M.
1979 Afghanistan: the Beginning of a New Era. World Marxist Review 22:103-109.

2298 Ziring, Lawrence
1981 Iran, Turkey, and Afghanistan: A Political Chronology. New York: Praeger. Pp. 230.

2299 Zurrer, Werner
1973 Die Sowjetisch-Afghanischen Bezienhungen und Grossbritannien 1918-1926 [Soviet-Afghan Relations and Great Britain 1918-1926]. Jahrbucher fur Geschichte Osteuropas 21(2):196-249.

VII. ECONOMIC STRUCTURE

Agriculture; industry; trade; finance;
taxation; handicrafts; labor force

Here is another vitally important subject on which contemporary materials are inadequate for a real understanding of what is going on in the country and of the goals and progress of economic development. Some of the difficulty stems from the lack of reliable official statistics, or the assumed unreliability of those statistics which are obtainable. Figures and studies having to do with finance and taxation are very hard to find. Articles relating to labor are almost nonexistent, due in large part to the absence of labor unions and other labor organizations.

It is indeed fortunate that it has been possible to include a fair number of unpublished reports and studies which shed a clear and detailed light into obscure aspects of the economic structure.

2300   'Abdul Majid Khan
      1949   Mushkilat-i Iqtisadi va Mujadaleh ba Anha [Economic Difficulties and Contending with Them]. Kabul: Matba'eh-yi 'umumi, 1328. Pp. 67.

2301   Abdul Rahim-zai, Abdul Malik and Associates
      1955   Economic Report of Afghanistan. Unpublished report. Istanbul. Pp. 41.

      A brief review by the Minister of Finance of economic developments from 1919 on, with an optimistic description of new government-sponsored projects and new policy. Valuable as an official document.

2302   Afghan Financial Statistics
      1964   Kabul: The Bank of Afghanistan, Research Department.

      The first number of this monthly publication appeared in August 1964.

2303   Afghan Progress in the Third Year of the Plan
      1960   London: Information Bureau, Royal Afghan Embassy. Pp. 104.

      A well-illustrated, comprehensive account of progress on the First Five Year Development Plan between September 1958 and September 1959.

VII. ECONOMIC STRUCTURE

2304   Afghan Progress in the Fifth Year of the Plan
            1961 London: Information Bureau, Royal Afghan Embassy.
              Pp. 92.

            A well-illustrated, comprehensive account of progress on
            the First Five Year Development Plan for the year ending
            September 1961.

2305   Afghanistan [Afghanistan]

            1928 Bulletin du Chambre de Commerce France-Asiatique,
              numéro special. Pp. 48.

            A publication commemorating the visit of Amanullah to
            Paris and including a number of brief articles on such
            subjects as Karakul sheep, Kabul, and railroads in
            Afghanistan.

2306   Afghanistan
            1939 Bihtar ast Yak Manlaket-i San'ati Bashad ya
              Zira'ati? [Afghanistan; Should it be an Industrial or
              Agricultural Country?]. Kabul: Matba'eh-yi 'umumi,
              1318. Pp. 178.

            A publication in Dari issued by the Ministry of National
            Economy, in which several local figures discuss the impli-
            cations of the title.

2307   Afghanistan
            1941 The Country and its Resources. Bulletin of
              International News 18 (1907-1921). London.

2308   Afghanistan
            1950 Summary of Basic Economic Information. Commerce
              Department. International Reference Service 7(68):1-4.
              Washington: U.S. Government Printing Office.

2309   Afghanistan
            1965 Structure Economique et Sociale. Commerce Extérieur
              [Afghanistan: Economic and Social Structure. Foreign
              Trade]. Lausanne: Office Swisse d'Expansion
              Commerciale. Pp. 83; bibliography; mimeographed.

2310   Da Afghanistan Bank
            1950 Kabul. Condensed Statement of the Accounts for the
              Year 1328. (Ended March 20, 1950)

VII. ECONOMIC STRUCTURE

>Lacks date and place of publication. Contains 5 unnumbered pages in English and the same number in Dari. Assumed to be an annual publication and of definite value for its presentation of hard-to-find data.

2311 Afghanistan as a Source for Crude Drugs and Essential Oils
1946 Commerce Department. (Industrial Reference Service, December, Vol. 4, Pt. 2, no. 133.) Washington: U.S. Government Printing Office. Pp. 2.

2312 Afghanistan's Economic Development Plan and Her Current Difficulties
1949 Unpublished Report. Ministry of National Economy. Washington. Pp. 236.

>Reviews postwar economic changes and presents details of the Five Year Plan (1949-1953) set up by the then Minister of National Economy (1932-1950), Abdul Madjid.

2313 Afghanistan's Foreign Trade (Revised) 1335 through 1340
1963 Kabul: Statistical Department, Ministry of Commerce. Pp. 47.

2314 Afghanistan's Foreign Trade 1335 Through 1342 (March 21, 1956 Through March 20, 1964)
1965 Kabul: Statistical Department, Ministry of Commerce. Pp. 154.

2315 Afghanistan's Reclamation Program
1948 Reclamation Era 34:55-56. Washington.

2316 Ahmed, Akbar S.
1978 The Economic and Social Organization of Selected Mohmand Pukhtun Settlements. Unpublished Ph.D. Dissertation. University of London. Pp. 549.

2317 Aitchison, James Edward T.
1891 Notes to Assist in a Further Knowledge of the Products of Western Afghanistan and of North-Eastern Persia. Transactions of the Botanical Society of Edinburgh 18:1-228.

2318 Akram, Mohammad
1948, 1949 L'Agriculture en Afghanistan [Agriculture in Afghanistan]. Afghanistan 3(4):50-52; 4(1):26-29.

>A brief survey touching on climate, methods of irrigation, and local types of wheat, barley, and rice.

VII. ECONOMIC STRUCTURE

2319 Alekseenkov, P.
1933 Agrarnyi vopros v Afganskom Turkestane [Agricultural Question in Afghan Turkestan]. Moscow: Mezhdunarodnyi Agrarnyi Institut. Pp. 107; map.

2320 Ali, Mohammad
1946 Commercial Afghanistan. Delhi. Pp. ii, 70; appendices; sketch map.

Short sections deal with flora and fauna, minerals, commerce and industry, exports, imports, banking regulations and customs regulations. Given the scarcity of reliable information on most of these subjects, all are of value. Among the useful appendices is a list of 87 Afghan business firms, with their addresses, type of business, and capitalization, and also a list of newspapers and periodicals published in the country.

2321 Amat, Barthelemy
1976 L'organisation paysanne pour la distribution de l'eau pour l'irrigation, dans les villages de la steppe: L'institution du Mirab. Afghanistan Journal 3(3):86-90.

2322 Amerkhail, Najibullah
1972 Management Problems of Industrial Enterprises in the Middle East, with Special Reference to Afghanistan. Unpublished Ph.D. Dissertation. University of Bonn.

2323 Amini, Naim
1977 Möglichkeiten und Grenzen der Industrialisierung eines unterentwickelten Raumes: dargestellt am Beispiel Afghanistan. (Possibilities and Limitations of the Industrialization of an Underdeveloped Area: Demonstrated by the Example of Afghanistan.) Unpublished Ph.D. Dissertation. University of Bonn. Pp. 163.

2324 Arens, H. J.
1974 Die Stellung der Energiewirtschaft im EntwicklungsporeB Afghanistans. Afghanische Studien 13:1-396.

2325 Arens, H. J.
1975 Die Energieversorgung in Afghanistan. Afghanistan Journal 2(1):12-19. Photos.

VII. ECONOMIC STRUCTURE

2326 Arens, H. J.
1976 Zur Problematik der Regionalisierung in Entwicklungslandern, dargestellt am Beispiel Afghanistan. Afghanische Studien 14:54-74.

2327 Ashrafi, Naim
1975 Neue Tendenzen der Wirtschaftsordnung und des Wirtschaftsrechts in der Republik Afghanistan seit dem Umsturz vom 17-7-1973. Orient 16(4):131-148.

New tendencies of economic planning and economic law in the Republic of Afghanistan after the coup d'etat on 17-7-1973.

2328 Asiel, Murad Ali
1974 Economic Analysis of Water Resources Projects in Developing Countries: A Case Study of the Helmand-Arghandab Valleys Projects in Afghanistan. Unpublished Ph.D. Dissertation. University of Colorado at Boulder. Pp. 734.

An assessment of the criterion which have been applied to project analysis in developing countries and the application of revised criteria in the expost analysis of large development projects in Afghanistan.

2329 Asiel, Murad A. and Gerhard Schmitt-Rink (eds)
1979 Aussenhandel und Terms of Trade Afghanistans 1961-1975. Bochum: Studienverlag N. Brockmeyer. Pp. 194.

2330 Assad, M. N.
1978 Evaluation of Fixed Assets and Working Capital According to Commercial Code and Income-tax Law of Afghanistan. Zeitschrift fur Betriebswirtschaft 48(11):971-977.

2331 Babakhodzaev, M. A.
1975 Ocherki Sothialno-Ekonomicheskoi i Politicheskoi Istorii Afghanistana (Koneth XIX B.). [Work on the Socio-Economic and Political History of Afghanistan to the end of the Nineteenth Century]. Tashkent: Uzbek SSR Academy of Sciences. Pp. 196.

A materialist analysis of the socio-economic and political history of Afghanistan to the end of the rule of Abdul Rahman.

VII. ECONOMIC STRUCTURE

2332 Bahram, Ghulam M.
1977 The Role of the Extension Supervisor as Perceived by Extension Personnel in Afghanistan. Unpublished Ph.D. Dissertation. University of Wisconsin-Madison. Pp. 236.

A study of the role of the Afghan extension supervisors as perceived by extension personnel.

2333 Baker, Henry D.
1915 British India. With Notes on Ceylon, Afghanistan and Tibet. Washington: U.S. Government Printing Office. Pp. 638; map.

This work—Special Consul Report No. 72 of the Department of Commerce—contains scarce economic data for the period in question, including statistical tables. Pages 533-561 are devoted to Afghanistan.

2334 Baldus, R. D.
1979 Starting Cooperative Development in Afghanistan. Internationales Asienforum 10(1-2):39-51.

2335 Balland, D.
1973 Le coton en Afghanistan. Revue Geographique de l'Est 13(1-2):17-75.

2336 Balland, D.
1973 Une nouvelle generation d'industries en Afghanistan. Contribution a l'etude de l'industrialisation du Tiers-Monde. Bulletin de la Societe Languedocienne de Geographie 7(1).

2337 Banoory, Syed Ahmad Shah
1974 Moglichkeiten und Probleme der Kapitalbildung in Mittelasien. Unpublished Ph.D. Dissertation. University of Bonn.

2338 Baron, Lloyd I.Z.
1975 The Water Supply Constraint: An Evaluation of Irrigation Projects and Their Role in the Development of Afghanistan. Unpublished Ph.D. Dissertation. McGill University.

Expost evaluation of Russian and American irrigation projects designed to alleviate the water supply constraints in Afghanistan along with an exante analysis of incremental investments.

VII. ECONOMIC STRUCTURE

2339 Basic Data on the Economy of Afghanistan
1955 Unpublished report. U.S. Department of Commerce. World Trade Information Service, Part 1, nos. 55-74. Washington: U.S. Government Printing Office. Pp. 11.

Up-to-date, detailed information on Afghan foreign trade. All values are given in U.S. dollars.

2340 Basic Statistics of Afghanistan
1962 Kabul: Ministry of Planning, Statistics and Research Department. Pp. 36.

2341 Basso, Jacques
1972 La cooperation culturelle scientifique et technique entra la France et l'Afghanistan: Etat des Travaux. Cooperationes Internationales 5:49-65.

2342 Bernardin, Marc
1972 Enseignement et aide internationale en Afghanistan. Cooperationes Technologique 3:35-42.

2343 Bogdanov, L.
1928 The Afghan Weights and Measures. Journal and Proceedings of the Asiatic Society of Bengal n.s. 24:419-435.

Discusses and describes the systems of weights and measures in use in Afghanistan prior to 1925 (the date on which the country theoretically adopted the metric system).

2344 Bresse, L.
1926 Dans l'Asie que s'éveille. Découverte d'une mine de pétrole en Afghanistan et grands tra vaux d'irrigation dans la région de Caboul [In Awakening Asia. Discovery of an Oil Source in Afghanistan and Great Irrigation Works in the Region of Kabul]. Paris: Correspondance d'Orient. Pp. 256-258.

2345 Burger, W.
1963 Community Development in Afghanistan. Mens En Mij 38(5):368-383.

2346 Buscher, Horst
1969 Die Industriearbeiter in Afghanistan. Meisenheim: Verlag Anton Hain.

VII. ECONOMIC STRUCTURE

2347 Buscher, Horst
    1969 Die Industriearbeiter in Afghanistan. Eine Studie zur gesellschaftspolitischen Problematik sozial schwacher Bevolkerungsschichten in Entwicklungslandern. Meisenheim: Anton Hain Verlag. Pp. 160.

2348 Buscher, H., N. Assad, and H. Berger
    1977 Betriebswirtschaftliche Probleme in Afghanischen Industrieunternehmen. Afghanische Studien 17. Meisenheim: Anton Hain Verlag.

2349 Casimir, M. J., R. P. Winter and Bernt Glatzer
    1980 Nomadism Remote Sensing: Animal Husbandry and the Sagebrush Community in a Nomad Winter Area in Western Afghanistan. Journal of Arid Environments 3.

2350 Centlivres, Pierre
    1976 Structure et evolution des bazars du Nord Afghan. In Aktuelle Probleme der Regionalentwicklung und Stadtgeographie Afghanistans. Edited by E. Grötzbach. Meisenheim: Anton Hain Verlag. Pp. 119-145.

2351 Cervinka, Vladimir
    1950 Afghanistan: Structure économique et sociale. Commerce extérieure [Afghanistan. Economic and Social Structure. Foreign Commerce]. Lausanne: Office Suisse d'Expansion Commerciale, Zürich et Lausanne. Pp. 83; bibliography; sketch map. (The author also used V. Cervin as his name.)

    The author, a social scientist, was resident in Afghanistan between 1938 and 1944. His article represents a particularly well-informed summary of the inadequately documented internal economic situation. Current economic and financial problems are analyzed and future developments outlined.

2352 Chernyakovskaya, Neonila Ivanovna
    1965 Razvitiye promyshlennosti i polozheniye rabochego klassa Afganistana [Development of Industry and Position of the Working Class of Afghanistan]. Moscow: Nauka (Glav. red. Vostochnoy Literatury). Pp. 168.

2353 Cressey, G. B.
    1958 Qanats, Karez, and Foggaras. Geographical Review 48:27-44.

VII. ECONOMIC STRUCTURE

2354   Dada, H., and L. Pickett
       1969   1968 Supplement to the Bibliography of Material Dealing with Agriculture in Afghanistan. Kabul.

2355   Data Book (South Asia)
       1943   Department of State. Office of Intelligence Research. IR-6310. September.

       Afghanistan is treated on pages 95-108, the material including a statistical summary covering vital facts and figures and a series of tables presenting financial and economic information.

2356   Davidov, Alexandr D.
       1964   Selskaya Obshina u Hazareithev Tsentralnogo Afganistana. Kratkie Soobsheniya Instituta Narodov Azii 77.

2357   Davidov, Aleksandr D.
       1962   Razvitiye Kapitalisticheskikh otnosheniy v zemledelii Afganistana [Development of Capitalistic Relations in Afghan Agriculture]. Moscow: Izdatel'stvo Vostochnoy Literatury. Pp. 160.

2358   Davidov, Aleksandr D.
       1963   O sel'skoy obshchine i yeye Khozyaystvennom znachenii v Afganistane [The Rural Commune and its Economic Significance in Afghanistan]. In Voprosy Ekonomiki Afganistana. Moscow: Izdatel'stvo Vostochnoy Literatury. Pp. 57-124.

2359   Davidov, Alexandr D. and N. Chernakhovskaya
       1973   Afganistan [Afghanistan]. Moscow: Mysl. Pp. 162.

       A description and analysis of economic development achievements, problems, prospects, and potentialities of Afganistan over the past two decades.

2360   Dawar, Heider
       1971   Die Bedeutung der Zollpolitik fur die industrielle Entwicklung wirtschaftlich zuruckgebliebener Raume: Dargestellt am Beispiel Afghanistans. [The Importance of Customs Policies for the Industrial Development of Economically Backward Areas: Described in the Case of Afghanistan]. Unpublished Ph.D. Dissertation. University of Bonn. Pp. 199.

VII. ECONOMIC STRUCTURE

2361 Deutsch, K.
    1975 Republik Afghanistan. Zum Machtwechsel in einem Entwicklungsland des Orients. Geographische Rundschau 10:403-415.

2362 Development Program
    1953 Unpublished report. Government of Afghanistan. San Francisco. Pp. 90; maps; diagrams.

    A report (with eleven separate appendices) intended for those concerned with finance, administration, engineering, and construction, to present an over-all analysis of land and water resources of the Helmand and Arghandab Valleys and to evaluate their economic potential. Also includes a tentative long-range program for the ultimate development of the area and a more specific plan for development within the next few years. Includes a history of the organizations established by the Afghan government to administer development programs.

2363 Dost, M. Anwar
    1978 Die Bedeutung offentlicher Betriebe in einem Entwicklungsland: dargestellt am Beispiel Afghanistans [The Importance of Public Utilities in a Developing Country: Described Through the Example of Afghanistan]. Unpublished Ph.D. Dissertation. Universität Köln. Pp. 227.

2364 Dupaigne, Bernard
    1974 Un artisan d'Afghanistan: sa vie, ses problemes, ses espoirs [A Craftsman in Afghanistan: His Life, Problems, and Hopes]. Objets et Mondes 14(3):143-170.

2365 Dupaigne, Bernard
    1977 Du Karez aux puits dans le Nord de l'Afghanistan. Revue Geographique de l'Est 17(1-2):27-36.

2366 Eberhard, Wolfram
    1967 Labour Sources for Industrialization: The Case of Afghanistan. In Settlement and Social Change. By Wolfram Eberhard. Hong Kong: Hong Kong University Press. Pp. 415-438.

2367 Eckensberger, Lutz H. and Gunter F. Schneider
    1973 Identifikation mit Change Agents als eine Voraussetzung fur Geplanten Sozialen Wandel: Eine Untersuchung des Lehrpersonals Technisch-Gewerblicher Ausbildungsstatten in Afghanistan [Identification with Change Agents as a Preliminary Condition for Planned

VII. ECONOMIC STRUCTURE

Social Change: An Investigation of the Staff Instructor in Institutes of Technico-Professional Instruction in Afghanistan]. Die Dritte Welt 2(2):187-220.

2368   Economic Review of Afghanistan, 1949
    1950 Commerce Department. (International Reference Service, August 1950, vol. 7, no. 90.) Washington: U.S. Government Printing Office. Pp. 3.

2369   Economic Studies
    1961- A periodical which first appeared in 1961, published by the Faculty of Economics of Kabul University. The title is given in English on the cover; the text is in Dari and Pushtu.

2370   Economic Survey of Asia and the Far East, 1954
    1955 Economic Bulletin for Asia and the Far East 5(4). Bangkok: United Nations. Pp. 223.

    Chapter 6 (pages 57-64) reviews economic and financial progress in Afghanistan during the postwar period. Contains hard-to-get official data--partly unreliable.

2371   Ekker, Martin H.
    1952 Economic Aspects of Development of Afghanistan. United Nations. Pp. 69.

    Prepared by a Dutch economist under the auspices of the U.N. Technical Assistance Administration at the end of one year of service as economic advisor. Contains reliable financial data and a critical appraisal of major development projects and of government economic policy and administration.

2372   Eltezam, Zabioullah A.
    1966 Afghanistan's Foreign Trade. Middle East Journal 20(1):95-103.

2373   Eltezam, Zabioullah A.
    1967 Problems of Economics Development and Resource Allocation in Afghanistan. Unpublished Ph.D. Dissertation. Wayne State University. Pp. 199.

    Analysis of the problems of economic development in Afghanistan with emphasis on agricultural, industrial, and trade sectors.

VII. ECONOMIC STRUCTURE

2374 The Em-Kayan
n.d. Morrison-Knudsen Co., Inc., Boise, Idaho.

This monthly magazine contains occasional short articles, generously illustrated, of such projects of Morrison-Knudsen Afghanistan, Inc., as the Kajakai Dam, the Arghandab Dam, and the Boghra canal system.

2375 Erhard, F.
1973 Bevolkerungsprobleme der Grenzgebiete zwischen Iran, Afghanistan und Pakistan. Orient 14(3):126-136.

2376 Eskilsson, Enar
n.d. Report on Coordinating the Development of Afghanistan's Energy Resources. No publisher. Pp. 85; 23 tables; mimeographed.

2377 Etienne, Gilbert
1971 Possibilities et Limites de L'Agriculture Traditionnelle: Le Cas d'un Village Afghan [Possibilities and Limits of Traditional Agriculture: The Case of an Afghan Village]. Revue de Psychologie des Peuples 26(1):11-24.

2378 Farhang, Amin
1974 Die soziookonomischen Aspekte der Entwicklungsplanung: Dargestellt am Beispiel Afghanistans. [The Socioeconomic Aspects of Development Planning: Presented in the Case of Afghanistan]. Unpublished Ph.D. Dissertation. Köln University, Köln. Pp. vi, 346, xv.

2379 Farouq, Ghulam
1973 Socio-economic Aspects of Land Settlement in the Helmand Valley, Afghanistan. Unpublished M.A. Thesis. American University of Beirut.

2380 Ferdinand, Klaus
1959 Ris. Traek af dens dyrkning og behandling i Østafghanistan [Rice. Aspects of Cultivation and Treatment in East Afghanistan]. Kuml. Pp. 195-232. (Aarhus, Denmark)

2381 Ferdinand, Klaus
1963 The Horizontal Windmills of Western Afghanistan. Folk 5:71-89.

VII. ECONOMIC STRUCTURE

2382   Ferdinand, Klaus
        1967 The Horizontal Windmills of Western Afghanistan: An Additional Note. Folk 8-9:83-88.

2383   Ferdinand, Klaus
        1969 Nomadism in Afghanistan. In Viehwirtschaft und Hirtenkultur. Edited by D. Foldes. Budapest.

2384   Field, Neil C.
        1954 The Amu Darya: A Study in Resource Geography. Geographical Review 44:528-542.

        A study of proposed methods of developing the use of the water of this great river dividing Afghanistan and the U.S.S.R. and an examination of the international problems which such development would involve.

2385   Fischer, Dieter
        1970 Waldverbreitung im ostlichen Afghanistan. Meisenheim: Anton Hain Verlag. Pp. 160.

2386   Fitter, Jorn C.
        1973 Der Einfluss der Verkehrsinvestitionen auf die wirtschaftliche Entwicklung Afghanistans. Meisenheim: Anton Hain Verlag. Pp. 146.

2387   Forsberg, A.
        1976 Luy Bagh och Shin Kaley - en sociokonomisk studie av tvo byar i södra Afghanistan [A Socio-economic Study of Two Villages in Southern Afghanistan]. Uppsala: Institute of Cultural Geography, University of Uppsala. Pp. 116; photos; illustrations.

2388   Forsberg, A. and T. Holma
        n.d. PACCA - Programme on Agricultural Co-operatives and Credit in Afghanistan. Uppsala University. Pp. 40. (in Swedish)

2389   Franck, Dorothea Seelye and Peter G. Franck
        1950 Economic Review: The Middle East Economy in 1949. Middle East Journal 4(2):228. Washington.

        A short factual paragraph, in a long article, on the drop in Afghanistan's imports and exports for 1949 and the reasons for this.

2390   Franck, Peter G.
        1949 Problems of Economic Development in Afghanistan. Middle East Journal 3(3):293-314; 421-440.

VII. ECONOMIC STRUCTURE

>Important study by an American economic consultant and teacher who was advisor to the Afghan Ministry of National Economy in 1948-1950. Supported by reliable and difficult-to-obtain financial and economic data. The first installment deals with the impact on the local situation of international conditions and the second with planning and finance.

2391 Franck, Peter G.
1954 Afghanistan: A New Day is Dawning. Middle East Report 7(6):3 unnumbered pages. Washington.

>Extremely condensed survey, with emphasis upon financial and economic problems and projected solutions.

2392 Franck, Peter G.
1954 Obtaining Financial Aid for a Development Plan. The Export-Import Bank of Washington Loan to Afghanistan. (Printed for the Use of the Committee on Banking and Currency.) Washington: U.S. Government Printing Office. Pp. 55; list of documents consulted.

>An account, by the American economic advisor to the Afghan Ministry of National Economy in 1948-1950, of the steps involved in obtaining a development loan of $21 million, and with an interesting appraisal of the results of this expenditure.

2393 Franck, Peter G.
1955 Foreign Aid and Economic Development in Afghanistan. Unpublished Ph.D. Dissertation. University of California, Berkeley. Pp. 105.

2394 Franck, Peter G.
1955 Technical Assistance Through the United Nations--the Mission in Afghanistan 1950-1953. In Hands Across Frontiers. Edited by Howard M. Teaf and Peter G. Franck. Ithaca: Cornell University Press. Pp. 13-61.

>Describes United Nations operations and evaluates results, based on interviews and unpublished field reports.

2395 Franck, Peter G.
1956 Economic Progress in an Encircled Land. Middle East Journal 10(1):43-59; sketch map of the Helmand Valley; tables.

VII. ECONOMIC STRUCTURE

>Evaluates changes in budget, trade, private and public investments, economic organization, and international aid programs since 1947.

2396 Franck, Peter G.
>1960 Afghanistan Between East and West. Washington, D.C.: National Planning Association. Pp. 86.

>A report on the economics of competitive coexistence, including material on trade, economic development, and political relations with the United States and the U.S.S.R.

2397 Franz, Erhard
>1972 Zur Gegenwaertigen Verbreitung und Grupperiung der Turkmenen in Afghanistan. Baessler-Archiv 20:191-236.

2398 Franz, E.
>1973 Bevoelkerungsprobleme den Grengsgebeite Zwischen Iran, Afghanistan und Pakistan. Orient 14(3):126-136.

2399 Fritz, Dale B.
>1962 Simple Tools for Social Progress. The Asia Foundation. Program Bulletin 22:4-6.

>Report by an American adviser on the introduction and local manufacture of turning plows, seed drills, inertia pumps, and fly-shuttle looms.

2400 Fröhlich, Dieter
>1970 Nationalismus und Nationalstaat in Entwicklungslaendern: Probleme der Integration Ethnischer Gruppen in Afghanistan [Nationalism and the National State in Developing Countries: Problems of Integration of Ethnic Groups in Afghanistan]. Meisenheim am Glan: Verlag Anton Hain. Pp. 250.

>Chapters by two writers on problems of ethnic integration in Afghanistan. This is volume number three in the Afghanische Studien series with L. Fischer, K. Jettmar, R. Koenig, W. Kraus, and C. Rathjens as general editors.

2401 Fry, Maxwell J.
>1974 The Afghan Economy: Money, Finance and the Critical Constraints to Economic Development. Leiden; Social, Economic and Political Studies of the Middle East. Netherlands: E. J. Brill. Pp. x, 332; 128 f.

VII. ECONOMIC STRUCTURE

2402 Fry, Maxwell J.
1976 Purchasing-Power-Parity Application to Demand for Money in Afghanistan. Journal of Political Economy 84(5):1133-1138.

2403 Furdoonjee, Nowrozjee
1838 Report on the Weights, Measures, and Coins of Cabul, and Bukhara. Journal of the Asiatic Society of Bengal 7:392-900.

Tables, with short remarks and explanations, of weights, measures and coins of Kabul, Bokhara (and Peshawar), with their corresponding values in English and Indian measures, weights, and coins.

2404 Furse, P. and P.
1968 Afghanistan 1966. Journal of the Royal Horticultural Society XCIII (1):20-30; XCIII (2):92-97; XCIII (3):114-124.

2405 Gattinara, Giancarlo Castelli
1968 L'Attivita Commerciale dei Nomadi Dell'Afghanistan [The Commercial Activity of the Nomads of Afghanistan]. Rassegna Italiana di Sociologia 9(3):499-514.

2406 Gaube, Heinz
1977 Innenstadt - Aussenstadt. Kontinuitat und Wandel im Grundriss von Herat (Afghanistan) zwischen dem 10. und 15. Jahrhundert. In Beitrage zur Geographie orientalischer Stadte und Markte. Edited by Gunther Schweizer. Wiesbaden: Ludwig Reichert. Pp. 213-240.

2407 Gentelle, Pierre
1979 L'Afghanistan et l'aide internationale de 1950 a 1978. Tiers Monde 20(10/12):863-869.

2408 Gerken, E.
1974 Population, Agricultural Productivity, and Employment in Rural Nonagricultural Sector - Interpreting Observations in Paktia-Afghanistan. Internationales Asienforum 5(2):195-208.

2409 Ghaussi, M. Aref
1953 Afghan Carpet Industry. Afghanistan 8(4):42-45.

The chief characteristics of Afghan carpets, described so that the reader may be able to distinguish them from other oriental carpets.

VII. ECONOMIC STRUCTURE

2410 Ghaussi, M. Aref
1954 Some Facts about Three Important Handicrafts of Afghanistan. Afghanistan 9(2):22-26.

The process of cotton-weaving, and its cost; silk-weaving; and the long, painstaking method of carpet-weaving.

2411 Ghaussi, M. Aref
1960 Dictionary of Economics. English-Persian. Kabul. Pp. 143 and 105. Mimeographed. (1339 A.H.)

2412 Ghaussy, A. Ghanie
1975 Grundzuge des vierten Entwicklungsplanes in Afghanistan. Afghanistan Journal 2(3):112-118.

2413 Gilli, A.
1977 Die Waldgebiete im Osten Afghanistans. Feddes Repertorium 88:375-387.

2414 Ginnever, O. R.
1944 Cotton in Afghanistan. Geographical Journal 104:212-213.

The tentative results obtained from planting American type cotton, obtained by the Afghan government from the USSR.

2415 Glaister, G. S.
1979 Village Road Construction in Afghanistan: Appropriate Technology and Management. Transport and Communications Bulletin of Asia and Pacific 53:14-20.

2416 Glatzer, B.
1977 Nomaden von Gharjistan. Wiesbaden.

2417 Glaubitt, Klaus
1979 Effekte staalicher Aktivitat in Entwicklungslandern. Analyse realer und monetarer Probleme Afghanistans. Tubingen und Basel: Horst Erdmann Verlag. Pp. 261.

2418 Glaubitt, K., F. Saadeddin and B. Schafer
1977 Government Revenues and Economic Development of Afghanistan. Afghanistan Journal 4(1):20-25.

2419 Glaubitt, K., F. Saadeddin, B. Schafer, unter Mitarbeit von J. Kanne
1975 Das System der Staatseinnahmen und seine Bedeutung fur die Wirtschaftsentwicklung Afghanistans. Afghanische Studien 10. Pp. 106.

VII. ECONOMIC STRUCTURE

2420 Golovin, Y. M.
  1962 Afganistan, ekonomika i vneshnyaya torgovlya [The Economy and External Trade of Afghanistan]. Moscow: Vneshtorgizdat. Pp. 168.

  Chapters are devoted to industry, agriculture, transport, finance, and foreign trade, with emphasis on Afghan-Soviet relations.

2421 Golovin, Y. M.
  1962 Sovetskiy soyuz i Afganistan. Opyt ekonomicheskogo sotrudichestva [The Soviet Union and Afghanistan. Economic Cooperation]. Moscow: Izdatel'stvo Vostochnoy Literatury. Pp. 102; bibliography.

2422 Gouttiere, Thomas E.
  1980 U.S. Government Assistance to Afghan Refugees in Pakistan. Afghanistan Journal 7(4):159.

2423 Greene, Brook A. and F. Khayruddin Fazl
  1974 Selected Socio-economic Characteristics of Kohistan and Panjsher Districts, Kapisa Province, Afghanistan. Beirut: Faculty of Agricultural Sciences, American University of Beirut. Pp. 74.

2424 Grötzbach, Erwin
  1969 Economic Processes and Their Regional Differentiation in the Hindu Kush, Afghanistan. The Geographical Review of Afghanistan 7(2):1-7.

2425 Grötzbach, Erwin
  1972 Kulturgeographischer Wandel in Nordost-Afghanistan seit dem 19. Jahrhundert. Afganische Studien Bd. 4, Meisenheim am Glan.

2426 Grötzbach, Erwin
  1976 Periodische Markte in Afghanistan. Erdkunde 30(1):15-19.

2427 Grötzbach, Erwin
  1979 Stadte und Basare in Afghanistan. Eine stadtgeographische Untersuchung. Wiesbaden: Ludwig Reichert. Pp. 221.

2428 Grolimund, Kurt
  1981 Die Wirtschaftliche Struktur und Situation von Afghanistan. Hoeheren Wirtschafts und Verwaltungsschule 4. Pp. 43.

VII. ECONOMIC STRUCTURE

2429 Gul, Azam and Lloyd Picket
     1966 An Agronomic Survey in Six Eastern Provinces of Afghanistan. Kabul: Faculty of Agriculture, Kabul University. Pp. 82.

2430 Gurevich, Naum M.
     1959 Vneshnyaya torgovlya Afganistana do Vtoroy Mirovoy Voyny [Foreign Trade of Afghanistan before World War II]. Moscow: Izdatel'stvo Vostochnoy Literatury. Pp. 223; bibliography.

     A survey from the early nineteenth century, with emphasis on the years after 1919.

2431 Gurevich, Naum M.
     1962 Gosudarstvennyy sektor v ekonomike Afganistana [Government Business Enterprises in the Afghan Economy]. Moscow: Izdatel'stvo Vostochnoy Literatury. Pp. 110.

2432 Gurevich, Naum M. (ed)
     1963 Voprosy ekonomiki Afganistana [The Problems of Afghanistan's Economy]. Moscow: Izdatel'stvo Vostochnoy Literatury. Pp. 248.

     Articles by the editor and four other specialists on the following subjects: The Question of Transit in Afghanistan's Economy and Policy, On the Agricultural Commune and its Economic Importance in Afghanistan, On the Question of Training National Technical Cadres in Afghanistan, The Economic Position of the Imperialist States in Present Day Afghanistan, and Export Articles of Afghanistan's Economy, 1939-1960.

2433 Hafisi, Abdul Satar
     1974 Geologische-petrographische Untersuchung des chromitfuhrenden Ultrabasitmassivs vom Logal Tal (Sudlich von Kabul). [A Geological and Petrological Investiation of the Chromite-Bearing Ultrabasite Massif of the Logar Valley, South of Kabul]. Unpublished Ph.D. Dissertation. University of Bonn. Pp. 113.

2434 Haider, Habib
     1976 Contribution a l'etude de la commercialisation des produits agrocoles en Afghanistan. [Contribution to the Study of the Commercialization of Agricultural Produce in Afghanistan]. Unpublished Ph.D. Dissertation. University of Paris IV (Paris-Sorbonne). Pp. xiv, 330.

VII. ECONOMIC STRUCTURE

2435 Hakimi, Abdul Karim
  1958 Masa'ile Iqtisadi-yi Ma [Our Economic Problems]. Kabul: Matba'eh-yi doulati. Pp. 54. (1337 A.H.)

  A number of essays on Afghan economy. In Dari.

2436 Helmand Valley Industrial Survey--Phase I
  1955 Unpublished Report. International Engineering Company. San Francisco. Pp. 175; maps.

  First survey and appraisal of industrial activities in the Helmand Valley, followed by an optimistic analysis of markets contributing to potential expansion of industry in an area of 100,000 square miles (2/5 of Afghanistan).

2437 Hinrichs, Harley H.
  1962 Certainty as Criterion: Taxation of Foreign Investment in Afghanistan. National Tax Journal 15(2):139-154.

2438 Hoff, Hellmut
  1963 Die deutsch-afghanischen Wirtschaftsbeziehungen [German-Afghan Economic Relations]. Orient 4(3):98-99.

2439 Hondrich, Karl Otto
  1964 Die Einstellung Afghanischer Studenten zum Sozialen Wandelversuch einer Empirischen Studie in einem Wirtschaftlich Unterentwickeltenland [The Attitude of Afghanistan Students Towards Social Change - An Attempt at an Empirical Study in an Economically Underdeveloped Country]. Koelner Z. Soziol. Soz-Psychol. 16(4):703-726.

2440 Hoshmand, Ahmad Reza
  1978 Economic Cooperation Between Afghanistan, Iran, and Pakistan: An Application of Customs Union Theory. Unpublished Ph.D. Dissertation. University of Maryland. Pp. 212.

  Investigates application of the theory of customs union to the three countries. A study on an exante basis in terms of trade creation, trade diversion and welfare.

2441 Hoshmand, A. Reza
  1981 Customs Union for Afghanistan, Iran, and Pakistan: A Reassessment of Options. Journal of South Asian and Middle Eastern Studies 5(1):3-9.

VII. ECONOMIC STRUCTURE

In light of the current conditions in Central and South Asia the author reassesses his earlier proposal for an economic cooperation through customs union between Afghanistan, Iran, Pakistan. See above.

2442 India
n.d. Trade Agency, Kabul. Report. 1st--1937/38. Delhi: Manager of Publications. Pp. v.

Publication of the Department of Commercial Intelligence and Statistics (India), Calcutta.

2443 Indian Institute of Foreign Trade
1972 Marketing Research Division Export Prospects of Select Indian Products in Afghanistan. New Delhi: Indian Institute of Foreign Trade. Pp. v, 233.

2444 Industrial Development in Afghanistan
1965 A Forward Look. Robert R. Nathan Associates. Pp. 77; mimeographed.

2445 Iqtisad [Economics]
1931- An illustrated monthly periodical which first appeared in 1931.

Sponsored by the Ministry of National Economy, the articles are in Dari, Pushtu, and English. The periodical has appeared irregularly, and its title has other forms.

2446 Ishida, O.
1980 Japanese Researcher Reports from Inside Afghanistan. Business Japan 25(10):31.

2447 Janata, Alfred
1975 Kantholzexport nach Pakistan. Afghanistan Journal 2(2):73. Map; photo.

2448 Janata, Alfred
1963 Die landwirtschaftliche Struktur Afghanistans [The Agricultural Structure of Afghanistsn]. Bustan 3:36-40. Vienna.

2449 Jeanneret, Andre
1965 A propos de toiles imprimees et peintes desrinees a la chasse aux perdrix en Afghanistan. Baessler Archiv 13:115-126.

VII. ECONOMIC STRUCTURE

2450   Jeanneret, Andre
        1974 Contribution a l'etude des Boulangers de Kaboul.
              Afghanistan Journal 1(2):37-44. Photos; illustrations.

2451   Jensch, Werner
        1971 Die Afghanischen Entwicklungsplane vom Ersten Biszum
              Dritten Plan. Unpublished Ph.D. Dissertation. Bochum
              University. Pp. 390.

2452   Jentsch, Christoph
        1973 Das Nomadentum in Afghanistan. Meisenheim: Anton
              Hain Verlag. Pp. 242.

2453   Kajakai Report and its Relation to the Development of the
              Helmand Valley
        1949 Unpublished Report. International Engineering
              Company. Washington. Pp. 50; map.

        Appraises economic returns from harnessing the Helmand
        River and irrigating 550,000 acres. Served to justify the
        1950 U.S. dollar loan request from the U.S. Export-Import
        Bank.

2454   Kamal, Abdul Hadi
        1954 Das Agrarland Afghanistan und seine Zukunft [The
              Farm Land of Afghanistan and its Future]. Zurich.

2455   Kamrany, Nake M.
        1962 The First Five-Year Plan of Afghanistan (1956-1961):
              An Economic Evaluation. Ph.D. Dissertation. University
              of Southern California. Pp. 250.

        An assessment of the contributions and drawbacks of the
        first five-year development plan of Afghanistan.

2456   Kamrany, Nake M.
        1969 Peaceful Competition in Afghanistan: American and
              Soviet Models for Economic Aid. Washington:
              Communication Services Corporation. Pp. ix, 125.

        A slightly revised version of the Ph.D. dissertation of
        the author. Descriptive and based upon inconclusive
        second-hand data. The work fails to develop a critical
        understanding and comparison of American and Soviet models
        for development, particularly as far as these models stand
        up to the backdrop of the Afghan society and culture.

VII. ECONOMIC STRUCTURE

2457 Kanne, Jürgen
1974 Interne Investitionsfinanzierung in Afghanistan. [Internal Financing of Investments in Afghanistan]. Unpublished Ph.D. Dissertation. University of Bochum. Pp. xiv, 641.

2458 Kanne, Jürgen
1976 Die Rolle des Bankwesens im Entwicklungsprozess Afghanistans. Afghanistan Journal 3(1):22-27.

2459 Karhanah [Agriculture]
1952- The quarterly publication of the Department of Agriculture, which first appeared at Kabul in 1952. The articles are in Pushtu and Dari.

2460 Kayoumi, A. H.
1966 La Banque Centrale d'Afghanistan et son Role dans le Development du Pays. Ph.D. Thesis. University of Neuchatel. Pp. 140.

2461 Khan, Ghani Mohammad
1972 Afghanistan's Transit Trade Through Pakistan and the Unrecorded Transactions at Landikotal. Peshawar: Board of Economic Enquiry, NWFP, University of Peshawar. Pp. ii, 29.

2462 Kherad, Akbar
1971 La politique de cooperation financiere et technique de l'Afghanistan. [Afghanistan's Policy of Financial and Technical Cooperation]. Unpublished Ph.D. Dissertation. Panthern-Sorbonne (Paris I). Pp. 414.

2463 Khodjayev, M. A. Baba
1972 The Question of the Formation of an all-Afghan Market and the Trade and Industrial Policy Pursued by Amir Abdul Rahman. Afghanistan 25(2):42-48.

2464 Kohzad, Ahmad Ali
1948 Le lapis-lazuli et son rôle dans les relations de l'Ariana avec les pays de l'Asie [Lapis-lazuli and its Role in the Relations of Aryana with the Countries of Asia]. Afghanistan 3(4):1-2.

Locates the mines in the country and tells of finds of worked lapis-lazuli in ancient sites in Iran, Iraq, and Egypt.

VII. ECONOMIC STRUCTURE

2465   König, Rene
        1971 Die Nan-Baecker in Afghanistan: Ueberlegungen zu
           Einem Fall isolierter Arbeitsteilung [The Nan Bakers in
           Afghanistan: Considerations on a Case of Isolated
           Division of Labor]. Kölner Zeitschrift fuer Soziologie
           und Sozial-psychologie 23(2):304-326.

2466   Köster, Ulrich
        1973 Institutionelle Massnahmen zur Verbesserung der
           Marktstruktur von Weizen in Afghanistan. Z. Ausl.
           Landw. 12:222-233.

2467   Kohzad, Ahmad Ali
        1949 Shah Shamiran et le Raisin [Shah Shamiran and the
           Grape]. Afghanistan 4(3):45-48.

        Notes on ancient mentions of vineyards in Afghanistan are
        followed by a story of the legendary discovery of the
        grape vine in the reign of Shah Shamiran.

2468   Kohzad, Ahmad Ali
        1953 "Nimrouz" ou le bassin inférieur de l'Hilmend
           ["Nimrouz" or the Lower Basin of the Helmand].
           Afghanistan 8(4):46-50.

        Ancient and modern evidence to prove that the lower valley
        of the Helmand was--before the invasion of Timur--fertile
        and well irrigated and that it may, under the government's
        efforts to recolonize and irrigate, be so again.

2469   Kraus, Rudiger W. H.
        1973 Siedlungspolitik und Erfolg: dargestellt an
           Siedlungen in den Provinzen Hilmend und Baghlan,
           Afghanistan [Settlement Policy and Success: Exemplified
           by Settlements in the Provinces of Hilmend and Baghlan,
           Afghanistan]. Unpublished Ph.D. Dissertation. Giessen
           University. Pp. 150.

2470   Kraus, Willy (ed)
        1972 Steigerung der landwirtschaftlichen Produktion und
           ihre Weiterverarbeitung in Afghanistan. Meisenheim:
           Anton Hain Verlag. Pp. 152.

2471   Labour Legislation in Afghanistan
        1948 International Labour Review 57:83-85.

VII. ECONOMIC STRUCTURE

A summary of the labor regulations issued in the Royal Order of January 16, 1946. The regulations deal with wages, hours, accident compensation, social security, and health.

2472 Lakanwal, Abdul Ghafar
1978 Situationsanalyse landwirtschaftlicher Beratungsprogramme in Entwicklungslander. Methodische Probleme, dargestellt an Beratungsprogrammen zur Forderung von Kleinlandwirten in Paktia (Afghanistan). Sozialokonomische Schriften zur Agrarentwicklung 30. Saarbrucken, Breiterbach. Pp. viii, 283.

2473 Lapparent, Albert F. de
1975 La montagne du fer d'Hajigak en Afghanistan Central. Afghanistan Journal 2(1):8-11. Map; photos.

2474 The Law of Commerce (Commercial Law of Afghanistan)
n.d. Kabul: Public Administration Service, USAID. Not paged, mimeographed.

A translation of the law of 1955.

2475 Lieberman, Samuel S.
1980 Afghanistan: Population and Development in the "Land of Insolence." Population and Development Review 6(2):271-298.

2476 Mahmoud, Shah
1967 The Contribution of Foreign Trade to the Economy of Afghanistan 1947-1963. Unpublished Ph.D. Dissertation. Columbia University. Pp. 325.

A study of the importance of international trade for Afghanistan. Detailed examination of important changes which have occurred in Afghan international trade since World War II.

2477 Mangal, S. M.
1973 Nekotorye problemy sotsial'no-ekonomicheskogo razvitiia Afganistana [Several Problems in the Socio-Economic Development of Afghanistan]. Unpublished Ph.D. Dissertation. Moskovskii gosudarstvennyi universitet.

2478 Masannat, George S.
1969 Development and Diplomacy in Afghanistan. Journal of Asian and African Studies 4(1):51-60.

VII. ECONOMIC STRUCTURE

2479 McArthur, I. D., Sarwar Sayad, and Maqsood Nawin
1979 Rangeland Livestock Production in Western Afghanistan. Journal of Arid Environments 2(2):163-179.

2480 McChesney, Robert D.
1968 The Economic Reforms of Amir Abdul Rahman Khan. Afghanistan 21(3):16-28.

2481 Mehrabi, Shah M.
1978 An Analysis and Evaluation of Economic and Education Sectors in Afghanistan. Unpublished Ph.D. Dissertation. University of Cincinnati. Pp. 282.

2482 Meuer, Gerd
1980 Afghanistan und die Dritte Entwicklungsdekade: neue Strategien fur alte Probleme? Neue Ges. 27(5):388-392.

2483 Michel, Aloys A.
1959 The Kabul, Kunduz, and Helmand Valleys and the National Economy of Afghanistan. Unpublished Ph.D. Dissertation. Columbia University. Pp. 441.

2484 Michel, Aloys A.
1960 The Kabul, Kunduz, and Helmand Valleys and the National Economy of Afghanistan. Washington, D.C.: National Academy of Sciences. Pp. 441; bibliography; maps.

A detailed account, based upon first-hand observations, of present and proposed irrigation and power projects in major river valleys.

2485 Michel, Aloys A.
1961 Foreign Trade and Foreign Policy in Afghanistan. Middle Eastern Affairs 12(1):7-15.

An analysis of the country's foreign trade, reflecting an increasing dependence on the U.S.S.R.

2486 Michel, Aloys A.
1972 The Impact of Modern Irrigation Technology in the Indus and Helmand Basins of Southwest Asia. In The Careless Technology. Edited by M. T. Farver and J. P. Milton. New York. Pp. 257-275.

2487 Miner, Thomas H. and Associates, Inc.
1968 Developing the Herb Industry in Afghanistan. Prepared for Ministry of Commerce, Afghanistan. Project 306-11-990-087. Kabul: UAID.

VII. ECONOMIC STRUCTURE

2488   Ministry of National Economy
        1951 The Economic Year Book. A Summary of the Economic Activities in Afghanistan during the Year 1329 (1950) Compiled by Yusuf Aina. Kabul. Pp. 96. (English summary translation provided.)

        The English section is too short to give more than the briefest outline of financial and economic activities.

2489   Ministry of Planning
        1959 Survey of Progress. 1959. Four volumes with volume one in two parts. Kabul: Government Printing House.

        Mimeographed report, each volume containing sections in Persian and in English; the pages are not numbered consecutively.

2490   Ministry of Planning
        1960 Survey of Progress. 1960. Kabul: Military Printing Press. Pp. 215; 90 tables; map.

        Comprises the third annual report on the First Five Year Development Plan. Part I is a progress report of the activities of the ministries, Part II an analytical review of significant economic and social developments, and Part III a series of statistic tables. The report was also published in Pushtu and in Dari.

2491   Ministry of Planning
        1963 Survey of Progress. 1961-62. Kabul: Government Printing House. Pp. 83; 51 pages of tables and charts.

        A review of activity under the First Five Year Plan, 1956-1961.

2492   Ministry of Planning
        1969 Survey of Progress 1968-1969. Kabul: Department of Statistics, Ministry of Planning. Pp. 132.

2493   Ministry of Planning
        1970 Survey of Progress 1969-1970. Kabul: Department of Statistics, Ministry of Planning. Pp. 159.

2494   Ministry of Planning
        1971 The Third Five Year Economic and Social Plan of Afghanistan. Kabul: Government Printing Press. Pp. 305.

VII. ECONOMIC STRUCTURE

2495   Ministry of Planning
            1972 Statistical Pocketbook. Kabul: Department of
                Statistics, Ministry of Planning.

2496   Ministry of Planning
            1972 Survey of Progress 1970-71. Kabul: Department of
                Statistics, Ministry of Planning.

2497   Ministry of Planning
            1977 First Seven Year Economic and Social Development
                Plan, 1976/77-1982/83. Kabul: Government Printing
                Press.

2498   Mirzoyan, S.
            1964 Uspekhi Khozyaystvennogo razvitiya Afganistana
                [Successes of Economic Development in Afghanistan].
                Mirovaya Ekonomika i Mezhdunarodnyye Otnosheniya 11:98-
                100. Moscow.

2499   Mohammed, Ali
            1949 Karakul as the Most Important Article of Afghan
                Trade. Afghanistan 4(4):48-53.

        Traces the early use of Karakul and its history as an item
        of commerce, lists sales of skins in recent years, and
        outlines steps which should be taken to improve the
        marketing of this item.

2500   Moir, M. C.
            1943 Afghanistan--Crossroads of Asia; Gateway to India.
                Foreign Commerce Weekly 9:10-15.

        Itemizes the initial steps taken toward a modern economy
        through industrialization and the expansion of irrigation
        facilities.

2501   Mokhtarzada, Mohammed Taufiq
            1972 Entstehung und Entwicklung der deutsch-afghanischen
                Beziehungen unter besonderer Berucksichtigung der
                Entwicklungshilfe der Bundesrepublic Deutschland fur
                Afghanistan wahrend der ersten Entwicklungsdekade. [The
                Emergence and Development of Afghani-German Relations
                with Particular Regard to the Development Aid of the
                Federal Republic of Germany Extended to Afghanistan
                during the First Decade of Her Development].
                Unpublished Ph.D. Dissertation. Freie University
                Berlin. Pp. 232.

VII. ECONOMIC STRUCTURE

2502 Moos, Irene von
1980 Die Wirtschaftliche Veraeltnisse im Munjan-Tal und der Opiumgebrauch der Bevoelkerung. Leistal: Biblitheca Afghanica, Schriftenreinhe 1. Pp. 64.

The first in the Swiss Afghanistan Archive's entries. Deals with general socio-economic conditions in the Munjan Valley and focuses on the use of opium in the region.

2503 Muhammad Kabir Khan Ludin
1948 Afghan Government Views: The Kabul River Valley Development. Afghanistan 3(4):44-49; map.

A summary account of numerous planned projects to utilize the water of the Kabul River for irrigation and power. Since the time of writing, the largest project, the Sarobi dam, has gone steadily forward.

2504 Muhiddinov, I.
1975 Zemledelie Pamirskikh Tadjikov Vakhana N Ishkashima. B XIX - Nachalne XX B.: Istoriko-Etnograficheskii Ocherk. [The Agriculture of Pamir Tajiks of Wakhan and Ishkashim, Nineteenth Century to the Beginning of the Twentieth Century]. Moscow: USSR Academy of Sciences. Pp. 127.

An ethnohistoric work dealing with agricultural technology and plant cultivation among the Tajiks of Wakhan and Pamir during the nineteenth century and the beginning of the twentieth century. Of interest to students of ethnography and economics of Tajiks.

2505 Munneke, Roelof J.
1980 The Bazaar in Market-Towns in Northern Afghanistan. Afghanistan Journal 7(4):146-147.

2506 Munneke, Roelof J.
1980 The Bazaar in Market-Towns in Northern Afghanistan: Methods of Presentation. In From Field-Case to Show Case. Edited W. R. Gulik. Amsterdam: Gieben. Pp. 85-96.

2507 Nadjibi, Azis S. A.
1974 Projektanalyse fur Industrieprojekte in Entwicklungslandern, dargestellt am Beispiel Afghanistans. [Project Analysis for Industrial Projects in Developing Countries, Demonstrated in the Case of Afghanistan.] Unpublished Ph.D. Dissertation. University of Bonn. Pp. 236.

VII. ECONOMIC STRUCTURE

2508   Nagler, Horst
        1969 Privatinitiative beim Industrieaufbau in Afghanistan. [Private Initiative in the Building up of Industry in Afghanistan]. Unpublished Ph.D. Dissertation. University of Bochum. Pp. 270.

2509   Najafi, Fazil Tawab
        1977 Proposed Karachi-Rasht Railway System (KRR) and its Impacts on the Development of Afghanistan, Iran and Pakistan. Unpublished Ph.D. Dissertation. Virginia Polytechnic Institute and State University. Pp. 285.

        Analysis of the developmental impact of a proposed international railway system especially through the Afghanistan/Pakistan region. Study of the socio-economic characteristics of Afghanistan/Pakistan in comparison to Uganda, Kenya, Tanzania, and Switzerland, West Germany, France.

2510   Nazar, Ata Mohammad
        1979 Risk Avoidance in the Operation of a Water Supply System (Qalagai Project in Afghanistan). Unpublished Ph.D. Dissertation. Colorado State University. Pp. 323.

        Discusses the operational criteria based on engineering analysis which was to provide irrigation water and generate hydro-electric energy as a result of the Qalagai Project.

2511   Nedeltcheff, Nicolaff
        1929 Le mouton "Kerekul" [The Karakul Sheep]. Lyon: Bosc et Rieu. Pp. 79.

2512   Neubauer, H. F.
        1954 Bemerkungen uber das Vorkommen wilder Obstsorten in Nuristan. Angew. Bot. 28:81-88.

2513   Neubauer, H. F.
        1974 Die Nuristanrebe, Herkunft der Edelrebe und Ursprung des Weinbaues. Afghanistan Journal 1(2):32-36.

2514   Nicollet, Serge
        1972 L'elevage dans la province Afghane de Caboul. [Animal Husbandry in Kabul Province, Afghanistan]. Unpublished Ph.D. Dissertation. University of Paris XII (Paris-Val-de-Marne). Pp. 120.

VII. ECONOMIC STRUCTURE

2515 Nikitine, Basile
    1932 La structure - économique de l'Afghanistan [The Economic Structure of Afghanistan]. Paris: Société d'Études et d'Informations Économiques. (Mémoires et Documents). Pp. 29.

    A sound, rather thorough study, with a certain emphasis on a projection of the economic development of the country.

2516 Nogge, G. and J. Niethammer
    1976 Die Vogel auf den Basaren von Kabul und Charikar. Afghanistan Journal 3(4):150-157. Photos; tables.

2517 Noor, Abdul Sami
    1973 Die Rolle des Aussenhandels in der wirtschaftlichen Entwicklung Afghanistans [The Role of Foreign Trade in the Economic Development of Afghanistan]. Unpublished Ph.D. Dissertation. University of Bonn. Pp. 237.

2518 Noorzoy, M. Siddiq
    1976 Planning and Growth in Afghanistan. World Development 4:761-773.

2519 Noorzoy, M. Siddiq
    1977 An Analysis of the Afghan Foreign and Domestic Private Investment Law of 1974. Afghanistan Journal 4(1):29-30.

2520 Noorzoy, M. Siddiq
    1979 The First Afghan Seven Year Plan 1976/77-1982/83: A Review of Some Comparisons of the Objectives and Means. Afghanistan Journal 6(1):15-23.

2521 Norvell, Douglass G., Mohammad Yussof Hakimi, Mohammad Naim Dindar
    1973 Markets and Men in Afghanistan. Washington, D.C.: Agency for International Development. Pp. iv; 118; plates.

    A description and analysis of marketing conditions and possiblities in Afghanistan.

2522 Oesterdiekhoff, Peter
    1977 Hemmnisse und Widerspruche in der Entwicklung armer Lander: Darstellung am Beispiel Afghanistans. [Obstacles and Contradictions in the Development of Poor Countries: Shown Through the Example of Afghanistan]. Ph.D. Dissertation. University of Bremen. Pp. 695.

VII. ECONOMIC STRUCTURE

2523 Oksendahl, Wilma
1961 Business Education for Afghan Women. The Asia Foundation (Program Bulletin) 19:5-7.

First-hand report by an American adviser at Kabul.

2524 Pangeh [Bank]
1941- A monthly, largely in Persian, published at Kabul since 1941 by the National Bank of Afghanistan.

2525 Pastidis, S. L.
1964 Summary of Literature on Food and Agricultural Marketing in Afghanistan. Kabul: no publisher. Pp. 14; mimeographed.

A descriptive listing of some 56 ephemeral reports by the author.

2526 Paul, Arthur
1963 Role of Trade in Afghanistan's Development. Asia Foundation (Program Bulletin) 29:1-5.

2527 Peasant Life in Afghanistan
1945 Moslem World 35:259.

A short article on farms and farmers, presented anonymously.

2528 Pedersen, Gorm
1981 Socio-Economic Change Among a Group of East Afghan Nomads. Afghanistan Journal 8(4):115-122.

2529 Pikulin, M. G.
1961 Razvitiye natsional'noy ekonomiki i kul'tury Afganistana 1955-1960 [The Development of National Economy and Culture in Afghanistan 1955-1960]. Tashkent: Izdatel'stvo Akademii Nauk Uzbekskoy S.S.R. Pp. 151; bibliography.

Largely concerned with the course of the First Five Year Plan. Material on cultural progress and on the need to eliminate feudalism in the society.

2530 Planhol, Xavier de
1973 Lineamenti generali del commercio della neve nel Mediterraneo e nel Oriente. Bollettino della Societa Geografica Italiana 10(2):315-339.

VII. ECONOMIC STRUCTURE

2531 Planhol, Xavier de
1974 Le Commerce de la Neige en Afghanistan. Revue de Geographie Alpine 72(2):269-276.

2532 Polyak, A. A.
1964 Ekonomicheskiy stroy Afganistana; ocherki [Economic System of Afghanistan; Essays]. Moscow: Nauka. Pp. 161.

2533 Poulton, Robin and Michelle
1981 Prospects for Afghanistan's Economy. The World Today 34(5):182-187.

2534 Preparing Shipments to Afghanistan
1950 International Reference Service, Foreign and Domestic Commerce Bureau, U. S. Department of Commerce 7(116):4.

2535 Project Progress Report
1961 United States Operations Mission to Afghanistan. June 30, 1961. Kabul: Program Office, USOM. Pp. 157.

A mimeographed report which includes an historical analysis of the American aid program, a description of individual projects, and a list of contractors employed on the projects.

2536 Putnam, B. H., and J. J. Van Belle
1978 Monetary Approach to Afghanistan's Flexible Exchange-Rate. Journal of Money, Credit and Banking 10(1):117-118.

2537 Qaderi, M. Zaher
1977 An Assessment of Agricultural Competencies Possessed and Needed by Beginning Agricultural Workers in Afghanistan. Unpublished Ph.D. Dissertation. Pennsylvania State University. Pp. 167.

Assesses the competencies of beginning agricultural workers in Afghanistan to develop recommendations for the improvement of the curriculum in the College of Agriculture, Kabul University.

2538 Rao, Aparna
1979 Les Ghorbat: Contribution a L'etude Economique et Sociale d'un Group "Jat" d'Afghanistan. Unpublished Ph.D. Dissertation. University of Paris. Pp. 492.

VII. ECONOMIC STRUCTURE

2539   Rathjens, C.
            1975 Witterungsbedingte Schwankungen dur Ernahrungsbasis
                in Afghanistan. Erdkunde 29(3):182-188.

2540   Reinhard, Gregor M.
            1968 Strategic Problems of the Indian Ocean Area: The
                Iran-Afghanistan-Pakistan Sector of the International
                Frontier. Unpublished Ph.D. Dissertation. Catholic
                University of America. Pp. 431.

        An analysis of conflicting strategies of the great powers
        to establish control over the Iran-Pakistan border,
        especially over the overland routes leading through this
        sector to the Persian Gulf and the Indian Ocean.

2541   Reinshagen, Heide and Lutz H. Eckensberger
            1976 Manual Labor or Educational/Intellectual Require-
                ments as Determinants of Occupational Prestige in
                Afghanistan: A Critical Investigation. Journal of
                Vocational Behavior 8(3):275-283.

2542   Reisner, Igor Mikhailovich
            1953 Afghanistan; ekonomiko-geograficheskaia kharakteris-
                tika [Afghanistan; Economic-Geographic Characteristics].
                Moscow: Gosudarstvennoe izdatel'stvo geografischeskai
                literatury. Pp. 67; map.

        A revision of a book entitled Afghanistan, published by
        the same author in 1939. More stress is placed on
        economic factors, and the material has been brought up-to-
        date.

2543   Reisner, Igor Mikhailovich
            1954 Razvitie Feodalizma i Obrazovanie Gosudarstva u
                Afganstev. [The Emergence of Feudalism and the
                Establishment of the Feudal State Among the Afghans].
                Moscow: USSR Academy of Sciences. Pp. 210.

        A study of the formation of State-systems in Afghanistan.
        Concludes that feudalism appeared in Afghanistan after the
        twelfth century.

2544   Report on Development of the Arghandab Area
            1949 Unpublished report. International Engineering
                Company. Washington. Pp. 16; tables; maps.

VII. ECONOMIC STRUCTURE

Describes the agricultural potential of year-round irrigation of the fertile southwestern valley. Served to justify part of the 1950 loan from the U.S. Export-Import Bank.

2545   Report on Development Program of Government of Afghanistan
       1955 Unpublished report. International Engineering Company. San Francisco. Pp. 48; map.

Introduced by a letter of transmittal from the Helmand Valley Authority, this report served as the formal loan application filed in November 1953 with the U.S. Export-Import Bank. It summarizes irrigation construction work since 1946 and appraises six new projects in the Arghandab and Helmand valleys and a major road-building program.

2546   Report to the Government of Afghanistan on Handicrafts and Small-Scale Industries
       1954 Unpublished report. International Labor Organization. Geneva. Pp. 67.

Prepared by a technical expert serving under U. N. Technical Assistance Administration, from February 1953 to January 1954. Describes home weaving and the cotton, wool, silk and carpet industries, and appraises the economic potential of expanded handicraft activities.

2547   Report of the Helmand River Delta Commission
       1951 Unpublished report. Washington: U.S. Department of State. Pp. 151; map of Sistan.

Describes agricultural and hydrological features of the Sistan basin as background for the dispute over division of the Helmand River water between Iran and Afghanistan. Contains data not available elsewhere. Prepared by a U.S. engineer, on behalf of an international arbitration commission after a 1950 field trip.

2548   Report on Proposed Cement Factory near Kabul, Afghanistan
       1948 Unpublished report. International Engineering Company. San Francisco. Pp. 13; sketches.

Appraises the need for and the feasibility of a cement plant with 60,000 tons annual capacity.

2549   Report on Proposed Trunk Highways (Afghanistan)
       1949 Unpublished report. International Engineering Company. San Francisco. Pp. 23; maps.

VII. ECONOMIC STRUCTURE

>Describes the economic role of the existing Qandahar-Kabul-Torkham route and the potential benefits of its reconstruction.

2550 Resai, Mohammed Ismail
1958 Struktur und Entwick- lungsmöglichkeiten der Wirtschaft von Afghanistan [The Structure and Development Potentials of the Economy of Afghanistan]. Bonn. Pp. 101; bibliography.

A doctoral dissertation, privately printed by the author, based largely upon European sources rather than research in Afghanistan.

2551 Reut, Marguerite
1976 L'elevage du ver a soie en Afghanistan et l'artisanat de la soie a Herat [The Raising of Silkworms in Afghanistan and the Silk Industry in Herat]. Unpublished Ph.D. Dissertation. Sorbonne-Nouvelle (Paris III). Pp. iv, 283.

2552 Reut, Marguerite
1979 La Production de la Soie a Herat. Studia Iranica 8(1):107-116.

2553 Rhein, Eberhard
1964 Hilfe für Afghanistan aus Ost und West [Aid for Afghanistan from East and West]. Aussenpolitik 15(8):557-564.

2554 Rhein, Eberhard and A. Ghanie Ghaussy
1966 Die Wirtschaftliche Entwicklungen Afghanistans. 1880-1965 [The Economic Development of Afghanistan. 1880-1965]. Köln/Opladen: C. W. Leske. Pp. 208; bibliography.

2555 Rosenbaum, H.
1975 Das Afghanistan-Archiv des Instituts fur Entwicklungsforschung und Entwicklungspolitik der Ruhr-Universitat Bochum. Afghanistan Journal 2(4):151-152.

2556 Rosset, Louis-Felicien
1946 Afghan Marble. Afghanistan 1(2):4-11.

Lists local sites and types and describes the Kabul marble works.

VII. ECONOMIC STRUCTURE

2557 Rozhevits, R.
1928 IU. Novye Dannye po Flore zlakov Afganistana [New Materials on the Cereal Family of Afghanistan]. (In Russian, with French Summary.) Bulletin of Applied Botany of Genetics and Plant Breeding 19(1):121-126. Leningrad.

The French summary, Nouveaux matériaux sur la flore des graminées de l'Afghanistan, begns on page 125--a list of 20 cereal specimens found in Afghanistan. An entirely new species, Oryzopsis Vavilovi Roshev, is described in Latin on page 123.

2558 Samii, Said
1974 Wandlungen in der Sozialstruktur der Bevolkerung Afghanistans in Entwicklungsprozess 1950 bis zur Gegenwart. [Changes in the Social Structure of the Afghan Population During the Course of Development, 1950 to Present]. Unpublished Ph.D. Dissertation. Köln University. Pp. 282.

2559 Samini, A.
1961 Zustand und Entwicklungsmöglichkeiten der Wirtschaft Afghanistans unter besonderer Berücksichtigung der Landwirtschaft [The Condition and the Development Potential of Afghanistan's Economy Under the Special Aspect of Farming]. Bonn.

2560 Sawari, M. Sadiq
1974 Afghanistan Zwischen Tradition und Modernisierung. Europaische Hochschulschriften, Reihe 31(2):1-312.

2561 Schafer, Bernd
1974 Schmuggel in Afghanistan. Afghanistan Journal 1(2):27-31.

2562 Schwarzenbach, Annemarie Clark
1940 Afghanistan in Transition. Geographical Magazine 11:326-341; map. London.

Condensed account of a trip taken throughout much of Afghanistan in 1939, with attention centered on the efforts at industrialization of the country.

2563 Schwob, Marcel
1955 The Economic Challenge in Afghanistan. United Nations Review 2:25-27.

VII. ECONOMIC STRUCTURE

        An outline of plans for charting and developing mineral and economic resources with the assistance of various agencies of the United Nations.

2564 Scoville, James G.
      1974 Afghan Labor Markets: A Model of Interdependence. Industrial Relations 13(3):274-287.

2565 Second Five Year Plan
      1963 1341-45 (March 1962-March 1967). Kabul: Government Printing House. Pp. 100.

      Prepared by the Ministry of Planning.

2566 Seifert, Bruno
      1929 Der Anteil Deutschlands an der wirtschaftlichen Entwicklung Afghanistans, von Bruno Seifert; hrsg. in Verbindung mit der Deutschen Akademie München und dem Institut für mittel-und südosteuropaische Wirtschaftsforschung an der Universität Leipzig [Germany's Participation in the Economic Development of Afghanistan, by Bruno Seifert; Published in Connection with the German Academy of Munich and the Institute for Middle-and-Southeast European Economic Research at the University of Leipzig]. Stuttgart: Ausland und Heimat Verlagsaktiengesellschaft. Pp. 66; map.

      The author's Ph.D. Dissertation.

2567 Semin, A.
      1954 Sovetsko-afganskie ekonomicheskie otnosheniia [Soviet-Afghan Economic Relations]. Vneshniaia Torgovlia 24(5):1-6. Moscow.

2568 Sérignan, Claude
      1960 Le plan quinquennal Afghan [The Afghan Five Year Plan]. Orient 4:77-96.

      An analysis of the First Five Year Development Plan.

2569 Shah, S. M.
      1946 Trade with Afghanistan. Lahore: Ripon Printing Press. Pp. vii, 103; appendices; folding map.

VII. ECONOMIC STRUCTURE

Some ten brief chapters deal with communications, education, press, exports, imports, banks and currency, business concerns, commerce, and related subjects. The author notes that "since the Afghan Government does not publish any trade returns, the various figures . . . cannot be calculated as unassailable."

2570 Shah, S. M.
1948 Afghan General and Commercial Directory 1327 (1948-49). Karachi: Himaliya Press. Pp. iv, 170; folding map.

The author, a Pakistani associated with the Ministry of Commerce at Karachi, claims that this is the first such publication on Afghanistan. It features hard-to-find information on such subjects as names and positions of government officials, schools and teachers, writers and publications, a street guide to Kabul, and a considerable variety of miscellaneous information.

2571 Shalizi, Abdussattar
1950 The Text of Mr. Shalizi's Speech in the Plenary Session of the Asian Regional Conference at Nuwara Eliya, Ceylon. Afghanistan 5(1):33-39.

The Afghan General Director of Labor sets forth Afghanistan's hopes and work in the labor field and endorses the program of the International Labor Organization.

2572 Shalizi, Abdussattar
1963 Problems and Characteristics of Afghanistan's Internal Development. Review of International Affairs 14:6-10.

2573 Shirreff, David
1977 Afghanistan Development: Seven-Year Plan Leans Heavily on Foreign Aid. Middle East Economic Digest 21:3-4.

2574 Shirreff, David
1977 Afghanistan: Big Powers No Longer Compete as Big Spenders. Middle East Economic Digest 21:7-8.

2575 Shirreff, David
1977 Afghanistan: Landlocked Exporters Aim For New Markets. Middle East Economic Digest 21:12.

VII. ECONOMIC STRUCTURE

2576   Singer, Andre
        1973 Tribal Migrations on the Irano-Afghan Border. Asian Affairs 60(2):160-165.

2577   Singer, Andre
        1976 Problems of Pastoralism in the Afghan Pamirs. Asian Affairs 63(2):156-160.

2578   Snoy, Peter
        1962 Die Kafiren. Formen der Wirtschaft und geistigen Kultur. Dissertation. Frankfort am Main.

2579   Stevens, Ira Moore and K. Tarzi
        1965 Economic and Agricultural Production in Helmand Valley. Denver: U.S. Department of the Interior (Bureau of Reclamation). Pp. xii, 101.

2580   Stewart, Ruth W.
        1961 Caravan Trade in Asia With Special Reference to Afghanistan. Kabul: Communications Media Division, USOM/A. Not paged; mimeographed; maps; bibliography.

        Includes a Dari translation of the English text.

2581   Stilz, D.
        1974 Entwicklung und Struktur der Afghanischen Industrie. Afghanische Studien 11. Meisenheim: Anton Hain Verlag. Pp. 116.

2582   Strand, Richard F.
        1975 The Changing Herding Economy of the Kom Nuristani. Afghanistan Journal 2(4):123-134. Map; photos.

2583   Strany Vostoka
        1936 Ekonomicheskii spravochnik. 2. Srednyi Vostak. Afghanistan pod redaktsiei I. M. Reisnera [Countries of the East. An Economic Bulletin. 2. The Middle East. Afghanistan]. Edited by I. M. Reisner. Moscow: Vsesoiuznaia torgovaia palata. Pp. 207-325.

        A work that was superseded by the work on Afghanistan published by the editor in 1953. See no. 2542.

2584   Strathmann, Heribert
        1980 Haendler und Handwerker als Soziales Segment in Afghanistan. [Merchants and Craftsmen as Social Segments in Afghanistan]. Meisenheim: Anton Hain Verlag. Pp. 378.

VII. ECONOMIC STRUCTURE

2585 Survey of Progress 1962-64
      1964 Kabul: Education Press. Pp. 152; mimeographed.

      Prepared by the Department of Statistics and Research, Ministry of Planning.

2586 Survey of Progress 1964-65
      1965 Kabul: Government Printing Press. Pp. 58; 46 pages of tables.

2587 Survey of Progress 1968-69
      1969 Department of Statistics, Ministry of Planning. Kabul.

2588 Survey of the Tourism Industry in Afghanistan
      1965 Chicago: Thomas H. Miner and Associates. Pp. 383; bibliography.

2589 Swayze, Francis J.
      n.d. Foreign Private Enterprise and Afghanistan. No publisher. Pp. 33 and Appendix; mimeographed.

      The Appendix contains the text, in English translation, of the Law Encouraging th Investment of Private Foreign Capital in Afghanistan, which was enacted in 1958.

2590 Tarzi, Rahimullah
      1970 La reconnaissance et l'execution des sentences arbitrales etrangeres dans le commerce international (Uznanie i wykonanie zagranicznych orzeczen arbitrazowych w handlu miedzynarodowym, ze szczegolnym uwzglednieniem arbitrazu handlowego w Afganistanie). [French and Polish: The Recognition and Execution of Foreign Arbitration in International Trade with Specific Reference to Arbitration in Afghanistani Trade]. Unpublished Ph.D. Dissertation. Uniwersytet Warszawski.

2591 Technical Cooperation Agreement Between United States and Afghanistan,
      1951 Signed in Kabul, February 7; Entered into Force February 7. U.S. State Department. (Treaties and Other International Acts Series 2210. State Publication 4166.) Washington: U.S. Government Printing Office. Pp. 3.

2592 The Third Five Year Economic and Social Development Plan of Afghanistan
      1967 Ministry of Planning. Kabul.

VII. ECONOMIC STRUCTURE

2593　Toepfer, Helmuth
　　　　1975　Oekonomische Verhaltensweisen von Familien mit landwirtschaftlichen Vollerwerbsbetrieben in Afghanistan (mit einem Simulationsmodell). Orient 16(2):147-163.

2594　Tromp, S. W.
　　　　1951　Report on the Oil Possibilities of North Afghanistan. Unpublished report. Kabul. Pp. 34; 5 appendices.

　　　　Detailed technical analysis of geological structure and oil seepages found in the Northern Provinces during a field trip in October-December 1950. Prepared under the auspices of the U.N. Technical Assistance Administration for the guidance of the oil development program.

2595　Uddin, Islam
　　　　1972　Agrargeographische Untersuchung in Guldara und Ghori als Beispiele fur Alt- und Jungsiedelland im Afghanischen Hindukush: Gegenuberstellung und Vergleich. [Agricultural and Geographical Investigation in Guldara and Ghori as Examples of Long and Recently Settled Areas in the Hindu Kush, Afghanistan: Contrast and Comparison]. Ph.D. Dissertation. Köln University. Pp. 121, x.

2596　United Nations, Economic Commission for Asia and the Far East
　　　　1961　Multi-purpose River Basin Development. Part 2D-Water Resources Development in Afghanistan, Iran, Republic of Korea and Nepal. Chapter I, Afghanistan. Bangkok.

2597　United States Department of Labor
　　　　1969　Labor Law and Practice in Afghanistan. Washington, D.C.: Bureau of Labor Statistics. Pp. 23.

2598　Vavilov, N. I. and D. D. Bukinich
　　　　1929　Zemledel'cheskiy Afganistan [Agricultural Afghanistan]. Supplement 33 to the Bulletin of Applied Botany, of Genetics and Plant Breeding. Leningrad. Pp. xxxii, 610; maps.

　　　　The full report of research in Afghanistan between 1924 and 1927 by experienced Soviet botanists. Several subjects were of major interest: the collection of plant

VII. ECONOMIC STRUCTURE

samples, study of the regularities in crop distribution on the Hindu Kush, investigation of agricultural technics, and a survey of agricultural resources. The work is uniquely valuable in its field, as is indicated by the important summary in English given on pages 535-610.

2599 Velter, Andre, Emmanuel Delloye, and Marie-Jose Lamothe
1979 Les Bazars de Kaboul. Paris: Hier et Demain. Pp. 255.

2600 Vizhdani, Abdul Vahid
1973 Perepis' naseleniia v SSSR i Afganistane. [A Census of the Population in the USSR and Afghanistan]. Unpublished Ph.D. Dissertation. Kievskii institut narodnogo khoziaistva. Kiev, Ukrain SSSR.

2601 Volin, M. E.
1950 Chromite Deposits in Logar Valley, Kabul Province, Afghanistan. Washington: U.S. Department of Interior, Bureau of Mines. Pp. 58.

Geological and economic appraisal (unfavorable) of 181,000 tons of chrome ores.

2602 Wade, Nicholas
1981 Afghanistan: The Politics of a Tragicomedy. Science 212(4494):521-523.

2603 Wald, Hermann-J. and Asis Nadjibi
1977 Landreform in Afghanistan. International Asienforum 8(1/2):110-123.

2604 Wegner, D. H. G.
1964 Nomaden- und Bauernteppiche in Afghanistan. Baessler-Archiv. Berlin.

2605 Wegner, D. H. G.
1965 Nomaden- und Bauernteppiche in Afghanistan. Baessler-Archiv 12. Berlin.

2606 Wiebe, Dietrich
1973 Grundlagen und Entwicklungsmoeglichkeiten der Industrie in Afghanistan. Orient 14:52-63.

2607 Wiebe, Dietrich
1973 Struktur und Funktion eines Serais in der Alstadt von Kabul. In Kulturgeographische Untersuchungen im Islamischen Orient. Edited by Reinhard Stewig and Horst-Gunter Wegner. Kiel: Schriften des Geographischen

VII. ECONOMIC STRUCTURE

       Instituts der Universitat Kiel 38. Pp. 213-240.
       An examination of the structure and function of Serais in Kabul.

2608   Wiebe, Dietrich
       1973 Some Considerations on the Municipal Structure of Large Afghan Cities, Illustrated by the Example of Kandahar. Comparative Legal Government 7(1):41-49.

2609   Wiebe, Dietrich
       1975 Zur Industriestruktur von Afghanistan. Geographisches Taschenbuch. Pp. 80-105.

2610   Wiebe, Dietrich
       1976 Die raumliche Gestalt der Alstadt von Kandahar. Ein kulturgeographischer Beitrag zum Probleme der partiellen Modernisierung. Afghanistan Journal 3(4):132-146. Maps; tables.

2611   Wiebe, Dietrich
       1976 Formen des ambulaten Gewerbes in Sudafghanistan. Erdkunde 30(1):31-44.

2612   Wiebe, Dietrich
       1976 Freizeitverhalten und Tourismus in Afghanistan. Ein Beitrag zur Fremdenverkehrsgeographie drittweltlicher Lander. Orient 17(1):141-157.

2613   Wiebe, Dietrich
       1977 Entwicklungsprojekte und soziookonomischer Wandel in Afghanistan. Munchen: Paderborn.

2614   Wiebe, Dietrich
       1979 Charikar - Entwicklungsprobleme eines Gross-stadtnahen Regionszentrums in Afghanistan. Afghanistan Journal 6(2):39-49.

2615   Wiebe, Dietrich
       1979 Die Afghanischen Arbeitskraftewanderungen in die Islamischen Staaten. Orient 20(2):96-100.

2616   Wiebe, Dietrich
       1979 Strukturwandlungen Afghanischer Mittelpunktsiedlungen unter dem Einfluss Auslandischer Infrastrukturprojekte. Erdkunde 33(3):204-215.

VII. ECONOMIC STRUCTURE

2617 Wiebe, Dietrich
    1979 Zum Strukturwandel Gross-stadtischer Geschaftszentren in Afghanistan, dargestellt an Beispielen aus Kabul und Kandahar. Kieler Geographische Schriften, Geografische Institut der Universitaet 50:417-426.

2618 Wiebe, Dietrich
    1981 Verkehrsausbau und Wirtschaftsentwicklung in Afghanistan [Transportation and Economic Development in Afghanistan]. Afghanistan Journal 8(2):43-54.

2619 Wirth, E.
    1974 Zum Problem des Bazars (suq, Carsi). Versuch einer Begriffsbestimmung und Theorie des traditionalen Wirtschaftszentrums der orientalisch-islamischen Stadt. Der Islam 51(2):203-260.

2620 Wirth, E.
    1975 Zum Problem des Bazars (suq, Carsi). Versuch einer Begriffsbestimmung und Theorie des traditionalen Wirtschaftszentrums der orientalisch-islamischen Stadt. Der Islam 52(1):6-46.

2621 Yakoub, M.
    1972 Etude hydrogeologique du bassin de Parwan, Afghanistan. [A Hydrogeological Study of the Parwan Basin, Afghanistan]. Unpublished Ph.D. Dissertation. University of Paris (Montpellier II). Pp. 180; appendices.

2622 Yoder, Richard Allen
    1978 Class, Security, and Fertility: A Social Organizational/Social Justice Perspective on Fertility Behavior in Afghanistan. Unpublished Ph.D. Dissertation. University of Pittsburgh. Pp. 138.

2623 Yusuf, Kaniz Fatima
    1959 Economic and Political Cooperation of Pakistan, Iran and Afghanistan. Unpublished Ph.D. Dissertation. Clark University. Pp. 234.

Deals with the distribution and ethnic homogeneity and economic activity of these three states with a discussion of the possibility of cooperation among the three countries.

VII. ECONOMIC STRUCTURE

2624 Zaman, Mohammed
  1951 L'Agriculture en Afghanistan et ses relations avec l'économie nationale [Agriculture in Afghanistan and its Relations to the National Economy]. Afghanistan 6(3):47-55.

  In developing her resources, Afghanistan must concentrate on agriculture rather than on industry, according to the author. He examines several factors influencing agricultural productivity, such as rainfall, climate, etc.

2625 Zaripov, Sh.
  1972 Proizvodetelnie Silie Selskogo Khoziaistva Covpremennogo Afganistana. [Productive Forces of Contemporary Agricultural Afghanistan]. Dushanbe: Tajikistan SSR Academy of Sciences. Pp. 146.

  Analysis of the agrarian economy and productive forces of present day Afghanistan.

2626 Zekrya, Mir-Ahmed Baray
  1976 Planning and Development in Afghanistan: A Case of Maximum Foreign Aid and Minimum Growth. Unpublished Ph.D. Dissertation. Johns Hopkins University. Pp. 222.

  A comprehensive study of Afghanistan's fifteen years of development experience in political and economic spheres as reflected in the application of last three five year plans.

2627 Zhowandai, Saleha
  1977 An Economic Analysis and Measurement of Afghanistan's Protection Structure. Unpublished Ph.D. Dissertation. University of Hawaii.

  An application of the theory of effective protection. Investigation and analysis of the protective effect of Afghanistan's tariff structure and other government policy measures.

2628 Zikria, Nazir Ahmad
  1972 Les facteurs du sous-developpement economique en Afghanistan. [The Factors of Economic Underdevelopment in Afghanistan]. Unpublished Ph.D. Dissertation. University of Paris VIII (Paris-Vincennes). Pp. 156.

VIII. LANGUAGES AND LITERATURE

Languages and dialects; lexicons; grammars;
dictionaries; literature in prose and
poetry; manuscripts and editions of
manuscripts; folklore; songs
and ballads; inscriptions

A significant number of items in this chapter are in the Dari or Pushtu languages. Works of this nature have been listed in the bibliography by Akram and in the catalogues of printed books by Edwards and Arberry; in fact Akram includes a number of elusive works printed in India in Pushtu during the nineteenth century which have not been included in this publication. However, many of the titles here given have not been listed elsewhere, since they represent works published in Afghanistan during the last 40 years. These titles reflect the efforts of an energetic group of modern Afghan scholars to promote the historical, literary, and sociological background of their country by means of original writings and by means of editions of neglected manuscripts. A royal decree of 1936 sparked the movement to bring Pushtu literature out of obscurity, and a great deal has been accomplished in this field under the sponsorship of the Pushtu Tolaneh, or Pushtu Society. In addition, the ancient and operative Code of the Pushtuns, or Pushtunwali, has been recorded and interpreted through the work of these scholars. It does seem amazing that in all the years when the British were engaged at close quarters with these tribal elements they did not collect material on the Pushtunwali; perhaps the omission was a deliberate one. In much the same way, the works of earlier writers who wrote in Dari but who remained almost unknown to the West have been recovered from oblivion. It may be some time before scholars in other countries take advantage of this source material.

Afghan scholars have written extensively in Pushtu for the periodical Kabul and in Dari for the periodical Aryana. It has not been feasible to index these two periodicals, but a real effort has been made to illustrate the scope of local writing by including in this bibliography a complete listing of all the articles that have been published in the periodical Afghanistan (No. 1) through 1954--all either in French or English. Of somewhat uneven merit, the titles of these articles appear within the various chapters of this publication.

One extensive classification of works written and printed in Afghanistan has been omitted from this bibliography, although the items have been carefully examined. These are the school texts, lithographed or printed at Kabul by the government and distributed free of charge to the students by the Ministry of Education. Some 90 texts which were reviewed fell into the following categories: history; history of Afghan literature; history of Islam; religion (Islam); ethics; grammar; arithmetic and algebra; physics; biology; chemistry; geography; astronomy; and natural sciences. Most numerous

VIII. LANGUAGES AND LITERATURE

were the grammars for teaching Dari and Pushtu, with second and third places taken by works on arithmetic and algebra and by works by foreign linguists concerned with Dari and Pushtu as spoken and written in Afghanistan.

It is of interest to note that local scholars, authors of textbooks, and figures in public life have contributed to the growing number of volumes of the Afghan Encyclopedia. If this work progresses, the Afghans will have available for the first time an exhaustive knowledge of the modern world. They will have the facility of moving from a remote past into the urgent present. In quite another way, the scholarly works in Dari and Pushtu may supply firm contacts with traditional cultural values, customs, and beliefs.

2629 Abayeva, T.
1958 Ob afganskom narodnom tvorchestve [On Afghan Folk Creativity]. Zvezda Vostoka 10:78-83.

Concerns the popular literature of the country, with examples of poetry.

2630 Da 'Abdul 'Ali Mostaghni Diwan [The Collected Works of 'Abdul 'Ali Mostaghni]
1959 Kabul: Pohani matba'eh. Pp. 160. (1338 A.H.)

Collection of Mostaghni's poems in Pushtu.

2631 Abdullah Khan, Malik al-Shu'ara' (ed)
1940 Kalid al-Sarf [The Key of Accidence]. Kabul: Matba'eh-yi 'umumi. Pp. 46. (1319 A.H.)

Poorly lithographed text in Dari of a work designed for classes in adult education.

2632 Abu Bakr, Ruqaiyah
1956 Golha-yi Khudrow [Wild Flowers]. Kabul. Pp. 86. (1335 A.H.)

Collection of poems in Dari.

2633 Afghan-navis, Abdullah
1960 Loghat-i 'Amiana-yi Farsi Afghanistan [A Dictionary of Colloquial Farsi in Afghanistan]. Kabul: Matba'eh-yi doulati. Pp. 176. (1340 A.H.)

The initial effort at compiling a dictionary of the spoken Dari of Afghanistan.

2634 Afghanistan: Evergreen EVR 002
n.d. A recorded miscellany of Afghan music.

VIII. LANGUAGES AND LITERATURE

2635 Afganskiy sbornik [Afghan Collection]
1959 Kratkiye Soobshcheniya Instituta Vostokovedeniya. Moscow. 33:137; 37:139.

2636 Afganskiye Skazki [A Collection of Afghan Tales]
1955 Moscow: Goslitizdat. Pp. 155.

Afghan folklore, legends, and fables in Russian translation, not identified as to sources.

2637 Ahmed, Akbar S.
1975 Mataloona: Pukhto Proverbs. Karachi: Oxford University Press. Pp. 59.

A very useful compendium of Pushtu proverbs collected by a professional anthropologist and a dynamic student and scholar of Pushtun Society and Culture.

2638 Alvad, Thomas and Lennart Edelberg
1953 The Nuristani Harp. Afghanistan 8(3):34-44; map.

A description of the harp found among the Safid Push Kafirs and its relation to other primitive harps, with a speculation that this may be the forerunner of the Sumerian harp.

2639 Archer, William Kay
1964 The Music of Afghanistan and Iran. Society for Asian Music. Pp. 2-9. Summer.

2640 Asadabadi, Mirza Lutfullah Khan
1926 Sharh-i Hal u Asar-i Sayyid-i Jamal al-Din-i Asadabadi [Life and Works of Sayyid Jamal al-Din Asadabadi]. Berlin: Orientalistischer Zeitschriftenverlag Iranschahr. Pp. 128.

The nephew of Sayyid Jamal al-Din writes of his uncle's life and gives a description of his literary works.

2641 Aslanov, M. G.
1963 O formirovanii afganskogo natsional'nogo yazyka [On the Formation of the Afghan National Language]. In Etnicheskiye protsessy i sostav naseleniya v stranakh Peredney Azii. Moscow-Leningrad: Izdatel'stvo Vostochnoy Literatury. Pp. 3-23.

Deals with prospects of Pushtu as the national language of Afghanistan.

VIII. LANGUAGES AND LITERATURE

2642 Aslanov, M. G.
    1966 Afghansko-Russkii Slovar: Pushtu [Afghan-Russian Dictionary: Pushtu]. Moscow: Soviet Encyclopedia Publications Department. Pp. 994.

    A Pushtu-Russian Dictionary containing 50,000 words.

2643 'Ata, Muhammad Mirza
    1952 Nava-yi Ma'arik [The Song of Battle-Fields]. Kabul: Matba'eh-yi 'umumi. Pp. 229. (1331 A.H.)

    Edited by Ahmad 'Ali Kohzad, the Dari manuscript now in the Kabul Museum was written in 1854 A.D.

2644 Athar, Qazi 'Abd al-Halim
    1963 Tir Hir Sho'aran [Forgotten Poets]. Peshawar: Peshawar University. Pp. 284; lithographed.

    A collection of poetry in Pushtu.

2645 Ayazi, Muhammad A'zam
    1939 Qava'd-i Pushtu [The Rules of Pushtu]. Kabul: Matba'eh-yi 'umumi. Pp. 224. (1318 A.H.)

    Pushtu grammar taught through the medium of a Dari text.

2646 Aybek, Zafer Hasan
    1973 Ubayd-Allah Sindhi in Afghanistan. Journal of the Regional Cultural Institute 6(3-4):129-136.

2647 Badakhshi, Shah Abdullah
    1953 Les langues du Pamir [The Languages of the Pamir]. Afghanistan 8(3):46-56.

    A discussion of the similarity between European languages and Sanskrit, due to their Aryan origin, and an identification of the Pamirs as "Aryan Vadje," the birthplace of the race; finally, a laudatory note on the Minister of Education's Dictionary of Afghan Languages.

2648 Badakhshi, Shah Abdullah
    1960 Da Afghanistan da Zino Zhibo u Lahjo Qamus [A Dictionary of Some Languages and Dialects of Afghanistan]. Kabul. Pp. 225. (1339 A.H.)

    The text is in Pushtu.

VIII. LANGUAGES AND LITERATURE

2649 Baghban, Hafizullah
1968 An Overview of Herat Folk Literature. Afghanistan 21(1):81-90; 21(2):51-62.

2650 Baghban, Hafizullah
1975 Afghanistan. In Folktales Told Around the World. Edited by Richard M. Dorson. Chicago: University of Chicago Press. Pp. 209-242.

Details and formally classifies five folktales from northwestern Afghanistan.

2651 Baghban, Hafizullah
1976 The Context and Concept of Humor in Magadi Theater. Unpublished Ph.D. Dissertation. Indiana University. Pp. 1296.

A most comprehensive study of the Magadi folk performances in light of their ethnohistory and as a folk-performing art in the Herat area of Afghanistan. Emphasis is placed on the style and symbolism of performance as they relate to the larger socio-cultural context.

2652 Beardsley, Charles
1959 The Naked Hills: Some Tales of Afghanistan. London: Peter Davies. Pp. 276.

Stories and true adventures as experienced by the author and his friends.

2653 Becka, Jiri
1978 Young Afghan Prose in Dari. Afghanistan Journal 5(3):102-104.

2654 Bedford, Jimmy
1973 Concise English-Afghan Dari Dictionary. Lahore: Ferozsons Ltd. Press. Pp. 222.

2655 Bedil, Mirza Abdul Qadir
1963 Robay'at [Quatrains]. Kabul: Matba'eh-yi ma'ref. Pp. 566. (1342 A.H.)

A companion volume to the collected poetry of Bedil.

2656 Bellew, Henry Walter
1867 A Dictionary of the Pukkhtu or Pukshto Language, in Which the Words are Traced to Their Sources in the Persian and Indian Languages. London: Thacker and Co. Pp. xi, 355.

VIII. LANGUAGES AND LITERATURE

The first part of this work gives Pushtu words in Arabic script and transliteration, their linguistic origins and their meaning in English. The second part gives English words with the Pushtu equivalent in transliteration only. Another edition was issued at Lahore in 1901.

2657 Bellew, Henry Walter
1867 A Grammar of the Pukkhto or Pukshto Language on a New and Improved System. London: W. H. Allen and Co. Pp. xii, 155.

An important early work, long one of the chief sources of information about the language, and still of value.

2658 Belyayev, Viktor M.
1960 Afganskaya narodnaya muzyka [Afghan Folk Music]. Moscow: Sovetskaya Kompozitor. Pp. 27.

History and criticism of Afghan folk music. Included in text are Afghan folk dance music, folk songs, and dances.

2659 Benava, Abdul Raouf
1944 Pushtani Mirmani [Pushtun Ladies]. Kabul: Matba'eh-yi 'umumi. Pp. 256. (1323 A.H.)

Studies on a number of Afghan women in Pushtu.

2660 Benava, Abdul Raouf
1946 Da Ghanamu Wazhi [The Wheat Stalk]. Kabul: Matba'eh-yi 'umumi. Pp. 31. (1325 A.H.)

A poem in Pushtu describing the crowning of Ahmad Shah.

2661 Benava, Abdul Raouf (ed)
1946 Da Pir Muhammad Kakar Diwan [The Divan of Pir Mohammed Kakar]. Kabul: Matba'eh-yi 'umumi. Pp. 142. (1325 A.H.)

The collected works in Pushtu of a scholar who was the first grammarian of that language and who died in 1781 A.D.

2662 Benava, Abdul Raouf
1946 Fleurs de folk-lore afghan: hymnes nuptiaux de la littérature populaire [Flowers of Afghan Folk-Lore: Marriage Hymns of Folk Literature]. Afghanistan 1(4):44-48.

VIII. LANGUAGES AND LITERATURE

A number of quatrains in Pushtu are given in Arabic script and in translation.

2663 Benava, Abdul Raouf
1947 Adabi Funun [Literary Modes]. Kabul: Matba'eh-yi 'umumi. Pp. 106. (1326 A.H.)

An original work in Pushtu.

2664 Benava, Abdul Raouf (ed)
1949 Da Rahman Baba Diwan [The Divan of Rahman Baba]. Kabul: Matba'eh-yi 'umumi. Pp. 210. (1328 A.H.)

The collected works in Pushtu of a member of the Muhmand tribe who lived in 1632-1706 A.D. His verses are widely employed for taking auguries.

2665 Benava, Abdul Raouf
1950 Khushhal Khattak Tseh wayiy [What Does Khushhal Khattak Say?]. Kabul: Matba'eh-yi 'umumi. Pp. 158. (1329 A.H.)

Selections from the famous Pushtu poet, emphasizing his feelings of national independence and pride.

2666 Benava, Abdul Raouf (ed)
1952 Da Kazem Khan Shayda Diwan [The Divan of Kazem Khan Shayda]. Kabul: Matba'eh-yi 'umumi. (1331 A.H.)

The collected works of an eighteenth-century Pushtu poet.

2667 Benava, Abdul Raouf
1954 Les poétesses de l'Aryana [The Poetesses of Aryana]. Afghanistan 9(3):49-55.

Some verses (translated into French) taken from the songs of Aryan poetesses which appear in the Vedic books.

2668 Benava, Abdul Raouf
1957 Da Hannan Diwan [The Divan of Hannan]. Kabul: Matba'eh-yi doulati. Pp. 244. (1336 A.H.)

The collected works in Pushtu of the poet Hannan.

2669 Benava, Abdul Raouf
1958 Landai [Couplets]. Kabul: 'Askari matba'eh. Pp. 176. (1337 A.H.)

VIII. LANGUAGES AND LITERATURE

>On each page a Pushtu couplet, with translations into Dari and English. Many full-page illustrations in color, related to the subject matter of the verse.

2670 Benava, Abdul Raouf
1968 Awsani Likwal [Story Writing]. Three volumes. Kabul: Government Printing.

2671 Benava, Abdul Raouf, Abdul Hai Habibi, and Sayyid Qasem Rishtiya (trans)
1947 Da Darmesteter Pushtu Tsirrani [The Researches of Darmesteter in Pushtu]. Kabul: Matba'eh-yi 'umumi. Pp. 112. (1326 A.H.)

A translation into Pushtu of Darmesteter's Pushtu grammar.

2672 Biddulph, C. E.
1890 Afghan Poetry of the Seventeenth Century--Being Selections From the Poems of Khush Hal Khan Khatak. With Translation and Grammatical Introductions. London: K. Paul, Trench, Trubner and Co., Ltd. Pp. xvii, 120 and 74.

The introduction sets the background of the second half of the seventeenth century, when the Pushtun poet in question was active. This is followed by a grammatical section dealing with Pushtu grammar and vocabulary, and then come the poems themselves--presented in Pushtu and English translation.

2673 Bing, J. M.
1980 Linguistic Rhythm and Grammatical Structure in Afghan Persian (Dari). Linguistic Inquiry 11(3):437-463.

2674 Bivar, A. D. H.
1953 The Hephthalite Inscriptions of Uruzgan. Afghanistan 8(4):1-4.

On two inscriptions carved in Hephthalite Greek script on limestone blocks in an unknown language--their tentative translation and possible date (around 500 A.D.).

VIII. LANGUAGES AND LITERATURE

2675 Blumhardt, J. F. and D. N. MacKenzie
    1965 Catalogue of Pashto Manuscripts in the Libraries of the British Isles. Bodleian Library, The British Museum, Cambridge University Library, India Office Library, John Rylands Library, School of Oriental and African Studies. Trinity College, Dublin: British Museum. Pp. xii, 147.

2676 Bogdanov, L.
    1930 Stray Notes on Kabuli Persian. Journal and Proceedings of the Asiatic Society of Bengal n.s. 26:1-25.

A detailed and thoroughly informed study, which describes the differences between the Dari spoken in Iran and in Afghanistan. Includes a lengthy vocabulary.

2677 Bonelli, Luigi
    1928-29, 1930, 1931, 1936 Appunti fonetici sul volgare persiano di Kabul [Phonetic Features of the Persian Vernacular of Kabul]. Annali del Reale Instituto Orientale di Napoli 1:5-14; 2:24-26; 4:20-33; 8:43-53.

Notes on the sounds and grammar, with a fairly extensive glossary of items that struck the author as dialectal peculiarities. Based on work with Afghan students in Italy.

2678 Bray, Denys
    1913 The Life-History of a Brahui. London: Royal Asiatic Society. Pp. 172.

An autobiographical account of a Brahui dealing primarily with birth, childhood, betrothel, marriage, sickness, death, burial, mourning, evil spirits, and notions of life after death.

2679 Buddruss, Georg
    1959 Beitrage zur Kenntnis der Pashai-Dialekte. Abhandlungen fur die Kunde des Morgenlandes 33(2). Wiesbaden.

2680 Buddruss, Georg
    1960 Die Sprache von Wotapur und Katarqala; linguistische Studien im Afghanischen Hindukusch [The Language of Wotapur and Katarqala; Linguistic Studies in the Afghan Hindukush]. University of Bonn. Pp. 144; map.

VIII. LANGUAGES AND LITERATURE

2681 Buddruss, Georg
1978 Georg Morgenstierne 1892-1978. Afghanistan Journal 5(3):109-111.

2682 Bukhari, Farigh and Reza Hamadani
1977 Rahman Baba. Islamabad: National Institute of Folk Heritage. Pp. 160.

A collection of Rahman Baba's poetry in Pushtu with Urdu notes and introduction.

2683 Burhan, M. Esmael
1972 Bilingual Education for Afghanistan. Unpublished Ph.D. Dissertation. University of Texas at Austin. Pp. 161.

Concerned with the teaching and learning of Pushtu and Dari as second languages in Afghanistan.

2684 Caillou, Alan
1972 Afghan Assault. New York: Pinnacle Books. Pp. 187.

A crude fiction about American Mercenary forces who succeed in defeating an anti-Democracy social element in Afghanistan.

2685 Central Asian Review
1966 The Development of Pushtu as the National and Literary Language of Afghanistan. Central Asian Review 14(3):210-220.

English summary translation of a Russian work on this problem by N. A. Davidov which appeared in 1965.

2686 Chand Kitab-i Khatti va Chapi Marbut ba Tarikh-i Afghanistan [Some Manuscripts and Printed Books Connected with the History of Afghanistan]
1954 Aryana 12(4):181-186.

An informed review of some primary and secondary works on Afghan history.

2687 Charpentier, Joel
1928 Some Remarks on Pashto Etymology. Acta Orientalia 7:180-200.

Notes on the derivation of 51 Pashto words. Georg Morgenstierne's comments follow the Charpentier article, beginning on page 198.

VIII. LANGUAGES AND LITERATURE

2688 Chavarria-Aguilar, Oscar L.
   1962 Pashto Basic Course. Ann Arbor: University of Michigan. Pp. 195.

2689 Chavarria-Aguilar, Oscar L.
   1962 Pashto Instructor's Handbook. Ann Arbor: University of Michigan. Pp. 73.

2690 Chavarria-Aguilar, Oscar L.
   1962 A Short Introduction to the Writing System of Pashto. Ann Arbor: University of Michigan. Pp. 22.

2691 Cook, Nilla C.
   1947 La terre d'Ariana [The Land of Aryana]. Afghanistan 2(1):1-6.

   Unsubstantial reveries inspired by passage through Herat, Qandahar, and Ghazni.

2692 Cook, Nilla C.
   1954 Songs of Kabul. Afghanistan 9(2):54-58.

   English verses on poetic aspects of Kabul life and Afghan history.

2693 Curiel, Raoul
   1954 Inscriptions de Surkh Kotal [Inscriptions of Surkh Kotal]. Journal Asiatique 242:189-205.

   A detailed study of very fragmentary inscriptions cut in Greek characters into limestone and in an unidentified eastern middle-Iranian language.

2694 Darmesteter, James
   1888 Inscriptions de Caboul [Inscriptions in Kabul]. Journal Asiatique 8(11):491-503.

   Contains the texts of inscriptions and their translations, the inscriptions being on Babur's tomb and adjacent ones.

2695 Darmesteter, James
   1888-1890 Chants populaires des Afghans, recueillis par James Darmesteter [Folk-Songs of the Afghans, Collected by James Darmesteter]. 2 vols. Paris: Imprimerie nationale. Pp. (1) xii; (2) ccxviii; 228.

VIII. LANGUAGES AND LITERATURE

>A discussion of the language, history, and origin of the Afghans, followed by a study of the popular literature of the country. Songs in the categories of history, religion, story, and love are given in text and in French translation.

2696 Darmesteter, James
1890 La grande inscription de Qandahar [The Great Inscription at Qandahar]. Journal Asiatique 8(15):195-230.

>Contains a detailed record and translation of carved inscriptions in the neighborhood of Qandahar, the inscriptions are of historical importance. Dari texts are given in Arabic characters. Includes bibliographical notes relating to Qandahar.

2697 Davidson, John
1902 Notes on the Bashgali (Kafir) Language. Calcutta.

2698 De Croze, J. Berjane
1946 Aryana; Chanson libre [Aryana; Free Song]. Afghanistan 1(4):18-21.

>Poetry and aphorisms from the cultivated pen of the Countess de Croze.

2699 Dehoti, A. P. and N. N. Ershov
1949 Russko-Tadzikskii Slovar [Russian-Tajiki Dictionary]. Moscow and Staliabad: USSR Academy of Sciences. Volume I. Pp. 967.

>A Russian-Tajiki dictionary containing about 45,000 words. In cyrillic.

2700 Dianous, Hugues Jean de
1963-1964 La litterature afghane de langue persane [Afghan Literature in the Persian Language]. Orient 26:47-63; 31(137-171.

>A serious, valuable study. The first part deals with the earlier centuries of Islam and the second covers material of the present century. Translations into foreign languages are included.

2701 Dilthey, Helmtraut
1971 Versammlungsplaetze in Dardo-Kafirischen Raum. Wiesbaden: Otto Harrassowitz. Pp. ix, 212.

VIII. LANGUAGES AND LITERATURE

2702 Diwan-i Ahmad Shah Abdali [Collected Works of Ahmad Shah Abdali]
1963 Peshawar: Peshawar University. Pp. 263; lithographed.

Pushtu poetry ascribed to a ruler of Afghanistan.

2703 Dor, Remy
1976 Orature du Nord-Est Afghan I. Les Kirghiz du Pamir. Turcica-Revue d'Etudes Torques 8(1):87-116.

2704 Dorn, Bernhard
1847 A Chrestomathy of the Pushtu or Afghan Language to Which is Subjoined a Glossary in Afghan and English. St. Petersburg. Pp. x, 260.

Excerpts from a variety of written works with notes and glossary.

2705 Dorofeyeva, L. N.
1955 Opiet Leksiko-Grammaticheskoi Kharakteristiki Kabuli. Moscow: Autoref Kand Des.

2706 Dorofeyeva, L. N.
1960 Yazyk Farsi-Kabuli [The Farsi-Kabuli Language]. Moscow: Izdatel'stvo Vostochnoy LIteratury. Pp. 83.

2707 Dost, Dost M.
1975 The Languages and Races of Afghanistan. Kabul: Ministry of Education.

2708 Dulling, G. K.
1973 The Hazaragi Dialect of Afghan Persian. Central Asian Monographs Number 1. Central Asian Research Centre: London.

2709 Dupree, Louis
1979 Functions of Folklore in Afghan Society. Asian Affairs 66(1):51-61.

2710 Dupree, Nancy Hatch
1974 An Interpretation of the Role of the Hoopoe in Afghan Folklore and Magic. Folklore 85:173-193.

Explores Afghan legends in terms of how they define the hoopoe's (Upupa epops) personality and how society uses them to re-enforce certain cultural values.

VIII. LANGUAGES AND LITERATURE

2711 Dvoryankov, N. A.
    1958 O glavnykh chlenakh predlozheniya s ergativnoy konstruksiyey v Pashto [On the Main Elements of a Sentence Containing the Ergative Construction in Pushtu]. Sovetskoye Vostokovedeniye 5:103-108.

2712 Dvoryankov, N. A.
    1960 Yazyk Pushtu [The Pushtu Language]. Moscow: Izdatel'stvo Vostochnoy Literatury. Pp. 99; bibliography.

2713 Dvoryankov, N. A.
    1963 Pashto Dialects: The Literary Languages in Afghanistan. XXVI International Congress of Orientalists. Moscow.

2714 Dvoryankov, N. A.
    1965 The Development of Pushtu as the National and Literary Language in Afghanistan. Central Asian Review 14(3):210-220.

2715 Dzhabbarov, I. M.
    1971 Nekotoye Etnograficheskiye Materialy v Uzbekskoi Versii Eposa "Alpamysh" [Some Ethnographic Materials in the Uzbek Version of the Epic Poem "Alpamysh"]. Sovetskaya Etnografiya 46(2):128-133.

2716 Dzhafarova, A. A.
    1954 Feraidoun. Afghanistan 9(2):51-53.

Feraidoun or Taritouna, was a great hero of the Avesta, who drove the Semitic conqueror from the Aryan Kingdom of Peshadi and established himself as king.

2717 Dzhafarova, A. A.
    1964 Istoricheskaya tema v literature Afganistana, (na yazyke farsi) [The Historical Theme in the Literature of Afghanistan (in Persian)]. Kratkiye Soobshcheniya Instituta Narodov Azii. Moscow. Vol. 65:71-79.

2718 Efimov, V. A.
    1965 Yazik Afganskikh Hazara. Yakaulongskii Dialect. Moscow: USSR Academy of Sciences.

2719 Elfenbein, J. H.
    1966 The Baluchi Language. A Dialectology with Texts. The Hague: E. J. Brill. Pp. iv, 48; sketchmaps.

VIII. LANGUAGES AND LITERATURE

2720 Elham, Mohammed Rahim (trans)
1961 Da Pushtu Gramar [A Grammar of Pushtu]. Kabul. Pp. 215. (1340 A.H.)

A translation into Pushtu of Penzl 1955. See no. 2940.

2721 Enevoldsen, Jens
1971 Pashto Proverbs and Landeys in English and Danish. Denmark.

2722 English-Pashto Dictionary
1975 Kabul: Ministry of Education, Pashto Academy.

2723 Ethe, Hermann
1897 Die Tafelrunde Sultan Mahmuds und seiner unmittelbaren Nachfolger [The Round Table of Sultan Mahmud and His Immediate Successors]. Grundriss der Iranischen Philologie, Pt. 1, pp. 223-233. Strasbourg: Karl J. Trubner.

An examination of the literary activity at the court of Mahmud of Ghazni, and his successors, by a noted cataloguer of Persian manuscripts. See also no. 2740.

2724 Evans-Von Krbek, Jeffrey Hewitt Pollitt
1977 The Social Structure and Organization of a Pakhto Speaking Community in Afghanistan. Unpublished Ph.D. Dissertation. Durham University. Pp. 355.

2725 Farhadi, Abdul Ghafur Rawan
1955 Le persan parlé en Afghanistan. Grammaire du Kaboli [The Spoken Persian of Afghanistan. A Grammar of Kabuli]. Paris: C. Klincksieck. Pp. 150; 44.

A mimeographed publication by a young Afghan scholar who treats the subject more intensively than in earlier works. The second section of the work illustrates quatrains of local poetry in transliteration and translation.

2726 Farhadi, Abdul Ghafur Rawan (trans)
1962 Zendigi-yi Khwaja 'Abdullah Ansari [The Life of Khwaja 'Abdullah Ansari]. Kabul: Matba'eh-yi doulati. Pp. 196. (1341 A.H.)

A translation into Dari of a work by Pére S. de Beaurecueil.

VIII. LANGUAGES AND LITERATURE

2727 Farhadi, Abdul Ghafur Rawan
   1969 Die Sprachen von Afghanistan. In Zentralasiatische Studien des Seminar Fuer Sparch und Kulturwissenschaft Zentralasiens de Universitat Bonn. No. 3. Wiesbaden.

2728 Farhadi, Abdul Ghafur Rawan
   1970 Languages. In Kabul Times Annual. Kabul: Government Printing House. Pp. 121-124.

   A brief discussion of linguistic diversity in Afghanistan.

2729 Farhadi, Abdul Ghafur Rawan
   1974 Razgovornyi Farsi v Afganistane [Spoken Farsi in Afghanistan]. Translated from French. Moscow: Nauka. Pp. 210.

2730 Farhang, Mir Muhammad Sadiq
   1955 Saffarian [Saffarids]. Kabul: Matba'eh-yi 'umumi. Pp. 40. (1334 A.H.)

   A short account in Dari of the Saffarid rulers.

2731 Fozilov, Mullojon
   1975 Farhangi Zarbulmasal, Maqol va Aforizmhoi Tajiki o Farsi [Dictionary of Tajiki and Farsi Proverbs and Sayings]. Dushanbe: Irfon. Volume I. Pp. 367.

   A comprehensive work on the subject covering a number of dialectical variations in Persian, Dari, and Tajiki.

2732 Fozilov, Mullojon
   1977 Farhangi Zarbulmasal, Maqol va Aforizmhoi Tajiki o Farsi [Dictionary of Tajiki and Farsi Proverbs and Sayings]. Dushanbe: Irfon. Volume II. Pp. 583. See above.

2733 Fraser, George MacDonald (ed)
   1969 Flashman: From the Flashman Papers 1839-1842. New York: New American Library. Pp. 252.

   The famous Flashman provides a semi-fictional account of the first Anglo-Afghan War, particularly the British attempt at leaving Afghanistan. For a fiction work the book contains a good deal of historical and factual material as seen from the British perspective. Entertaining and partially informing.

VIII. LANGUAGES AND LITERATURE

2734 Freeman, Antonyi
1965 The Music of Kabul. Asia Foundation, Program Bulletin 34:1-3.

2735 Friedl, E.
1965 Traeger Medialer Begabung im Hindukusch und Karakorum. Acta Ethnologica et Linguistica 8.

2736 Gablentz, H. C. von der
1866 Ueber die Sprache der Hazaras und Aimaks [On the Speech of the Hazaras and Aimaqs]. Zeitschrift der Deutschen Morgenländischen Gesellschaft 20:326-335.

As evidence that the Aimaqs and Hazaras are of Mongol origin, a short vocabulary, giving the Mongol word, its German translation, and variants in Central Asian dialects is provided. A group of sentences is treated in the same way.

2737 Geiger, Wilhelm
1893 Etymologie und Lautlehre des Afghanischen [Etymology and Phonology of the Afghan Language]. Munich: Verlag der Akademie. Pp. 56.

Systematic exposition of the place of Pushtu phonology in the historical development of Iranian languages.

2738 Geiger, Wilhelm
1898-1932 Die Sprache der Afghanen [The Language of the Afghans]. In Grundriss der Iranischen Philologie, 1, Pt. 2. Strasbourgh: Karl J. Trubner. Edited by Wilhelm Geiger and Ernst Kuhn. Pp. 201-230.

Condensed description of the language, making full use of previously published books and articles.

2739 Gerasimova, A. S.
1961 Obshchestvennyye motivy v sovremennoy literature Afganisana [Social Trends in the Modern Literature of Afghanistan]. Moscow: Izdatel'stvo Vostochnoy Literatury. Pp. 159.

2740 Gerasimova, A. S.
1974 Sud'by Afganskogo Rasskaza 60-KH Godov [The Fate of the Afghan Short Story in the 1960's]. Narody Azii i Afriki 1:104-110.

VIII. LANGUAGES AND LITERATURE

2741 Gerasimova, A. S. and G. F. Girs (eds)
1963 Literatura Afganistana [The Literature of Afghanistan]. Moscow: Izdatel'stvo Vostochnoy Literatury. Pp. 194.

2742 Ghawareh Ash'ar da Gol Pacha Olfat [Choice Poetry of Gol Pacha Olfat]
1955 Kabul. Pp. 256. (1334 A.H.)

Poetry in Pushtu.

2743 Ghulami, Muhammad Ghulam
1957 Jangnameh [A Story of Combat]. Kabul: Matba'eh-yi doulati. Pp. 210. (1336 A.H.)

A long poem in Dari, dealing with the resistance to foreign invaders between 1839 and 1842.

2744 Gilbertson, George Waters
1932 The Pakhto Idiom: A Dictionary. 2 vols. Hertford: Stephen Austin and Sons, Ltd. Pp. (1) xv, 496; (2) 497-964; bibliography.

A most extensive English-Pushtu dictionary ("eastern dialect" only), with the meaning and usage of each word illustrated by one or more Pushtu sentences in Arabic script, transliteration, and translation. The bibliography includes a list of words in and on the Pushtu language.

2745 Girs, G. F.
1963 Stikhi poetov Afganistan [Verses From the Poets of Afghanistan]. Moscow: Izdatel'stvo Inostrannoy Literatury. Pp. 105.

Translations into Russian from poems in Dari and Pushtu.

2746 Glassman, Eugene H.
1972 Conversational Dari: Introductory Course in Dari. Kabul: Language and Orientation Committee, International Afghan Mission. Pp. xviii, 375.

2747 Gochenour, Theodore S.
1965 The Landdey, Mirror of the Pashtuns. Viewpoints 5(6):22-29.

Concerns a poetic form, two nonrhyming lines more frequently sung than recited. Examples are given in Pushtu script, transliteration, and translation.

VIII. LANGUAGES AND LITERATURE

2748 Goodwin, Buster
1969 Life Among the Pathans (Khattaks). Tollesbury, Essex: The Owl Printing Company. Pp. 155.

Life story of the author as lived among the Khattaks. Goodwin chose to live among the Khattaks on a permanent basis after the British left India.

2749 Gordon, B. E. M. (ed)
1902 Translation of the Ganj-i-Pukhto into the Khowar Dialect. By Khan Sahib Abdul Hakim Khan. Calcutta: Office of the Superintendent of Government Printing, India. Pp. 67.

A collection of tales in colloquial Pushtu.

2750 Grierson, George Abraham
1903 The Languages of India: Being a Reprint of the Chapter on Languages Contributed by George Abraham Grierson to the Report on the Census of India, 1901, Together with the Census Statistics of Languages. Calcutta: Office of the Superintendent of Government Printing, India. Pp. 146; maps; tables.

A study of the languages and their families. Pages 43-93 deal with the Aryan subfamily of the Indo-European family. Pushtu is treated on pages 46-47. Tables show the number of persons speaking each language.

2751 Grierson, George Abraham (ed)
1921 Linguistic Survey of India, vol. 10. Specimens of the Languages of the Iranian Family. Calcutta: Office of the Superintendent of Government Printing. Maps.

Grierson both edited the volume and wrote all the descriptive material. Includes brief but highly informative introductions to Iranian languages in general and for Pushtu. Specimens and comments for over a dozen varieties of Pushtu and for two out-of-the-way Dari dialects. Good map of the distribution of Pushtu. Also contains a description of the Pamir languages (called Ghalchah), with a map showing their distribution.

2752 Grierson, George Abraham
1921 Part II. Dardic, or Pisacha Languages. *In* Linguistic Survey of India, vol. 8. Calcutta: Superintendent of Government Printing.

VIII. LANGUAGES AND LITERATURE

2753 Habibi, Abdul Hai
1938 Paygham-i Shahid [The Message of the Martyr]. Kabul: Matba'eh-yi 'umumi. Pp. 27. (1317 A.H.)

The work comprises poems written by the author and dedicated to the ruler; the poems deal with contemporary problems and subjects.

2754 Habibi, Abdul Hai (ed)
1941 Pushtana Shuara, 300 A.H. to 1200 A.H. [Pushtu Poets, 300 A.H. to 1200 A.H.]. Kabul: Umumi Matba'a. Pp. 394.

Includes biographic notes and samples of poetry and writings for 179 Pushtun poets during the period covered. Published in 1320 A.H. In Pushtu.

2755 Habibi, Abdul Hai
1946 The Oldest Poems in Pashto, or The Oldest Pashto Poet, Amir Krore Jahan Pahlawan. Afghanistan 1(1):9-15.

A brief account of the Sori tribes, followed by a description of the subject of the article, a ruler of the Sori dynasty of the eighth century. The article closes with a translation of a short passage from an epic.

2756 Habibi, Abdul Hai
1946 Da Pushtun de Adabiyatu Tarikh [The History of Pushtu Literature]. Kabul: Matba'eh-yi 'umumi. Pp. 137. (1325 A.H.)

A study of the subject in Pushtu by the then Dean of the Faculty of Literature.

2757 Habibi, Abdul Hai
1962 Pushtu wa Loyikan-i Ghazneh; Yek Tahqiqe Jadid dar Tarikh aw Adabiyate Pushtu wa Tarikhe Ghaznah [Pushtu and the Loyaks of Ghaznah; a New Inquiry into the History and Literature of Pushtu and the History of Ghaznah]. Kabul: Matba'eh-yi doulati. Pp. 154. (1341 A.H.)

VIII. LANGUAGES AND LITERATURE

2758 Habibi, Abdul Hai
1963 Zaban-i do Hazar Sol Qabl-i Afghanistan ya Madar-i Zaban Dari Tohalqa-i Siyah va Sorkh Kutal-i Baghlan [The Language of Afghanistan Two Thousand Years Ago, or The Mother of the Dari Language Converged at Siah and Sorkh Kutal-i Baghlan]. Kabul: Doulati matba'eh. Pp. 140. (1342 A.H.)

2759 Habibi, Abdul Hai
1967-68 Paxto Literature at a Glance. Afghanistan 20(3):45-54; Afghanistan 20(4):51-64; Afghanistan 21(1):53-57.

2760 Habibi, Abdul Hai
1971 A Short History of Calligraphy and Epigraphy in Afghanistan. Kabul: The Historical and Literary Society of Afghanistan. (Text in Dari)

2761 Hamid, 'Abdul Razaq
1959 Bahar-i Sa'adat [The Spring of Happiness]. Kabul: Matba'eh-yi doulati. Pp. 138. (1338 A.H.)

A collection of Pushtu poems.

2762 Hanley, Barbara
1970 English-Pushtu Dictionary. Kabul. Pp. 259.

2763 Hasan, Ya'qub
1939 Pushtu az Nazar-i Fiqh al-Lugheh [Pushtu From the Grammatical View Point]. Kabul: Matba'eh-yi 'umumi. Paged as 201-310. (1318 A.H.)

A lithographed work in Persian.

2764 Hashimbekov, X.
1971 Problema Evropeizmov B Terminologii Afganskogo Dari [Problem of European Terminology in Afghan Dari]. In Indiiskaya i Iranskaya Filologiya. Vaprosie Leksiki. Moscow: USSR Academy of Sciences. Pp. 116-126.

2765 Heissig, W.
1969 Der Moghol-Dichter 'Abd al-Qadir, Zentralasiatische Studien 3:431-438.

2766 Henderson, Michael M. T.
1975 Diglossia in Kabul Persian Phonology. Journal of the American Oriental Society 95:651-654.

VIII. LANGUAGES AND LITERATURE

2767 Henning, W. B.
    1957 The Inscriptions of Tang-i Azao. Bulletin of the School of Oriental and African Studies 20:335-342.

    Rock-cut inscriptions in Persian, written in the Hebrew script and dated to 1351 A.D.

2768 Herati, Muhammad Hashim Omidvar
    1962 Diwan-i Khalilullah Khalili [The Divan of Khalilullah Khalili]. Tehran: Haidari. Pp. 306. (1341 A.H.)

    A collection of the poet's work in Dari, with commentaries and appreciations by scholars in Iran.

2769 Heravi, Ghulam Riza Mayil
    1962 Ma'refi: Ruznameh-ha; Jaraid; Majalat-i Afghanistan [Introduction: Newspapers; Periodicals; Magazines of Afghanistan]. Kabul: Doulati matba'eh. Pp. 144; index. (1341 A.H.)

    Uniquely valuable documentation in Dari; each item is described at some length.

2770 Heravi, Ghulam Riza Mayil
    1965 Sharh Hal va Athar-i Amir Husayn Ghuri Heravi Motavaffa 718 [An Account of the State and Remains of Amir Husayn Ghuri Heravi, Deceased in 718]. Kabul: Vizarat-i etala'at va Kultur. Pp. 124. (1344 A.H.)

    A recent edition of a renowned book of learning.

2771 Heravi, Shaykh al-Islam Khwajeh 'Abdullah Ansari
    1962 Tabaqat al-Sufiyeh [Compendium of Sufism]. Kabul: Matba'eh-yi doulati. Pp. 738. (1341 A.H.)

    An edition in Dari of a work written in 1088 A.D., compiled from three manuscripts by Abdul Hai Habibi.

2772 Herbert, Raymond J. and Nicholas Poppe
    1964 Kirghiz Manual. Uralic and Altaic Series, Volume 33. Bloomington: Indiana University. Pp. 1.

2773 Hesche, Wolfram, Wolf-Dieter Hildebrant and Andreas Thermann
    1979 Das Mogoli in Badakhschan (Afghanistan). Central Asiatic Journal 23(3/4):176-236.

    A structural sketch and a word list of Mogholi language in Afghanistan.

VIII. LANGUAGES AND LITERATURE

2774 Hodge, C. T.
 1954 Spoken Pashto. Unit 1. Pronunciation. Washington: Foreign Service Institute, U.S. Department of State.

 A description, pedagogically oriented, of the phonemes of Pushtu as spoken in the Wardak region.

2775 Howell, Evelyn and Olaf Caroe (trans)
 1963 The Poems of Khushal Khan Khattak. Peshawar: University of Peshawar. Pp. xiv, 98.

 The texts of the poems in Pushtu, accompanied by translations into English.

2776 Hughes, Thomas P. (ed)
 1882 Ganj-i-Pukhto, or Pukhto Treasury. London: W. H. Allen and Co. Pp. iv, 128.

 A reader and glossary based on the conversational usage of uneducated Pushtu speakers (eastern dialect), published as a government textbook for examinations in Pushtu.

2777 Hughes, Thomas P. (ed)
 1893 The Kalid-i-Afghani, Being Selections of Pushtu Prose and Poetry for the Use of Students. Lahore: Munshi Gulab Singh and Sons. Pp. iii, 418.

 Includes prose material in Pushtu from the Ganj-i-Pushtu, the Tarikh-i-Mahmud-i-Ghaznavi, and the Tarikh-i-Murassa; also poetry from the Qissa Shahzada Bahram, Diwan-i-Abdul Rahman, Diwan-i-Khushhal Khan, and the Chaman-i-Benazir; all in Pushtu. There appears to have been an edition of this collection published as early as 1872 at Peshawar and printed by the Panjab Educational Press at Lahore: it is very rare.

2778 Iakubova, E. S.
 1975 "Divan" Akhmad shakha Durrani kak istochnik po istorii iazyka pashto i afganskoi literatury (po tashkentskoi rukopisi) [The Divan of Ahmad Shah Duranni as a Source for the History of Pashto and Afghan Literature (According to a Tashkent Manuscript)]. Unpublished Ph.D. Dissertation. Institut vostokovedeniia Akademii nauk Uzbekskoi, SSR. Tashkent.

VIII. LANGUAGES AND LITERATURE

2779   Imam al-Din, S. M. (ed)
        1960-1962 Tarikh-i-Khan Jahani wa Makhzan-i-Afghani, of
            Khwajah Ni'mat Allah ibn Khwajah Habib Allah of Herat
            (Persian text). Dacca: Asiatic Society of Pakistan.
            Two vls., pp. (1) 93 and (2) 897.

2780   Iqbal, Sir Mohammad
        1928 Khushhal Khan Khattack--the Afghan Warrior--Poet.
            Islamic Culture 2:485-494. Hyderabad.

        A renowned poet and philosopher of modern Islam steps out
        of his field and borrows the efforts of another scholar.
        Observations on the seventeenth-century poet are followed
        by examples taken from Raverty's translations (see no.
        2967). Verses quoted include striking characterizations
        of the Afghans, Persians, Hazaras, etc.

2781   Iqbal, Sir Mohammad
        1934 Musafir [The Traveller]. Lahore: Gilani. Pp. 217.
            (1313 A.H.)

        A lithographed account in Dari verse by a noted poet and
        reformer of Islam. The work deals with a visit made to
        Kabul in 1933 and includes poetry written on that
        occasion.

2782   'Ismati, Ma'sumeh
        1955 Khushhal Khattak Kist [Who is Khushhal Khattak?].
            Kabul: Matba'eh-yi 'umumi. Pp. 158. (1334 A.H.)

        A biography in Dari of the Pushtun poet.

2783   Ivanov, W. (trans)
        1964 The Works of Khayr-Khwar of Herat. Bombay: Ismaili
            Society (Series D., no. 16).

        The Dari text of the Tasnifat-i-Khayr-Khwah-i Herat was
        published by the Ismaili Society in 1961, as Series D.,
        no. 13.

2784   Iwamura, S. and H. F. Schurmann
        1954 Notes on Mongolian Groups in Afghanistan. In Silver
            Jubilee of the Zinbun Kagaku Kenkyusyo Kyoto University,
            Kyoto. Pp. 478-515.

2785   Iz Afganskoy Poezii [From Afghan Poetry]
        1955 Moscow: Gosudarstvennoye izdatel'stvo Khudozhest-
            vennoy literaturï. Pp. 223.

VIII. LANGUAGES AND LITERATURE

The Pushtu and Dari poetry of Khushhal Khattak and others, in Russian translation.

2786 Jami, Nur al-Din Abdul Rahman
1965 Tajlil-i panjsad va Panjahomin Sal-i Tavallod-i Nur al-Din Abdul Rahman Jami [On the Occasion of the 550th Year of the Birth of Nur al-Din Abdul Rahman Jami]. Kabul: Matba'eh-yi doulati. Pp. 108. (1344 A.H.)

2787 Jan, Qazi Ahmad
1917 How to Speak Pushtu. Lahore. Pp. 109.

Morgenstierne describes this work as "small, but very useful."

2788 Janata, Alfred
1962-1963 Die Bevoelkerung von Ghor. Archiv fuer Voelkerkunde 18:7-11.

2789 Janata, Alfred
1971 On the Origin of the Firuzkuhi in Western Afghanistan. Archiv fuer Voelkerkunde 25:57-65.

2790 Jarring, Gunnar
1933 Studien zu einer osttürkischen Lautlehre [Studies Toward an East Turkish Phonology]. Lund: Borelius. Pp. 1, 53; facsimile of manuscript fragment.

Part I is a technical phonological study of the East Turki dialect. Part II contains texts in Turkish script, footnoted and explained in German, and transliterated texts with translations in German on the facing pages.

2791 Jarring, Gunnar
1937 The Uzbek Dialect of Qilich (Russian Turkestan). With Texts and Glossary. Lund: Lunds universitets arsskrift, N. F. Ard. 1. 33(3):i, 56; list of works quoted.

The author discusses first the divisions and subdivisions of the Uzbek dialects, then, concentrating on that of Qilich, explains briefly some points of phonetics and grammar. The texts--one folk-tale and two poems (transliterated)--are translated into English. The glossary follows the translations.

VIII. LANGUAGES AND LITERATURE

2792 Jarring, Gunnar
1938 Uzbek Texts From Afghan Turkestan with Glossary. Lund: Lunds universitets arsskrift, N. F. Ard 1. 34(2):iii, 246; list of works quoted.

This is a series of eighteen stories, three miscellaneous texts and some proverbs, all given in transliteration and translated into English. There is a large glossary and an index of the supposed non-Iranized equivalents to the Iranized words appearing in the glossary. The dialect represented is the Uzbek speech of the town of Andkhui.

2793 Javid, Ahmad
1964 Afsanahai Qadim-i Shahr-i Kabul [Old Legends of the City of Kabul]. Kabul: 'Ameh. Pp. 82. (1343 A.H.)

2794 Kabul Times Annual
1970 Kabul: Kabul Times Publishing Agency. Pp. 400 + the 1964 constitution of Afghanistan.

Includes brief sketches on Afghan geography, economy, press, languages, and short descriptions of the various provinces of Afghanistan. Some charts, illustrations, and maps are included.

2795 Kessel, Joseph
1968 The Horsemen. New York: New American Library. Pp. 416.

A dramatization of the game of Buzkashi. Although an interesting novel, the book contains many inaccuracies about the social and cultural plane as well as about the game of Buzkashi. A good example of a half-baked novel.

2796 Khadem, Qiyam al-Din
1945 Bayazid Rushan [Bayazid Rushan]. Kabul: Matba'eh-yi 'umumi. Pp. 164. (1324 A.H.)

An account in Pushtu of an eighteenth-century Sufi who opposd the Moghuls and whose sect was attacked by Akhund Darvizeh Ningarhari (see no. 1764).

2797 Khadem, Qiyam al-Din
1947 Ruhi Goluneh [Wild Flower]. Kabul: Matba'eh-yi 'umumi. Pp. 152. (1326 A.H.)

An original work in Pushtu.

VIII. LANGUAGES AND LITERATURE

2798   Khadem, Qiyam al-Din
        1948   Da Pushtu Keli [The Pushtu Key]. Kabul: Matba'eh-yi 'umumi. Pp. 62. (1327 A.H.)

        One of a series designed for the use of government officials engaged in learning Pushtu.

2799   Khadem, Qiyam al-Din (trans)
        1954   Makarim al-Akhlaq [Noble Ethics]. Kabul: Matba'eh-yi 'umumi. Pp. 317. (1333 A.H.)

        A translation from Arabic into Pushtu of a work on ethics by Shaykh 'Abd al-Qader al-Moghrabi.

2800   Khalili, az Ash'ar-i Ostad [From the Poems of Ostad Khalili]
        1961   Kabul: Doulati matba'eh. Pp. 502. (1340 A.H.)

2801   Khalili, Khalilullah
        1954   Muntakhabat-i Ashiar [Selections of Poetry]. Kabul: Matba'eh-yi 'umumi. Pp. 83. (1333 A.H.)

        Selections representing a number of contemporary Afghan poets who write in Persian.

2802   Khalili, Khalilullah
        1955   Fayz-i Quds [Divine Grace]. Kabul: Matba'eh-yi 'umumi. Pp. 102. (1334 A.H.)

        The text, in Dari, is a study of Dari poetry by a contemporary Afghan scholar and former secretary of the Council of Ministers.

2803   Khalili, Khalilullah (ed)
        1959   Kolliyat-i Hakim Sana'i [The Collected Works of Hakim Sana'i]. Kabul: Matba'eh-yi doulati. (1338 A.H.)

        The Dari text of the poems of an author of the Ghaznavid period.

2804   Khan, Qazi Rahimullah
        1938   The Modern Pushto Instructor. Peshawar.

2805   Khasteh, A. (ed)
        1960   Mo'asiren Sokhanvar [Contemporary Writers]. Kabul: Doulati matba'eh. Pp. 363. (1339 A.H.)

        An anthology of living Afghan poets writing in Dari, including biographical data and photographs of the authors.

VIII. LANGUAGES AND LITERATURE

2806   Khushhal Khan Khattak
            1956 Muntakhabat: Kushhal Khan Kotok. Translated by
                Said Anwarulhaq. Peshawar: Pushto Academy, University
                of Peshawar. Pp. 641. (Text in Pushtu and Urdu.)

2807   Kieffer, Charles M.
            1975 Les parlers de la vallee du logar-Wardak
                (Afghanistan), etude de dialectologie iranienne [The
                Dialects of the Valley of Logar-Wardak (Afghanistan):
                Study of Iranian Dialectology]. Unpublished Ph.D.
                Dissertation. University of Paris III (Sorbonne-
                Nouvelle). Pp. x, 386.

2808   Kieffer, Charles M.
            1977 The Approaching End of the Relict Southeast Iranian
                Languages Ormuri and Paraci in Afghanistan. Linguistics
                191:71-100.

2809   Kieffer, Charles M. and S. Sana
            1979 Fragments Pasto, Persans et Arabes de Malte. I.
                Liste de debiteurs en Pasto. Journal Asiatique 267:357-
                371.

2810   Kisilova, L. N.
            1973 Ocherki Po Leksikologii Yazika Dari [Work on the
                Lexicology of Dari]. Moscow: USSR Academy of Sciences.

2811   Kisilova, L. N. (comp)
            1978 Dari-Russian Dictionary. Moscow: Russian Languages
                Publishing Agency.

        The dictionary includes 21,000 basic spoken and popular
        words used by the Kabul citizens.

2812   Kohzad, Ahmad Ali
            1946 Alexandre en Afghanistan. Pièce en quatre actes
                [Alexander in Afghanistan. A Play in Four Acts].
                Afghanistan 1(3):10-23; 1(4):1-17.

        Alexander meets local chieftains who tell him of their
        habits and customs.

2813   Kohzad, Ahmad Ali
            1949 Drama of Islam: A Comedy. Afghanistan 4(1):45-67.

        A turgid, involved description of a pageant in which
        colonization, the new nation of Pakistan, and the Afghan
        tribes are intermingled.

VIII. LANGUAGES AND LITERATURE

2814   Kohzad, Ahmad Ali
       1952 Parwati: jeune montagnarde de la région de Gomal
       [Parwati: A Young Mountain Woman of the Gomal Region].
       Afghanistan 7(1):42-49.

       The Aryan legend of a beautiful princess and her lover who
       had to seek his fortune.

2815   Kohzad, Ahmad 'Ali (ed)
       1953 Guldastah-yi 'Ishq [Nosegay of Love]. Kabul:
       Matba'eh-yi 'umumi. Pp. 14. (1331 A.H.)

       A commemorative souvenir in Dari to mark the 700th
       anniversary of Maulana Jalal al-Din Balkhi.

2816   Kohzad, Ahmad Ali
       1953 Mawlana Djallal-ud-Din Balkhi [Maulana Jalal al-Din
       Balkhi]. Afghanistan 8(1):60-63.

       Commemorating the 700th anniversary of his death, a
       biography of an Islamic mystic and philogopher of the
       thirteenth century A.D. See no. 2815.

2817   Kohzad, Ahmad Ali
       1953 Zarir et Yatkazarizan [Zarir and Yatkazarizan].
       Afghanitan 8(1):53-59.

       On the Aryan hero Zarir, younger brother of the Bactrian
       ruler Aspah, and the epic of his deeds, Yatkazarizan.

2818   Kohzad, Mohammad Nabi
       1951 Afghanistan Crocevia dell'Asia [Afghanistan,
       Crossroads of Asia]. Afghanistan 6(2):40-43.

       An appreciation of Caspani and Cagnacci's Afghanistan
       Crocevia dell'Asia, quoting the Preface, by the Italian
       Ambassador Plenipotentiary in Afghanistan, in full.

2819   Kohzad, Mohammad Nabi
       1951 Akbar Nameh. Afghanistan 6(4):59-61.

       The announcement of a book, a collection of poetry,
       concerned with the past 150 year of Afghan history.

2820   Kohzad, Mohammad Nabi
       1954 Un nouvel ouvrage "Légendes et coutumes afghanes"
       [A New Work "Afghan Legends and Customs"]. Afghanistan
       9(1):55-57.

VIII. LANGUAGES AND LITERATURE

A note on the appearance of Legendes et coutumes afghanes, containing a mention of the Hackins' work in Afghanistan and a list of the book's contents.

2821 Koshan, Ghulam Hazrat (ed)
    1965 Pazhwak, Abdur-Rahman. Gulhai Andesha [Flowers of Sorrow]. Kabul: Ministry of Education Press. Pp. 159.

A collection of poems in Pushtu.

2822 Kovusov, Anna, Yakovom Kozlovskiy (trans)
    1964 Afganskiye Vstrechi [Meetings in Afghanistan]. Sovetskiy Pisatel'.

Verse by a Turkoman poetess, translated into Russian. Some poems tell of the friendliness of the Afghan people, others are based on Afghan folklore.

2823 Kratkii afgansko-russkii slovar'
    1950 Sostavil P. B. Zudin. Pod redaktsiei chlena-korrespondenta AK. S.S.S.R. Prof. E. E. Bertel'sa [Short Afghan-Russian Dictionary. Compiled by P. B. Zudin. Edited by the Corresponding Member of the Academy of the U.S.S.R. Professor E. E. Bertels]. Moscow: Gosudarstvennoe izdatel'stvo inostrannykh i natsional'nykh slovarei. Pp. 568.

A very useful work. The material is up-to-date, and there is a valuable grammatical sketch. Based in part on native Afghan dictionaries, with Pushtu entries given in Arabic script and in Cyrillic transliteration.

2824 Kratkii voennyi persidsko-russkii slovar'
    1954 S prilozheniem voennogo slovaria Kabuli. Sostavili L. S. Peisikov, N. P. Savchenko, S. d. Smirnov. Pod. red. N. P. Savchenko. Okolo 10,000 slov i terminov [Short Persian-Russian Military Dictionary with a Supplementary Military Glossary in the Kabuli Language]. Moscow: Gosudarstvennoe izdatel'stvo inostrannykh i natsional'nykh slovarei. Pp. 334.

2825 Kushev, V. V.
    1976 Opisanie Rukopisei na yaieke Pashto Instituta Vostokobedeniya [Description of Pushtu Manuscripts at the Oriental Institute]. Moscow: USSR Academy of Sciences. Pp. 136.

VIII. LANGUAGES AND LITERATURE

Describes twenty-three (newly acquired manuscripts) housed in the Pushtu collection of the Oriental Institute, USSR Academy of Sciences in Moscow.

2826 Kushkaki, Burhan al-Din
1939 Peh Pateh da Pattu Platenay [In Secrecy to Search for Secrets]. Kabul: Matba'eh-yi 'umumi. Pp. 272. (1318 A.H.)

An original work in Pushtu.

2827 Laheeb, Nasratullah
1977 A Linguistic Investigation of Uzbek Dialects in Afghanistan. Unpublished Ph.D. Dissertation. University of Washington. Pp. 220.

2828 Laugier de Beaurecueil, S. de
1964 Manuscripts d'Afghanistan [Manuscripts of Afghanistan]. Cairo: Imprimerie de l'Institut francais d'archéologie Orientale. Pp. xiii, 420.

2829 Lazard, Gilbert
1963 La Langue de plus ancient monuments de la prose persane [The Language of the Oldest Examples of Persian Prose]. Paris: Klincksieck. Pp. 535; indices.

2830 Lebedev, Konstantin A.
1956 Grammatika yazyka pushtu [Grammar of the Pushtu Language]. Moscow: IIMO. Pp. 223.

2831 Lebedev, Konstantin A.
1961 Karmannyy russko-Afganskiy slovar' [Russian-Afghan Pocket Dictionary]. Moscow: GIS. Pp. 752.

2832 Lebedev, Konstantin A., Z. M. Kalinina, and L. S. Yatsevich
1963 Uchebnik afganskogo yazyka (Pushtu) [Textbook of the Afghan Language (Pushtu)]. Moscow: IIMO. Pp. 236.

2833 Lebedev, K. A., L. S. Yathevich and Z. M. Kalinina
1973 Russko-Afganskii Slovar: Pushtu [Russian-Afghan Dictionary: Pushtu]. Moscow: Soviet Encyclopedia Publications Department. Pp. 872.

A Russian-Pushtu Dictionary containing 32,000 words.

2834 Leech, R.
1838 A Vocabulary of the Language of the Moghal Aimaks. Journal of the Royal Asiatic Society of Bengal 7:785-787.

VIII. LANGUAGES AND LITERATURE

A short vocabulary, with a few sentences (all transliterated) translated into English.

2835 Leech, R.
1839 Grammar of the Pashto or Afghanee. Journal of the Asiatic Society of Bengal 8:1-16.

2836 Lentz, Wolfgang
1937 Ein Lateinalphabet für das Paschto [A Latin Alphabet for Pushtu]. Berlin: A. Eeine. Pp. 12.

A technical study of little apparent practical value.

2837 Literaturovedeniye. Indiya, Pakistan, Afganistan [History of Literature. India, Pakistan, Afghanistan]
1965 Kratkiye Soobshcheniya Instituta Narodov Azii 80:1-188. Moscow.

2838 Lorenz, Manfred
1979 Lehrbuch des Pashto (Afganisch). Leipzig: VEB Verlag Enzyklopadie. Pp. 303.

2839 Lorimer, David Lockhart Robertson
1915 Pashtu Part I. Syntax of Colloquial Pashtu, with Chapters on Persian and Indian Elements in the Modern Languages, by Major D. L. R. Lorimer. Oxford: The Clarendon Press.

In spite of the title, the book is a complete grammar (of "Northeastern Pushtu"), not just a study of syntax. The alphabet is explained, but the bulk of the book uses only transliteration. Part II, which was to deal with historical matters, never appeared.

2840 Lorimer, David Lockhart Robertson
1922 The Phonology of the Bakhtiari, Badakhshani, and Madaglashti Dialects of Modern Persian. With Vocabularies. London: Royal Asiatic Society. Pp. xi, 205.

Part II, on the Badakhshani and Madaglashti dialects, pages 127-205, contains material on the phonology and morphology, brief sample texts, and a vocabulary of the dialect of Dari spoken in the northeastern corner of Afghanistan. The author, a member of the Foreign and Political Department of the Government of India, collected the material in the field.

VIII. LANGUAGES AND LITERATURE

2841 Lorimer, J. G.
1902 Grammar and Vocabulary of Waziri Pashto. Calcutta: Office of the Superintendent of Government Printing, India. Pp. x, 345.

The only extensive treatment of a dialect as such (other than Peshawar or Qandahar) without reference to the literary norm.

2842 Lowenthal, R.
1860 Is the Pushto a Semitic Language? Journal of the Asiatic Society of Bengal 29:323-345.

2843 MacKenzie, D. N. (trans)
1965 Poems From the Divan of Khushal Khan Khattak. London: George Allen and Unwin Ltd. Pp. 258.

2844 Majmu'eh-yi Ash'ar-i Vajid
1953 Bakhsh-i Chaharum [A Collection of Poems by Vajid. Part Four]. Fayzabad: Matba'eh-yi Badakhshahan. Pp. 110. (1332 A.H.)

A collection of modern Persian poetry in the dialect of the region.

2845 Majruh, Sayyid Shams al-Din
1958 Montakhab Sha'arunah [Selected Poems]. Kabul: Matba'eh-yi doulati. (1337 A.H.)

Poems in Pushtu.

2846 Martin, Thomas J. (comp)
1977 North American Collections of Islamic Manuscripts. New York: G. K. Hall and Co., American Council of Learned Societies. Pp. xvii, 96.

2847 Massé, Henri
1939 L'Académie afghane et ses publications. Appendice: La presse en Afghanistan [The Afghan Academy and its Publications. Appendix: The Press in Afghanistan]. Revue des Études Islamiques 13:180-199.

On the occasion of the opening of the ninth year of publication of the periodical Kabul, a French scholar reviews the work of the sponsoring academy. Notices of publications issued by the Academy are followed by summaries of articles on education, music, and folklore from Kabul, and, finally, by a list of newspapers and periodicals which have appeared in Afghanistan.

VIII. LANGUAGES AND LITERATURE

2848 Masson, Charles
1848 Legends of the Afghan Countries, in Verse: With Various Pieces, Original and Translated. London: J. Madden. Pp. vii, 328.

An early attempt at compiling folktales in Afghanistan. In the absence of any other comprehensive work, this is an important source for its subject.

2849 Ma'sumi N. and M. Kholov (comps)
1965 Namuneh Fol'klori Khalqhoi Afghanistan. Ruboiat va Surudho [Samples of Afghan Popular Folklore. Verses and Songs]. Dushanbe: Irfon. Pp. 320.

A publication in contemporary Tajik script containing 895 short verses, 135 landay, and 22 songs--all in Dari. A second edition was published in 1966.

2850 Maylon, F. H.
1913 Some Current Pushtu Folk Stories. Memoirs of the Asiatic Society of Bengal 3:355-405. Calcutta.

Some ten Pushtu folk stories are given in translation by a British officer; the selection illustrates varieties of the dialects of the Orakzai, Afridi, and Yusufzai ethnic elements.

2851 Mel'nikova, G. (ed)
1958 Skazki i stikhi Afganistan [Tales and Verse From Afghanistan]. Moscow: Gosudarstvennoe Izdatel'stvo Khudozhestvennoy literaturi. Pp. 311.

2852 Merganov, S.
1973 Iazyk i poetika afganskikh (pashto) poslovits i pogovorok [The Language and Poetry of Afghan (Pushtu) Proverbs and Sayings]. Unpublished Ph.D. Dissertation. Institut Vostokovedeniiia Akademii nauk SSSR.

2853 Michener, James A.
1963 Caravans. New York: Random House. Pp. 370.

A romantic novel with the plot set up in Afghanistan. Offers interesting "Michenerian" insights about the people and culture of the country.

VIII. LANGUAGES AND LITERATURE

2854 Mills, Margaret Ann
1978 Cupid and Psyche in Afghanistan: An International Tale in Cultural Context. New York: Afghanistan Council, The Asia Society. Occasional paper no. 14. Pp. 28.

The author tries to demonstrate the relationship of an Afghan folktale, Xasteh Xomar to the tales of Beauty and the Beast and Cupid and Psyche.

2855 Mills, Margaret Ann
1978 Oral Narrative in Afghanistan: The Individual in Tradition. Unpublished Ph.D. Dissertation. Harvard University. Pp. 484.

A structural analysis of folktales from Northwest Afghanistan based upon fieldwork in Herat.

2856 Miran, M. Alam
1969 Major Problems of Dari Speakers in Mastering Pashto Morphology. M.A. Thesis. University of Texas.

2857 Miran, M. Alam
1974 Some Linguistic Difficulties Facing Dari Speakers Learning Pashto. New York: Afghanistan Council, the Asia Society. Occasional paper no. 7. Pp. 30.

2858 Miran, M. Alam
1975 Naming and Address in Afghan Society. Arlington, Virginia: Center for Applied Linguistics. Pp. 26.

2859 Miran, M. Alam
1975 Sociolinguistic Factors Affecting Primary Education in Afghanistan: A Consideration of Aspects of Multilingualism and National Education Policy. Unpublished Ph.D. Dissertation. University of Texas at Austin. Pp. 230.

Concerned with the establishment of the bilingual and literacy educational programs and the development of national unity among different ethnic groups in Afghanistan through these programs.

2860 Miran, M. Alam
1977 The Functions of National Languages in Afghanistan. New York: Afghanistan Council, The Asia Society. Occasional paper no. 11. Pp. 10.

VIII. LANGUAGES AND LITERATURE

>The linguistic diversity of Afghanistan as it relates to the problems of socio-cultural integration is discussed.

2861 Miran, M. Alam
1977 Language Planning in Afghanistan. Sociolinguistics Newsletter 8(1):18-22.

2862 Miran, M. Alam
1977 Sociolinguistic Factors in Afghanistan. Afghanistan Journal 4(3):122-127.

2863 Montakhabat-i Khushhal Khan Khattak [Selections From Khushhal Khan Khattak]
n.d. Peshawar: Peshawar University. Pp. 320; index.

>Pushtu poetry, with translations into Urdu.

2864 Morgenstierne, Georg
1926 Report on a Linguistic Mission to Afghanistan. Oslo: H. Aschehoug and Co. Pp. 100.

>This publication is Volume I-2 in Series C of the Instituttet for Sammenlignende Kulturforskning. Includes remarks on Pushtu and Dari spoken in Afghanistan and more detailed treatment of several languages of northeastern Afghanistan. The highly technical nature of the study is somewhat alleviated by the presence of an unusual and valuable bibliography, a linguistic sketch map of northeastern Afghanistan, and a sketch map of Pashai dialect boundaries. The author visited the area in 1924.

2865 Morgenstierne, Georg
1927 An Etymological Vocabulary of Pashto. Oslo: I kom. hos Jacob Dybwad. Pp. 120.

>Restricted chiefly to words for which cognates can be found in Indo-Iranian languages, and includes a few loanwords where they "present phonetic features of interest."

2866 Morgenstierne, Georg
1929 Indo-Iranian Frontier Languages. I. Parachi and Ormuri. Oslo: H. Aschehoug and Co. Pp. 419.

>The publication is Volume 11 in Series B of the Instituttet for Sammenlignende Kulturforskning. It includes a grammar and phonology for each language, with transliterated and translated texts of stories, poems and vocabularies.

VIII. LANGUAGES AND LITERATURE

2867 Morgenstierne, Georg
   1929 The Language of the Ashkun Kafirs. Norsk Tidsskrift for Sprogvidenskap 2:192-289.

   The possible origins of the language, a grammar and texts, transliterated with interlinear translations. A lengthy vocabulary defines words and gives corresponding words in other languages and dialects.

2868 Morgenstierne, Georg
   1931 The Wanetsi Dialect of Pashto. Norsk Tidsskrift for Sprogvidenskap 4:156-175.

   This dialect of Pushtu is so divergent that it probably should be regarded as a separate language.

2869 Morgenstierne, Georg
   1932 Report on a Linguistic Mission to North-Western India. Oslo: H. Aschehoug and Co. Pp. 76; maps.

   The publication is Volume III-1 in Series C of the Instituttet for Sammenlignende Kulturforskning. The work was carried on in 1929, principally in Chitral but with the employment of cross-border informants on such languages spoken within Afghanistan as Tirahi, Ashkun, Pashai, Waigeli, and Prasun. One map of the region north of the Kabul River indicates language localities on both sides of the frontier.

2870 Morgenstierne, Georg
   1934 Additional Notes on Ashkun. Norsk Tidsskrift for Sprogvidenskap 7:56-115.

   Additions to, and corrections of, The Language of the Ashkun Kafirs, with texts and vocabulary. See no. 2867)

2871 Morgenstierne, Georg
   1934 Note on the Khetrani Dialect of Lahnda. Acta Orientalia 13:173-175.

   A short list of words collected from a Khetran whom the author met briefly.

2872 Morgenstierne, Georg
   1934 Notes on Tirahi. Acta Orientalia 12:161-189.

   A few additions and corrections to the knowledge of Tirahi, with vocabulary.

VIII. LANGUAGES AND LITERATURE

2873   Morgenstierne, Georg
        1938 Indo-Iranian Frontier Languages. II. Iranian Pamir
              Languages (Yidgha-Munji, Sanglechi-Ishkashmi, and
              Wakhi). Oslo: H. Aschehoug and Co. Pp. xxiv, 630; map.

        The publication is Volume 35 of Series B of the
        Instituttet for Sammenlignende Kulturforskning. The
        author covers phonology, morphology texts, and a
        comparative vocabulary of these little-known languages.
        Includes references to all previously published studies.

2874   Morgenstierne, Georg
        1940 Archaisms and Innovations in Pashto Morphology.
              Norsk Tidsskrift for Sprogvidenskap 12:88-114.

2875   Morgenstierne, Georg
        1944 Indo-Iranian Frontier Languages. III. The Pashai
              Language. 2. Texts and Translations. With Comparative
              Notes on Pashai Folktales by Reidar Th. Christiansen.
              Oslo: H. Aschehoug and Co. Pp. xxxviii, 304.

        The publication is Volume 40 of Series B of the
        Instituttet for Sammenlignende Kulturfoskning. Pashai,
        belonging to the Dardic group of Indo-Aryan languages, is
        spoken in the hill country northeast of Kabul. Collected
        in 1924, the prose examples are of five dialects and
        stress fairy tales. Some fifteen dialects are represented
        in examples of poetry, in which poems of vendetta
        predominate over the epic and lyric.

2876   Morgenstierne, Georg
        1949 The Language of the Prasun Kafirs. Norsk Tidsskrift
              for Sprogvidenskap 15:188-334.

2877   Morgenstierne, Georg
        1956 Indo-Iranian Frontier Languages. III. The Pashai
              Language. 3. Vocabulary. Oslo: H. Aschehoug and Co.
              Pp. xi, 232.

        The supplement to no. 2875.

2878   Morgenstierne, Georg
        1970 Istalif and Other Place-Names of Afghanistan.
              Bulletin of the School of Oriental and African Studies
              333:350-352.

2879   Morgenstierne, Georg
        1970 Notes on Bactrian Phonology. Bulletin of the School
              of Oriental and African Studies 333:125-131.

VIII. LANGUAGES AND LITERATURE

2880   Morgenstierne, Georg
        1973 Irano-Dardica. Wiesbaden: Ludwig Reichert Verlag. Pp. 388; index.

2881   Morgenstierne, Georg
        1973 Indo-Iranian Frontier Languages, III/1, 2, 3: The Pashai Language (second edition). The Institute for Comparative Research in Human Culture.

2882   Morgenstierne, Georg
        1974 Report on a Linguistic Mission to Northwestern India. (Original 1932.) Karachi: Indus Publications. Pp. 74, maps, plates, illustrations, bibliography.

Includes a discussion of the Dardic languages of Afghanistan.

2883   Morgenstierne, Georg
        1975 Volksdichtung in Afghanistan. Afghanistan Journal 2(1):2-7.

2884   Morgenstierne, Georg and James A. Lloyd
        1928 Notes on the Pronunciation of Pashto (Dialect of the Hazara District). London: Institute Bulletin of the Society of Oriental Studies 5:53-63.

Careful, phonetic description of the speech of an informant in England, with IPA transcriptions of the examples.

2885   Muhammad Hotak ibn Da'ud Khan
        1944 Putah Khazaneh [The Secret Treasure]. Edited by Abdul Hai Habibi. Kabul: Matba'eh-yi 'umumi. Pp. 290. (1323 A.H.)

In this work written in Pushtu in 1729 A.D. the author gives biographies of some 51 contemporaries and traces the development of Pushtu poetry from earlier periods.

2886   Mumand, Muhammad Gol
        1937 Pushtu Sind Ya'ni Awwalin Qamus afghani [Pushtu Stream, or The First Afghan Dictionary]. Kabul: Matba'eh-yi 'umumi. Pp. (1) 399; (2) 366. (1316 A.H.)

Two volumes in Pushtu, bound as a single volume.

VIII. LANGUAGES AND LITERATURE

2887   Mumand, Muhammad Gol
1938 Da Pushtu da Zhebay Liyarah [The Path of the Pushtu Language]. Balkh. Pp. 239, 156. (1317 A.H.)

A grammar of the Pushtu language.

2888   Mumand, Muhammad Gol
n.d. Melli Hindara [National Mirror]. Kabul: Matba'eh-yi 'umumi.

A collection of stories about the courage of the Afghans.

2889   Murphy, Christopher
1974 Abdulla Qodirij: His Works and His Role in Uzbek Literature. Unpublished Ph.D. Dissertation. University of Washington. Pp. 305.

2890   Music, Afghanistan
n.d. Afghanistan: Music in Kabul. Lyrichord. LIST 7259-B (Record).

2891   Music, Afghanistan
1969 An Anthology of Oriental Music. Afghanistan: Music of the Uzbeks. AST-4001 (Record).

2892   Music, Afghanistan
1970 An Anthology of Oriental Music. Afghanistan: Music of the Pashtoons, Heratis and Kazakhs. AST-4004 (Record).

2893   Music, Afghanistan
1972 An Anthology of Oriental Music. The Music of Afghanistan: Music of the Tajiks. AST-4007 (Record).

2894   Music, Afghanistan
1973 Afghanistan: Music From the Crossroads of Asia. Explorer Series. H-72053-B (Record).

2895   Music, Afghanistan
1976 Dupaigne, B. Musiques classiques and populaires d'Afghanistan. Anthologie de la musique des peuples (AMP 72901). Societe Francaise de Productions Phonographiques (SFPP). Paris. (Record)

2896   Music, Afghanistan
n.d. Radio Kabul. Ethnic Folkways Library. Folkways FE-4361 (Record).

VIII. LANGUAGES AND LITERATURE

2897 Music, Afghanistan
n.d. A Musical Anthology of the Orient (UNESCO Collection). Musurgia BM30, Afghanistan, L2003 (Record).

2898 Music, Afghanistan
n.d. Musique folklorique d'Afghanistan [Folklore Music of Afghanistan]. BAM, Paris LD337 (Record).

2899 Muwlani, M. Sarwar (comp)
1971 Shi'r-e Mu'asir-e Afghanistan [Contemporary Poetry of Afghanistan]. Tehran: Intisharat-i Zar. Pp. viii; 175.

2900 Naby, Eden
1975 Transitional Central Asian Literature: Tajik and Uzbek Prose Fiction From 1909 to 1932. Unpublished Ph.D. Dissertation. Columbia University. Pp. 266.

Analysis and examination of transitional Tajik and Uzbek literature in Soviet Central Asia.

2901 Najaf 'Ali Khan
1924 Tuhfeh-yi Amaniyeh [Gift of Amanullah]. Lahore: Karimi. Pp. 72.

A lithographed poem in Dari, celebrating the accession to the throne of Amir Amanullah.

2902 Najib-ullah
1951 Abouraihan Al-Beiruni and His Time. Afghanistan 6(1):17-27.

About a phenomenal scholar at the court of Sultan Mahmud.

2903 Najib-ullah
1951 Speech Delivered by Dr. Najib-ullah Khan. Afghanistan 6(4):52-58.

On the importance of the Urdu language and the Khorasan school of poetry in Afghan-Indian cultural relations.

2904 Najib-ullah
1963 Islamic Literature, An Introductory History with Selections. New York: Washington Square Press. Pp. 441.

A descriptive study by the late Afghan diplomat and scholar. Includes material from Afghanistan.

VIII. LANGUAGES AND LITERATURE

2905 Nawis, Abdullah Afghan
    1957 Afghan qamus. Farsi peh pushtu [Afghan Dictionary. Persian into Pushtu]. Kabul. Vol 1:133; 2:128; 3:124. (1336 A.H.)

2906 Nawis, Abdullah Afghan
    1961 Loghat 'Amianah-yi Farsi Afghanistan [Dictionary of the Popular Persian of Afghanistan]. Kabul: Matbu'atu Mostaqel Riassat. Pp. 592. (1340 A.H.)

A work dealing with the colloquial dialect of the country.

2907 Ne'matulloev, H. and R. Hoshim (eds)
    1958 Namunai Ash'ori Shoironi Afghan [Samples of the Poetry of Afghan Poets]. Stalinabad: Nashriati Davlatii Tojikiston. Pp. 184.

The poems, in Dari, are given in contemporary Tajik script.

2908 Ne'matulloev, H. and R. Hoshim (eds)
    1959 Namuneh-yi Ash'ar-i Sha'iran-i Afghan [Samples of the Poetry of Afghan Poets]. Stalinabad: Nashriat-i Dovlatii. Pp. 296.

The poems, in Dari, are given in Arabic script.

2909 Nilsen, Don L. F.
    1977 Kabul Sign Language: A Historical Perspective. Afghanistan Journal 4(4:149-154.

2910 Niyazov, H. N.
    1979 Description of Persian and Tajik Manuscripts of the Institute of Oriental Studies. Vol. 5. Moscow: Institute of Oriental Studies, USSR Academy of Sciences. (In Russian.)

2911 Nohsadumin Sal-i Wafat-i Khwajeh 'Abdullah Ansari Heravi [The Nine Hundredth Year of the Death of Khwajeh 'Abdullah Ansari Heravi]
    1962 Kabul: Matba'eh-yi Wizarat-i, Matbuat. Pp. 216. (1341 A.H.)

A commemorative volume, in Dari.

VIII. LANGUAGES AND LITERATURE

2912   Nuri, Muhammad Gol (ed)
       1941   Da Pushtu Istilahat aw Muhawari [The Colloquial Expressions Used in Conversation]. Kabul: Matba'eh-yi 'umumi. Pp. 392. (1320 A.H.)

       Expressions in Pushtu, arranged under alphabetical headings.

2913   Nuri, Muhammad Gol
       1948   Matalunah [Proverbs]. Kabul: Matba'eh-yi 'umumi. Pp. 156. (1327 A.H.)

       Arranged in alphabetical order are some 1900 popular proverbs and sayings in Pushtu.

2914   Nuri, Nur Ahmad
       1947   Gulshan-i Emarat [Flowering of Court Life]. Kabul: Doulati matba'eh. Pp. 166. (1335 A.H.)

       Account of life in the courts of the nineteenth-century rulers of Afghanistan, in Dari.

2915   Obidov, Usmanjon
       1977   Shevai Jabulus-siroj, Afganistani Shimoli [The Dialect of Jabulsiroj, northern Afghanistan]. Dushanbe: Tajikistan SSR Academy of Sciences. Pp. 236. (In Tajiki)

       A discussion of the phonology, morphology, syntax, and lexemes of Dari as spoken in Jabusiroj, Afghanistan. In Cyrillic. Some transcriptions in Latin characters. Includes a word list.

2916   Olfat, Gol Pacha
       1942   Loghawi Tsiranah [Philological Research]. Kabul: Matba'eh-yi 'umumi. Pp. 84. (1321 A.H.)

       A work in Pushtu, which traces the origin of root words of that language to Sanskrit.

2917   Olfat, Gol Pacha
       1948   'Oli Afkar [Great Thoughts]. Kabul: Matba'eh-yi 'umumi. Pp. 58. (1327 A.H.)

       A collection of Pushtu poetry.

VIII. LANGUAGES AND LITERATURE

2918 Olfat, Gol Pacha
1949 Tseh Likal ya Lik Puhah [Writing and the Art of Writing]. Kabul: Matba'eh-yi 'umumi. Pp. 96. (1328 A.H.)

A study in Pushtu dealing with the literary writing styles of that language.

2919 Olfat, Gol Pacha
1953 Adabi Bahsunah [Literary Discussions]. Kabul: Matba'eh-yi 'umumi. Pp. 132. (1332 A.H.)

A contemporary work in Pushtu.

2920 Olfat, Gol Pacha
1955 Ghorah Ash'ar [Selected Poems]. Kabul: Matba'eh-yi 'umumi. Pp. 256. (1334 A.H.)

A collection of poems in Pushtu.

2921 Olfat, Gol Pacha
1956 Lwer Khiyalunah aw Zhwar Fikrunah [High Ideas and Deep Thoughts]. Kabul: Matba'eh-yi 'umumi. Pp. 97. (1335 A.H.)

2922 Olfat, Gol Pacha
1956 Mantiq [Logic]. Kabul: Matba'eh-yi 'umumi. Pp. 53. (1335 A.H.)

A short introduction to logic, written in Pushtu.

2923 Olfat, Gol Pacha
1957 Neshruneh [Prose]. Kabul: Matba'eh-yi 'umumi. Pp. 118. (1336 A.H.)

A collection of prose writings in Pushtu.

2924 Olfat, Gol Pacha
1962 Da Zrah Waina [The Lament of the Heart]. Kabul: Pohani matba'eh. Pp. 122. (1341 A.H.)

A collection of poems in Pushtu.

2925 Oransky, I. M.
1979 Iranian Languages in Historical Interpretation. Moscow: Institute of Oriental Studies, USSR Academy of Sciences. Pp. 237. (In Russian)

VIII. LANGUAGES AND LITERATURE

2926 Ostrovskii, B. Y.
1971 Distributsiya Variantov Morfem v Kabulskom Dialektiki [Distribution of Variant Morpheme in the Kabul Dialect]. In Iranskaya Filologiya. Moscow: USSR Academy of Sciences. Pp. 54-67.

2927 Ostrovskii, B. Y.
1971 Nekotie Fonologicheskie Osobbennosti Razgovornogo Kabuli. Narodie Azii i Afriki 5:143-145.

2928 Paktiyani, N. M. (ed)
1960 Palwasha. Da 'Abd al-Ghani Khan Ghani Asha'ar [Radiance. The Poems of 'Abd al-Ghani Khan Ghani]. Kabul. Pp. 236. (1339 A.H.)

A collection of poems in Pushtu.

2929 Panj Ganj [Five Treasures]
1934 Kabul: Manzum 'Amm-i Barqi Paris. Pp. 72. (1353 A.H.)

A lithographed edition of the very popular and frequently reproduced school text in Dari. Contains poetry and passages on religion and ethics from such sources as Sa'di, the Mahmud-nameh, the Pand-nameh of 'Attar, and the Nam-i Haq.

2930 Parker, Barrett and Ahmad Javid
1970 A Collection of Afghan Legends. Kabul: Afghan Books. Pp. 119.

A collection of 24 tales from Afghanistan (Kabul and vicinity) with no analysis. Most stories are brutally abridged.

2931 Pasarlani Mosha'erah [Poetry on Spring]
n.d. Kabul: Matba'eh-yi 'umumi. Pp. 32.

Short selections of Pushtu by more than a score of contemporaries.

2932 Pazhwak, Abdul Rahman (ed)
1946 The Lovers of Dilaram. Translated by Abdul Satar Shalizi. Afghanistan 1(2):35-45.

A romantic and tragic tale of young love: no indication of its original literary source.

VIII. LANGUAGES AND LITERATURE

2933   Pazhwak, Abdul Rahman
        1957 Afsana-ha-yi Mardom [Folktales]. Kabul. Pp. 87.
          (1336 A.H.)

        A work in Dari by an Afghan scholar-diplomat.

2934   Pazhwak, Abdul Rahman
        1965 Golha-yi Andisheh [The Flowers of Reflection].
          Kabul: Pohani Matba'eh. Pp. 159. (1344 A.H.)

        Contemporary poetry in Dari.

2935   Pazhwak, Muhammad Din (ed)
        1955 Pushtuni Sandarai [Pushtu Songs]. Kabul: Matba'eh-
          yi 'umumi. Pp. 398. (1334 A.H.)

        The first volume of a two-volume collection.

2936   Pazhwak, Muhammad Din
        1956 Pushtu Neshrunah [Pushtu Prose]. Kabul: Matba'eh-yi
          'umumi. Pp. 122. (1335 A.H.)

2937   Penzl, Herbert
        1950 On the Cases of the Afghan (Pashto) Noun. Word
          6:70-73.

        A study of the three Pushtu cases: direct, oblique, and
        vocative.

2938   Penzl, Herbert
        1951 Afghan Descriptions of the Afghan (Pashto) Verb.
          Journal of the American Oriental Society 71:97-110.

        An analysis of the descriptions of the verb form as they
        appear in native grammars of Pushtu.

2939   Penzl, Herbert
        1954 Orthography and Phonemes in Pashto (Afghan).
          Journal of the American Oriental Society 74:74-81.

        Study of the correlation between Pushtu orthography and
        phonemes, with valuable comments on dialect differences
        and views of the native grammarians.

2940   Penzl, Herbert
        1955 A Grammar of Pashto: A Descriptive Study of the
          Dialect of Kandahar, Afghanistan. Washington: American
          Council of Learned Societies. Pp. 169.

VIII. LANGUAGES AND LITERATURE

>Material collected by the author, an American linguist, at Qandahar in 1948 forms the basis of a grammar in which structure is emphasized. Very useful introduction on the present status of the language.

2941 Penzl, Herbert
 1961 Western loanwords in modern Pashto. Journal of the American Oriental Society 81:43-52.

>A list of these words, indicating that more of those in current usage for scientific terms come from Arabic and Dari.

2942 Penzl, Herbert
 1962 A Reader of Pashto. Ann Arbor: University of Michigan. Pp. 274.

>A reader prepared under contract between the University of Michigan and the United States Office of Education. The text includes 31 selections in script, in transliteration, and in translation, with glossaries and exercises.

2943 Phillott, Lieutenant Colonel D. C.
 1919 Higher Persian Grammar, Showing Differences Between Afghan and Modern Persian, with Notes on Rhetoric. Calcutta: Baptist Mission Press. Pp. xii, 937.

2944 Plowden, Trevor Chichele (trans)
 1893 Translation of the Kalid-i-Afghani, the Text Book for the Pakkhto Examination, with Notes. Lahore: Munshi Gulab Singh and Sons, 2nd edition. Pp. 427; genealogical tables.

>A translation of the texts edited by Thomas P. Hughes. See no. 2780.

2945 Popalzai, Aziz al-Din Vakili
 1963 Honar Khat dar Afghanistan dar do Qarn-i 'Akher [The Art of Calligraphy in Afghanistan in the Last Two Centuries]. Kabul: Doulati matba'eh. Pp. 219. (1342 A.H.)

>A work in Dari, generously illustrated with specimens of calligraphy.

VIII. LANGUAGES AND LITERATURE

2946   Popay Ressena, by H. L. O.
        1954 Afghanistan 9(2):48-50.

        On a description in the Avesta of a mountain chain known
        to the Aryans as Popai Ressena, and to the Greeks as
        Paropamisus.

2947   Pourhadi, I. V.
        1976 Afghanistan's Press and its Literary Influence.
        Afghanistan Journal 3(1):28-34.

2948   Prentice, Verna Russillo
        1977 The Illustration of Sa'di's Poetry in Fifteenth
            Century Herat. Unpublished Ph.D. Dissertation. Harvard
            Univerity. Pp. viii, 154; plates.

        Sa'di was a thirteenth century Persian poet.

2949   Pushtani Arman [The Desire of the Pushtuns]
        1955 Kabul: Matba'eh-yi 'umumi. Pp. 111. (1334 A.H.)

        An anthology of some 60 examples of patriotic and
        inspirational poetry in Pushtu by both early and
        contemporary writers.

2950   Da Pushtu Munazareh Peh Kabul Radio Kshay [The Prose Contest of
            Pushtu Over Radio Kabul]
        n.d. Kabul: Matba'eh-yi 'umumi. Pp. 46.

        A collection of discourses delivered in Pushtu by some 16
        officials, writers, and members of the staff of Radio
        Kabul.

2951   Pushtu Qamus [Pushtu Dictionary]
        1952-1954 2 vols. Kabul: Matba'eh-yi 'umumi. Pp. 995.
            (1331-1333 A.H.)

        A very valuable Pushtu-Dari dictionary.

2952   Qamus-i Jughrafiya'i-yi Afghanistan [Dictionary of the
            Geography of Afghanistan]
        1956-1960 Kabul: Matba'eh-yi doulati. (1335-1339 A.H.)

        A Pushtu edition of this four-volume work in Dari began to
        appear in 1962.

VIII. LANGUAGES AND LITERATURE

2953 Qandahari, Taleb (ed)
n.d. Ash'ar-i Vasel [Poems of Vasel]. Kabul: Doulati matba'eh. Pp. 130.

Vasel was a lyric poet, writing primarily between 1920 and 1930. He was the secretary of Amir Abdul Rahman.

2954 Qandahari, Taleb (ed)
1964 Azad Kabuli, Muntakhabat-i Ash'ar [Azad Kabuli. Selections of Poetry]. Kabul: Doulati matba'eh. Pp. 153. (1343 A.H.)

2955 Rafiq, Muhammad
1939 Dweh Sareh Mayen Wrunnah [Two Loving Brothers]. Kabul: Matba'eh-yi 'umumi. Pp. 140. (1318 A.H.)

A work in Pushtu.

2956 Raheen, Sayyed Makhdom (ed)
1967 Selected Works of Sayyed Jamaluddin al-Afghani. Kabul: Baihaqi Publishing House. Pp. 170. (1355 A.H.)

A collection of articles, letters, and poems.

2957 Rahimi, M. V. and L. V. Uspenskoi
1954 Tadziksko-Russkii Slovar [Tajiki: Russian Dictionary]. Moscow: Tajikistan SSR Academy of Sciences. Pp. 528.

A Tajiki-Russian dictionary containing about 40,000 words. In Cyrillic.

2958 Rahman, Abdul Rahman
1963 Diwan Adbdul Rahman. Translated by Amir Hamza Shinwari. Peshawar: University of Peshawar. Pp. 285. (Text in Urdu and Pushtu).

2959 Rahmani, Magdalene
1947 Rabea-i-Balkhi [Rabea-i Balkhi (Afghan Poetess)]. Afghanistan 2(3):17-21.

An account of the tragic life of the tenth-century poetess, with one sample of her verse.

2960 Rapp, E. L.
1965 Die Judisch-Persisch-Hebräischen Inschriften aus Afghanistan [The Jewish-Persian-Hebrew Inscriptions From Afghanistan]. Munich: J. Kitzinger. Pp. 77; bibliography.

VIII. LANGUAGES AND LITERATURE

2961 Rahmani, Mageh
1952 Pardeh-Nishinan-i Sukhanguy [Veiled Speakers]. Kabul Matba'eh-yi 'umumi. Pp. 94. (1331 A.H.)

An anthology of Dari prose and poetry from various periods.

2962 Rahmany, Magdalina
1952 Deux poétesses Afghanes du XIIIe siècle [Two Afghan Poetesses of the Thirteenth Century]. Afghanistan 7(1):39-41.

Short biographies of 'Aaiysha, an Afghan court poetess, and Mahjoube, a very gifted woman.

2963 Rashad, Abdul Shukur
1957 Lodi Pushtaneh [Lodi Pushtuns]. Kabul: Matba'eh-yi doulati. Pp. 425. (1336 A.H.)

A work in Pushtu about the Lodi dynasty.

2964 Raun, Alo
1969 Basic Course in Uzbek. Indiana University Publications: Uralic and Altaic Series, Volume 59. Bloomington: Indiana University. Pp. 271.

2965 Raverty, Henry George
1860 A Dictionary of the Pukhto, Pushto, or Language of the Afghans; London: William and Norgate. (2nd edition) Pp. xxiv, columns 1166.

2966 Raverty, Henry George (ed)
1860 The Gulshan-i-Roh: Being Selections, Prose and Poetical, in the Pushto, or Afghan Language. Edited by Captain H. G. Raverty. London: Longman, Green, Longman and Roberts. Pp. viii, 408.

This "Mountain Bouquet" contains what the editor considered to be the most characteristic examples of the great writers of Pushtu poetry and prose.

2967 Raverty, Henry George
1864 On the Language of the Siah posh Kafirs, with a short list of words to which are added specimens of Kohistani, and other dialects spoken on the northern border of Afghanistan. Journal of the Asiatic Society of Bengal 33:267-278.

VIII. LANGUAGES AND LITERATURE

2968   Raverty, Henry George
        1867 A Grammar of the Puk'hto, Pus'hto, or Language of
              the Afghans. London: William and Norgate, 3rd edition.
              Pp. x, 204.

        Attempts to include all dialects, but is based chiefly on
        literary works. Contains a lengthy introduction. Now
        antiquated. The first edition appeared in 1855 and the
        second in 1860.

2969   Raverty, Henry George (trans)
        1867 Selections From the Poetry of the Afghans, From the
              XVIth to the XIXth-Century, Literally Translated From
              the Original Pushtoo. London: William and Norgate.

        The translation of the collection, Gulshan-i-Roh, made by
        the same author. See no. 2966.

2970   Rishtin, Sadiqullah (ed)
        1942 Pushtana Shuara, 1200 A.H. to 1300 A.H. [Pushtun
              Poets, 1200 A.H. to 1300 A.H.]. Kabul: Umumi Matba'a.
              Pp. 287.

        Includes biographic notes and samples of poetry and
        writings for 55 Pushtun poets during the period.
        Published in 1321 A.H. In Pushtu.

2971   Rishtin, Sadiqullah
        1946 Da Pushtu da Adab Tarikh [The History of Pushtu
              Literature]. Kabul: Matba'eh-yi 'umumi. Pp. 190.
              (1325 A.H.)

        A history of this literature written in Pushtu.

2972   Rishtin, Sadiqullah
        1947 Da Pushtu Ishtiqaquneh aw Terkibunah [The
              Derivatives and Compounds of Pushtu]. Kabul: Matba'eh-
              yi 'umumi. Pp. 94. (1326 A.H.)

        An important work in Pushtu.

2973   Rishtin, Sadiqullah
        1947 Pushtu Keli [The Pushtu Key]. Kabul: Matba'eh-yi
              'umumi. Pp. 59. (1326 A.H.)

        One of a series of Pushtu grammars designed for the use of
        government officials engaged in learning Pushtu.

VIII. LANGUAGES AND LITERATURE

2974 Rishtin, Sadiqullah (ed)
  1947 Wish Zalmayan [Enlightened Youth]. Kabul. Pp. 191. (1326 A.H.)

  A collection of Dari and Pushtu poetry and prose by young Afghans.

2975 Rishtin, Sadiqullah
  1948 Pushtu Gramar [Pushtu Grammar]. Kabul: Matba'eh-yi 'umumi. Pp. 184. (1327 A.H.)

  A grammar in Pushtu, with English headings for the subdivisions of the text.

2976 Rishtin, Sadiqullah
  1951 Naway Zhwand [The New Life]. Kabul: Matba'eh-yi 'umumi. Pp. 181. (1330 A.H.)

  A work dealing with Pushtunistan and written in Pushtu.

2977 Rishtin, Sadiqullah (ed)
  1952 Da Abdul Hamid Mumand Diwan [The Divan of Abdul Hamid Mumand]. Kabul: Matba'eh-yi 'umumi. Pp. 154. (1331 A.H.)

  The work of a Pushtu poet who was active in 1725 A.D.: this Diwan is known as the Dur-o-Marjan.

2978 Rishtin, Sadiqullah (ed)
  1952 Pushtaneh sho'ara [Pushtu Poets]. Kabul: 'Umumi matba'eh. Pp. 283. (1331 A.H.)

  A collection of Pushtu verses by different Pushtu poets.

2979 Rishtin, Sadiqullah (ed)
  1953 Da Baha'i Jan Kolliyat [The Collected Works of Bahai Jan]. Kabul: Matba'eh-yi 'umumi. Pp. 134. (1332 A.H.)

  The poetry in Pushtu of Bahai Jan Sahibzadeh, who was living at Qandahar.

2980 Rishtin, Sadiqullah (ed)
  1954 Baz Nameh da Khushhal Khan Khattak [The Book of Falconry of Khushhal Khan Khattak]. Kabul: Matba'eh-yi 'umumi. Pp. 67. (1332 A.H.)

  An edition of one of the major works of the famous Afghan poet; a mathnawi in Pushtu.

VIII. LANGUAGES AND LITERATURE

2981 Rishtin, Sadiqullah
   1960 Da Zhwand Sandareh [Song of Life]. Kabul. Pp. 118. (1339 A.H.)

   A work in Pushtu.

2982 Rishtin, Sadiqullah and Gholam Rahman Jarar (eds)
   1952 Pushtu Qesi [Pushtu Stories]. Kabul: Matba'eh-yi 'umumi. Pp. 164. (1331 A.H.)

   A collection of stories in Pushtu.

2983 Roos-Keppel, George Olof (trans)
   1905 Translation of the Ganj-e-Pakhtu. Lahore: Anglo-Sanskrit Press. Pp. 94.

   Rare English translation of the "Pakhtu Treasury," composed by Ahmad Maulavi.

2984 Roos-Keppel, George Olof
   1943 A Manual of Pushtu, by Major G. Roos-Keppel and Qazi Abdul Ghani Khan. London: Oxford University Press. Pp. xii, 310.

   A contemporary reworking of a manual first published in 1901. Based on actual usage, written and spoken, of Peshawar. Includes a grammar, sections on composition and exercises, and a large collection of useful colloquial sentences. No transliteration.

2985 Rossi, Adriano V.
   1979 Iranian Lexical Elements in Brahui. Naples: Instituto Universitario Orientale (Series Minor, Volume 8). Pp. 422.

2986 Safee, M. Naim Janbaz
   1973 Farhang-i Istilahat-i Lisan-i Englisi Dari [English-Dari Daily Idioms Dictionary]. Kabul: Government Printing. Pp. 269.

2987 Saldjouqui, Fekri
   1954 Ostad Banay Heravi. Afghanistan 9(3):18-21.

   On a famous poet, musician, mathematician, astrologer, and architect, a native of Herat.

2988 Saleh Muhammad Khan
   1934 Khud Amuz-i Pushtu [Pushtu Self-Taught]. Qandahar. (1313 A.H.)

VIII. LANGUAGES AND LITERATURE

2989   Saleh Muhammad Khan
            1937 Pushtu zeba [Pushtu Language]. Kabul: 'Umumi
               matba'eh. Pp. 100; lithographed. (1316 A.H.)

2990   Saljuki, Fekri
            1961-1963 Kolliyat-i Mirza Abd al-Qader Bedil [Collected
               Works of Mirza Abd al-Qader Bedil]. Kabul: Matba'eh-yi
               ma'ref. 1:1198 (1340 A.H.); 2 (1341 A.H.); 3 (1342
               A.H.).

            A definitive edition of the works of Bedil, widely
            regarded as the leading mystic poet of Afghanistan.

2991   Saljuqi, Salah al-Din
            1955 Afkar-i Sha'ar [Thoughts of Poets]. Kabul:
               Matba'eh-yi. Pp. 137. (1334 A.H.)

            A commentary on selected poems in Dari.

2992   Saljuqi, Salah al-Din
            1963 Naqd-i Bedil [The Wealth of Bedil]. Kabul: Pohani
               matba'eh. Pp. 571. (1342 A.H.)

            A commentary and biography by the editor of Bedil's
            collected works, in Dari.

2993   Serraj, Mahbub
            1961 Maulana Balkhi va Pedarash [Maulana Balkhi and His
               Father]. Kabul: Matba'eh-yi doulati. Pp. 142. (1340
               A.H.)

            A study of the effect on his poetry of paternal education.

2994   Shafeev, D. A.
            1955 Kratkiy grammaticheskiy ocherk afganskogo yazyka
               [Short Essay on Afghan Language Grammar]. In Russko-
               afganskiy slovar' 1035-1174. Edited by P. B. Zudin.
               Moscow: GIS.

            Sketch of the phonology, morphology, and syntax of Western
            Pushtu, with Arabic script and phonemic transcriptions.

2995   Shafeev, D. A.
            1964 A Short Grammatical Outline of Pashto. Bloomington:
               University of Indiana. Pp. 89.

            An edited translation by H. H. Paper of the original
            Russian.

VIII. LANGUAGES AND LITERATURE

2996 Shah, Idries
1966 The Exploits of the Incomparable Mulla Nasrrudin. London: Jonathan Cape. Pp. 160.

Mulla Nasrruddin stories are common throughout Afghanistan. This volume offers 100 such stories. Although there are a number of other items on Mulla Nasrruddin stories, this item has been chosen for compactness and the absence of local context.

2997 Da Shams al-Din Kakar Diwan [The Diwan of Shams al-Din Kakar]
1954 Kabul: Matba'eh-yi 'umumi. Pp. 169. (1333 A.H.)

The collected poems in Pushtu of a son of Pir Muhammad Kakar.

2998 Shibli, Nu'mani
1947 Da Sirat al-nabi Mustatab Kitab [The Book of the Biography of the Prophet]. Kabul: Matba'eh-yi 'umumi. Pp. 448. (1326 A.H.)

A translation of the well-known Arabic work into Pushtu by Burhan al-Din Kushkaki.

2999 Shoironi Afgoniston
1958 Obraztsy stikhov souremennykh poetov Afganistana [Shoironi Afghanistan; Verses of Contemporary Afghan Poets]. Stalinabad, USSR: Tajikistan SSR Academy of Sciences.

The text is in Tajiki. Cyrillic script.

3000 Shpoon, Saduddin
1968 Paxto Folklore and the Landey. Afghanistan 20(4):40-50.

3001 Shpoon, Saduddin
1972 Landeys From Afghanistan. Asia 25:4-7.

3002 Shpoon, Saduddin
1975 Ajab Khan: Memoirs of an Afridi Tribesman (Translated From Pushto by Saduddin Shpoon). The Malahat Review 33:49-63.

VIII. LANGUAGES AND LITERATURE

>This is the first installment of the biography of an Afridi Pushtun tribesman. Ajab Khan was witness to several political and historical events in the Pushtun area. He also offers some original native glimpses into Pushtun life and culture. Unfortunately, the Malahat Review nor (to my knowledge) another publication carried the balance of the biography.

3003 Shukrolla, Aripov
1977 Thikl Proizvedenii Abdul-Raufa Benava: Gorestnei Razmieshleniya [Cycle of Works of Abdul Rauf Benava: Mournful Reflections]. Dushanbe: Tajikistan SSR Academy of Sciences. Pp. 135.

A literary analysis of the works of some of the poetry and writings of Abdul Raouf Benava.

3004 Shukurov, M. S. et al.
1969 Farhangi Zaboni Tojiki [Dictionary of the Tajik Language]. Volume I, A-O. Moscow: Soviet Encyclopedia Publications Department. Pp. 951.

About 45,000 Tajik words. A literary dictionary of Tajiki. Illustrated with Tajik poetry and proverbs. In Cyrillic.

3005 Shukurov, M. S. et al.
1969 Farhangi Zaboni Tojiki [Dictionary of the Tajik Language]. Volume II, P-J. Moscow: Soviet Encyclopedia Publications Department. Pp. 949.

About 45,000 Tajik words. A literary dictionary of Tajiki. Illustrated with Tajik poetry and proverbs. In cyrillic.

3006 Sidqi, Muhammad Usman
1964 Sorud-i hasti [Songs of Existence]. Kabul: Doulati matba'eh. Pp. 127. (1343 A.H.)

Short poems composed in Kabul, New York, and other places.

3007 Sigel, Carol Ann
1974 A Cultural Analysis of Afghan Folktale Themes. New York: Afghanistan Council, The Asia Society. Occasional paper no. 8. Pp. 22.

3008 Sigel, Carol Ann
1974 Children Folktales in Afghanistan. Unpublished M.A. Thesis. American University of Beirut.

VIII. LANGUAGES AND LITERATURE

3009 Singh, Prabhjot-Kaur (Mrs. Narenderpal)
1963 Kandahari Hava. New Delhi: Vidya Prakashan Bhavan. Pp. 145.

A comparative study of Afghan Dari and Punjabi folk songs. In Punjabi, in Gurmukhi script, with translations of some quatrains (chahar-baiti) from Afghan Dari.

3010 Sjoberg, Andrée F.
1963 Uzbek Structural Grammar. Uralic and Altaic Series, Volume 18. Bloomington: Indiana University. Pp. 115.

3011 Skazki, Basni i Legendy Beludzhei [Baluchi Tales, Fables and Legends]
1974 Translated from English. Moscow: Nauka. Pp. 176.

3012 Sobman, Ali M.
1976 A Collection of Afghan Folklore. Kabul: Ministry of Education.

3013 Sokolova, V. S.
1953 Pamir Yazyki [Pamir Languages]. In Ocherki po fonetike iranskikh jasykov 2:81-240. Moscow: Izdatel'stvo Akademiia Nauk.

3014 Sourdel, Dominique
1963-1964 Un trésor de dinars Gaznawides et Salgulcides découvert en Afghanistan [A Treasure of Ghaznavid and Seljuk Dinars Found in Afghanistan]. Bulletin d'Études Orientales de l'Institut Français de Damas 18:197-208; plates.

Description and analysis of a find of coins and jewelry discovered near Qunduz.

3015 Sovremennyye Literaturnyye Yazyki stran Azii [The Modern Literary Languages of Asia]
1965 Moscow.

Includes a chapter by N. A. Dvoryankov, "The Development of Pushtu as the National and Literary Language of Afghanistan."

3016 Spiegelman, J. M. and J. Ling
1972 Shaer of Afghanistan. New York: Messner.

3017 Spooner, Brian
1967 Notes on the Baluchi Spoken in Persian Baluchistan. Iran 5:51-72.

VIII. LANGUAGES AND LITERATURE

3018   Stern, S. M.
        1949 A propos de l'inscription juive de l'Afghanistan [Concerning the Hebrew Inscription of Afghanistan]. Journal Asiatique 237:47-49.

        Concerns an inscription of 739 A.D., its probable arrangement, with a reproduction and translation.

3019   Strand, Richard F.
        1973 Notes on the Nuristani and Dardic Languages. Journal of the American Oriental Society 93(3):297-305.

3020   Tarakai, Noor Mohammed
        1957 Da Bang Musafarat [The Journey of Opium]. Kabul: Pashtu Tolana. (1336 A.H.)

3021   Tarzi, Mahmud (trans)
        1912 Siyahet dar Jaww-i Hava [Trip in the Skies]. Kabul: 'Inayet. Pp. 219. (1331 A.H.)

        A translation into Dari of Jules Verne's "Trip to the Moon." Published in 1331 A.H. Lunar year.

3022   Tarzi, Mahmud (trans)
        1913 Jazireh-yi Pinhan [The Hidden Island]. Kabul: 'Inayet. Pp. 479. (1332 A.H.)

        A translation into Dari of the work of the same title by Jules Verne. Published in 1332 A.H. Lunar year.

3023   Tarzi, Mahmud
        1913 Rauzeh-yi Hikam [The Garden of Wise Sayings]. Kabul: 'Inayet. Pp. 158. (1331 A.H.)

        A collection of political, moral, and literary essays in the Dari language.

3024   Tarzi, Mahmud
        1913 Az har dahan sukhani va az har chaman samani [From Every Mouth a Word and From Every Garden a Jasmine]. Kabul: 'Inayet. Pp. 268. (1331 A.H.)

        A lithographed work containing a variety of noteworthy selections in Dari prose and poetry. Published in 1331 A.H. Lunar year.

3025   Tegey, Habibullah
        1966 Modern Linguistics and Linguistic Problems. Kabul: Pashtu Academy. Pp. 128. (In Pushtu).

VIII. LANGUAGES AND LITERATURE

3026 Tegey, Habibullah
1975 A Study of Pushto Clitics and Implications for Linguistic Theory. Studies in the Linguistic Sciences 5(1):154-196.

3027 Tegey, Habibullah
1975 The Interaction of Phonological and Syntactic Processes: Examples From Pushto. Chicago: Papers from the Eleventh Regional Meeting, Chicago Linguistic Society. Pp. 571-582.

3028 Tegey, Habibullah
1977 Ergativity in Pushto. In Linguistic Method: Papers in Honor of Herbert Penzl. Edited by I. Rauch et al. The Hague: Peter de Ridder.

3029 Tegey, Habibullah
1977 The Grammar and Clitics: Evidence From Pashto and Other Languages. Ph.D. Dissertation. University of Illinois. Pp. 284.

Extensive examination of clitics in Pushtu and other languages to find answers to the questions about the grammar of clitics.

3030 Tegey, Habibullah
1978 The Grammar and Clitics: Evidence From Pashto (Afghani) and Other Languages. Kabul: International Center for Pashto Studies. Pp. 278.

3031 Trumpp, E.
1867, 1869 Die Verwandtschaftsverhältnisse des Pasto [The Relationships of Pushtu]. Zeitschrift der deutschen morgenländischen Gesellschaft 21:10-155, 1-93.

3032 Trumpp, E.
1873 Grammar of the Pasto or Language of the Afghans. London and Tübingen: Trubner and Co.

Sometimes regarded as the standard grammar, it is based exclusively on literary sources, with no indication of current spoken usage. The presentation is extremely scholarly, with a great parade of philological learning, but the author's comparative and historical conclusions are in large part erroneous.

VIII. LANGUAGES AND LITERATURE

3033 Vajid, Muhammad Qasim
1952 Marg-i Farhad [Death of Farhad]. Fayzabad: Matba'eh-yi Badakhshan. Pp. 64. (1331 A.H.)

The familiar tale, in Dari, of Khosrow, Farhad, and Shirin.

3034 Vakil, Fazl Muhammad
1951 Da Pushtu zhabe land gramar [The Short Grammar of the Pushtu Language]. Kabul. Pp. 64; bibliography. (1330 A.H.)

3035 Vittor, Frank
n.d. The Literary School of Herat in the Timurid Period. Unpublished Ph.D. Dissertation. University of California, Berkeley.

3036 Waish, Raz Mohammed
1958 Pashtu Books. Kabul: Government Printing House. Pp. 258.

Contains a partial list of Pushtu books and manuscripts available in the various libraries and collections in Kabul. Translation of no. 3037.

3037 Waish, Raz Mohammed
1958 Pushtu Kitabuneh [Pushtu Books]. Kabul: Matba'eh-yi doulati. Pp. 236. (1337 A.H.)

A useful selected annotated bibliography of some 405 works in Pushtu available in Kabul libraries.

3038 Wazhma [Fragrance]
1960 Bimonthly Pushtu magazine published by the Faculty of Letters and Humanities, Kabul University. First appeared in 1960.

3039 Wei, Jacqueline
1962 Dialectal Differences Between Three Standard Varieties of Persian: Tehran, Kabul, and Tajik. Arlington, Virginia: Center for Applied Linguistics. Pp. 51.

3040 Weiers, Michael
1975 Die Sprache der Hazara und der Mongolen von Afghanistan in lexikostatistischer Sicht. Afghanistan Journal 2(3):98-102.

VIII. LANGUAGES AND LITERATURE

3041 Wilson, J. Christy, Jr.
1955 An Introduction to Colloquial Kabul Persian. Presidio of Monterey, California: Army Language School. Pp. 58.

A brief account of the vocabulary and constructions, most useful for foreigners wishing to speak Dari at Kabul, but complicated by the use of confusing symbols for many letters of the alphabet.

3042 Wutt, Karl
1980 Pashai: Landschaft-Menschen-Architectur. Graz, Austria: Academische Druck. Pp. 120.

Deals with the geography, society, and architecture of the Pashai speakers of Afghanistan.

3043 Yaqubi, M. Din
1962 Transliteration System for Geographical Names in Afghanistan. Kabul: Ministry of Mines and Industry. Pp. 9.

A useful pamphlet, with parallel columns in English and in Dari.

3044 Zachova, Eliska
n.d. Die Fee aus dem Granatapfel und andere afghanische Märchen [The Fairy From the Pomegranate and Other Afghan Stories]. Prague. Pp. 95.

3045 Zamir, Muhammad Hasan (ed)
1956 Pushtuni Sandarai [Pushtun Songs]. Kabul: Matba'eh-yi 'umumi. Pp. 302. (1335 A.H.)

The second volume of a two-volume collection.

3046 Zawak, Muhammad Din
1955 Khushhal Khan Khattak Kist? [Who is Khushhal Khan Khattak?]. Kabul: Matba'eh-yi doulati. Pp. 158. (1334 A.H.)

3047 Zudin, P. B.
1950 Kratkiy Afgano-russkiy slovar' [Short Afghan-Russian Dictionary]. Moscow: GIS. Pp. 568.

Condensed version of no. 2823.

VIII. LANGUAGES AND LITERATURE

3048   Zudin, P. B. (ed)
            1955 Iz afganskikh pesen i stikhov [From Afghan Songs and
                Poetry]. Moscow: Goslitizdat. Pp. 224.

        Translations into Russian from Dari and Pushtu.

3049   Zudin, P. B.
            1955 Russko-afganskiy slovar' [Russian-Afghan
                Dictionary]. Moscow: GIS. Pp. 1176.

        Defines about 12,000 words and includes a gazetteer.
        Pushtu words are given in Arabic script and Cyrillic
        transliteration.

3050   Zyar, Mojaver Ahmad
            1974 Die Nominalkomposita des Paschto [The Nominal
                Composita of Pashto]. Unpublished Ph.D. Dissertation.
                University of Bern. Pp. ii, 117.

IX. ART AND ARCHAEOLOGY

Archaeology; historical monuments and sites; excavation
reports and publications; art; history of art;
material culture; architecture; numismatics

In this section, a significant number of the titles reflect the work of la Délégation archéologique française en Afghanistan. In 1921 the French government secured a virtual monopoly of archaeological excavation in the country, and since then their work, which began the following year, has gone steadily forward. Numerous volumes and many more articles reflect work at Buddhist and Muslim sites. The listing of this material is not exhaustive. During the past two decades the ancient sites (historic and prehistoric) of the country have been opened to scholars from other countries, and some indications of this fact appear in the works listed here. The steadily increasing concern of the Afghans with their own cultural and artistic heritage is finding expression in the numerous articles which have appeared in the periodical Afghanistan: many of them were initially written for Kabul or Aryana.

Given the fact that material on Afghan numismatics is scattered and relatively unknown, a special effort was made (by the author of the first three editions of this bibliography) to collect pertinent references on this subject.

3051   Agresti, Henri
        1970 Rock Drawings in Afghanistan. Miami: Field Research Projects of the University of Miami (Occasional Paper No. 14). Pp. 51.

3052   Allchin, F. R. and Norman Hammond (eds)
        1978 The Archaeology of Afghanistan from Earliest Times to the Timurid Period. New York: Academic Press. Pp. xxiii; 451, illustrated.

A comprehensive work synthesizing major research findings and developments in the archaeology of Afghanistan. Written by various authors, the chapters cover geography, the palaeolithic, the later prehistoric period, the early historic period, the pre-Muslim period, from the rise of Islam to the Mongol invasion, and from the Mongol invasion to the rise of the Moghols. A comprehensive bibliography is provided.

IX. ART AND ARCHAEOLOGY

3053   Allen, Terry
        1980 A Catalogue of the Toponyms and Monuments of Timurid Herat. Cambridge, MA: Studies in Islamic Architeture, Harvard University and Massachusetts Institute of Technology. Pp. 259.

3054   Auboyer, Jeannine
        1950 Joseph Hackin (1886-1941): In Memoriam. Afghanistan 5(3)1-9; bibliography.

        A biographical sketch, an appreciation of Hackin's archaeological work, and a tribute to the man himself.

3055   Auboyer, Jeannine
        1968 The Art of Afghanistan: Photographs by Dominique Darbois (translated from the French by Peter Kneebone). Feltham: Hamlyn. Pp. 75.

3056   Bacharach, Jere L.
        1976 Andarab and the Banijurids. Afghanistan Journal 3(4):147-150.

3057   Baily, John
        1977 Movement Patterns in Playing the Herati Dutar. In The Anthropology of the Body. Edited by J. Blacking. New York: Academic Press. Pp. 275-330.

3058   Bamborough, Philip
        1979 Antique Oriental Rugs and Carpets. Poole, Dorset: Blandford Press. Pp. 192

3059   Barger, Evert
        1939 Exploration of Ancient Sites in Northern Afghanistan. Geographical Journal 93:377-398; map.

        Summary account of travels made in 1938 in the region of the Oxus Valley in Northeastern Afghanistan, with description of archaeological sites studied by the French mission.

3060   Barger, Evert
        1939 Opening a Rich New Field of Archaeological Research in Central Asia: The Pioneer Exploration of the Oxus Territories in Northern Afghanistan by the First British Expedition in the Country. Illustrated London News (April):682-683.

IX. ART AND ARCHAEOLOGY

>A brief account of an exploratory expedition to investigate mounds that may contain Greek cities, with photographs of the mounds and artifacts. By the leader of the expedition, a lecturer in the University of Bristol.

3061 Barger, Evert
　　　1944 Some Problems of Central Asian Exploration. Geographical Journal 103(1/2):1-18; map.

>On the difficulties of dating and correlating archaeological evidence into an adequate history of early Afghanistan. The author sees promise in the finds in Bactria.

3062 Barthoux, J.
　　　1929 Les institutions françaises en Afghanistan, écoles et travaux archęologiques [The French Institutions in Afghanistan, Schools and Archaeological Undertakings]. L'Europe Nouvelle 569:16-17.

3063 Barthoux, J
　　　1930 Les fouilles de Hadda. Figures et figurines [Excavations at Hadda. Figures and Figurines]. Paris and Brussels: Les Editions G. Van Oest.

>Part of the series: Mémoires de la Délégation archéologique française en Afghanistan (vol. 4, Pt. 3). The album of 112 plates illustrates nearly 500 pieces of sculpture excavated at Hadda.

3064 Barthoux, J.
　　　1933 Les fouilles de Hadda. Stupas et sites [Excavations at Hadda. Stupas and Sites]. Paris and Brussels: Les Editions G. Van Oest, 1933. Pp. 213.

>Also part of the series: Mémoires de la Délégation archéologique française en Afghanistan (vol. 4, Pts. 1 and 2). Description of the stupas studied by the author, together with analysis and classification of types of these monuments.

3065 Bauer, W. and Alfred Janata
　　　1974 Kosmetik, Schmuck, und Symbolik in Afghanistan. Archiv fuer Voelkerunde 28:1-43.

3066 Bechhoefer, William B.
　　　1975 Serai Lahori: Traditional Housing in the Old City of Kabul. College Park, Maryland: School of Architecture, University of Maryland. Pp. 42.

IX. ART AND ARCHAEOLOGY

>Primarily a series of sketches and drawings of various types of household architecture found in an old section of the city of Kabul.

3067   Bechhoefer, William B.
>1977 The Role of Squatter Housing in the Urbanization of Kabul. Afghanistan Journal 4(1):3-8.

3068   Bechhoefer, William B.
>1977 Architectural Education in Afghanistan. Afghanistan Journal 4(4):147-149.

3069   Bechhoefer, William B.
>1977 Architectural Education in Developing Nations: Case Studies in Tunisia and Afghanistan. Journal of Architectural Education 30(4):19-22.

3070   Bergmann, Horst, Rupert Geiswinkler, and Wolfgang Nairz
>1978 Mit Seil und Drachen im Hohen Hindukusch. Afghanistan Journal 5(2):74-78. Photos

3071   Bernard, Paul
>1967 Ai Khanum on the Oxus: A Hellenistic City in Central Asia. London. Proceedings of the British Academy.

3072   Bernard, Paul
>1973 Fouilles D'Ai Khanoum (Campanes 1965, 1966, 1967, 1968). Memoires De La Delagation Archeologique Française En Afghanistan. Paris: Editions Klincksieck, 1973. Volume I. Pp. 246 text and illustrations. Volume II, 143 tables, illustrations and drawings.

3073   Berre, Marc Le and Daniel Schlumberger
>1964 Observations sur les Remparts de Bactres [Observations on the Ramparts of Balkh]. Paris: Libraire C. Klincksieck. Pp. 104; plates.

>A separate publication of Pt. 3 of Volume 19, Mémoires de la Délégation archéologique française en Afghanistan.

3074   Biography of Some Member of the Danish Mission
>1948 Afghanistan 3(3):38-42.

>Sketches, with photographs, of four of the members and brief lists of their publications.

IX. ART AND ARCHAEOLOGY

3075   Bivar, A. D. H.
            1954 Fire-Altars of the Sassanian Period at Balkh.
            Journal of the Warburg and Courtauld Institute 17:182-
            183. (London.)

3076   Bivar, A. D. H.
            1966 Seljuqid Ziyarets of Sar-i-Pul (Afghanistan).
            Bulletin of the School of Oriental and African Studies
            29(1):57-63.

3077   Bivar, A. D. H.
            1974 A Mongol Invasion Hoard From Eastern Afghanistan.
            In Near Eastern Numismatics, Iconography, Epigraphy and
            History: Studies in Honor of George C. Milas.
            Beyrouth. Pp. 369-381.

3078   Bivar, A. D. H.
            1977 The Inscription of Salar Khalil in Afghanistan.
            Journal of the Royal Asiatic Society 2:145-149.

3079   Blanc, Jean-Charles
            1976 Afghan Trucks. New York: Stonehill Publishing Co.
            Pp. 107.

3080   Bobolyubov, A. A.
            1973 Carpets of Central Asia. (Revised). The Crosby
            Press.

3081   Bombaci, Alessia
            1959 Summary Report on the Italian Archaeological Mission
            in Afghanistan I. Introduction to the Excavations at
            Ghazni. East and West 10(1/2):3-22.

3082   Bourgeois, Jean-Louis
            1980 Welcoming the Wind. Natural History. November:70-
            75.

            An illustrated article about wind-catcher technology in
            southwestern and southern Afghanistan.

3083   Brandenburg, D.
            1977 Herat: Eine Timuridische Hauptstadt. [A Timurid
            Capital City]. Graz, Austria: Akademische Druck Verlag.

3084   Bruno, Andrea
            1962 The Planned and Executed Restoration of Some Monu-
            ments of Archaeological and Artistic Interest in
            Afghanistan. East and West 13(2-3):99-185.

IX. ART AND ARCHAEOLOGY

3085   Bruno, Andrea
       1979 Das Minarett von Jam [The Minaret of Jam]. Die
       UNESCO hilft an der Restaurierung eines afghanischen
       Benkmals. UNESCO-Kurier 20(10):32-34.

3086   Bucherer-Dietschi, Paul A.
       1975 Ein Freilichtmuseum in Afghanistan. Afghanistan
       Journal 2(3):103-104.

3087   Buddruss, Georg and G. Djelani Davary
       1980 Zu zwei Dari-Inschriften aus dem Wakhan.
       Afghanistan Journal 7(3):109-111.

3088   Burgess, James
       1978 The Gandhara Sculptures. Delhi: Bharatiya Publishing House. Pp. 25; 28 plates.

3089   Byron, Robert
       1935 The Shrine of Khwaja Abu Nasr Parsa at Balkh.
       Bulletin of the American Institute for Persian Art and
       Archaeology 4(1):12-14. New York.

       Summary description of the damaged, late fifteenth-century structure, and brief mention of the saintly figure there enshrined.

3090   Byron, Robert
       1937 The Road to Oxiana. London: Macmillan and Co., Ltd. Pp. 341.

       By the late British scholar of history and the arts. One third of the book is a published travelogue of northern and eastern Afghanistan in 1934, with excellent accounts of important architectural monuments. A second edition appeared in 1950.

3091   Caroe, Olaf
       1973 The Gauhar Shad Musalla (Mosque) in Herat. Journal of the Royal Central Asian Society 60(3):295-298.

3092   Casal, Jean Marie
       1952 Mundigak: Une site de l'âge du bronze en
       Afghanistan [Mundigak: A Bronze Age Site in
       Afghanistan]. Afghanistan 7(4):41-48.

       The excavation of the mound, with an enumeration of the finds at each level.

IX. ART AND ARCHAEOLOGY

3093   Casal, Jean Marie
        1963 Fouilles de Mundigak [The Excavations at Mundigak]. Paris: Mémoires de la Délégation archéologique française en Afghanistan. Volume 1 text, pp. 260; vol. 2, 188 plates.

        Describes an early site near Qandahar.

3094   Casimir, M. J. and B. Glatzer
        1971 Sah-i Mashad; a Recently Discovered Madrasah of the Ghurid Period in Gargistan (Afghanistan). East and West 21:53-68.

3095   Caspani, P. E.
        1946 Lahore-Delhi. Afghanistan 1(1):39-40.

        Locates the site of ancient Gorydale and points out its latter-day derivation in local speech.

3096   Caspani, P. E.
        1946 Les premiers contacts entre la Chine et l'Afghanistan et les origines de la Route de la Soie [The First Contacts between China and Afghanistan and the Origins of the Silk Route]. Afghanistan 1(3):30-35.

        Deals with the contacts established in the second century A.D. as reflected by Chinese writers.

3097   Caspani, P. E.
        1946 La promenad archéologique de Kaboul [The Archaeological Tour of Kabul]. Afghanistan 1(4):35-43.

        Describes ancient remains and monuments to be seen within a distance of 10 kilometers from Kabul and along the main highway toward Jalalabad.

3098   Caspani, P. E.
        1946 The Walls of Kabul. Afghanistan 1(2):31-34.

        A tour of these walls, supplemented by historical data.

3099   Caspani, P. E.
        1947 Le Nau-Bahur de Balkh [The Nau-Bahur of Balkh]. Afghanistan 2(1):45-50.

        Summary description of the most conspicuous ruins of ancient Balkh.

IX. ART AND ARCHAEOLOGY

3100　　Centlivres, Pierre
　　　　　　1972　Les Instruments de Musique de Perse et d'Afghanistan au Department d'ethnographie du Musee d'Histoire de Berne.　Jahrbuch 51-52:305-320.

3101　　Centlivres, Pierre and Micheline Centlivres-Demont
　　　　　　1977　Chemins d'Ete, Chemins d'hiver entre Darwax et Qataghan (Afghanistan du nord-est).　Afghanistan Journal 4(4):155-163.　Maps; photos.

3102　　Centlivres, Micheline and P. Calottes
　　　　　　1968　Mitres et Toques.　Bulletin Annuel du Musée et Institute d'Ethnogrpahie de la Ville de Genéve 11:11-46.

3103　　Centlivres-Demont, Micheline
　　　　　　1975　Les Peintures sur Caminons en Afghanistan.　Afghanistan Journal 2(2):60-64.　Photos.

3104　　Centlivres-Demont, Micheline
　　　　　　1976　Popular Art in Afghanistan. (Translated from the French by Robin R. Charleston).　Graz, Austria: Academische Druck-u Verlaganstalt.　Pp. 64; map and illustrations.

　　　　　　Includes text and illustrations of popular Afghan art work on trucks, Mosques and tea houses.

3105　　Centlivres-Demont, Micheline
　　　　　　1977　Volkskunst in Afghanistan: Malereien an Lastwagen, Moscheen und Teehaeusern [Folk Art in Afghanistan: Painting on Trucks, Mosques and Tea Houses].　Graz, Austria: Akademische Druck-u Verlaganstalt.　Pp. 72.

3106　　Chandra, Pramod
　　　　　　1976　Das Papageienbuch.　Este vollstandige Faksimile-Ausgabe einer Moghul-Handschrift.　Afghanistan Journal 3(4)130-131.

3107　　Charpentier, C. J.
　　　　　　1977　The Making of Karakul-Caps.　Afghanistan Journal 4(2):76-78.　Photos.

3108　　Chirvani, A. S. Melikian
　　　　　　1970　Eastern Iranian Architecture: Apropos of the Ghurid Parts of the Great Mosque of Herat.　Bulletin of the School of Oriental and African Studies 333:322-327.

IX. ART AND ARCHAEOLOGY

3109   Choukour, Simonne
1949   Exposition de peinture de la Société All India Fine Arts and Crafts [Exhibition of Painting of the All India Fine Arts and Crafts Society]. Afghanistan 4(2):52-57.

Description, commentary, and illustrations give ample coverage to an exposition.

3110   Clark, H.
1922   Bokhara, Turkoman and Afghanistan Rugs. London: John Lane. Pp. 122.

3111   Combaz, Gisbert
1937   L'Inde et l'Orient Classique. 2 vols Paris: Libraire orientaliste Paul Geuthner. Pp. (1)264; (2)165 plates.

An exhaustive examination of the influences of Indian and late classical art upon each other, with many illustrations of art objects and monuments from within the limits of Afghanistan.

3112   Combe, E., J. Sauvaget, G. Wiet, et al., (eds)
1931-1945   Répertoire chronologique d'épigaphie arabe [Chronological Inventory of Arabic Epigraphy]. 13 vols. Cairo: Imprimerie de l'Institute française d'archéologie orientale. 1(Moslem year):1-243; 2:243-258; 3:285-320; 4:320-354; 5:354-386; 6:386-425; 7:425-485; 8:485-550; 9:550-601; 10:601-626; 11(1):627-636; 627-636; 11(2):637-653; 12:653-680; 13:680-705.

An invaluable work containing the texts of inscriptions in Arabic script and with translations into French.

3113   Curiel, Raoul and G. Fussman
1965   Le Trésor Monetaire de Qunduz [The Monetary Treasure of Qunduz]. Paris: Mémoires de la Délégation archéologique française en Afghanistan.

3114   Curiel, Raoul and Daniel Schlumberger
1953   Trésors monétaires d'Afghanistan [Monetary Treasures of Afghanistan]. Paris: Imprimerie Nationale. Pp. 130.

The publication is Volume 14 of the Mémoires de la Délégation archéologique française en Afghanistan, and deals with three hoards of early coins found in that country. One was of Greek coins from the Achaemenid period; the second of Indian, Greek, and Indo-Greek coins of the fourth century B.C. to the third century A.D.; and

IX. ART AND ARCHAEOLOGY

the third of a collection of Sassanian and Kushano-Sassanian coins of utmost scholarly importance. The work concludes with a complete list of the Sassanian and Kushano-Sassanian coins found in Afghanistan and with a list of historical sources relating to the city of Kabul.

3115 Dagens, B., M. Le Berre, and Daniel Schlumberger
1964 Monuments Préislamiques d'Afghanistan [Pre-Islamic Monuments of Afghanistan]. Paris: Mémoires de la Délégation archéolgique française en Afghanistan. Pp. 104; 19 figures; 45 plates.

The three parts cover Buddhist sculpture, Buddhist monasteries in the Foladi Valley, and the walls of Balkh.

3116 Dales, George F.
1965 A Suggested Chronology for Afghanistan, Baluchistan, and the Indus Valley. In Chronologies in Old World Archaeology. Edited by Robert W. Ehrich. Chicago: University of Chicago Press. Pp. 257-284.

3117 Dales, George F.
1972 Prehistoric Research in Southern Afghan-Seistan. Afghanistan 24(4):14-40.

3118 Dales, George
1977 New Excavations at Nadi-i Ali (Sorkh Dagh), Afghanistan Research Monograph 16, Center for South and Southeast Asia Studies. Berkeley: University of California.

3119 Dames, M. Longworth
1888 Coins of the Durranis. Numismatic Chronicle (Third Series) 8:325-363; plate. London.

A short account of the kings of the Durrani dynasty and their mints and coins. The paper includes a series of Persian couplets taken from the coins, a chronological table of the dynasty, a list of the kings, a genealogical table, a catalogue of coins, and an index of mints. Addenda and corrigenda to the article appear in the Numismatic Chronicle (Third Series) Volume 9, 1889.

3120 Davary, G. Djelani
1977 A List of Inscriptions of the pre-Islamic Period from Afghanistan. Studien zur Indologie & Iranistik 3:11-22.

IX. ART AND ARCHAEOLOGY

3121 Davary, Djelani and Hanna Erdmann
1977 Die Moschee von Takhta Pol in Nordafghanistan.
Afghanistan Journal 4(3)100-110. Map; plates.

3122 Davis, Richard Shope
1974 The Late Paleolithic of Northern Afghanistan
Unpublished Ph. D. Dissertation. Columbia University.

One of the first synthesis of the available late
paleolithic data from Afghanistan. The thesis argues that
the late paleolithic sequence in Northern Afghanistan
represents a primarily autocthonous cultural development.

3123 Davis, Richard S., Vadim A. Ranov and Andrey E. Dodonov
1980 Early Man in Soviet Central Asia. Scientific
American, December:130-137.

A brief archaeological report of recent findings of stone
tools of the hunters and gatherers in Tajik-SSR during the
lower paleolithic.

3124 De Croze, Joel
1947 Les empires afghans des Indes et leur style
architecturel [The Afghan Empires of India and their
Architectural Style]. Afghanistan 2(1):7-15: 2(2):1-7.

A visitor to Afghanistan searches for architectural proto-
types of structures erected in India. Interest then
switches to the monuments erected in India under the
Afghan kings.

3125 Demont, Micheline and Pierre Centlivres
1967 Poteries et potiers d'Afghanistan. Bulletin Annuel
du Musée et Institut d'Ethnographie de la Ville de
Genève 10:23-67.

3126 Deydier, Henri
1950 Contribution al'étude oe l'art du Gandhara [Contri-
bution to the Study of Gandharan Art]. Paris: Libarire
d'Amérique et d'Orient, Adrien-Maisonneuve. Pp. xxviii,
325; 5 maps.

A detailed work, reflective of exhaustive labor by a young
French scholar, the study is a critical and analytical
bibliography of all material published on the so-called
Gandharan art between 1922 and 1949. Most of the sites
discussed are within the frontiers of Afghanistan.

IX. ART AND ARCHAEOLOGY

3127   Diemberger, A.
            1978 Hindukusch-Hindu Raj. In Sondernummer der Oster-
                reichischen Alpenzeitung, Folge 1421, September/Oktober.
                Wien: Osterreichischer Alpehklub. Pp. 83-126.

3128   Dor, R.
            1975 Contribution a l'etude des Kirghiz du Pamir Afghan.
                Paris.

3129   Dor, R.
            1976 Lithoglyphes du Wakhan et du Pamir. Afghanistan
                Journal 3(4):122-129. Map; plates.

3130   Drewnjaja Baktrija 2 (La Bactriana Ancienne, 2)
            1979 Materiaux de l'Expedition Archeologique afghano-
                Sovietique Moscow: Academie des sciences de l'URSS,
                Institut d'Archeologie.

3131   Dupaigne, Bernard
            1968 Apercu sur quelques techniques Afghanes. Objets et
                Mondes 7(1):84.

3132   Dupaigne, Bernard
            1970 Chique et tabatieres de courges gravees en
                Afghanistan. Objets et Mondes, 15:57-68.

3133   Dupaigne, Bernard
            1974 Un Artisan d'Afghanistan, Sa vie, ses Problems, ses
                Espoirs. Objects et Mondes 14(3):143-170.

3134   Dupaigne, Bernard
            1975 The Ikats of Uzbekistan. In The Textiles and Life
                of the Nomadic and Sedentary Uzbek Tribes of Central-
                Asia. Edited by David Lindahl and Thomas Knorr.
                Uzbek: Basel. Pp. 50-52.

3135   Dupaigne, Bernard
            1978 Le Grand art Decoratif des Turkmenes. Objets et
                Mondes 18(1):3-30.

3136   Dupree, Louis B.
            1951 Preliminary Field Report on Excavations at Shamshir
                Ghar, Koh-i-Duzd, and Deh Morasi Ghundai (Southwestern
                Afghanistan). Afghanistan 6(2):22-31; (3):30-35; map;
                chart of excavation.

IX. ART AND ARCHAEOLOGY

An explanation of the archaeological methods used and a description of the finds, with very tentative conclusions, in the cave called Sahmshir Ghar. Part II deals with the excavation of Deh Morasi Ghundai, a prehistoric mound in southwestern Afghanistan.

3137 Dupree, Louis B.
1954 Shamshir Ghar: Historic Cave Site in Kandahar Province, Afghanistan. Ph. D. Dissertation. Harvard University. Pp. 618. See no. 3142.

Archaeological, material culture sequence for the fourth to thirteenth century A.D. for a cave cite near the village of Badwan, South Central Afghanistan.

3138 Dupree, Louis B.
1956 Afghanistan Between East and West: Second Century B.C. to 122 A.D. Royal Central Asian Society Journal 43(1):52-60.

3139 Dupree, Louis B.
1956 Shamshir Ghar, a Historic Cave Site in Kandahar Province (Afghanistan). Arts Asiatiques 3(3):195-206.

Excavations of a large cave near Kandahar, which yielded artifacts from the third through the twelfth centuries A.D. See no. 3136 and 3137.

3140 Dupree, Louis B.
1956 Shamshir Ghar: A Historic Cave in Afghanistan. Orientalistische Literaturzeitung 7/8:293-296.

3141 Dupree, Louis B.
1957 Shamshir Ghar-A Cave in Afghanistan. Archaeology 10(2):108-116.

3142 Dupree, Louis B.
1958 Shamshir Ghar: Historic Cave Site in Kandahar Province, Afghanistan. Anthropological Papers of the American Museum of Natural History 46(2):137-312.

Detailed report of excavation conducted in 1951, including plates, diagrams, and tables. See no. 3137.

3143 Dupree, Louis B.
1958 Shamshir Ghar. Afghanistan 13(2):27-32.

IX. ART AND ARCHAEOLOGY

3144   Dupree, Louis B.
        1960 An Archaeological Survey of Northern Afghanistan.
           Afghanistan 15(3):13-15.

3145   Dupree, Louis B.
        1963 Deh Morasi Ghundai: A Chalcolithic Site in South-
           Central Afghanistan. Anthropological Papers of the
           American Museum of Natural History 50(2):59-136.

        Detailed report of the excavations in 1951, with plates,
        diagrams, maps, and contributions by specialists.
        Includes a bibliography.

3146   Dupree, Louis B.
        1967 The Prehistoric Period of Afghanistan. Afghanistan
           20(3):8-27.

3147   Dupree, Louis B.
        1968 The Oldest Sculptured Head? Natural History
           77(5):26-27; plate.

3148   Dupree, Louis B.
        1969 Archaeology: Recent Research in Afghanistan.
           Explorers Journal 47(2):84-93.

3149   Dupree, Louis B.
        1970 Stone Age Archaeology in North Afghanistan. VII
           Congress International Sciences Anthropologiques et
           Ethnologiques (Moscow) 5:406-417.

3150   Dupree, Louis B. (in collaboration with J. Lawrence Angel and
           Others)
        1972 Prehistoric Research in Afghanistan (1959-1966).
           Philadelphia: American Philosophical Society. Pp. 84.

3151   Dupree, Louis B.
        1975 New Palaeolithic Localities Near Dasht-i-Nawur.
           Afghanistan Journal 2(3):105-107.

3152   Dupree, Louis B.
        1976 Results of a Survey for Palaeolithic Sites in Dasht-
           i-Nawur. Afghanistan 29(2):55-63; 29(3):13-37.

3153   Dupree, Louis B. and Richard S. Davis
        1974 The Lithic and Bone Implements From Aq Kupruk and
           Dara-i-Kur. Afghanistan 26(4):52-74: 27(1):35-54.

IX. ART AND ARCHAEOLOGY

3154   Dupree, Louis B. and Klaus Fischer
       1961   Preliminary Report on the Discovery of a "Prehistoric" Valley in Central Afghanistan. International Conference on Asian Archaeology. New Delhi: Archaeological survey of India. Pp. 32-33.

3155   Dupree, Louis, P. Gouin, N. Omer
       1971   The Khosh Tapa Hoard From Afghanistan. Archaeology 24(1):28-34.

3156   Dupree, Louis, P. Gouin, N. Omer
       1971   The Khosh Tapa Hoard From Northern Afghanistan, with Addenda. Afghanistan 24(1):44-54.

3157   Dupree, Louis and Bruce Howe
       1963   Results of an Archaeological Survey for Stone Age Sites in Northern Afghanistan. Afghanistan 18(2):1-15.

3158   Dupree, Louis and C. Kolb
       1975   Ceramics From Aq Kupruk, Darra-i-Kur, and Hazar Gusfand. Afghanistan 27(4):47-69.

3159   Dupree, Louis, Laurence H. Lattman, Richard S. Davis
       1970   Ghar-i Mordeh Gusfand (Cave of the Dead Sheep): A New Mousterian Locality in Northern Afghanistan. Science 167(3925):1610-1612.

3160   Dupree, Nancy Hatch
       1977   Early Twentieth Century Afghan Adaptations of European Architecture. Art and Archaeology Research Papers 11:15-21.

3161   Dupree, Nancy Hatch and Louis Dupree
       1974   The National Museum of Afghanistan: A pictorial Guide. Kabul: Afghan Tourist Organization. Pp. 115.

3162   Edelberg, Lennart
       1957   Fragments d'un stupa dans la vallée du Kunar en Afghanistan [The Remains of a Stupa located in the Kunar Valley of Afghanistan]. Arts Asiatiques 4(3):199-207.

3163   Eggermont, P. H. L. and J. Hoftijzer (eds)
       1962   The Moral Edicts of King Asoka. Including the Greco-Aramaic Inscription of Kandahar and Further Inscriptions of the Maurian Period. The Hague: E. J. Brill. Pp. 48.

IX. ART AND ARCHAEOLOGY

3164   Eiland, Murray L.
            1973 Oriental Rugs from Western Collections Featuring a
                Comprehensive Display of Turkoman Rugs. Berkeley.

3165   Eiland, Murray L.
            1973 Oriental Rugs. New York: New York Graphic Society.

3166   English, Paul Ward
            1968 The Origin and Spread of Qanats in the Old World.
                Proceedings of the American Philosophical Society
                112(3):170-181.

        Although the work is based on research near Kirman, Iran,
        the article illustrates these subterranean tunnel-wells
        which are common in parts of Afghanistan and their
        importance for the history of irrigation technology and
        agriculture in Southwest Asia.

3167   Ershov, N. N. and Z. A. Shirokov
            1969 Albom Odezdie Tadzikov. (Album of Tajik Costumes).
                Dushanbe: Tajikistan SSR Academy of Sciences. Pp. 34.

        Contains drawings and paintings of various national
        costumes of Tajiks during the nineteenth and twentieth
        centuries. The text is in Tajiki, Russian, and English.
        Forty paintings and seven sheets of sketches and drawings
        of pattern-cuts are provided.

3168   Ettinghausen, Richard
            1951 Muslim Art in Western Eyes. Afghanistan 6(3):43-46.

        The adaptation of Muslim motifs in European art and the
        study of Muslim art by European and American scholars.

3169   Exhibition of Ancient Art of Afghanistan
            1936   Tokyo. Pp. 34; unnumbered plates.

        Catalogue of an exhibition of treasures from the Kabul
        Museum. Text in Japanese and English.

3170   Faegre, Torvald
            1979 Tents - Architecture of the Nomads. London: John
                Murray. Pp. viii, 167.

        A useful discussion and description of nomad tents in
        Central and Southwest Asia, including Afghanistan.

IX. ART AND ARCHAEOLOGY

3171 Fairservis, Walter A., Jr.
  1950 Archaeological Research in Afghanistan. Transactions of the New York Academy of Sciences 2(12):172-174.

  Report of a survey expedition to investigate prehistoric sites in Afghanistan.

3172 Fairservis, Walter, A., Jr.
  1950 Archaeological Research in Afghanistan. Afghanistan 5(4):31-34.

  Report of a survey expedition to investigat prehistoric sites in Afghanistan.

3173 Fairservis, Walter A., Jr.
  1950 Exploring the "Desert of Death." Natural History 59(6):246-253; map.

  The story of an expedition into Afghanistan to search for prehistoric sites. The article describes modern Afghanistan and the ghost city of Peshawarun. Mr. Fairservis served as a Special Field Assistant in the Department of Anthropology of the American Museum of Natural History.

3174 Fairservis, Walter A., Jr.
  1951-1952 Journey to 4000 B.C. Three parts. Collier's 128(25):22 f.; (26):23 f.; 129(1):32 f. December 22, December 29, 1951; January 5, 1952.

  A popular account of the expedition in Afghanistan under the auspices of the American Museum of Natural History and headed by Mr. Fairservis. The article is the story of the expedition's troubles and adventures; the few reports of archaeological research are elementary.

3175 Fairservis, Walter A., Jr.
  1961 Archaeological Studies in the Seistan Basin of Southwestern Afghanistan and Eastern Iran. Anthropological Papers of the American Museum of Natural History. New York: American Museum of Natural History. Pp. 128; plates.

3176 Fairservis, Walter A. Jr.
  1971 The Roots of Ancient India. New York: MacMillan, Pp.482; maps; illustrations.

  Covers detailed descriptions of many archeological sites in Afghanistan.

IX. ART AND ARCHAEOLOGY

3177   Ferdinand, Klaus
            1975 The Ethnological Collection of Mosegard Museum
                (Aarhus University). Folk 16-17:475-487.

3178   Fischer, Klaus
            1967 Zur Lage von Kandahar an Landverbindungen zwischen
                Iran und Indien. Bonner Jahrbücher 167:129-232.

3179   Fischer, Klaus
            1969 Preliminary Remarks on Archeological Survey in
                Afghanistan. Zentralasiatische Studien 3:327-409.

3180   Fischer, Klaus
            1974 Nimruz: Archaeologische Landesaufnahme in Sudwest-
                Afghanistan. Bonn: Rudolf Habelt Verlag. Pp. 437.

3181   Flury, Samuel and Andre Godard
            1925 Ghazni (premiers résultats de la mission archéo-
                logique française en Afghanistan) [Ghazni (First Results
                of the French Archaeological Mission in Afghanistan)].
                Paris. Pp. 33.

            Includes a study of the Arabic inscriptions of the
            surviving monuments by Flury and a discussion of the
            topography of Ghazni by Godard.

3182   Flussman, Gerard and Marc Le Berre
            1976 Monuments Bouddhiques de la Region de Caboul I: Le
                monastere de Gul Dara. Mémoires de la Délégation
                Archéologique Française en Afghanistan. Volume 22.
                Paris.

3183   Foucher, Alfred
            1905-1922 L'Art greco-bouddhique du Gandhara. Etude sur
                les origines de l'influence classique dans l'art
                bouddhique de l'Inde et de l'Extrême-Orient [The Greco-
                Buddhist Art of Gandhara. A Study of the Origins of the
                Classical Influence on the Buddhist Art of India and of
                the Far East]. 2 vols. Paris: Ernest Leroux, Pp.
                1:639; 2:400.

            Two volumes, published years apart, bring together a
            meticulous method and an analysis of the monuments of
            their historical traditions.

IX. ART AND ARCHAEOLOGY

3184 Foucher, Alfred
1942-1947 La veille de l'Inde, de Bactres à Taxila [The Ancient route from India, from Bactria to Taxila]. 2 vols. Paris. Pp. 1:1-173; 2:174-426; maps; charts; reconstructions; plates; index-lexicon.

Volume 1 deals with the geography and archaeology: Volume 2 with the history of the Route. Lengthy, but informed and evocative. Together, these two volumes form Volume 1 in the series: Mémoires de la Délégation archéologique française en Afghanistan.

3185 Fouchet, Maurice
1931 Notes sur l'Afghanistan. Oeuvre posthume. Preface de J. Hackin [Notes on Afghanistan. Posthumous Work. Preface by J. Hackin]. Paris: Editions Maisonneuve. Pp. 228.

Posthumous work of the first French Minister to Afghanistan, who served in 1923 and in 1924 until his early death. A general survey, with emphasis on archaeological sites and still more on the program and the efforts of King Amanullah. Kabul and its environs are also described at some length.

3186 Fouilles d'Ai Khanoum I
1973 Campagnes 1965, 1966, 1967, 1968. Texte et Figures; Planches - Rapport preliminaire publie sous la direction de Paul Bernard. Paris. Mémoires de la Délégation Archéologique Française en Afghanistan, Tome XXI.

3187 Frances, Jack
1973 Tribal Rugs from Afghanistan and Turkestan. London: Frances of Piccadilly. Pp. iv, 64.

3188 Francfort, Henri-Paul
1976 Les fortifications en Asie centrale des Achemenides aux Kouchans. [Fortifications in Central Asia from the Achaemenids to the Kushans]. Unpublished Ph.D. Dissertation. University of Paris I (Pantheon-Sorbonne), Pp. 390.

3189 Francfort, Henri-Paul
1979 Les Palettes du Gandhara (Mémoires de la Délégation Archéologique Française en Afghanistan, tome XXIII.) Paris: Diffusion de Boccard. Pp. 104.

IX. ART AND ARCHAEOLOGY

3190 Franz, Erhard
    1972 Zur Gegenwartigen Verbreitung und Gruppierung der Turkmenen in Afghanistan. Baessler-Archiv 20:191-238.

3191 Franz, Erhard
    1979 Die Mauri bei Herat. Bemerkungen zu einer kleinen Volksgrupper in Afghanistan. Sociologus 29(2):168-177.

3192 Franz, Heinrich Gerhard
    1977 Buddhistische Kultstatten in Sowjetisch-Zentralasien. Bemerkungen zu neuren Ausgrabungen der sowjetischen Archaologie. Afghanistan Journal 4(2):66-73. Photos; illustrations.

3193 Franz, Heinrich Gerhard
    1977 Der Buddhistische Stupa in Afghanistan. Ursprunge und Entwicklung (Teil 1). Afghanistan Journal 4(4):131-143; plates.

3194 Franz, Heinrich Gerhard
    1978 Der Buddhistische Stupa in Afghanistan. Ursprunge und Entwicklung (Teil 2). Afghanistan Journal 5(1):26-38. Photos; drawings; plates.

3195 Franz, Heinrich Gerhard
    1978 Das Chakri Minar als Buddhistische Kultsaule. Afghanistan Journal 5(3):96-101; plates.

3196 Franz, Heinrich Gerhard
    1979 Erste Mongraphie zur Archaologie Afghanistans. Afghanistan Journal 6(4):109-116; plates; drawings.

3197 Franz, Heinrich Gerhard
    1980 Buddhistische Kunst und Kultur entland der "Seidenstraße". Afghanistan Journal 7(1):23-29.

3198 Franz, Heinrich Gerhard
    1981 Buddhistische Kunst und Kultur Entlang der "Seidenstraße". Afghanistan Journal 8(3):96-101; plates.

3199 Franz, Heinrich Gerhard
    1981 Buddhistische Kunst und Kultur Entlang der "Seidenstraße". Afghanistan Journal 8(4):123-131.

3200 Freitag, H.
    1972 Interesting and New Labiatae and Capparidaceae Afghanistan (Beitrage zur Flora und Vegetation Afghanistans III). Notes From the Royal Botanic Garden 31:351-537. Edinburgh.

IX. ART AND ARCHAEOLOGY

3201   Frey, W.
           1972 Beitrage zur Moosflora Afghanistans II: Die
           Pleurokarpen Laubmoose. The Bryologist 75:125-135.

3202   Fry, Richard N.
           1946 Notes on the History of Architecture in Afghanistan.
           Arts Islamica 11-12:200-202.

           Brief discussion of the earlier sites of Kabul and an
           account of a decorative column and stupa near present-day
           Kabul.

3203   Fry, Richard N.
           1948 Two Timurid Monuments in Herat. Artibus Asiae
           11:206-213.

           Descriptions of the principal mosque (Masjid-iJami') and
           the extensive shrine of Khwaja 'Abdullah Ansari,
           accompanied by numerous illustrations and a plan of the
           mosque.

3204   Fry, Richard N.
           1954 An Epigraphical Journey in Afghanistan. Archaeology
           7:114-118.

           The search for and discovery of a Parthian rock
           inscription at Tang-i-Azao, west of Herat. More space is
           devoted to the trials of the trip by car than to the
           inscription.

3205   Fussman, G. and M. Le Berre
           1976 Monuments Bouddhiques de la Région de Caboul.
           (Tome) 1: Le Monastère de Gul Dara. Mémoires de la
           Délégation Archéologique Française en Afghanistan 22.
           Paris.

3206   Fussman, G.
           1973 Daniel Schulmberger, 1904-1972. Bulletin de l'Ecole
           Française d'Extreme-Orient 60:411-422.

3207   Gans-Ruedin, E.
           1975 Antique Oriental Carpets. Kodansha International.

3208   Gardin, J. C.
           1957 Céramiques de Bactres [Ceramics of Bactria (Balkh)].
           Paris: Mémoires de la Délégation Archéologique Française
           en Afghanistan 15:129; 38 figures; 24 plates.

IX. ART AND ARCHAEOLOGY

3209   Gardin, J. C.
            1963   Lashkari Bazar. Une Residence Royale Ghazneivde.
               II. Céramiques et Monnais de Lashkari Bazar et Bost
               [Lashkari Bazar. A Royal Ghaznavid Residence. II.
               Ceramics and Coins of Lashkari Bazar and Bust].
               Paris: Mémoires de la Délégation Archéologique Française
               en Afghanistan 18:220; 30 plages; 56 illustrations.

3210   Gardner, Percy
            1886   The Coins of the Greek and Scythnic Kings of Bactria
               and India in the British Museum. London: Stuart Poole.
               Pp. lxxvi, 193; xxxii; plates.

3211   Gardner, Percy
            1887   New Greek Coins of Bactria and India. Numismatic
               Chronicle (Third Series) 7:177-181; plate.

        A description of a coin found in Bokhara, and of the
        evidence through which the author ascribes it to a Greek
        king of the second century B.C.

3212   Gerken, E.
            1974   Population, Agriculture Productivity and Employment
               in the Rural Nonagricultural Sector: Interpreting
               Observations in Paktia, Afganistan. Internationales
               Asienforum 5(3):195-208.

3213   Gettens, Rutherford J.
            1937   The Materials in the Wall Paintings of Bamiyan,
               Afghanistan. Technical Studies in the Field of the Fine
               Arts 6(3):186-193.

        Discusses the technique which was tempera with an animal
        glue binder and not true fresco. The earths employed to
        produce seven colors are identified.

3214   Ghrishman, Roman
            1939   Fouilles de Nad-Ali, dans le Seistan afghan
               [Excavations at Nad-Ali in Afghan Sistan]. Revue des
               Arts Asiatiques 13:10-12.

        First account of the preliminary explorations of a
        remotely situated prehsitoric site.

3215   Ghrishman, Roman
            1946   Begram, recherches archéolgiques et historiques sur
               les Kouchans [Begram, Archaeological and Historical
               Research on the Kushans]. Cairo: Institut français
               d'archéologie orientale. Pp. xiv, 277.

IX. ART AND ARCHAEOLOGY

>The publication is Volume 12 in the Mémoires de la Délégation Archéologique Française en Afghanistan. The author describes the site and the excavations, and then displays solid erudition in a numimatic study, a new chronology of the Kushan kings, and a reconstruction of the history of the Kushans.

3216 Ghrishman, Roman, and T. Ghrishman
1948 Les Choinites-Hephtalites. Cairo: Mémoires de la Délégation Archéologique Française en Afghanistan 13:156.

3217 Glatzer, Bernt
1973 The Madrasah of Shah-i-Mashhad in Badghis. Afghanistan 25:46-68.

3218 Glatzer, Bernt
1980 Das Mausoleum und die Moschee des Ghoriden Ghiyath ud-Din in Herat. Afghanistan Journal 7(1):6-22; plates.

3219 Gnoli, Gherardo
1964 Le Iscrizioni Giudeo-Persiane del Gur (Afghanistan) [The Jewish-Persian Inscription of Gur (Afghanistan)]. Rome: Instituto Italiano per il Medio ed Estremo Oriente. Pp. 70; 8 plates; bibliography.

>An inscription, cut on a rock, dating from the late twelfth or early thirteenth century.

3220 Godard, Andre and Joseph Hackin
1928 Les Antiquités bouddhiques de Bamiyan [The Buddhist Antiquities of Bamian]. Paris and Brussels: Les Editions G. Van Oest. Pp. 113; 98 plates; short bibliography.

>This documentary work by two French archaeologists is the second volume of the series: Mémoires de la Délégation archéologique Française en Afghanistan. Later study at the site by Hackin served to augment this initial research.

3221 Goetz, Hermann
1957 Late Gupta Sculpture in Afghanistan: The "Scorretti Marble" and Cognate Sculptures. Arts Asiatiques 4(1):13-19.

3222 Golombek, Lisa
1969 Abbasid Mosque at Balkh. Oriental Art 15:173-189.

IX. ART AND ARCHAEOLOGY

3223 Golombek, Lisa
   1969 The Timurid Shrine at Gazur Gah. Toronto: Royal Ontario Museum. Pp. 227; plates.

3224 Golombek, Lisa
   1971 The Chronology of Turbat-i Shaykh Jam. Iran 9:27-44.

3225 Goya, Sarwar
   1946 The Green Dome, or the Mausoleum of the Timurid Princes. Afghanistan 1(1):16-19.

   Concerns the mausoleum which the wife of Shah Rokh, Gowhar Shad, erected at Herat between 1417 and 1437 A.D.

3226 Gratzl, Karl
   1978 Petroglyphen im Wakhan und im 'Großer Pamir'. In Großer Pamir. Edited by Karl Gratzl. Graz, Austria: Akademische Druck Verlag.

3227 Gratzl, Karl
   1980 Die Sammlung Prokot. Afghanistan Journal 7(1):33-34; plates.

3228 Grousset, Rene
   1950 Un savant français; Joseph Hackin [A French Scholar; Joseph Hackin]. Afghanistan 5(4):1-12.

3229 Gullini, Giorgio
   1960 Attività acheologica italiana in Asia. Mostra dei risultati delle missioni in Pakistan e in Afghanistan 1956-1959. Torino, Galleria Civica d'arte moderna. Pp. 78; 35 plates.

   The catelogue of an exhibition at Turin, which describes the excavations at Ghazni and illustrates thirteen of the objects found.

3230 Gullini, Giorgio
   1961 L'Afghanistan dalla Preistoria all'Islam. Capolavori de Museo di Kabul [Afghanistan From Prehistory Until Islam. Masterpieces of the Kabul Museum]. Turin: Galleria Civica d'arte moderna. Pp. 171; 67 plates; bibliography.

3231 Gupta, S. P.
   1979 Archaeology of Central Asia and the Borderlands. Delhi: B. R. Publishing Corporation. Volume I, pp. 194. Volume II, pp. 341.

IX. ART AND ARCHAEOLOGY

Includes summary archaeological material on Northern Afghanistan and Southern Afghanistan in relation to India, Iran, and Central Asia.

3232 Habib, Abdul Haq
1971 A Short History of Calligraphy and Epigraphy in Afghanistan. Kabul: The Historical and Literary Society of Afghanistan Academy. (Translated from Dari.)

3233 Hackin, Joseph
1935 Répartitions des monnaies anciennes en Afghanistan [The Distribution of Ancient Coins in Afghanistan]. Journal Asiatique 226:287-292; map.

On the sites of major coin discoveries, with a map showing the places where coins (and what kind of coins) are plentiful.

3234 Hackin, Joseph
1937 Asar-i 'Atiqeh-yi Kotal-i Khayr Khaneh-yi Kabul [Ancient Remains of Kotal-i Khair Khaneh at Kabul]. Kabul: Matba'eh-yi 'umumi. Pp. 51. (1316 A.H.)

A translation into Dari by Sayyed Qasim Rishtiya of a publication in French.

3235 Hackin, Joseph
1950 L'Art bouddhique de la Bactriane et les origines de l'art greco-bouddhique [Buddhist Art of Bactria and the Origins of Greco-Buddhist Art]. Afghanistan 5(1):1-9.

Examination of masks taken from excavations in Bactria to show that Greco-Buddhist art rose in Bactria toward the end of the Greek domination.

3236 Hackin, Joseph
1950 The Buddhist Monastery of Fonduqistan. Afghanistan 5(2):19-35.

Detailed descriptions of painting and statuary found in the Buddhist sanctuary at Fonduqistan.

3237 Hackin, Joseph
1951 Les fouilles de Begram [The Excavations of Begram]. Afghanistan 6(4):1-10.

Examples of Hellenistic, Greco-Roman, Indian, and Chinese art execavated at Begram, with a note on the historical

IX. ART AND ARCHAEOLOGY

>circumstances (first and second centuries A.D.) which made such a collection possible.

3238 Hackin, Joseph and Joseph Carl
>1933 Nouvelles recherches archéologiques à Bamiyan [New Archaeological Research at Bamian]. Paris and Brussels: Les Editions G. Van Oest. Pp. 90; 84 plates.

>This volume, the third of the series: Mémoires de la Délégation archéologique Française en Afghanistan, continues the study presented in the second work of this series. See no 3220.

3239 Hackin, Joseph and Joseph Carl
>1936 Recherches archéologiques au Col de Khair Khaneh prés de Kabul [Archaeological Research at the Pass of Khair Khaneh near Kabul]. Paris: Les Editions d'Art et d'Histoire. Pp. 34; plates.

>Volume 7 in the Mémoires de la Délégation archéologique Française en Afghanistan. It is collected with the excavation of three sancutaries, built on the roof of still another, and dated in the fifth century A.D. There is much attention given to the principal piece of scuplture, a white marble representation of a sun god.

3240 Hackin, Joseph, Andrea Godard and Yedda Godard
>1936 Asar-i 'atiqeh-yi Buda'i Bamiyan [Antiquities of Ancient Buddhist Bamian]. Kabul: Matba'eh-yi 'umumi. Pp. 87, 3. (1315 A.H.)

>A translation into Dari by Admad 'Ali Khan, of the original work in French. The original illustrations are reprinted.

3241 Hackin, Joseph and R. Hackin
>1939 Bamian, Furher zu den Buddhistischen Hohlenklosern und Kolossalstatuen. Paris.

3242 Hackin, Joseph and R. Hackin
>1939 Recherches archéologiques à Begram [Archaeological Reserach at Begram]. 2 vols. Paris: Les Editions d'Art et d'Histoire. 1, pp. 137; 2, pp. 88; plates; maps.

>Volume 9 in the Mémoires de la Délégation archéologique Française en Afghanistan. Volume 1 is largely a catalogue of the objects found in the ancient city identified as Alexander's Nicea. An introductory chapter discusses the excavation and the finds, particularly the carved ivories.

IX. ART AND GEOGRAPHY

3243 Hackin, J., J. Carl, and J. Meunie
1959 Diverses recherches archeologiques in Afghanistan (1933-1940). Mémoires de la Délégation archéologique Française en Afghanistan. Volume 8. Paris.

3244 Hallet, Stanley Ira
1973 Afgahnistan's Hot Rods. Architecture Plus:32-37.

3245 Hallet, Stanley and Rafi Samizay
1973 The Yurt of Afghanistan. Utah Architect 52:11-13.

3246 Hallet, Stanley Ira and Rafi Samizay
1975 Nuristan's Cliff-Hangers. Afghanistan Journal 2(2):65-72; photos; line drawings.

3247 Hallet, Stanley Ira and Rafi Samizay
1980 Traditional Architecture of Afghanistan. New York: Garland STPM Press. Pp. 202; bibliography.

A pioneering work in English about the indigenous architecture of Afghanistan. The book includes excellent discussion of the various house architecture and their distribution throughout the country. Useful supplementary drawings and pictures are included. A must source for the students of Afghan residential architecture.

3248 Hamidi, Hakim
1967 A Catalog of Modern Coins of Afghanistan. Kabul: Ministry of Finance. Pp. vii, 43.

3249 Hanne, Mormann and Erich Ploger
1978 Buskaschi in Afghanistan. Luzern and Frankfurt: M. Bucher. Pp. 132.

3250 Hedge, I. C. and P. Wendelbo
1972 Studies in the FLora of Afghanistan XIII: Various New Taxa and Records. Notes From the Royal Botanic Garden 31:331-350. Edinburgh.

3251 Hennequin, Gilles
1970 Grandes monnaies Samanides et Ghaznavides de l'Hindu Kush 331-421 A.H. Etude Numismatique et Historique. Annales Islamologiques 9:127-177.

3252 Herzfeld, Ernst
1930 Kushano-Sasanian Coins. In Memoirs of the Archaeological Survey of India, No. 38. Calcutta: Government of India, Central Publication Branch. Pp. 51; plates.

IX. ART AND GEOGRAPHY

        A discussion of the evidence for a new chronological arrangement and dating of known coins of the Sassanian-Kushan period. Includes a list of coins, with a description of each.

3253   Higuchi, T. and S. Kuwayamy
        1972 The Kyoto University Archaeological Misison to Central Asia. Kyoto: The Archaeological Survey of Kyoto University in Afghanistan 1970, 1972. Pp. 27.

3254   Hirche, Elke
        1979 Tochter zahlen nicht. Ein Madchenschicksal aus Afghanistan. Gottingen: W. Fischer Verlga. Pp. 192.

3255   Hlopin, I. N.
        1974 Ancient Farmers in the Tedzen Delta. East and West, New Series 24(1-2):51-87.

3256   Hlopina, L. I.
        1972 Southern Turkmenia in the Late Bronze Age. East and West 22(3-4):199-214.

3257   Hoerburger, Felix
        1968 Supplementary Jingling in the Instrumental Folk Music of Afghanistan. Journal of the IFMC 20:51-54.

3258   Hoerburger, Felix
        1969 Volksmusik in Afghanistan, nebst einem Exkurs uber Qor'an-Rezitation und Thora-Kantillation in Kabul [Folk Music in Afghanistan, With a Discussion of Qur'an Recitation and Torah Cantillation in Kabul]. Regensburg: Bosse.

3259   Howarth, T. G. und D. Povolny
        1973 Beitrage zur Kenntnis der Fauna Afghanistans: Rhopalocera, Lepidoptera. Acta Musei Moraviae 58:131-158.

3260   Hughes, D.
        1967 Finger Dematoglypics from Nuristan, Afghanistan. Man 2(1):119-25.

3261   Huyn, Hans Graf
        1980 Fuenf vor Zqoelf--Die Welt Nach Afghanistan. Wien-Muenchen: Fritz Molden. Pp. 274.

3262   Irwin, John
        1973 "Asokan" Pillars: a Reassessment of the Evidence. Burlington Magazine 115:706-720.

IX. ART AND GEOGRAPHY

3263   Itemadi, Guya
            1953 The General Mosque of Herat. Afghanistan 8(2):40-
            50.

        A history of the mosque, with the various traditions of
        its building, and accounts of its reconstruction and
        redecoration.

3264   Jacquet, E.
            1836, 1837, 1839 Notice et mémoires sur les découvertes
            faites par le Dr. Honigberger en Afghanistan [A Notice
            and Records of the Discoveries Made by Dr. Honigberger
            in Afghanistan]. Journal Asiatique, (Third Series)
            2:234-277; 4:401-440; 7:385-404.

        The beginning of archaeological research in Afghanistan.
        A German doctor found his way into the country sometime
        after 1815 and--under the protection of the Afghan
        government--excavated and looted stupas and other sites.
        This material stems from his own account of these
        adventures and is often lively reading.

3265   Janata, Alfred
            1974 Die Afghanistan-Sammlungen des Museums fur
            Volkerkunde in Wien. Afghanistan Journal 1(1):5-12.

3266   Janata, Alfred
            1975 Beitrag zur Volkerkunde Afghanistans. Archiv fur
            Volkerkunde 29:7-36.

3267   Janata, Alfred
            1978 Ikat in Afghanistan. Afghanistan Journal 5(4):130-
            139; plates.

3268   Janata, Alfred
            1980 Schmuck in Afghanistan (Jewelry in Afghanistan).
            Graz, Austria: Akademische Druck Verlag. Pp. 212.

        A pioneering work on folk jewelry and ornamentation in
        Afghanistan. Profusely illustrated.

3269   Japan-Afghanistan Joint Archeological Survey in 1978
            1980 The committee of the Kyoto University Archeological
            Mission to Central Asia 1980, Kyoto University. Pp. 26.

3270   Jettmar, Karl
            1972 Die Steppenkulturen und die Indoiraneir des
            Plateaus. Iranica Antique 9:65-93.

IX. ART AND GEOGRAPHY

3271   Jettmar, Karl
        1978 Auf den Spuren der Indoiranier? Bronzezeitfunde
            sowjetischer Archaologen in Nordwest-Afghanistan.
            Afghanistan Journal 5(3):87-95; maps; plates; illustra-
            tions.

3272   Johnston, R. H., and K. G. Hussain
        1974 Master Afghan Potter, an Anlytical and Synthesizing
            Study with Some Archaeological Overtones. American
            Journal of Archaeology 78(2):168-169.

3273   Jones, H. McCoy and Jeff W. Boucher
        1972 Weavings of the Tribes in Afghanistan. Washington,
            D.C.

3274   Jones, H. McCoy and Jeff W. Boucher
        1973 Tribal Rugs From Turkmenistan. Washington, D.C.

3275   Jones, Schuyler
        1981 A Kuna Urei in the Victoria and Albert Museum.
            Afghanistan Journal 8(4):138-139.

3276   Kalus, L.
        1979 La Collection des Monnaies Islamiques du Musee de
            Kaboul. Afghanistan Journal 6(2):50-53; plates.

3277   Karmysheva, B. Kh.
        1969 Arten der Viehhaltung in den Sudbezirken von
            Usbekistan and Tadshikistan. Viehwirtschaft und
            Hirtenkultur (Budapest):112-126.

3278   Katz, Tami Beth
        1974 Report on Housing on Koh-i-Asmai. Unpublished
            manuscript. College Park: School of Architecture,
            University of Maryland.

3279   Kazimee, Bashir A.
        1977 Urban-Rural Dwelling Environments: Kabul,
            Afghanistan. Cambridge: School of Architecture,
            Massachusetts Institute of Technology.

3280   Khalili, Khalilullah
        n.d. 'Arámgah-i Bubar [The Resting Place of Babur].
            Kabul: Matba'eh-yi 'umumi. Pp. 70.

        A description in Dari of the site on the outskirts of
        Kabul.

IX. ART AND GEOGRAPHY

3281 Kieffer, Charles M.
      1960 Le minaret de Ghiyath al-Din a Firouzkoh. Afghanistan 15(4):16-60.

3282 Kieffer, Charles M.
      1975 Wardak, Toponyme et Ethnique d'Afghanistan. Acta Iranica 4:476-483.

3283 King, L. White
      1896 History and Coinage of the Barakzai Dynasty of Afghanistan. Numismatic Chronicle, (Third Series) 16:277-344; plates.

The article is intended as a continuation of M. Longworht Dames' Coins of the Durranis (see no. 3119). It is a fairly comprehensive account of the decline of the Durrani dynasty and the rise of the Barakzai, with biographical sketches of the most prominent members of the family; some generalizations about their coinage and descriptions of the coins, quotations from the coins and a catalogue of coins. The author spend "a long residence on the northwest frontier of India . . . [and] had opportunities of meeting many members of both the Royal Families (Durrani and Barakzai)."

3284 Kingsley, Bonnie M.
      1981 The "Chitrali"--A Macedonian Import to the West. Afghanistan Journal 8(3):90-93; plates.

3285 Klass, Rosanne
      1981 Missing in Action: Treasures of Afghanistan. Asia (March-April):27-35.

The article charges that the Soviets have shipped valuable artifacts from the Kabul Museum. Some well-established American authorities have refuted this specific charge.

3286 Klimberg, Deborah S.
      1975 Bamiyan in the Development of the Arts of Afghanistan. Unpublished Ph.D. Dissertation. Harvard University.

3287 Klimburg, M.
      1960 Blick auf Ghor. Du Zurich 231:41-50.

IX. ART AND GEOGRAPHY

3288   Klimburg-Salter, Deborah Elizabeth
         1976 Buddhist Painting of the Hindu Kush: Bamiyan, Fondukistan, Foladi, Kakrak. Unpublished Ph. D. Dissertation. Harvard University. Pp. xvii, 312; figures.

3289   Knobloch, Edgar
         1981 Survey of Archaeology and Architecture in Afghanistan. Part I: The South-Ghazni, Kandahar and Sistan. Afghanistan Journal 8(1):3-20.

3290   Kohl, Philip (ed)
         1981 The Bronze Age Civilization of Central Asia: Recent Soviet Discoveries. Armonk, N.Y.: M. E. Sharpe Inc.

         Covers recent Soviet archaeological findings in southern Soviet Union and northern Afghanistan. Provides a much needed account of the cultural history of the area.

3291   Kohzad, Ahmad Ali
         1938 Begram [Begram]. Kabul: Matba'eh-yi 'umumi. Pp. 108. (1317 A.H.)

         An account in Dari of the site, the excavations conducted by the French archaeological mission, and a description of the important finds.

3292   Kohzad, Ahmad Ali
         1938 Maskukat-i qadim-i Afghanistan [Ancient Coins of Afghanistan]. Kabul: Matba'eh-yi 'umumi. Pp. 40; plates of coins. (1317 A.H.)

         Valuable study in Dari of coins issued by the pre-Islamci rulers of the area, with emphasis upon the Greco-Bactrian coinage.

3293   Kohzad, Ahmad Ali
         1948 La statuaire au Nouristan et le travail sur bois [Nuristan Statuary and Woodwork]. Afghanistan 3(3):1-4.

         A brief discussion of the types of carving, illustrated with several examples.

3294   Kohzad, Ahmad Ali
         1948 Les travaux sur métal de l'époque ghaznevide [The Metal Work of the Ghaznavid Period]. Afghanistan 3(3):24-32.

IX. ART AND GEOGRAPHY

> The director of the Kabul Museum discusses some of the earliest dated pieces of Islamic metalwork, attributes a number to Afghan soil, and describes pieces from Ghazni which are now in the Kabul Museum.

3295 Kohzad, Ahmad Ali
 1949 Lashkargah (camp militaire) [Lashkargah (Military Camp)]. Afghanistan 4(1):30-35.

> Describes the Ghaznavid site, adjacent to Bust at the confluence of the Helmand and Arghandab rivers, and announces forthcoming excavations by the French mission.

3296 Kohzad, Ahmad Ali
 1949 Marnejan Hill. Afghanistan 4(4):24-26.

> A mound on the eastern outskirts of Kabul yielded a collection of very early Greek coins, a horde of Sassanian coins, and statuary from two Buddhist temples.

3297 Kohzad, Ahmad Ali
 1949 Premiers échantillons de la peinture ghazneivde [Fist Examples of Ghaznavid Painting]. Afghanistan 4(2):48-51.

> Enthusiastic comment on discoveries made in the excavations at Lashkari Bazaar.

3298 Kohzad, Ahmad Ali
 1950 The Tour of the Archaeological Mission of the American Museum of Natural History in Afghan Seistan. Afghanistan 5(1):29-32.

> An indignant refutation of "reports of a lost Afghan city" that were circulated by "American romance-hunting periodicals."

3299 Kohzad, Ahmad Ali
 1951 Uniformes et armes des gardes des Sultans de Ghazna [Uniforms and Arms of the Sultans' Guard at Ghazni]. Afghanistan 6(1):48-53.

> On the eleventh-century murals found in the Audience Chamber of the Palace at Lashkari Bazaar--a discussion of the costume worn by the pictured guardsmen and an attempt to place them within the framework of Central Asian painting traditions.

IX.   ART AND GEOGRAPHY

3300   Kohzad, Ahmad Ali
        1952 Four Months' Visit to Museums in the United States.
           Afghanistan 7(2):1-8.

        Mr. Kohzad's impressions of the leading museums of the
        United States, in relation to collections of objects from
        the Afghan-Iranian plateau region.

3301   Kohzad, Ahmad Ali
        1952 L'Influence artistique de l'art de l'Afghanistan
           ancien en Chine et en Asie centrale [The Artistic
           Influence of Ancient Afghan Art on China and Central
           Asia]. Afghanistan 7(2):42-53.

        On early Afghan art, particularly Greco-Buddhistic, and
        its spread into China.

3302   Kohzad, Ahmad Ali
        1953 Arms of the Arian(s) Heroes in Avesta Period.
           Afghanistan 8(3):27-33.

        The weapons of ancient heroes as described in the Avesta,
        the names of which, with slight variations, have survived
        into current use.

3303   Kohzad, Ahmad Ali
        1953 Gardien de la ville de Capici et ses armoires [The
           Guardian of the City of Kapici and his Symbols].
           Afghanistan 8(2):18-21.

        On the patron god of the old city of Kapici, who appeared
        on coins as an elephant's head.

3304   Kohzad, Ahmad Ali
        1953 Lashkargah [Lashkargah]. Kabul: Matba'eh-yi 'umumi.
           Pp. 152. (1332 A.H.)

        An account, in Dari, of the site currently under
        excavation by the French archaeological mission.

3305   Kohzad, Ahmad Ali
        1953 Le plus ancien temple de Bamyan [The Most Ancient
           Temple of Bamian]. Afghanistan 8(2):58-64.

        The oldest temple yet found at Bamian, dated in the third
        century A.D., and its sculpture and paintings. A poor
        English translation appears in the same number, on pages
        12-17.

IX. ART AND GEOGRAPHY

3306   Kohzad, Ahmad Ali
1953 Recherches archéologiques en Afghanistan [Archaeological Research in Afghanistan]. Afghanistan 8(2):1-11.

A report on 30 years of archaeological reseearch, with notes on the major excavations at Hadda, Kapici, Bamiyan, Balkh, and Lashkari Bazaar.

3307   Kohzad, Ahmad Ali
1953 Recherches archéologiques à Sorkh Kotal situé dans le dsitrict de Ghori [Archaeological Research at Surkh Kotal in the District of Ghor]. Afghanistan 8(2):51-57.

On the inscriptions and remains discovered by M. Daniel Schlumberger, and thought to be Kushanid. The inscriptions, though in Greek letters, were in a language not Greek, and have not yet been identified.

3308   Kohzad, Ahmad Ali
1953 Le Temple de Sakawand [The Temple of Saqawand]. Afghanistan 8(1):34-42.

On the prosperous cult of the sun god practiced in the once-flourishing city of Saqawand, in the district of Logar.

3309   Kohzad, Ahmad Ali
1954 Recherches archéologiques et monuments anciens en Afghanistan--le musée de Kaboul [Archaeological Research and Ancient Monuments in Afghanistan--the Museum of Kabul]. Afghanistan 9(4):1-18.

A survey of archeological research done in Afghanistan, with descriptions of the imporant excavations and of the finds that are in the Kabul Museum.

3310   Kohzad, Ahmad Ali
1955 Rahnuma-yi Bamiyan [Guide to Bamian]. Kabul: Matba'eh-yi 'umumi. Pp. 50. (1334 A.H.)

3311   Kohzad, Mohamad Nabi
1946 L'Inauguration du Salon d'Automme à Kaboul [The Inauguration of the Autumn Salon at Kabul]. Afghanistan 1(4):30-34.

An exposition of works by local painters, nearly all of which illustrated an episode of Afghan history.

IX. ART AND GEOGRAPHY

3312 Kohzad, Mohamad Nabi
1949 Trois jours à Lashkari-Bazar [Three Days at Lashkari-Bazaar]. Afghanistan 4(3):60-62.

A local observer describes finds made in the second period of the first season's excavations at the site--notably decorated and inscribed brickwork.

3313 Kohzad, Mohamad Nabi
1953 Un ouvrage afghan sur Lashkargah [An Afghan Work on Lashkargah]. Afghanistan 8(3):57-59.

A congratulatory review of Ahmad Ali Kohzad's book on Lashkari-Bazaar.

3314 Kolb, C. C.
1977 Imitation Arretine Pottery in Northern Afghanistan. Current Anthropology 18(3):536-538.

3315 Konieczny, M. G.
1979 Textiles of Baluchistan. London: British Museum. Pp. 77; illustrations; bibliography.

3316 Kostka, Robert
1974 Die stereophotogrammetrische Aufnahme des Großen Buddha in Bamiyan. Afghanistan Journal 1(3):65-74. Photographs; line drawings.

3317 Kruglikova, I. T.
1976 Afganskaya ekspediciya. In Archeologiceskie otkrytiya 1975 goda. Pp. 581-583. Moscow.

3318 Kruglikova, I. T.
1977 Sovetsko-Afghanskaya ekspediciya. In Archeologiceskie otkrytiya 1976 goda. Pp. 589-590. Moscow.

3319 Kruglikova, I. T., V. I. Sarianidi, and G. A. Pugacenkova
1975 Sovetsko-Afghanskaya ekspediciya. In Archeologiceskie otkrytiya 1974 goda. Pp. 559-561. Moscow.

3320 Kusmina, Jelena
1980 Die Alten Bodenbauer Afghanistans. Afghanistan Journal 7(4):119-125.

3321 Lal, M.
1834 A Brief Description of Herat. Journal of the Asiatic Society of Bengal 3:16-18.

IX. ART AND GEOGRAPHY

3322   Lamber-Karlovsky, C.
            1967 Archeology and Metallurgical Technology in Prehistoric Afghanistan, India, and Pakistan. American Anthropologist 69(2):145-62.

3323   Lentz, Wolfgang
            1937 Uber einige Fragen der materiellen Kultur von Nuristan. Zeitschrift fur Ethnologie 69.

3324   Leshnik, Lorenz S.
            1967 Kushano-Sassanian ceramics from Central Afghanistan: A Preliminary Note. Berliner Jahrbuch für Vor-und Frühgeschicte 7:311-34.

3325   Leshnik, Lorenz S.
            1968 Ghor, Firuzkoh and the Minar-i-Jam. Central Asiatic Journal 12(1):38-49.

3326   Lezine, A.
            1964 Trois Stupa de la Région de Caboul [Three Stupas in the Kabul region]. Artibus Asiae 27(1/2):24.

3327   Mackenzie, D. N. (ed)
            1976 The Buddhist Sogdian Texts of the British Library. (Acta Iranica 10). Leiden: E. J. Brill. Pp. 200; plates.

3328   Manchester Guardian
            1953 On the Fringe of the Indus. Afghanistan 8(1):43-46.

        A note reprinted from the Manchester Guardian on Jean Marie Casal's excavations in the mound called Mundigak--describing briefly the finds at successive levels.

3329   Mandel'shtam, A. M.
            1954 O nekotorykh rezul'tatakh raboty Frantsuzskoi arkheologicheskoi missii v Afganistane [Some Results of the Work of the French Archaeological Mission in Afghanistan]. Sovetskaia Arkheologiia 21:415-429. Moscow.

3330   Maricq, André and Gaston Wiet
            1959 Le Minaret de Djam [The Minaret of Jam]. Paris: C. Klincksieck. Pp. 90; xvi plates; index.

        Volume 16 of the Mémoires de la Délégation archéologique Française en Afghanistan is concerned with the discovery of the capital of the Ghorid rulers, with special emphasis on its lofty minaret.

IX. ART AND GEOGRAPHY

3331 Martin, D. R.
1961 Further Postal History of the Second Afghan War, 1878-81 with Kandahar and Baluchistan, 1881-87. Bath: Postal History Society. Pp. 41.

3332 Martin, D. R.
n.d. Postal History of the First Afghan War, 1838-42. Bath: Postal History Society.

3333 Matheson, Sylvia
1961 Time Off to Dig; Archaeology and Adventus in Remote Afghanistan. London: Olhams Press Ltd. Pp. 286; index.

A chatty, pleasantly informative account of excavations in 1955 at Mundigak, near Qandahar, and of impressions of the country.

3334 Matson, F. R.
1973 Glazed Pottery of Afghanistan - Variations on a Theme. American Journal of Archaeology 77(2):219-220.

3335 Mauelshagen, L. and D. Morgenstern
1973 Geodatische Arbeiten bei archaologischen Untersuchungen der Ruinenfelder von Afghanisch-Sistan. Vermessungswesen und Raumordnung 35:253-268.

3336 Mauelshagen, L., D. Morgenstern and K. Tonnessen
1973 Photogrammetrische und klassische Archaometrie in Afghanisch-Sistan. Allgemeine Vermessungsnachrichten 11, 426-438.

3337 May, C. J. D.
1964 How to Identify Persian Rugs and Other Oriental Rugs. G. Bell & Sons.

3338 Melikian-Chirvani, A. S.
1969 La plust ancienne mosquee de Balkh. Arts Asiatiques 20:3-20.

3339 Melikian-Chirvani, A. S.
1970 Eastern Iranian Architecture: A Propos of the Ghurid Parts of the Great Mosque of Herat. Bulletin of the London School of Oriental and African Studies 33:322-327.

3340 Mémoires de la Délégation Archéologique Française en Afghanistan
1978 Tome 18, Lashkari Bazare, Une residence Royale Ghaznavide et Ghoride. 3 volumes. Volume I: L'Architec-

IX. ART AND GEOGRAPHY

        ture, par Daniel Schlumberger avec la collaboration de Marc le Berre, Pp. 110; Volume II: Le decor non Figuratif et les inscriptions, par Janinine Sourdel-Thomine, Pp. 77; Volume III: Tafelband: Planches, 152 Tafeln. Paris: Boccard.

3341   Meunie, Jacques
        1942 Shotorak. Paris: Les Éditions d'Art et d'Histoire. Pp. 74; plates; sketch map.

        Volume 10 in the Mémoires de la Délégation Archéologique Française en Afghanistan. The excavation of a Buddhist monastery--its stupas, sculpture and decorative motifs--with a discussion of the cultural elements found there and their influence.

3342   Michaud, Roland and Sabrina
        1980 Afghanistan: Paradise Lost. New York: Vendome Press. Pp. 23; 98 color photographs.

        Includes brief outline text about general conditions in the various provinces in Afghanistan. The accompanying photographs are representative and of excellent professional and artistic quality. The photographs represent land, life, and society in Afghanistan. A technical error (plate 187): Shar-i-Gholghola (Shahr-i Gholghola) is located in Bamian Province not in the province of Nimruz.

3343   Michiner, Michael
        1973 The Multiple Dirhams of Medieval Afghanistan. London: B. A. Seaby Ltd. Pp. 152; 29 plates; 4 maps.

3344   Mitchiner, Michael
        1974 The Dirhems of Medieval Afghanistan. London.

3345   Mizuno, Seiichi (ed)
        1962 Haibak and Kashmir-Smast Buddhist Cave-Temples in Afghanistan and Pakistan Surveys in 1960. Kyoto: Kyoto University. Pp. 107.

3346   Momal, C.
        1949 Exposition Simonne Choukour sur le haut patronage de S. E. l'Ambassadeur de France en Afghanistan [Simonne Choukour Exhibition, under the Patronage of His Excellency the French Ambassador to Afghanistan]. Afghanistan 4(2):45-47.

        Describes a number of paintings in an exhibition of the work of a French-trained artist.

IX. ART AND GEOGRAPHY

3347   Morgan, J. de
1923-1936 Manuel de numismatique orientale de l'antiguité et du moyen âge. Publication achevée sous la direction de K. J. Basmadjian. Vol. 1 [Handbook of Oriental Numismatics of Antiquity and the Middle Ages. Published under the Direction of K. J. Basmadjian. Vol. 1]. Paris: Paul Geuthner. Pp. 480; maps; bibliogrpahies.

Chapters IX, X, XI, and XV deal in a general way with the history and coinage of ancient and medieval Afghanistan.

3348   Moskova, V. G.
1970 Carpets of the Peoples of Central Asia. (In Russian). Moscow: Nauka.

3349   Musée Guimet
1951 Exposition d'art asiatique: Chine, Asie centrale, Afghanistan [Guimet Museum. Exhibition of Asiatic Art: China, Central Asia, Afghanistan]. Afghanistan 6(1):28-40.

A description of the contents of the exhibit.

3350   Musée National d'Afghanistan, Kaboul
1961 Guide du Visiteur [National Museum of Afghanistan, Kabul. Visitor's Guide]. Kabul. Pp. 31; mimeographed.

3351   Mustamandi, S.
1968 A Preliminary Report on the Excavations of Tapa-i-Shotur in Hadda. Afghanistan 21(1):58-59.

3352   Mustamandi, S.
1968 The Fish Porch. Afghanistan 21(2):68-80.

3353   Mustamandi, S.
1969 La fouille de Hadda. Comptes Rendus d'Académie des Inscriptions et Belles Lettres. Pp. 119-30.

3354   Mustamindi, S.
1974 The Herakles of Hadda. Afghanistan 24(4):75-77.

3355   Mustamandi, S. and M.
1968 The Excavation of the Afghan Archaeological Mission in Kapisa. Afghanistan 20(4):67-69.

3356   Mustamandi, S. and M.
1969 Nouvelles fouilles à Hadda (1966-1967) par l'institut Afghan d'archaeologie. Arts Asiatiques 19:15-36.

IX. ART AND GEOGRAPHY

3357 Naimi, Ali Ahmad
    1946 Afghan Calligraphy, Illumination and Miniature-Work in the 9th Century A. H. Afghanistan 1(1):33-38.

Deals with the artists of the Herat school of art who were active under the Timurid ruler.

3358 Naimi, Ali Ahmad
    1948 Behzad. Afghanistan 3(2):63-66.

Sketchy account of the life and work of the greatest miniaturist; with bibliographical notes.

3359 Naimi, Ali Ahmad
    1948 Une famille d'artistes [A Family of Artists]. Afghanistan 3(3):43-46.

A brief resumé of the life and works of two younger relatives of the noted miniaturist, Behzad.

3360 Naimi, Ali Ahmad
    1948 Boste [Bust]. Afghanistan 3(4):14-16.

An historical account of the site at the confluence of the Helmand and Arghandab rivers, with citations from local, early historians.

3361 Naimi, Ali Ahmad
    1949 Ostad Mohammadi. Afghanistan 4(1):1-3.

Discusses a contemporary of the miniaturist Behzad, and gives a brief checklist of his surviving works.

3362 Naimi, Ali Ahmad
    1952 Les monuments historiques et les mausolées de Ghazni [The Historic Monuments and Mausoleums of Ghazni]. Afghanistan 7(2):9-12.

A short history of Ghazni and descriptions of the principal tombs and monuments.

3363 Naumann, C.
    1973 Ein ehemaliges Wilkyak-Vorkommen im Afghanischen Pamir. Bonn, zool. Beitr. 24:249-253.

3364 Naumann, C. and J. Niethammer
    1973 Zur Saugetierfauna des afghanischen Pamir und Wakhan. Bonn. zool. Beitr. 24:237-248.

IX. ART AND GEOGRAPHY

3365   Naumann, C. and G. Nogge
        1973 Die Großauger Afghanistans. Z. Kolner Zoo 16:79-93.

3366   Niethammer, G.
        1973 Zur Vogelwelt des Afghanischen Pamir und des Darwaz. Bonn. zool. Beitr. 24:270-284.

3367   Nogge, G.
        1973 Ornithologische Beobachtungen im Afghanische Pamir. Bonn. zool. Beitr. 24:254-269.

3368   Noheb, Abdul Karim (trans)
        1978 Buddhist Records of the Western World (Pashto) Kabul: Ministry of Education. (Original in Pushtu).

3369   Noonan, Thomas S.
        1944 Medieval Islamic Copper Coins from European Russian and Surrounding Regions: The Use of the Fals in Early Islamic Trade with Eastern Europe. JAOS 94:448-53.

3370   O'Bannon, George W.
        1974 The Turkoman Carpet. Duckworth.

3371   O'Bannon, George W.
        1977 The Saltiq Ersari Carpet. Afghanistan Journal 4(3):111-121; plates; line drawings; chart.

3372   O'Kane, B.
        1979 Taybad, Turbat-i Jam and Timurid Vaulting. Iran 17:87-104.

3373   Omar, Gholam
        1949 Commentaire sur les résultats des derniers fouilles archéologiques françaises en Afghanistan [Comment on the Results of the Latest French Archaeological Excavations in Afghanistan]. Afghanistan 4(1):19-29.

        A review of the results of the excavations at Begram.

3374   Orazi, Roberto
        1977 The Mausoleum of Muhammad Sharif Khan Near Ghazni: Architectural Survey With a View to Restoration. East and West 27:255-276.

3375   Oudenhoven, Nico J. A. Van
        1979 Indigenous Games for Development Education. UNICEF Development Education Paper No. 9.

IX. ART AND GEOGRAPHY

3376 Oudenhoven, Nico J. A. Van
1980 Common Afghan "Street" Games and Child Development. Afghanistan Journal 7(4):126-138.

3377 Paruck, Furdoonjee D.
1924 Sassanian Coins. Bombay: The Times Press. Pp. xx, 536; tables; map; bibliography.

An exhaustive study of the history and coinage of the Sassanian kings. It contains a history of each reign and a note on its coinage; extensive tables, with explanations, of mint-monograms; a glossary of the words used in inscriptions, with a discussion of each word; a catalogue of coins arranged under kings and a Sassanian bibliography.

3378 Patterson, Frank E.
1964 Afghanistan, its Twentieth Century Postal Issues. New York, Collectors Club. Pp. 208.

An example of arduous research conducted at Kabul from 1946 through 1949.

3379 Picken, L. E. R.
1974 An Afghan Quail-Lure of Typological and Accoustic Interest. Studia Instumentomum Musicae Popularis 3:172-175; 183-285.

3380 Pisarcheik, A. K. and N. N. Eroshov (eds)
1973 Materialnaya Kultura Tadjikov Verkhobev Zeravshana. (Material Culture of the Tajiks of the Upper Reaches of Zerafshan). Dushanbe: Tajikistan SSR Academy of Sciences. Pp. 297.

A material culture description of the Tajiks of the upper regions of the Zerafshan valley. Of interest to scholars interested in the traditional material culture and society of Tajiks.

3381 Poole, Reginald Stuart
1887 The Coins of the Shahs of Persia, Safavis, Afghans, Efsharis, Zands, and Kajars. London and Paris. Pp. xcvi, 336; chronological and genealogical tables; plates; indices.

A catalogue of the coins of the Shahs of Persia in the British Museum including those of the Afghans Mahmud and Ashraf (pages 64-68) and Azad Khan (page 130). An introductory chapter expalins the chronology of the rulers

IX. ART AND GEOGRAPHY

and their use of inscriptions, with some couplets reproduced in Persian and translated into English couplets.

3382   Pope, Arthur Upham
1935 The Mosque at Qal'a-i-Bist. Bulletin of the American Institute for Persian Art and Archaeology 4:7-11.

A brief description and the first good photographs to be published of the remains of this early Muslim structure, probably the arch of the entrance portal of a monumental structure of about 1000 A.D.

3383   Prinsep, Henry Thoby
1974 Historical Results From Bactrian Coins and Other Discoveries in Afghanistan: Based on the Notebooks and the Coin-cabinet of James Prinsep. Chicago: Ares Publishers. Pp. iv, 124.

3384   Prinsep, James
1838 Additions to Bactrian Numismatics and Discovery of the Bactrian Alphabet. Journal of the Asiatic Society of Bengal 7:636-655.

A description of some new coins and a theory of the Bactrian alphabet, giving the letters with English equivalents and explanations. A table shows the names of the kings in Bactrian, Greek, and English.

3385   Pugachenkova, G. A.
1963 Iskusstvo Afganistan [Culture of Afghanistan]. Moscow: Iskusstvo. Pp. 248.

A well-illustrated survey of the arts and architecture of the country from pre-Islamic times.

3386   Pugachenkova, G. A.
1968 Les monuments peu connus de l'architecture medieval de l'Afghanistan. Afghanistan 21(1):17-52.

3387   Pugachenkova, G. A.
1969-70 The architecture of Central Asia at the time of the Timurids. Afghanistan 22(3-4):15-27.

IX. ART AND GEOGRAPHY

3388 Pugachenkova, G. A.
 1973 Izucheniye Kultury Baktriiskikh Gorodov v Yuzhnom Uzbekistane [Study of the Culture of the Bactrian Cities in Southern Uzbekistan]. Vestnik Akademii Nauk SSSR 43(3):70-78.

3389 Rainey, Froelich
 1953 Afghanistan; Reconnaissance Summer, 1953. University Museum Bulletin 17:40-56. Philadelphia.

3390 Reut, M.
 1973 Le Verre Soufflé de Herat. Studia Iranica 2(1):97-111.

3391 Rice, Frances M.
 1971 Art in Afghanistan: Objects From the Kabul Museum. London: Allen Lane. Pp. x, 93.

3392 Ritter, C.
 1838 Die Stupas (Topes) und die Colosse von Bamiyan. Berlin.

3393 Robert, L.
 1968 De Delphes à l'Oxus, Inscriptions Grecques nouvelles de la Bactriana. Comptes Rendus d'Académie des Inscriptions et Belle Lettres: pp. 416-58.

3394 Rodgers, Charles J.
 1885 The Coins of Ahmad Shah Abdalli or Ahmad Shah Durrani. Journal of the Asiatic Society of Bengal 54:67-76.

 The use of coins to illustrate the ruler's invasions of India.

3395 Rogers, Millard
 1942 An Ivory Sardula From Begram. Artibus Asiae 15:5-9.

 This sardula, an animal with the body of a lion and the beak of a parrot, is in the Kabul Museum. The author ascribes it to the middle of the first century A.D.

3396 Rosenfield, John M.
 1966 The Dynastic Arts of the Kushans. Berkeley: University of California. Pp. 544; bibliography; index; over 200 illustrations.

IX. ART AND GEOGRAPHY

> Traces the political history of the Kushans, using numismatic and epigraphic sources. Analyzes the arts, relating them to western Asia and the Roman empire.

3397 Rowland, Benjamin, Jr.
1946 The Dating of the Sassanian Paintings at Bamiyan and Dukhtar-i-Hushirvan. Bulletin of the Iranian Institute 6-7:35-42.

> Assigns the paintings to the period of Khrusraw II--early seventh century--and to nominal Buddhists still retaining the Sassanian artistic heritage.

3398 Rowland, Benjamin, Jr.
1949 The Hellenistic Tradition in Northwestern India. Art Bulletin 31:1-10.

> A leading American art historian discusses the survival of first-century Hellenistic forms in fifth-century sculpture at Hadda and other sites. He is critical of certain of the opinions of members of the French archaeological mission in Afghanistan.

3399 Rowland, Benjamin, Jr.
1965 A Cycle of Gandhara. Bulletin of the Boston Museum of Fine Arts 62:114-129.

> Excellent account of the Gandhara schools of art and their monuments in Afghanistan and Pakistan.

3400 Rowland, Benjamin, Jr.
1976 Ancient Art From Afghanistan: Treasures of the Kabul Museum. New York: Arno Press. Pp. 144

> The catalogue of a traveling exhibition.

3401 Rowland, B. and F. Rice
1971 Art in Afghanistan. Objects from the Kabul Museum. Coral Gables: University of Miami.

3420 Sakata, Hiromi Lorraine
1976 The Concepts of Music and Musician in Three Persian-Speaking Areas of Afghanistan. Unpublished Ph.D. Disseration. University of Washington. Pp. 295.

IX. ART AND GEOGRAPHY

>Explores the concept of music and musicians in three Dari speaking areas of Afghanistan and examines the relationship between the conditions which determine the concepts and material aspects of musical phenomenon in these areas.

3403   Sakata, Lorraine
        1977 Afghan Musical Instruments: The Rabab. Afghanistan Journal 4(4):144-146; plates.

3404   Sakata, Lorraine
        1978 Afghan Musical Instruments: The Danbura. Afghanistan Journal 5(2):70-73; plates.

3405   Sakata, Lorraine
        1978 Afghan Musical Instruments: Dutar and Tanbur. Afghanistan Journal 5(4):150-152; plates.

3406   Sakata, Lorraine
        1979 Afghan Musical Instruments: Ghichak and Saroz. Afghanistan Journal 6(3):84-86; plates.

3407   Sakata, Lorraine
        1979 Afghan Musical Instruments: The Nai. Afghanistan Journal 6(4):144-146; plates.

3408   Sakata, Lorraine
        1980 Afghan Musical Instruments: Drums. Afghanistan Journal 7(1):30-32; plates.

3409   Sakata, Lorraine
        1980 Afghan Musical Instruments: Sorna and Dohl. Afghanistan Journal 7(3):93-96; plates.

3410   Sakata, Lorraine
        1980 Afghan Musical Instruments: Chang. Afghanistan Journal 7(4):144-145; plates.

3411   Saljooki, F.
        1967 The Complete Copy of the Ancient Inscription of the Ghiassuddin Grand Mosque in Herat. Afghanistan 20(3):78-80.

3412   Samizay, M. Rafi
        1974 Herati Housing of Afghanistan. Ekistics 38(227):247-251.

IX. ART AND GEOGRAPHY

3413   Samizay, M. Rafi
            1974 Urban Growth and Residential Prototypes in Kabul, Afghanistan. Cambridge: MIT School of Architecture and Planning. Pp. 97.

3414   Sarianidi, V. I.
            1974 Baktrija v epochu bronzy. Sovetskaja Archeologiya 4:49-71.

3415   Sarianidi, V. I.
            1976 Issledovnia pamyatnikov daslinskogo oazisa. Sbornik "Drevnyaya Baktriya." Pp. 21-86. Moscow.

3416   Sarianidi, V. I.
            1976 Pecati - amulety Murgabskogo stilya. Sovetskay archeologiya 1:42-68.

3417   Sarianidi, V. I.
            1977 Ancient Bactria: New Aspects of an Old Problem. International Symposium on Ethnic Problems of the Ancient History of Central Asia, Dushanbe, October 17-22, 1977. (Abstract of papers presented by Soviet scholars.) Pp. 43-467. Moscow.

3418   Sarianidi, V. I.
            1977 Drevnie semledel'cy Afghanistana. Moscow.

3419   Sarianidi, V. I.
            1977 Pamjatniki monumental'noj architektury Baktrii. Sovetskaya archeologiya 1:203-224.

3420   Sarianidi, V. I.
            1979 Die Schatze der Kuschanen-Konige. Afghanistan Journal 6(4):121-132.

3421   Sarianidi, Viktor
            1980 The Treasure of the Golden Mound. Archaeology 33(3):31-41.

            A brief discussion and illustration of the recent archaeological finds at Yemshi-tepe in northern Afghanistan by Soviet archaeologists. The site dates to the period of the Bactrian Empire in Central Asia.

3422   Sarianidi, V. I., N. N. Terechova, and E. N. Cernych
            1977 O ranney metallurgii i metalloobrabotke drevney Baktrii. Sovetskaya archeologiya 2:35-42.

IX. ART AND GEOGRAPHY

3423 Sauvaget, J.
1941-46 Glanes d'epigraphie Arabe. Revue des Etudes Islamiques 14:17-29. Paris.

3424 Scerrato, Umberto
1959 Summary Report on the Italian Archaeological Mission in Afghanistan. (II) The First Two Excavation Campaigns at Ghazni, 1957-1958. East and West 10(1-2):23-55.

3425 Scher, J. A.
1980 Petroglifi sredney i zentralnoy Asii [Petroglyphs of Central Asia]. Moscow: Nauka. Pp. 328.

3426 Schlumberger, Daniel
n.d. Surkh Kotal and the Ancient History of Afghanistan. London: The Afghan Information Bureau. Pp. 24.

3427 Schlumberger, Daniel
1947 L'Exploration archéologique de l'Afghanistan: Résultats acquis et perspectives d'avenir [Archaeological Exploration of Afghanistan: Results Achieved and Prospects of the Future]. Afghanistan 2(4):1-23.

A sketch of the geography and early history of the country is followed by a very informative account of major archaeological sites and by a summary of excavations already carried out.

3428 Schlumberger, Daniel
1949 Archaeology in Afghanistan. Work of the French Archaeological Delegation. Archaeology 2(1):11-16.

Mr. Schlumberger, Director of the French Archaeological Delegation in Afghanistan since 1946, gives a very brief but clear and abundantly illustrated summary of more than a score of years of digging by French scholars.

3429 Schlumberger, Daniel
1949 Les fouilles de Lashkari Bazar: Recherches archéologiques sur l'époque ghazneivide [The Excavations at Lashkari Bazaar: Archaeological Research on the Ghaznavid Era]. Afghanistan 4(2):34-44.

Discusses the history of the site and its present topography and describes the first season of excavation.

IX. ART AND GEOGRAPHY

3430   Schlumberger, Daniel
        1950 Les fouilles de Lashkari Bazar [The Excavations of Lashkari Bazaar]. Afghanistan 5(4):46-56.

        The excavation of the Great Palace and the Audience Chamber, with a description of the mural paintings of the Sultan's Guard; and of the Central Palace and the Bazaar, with a note on what remained to be done.

3431   Schlumberger, Daniel
        1950 The Ghaznavid Palace of Lashkari-Bazar. Illustrated London News 216:458-462. March 25.

        The initial acocunt of the highly successful excavations of an eleventh-century Muslim palace, situated on the banks of the Helmand River in southwestern Afghanistan.

3432   Schlumberger, Daniel
        1952 La grand mosquée de Lashkari Bazar [The Great Mosque of Lashkari Bazaar]. Afghanistan 7(1):1-4.

        The finding and dating of the twice-built mosque.

3433   Schlumberger, Daniel
        1952 Le temple de Surkh Kotal en Bactraine [The Temple of Surkh Kotal in Bactria]. Journal Asiatique 240:433-453.

        Initial scholarly report of the excavation of the first Hellenistic type of structure to be discovered within the boundaries of Afghanistan.

3434   Schlumberger, Daniel
        1954 Surkh Kotal: A Late Hellenistic Temple in Bactria. Afghanistan 9(2):41-47.

        A further report on the Greco-Iranian temple which contains the fire-altar of an unknown Iranian cult.

3435   Schlumberger, Daniel
        1954 Surkh Kotal: Un site archéologique d'époque kouchane en Bactriane [Surkh Kotal: An Archaeological Site of the Kushan Epoch in Bactria]. Afghanistan 9(1):44-54.

        The discovery and excavation of a Fire-Sanctuary evidently belonging to the Great Kushan epoch. It is the first of its kind to be found, and appears to be the seat of an Iranian cult, not yet identifed.

IX. ART AND GEOGRAPHY

3436   Schlumberger, Daniel
        1954 Le temple de Surkh Kotal en Bactriane (II) [The Temple of Surkh Kotal in Bactria (II)]. Journal Asiatique 242:161-187.

        Continues the account given in an earlier number of this periodical of the uncovering the temple site. See no. 3433.

3437   Schlumberger, Daniel et al.
        1978 Lashkari Bazar, une Presidence Royale Ghaznevide et Ghoride. Mémoires de la Délégation Archéologique Française en Afghanistan 18. 3 Bande. Paris.

3438   Schlumberger, Daniel and P. Bernard
        1965 Ai Khanum. Bulletin de Correspondence Hellenique 89:590-657.

        A preliminary report on a first season of excavation at Ai Khanum, a Bactrian site on the Amu Darya River.

3439   Sedqi, Osman
        1948 Un Aperçu d'histoire de l'art afghan [A Glance at the History of Afghan Art]. Afghanistan 3(4):53-56.

        A sketch which covers too many centuries in too few pages to be of real value or interest.

3440   Seherr-Thoss, Sonia P.
        1968 Design and Color in Islamic Architecture; Afghanistan, Iran, Turkey. Washington: Smithsonian Institution Press. Pp. 312.

3441   Shahrani, F.
        1973 The History of Fine Arts in Afghanistan. Afghanistan 26(3):17-22.

3442   Shairzay, Arsallah
        1973 Report on Housing in Kart-i Sakhi. (Mimeographed manuscript.) Kabul: Department of Architecture, Faculty of Engineering, Kabul University.

3443   Shakur, M. A.
        1947 A Dash Through the Heart of Afghanistan. Being Personal Narrative of an Archaeological Tour with the Indian Cultural Mission. Peshawar: Imperial press. Pp. 126; folding sketch map; sketch plans of Balkh and Quandahar.

IX. ART AND GEOGRAPHY

> The mission, of which the author, Curator of the Peshawar Museum, was a member, travelled extensively by car and visited such notable sites as Bamian, Balkh, Begram, Mazar-i Sharif, Ghazni, and Qandahar.

3444 Sibtain, Syed N.
1981 To Build a Village. Afghanistan Journal 8(3):79-89.

3445 Le site archéologique de Bamiyan
1934 Guide du visiteur [The Archaeological Site of Bamiyan. Visitor's Guide]. Paris: Les Éditions d'Art et d'Histoire. Pp. 60.

> Succinct, reliable description of the Buddhas and the painted grottoes at Bamian, published by la Délégation archéologique française en Afghanistan.

3446 Slobin, Mark Sheldon
1969 Instrumental Music in Northern Afghanistan. Ph.D. Dissertation. University of Michigan. Pp. 325.

> Study of Music in northern Afghanistan--music as a part of town life, musical instruments of the North, the musical styles of the region. The introductory chapter provides ethnographic and geographic data about the area under study.

3447 Slobin, Mark
1970 Music and the Structure of Town Life in Northern Afghanistan. Ethnomusicology 14(3):450-458.

> A prize-winning paper dealing with the relationshp of music to socio-economic distinctions. A typology of towns (in northern Afghanistan), based on their functions as marketing, administrative, and industrial centers is developed.

3448 Slobin, Mark
1970 Persian Folksong Texts From Afghan Badakhshan. Iranian Studies 3(2):91-103.

3449 Slobin, Mark
1971 Rhythmic Aspects of the Tajik Maqam. Ethnomusicology 15(1):100-104.

3450 Slobin, Mark
1975 Buz-baz: A Musical Marionette of Northern Afghanistan. Asian Music 6:217-224.

IX. ART AND GEOGRAPHY

3451 Slobin, Mark
       1976 Music in the Culture of Norther Afghanistan. Tucson: University of Arizona Press. Pp. xiv; 297.

       An ethnomusicological thesis on music of northern Afghanistan. The book includes some ethnographic material on the societies of northern Afghanistan. See no. 3446.

3452 Smith, Vinzenz A.
       1911 The Monolithic Pillars or Columns of Ashoka. Zeitschrift der Deutschen Morgenlandischen Gesellschaft 65:221-233.

3453 Snellgrove, David (ed)
       1978 The Image of the Buddha. Kodansha International/ UNESCO. Pp. 482; plates.

3454 Sourdel, Dominique
       1953 Inventaire de Monnaies Musulmanes Anciennes du Musée de Caboul [Catalogue of the Old Muslim Coins of the Kabul Museum]. Cairo: Institut Fraçais de Damas. Pp. 145; 6 plates.

3455 Sourdel-Thomine, J.
       1960 L'art guride d'Afghanistan. A propos d'un livre recent. Arabice 7:273-280.

3456 Spooner, Brian
       1973 Afghan Carpets Today. Expedition (Spring).

3457 Stark, Freya
       1970 The Minaret of Djam: An Excursion in Afghanistan. London: J. Murray Co. Pp. 99; 48 plates.

3459 Stewart, Rebecca M.
       1974 The Tabla in Perspective. Unpublished Ph. D. Dissertation. University of California at Los Angeles. Pp. 444.

3458 Strzygowski, Joseph
       1932 The Afghan Stuccos of the N. R. F. Collection. New York: Stora Art Gallery. Pp. 30.

       A discussion of some 46 Greco-Buddhist statues found near Tashqurghan and displayed at the Nouvelle Revue Française gallery at Paris.

IX. ART AND GEOGRAPHY

3460 Stuckert, Ruedi
 1980 Der Baubestand der Masjid-al-Jami in Herat 1942/43. Afghanistan Journal 7(1):3-5; drawings.

3461 Szabo, Albert and Brenda Dyer Szabo
 1978 Preliminary Notes on the Indigenous Architecture of Afghanistan. Cambridge: Department of Architecture, Harvard University. Pp. 73.

 Preliminary review of the dwelling types investigated throughout Afghanistan during 1974-1976.

3462 Taddei, Maurizio
 1968 Tapa Sardar, First Preliminary Report. East and West 18:109-124.

3463 Taddei, Maurizio and Giovanni Verardi
 1980 Tapa Sardar--Second preliminary report. East and West 28(1-4):33-135.

3464 Tarzy, Zemaryalai
 1977 L'architecture et le Decor Rupestre des Grottes de Bamiyan (Bibliotheque du Centre de Recherches sur L'Asie Centrale et La Haute-Asie. Archeologie en Asie Centrale et en Afghanistan, I). 2 vols. Paris: Imprimerie National. 1:201; 2:166.

3465 Terry, Allen
 1980 A Catalogue of the Toponyms and Monuments of Timurid Herat. Cambridge: Program for Islamic Architecture at Harvard University and Massachusetts Institute of Technology. Pp. 293.

3466 Togan, Z. V.
 1970 The Topography of the Balkh Town to the Middle of the Seventeenth Century. Central Asiatic Journal 14:277-288.

 A historical reconstruction of the various cultural traditions at Balkh. Includes the Dari text of Mahmud ibn Vali Tinish in his Abdullah-Nama about the topography of Balkh.

3467 Tosi, Maurizio
 1968 Excavations at Shahr-i-Sokhta. East and West 18(1-2):9-66.

IX. ART AND GEOGRAPHY

3468   Tosi, Maurizio
       1969   Excavations at Shahr-i Sokhta. Preliminary Report of the Second Campaign, September-December 1969. East and West 19(3-4):283-386.

3469   Tosi, Maurizio and Rauf Wardak
       1972   The Fullol Hoard: A New Find From Bronze-Age Afghanistan. East and West 22(102):9-17.

3470   Trousdale, William
       1965   Rock Engravings From the Tang-i Tizao in Central Afghanistan. East and West 15(3-4).

3471   Tucci, G.
       1968   Oriental Notes IV: The Syncretistic Image of Mazar-i-Sharif. East and West 18(3-4):293-94.

3472   Uyehara, Cecil H. (Comp)
       1974   Afghan Stamps: An Annotated Bibliography, Part I & II. Journal of the Society for Philatelic Americans. September-October.

3473   Veradi, Giovanni
       1977   Notes on Afghan Archaeology II: Ganesha Seated on Lions, a New Shahi Marble. East and West 27:277-283.

3474   Veradi, Giovanni
       1977   Report on a Visit to Some Rock-Cut Monasteries in the Province of Ghazni. East and West 27:129-150.

3475   Veradi, Giovanni
       1979   The Buddhist Cave Complex of Homay Qal'a. In South Asian Archaeology. Leiden: Brill. Pp. 119-126.

3476   Wald, H. J.
       1973   Tawa-Khana (Floor Heating) in Afghanistan. Zeitschrift fur Ethnologie 98(2):287-290.

3477   Watts, Donald J.
       1981   Recurrent Patterns in Traditional Afghan Settlements. Afghanistan Journal 8(2):66-72; plates.

3478   Wegner, D. H. G.
       1964   Rugs of the Nomads and Farmers in Afghanistan. Baesserl-Archiv. Bonn.

3479   Weiers, M.
       1972   Die Sprache der Moshol der Provinz Herat in Afghanistan. Sprachmaterial Grammatik-Wortliste. Bonn.

IX. ART AND GEOGRAPHY

3480   Wheeler, Mortimer
       1946 Troissemaines en Afghanistan [Three Weeks in
         Afghanistan]. Afghanistan 1(4):49-50.

       Very brief report by the head of an archaeological mission
       which came from India to travel through Afghanistan.

3481   Wheeler, R. E. Mortimer
       1947 Archaeology in Afghanistan. Antiquity 21:57-65.

       An account of the Indian mission sent to visit
       archaeological sites in Afghanistan. Mr. Wheeler, then
       Director-General of Archaeology in India, was a member of
       the Mission.

3482   Whitehead, Richard Bertram
       1923 Notes on Indo-Greek Numismatics. Numismatic
         Chronicle (Fifth Series) 3:294-343.

       The author, an amateur coin collector in India for many
       years, was inspired by a find of Indo-Bactrian
       tetradrachms at Kabul in 1917 to undertake this first
       extensive survey of the subject.

3483   Whitehead, Richard Bertram
       1936 The Coins of Nadir Shah and the Durrani Dynasty.
         Journal of the Royal Asiatic Society of Bengal.
         Letters. Numismatic Supplement 46 2(3):107-110.

       A note on some Durrani coins not listed in that author's
       Catalogue of the Coins of Nadir Shah and the Durrani
       Dynasty.

3484   Wilson, Horace Hayman
       1841 Ariana Antiqua. A Descriptive Account of the
         Antiquities and Coins of Afghanistan: With a Memoir on
         the Buildings Called Topes, by C. Masson, Esq.
         London: Published under the Authority of the Honorable
         the Court of Directors of the East India Company. Pp.
         xvi, 452.

       Important as a pioneering effort into the ever-broadening
       field of the archaeology of Afghanistan. For "topes," read
       "stupas."

3485   Wolfart, Reinhard and Hanspetter Wittekindt
       1980 Geologie van Afghanistan. Berlin-Stuttgart:
         Gebrueder Borntraeger. Pp. 500.

IX. ART AND GEOGRAPHY

3486　Wolfe, Nancy Hatch
　　　　1963　The Valley of Bamiyan. Kabul: Defense Ministry
　　　　　Printing Department. Pp. 79; bibliography.

3487　Wolfe, Nancy Hatch
　　　　1965　An Historical Guide to Kabul. Kabul: Education
　　　　　Press. Pp. 171; maps.

　　　An historical introduction, followed by five detailed
　　　tours of the city.

3488　Wolfe, Nancy Hatch
　　　　1966　Herat: A Pictorial Guide. Kabul: Education Press.
　　　　　Pp. 66.

　　　An illustrated history and guide, with a map of the city.

3489　Wright, P. W. M.
　　　　1981　Bricks: An Account of the Production of Bricks in
　　　　　the Kabul Region During the Late 1970s and Early 1980s.
　　　　　Afghanistan Journal 8(4):132-137: plates.

3490　Wustenfeld, H. F. and E. Mahler
　　　　1961　Wustenfeld-Mahlersche Vergleichungs-tabellen zur
　　　　　Muslimischen und Iranischen Zeit-rechnung. 3. Aufl.,
　　　　　neu bearb. Wiesbaden: Convb. B. Spoler.

3491　Wutt, Karl
　　　　1976　Uber Zeichen und Ornamente der Kalash in Chitral.
　　　　　Archiv fur Volkerkunde 30:137-173.

3492　Wutt, Karl
　　　　1977　Zur Bausubstanz des Darrah-e Nur. Afghanistan
　　　　　Journal 4(2):54-65; plates.

3493　Yate, Charles E.
　　　　1887　Notes on the City of Herat. Journal of the Asiatic
　　　　　Society of Bengal 56(1):84-106.

　　　Includes notes on the art and historical monuments of
　　　Herat.

3494　Young, Rodney S.
　　　　1954　Afghanistan Reconnaissance. Archaeology 7:51-52.

　　　Describes field work carried on in the summer of 1953 by a
　　　group from the University Museum of the University of
　　　Pennsylvania. Records surface observations, digging at
　　　Qunduz, and putting down trial trenches at Balkh.

IX. ART AND GEOGRAPHY

3495   Young, Rodney S.
        1955 The South Wall of Balkh-Bactra. American Journal of Archaeology 59:267-76.

3496   Zestovski, P. I.
        1948 Esquisses architecturales de l'Afghanistan [Architectural Sketches of Afghanistan]. Afghanistan 3(2):38-62.

        A topographical description of the site of Bamian, accompanied by reproductions of surveys, of plans, and of sketches of monuments and ruins.

3497   Zestovski, P. I.
        1949 Esquisses d'architecture afghane: Herat, Kaboul-Herat [Sketches of Afghan Architecture: Herat, Kabul-Herat]. Afghanistan 4(3):1-25; bibliography.

        An interesting and valuable article on Herat and its vicinity by a European engineer. A description of the town is followed by an extended historical notice. Eighteen pen drawings--including a plan of Herat and a plan of the Masjid-i Jami' are included.

3498   Zestovski, P. I.
        1950 L'Oasis de Sultan Bakva [The Oasis of Sultan Bakva]. Afghanistan 5(3):41-51.

        A description of the oasis, its crumbled mosque and nomad cemetery; of the town and cemetery of Farah; and of a nomad caravan.

3499   Zipper, Kurt
        1975 Teppiche aus Afghanistan. Afghanistan Journal 2(2):43-52; plates.

3500   Zipper, Kurt
        1976 Neue Wege der Mustergestaltung und Ornamentierung im Afghanische Teppich. Afghanistan Journal 3(3):105-109.

INDEX

A

Abaeva, T. G., 727
Abawi, Ahmad Omer, 1902
Abayeva, T., 2629
Abbas, Agha (of Shiraz), 153
Abd al-Karim 'Alavi, 728, 729
Abd al-Qudoos, 1538
Da Abdul 'Ali Mostaghni Diwan, 2630
Abdul Majid Khan, 2300
Abdul Rahim-zai, Abdul Malik, 2301
Abdul Rahman, Amir, 730, 1539, 1540, 1541
Abdullah Khan, Malik al-Shu'ara, 2631
Abidi, A. H. H., 1903
Abu Bakr, Ruqaiyah, 2632
Academy of Sciences, USSR, 1
Adamec, Ludwig W., 731, 732, 733, 734, 735, 736, 737, 738, 1904, 1905, 1906
Adelman, Kenneth L., 1907
Adye, John, 740
Adye, Sir John Miller, 739
Aerial Bombardment of the Tribal Area, 1908
Afgánistán: Zeměpisný, Hospodářský, Politický a Kulturní Přehled, 11
Afganskiy sbornik, 2635
Afganskiye Skazki, 2636
Afghan Financial Statistics, 2302
Afghan Geological Survey Department, 154
al-Afghan, Jamal al-Din, 741
Afghan-navis, Abdullah, 2633
The Afghan-Pakistan Conflict, 1909
Afghan Progress in the Third Year of the Plan, 2303
Afghan Progress in the Fifth Year of the Plan, 2304
Afghan Student News, 1542
Afghan Studies, 2
Afghanistan, 742, 1543, 2307
L'Afghanistan, 2305
Afghanistan and Pakistan, 1914
Afghanistan at a Glance, 7
Afghanistan Ariana, 1544
Afghanistan as a Source for Crude Drugs and Essential Oils, 2311
Da Afghanistan Bank, 2310
Da Afghanistan Bank Majelah, 1545
Afghanistan Council, Asia Society, 4, 1233
Afghanistan Dar Hal-i Pishraft va Tariqi, 6
Afghanistan dar Dawrah-1 Hekumati-i Enqalabi, Hut 1341-Mizan 1344, 1910
Afghanistan Journal, 8

Afghanistan, Laws, Statutes, etc., 1911, 1912
Afghanistan Moderne, 1913
Afghanistan News, 9
L'Afghanistan Nouveau, 1546
Afghanistan Present and Past, 12
Afghanistan, Quarterly Publication, 3
Afghanistan Studies, 10
Afghanistan, The Truth About, 1915
Afghanistan: Bihtar ast Yak Mamlakat-i San'ati Bashad ya Zira'ati, 2306
Afghanistan: Development in Brief, 5
Afghanistan: Evergreen EVR 002, 2634
Afghanistan: Official Standard Names, 155
Afghanistan: Structure Economique et Sociale, 2309
Afghanistan: Summary of Basic Economic Information, 2308
Afghanistan's Economic Development Plan and Her Current Difficulties, 2312
Afghanistan's Foreign Trade (Revised) 1335 through 1340, 2310
Afghanistan's Foreign Trade 1335 through 1342, 2314
Afghanistan's Reclamation Program, 2315
Agresti, Henri, 3051
Ahadyar, Niaz M., 1547
Ahang, Mohammed Kazem, 13, 14, 1548
Ahlan Bikum fi Afghanistan, 15
Ahmad, A., 743
Ahmad, Fazl, 16
Ahmad, N. D., 745, 1917
Ahmad, Jamal-ud-din and Muhammad Abdul Aziz, 17
Ahmad Jan, 744
Ahmad, Mohammad B., 1916
Ahmad, Syed Barakat, 1918
Ahmadyar, M. Nabi, 1549
Ahmed, Akbar S., 1234, 1235, 1236, 1237, 1238, 1239, 1240, 1241, 1242, 1243, 1919, 2316, 2637
Ahmed, Feroz, 1920
Aitchison, C. U., 746
Aitchison, James Edward T., 156, 157, 2317
Akhramovich, Roman T., 747, 748, 749, 750, 751, 752, 1921, 1922
Akhramovich, R. T. and L. A. Erovchenkov, 18
Akhtar, S. A., 1550
Akram, Mohammad, 19, 158, 159, 160, 161, 2318
Alder, Garry J., 753, 754, 755
Alder-Karlsson, Gunnar, 1923
Alee, Shekh Khash, 162
Aleksandrov, I. and R. Akhramovich, 20
Alekseenkov, P., 2319
Alexander, Michael, 163
Alexandrescu-Dersca, M. M., 164
Algar, H., 1551

Ali Khan, Mohammed, 763
Ali, Majid A., 1924
Ali, Mirza Fazl, 756
Ali, Mohammad, 21, 22, 23, 24, 165, 757, 758, 759, 760, 761, 762, 1244, 1552, 1553, 2320
Ali Quili mirza, 764
Allan, N. J. R., 25
Allan, Nigel John Roger, 166
Allchin, R. R. and Hammond, 3052
Allen, R. A. and R. K. Ramazani, 765
Allen, Terry, 3053
Alvad, Thomas and Lennart Edelberg, 2638
Aman-i Afghan, 1554
Amat, Barthelemy, 2321
Amerkhail, Najibullah, 2322
Amin, Aminullah, 1555
Amin, Hamidullah and Gordon B. Schilz, 167
Amini, Naim, 2323
Amnesty International, 1925
Amoss, Harold L., 766, 1245, 1556
An Analysis of Several Recent Afghan Laws, 1926
Anderson, Jon W., 1246, 1247, 1248
Anderson, Jon W. and Richard F. Strand, 1249
Anderson, Steven C., 168
Anderson, Steven C. and Alan E. Leviton, 169, 170
Anderson, W., 171
Andreev, M. C., 1250, 1251
Andrew, Sir William Patrick, 767
Angar, 1557
Anis, 1558
Anonymous, 768, 769
Ansari, Mir Amin al-Din, 1559, 1560
Antoine, Giles, 770
Aperçu Général sur l'Afghanistan, 26
Aqa, Mir, 1561
Arabadzhyan, A. Z., 771
Arberry, A. J., 27
Arberry, A. J. and R. Landau, 1562
Archer, William Kay, 2639
Arefi, Abdul Ghafoor, 172, 772, 1252
Arends, A. K., 773
Arens, H. J., 2324, 2325, 2326
Arens, H. J., G. Braach, S. Gurtler, E. Nast, and W. Paszkowski, 173
Arez, G., 174, 175
Argyll, George Douglas Campbell, 774
Aristov, N. A., 176, 775, 1253
Armstrong, H. F., 1927
Arnold, Anthony, 1928
Arrowsmith, J., 177

Arshad, Muhammad Shah, 1563
Artamonov, E., 776
Artner, Stephen J., 1929
Arunova, Marianna R., 28
Aryana, 29
Aryana Da'iratu'l-Ma'arif, 30
Aryana Dayratulmuaref, 31
Asadabadi, Mirza Lutfullah Khan, 2640
Asas-namah, 1930
Ashe, Waller, 777
Ashida, K., 1564
Ashrafi, Naim, 2327
Asiel, Murad Ali, 2328, 2329
Aslanov, M. G., 2641, 2642
Aspaturian, Vernon V., 1931
Assad, M. N., 2330
Assadullah, Said, 1565
Ata, Mohammed Mirza, 2643
Ataulla, Qazi Khan Sahib, 778
Atayee, M. Ibrahim, 1932
Athar, Qazi Abdul Halim, 2644
Atkinson, James, 779
Atlantic Report, 32
Auboyer, Jeannine, 3054, 3055
Aurembou, Renee, 178
Ayazi, Mohammed Azam, 2645
Aybek, Zafar Hasan, 2646
Azoy, Geoffrey Whitney, 1254, 1255

B

Babakhodzaev, M. A., 2331
Babakhodzayev, A. Kh., 780
Babakhodzayev, Marat A., 781
Bacharach, Jere L., 3056
Bacon, Elizabeth E., 1256, 1257, 1258, 1259
Bacon, Elizabeth E. and Alfred E. Hudson, 782
Badakhshan, 1567
Badakhshi, Shah Abdullah, 783, 2647, 2648
Baghban, Hafizullah, 2649, 2650, 2651
Bahar, Malik al-Shu'ara, 784
Bahram, Ghulam M., 2332
Bailleau, Lajoinie S., 1568
Baily, John, 3057
Baker, Anne and Sir Ronald Ivelaw-Chapman, 785
Baker, Henry D., 2333
Bakhtiari, Abdullah, 1569
Baldus, R. D., 2334
Balikci, Asen, 1570, 1571

Balkh, 1572
al-Balkhi, Abu Bekr ibn 'Abdullah 'Umar ibn Da'ud al-Vayz Safi al-Din, 786
Balland, D., 1260, 2335, 2336
Ballis, William B., 787
Baloch, Inayatullah, 1933
Baloch, Mir Khuda Baksh Bijarani Marri, 1261
Balsan, Francois, 179, 180
Baltabeav, D., 1934
Baluch, M. S. K., 181
Baluchistan Through the Ages, 1935
Bamborough, Philip, 3058
Banawal, Juma Gul, 1573
Banerjee, J. M., 788
Banoory, Syed Ahmad Shah, 2337
Barfield, Thomas, 1263, 1264
Barfield, Thomas Jefferson, III, 1262
Barg-i Sabz, 1574
Baron, Lloyd I. Z., 2338
Barrat, J., 182
Barrat, Jacques, 1265
Barth, Fredrik, 1266, 1267, 1268, 1269, 1270, 1271, 1272, 1273, 1274
Barthold, Wilhelm, 789, 790
Bartholomew, John George, 33
Barthoux, J., 3062, 3063, 3064
Basic Data on the Economy of Afghanistan, 2339
Basic Facts on Afghanistan, 34
Basic Statistics of Afghanistan, 2340
Basso, Jacques, 2341
Baudet, Roger, 1575, 1576, 1577, 1578
Bauer, W. and Alfred Janata, 3065
Baum, F. L., 1579
Bayderin, Viktor A., 183
Bayhaqi, Abu al-Fazl Mohammad ibn Hasayn, 791
Beardsley, Charles, 2652
Bearth, P., 184
Beaurecueil, S. de Laugier de, 792
Bechhoefer, Sondra Howell, 1580
Bechhoefer, William B., 3066, 3067, 3068, 3069
Bechtel, Marilyn, 1937, 1938, 1939
Beck, Sebastian, 1581
Becka, Jiri, 35, 1582, 2653
Bedford, Jimmy, 2654
Bedil, Mirza Abd al-Qader, 2655
Beeston, Alfred F. L., 36
Bell, Marjorie Jewett, 1583
Bell, M. S., 793
Bellew, Henry Walter, 185, 186, 794, 795, 796, 1275, 1277, 2656, 2657
Belyayev, Viktor M., 2658

Benava, Abdul Raouf, 187, 188, 797, 798, 1940, 1941, 1942, 1943, 2659, 2661, 2662, 2663, 2664, 2665, 2666, 2667, 2668, 2669, 2670
Benava, Abdul Raouf and Abdul Hai Habibi, 2671
Benjamin, J. J., II, 1278
Bennet, Leiutenant, 799
Berger, Evert, 3059, 1435, 3061
Berger, Nina, Ursullah Schillinger, and Rolf Sator, 37
Bergmann, Horst, 3070
Berke, Zuhdi, 1584, 1585
Bernard, P., 800, 801, 802, 3071, 3072
Bernardin, Marc, 2342
Bernhardt, P., 189
Bernstein, Carl, 1944
Berre, Marc Le and Daniel Schlumberger, 3073
Besant, Annie Wood, 803
Beugel, Ernst van der, 1945
Bhaneja, Balwant, 1946
Bibliografiiă Avganistana, 38
Bibliografiya Afganistana: Literatura na Russkom Yazyka, 39
Bibliographical Survey of the Soviet Literature on Afghanistan 1918-1967, 40
Bibliographie Geographique Internationale, 41
Bibliography of Asian Studies, 42
Bibliography of Recent Soviet Source Material on Soviet Central Asia and the Borderlands, 43
Bibliography of Russian Works on Afghanistan, 44
Bibliography on Afghanistan Available in Kabul Libraries, 45
Bibliotheca Afghanica, 46
Bidar, 1586
Biddulph, J., 1279
Biddulph, C. E., 2672
Biddulph, M. A., 190
Bierman, John, 1947
Bigham, Mir 'Abdul Rashid, 1587
Bing, J. M., 2673
Binkowski, Andrej, 191
Biography of Some Members of the Danish Mission, 3074
Biryukor, A., 804
Bisnek, A. G. and K. I. Shafrovskii, 47
Bivar, A. D. H., 2674, 3075, 3076, 3077, 3078
Blake, Stephen, 192
Blanc, Jean Charles, 1280, 3079
Blanford, H. F., 193
Blechman, Barry M. and Douglas M. Hart, 1948
Bleiber, F., 1588
Blumhardt, James Fuller, 48
Blumhardt, J. F. and D. N. MacKenzie, 2675
Bobolyubov, A. A., 3080
Bochkarev, P., 194

Boernstein-Bosta, F., and Mandana Baschi, 195
Boesen, Inger W., 1281
Bogdanov, L., 1589, 2343, 2676
Boldyrev, A. N., 805
Bolshaia Sovetskaia Entsiklopedia, 49
Bombaci, Alessia, 3081
Bonelli, Luigi, 2677
Bonine, Michael E., 50
Borcke, A. V., 1949
Bordet, P., 196
Borhani, Mo'in al-Din, 1590
Bosworth, Clifford Edmund, 806, 807, 808, 809, 810, 811
Bouillance de Lacoste, Emile Antoine, 197
Boukhari, Mir Abdoul Kerim, 812
Boulanger, M., 1591
Boulenger, P. M., 1592
Boulonger, Robert, 813
Bourgeois, Jean and Danielle, 1282
Bourgeois, Jean-Louis, 3082
Boutiere, A. and R. Clocchiatti, 198
Bouvat, Lucien, 199, 814
Braker, H., 1950
Brandenburg, D., 3083
Bravin, N. and I. Beliaev, 1283
Bray, Denys, 1284, 2678
Breckle, S. W., 200, 201, 202, 203, 204
Breckle, S. W. and U. Breckle, 207
Breckle, S. W. and W. Frey, 205, 206
Breckle, S. W. and W. Unger, 208
Breitenbach, Markus, 209
Brereton, J. M., 815
Bresse, L., 2344
Brides, Lord Saint, 1951
Broadfoot, J. S., 210, 1285
Broenner, Wolfram, 1952
Brown, Douglas, 211
Bruce, George, 816
Bruckl, Karl, 212
Bruggey, J., 213
Bruno, Andrea, 3084, 3085
Bucherer, P., 214
Bucherer, Paul A., 215
Bucherer-Dietsche, Paul A., 3086
Buchroithner, Manfred F., 216, 217
Buchroithner, M. F. and H. Kolmer, 218
Buchroithner, M. F. and S. M. Scharbert, 219
Buck, Alfred A., 1593
Buddruss, Georg, 2679, 2680, 2681
Buddruss, Georg and G. Djelani Davary, 3087

Bujtar, August von, 1953
Bukhari, Farigh and Reza Hamadani, 2682
Burger, W., 2345
Burgess, James, 3088
Burhan, M. Esmael, 2683
Burke, J., 51
Burkner, F. C., 220
Burnes, Alexander, 1286, 1594
Burrell, R. M. and Alvin J. Cottrell, 1954
Buscher, Horst, 2346
Buscher, H., N. Assad, and H. Berger, 2348
Bushev, P. P., 817
Butcher, George, 221
Buttiker, W., 222
Buultjens, Ralph, 1955
Byron, Robert, 3089, 3090

C

Çagatay, Babur and Andrée F. Sjoberg, 1287
Caillou, Alan, 2684
Caldwell, John Cope, 223
Canfield, Robert, 1291
Canfield, Robert L., 1289, 1290, 1292, 1293, 1956, 1957
Canfield, Robert LeRoy, 1288
Carless, Hugh, 1294
Carlsen, Bodil Hjerrild, 1595
Caroe, Olaf, 818, 1958, 1959, 3091
Casal, Jean Marie, 3092, 3093
Casimir, M. J. and B. Glatzer, 3094
Casimir, M. J., R. P. Winter and Bernt Glatzer, 2349
Caspani, E. and E. Cagnacci, 52
Caspani, P. E., 224, 819, 3095, 3096, 3097, 3098, 3099
Castagne, Joseph A., 820, 821, 1596, 1597, 1960
Catalogue of the Marathi, Gujarati, Bengali, Assamese, Oriya, Pushtu, and Sindhi Manuscripts in the Library of the British Museum, 53
Causes of the Afghan War, Being a Selection of the Papers Laid Before Parliament, With a Connecting Narrative and Comment, 822
Centlivres, Micheline and P. Calottes, 3102
Centlivres, Pierre, 1297, 1298, 1299, 1300, 1301, 1302, 2350, 3100
Centlivres, Pierre and Michelene Centlivres-Demont, 3101
Centlivres-Demont, Micheline, 1295, 3103, 3104, 3105
Central Asian Review, 54, 1303, 1304, 1598, 2585
Cervin, Vladimir, 1599
Cervinka, Vladimir, 2351
Chaffetz, D., 1961
Chakravarty, Suhash, 823
Champagne, David C., 1600
Chand Kitab-i Khatti va Chapi Marbut ba Tarikh-i Afghanistan, 2686

Chandra, Pramod, 3106
Chang, Y. C., 1962
Chapman, E. F., 824
Charpentier, C. J., 1305, 1306, 1307, 1308, 1963, 3107
Charpentier, Joel, 2687
Charter, David, 1964
Chatelier, A. le, 825
Chavarria-Aguilar, Oscar L., 2688, 2689, 2690
Cheryankovskaya, Neonila Ivanova, 2352
Chinoy, Mike, 1965
Chirvani, A. S. Melikian, 3108
Chishti, Imam al-Din Husayn, 826
Chokaiev, Mustafa, 827
Choukour, Simonne, 3109
Chretien, Jean-Pierre, 1966
Christensen, Asgar, 1309
Chu, Solomon, 1303
Chu, Solomon, Robert N. Hill, and Paul A. Martino, 1602
Chu, Solomon, Robert N. Hill and Saxon Graham, 1601
Chubin, Shahram, 1967
Churchill, Rogers Platt, 828
La Civilisation Iranienne (Perse, Afghanistan, Iran Extérieur), 829
Cizancourt, H. de, 225
Clark, H. Barbara, 3110
Clark, Juno-Ann, 1604
Clark, Richard J., 226
Clerk, C., 227
Cleveland, Harlan and Andrew J. Goodpaster with Joseph J. Wolf, 1968
Clifford, Mary Louise, 830
Clinch, Minty, 1605
Codrington, K. de B., 228
Cohen, R., 1969
Collin-Delavaud, M. C., 1310
Combaz, Gilbert, 3111
Combe, E., J. Sauvaget, and G. Wiet, 3112
Concerning a Statement Made by the Governor-General of Pakistan, 1970
Conolly, Arthur, 229, 230
Conolly, E., 231, 831
Constable, A. G., 832, 833
Constitution of Afghanistan, 1917
Cook, Nilla C., 2691, 2692
Correspondence Relating to Persia and Afghanistan, 834
Courcy, Kenneth de, 835
Cressey, George B., 232, 2353
Cresson, Rebecca A., 1606
Cummins, Ian, 1792
Cunningham, George, 1311
Curiel, R. and G. Fussman, 3113
Curiel, Raoul, 2693

Curiel, Raoul and Daniel Schlumberger, 3114
Current Afghan Observations on Pashtoonistan, 1873
Current Problems in Afghanistan, 55
Curriculum and Textbook Project (USAID/PTCCU), 1607
Curzon, George Nathaniel, 233, 234, 836
Cutler, J. C., 1608

D

Dada, H. and L. Pickett, 2354
Dagens, B., M. Le Berre, and Daniel Schlumberger, 3115
Dagher, Joseph A., 56
Dai, Shen-yu, 837
Daiwa, 1609
Dales, George F., 3116, 3117, 3118
Dallin, A., 1974
Daly, Kate, 1610
Dames, M. Longworth, 1312, 3119
Darmesteter, James, 1313, 2694, 2695, 2696
Data Book (South Asia), 2355
Datta, Bhupendra Nath, 1314
Davary, G. Djelani, 3120
Davary, Djelani and Hanna Erdmann, 3121
Davidov, Aleksandr D., 1315, 1316, 1611, 2356, 2357, 2358
Davidov, A., and N. Chernakhovskaia, 838, 2359
Davidson, John, 2697
Davies, C. Collin, 839
Davis, Richard Shope, 3122
Davis, Richard S., Vadim A. Ranov and Andrey E. Dodonov, 3123
Dawar, Heider, 2360
De Baer, Oliver R., 235, 236
Debeth, G. F., 1612, 1613, 1614
De Croze, J. Berjane, 237, 238, 1615, 2698
De Croze, Joel, 840, 3124
Defremery, M. C., 841
Dehoti, A. P. and N. N. Ershov, 2699
Delapraz, Alan and Micheline Delapraz, 239
Delloye, Isabelle, 1616
Delor, J., 1617
Demchenko, P., 1975
Democratic Republic of Afghanistan, 1976, 1977
Demont, M. and P. Centlivres, 3125
Denitch, B., 1978
Department of Mineral Exploratons, 240
Desio, A., 241, 244
Desio, A., E. Martina and G. Pasquare, 242
Desio, A., E. Tangiorgi and G. Ferrara, 243
Deutsch, K., 2361

Deutsche im Hindukusch: Bericht der Deutschen Hindukusch-Expedition 1935 der Deutschen Forschungsgemeinschaft, 57
Deutsches Orient-Institut, 1979
Development Program, 2362
Deydier, Henri, 3126
Dianous, Hugues Jean de, 1317, 1618, 2700
Dickson, W. E. R., 842
Dictionary of the Pathan Tribes on the Northwest Frontier of India, Compiled Under the Orders of the Quarter-Master General in India, 1318
Diemberger, A., 3127
Dieterle, Alfred, 843
Dietmar, Rudolf Georg, 844
Dietrich, Brandenburg, 245
Dil, Shaheen F., 1980
Dilthey, Helmtraut, 2701
Diver, Katherine Helen Maud, 246
Diwan Ahmad Shah Abdali, 2702
Djabarov, A., 1981
Djan-Zirakyar and Rahmat Rabi, 1982
Djilas, Milovan, 1983
Djouzdjani, 845
Dodwell, H. H., 846, 847
Doerrer, I., W. Gaebe, G. Hoehl and C. Jentsch, 247
Dollot, René, 58, 848
Dor, Remy, 248, 849, 1319, 1984, 1985, 2703, 3128, 3129
Dor, R. and C. M. Naumann, 850, 1320, 1321
Dorbieu, Paul-Louis, 1986
Dorn, Bernhard, 851, 2704
Dorofeyeva, L. N., 2705, 2706
Dost, Dost M., 2707
Dost, M. Anwar, 2363
Douglas, William O., 249
Drewnjaja Baktrija 2 (La Bactriane Ancienne 2), 3130
Drummond (Captain), 250
Duke, Joshua, 852
Dulling, G. K., 2708
Dunin, M. S., 251, 252
Dunsheath, J. and E. Baoillie, 253
Dupaigne, Bernard, 1619, 2364, 2365, 3131, 3132, 3133, 3134, 3135
Dupree, Ann, Louis Dupree and A. A. Motamedi, 59
Dupree, Louis, 60, 61 (AUSF Reports), 853, 854, 855, 856, 857, 858, 859, 1322, 1323, 1324, 1325, 1326, 1327, 1328, 1329, 1330, 1331, 1332, 1333, 1620, 1621, 1622, 1623, 1987, 1988, 1989, 1990, 1991, 1992, 1994, 1995, 1996, 1997, 1998, 1999, 2709, 3136, 3137, 3138, 3139, 3140, 3141, 3142, 3143, 3144, 3145, 3146, 3147, 3148, 3149, 3151, 3152
Dupree, Louis (in Collaboration with J. Lawrence Angel and Others), 3150

Dupree, Louis and Linette Albert, 62
Dupree, Louis and Richard S. Davis, 3153
Dupree, Louis and Nancy Hatch Dupree, 860, 1624
Dupree, Louis and Klaus Fischer, 3154
Dupree, Louis, P. Gouin and N. Omer, 3155, 3156
Dupree, Louis and Bruce Howe, 3157
Dupree, Louis and C. Kolb, 3158
Dupree, Louis, Lawrence H. Lattman and Richard S. Davis, 3159
Dupree, Nancy Hatch, 861, 862, 863, 1625, 1626, 1627, 1628, 1629, 1630, 1631, 1632, 2710, 3160
Dupree, Nancy Hatch and Louis Dupree, 3161
Durand, Algernon G. A., 2000
Durand, Sir Henry Marion, 864
Durrieu, M. G., 254
Dvoryankov, N. A., 63, 2711, 2712, 2713, 2714
Dzhabbarov, I. M., 2715
Dzhafarova, A. A., 1334, 2716, 2717
Dziegiel, Leszek, 2001

E

East India (Afghanistan), 865
East India (Military) Report on the Air Operations in Afghanistan Between December 12, 1928 and February 25, 1929, 866
Easterly, Edwin Michael, 1633
Ebadi, Samiia, 1634
Eberhard, Wolfram, 2002, 2366
Eckensberger, Lutz H. and Gunter F. Schneider, 1635, 2367
Economic Review of Afghanistan, 1949, 2368
Economic Studies, 2369
Economic Survey of Asia and the Far East, 1954, 2370
Edelberg, Lennart, 1335, 3162
Edelberg, Lennart and Schuyler Jones, 1336
Education in Afghanistan During the Last Half-Century, 1636
Educational Mission, 1637
Educational Statistics, Afghanistan, 1968/1347, 1638
Educational Statistics, Afghanistan, 1969, 1639
Edwards, Edward, 64
Edwardes, Herbert Benjamin, 1337
Efa, Francois, 255
Efimov, V. A., 2718
Eggermont, P. H. L. and J. Hoftijzer, 3163
Eiland, Murray L., 3164, 3165
Einzmann, Harald, 1338, 1640, 1641
Eiselin, Max, 256
Eisner, Curt and Clas M. Naumann, 257
Eiva, Andrew, 2003
Ekker, Martin H., 2371
Elfenbein, J. H., 2719

Elham, Muhammed Rahim, 2720
El-Hashimi, Sayed, 1642
Elias, N., 867
Elias, R., 868
Eliot, Theodore L., Jr., 2004
Elphinstone, Mountstuart, 65
Eltezam, Zabioullah A., 2372, 2373
The Em-Kayan, 2374
Emmanuel, W. F., 258
Enayat-Seraj, Khalilullah and Nancy Hatch Dupree, 869
Enevoldsen, Jens, 2721
Engert, Cornelius van H., 66
English Historian's Verdict on Durand Line, 2005
English-Pashto Dictionary, 2722
English, Paul, 259
English, Paul Ward, 3166
Enriquez, Colin M. D., 1339
Erhard, F., 2375
Ershov, N. N. and Z. A. Shirokov, 3167
Eskilsson, Enar, 2376
Essad Bey, Mohammed, 870
Ethe, Hermann, 67, 68, 2723
Ethe, Hermann and Edward Edwards, 69
Etienne, Gilbert, 2377
Ettinghausen, Richard, 3168
Evans, Hubert, 70
Evans-Von Krbek and Jeffrey Hewitt Pollitt, 2724
Exchange of Notes Between His Majesty's Government in the United Kingdom and the Government of Afghanistan Regarding Treaty Relations with Afghanistan, 871, 872
Exchange of Official Publications, 873
Exhibition of Ancient Art of Afghanistan, Tokyo, 3169
Eyre, Vincent, 874

F

Faegre, Torvald, 3170
Fairchild, Frank Louis, 1643
Fairservis, W. A., Jr., 875
Fairservis, Walter A., Jr., 3171, 3172, 3173, 3174, 3175, 3176
Falconer, H., 260
Far Eastern News Letter, 2006
Farhadi, Abdul Ghafur Ravan, 2725, 2726, 2727, 2728, 2729
Farhang, Amin, 2378
Farhang, Mir Muhammad Sidiq, 876, 2730
Farid, Ahmad, 71
Farid, F., 2007
Farouq, Ghulam, 2379
Farrukh, Mahdi, 72

Farsan, Nur Mohammed, 261
Faryab, 1644
Fayz Muhammad Khan Molla, 2008
Fazy, Robert, 1340
Fedorova, T. I., 262
Fenyvesi, C., 2009
Ferdinand, Klaus, 1341, 1342, 1343, 1344, 1345, 1346, 1347, 1348, 2380, 2381, 2382, 2383, 3177
Feroz, G. A., 1645
Ferrier, J. P., 263, 877
Field, Claud H., 1349
Field, Henry, 72
Field, Neil C., 2384
Finley, Mark, 1646
Firoz, M. M., 2010
Fischer, D., 264
Fischer, Dieter, 2385
Fischer, Klaus, 3178, 3179, 3180
Fischer, Ludolph, 1647
Fitter, Jorn C., 2386
Fletcher, Arnold, 878, 879
Fleury, Antoine, 880, 2011, 2012
Flohn, H., 265, 266
Flury, Samuel and Andre Godard, 3181
Flussman, Gerard and Marc Le Berre, 3182
Fly, C. L., 267
Fodor, Eugene and William Curtis, 1648
Foot, Rosemary, 2013, 2014
Forbes, Archibald, 881
Forbes, F., 268
Forbes, Rosita, 269
Forrest, George W., 271
Forsberg, A., 2387
Forsberg, A. and T. Holma, 2388
Forster, George, 270
Fostner, Ulrich, 272
Foucher, Alfred, 3183, 3184
Fouchet, Maurice, 3185
Fouilles d'Ai Khanaum I, 3186
Fountain, R., 2015
Fox, Ernest F., 273
Fox, John, 274
Fozilov, Mullojon, 2731, 2732
Frances, Jack, 3187
Francfort, Henri-Paul, 3188, 3189
Franck, Dorothea Seelye, 2016
Franck, Dorothea Seelye and Peter G. Franck, 2389
Franck, Peter G., 2390, 2391, 2392, 2393, 2394, 2395, 2396
Franz, Erhard, 1350, 1351, 2017, 2397, 2398, 3190, 3191

Franz, Heinrich Gerhard, 882, 1649, 3192, 3193, 3194, 3195, 3196, 3197, 3198, 3199
Fraser, George MacDonald, 2733
Fraser, Malcolm, 2018
Fraser-Tytler, Sir W. Kerr, 74, 275, 276, 2019
Freeman, Antonyi, 2734
Freitag, H., 277, 3200
Fremberg, Juergen, 1352
Frembgen, Juergen, 75
Frey, W., 278, 279, 3201
Frey, W. and W. Probst, 281
Frey, W., W. Probst and A. Shaw, 280
Friedl, E., 2735
Friendship and Diplomatic and Consular Representation, 883
Fritz, Dale B., 2399
Fröhlich, Dieter, 2020, 2400
Fromkin, David, 2021
Fry, Maxwell J., 2401, 2402
Fry, Richard N., 3202, 3203, 3204
Fucik, Julius, 1650
Fukuyama, Francis, 2022
Fulfalza'i (Popalzai), 'Aziz al-Din, 884
Fulfalza'i (Popalzai), 'Aziz al-Din Vakili, 885
Furdoonjee, Nowrozjee, 2403
Furnia, Arthur H., 1651
Furon, Raymond, 76, 282, 283, 1652, 1653
Furon, Raymond and Louis-Felicien Rosset, 284, 285
Furse, P. and P., 2404
Fussman, G., 3206
Fussman, G. and M. Le Berre, 3205

G

Gabert, G., 286
Gablentz, H. C. von der, 2736
Gabriel, Alfons, 287
Gafferberg, E. G., 1353, 1354
Gafurov, Bobodzan Gafurovich, 886
Gaisler, J., 288
Galkin, M., 289
Gandy, Christopher and Andre Singer, 1654
Gankovskii, Y. V., 887, 888
Ganns, O., 290
Gans-Ruedin, E., 3207
Gardin, J. C., 3208, 3209
Gardner, Alexander, 889, 890
Gardner, Percy, 3210, 3211
Garrity, Patrick J., 2023
Gattinara, Giancarlo Castelli, 2405

Gaube, Heinz, 2406
Gaulier, Simone, 891
Gavrilin, V., 892
Geerken, Hartmut, 291
Geiger, Wilhelm, 2737, 2738
General Atlas of Afghanistan, 292
Gentelle, Pierre, 2407
Gerasimova, A. S., 2739, 2740
Gerasimova, A. S. and G. F. Girs, 2741
Gerber, Alfred, 293
Gerken, E., 2408, 3212
Gettens, Rutherford J., 3213
Gevemeyer, Jan-Heeren, Wolfgang Holzwarth, and Hans G. Kippenberg, 294
Ghani, A. R., 77
Ghani, Ashraf, 1355, 2024
Da Gharbi Pakistan Yunitt (The Western Unit of Pakistan), 2025
Gharzi, General Muhammad Safar Vakil, 1356
Ghaussi, M. Aref, 1655, 1656, 2409, 2410, 2411
Ghaussy, A. Ghanie, 2412
Ghawarah Ash'ar da Gol Pacha Olfat (Choice Poetry of Gol Pacha Olfat), 2742
Ghrishman, Roman, 893, 3214, 3215
Ghirshman, R. and T. Ghirshman, 3216
Ghose, Dilip K., 894
Ghosh, Biswanath, 895
Ghosh, K. P., 2026, 2027
Ghubar, M., 1657, 2028
Ghubar, Mir Ghulam Muhammed, 896, 897, 898
Ghulami, Muhammad Ghulam, 2743
Gilbert, O., D. Jamieson, H. Lister, and A. Pendlington, 295
Gilbertson, George Waters, 2744
Gillett, Sir Michael, 2029
Gilli, A., 296, 2413
Ginnever, O. R., 2414
Girs, G. F., 2745
Glaesner, Heinz, 2030
Glaister, G. S., 2415
Glassman, Eugene H., 2746
Glatzer, Bernt, 1357, 1358, 2416, 3217, 3218
Glaubitt, Klaus, 2417
Glaubitt, K., F. Saadeddin, and B. Schafer, 2418, 2419
Gnoli, Gherardo, 3219
Gobar, Asad H., 1658, 1659, 1660
Gobj, Robert, 297, 899
Gochenour, Theodore S., 2031, 2747
Godard, Andre and Joseph Hackin, 3220
Godiksen, Lois Hansen, 1661
Goetz, Hermann, 3221
Goldman, Marshall I., 2032

Goldsmid, F. J., 298, 299, 900
Golombek, Lisa, 3222, 3223, 3224
Golovin, Y. M., 2420, 2421
Gonsior, Bernhard, 300
Goodwin, Buster, 2748
Gordon, B. E. M., 2749
Gordon, T. E., 301
Gortemaker, Manfred, 2033
Gosti iz Afganistan (Guests From Afghanistan), 1662
Gouttiere, Thomas E., 2422
Government of India, 901
Goya, Sarwar, 3225
Grassmuck, George and Ludwig W. Adamec with Frances H. Irwin, 78
Gratzl, Karl, 302, 303, 3226, 3227
Gray, John Alfred, 1663
Great Britain, Foreign Office, 902
Greene, Brook A. and F. Khayruddin Fazl, 2423
Gregorian, Vartan, 903, 904
Grenard, Fernand, 905
Grey-Wilson, C., 304
Grierson, George Abraham, 2750, 2751, 2752
Griesinger, W., 906
Griffith, Dr., 305, 306
Griffith, William E., 2034
Griffiths, John C., 907, 2035
Grodekov, N. I., 307
Grolimund, Kurt, 2428
Grötzbach, Erwin, 308, 309, 311, 312, 313, 314, 315, 316, 317, 908,
    2424, 2425, 2426, 2427, 2428
Grötzbach, E. and C. Rathjens, 310
Grötzbach, W., 318
Grousset, Rene, 3228
Gubanov, I. A., V. N. Pavlov, and M. C. Younos, 319
Gul, Azam, and Lloyd Picket, 2429
Gul, Mohammad, 909
Gullini, Giorgio, 3229, 3230
Gupta, Bhabani Sen, 2036
Gupta, Harl Ram, 910
Gupta, S. P., 3231
Gurash, 1664
Gurdon, B. E. M., 911
Gurevich, Aleksandr Mikhailovich, 320
Gurevich, Naum M., 2430, 2431, 2432
Gzerski, G., 321

H

Habberton, William, 912, 913
Habib, Abdul Haq, 3232
Habib, Mohammad, 914
Habibi, Abdul Hai, 915, 916, 917, 918, 919, 920, 2753, 2754, 2755, 2756, 2757, 2758, 2759, 2760
Habibi (Tabibi), Abdul Hakim, 921
Habibieyeh 1282-1322, 1665
Habibullah, Amir, 922
Habibullah, Sardar, 923
Hacker, J., 2037
Hackin, Joseph, 322, 1359, 3233, 3234, 3235, 3236, 3237
Hackin, Joseph and Joseph Carl, 3238, 3239
Hackin, J., J. Carl, and J. Meunie, 3243
Hackin, Joseph and Andrea Godard and Yedda Godard, 3240
Hackin, Joseph and R. Hackin, 3241, 3242
Hackin, Ria and Ahmad Ali Kohzad, 1360
Haddad, Nikulay, 1666
Hadiyah ba Dustan (A Gift to Friends), 1667
Haekel, Ingeborg, 323
Hafisi, Abdul Satar, 2433
Hafisi, A. S. and N. Osmani, 324
Haggerty, Jerome J., 2038
Hahn, Helmut, 325, 326
Haider, Habib, 2434
Hakim, Abdul, 1668
Hakimi, Abdul Karim, 2435
Halim, A., 924
Hall, Gus, 2039
Hall, Lesley, 79
Hallet, Stanley Ira, 3244
Hallet, Stanley and Rafi Samizay, 3245, 3246, 3247
Halliday, Fred, 2040, 2041, 2042, 2043, 2044, 2045
Hamada, M., 1669
Hamaoui, Ernest, 2047
Hambly, E. B., 925
Hambly, Gavin, 926
Hamid, Abdul Aziz, 1670, 2046
Hamid, 'Abdul Razaq, 2761
Hamid-Kashmiri, Hamid Allah, 928
Hamidi, Hakim, 3248
Hamilton, Angus, 327
Hamley, E., 929
Hameed-ud Din, 927
Hanifi, M. Jamil, 80, 1361, 1362, 1363, 1364, 1365, 1366, 2048
Hanley, Barbara, 2762
Hanna, Henry B., 930
Hannah, Norman B., 1671, 2049

Hanne, Mormann and Erich Ploger, 3249
Hanstein, Otfried von, 328
Haqiqate Inqilabe Saur (The Truth About the Saur Revolution), 1672
Haqiqate Sarbaz (The Truth of a Soldier), 1673
Harat, 1674
al-Haravi, Sayf ibn Muhammad ibn Ya'qub, 931
Harlan, Josiah, 932
Harris, Fred, 1675
Harrison, Selig S., 2050, 2051, 2052, 2053
Harmatta, J., 933
Hasan, K., 934
Hasan, Ya'qub, 2763
Hasan, Zubeida, 2054
Hashim Khan, Mir, 935
Hashimbekov, X., 2764
Hashimzai, Mohammed Qasem, 2055
Hashmat, A., 329
Hasrat, Aman Allah, 936
Hassas, Burhanoddin, 2056
Hasse, D., 330
Hassinger, Jerry D., 331, 332
Haughton, John C., 937
Hauner, Milan, 2057, 2058
Hauser, Ernest O., 938
Hautaluo, J. E. and R. J. Loomis, 1676
Hautsluoma, J. E. and V. Kasman, 333
Havelka, Jan, 334
Havelock, Henry, 939
Hawa, 1677
Hay, William R., 335, 336, 337
Hayden, H. H., 338
Hayward, G. S. W., 339
Hedge, I. C. and P. Wendelbo, 340, 3250
Heissig, W., 2765
Hekmat, Alim, 341
Heller, Mark, 2059
Helmand Valley Industrial Survey--Phase I, 2436
Henderson, Michael M. T., 2766
Hennequin, Gilles, 3251
Henning, W. B., 81, 2767
Hensman, Howard, 940
Henze, Dietmar, 941
Heras, Henri, 1678
Herati, Mohammed Hashim Omidvar, 2768
Herati, Mohammad Husayn, 942
Heravi, Ghulam Riza Mayel, 82, 83, 943, 2769, 2770
Heravi, Saifi, 944
Heravi, Shaykh al-Islam Khwajeh 'Abdullah Ansari, 2771
Heravy, Mir G. R. Ma'il, 1679

Herawi, Nayer, 945
Herberg, Werner, 342
Herbert, Raymond J. and Nicholas Poppe, 2772
Herbordt, O., 343
Herbordt, Oskar, 1680
Herbst, Dean Finley, 344
Herrlich, Albert, 1367
Herrmann, G., 345
Herzfeld, Ernst, 3252
Hesche, Wolfram, Wolf-Dieter Hildebrant and Andreas Thermann, 2773
Hess, A., 246
Heywad, 2060
Higuchi, T. and S. Kuwayamy, 3253
Hinrichs, Harley H., 2437
Hirche, Elke, 3254
Hlopin, I. N., 3255
Hlopina, L. I., 3256
Hobberton, W., 946
Hodge, C. T., 2774
Hoerburger, Felix, 3256, 3257
Hoff, Hellmut, 2438
Holden, E. S., 947
Holdich, Thomas Hungerford, 347, 348, 349, 350, 351, 948, 949, 1368
Hondrich, Karl Otto, 2439
Hoshmand, Ahmad Reza, 2440, 2441
Hough, Jerry F., 2061
Hough, W., 950
Houtsma, Martyn Theodor, 84
Howarth, T. G. and D. Povolny, 3259
Howell, Evelyn and Olaf Caroe, 2775
Howland, Felix, 352, 353
Hudson, Alfred E. and Elizabeth E. Bacon, 1369, 1681
Huffman, Arthur V., 1682
Hufford, Donald, 1683
Hughes, D., 3260
Hughes, Thomas P., 951, 2776, 2777
Humlum, Johannes, 354, 355
Hunte, Pamela A., 1370, 1371, 1372, 1373, 1684
Hunter, Edward, 356
Huntington, Ellsworth, 357
Huquq, 1685
al-Husaini, Mahmud (Al-Munshi ibn Ibrahim al-Djami), 952, 953
Hussain, Syed Shabir, 2062
Hussein, Mia, 358
Hutton, T., 359, 360, 361, 362
Huwyler, Edwin, 363, 1687
Huwyler, E. and I. V. Moos, 364, 1686
Huyn, Hans Graf, 3261
Hyman, Anthony, 2063, 2064

I

Iakubova, E. S., 2778
Iavorskii, I. L., 365
Ihlau, Olaf, 2065
Ilyas, M., N. Ali, M. I. Marshood, and K. Aziz, 1688
Imam al-Din, S. M., 2779
Imamuddin, S. M., 954
Imbeck, Klaus, 2066
Imperial Gazetteer of India, 85, 955
India, 2442
India Army, General Staff Branch, 956
India, Department of the Army, 1374
Indiya i Afganistana: Ocherki Istorii i Ekonomiki, 86
Indian Institute of Foreign Trade, 2443
Indian News Chronicle, 2067
Industrial Development in Afghanistan, 2444
Ingram, Edward, 2068, 2069
International Educational, 1689
Interview of Pierre Centlivres and Micheline Centlivres, 1375
In Whose Benefit?, 957
Iqbal, Sir Mohammad, 2780, 2781
Iqtisad, 2445
Iran, Afganistan i Sin'tszian (Zap-Kitai): Politiko-ekonomiches kie ocherki, 366
Irfan, 1690
Irons, William, 1376, 1377, 1378
Irwin, John, 3262
Irwin (Lieutenant), 367
Ishida, O., 2446
Islah, 1691
Ismati, Ma'sumeh, 2782
Istoriy Tadzhikskogo Naroda, 958
Itemadi, Guya, 3263
I'timadi, Muhammad Akbar Khan, 2070
Itifaqi-i Islam, 1692
Itihad, 1693
Itihad-i Mashriqi, 1694
Ivanov, W., 1379, 2783
Iven, H. E., 368
Iven, Walther, 369
Iwamura, S. and H. F. Schurmann, 2784
Iz Afganskoy Poezii, 2785

J

Jacquet, E., 3264
Jadeer, Habiburrahman, 2071
Jafri, Hasan Ali Shah, 2072
Jakel, K., 371, 2073
Jalabert, Louis, 959
Jalalabadi, Shir Ahmad, 960
James, Ben, 370
James, Eloise, 87
Jami, Nur al-Din Abdul Rahman, 2786
Jan, Qazi Ahmad, 2787
Janata, Alfred, 1380, 1381, 2447, 2448, 2788, 2789, 3265, 3266, 3267, 3268
Janata, Alfred and Reihanodin Hassas, 1382
Janssens, B. Busson de, 1695
Japan-Afghanistan Joint Archeological Survey in 1978, 3269
Jarring, Gunnar, 1383, 1384, 1696, 2790, 2791, 2792
Javid, Ahmad, 2793
Jawhar, Hassan Muhammad and Abd al-Hamid Baywami, 88
Jawzjani, Minhaj al-Din ibn Serraj al-Din Tabaqat-i Nasiri, 961
Jeanneret, Andre, 1385, 2449, 2450
Jean-Yves, Loude, 1386
Jeffrey, Thomas E., 1697
Jenkins, Robin, 1387, 1388
Jensch, Werner, 2451
Jentsch, Christoph, 372, 373, 1389, 1390, 2452
Jettmar, Karl, 89, 1391, 1698, 1699, 1700, 3270, 3271
Johnston, R. H. and K. G. Hussain, 3272
Jones, H. McCoy and Jeff W. Boucher, 3273, 3274
Jones, Paul S., 374
Jones, Sarah, 962
Jones, Schuyler, 90, 91, 1392, 1393, 2074, 3275
Jung, Chris L., 375

K

Kabir, Muhkammed, 2075
Kabul, 92
Da Kabul Kalani, 93
Kabul New Times, 1702
Da Kabul Puhantun Khabarunah, 1701
Kabul Times, 1703
Kabul Times Annual, 2794
Kaever, M., 376
Kajakai Report and its Relation to the Development of the Helmand Valley, 2453
Kakar, M. Aziz, 1704
Kakar, Hasan Kawun, 968

Kakar, M. Hasan, 963, 964, 965, 966, 967
Kalus, L., 3276
Kamal, Abdul Hadi, 2454
Kamali, Mohammad Hashim, 1705, 2076
Kamel, Dost Muhammad Khan, 969
Kamlin, M., 2077
Kamrany, Nake M., 2455, 2456
Kamrany, Nake M., Lois H. Godiksen, Eden Naby, and Richard N. Fry, 94
Kanne, Jürgen, 2457, 2458
Kapur, Harish, 970, 2078
Karhaneh, 2459
Karimi, A. R., 2079
Karmal, Babrak, 2080
Karmiesheva, B. X., 1394
Karmysheva, B. Kh., 3277
Karpov, G., 1395, 1396
Karpov, G. I. and P. V. Arbekov, 1397
Karutz, R., 377
Kasim, Jan Mohd., 378
Katrak, Sorab K. H., 379
Katz, Tami Beth, 3278
Kaye, E., 380
Kayeum, Abdul, 1706
Kayoumi, A. H., 2460
Kazemi, Shamsuzakir, 2081
Kazimee, Bashir A., 3279
Keddie, Nikki R., 971, 972
Kedourie, E., 973
Keiser, R. Lincoln, 1398, 1399, 1400, 1401
Kennan, George F., 2082
Kennedy, T. F., 1707, 1708
Kerr, Graham B., 1709, 1710
Kessel, Joseph, 95, 2795
Kessel, Joseph, Karl Flinker, and Max Klimburg, 381
Khadem, Qiyam al-Din, 1402, 2796, 2797, 2798, 2799
Khairzada, Faiz and Ralph H. Magnus, 2083
Khafi, Mirza Yaqub 'Ali, 974
Khalfin, N. A., 975
Khalfin, N. S., 976
Khalfin, Naftula, 2084
Khalid Khan, 2085
Khalil, Hakim Taj Mohamed, 2086
Khalil, Muhammad Ibrahim, 382, 977, 1711
Khalili, Afghan, 383
Khalili, az Ash'ar-i Ostad, 2800
Khalili, Khalilullah, 978, 2801, 2802, 2803, 3280
Khalil, Muhammad Ibrahim, 383
Khalilzad, Zalmay, 2087, 2088, 2089, 2090, 2091, 2092
Khalq, 1712

Khan, Ghani, 1403
Khan, Ghani Mohammad, 2461
Khan, Ghulam Mustafa, 979
Khan, Mohammed Said, 980
Khan, M. M. S. M., 981
Khan, Qazi Rahimullah, 2804
Khan, Rajah (of Cabool), 384
Khan, Said Alim S. H., 982
Khan, Subedar Muhammad Hussain, 983
Khanikoff, Nicolas de, 385
Khasteh, A., 2805
Khaturvatana (Torwayana), Najibullah, 984
Khawgiani, Mohammed Amin, 1713
Kherad, Akbar, 2462
Khidjayev, M. A. Baba, 2463
Khodzhayov, T. K., 1714
Khorasan, 1715
Khoroshkhin, A., 386
Khoshbeen, A. M., 1716
Khouri, Fred J., 2093
Khushhal Khan Khattak, 2806
Khwand-Amir, Ghiyas al-Din ibn Humam al-Din, 985
Kieffer, Charles M., 387, 986, 987, 1404, 1717, 2807, 2808, 2809, 3281, 3282
Kimche, Jon, 2094
King, David, 988
King, L. White, 3283
King, Peter, 388
Kingsbury, Patricia and Robert, 389
Kingsley, Bonnie M., 3284
Kisilova, L. N., 2810, 2811
Kisliakov, Nikolai Andreevich, 1406, 1407
Kisliakov, N. A. and A. I. Pershits, 1405
Kitamuro, S., 390
Klass, R. T., 2095
Klass, Rosanne, 391, 3285
Klein, I., 989
Klimberg, Deborah S., 3286
Klimburg, M., 3287
Klimburg-Salter, Deborah Elizabeth, 3288
Klimburg, Max, 990
Klockenhoff, H., 392
Klockenhoff, H. and G. Madel, 393
Kloft, W. and E. Kloft, 394
Kloft, W. and P. Schneider, 395
Knabe, Erika, 1408, 1718, 1719
Knoblock, Edgar, 3289
Knust, T. A., 396
Kohl, Philip, 3290

Kohzad, Ahmad Ali, 397, 398, 399, 400, 991, 992, 993, 994, 995, 996, 997, 998, 999, 1000, 1001, 1002, 1003, 1004, 1005, 1409, 1410, 1720, 1721, 1722, 1723, 1724, 2096, 2097, 2098, 2099, 2100, 2464, 2465, 2466, 2812, 2813, 2814, 2815, 2816, 2817, 3291, 3292, 3293, 3294, 3295, 3296, 3297, 3298, 3299, 3300, 3301, 3302, 3303, 3304, 3305, 3306, 3307, 3308, 3309, 3310
Kohzad, Mohamad Nabi, 3311, 3312, 3313
Kohzad, Mohammad Nabi, 401, 402, 403, 1006, 2818, 2819, 2820
Koie, M. and K. H. Reichinger, 404, 405
Kolb, C. C., 3314
Komarov, I., 1411
Konieczny, M. G., 3315
König, Rene, 2467
Konishi, Masatoshi, 406
Konow, Sten, 1007
Koshan, Ghulam Hazrat, 2821
Koshkaki, Mawlawi Borhan al-Din Khan, 1008
Köster, Ulrich, 2468
Kostka, Robert, 3316
Kovusov, Anna and Yakovom Kozlovskiy, 2822
Krader, Lawrence, 1412, 1413
Kratkii Afgansko-Russkii Slovar, 2823
Kratkii Voennyi Persidsko-Russkii Slovar, 2824
Kraus, Rudiger W. H., 2469
Kraus, Willy, 96, 408, 2470
Krause, Walter W., 407
Kreyberg, Leiv, 409
Kruglikova, I. T., 3317, 3318
Kruglikova, I. T., V. I. Sarianidi, and G. A. Pugacenkova, 3319
Kuhi, Muhammad Nasir, 410
Kuhn, Delia and Ferdinand Kuhn, 411
Kuhnert, Gerd, 412, 413
Kukhtina, T. I., 97
Kukhtina, Tat'yana I., 1725
Kukhtina, Tat'yana and A. K. Sverchevskaya, 98
Kulke, Holger, 414
Kulke, H. and W. Schreyer, 415
Kull, U. and S. W. Breckle, 416
Kullman, E., 417, 418
Kumar, B., 1009
Kundu, N., 1010
Kureischie, Azizullah, 1011
Kushan, G. Hazrat, 1012
Kushev, V. V., 2825
Kushkaki, Burhan al-Din, 419, 1013, 1014, 2826
Kushkaki, Burhan al-Din Khan, 420
Kusmina, Jelena, 3320
Kussmaul, Friedrich, 1414, 1415

L

L'Abeille, Lucerne, 2101
Labour Legislation in Afghanistan, 2471
Laheeb, Nasratullah, 2827
Lajoinie, Simone Bailleau, 1726
Lakanwal, Abdul Ghafar, 2472
Lal, Mohan, 421, 1015, 1016, 3321
Lamb, Harold, 1017
Land, D., 422
Lamber-Karlovsky, C., 3322
Lane-Poole, Stanley, 1018
Lang, J., 423
Lang, J. and H. Meon-Vilain, 424
Lansdell, Henry, 425
Lapparent, A. F. de, 426, 427, 2473
Lapparent, A. F. de and J. Blaise, 428
Latifi, 'Abdul Baqi, 1727
Laugier de Beaurecueil, S. de, 2828
The Law of Commerce, 2474
Lazard, Gilbert, 2829
Lebedev, Konstantin A., 2830, 2831
Lebedev, Konstantin A., Z. M. Kalinina, and L. S. Yatsevich, 2832, 2833
Lee, Vladimir, 1019
Leech, Major R., 1020
Leech, R., 429, 430, 431, 432, 433, 434, 2834, 2835
Le Fevre, Georges, 435
Le Fort, P., 436
Le Jeune, E., 2102
Lentz, Wolfgang, 99, 2836, 3323
Lentz, Wolfgang von, 1416
Le Roy, Marie, 437, 438
Lerzezynski, G. L., 2103
Leshnik, Lorenz S., 1021, 3324, 3325
Le Strange, Guy, 439
Levin, I. D., 2104
Levine, J. O., 1022, 1023
Lewis, Henry James, 2105
Lewis, Robert E., 440
Leyden, J., 1728
Lezine, A., 3326
Liberman, A. A., 1024
Lieberman, Samuel S., 2475
Ligeti, L., 1417, 1418
Linchevskii, I. A. and A. V. Prozorovskii, 441, 442
Linchevsky, I. A. and A. V. Prozorovsky, 443
Lindauer, G., 1729
Lindberg, K., 444, 1730

Lindholm, Charles, 1419, 1420, 1421, 1422, 1423, 1424
Lindholm, Charles and Cherry Lindholm, 1425
Lister, H., 445
Literaturovedeniye: Indiya, Pakistan, Afghanistan, 2837
Lival, Rahmatullah, 100
Labanov-Rostovsky, A., 1025
Lockhart, Laurence, 1026, 1027
Logofet, D. N., 1426
Lorenz, Manfred, 2838
Lorimer, David Lockhart Robertson, 2839, 2840
Lorimer, J. G., 2106, 2841
Lowenthal, R., 2842
Loy Pushtun, 2107
Ludin, Mohammad Kabir Khan, 2503
Lumsden, P., 446
Lumsden, Sir Peter, 1427
Lunt, J. D., 2108
Lushington, Henry, 1028
Luttwak, Edward N., 2109
Lys, M., 447
Lytle, Elizabeth Edith, 101

M

MacFadyen, D. R., 1731
MacGregor, C. M., 1029
MacGregor, G. H., 448
MacKenzie, C. F. and Sir H. M. Elliot, 1030
MacKenzie, D. N., 2843, 3327
MacKenzie, Franklin, 449
MacMahon, A. H., 450
MacMunn, George Fletcher, 1031
Macrory, Patrick A., 1032
Madadi, M. Akbar, 451
Magnus, Julius, 1732
Magnus, Ralph Harry, 2110, 2111
Mahfouz, Imza, 1733
Mahmoud, Shah, 2476
Mahran, G. H., T. S. M. A. El Alfy, and S. M. A. Ansary, 452
Maidan, I. G., 2112
Maillart, Ella K., 453
La Maison des Francais, 1734
Majmu'a-yi Sihat, 1735
Majmu'eh-yi Ash'ar-i Vajid, 2844
Majrouh, Sayd B., 1432
Majruh, Sayyid Shams al-Din, 2845
Malakhov, M., 1736
Malhotra, Joginder K., 2113
Malhotra, R. I., 1033

Malik, Hafeez, 1428
Malik al-Shu'ara, Bitab, 1337, 1338
Malleston, George Bruce, 1034, 1035
Manchester Guardian, 3328
Mandel'shtam, A. M., 3329
Mangal, S. M., 2477
Mann, Oskar, 1036
Manuchariants, Maiorov, Suderkin and Krekov, 454
Map, Afghanistan, 455
Map of Kabul, 457
Map, Persia and Afghanistan, 456
Maps, Afghanistan, 458
Maps of Afghanistan, 459
Maranjian, G., 1739
March of Pakhtoonistan, 2114
Maricq, André and Gaston Wiet, 3330
Markham, C. R., 460, 461, 462, 463
Markoroski, Bruno, 464
Marshall, D. N., 1037
Martin, D. R., 3331, 3332
Martin, Frank A., 1740
Martin, G., 1038
Martin, Ross J., 1741
Martin, Thomas J., 2846
Martino, Paul and Susan F. Schultz, 1742
Marvin, Charles, 465, 466
Masal'skii, F. I., 467
Masannat, George S., 2115, 2478
Masse, Henri, 2847
Massignon, Louis, 102
Masson, Charles, 468, 2848
Masson, Vadim M. and Vadim A. Romodin, 1039
Masson, V. and V. Sarianidy, 1040
Ma'sumi N. and M. Kholov, 2849
Matheson, Sylvia, 3333
Matson, F. R., 3334
Matthews, Herbert L., 1743
Mauelshagen, L. and D. Morgenstern, 3335
Mauelshagen, L., D. Morgenstern and K. Tonnessen, 3336
May, C. J. D., 3337
Maylon, F. H., 2850
Mayne, Peter, 2116
Mazhar, 'Ali, 469
McArthur, I. D., Sarwar Sayad, and Maqsood Nawin, 2479
McChesney, Robert D., 1041, 2480
McGeehan, Robert, 2117
McGovern, William M., 1042
McKeller, Doris, 1744
McNair, W. W., 470

Meakin, Annette M. B., 1429
Medvedev, Roy, 2118
Meher-Homji, V. M., R. K. Gupta and H. Freitag, 471
Mehnert, Klaus, 2119
Mehrabi, Shah Mohammad, 1745, 2481
Meissner, Boris, 2120, 2121
Mele, Pietro F., 472, 1746
Melia, J., 1043
Melikian-Chirvani, A. S., 3338, 3339
Melikian, L., A. Ginsberg, D. Cuceloglu, and R. Lynn, 1747
Melikian, Levon H. and A. Zaher Wehab, 1748
Mel'nikova, G., 2851
Memoires de la Delegation Archeologique Franḃaise en Afghanistan, 3340
Memoirs of Zehir-ed-din Muhammed Babur, Emperor of Hindustan, 1044
Mennessier, G., 473, 474
Menon, Rajan, 2122
Merganov, S., 2852
Merman, 1749
Messerschmidt, Ernst A. and Willy Kraus, 103
Meuer, Gerd, 2482
Meunie, Jacques, 3341
Meyer, Richard J., 1750
Michaelson, Karen L., 1430
Michaud, Roland and Sabrina, 475, 476, 1751, 3342
Michel, Aloys A., 477, 2483, 2484, 2485, 2486
Michel, Janine, 478
Michener, James A., 479, 1431, 2853
Michiner, Michael, 3343
The Middle East (yearly), 104
The Middle East and North Africa, 1980-81, 105
Middle East Journal, 106
Middle East Research and Information Project (89), 2123
Mieczkowski, Seiko, 2124
Mikhailov, K., 2125
Miles, C. V., 1045
Military Report, Afghanistan, 107
Miller, Charles, 1046
Miller, Constance O. and Edward M. Gilbert, 480
Mills, Margaret Ann, 2854, 2855
Minaev, I., 481
Miner, Thomas H. and Associates, Inc., 2487
Ministry of National Economy, 2488
Ministry of Planning, 2489, 2490, 2491, 2492, 2493, 2494, 2495, 2496, 2497
Miran, M. Alam, 2856, 2857, 2858, 2859, 2860, 2861, 2862
Mirazai, N. A. and S. W. Breckle, 482
Mirepois, Camille, 483, 1752
Mir-Khwand (Muhammad ibn Khwand-Shah ibn Mahmud), 1047
Mir Munshi, Sultan Mohammed Khan, 1048, 2126

Mirnov, L. and G. Polyakov, 2127
Mirzoyan, S., 2498
Misra, K. P., 2128
Missen, Francois, 2129
Mitchell, R., 484
Mitchiner, Michael, 3344
Mizuno, S., 1049, 3345
Mochtar, Said Gholam and Hartmut Geerken, 485
Modenov, S., 2130
Mohammed, Ali, 2499
Mohammad-Zoda, Kurbon and Muhabbat Shoh-Zoda, 1050
Mohebi, Ahmad Ali, 1051
Mohn, Paul, 486
Moir, M. C., 2500
Mokhtarzada, Mohammed Taufiq, 2501
Molesworth, Lieutenant-General George N., 1052
Momal, C., 3346
Monakhov, F. I., 487
Monier, M. Ibrahim, 1753
Monks, Alfred L., 2131
Montakhabat-i Khushhal Khan Khattak, 2863
Montgomerie, T. G., 488, 489, 490
Moorcroft, William and George Trebeck, 491
Moorish, C., 1053
Moos, Irene von, 2502
Morgan, Delmar E., 492
Morgan, J. de, 3347
Morgenstierne, Georg, 2864, 2865, 2866, 2867, 2868, 2869, 2870, 2871, 2872, 2873, 2874, 2875, 2876, 2877, 2878, 2879, 2880, 2881, 2882, 2883
Morgenstierne, Georg and James A. Lloyd, 2884
Morley, William Hood, 1054
Morrison, Ronald M. S. H. M., 1055
Moskova, V. G., 3348
Mo'tamedi, Ahmad Ali, 1433
Mouchet, J., 493
Mu'ahadeh Fi-mobayne Rus va Afghanistan, 2132
Mohammad 'Ali Khan, 494
Muhammad Abu'l-Fayz, 1056
Muhammad Hayat Khan, 1057
Muhammad Hotak ibn Da'ud Khan, 2885
Muhammad Husayn Khan, 495
Muhammad Kabir Khan Ludin, 2503
Muhammad Kabir ibn Shaykh Isma'il, 1058
Muhiddinov, I., 2504
Muhyi al-Din, 1059
Mukerjee, D., 2133
Mumand, Muhammad Gol, 1434, 2886, 2887, 2888
Munneke, R. J., 496

Munneke, Roelof J., 2505, 2506
Murphy, Christopher, 2889
Musée Guimet, 3349
Musée National d'Afghanistan, Kaboul, 3350
Music, Afghanistan, 2890, 2891, 2892, 2893, 2894, 2895, 2896, 2897, 2898
Mustafa, Zubeida, 2134, 2135
Mustamandi, S., 3351, 3352, 3353, 3354
Mustamandi, S. and M., 3355, 3356
Muwlani, M. Sarwar, 2899
Myrdal, Jan, 1060

N

n.a. (no author), 497, 498, 499, 500, 501, 502, 503, 504, 505, 506, 507, 1061
Naby, Eden, 2136, 2900
Nadjibi, Asis S. A., 2507
Nafisi, Sa'id, 1062
Nagler, Horst, 2508
Naim, Elizabeth, 1754
Naimi, Ali Ahmad, 1063, 1064, 1065, 3357, 3358, 3359, 3360, 3361
Naimi, M. Omar, 1066
Najaf, 'Ali Khan, 1755, 2901
Najafi, Fazil Tawab, 2509
Najibadadi, Akbar Shah Khan, 1067
Najibullah Khan, 1756, 2137, 2138, 2139, 2140, 2141, 2142, 2143, 2144, 2902, 2903, 2904
Nalivkin, I. D., 508
Nangarhar, 1757
Nariman, G. K., 509
Narimanov, 1068
al-Narshakhi, Abu Bakr Mohammed ibn Ja'far, 1069
Naseri, A., 510
Nash, Charles, 1070
National Assembly, 2145
Naumann, C., 3363
Naumann, Claus M., 511, 512
Naumann, C. and J. Niethammer, 513, 3364
Naumann, C. and G. Nogge, 514, 3365
Nauroz, K. M. and C. M. Naumann, 515
Nawis, Abdullah Afghan, 2905, 2906
Nayar, Kuldip, 2146
Nazar, Ata Mohammad, 2510
Nazari, Rahmatullah, 1758
Nazarov, X., 1071, 1072
Nazarrov, Haqnazar, 1073
Nazim, Muhammad, 1074, 1075
Neal, F. W., 2147

Nedeltcheff, Nicolaff, 2511
Negaran, Hannah (Pseudonym), 2148, 2149
Ne'matulloev, H. and R. Hoshim, 2907, 2908
Nemenova, R. L., 1435
Nendari, 1759
Nesterovich, S., 516
Neubauer, H. F., 517, 518, 519, 520, 2512, 2513
Neuhauser, Hans N. and Anthony F. DeBlase, 521
Newman, R. E., 1760
Neumann, Robert G., 2150
Newby, Eric, 522
Newell, Nancy Peabody and Richard S., 2151
Newell, Richard S., 2152, 2153, 2154, 2155, 2156, 2157, 2158
Newsletter, Afghanistan Council, 108
Newspapers, Magazines and Journals, 1761
Nicollet, Serge, 2514
Nida'-i Khalq, 1762
Niedermayer, Oskar von, 523, 524, 1076, 1077, 1436
Niethammer, G., 525, 526, 527, 3366
Niethammer, G. and J., 528
Niethammer, J., 529, 530, 531, 532, 533
Niethammer, J. and J. Martens, 534
Nikitine, Basile, 2515
Nilab, 1763
Nilsen, Don L. F., 2909
Ningarhari, Abd al-Karim ibn Makhdum, 1764
Nitecki, Mathew H. and Albert F. de Lapparent, 535
Niyazov, H. N., 2910
Nizam-namaeh-yi Tashkilat-i Asasi-yi Afghanistan, 1765
Nizam Nama-yi Tashkilate Assasi-yi Afghanistan, 2159
Nogge, G., 3367
Nogge, Gunther, 536, 537, 538, 539, 540, 541, 542, 543, 544
Nogge, G. and J. Niethammer, 2516
Nogge, Gunther and K. Nogge, 545
Noheb, Abdul Karim, 3368
Nohsadumin sal-i Vafat-i Khwajeh Abdullah Ansari Heravi, 2911
Nollau, Günther and Hans J. Wiehe, 1078
Noller, J. F., 2160
The Non-Pathan Tribes of the Valley of the Hindu-Kush, 1437
Noonan, Thomas S., 3369
Noor, Abdul Sami, 2517
Noorani, A. G., 2161
Noorzoy, M. Siddiq, 2518, 2519, 2520
Norris, J. A., 1079
Norvell, Douglass G., Mohammad Yussof Hakimi, Mohammad Naim Dindar, 2521
Notes on the Discovery of Hebrew Inscriptions in the Vicinity of the Minaret of Jam, 1080
Nukhovich, Eduard S., 1081

Nuri, Mohammed Gol, 2912, 2913
Nuri, Nur Ahmad, 2914
Nuristani, Mohammad Alam, 1438
Nur-Muhammad, Hafez, 1082
Nusraty, Mohammad Yonus, 109

O

O'Ballance, Edgar, 2162
O'Bannon, George W., 1766, 1767, 3370, 3371
Obidov, Usmanjon, 2915
Obruchev, Vladimir A., 546
Ocherki po novoi istorii stran Srednego Vostoka, 1083
O'Conner, Ronald W., 1768
Odell, Ernest, 2163
Oesterdiekhoff, Peter, 2522
Official History of Operations on the N. W. Frontier of India, 1936-37, 1084
O'Kane, B., 3372
Oksendahl, Wilma, 2523
Olfat, Gol Pacha, 2916, 2917, 2918, 2919, 2920, 2921, 2922, 2923, 2924
Oliver, Edward Emmerson, 1439
Olufsen, Ole, 547
Omar, Gholam, 3373
On Sir Zaferullah Khan's Statement, 2164
On Tabular Returns, 548
Open Doors, a Report on Three Surveys, 1769
Operations in Waziristan 1919-1920, 1085
Oransky, I. M., 2925
Orazi, Roberto, 3374
Oren, Stephen, 2165, 2166
Osetrov, N., 1086
Osipov, A. M., 1087
Osman, Shir Muhammad, 1088
Ostrovskii, B. Y., 2926, 2927
Oudenhoven, Nico J. A. van, 3375, 3376
Overholt, William, 2167
Ozaki, R. 2168

P

Pachter, H., 2169
The Pakhtun Question, 2170
Pakhtunistan, 2171
Pakhtunistan Day, 2172
Le Pakistan et la Ligue Musulmane, 2173
Paktiyani, N. M., 2928
Palwal, Abdul Raziq, 1089, 1090, 1091, 1092, 1093, 1094, 1095, 1440, 1441, 1770

Pamir, 1771
Pandey, Awadh B., 1096
Pandey, D. P., 1097
Pangeh, 2524
Panj Ganj, 2929
Panjshiri, Safdar, 1098
Papers Relating to Military Operations in Afghanistan, 1099
Papiha, S. S., D. F. Roberts, and A. G. Rahimi, 1772
Parker, Barret and Ahmad Javid, 2930
Paruck, Furdoonjee D., 3377
Parwan, 1772
Pasalani Mosha'areh, 2931
Pastidis, S. L., 2525
Pastner, Carroll McClure, 1442
Pastner, Stephen L., 1443, 1444, 1445, 1446, 1447
Pastner, Stephen L. and Carrol M. Pastner, 1448
Patterson, Frank E., 3378
Paul, Arthur, 2526
Payam-i Imruz, 1774
Payam-i Tandurusti, 1775
Payind, Mohammed Alam, 1776
Pazhwak, Abdur Rahman, 110, 2174
Pazhwak, Abdul Rahman, 2932, 2933, 2934
Pazhwak, Muhammad Din, 2935, 2936
Pearson, J. D., 111
Peasant Life in Afghanistan, 2527
Pedersen, Gorm, 2528
Peers, Ellis Edward, 1100
Pelt, M. M., J. C. Hayon, and C. Younos, 549
Penkala, Danuta, 1777
Pennell, Theodore L., 1449
Penzl, Herbert, 1778, 2937, 2938, 2939, 2940, 2941, 2942
Pernot, Maurice, 550
Peshereva, E. M., 1450
Peter of Greece and Denmark, Prince, 551, 1101, 1451, 1452
Petermann, August Heinrich, 1453
Philips, Cyril Henry, 1102
Philips, James, 2175
Phillott, Lieutenant Colonel D. C., 2943
Pickard, Cyril, 2176
Picken, L. E. R., 3379
Pikulin, M. G., 112, 1454, 2529
Pillsbury, Barbara L. K., 1779
Pisarcheik, A. K. and N. N. Eroshov, 3380
Planhol, Xavier de, 552, 553, 554, 1103, 2530, 2531
Planhol, Xavier de and Francois Denizat, 555
Plowden, Trevor Chichele, 2944
Pocket Guide to Afghanistan, 113
Podlech, D., 556, 557, 558

530

Podlech, D. and O. Anders, 559
Podlech, D. and O. Bader, 560
Point Four: Near East and Africa, 114
Polishchuk, A. I., 1780
Polyak, A. A., 2532
Pomeroy, William, 2177, 2178
Poole, Reginald Stuart, 3381
Popalzai, Aziz al-Din Vakili, 2945
Popay Ressena, 2946
Pope, Arthur Upham, 3382
Popowski, Jozeph, 1104
Postans, J., 561
Poullada, Leila, 115
Poullada, Leon B., 1781, 2179, 2180, 2181, 2182, 2183
Poulton, Robin and Michelle, 2533
Poulos, John W., 2184
Pourhadi, I. V., 1782, 2947
Pourhadi, Ibrahim V., 116, 117
Prentice, Verna Russillo, 2948
Preparing Shipments to Afghanistan, 2534
Price, M. Philips, 1783
Priestly, H., 1105
Prinsep, Henry Thoby, 3383
Prinsep, James, 3384
The Problem of Afghanistan, 1106
Project Progress Report, 2535
Proundlock, R. V., 562
Pugachenkova, G. A., 3385, 3386, 3387, 3388
Puget, A., 563
Pulyarkin, Valery A., 564
Pushtani Arman, 2949
Da Pushtu Munazareh peh Kabul Radio Kshy, 2950
Pushtu Qamus, 2951
Da Pushtunistan peh bab kay da Afghanistan Nazariyat, 2185
Pushtun Zhagh, 1784
Putnam, B. H. and J. J. Van Belle, 2536

Q

Qaderi, M. Zaher, 2537
Qamus-i a'lam-i Jughrafiya'i-yi Afghanistan, 565, 2952
Qandahari, Ghulam Morteza Khan, 1107
Qandahari, Taleb, 2953, 2954
Qanungo, K. R., 1108
Qasim, 'Ali Khan, 1109
Qawa'id-i Siraj al-Milleh dar Kharidari-yi Mal az Duval-i Kharijeh, 1785
Qur'an, The Holy, 1854
Qureshi, Saleem, 2186

R

Rafiq, Muhammad, 2955
Raheen, Sayyed Makhdom, 2956
Rahim, M. A., 1110
Rahimi, M. V. and L. V. Uspenskoi, 2957
Rahman, Abdul Rahman, 2958
Rahmani, Magdeline, 1786, 2959
Rahmani, Mageh, 2960
Rahmany, Magdalina, 1111, 2961
Rahmany, Magdaline, 1112
Rahmanzai, Abdul Moqim, 1787
Rahmati, Mohebullah, 566
Rahnuma-yi Qattaghan va Badakhshan, 567
Rahnuma-yi Tadavi va Viqayey az Maraz-i Trakhom, 1788
Rainey, Froelich, 3389
Ramati, Yohanan, 2187
Ramazani, R. K., 1113, 2188
Ramstedt, Gustav John, 568
Rand, Christopher, 1455, 2189
Rao, Aparna, 1456, 2538
Rao, J. Sambashiva, 1114
Rapp, Eugene Ludwig, 1115, 1116, 2962
Rashad, Abdul Shukur, 2963
Rashad, Shah Muhammad, 1789, 1790
Rasmi, Jarideh, 118
Rastogi, Ram S., 1117
Ratebzad, Anahita, 2190
Rathjens, C., 2539
Rathjens, Carl, 119, 569, 570, 571, 572, 573, 574, 575, 2191
Ratnam, Perala, 2192
Rattray, James, 576
Raufi, F. and O. Sickenberg, 577
Raun, Alo, 2964
Raunig, W., 578
Raverty, H. G., 1118
Raverty, Henry George, 579, 580, 581, 2965, 2966, 2967, 2968, 2969
Rawlinson, H. C., 582, 583, 584, 585, 586
Razi, Mohammad Houssain, 1791
Rebuff, 1119
Rechinger, K. H., 587
Rectanus, Earl Frank, 2193
Redard, Georges, 120, 1792
Regteren, C. O. van, 588
Reidsmit, E. R., 1793
Reinaud, M., 589
Reindke, Gisela, 1120
Reinhard, Gregor M., 2540

Reinshagen, Heide and Lutz H. Eckensberger, 2541
Reisner, Igor Mikhailovich, 590, 591, 1121, 2542, 2543
Reisner, Igor Mikhailovich and R. T. Akhramovich, 121
Reissner, Larissa, 1122
Relations of Afghanistan and the Soviet Union, 191-1969, 2194
Rellecke, Willy Clemens, 1457
Report on Development of the Arghandab Area, 2544
Report on Development Program of Government of Afghanistan, 2545
Report to the Government of Afghanistan on Handicrafts and Small-Scale Industries, 2546
Report of the Helmand River Delta Commission, 2547
Report on Proposed Cement Factory Near Kabul, 2548
Report on Proposed Trunk Highways, 2549
Reports of the Member States (UNESCO), 1794
Resai, Mohammed Ismail, 2550
Reshad, Ahmad, 1795
Reut, M., 2551, 2552, 3390
Reynolds, James, 1123
Rhein, Eberhard, 2553
Rhein, Eberhard and A. Ghani Ghaussy, 2554
Rice, Frances M., 3391
Ridout, Christine F., 2195
Riedl, H. and H. Freitag, 592
Rieu, Charles, 122, 123
Ringer, Karlernst, 593
Rishtin, Sadiqullah, 594, 1124, 2196, 2970, 2971, 2972, 2973, 2974, 2975, 2976, 2977, 2978, 2979, 2980, 2981, 2982
Rishtiya, Sayed Qasim, 595, 596, 1125, 1126
Rishtya, Sayed Qasim, 1796, 1797, 1798
Ritter, C., 3392
Robert, L., 3393
Roberts, Frederick Sleigh, 1st Earl of, 1127
Robertson, George S., 1458
Robinson, Nehemiah, 1459
Robson, Brian, 1128
Rodgers, Charles J., 3394
Rogers, Millard, 3395
Roghtia, 1799
Romodin, V. A., 124
Romodin, Vadim A., 1460
Roos-Keppel, George Olof, 1129, 2983, 2984
Rosenbaum, H., 2555
Rosenfield, John M., 3396
Rosenthal, Jerry E., 1800
Roskoschny, Hermann, 1130
Rosman, Abraham and Paula G. Rubel, 1461
Ross, Frank E., 597
Rosset, Louis-Felicien, 598, 599, 600, 601, 602, 603, 604, 605, 606, 607, 608, 1131, 1132, 2556

Rossi, Adriano V., 2985
Rothmemund, D., 1801
Roucek, Joseph S., 2197
Rowland, Benjamin, Jr., 3397, 3398, 3399, 3400
Rowland, B. and F. Rice, 3401
Roy, Nirodbhusan, 1133
Roy, Olivier, 2198, 2199
Royal Afghan Embassy, New Delhi, 2200
Rozhevits, R. U., 2557
Rubinstein, Alvin Z., 1134, 2201
Rubio Garcia, L., 2202, 2203, 2204, 2205, 2206
Rubio-Garcia, Leandro, 1135
Rudersdorf, Karl-Heinrich, 2207
Rybitschka, Emil, 609

S

Sablier, Edouard, 2208
Sachau, Edward and Hermann Ethe, 125
Sadoi Sharq, 1802
Safa, Muhammad Ibrahim, 1803
Safari, Hamid, 2209
Safee, M. Naim Janbaz, 1805, 2986
Safi, Abdul Qayum, 1804
Sahar, Hafiz, 1805
Sahraie, Hashem and Janet Sahraie, 1806
Saint-Brice, 1807, 1808
Sakai, T., H. Hajime, O. Norikazu, and Y. Ohba, 1462
Sakata, Hiromi Lorraine, 3402, 3403, 3404, 3405, 3406, 3407, 3408, 3409, 3410
Saldjouqui, Fekri, 2987
Sale, Lady Florentia, 1136
Saleh, Muhammad Khan, 2988, 2989
Salem, M. Zarif, 610
Salimi, Muhammad Arslan and Muhammad Shah Arshad, 1137
Salisbury, Harrison E., 1138
Saljooki, F., 3411
Saljuki, Fekri, 2990
Saljuqi, Fekri, 1139
Saljuqi, Salah al-Din, 1809, 1810, 1811, 1812, 2991, 2992
Sal-Nameh-yi Kabul, 126
Salzman, Philip C., 1463, 1464
Sami, Mahmud, 1813
Samii, Said, 2558
Samin, Abdul Quhar, 611
Samini, A., 2559
Samizay, M. Rafi, 3412, 3413
Samuelson, J., 1814
Samuelsson, Jan, 2210

Samylovskiy, I. V., 1815
Sana'i, 1816
Saraf, S. N., 1817
Sareen, Anuradha, 612, 2211
Sarianidi, V. I., 3414, 3415, 3416, 3417, 3418, 3419, 3420
Sarianidi, Victor, 3421
Sarianidi, V. I., N. N. Terechova, and E. N. Cernych, 3422
Sarif, Brigitte, 1818
Sarif, Gul Janan, 613, 1819
Sarwari, M. Sadiq, 1820
Sassani, Abul K., 1821
Sauvaget, J., 3423
Savad-i Mu'ahadeh-yi Dawlatayn-i 'Aliyatayn-i Afghanistan va-Iran, 1140
Sawari, M. Sadiq, 2560
Sawitzki, Hans-Henning, 614, 1822
Sayeed, Khalid B., 2212
Scerrato, Umberto, 3424
Schafer, Bernd, 2561
Schapka, U. and O. H. Volk, 615
Schefer, Charles H. A., 616
Scheibe, A., 617
Scher, J. A., 3425
Schimmel, A., 1823
Schinasi, May, 618, 619, 1141, 2213, 2214, 2215
Schlag nach über Iran, Afghanistan, Arabien and Indien, 127
Schlegelberger, Franz, 1826
Schlimm, Wolfgang, 620
Schlumberger, Daniel, 3426, 3427, 3428, 3429, 3430, 3431, 3432, 3433, 3434, 3435, 3436, 3437
Schlumberger, Daniel and P. Bernard, 3438
Schneider, Peter, 621, 1824, 1825
Schneider, P. and A. S. Djalal, 622
Schneider, P. and W. Kloft, 623
Schramm, Ryszard W., 624
Schurmann, H. F., 1465
Schwager, Joseph, 2216
Schwarz, Fred, 625
Schwarzenbach, Annemarie Clark, 1142, 2562
Schwob, Marcel, 2563
Scott, George Batley, 1466
Scott, Richard B., 1467
Scoville, James G., 2564
Scully, J., 626
The Second Afghan War (1878-80), 1143
Second Five Year Plan, 2565
Sedqi, Mohammad Osman, 627, 628, 629
Sedqi, Osman, 3439
See Afghanistan, 630
Segal, Gerald, 2217

Seherr-Thoss, Sonia P., 3440
Seifert, Bruno, 2566
Seifi, Aziz al-Rahman, 1144
A Select Bibliography: Asia, Africa, Eastern Europe and Latin America, 128
Selected Bibliography of Published Material on the Area Where Pushtu is Spoken: Afghanistan, Baluchistan and the North-West Frontier Province, 129
Sellman, Roger R., 631
Semin, A., 2567
Sera Miyasht, 1827
Seraj, Minhajuddin, 1145
Seraj-ul Akhbar, 1828
Serfaty, A., 632
Sérignan, Claude, 1829, 2568
Serraj, Mahbub, 2993
Shafeev, D. A., 2994, 2995
Shah, Aurang, 2218
Shah, Idries, 2996
Shah, S. I. A., 633
Shah, Sayad Amir, 2219
Shah Shoja' al-Molk Saduza'i, 1146
Shah Sirdar Ikbal Ali, 1147, 1148, 1468, 2220
Shah, S. M., 2569, 2570
Shahrani, E., 3441
Shahrani, M. Nazif, 1469, 1470
Shahrani, M. Nazif Mohib, 1471, 1472
Shairzay, Arsallah, 3442
Shakur, M. A., 1473, 3443
Shalinsky, Audrey C., 1474, 1475, 1476
Shalizi, Abdul Satar, 130
Shalizi, Abdussattar, 2571, 2572
Shalizi, Prita K., 131
Shamir, Haim, 1149
Da Shams al-Din Kakar Diwan, 2997
Shaniyazov, Karim Shaniazovich, 1477
Sharqawi, Muhammad 'Abd al-Mun'im, 132
Shchedrov, I., 2221
Shcherbinovsky, N., 1150
Sheehy, Ann, 1478
Shepperdson, M. J., 1479
Sheptunov, I., 634
Shibli, Nu'mani, 2998
Shir Muhammad Khan, 1151
Shirreff, David, 2573, 2574, 2575
Shoironi Afgonistan, 2999
Shor, Jean Bowie, 635
Shor, Jean Bowie and Franc Shor, 636
Shorish, M. Mobin, 2222, 2223, 2224

Shpoon, Saduddin, 3000, 3001, 3002
Shroder, John F., Jr., Cathleen M. DiMarzio, Dennis E. Bussom, and David Braslau, 637
Shukrolla, Aripov, 3003
Shukurov, M. S., 3004, 3005
Sibtain, Syed N., 3444
Siddiq, M., 1830
Siddiq, Mir Abdul Fatah, 1831
Siddiqi, I. H., 638
Siddiqi, Iqtidar Husain, 1152, 1153
Siddiqui, Nafis Ahmad, 1832
Siddons, Joachim H., 1154
Sidky, M. Habib, 2225
Sidqi, Mohammed 'Usman, 1155, 1156, 3006
Sigel, Carol Ann, 3007, 3008
Sigrist, Christian, 1480
Siiger, Halfdan, 639, 1481
Sikoyev, Ruslan, 2226
Simmons, J. S. and T. F. Whayne, 1833
Simpich, Frederick, 1834
Sinclair, Gordon, 640
Singer, Andre, 1482, 1483, 2576, 2577
Singh, Ganda, 1157, 1158
Singh, Narenderpal, 641
Singh, Prabhjot-Kaur, 3009
Sinha, Sri Prakash, 1836
Singhal, D. P., 1159
Sirat, Abdul Satar, 1836
Sircar, Joydeep, 642
Sistan, 1837
Le Site Archeologique de Bamiyan, 3445
Sivall, T. R., 643
Skinner, G. R., 2227
Shukrolla, Aripov, 3003
Shkurov, M. Sh., 3004, 3005
Sjoberg, Andree F., 3010
Skazki, Basni i Legendy Beludzhei, 3011
Slobin, Mark, 3447, 3448, 3449, 3450, 3451
Slobin, Mark Sheldon, 3446
Slousch, N., 1484
Smith, Harvey Henry, 133
Smith, Major C. B. E., 1160
Smith, R. B., 644
Smith, Vinzenz A., 3452
Snead, Rodman E., 645
Snesarev, A. E., 134, 646
Snellgrove, David, 3453
Snoy, Peter, 647, 1485, 1486, 2578
Sobman, Ali M., 3012

Sokolov-Strakhov, K., 648, 1161
Sokolova, V. S., 3013
Solovyov, Vladimir and Elena Klepikova, 2228
Sommer, Theo and Andreas Kohlschutter, 2229
Sonin, I. I., 649
Sonnenfeldt, Helmut, 2230, 2231, 2232
Soub, 1838
Sourdel, Dominique, 3014, 3454
Sourdel-Thomine, J., 3455
Sous la Direction de L'Equipe Ecologie et Anthropologie des Societes Pastorales, 1487
Sovetskoye Afganovedeniye za 40 let, 135, 136
Sovremennyye Literaturnyye Yazyki stran Azii, 3015
Spain, James W., 1488, 1489
Sperling, O., 1162
Spiegelman, J. M. and J. Ling, 3016
Spitler, J. F. and N. B. Frank, 1839, 1840
Spivack, M. R., 650
Splett, Oskar, 1841
Spooner, Brian, 1490, 1491, 1492, 3017, 3456
Sprenger, A. and Maulawi Mamluk al' Ali, 1163
Squire, Sir Giles, 1164
Sreedhar, 2233
Srivastava, M. P., 2234
Stack, Shannon Caroline, 1165, 2235
Stanishevskii, A. V., 137
Stanislaw, Miarkowski, 651
Stark, Freya, 3457
Starmuhlner, Ferdinand, 652
Stawiski, Boris, 1166
Steel, R., 2236
Stemuller, Camille Mirepois, 653
Stentz, Edward, 654, 655, 656
Stenz, Edward, 657
Stephen, O., 2237
Stephens, Ian, 2238
Steponov, I., 658
Stern, S. M., 3018
Steul, Willi, 1493, 1494, 2239
Stevens, Ira Moore and K. Tarzi, 2579
Stewart, C. E., 659
Stewart, Rebecca M., 3458
Stewart, Rhea Talley, 1167
Stewart, Ruth W., 2580
Stilz, D., 2581
Stoda, M. Ibrahim and Abdurrahman Palwal, 1168
Stolz, Karl, 1842
Stone, Russel A., Saxon Graham, and Graham Kerr, 1843, 1844
Storai, 1845

Storey, Charles A., 138
Strand, Richard F., 1495, 1496, 1497, 2582, 3019
Strany, Vostoka, 2583
Stratil-Sauer, G., 660
Strathmann, Heribert, 2584
Strauss, Franz Joseph, 2240, 2241
Strzygowski, Joseph, 3459
Stuckert, Ruedi, 3460
Stucki, Anneliese, 1498, 1499
Sullivan, Michael Gellinck, 1846
Sultan Muhammad ibn Musa Khan, 1169
Summerscale, Peter, 2242
Surkhakan va-Suret-i Tadabir-i Sihhi-yi An, 1847
Survey of Progress 1962-64, 2585
Survey of Progress 1964-65, 2586
Survey of Progress 1968-69, 2587
Survey of the Tourism Industry in Afghanistan, 2588
Swayze, Francis J., 2589
Sweetser, Anne T., 1848
Swidler, Nina Bailey, 1500, 1501
Swidler, Warren, 1502, 1503
Sykes, Christopher, 661
Sykes, Sir Percy M., 139, 1170, 1171
Szabo, Albert and Brenda Dyer Szabo, 3461

T

Tabibi, A. Hakim, 1172, 1173
Tabibi, Abdul Hakim, 2243, 2244
Taddei, Maurizio, 3462
Taddei, Maurizio and Giovanni Verardi, 3463
Tafsire Sharif, 1849
Tahir-Kheli, Shirin R., 2245, 2246
Taillardat, C. F., 140, 1174, 1850
Takharistan, 1851
Talboys, B. E., 2247
Tang, Peter S. H., 2248
Tanner, H. C., 662, 1504
Tanzi, Gastone, 663
Tapper, Nancy, 1505, 1506, 1507, 1508, 1509, 1510, 1511
Tapper, Richard, 1512, 1513, 1514, 1515, 1516
Tarakai, Noor Mohammed, 3020
Taraki, Muhammad Qadir, 1852
Taraki, M. Rasal, 1853
Taraki, Noor M., 2249, 2250, 2251
Tavakolian, Bahram, 1517
Tarikh-i Afghan, 1175
Tarikh-i Afghanistan, 1176, 1177
Tarikh-i Khayran, 1178

Tarikhe Sistan, 1179
Tarn, W. W., 1180
Tarzi, Mahmud, 664, 1181, 1182, 3021, 3022, 3023, 3024
Tarzi, Nangyalai, 2252
Tarzi, Rahimullah, 2590
Tarzy, Zemaryalai, 3464
Tate, George Passman, 665, 666, 667, 1183
Tavaquli, Ahmad, 1184, 1185
Tchardi-Wal, 2253, 2254, 2255, 2256
Technical Cooperation Agreement Between United States and Afghanistan, 2591
Tegey, Habibullah, 3025, 3026, 3027, 3028, 3029, 3030
Teicher, Howard, 2257
Temirkhanov, L., 1186
Temple, R. C., 668, 1187, 1518, 1519
Teplinskiy, Leonid B., 1188
Terenzio, Pio-Carlo, 1189
Terry, Allen, 3465
Thabet, Mohammed Ibrahim, 1190
Thakur, R., 2258
Thesiger, Wilfred, 1191, 1520
The Third Afghan War (1919), 1192
The Third Five Year Economic and Social Plan of Afghanistan, 2592
Thomas, Lowell J., 669
Thorburn, S. S., 1521, 2259
Thornton, Ernest, 1193, 1855
Threlkeld, Robert M., 1856
Tichy, Herbert, 670, 671, 672
Tilman, H. W., 673
Tissot, Louis, 1194
Todd (Major), 674
Toepfer, Helmuth, 2593
Togan, Z. V., 3466
Tolstov, C. P., T. A. Zdanko, C. M. Abramzona, N. A. Kisliakov, 1522, 1523, 1524, 1525
Tosi, M., 675
Tosi, Maurzio, 3467, 3468
Tosi, Maurzio and Rauf Wardak, 3469
Toynbee, Arnold, 677, 2260
Toynbee, Arnold J., 676, 1195, 1196, 1197
Trautman, Kathleen, 678
Trench, F., 679
Trever, K. V., 1198
Trinkler, Emil, 680, 681, 682
Tripathi, G. P., 1199
Tromp, S. W., 2594
Trosper, Joseph F., 1857
Trousdale, William, 3470

Trudy Sessii po Voprosam Istorii i Ekonomiki Afganistana, Irana, Turtsii, 141
Trumbull, David, 1858
Trumpp, E., 3031, 3032
Trussell, James and Eleanor Brown, 683, 1859
Tucci, Guiseppe, 1200
Tucci, G., 3471
Tulu'-i Afghan, 1860
Turri, E., 684
Tursunov, R., 2261

U

Uberoi, J. P. Singh, 1201, 1526, 1861, 2262
Uddin, Islam, 685, 2595
Uhlig, Helmut, 686
United Nations Economic Commission for Asia and the Far East, 2596
United States Department of Labor, 2597
Urdu-yi Afghan, 1862
Urmanova, Rukiya K., 1863
Usul-i Asasi-yi Dawlet-i Aliyeh-yi Afghanistan, 2263
Usul-i Vaza'if-i Dakhili-yi Riyaset-i Shura-yi Milli-yi Afghanistan, 2264
Usul-Nameh, 2265, 2266
Utas, Bo, 1864, 2267, 2268
Utbi, Muhammad, 1202
Uyehara, Cecil H., 3472

V

Vajid, Muhammad Qasim, 3033
Vakil, Fazl Muhammad, 3034
Vakil, Safar, 1527
Vakili, 'Aziz-al-Din, 687
Valenta, Jiri, 2269, 2270
Vali, Marshal Shah, 1204
Valiyan, 'Abd al-'Azim, 142
Vambery, Arminius, 688, 689, 690, 1528
Vanecek, Petr., 143
Van Praagh, D., 2271
Varma, B., 1207
Vastel, M., 2272
Vatan, 1865
Vaughan, J. L., 1203
Vaqi'at-i Durrani, 1205
Vaqi'at-i Shah Shuja', 1206
Vavilov, N. I. and D. D. Bukinich, 2598
Vayrynen, R., 2273

Velichkovsky, Y., 1866
Velter, Andre, Emmanuel Delloye, and Marie-Jose Lamothe, 2599
Verardi, Giovanni, 3473, 3474, 3475
Vercellin, Giorgio, 2274
Verchere, A. M., 691
Vertunni, Renato, 692
Vigne, Godfrey T., 693
Vinogradov, V. M., 2275
Viollis, Andrée, 1208
Visit Afghanistan, 694
Vittor, Frank, 3035
Vivekanadan, B., 2276
Vizhdani, Abdul Vahid, 2600
Vizhdani, Abdul Vakil, 1867
Voelkerkundliche Bibliographie, 144
Vogel, Renate, 1209
Voigt, Martin, 1529
Volin, M. E., 2601
Volk, O. H., 695, 696, 697
Volkov, Y., K. Gevorkyan, I. Mikhailenki, A. Polonsky, and V. Svetozarov, 2277
Volsky, D., 1210
Von Hentig, Werner Otto, 145
Voronin, A., 2278

W

Wade, Nicholas, 2602
Wafadar, K., 2279
Wagner, W., 698
Wagner, Wolfgang, 2280
Wahab Khan, Abdul, 699
Wahdat, 1868
Waish, Raz Mohammed, 3036, 3037
Wala, A. K., 1869
Wald, Hermann-J., and Asis Nadjibi, 2603
Wald, H. J., 3476
Waleh, Abdul H., 146, 1530
Waley, Arthur, 700
Wali, Shah, 1212
Walker, Philip F., 1211
Wallbrecher, Echard, 701
Walters, Royce Eugene, 1213
Walus, 1870
Warangah, 1871
Warburton, Robert, 1214
Ward, Francis Blackiston, III, 1872
Wardak, Guljan Wror, 1873
Warhurst, Geoffrey, 2281

Warner, Denis, 2282
Watkins, Mary Bradley, 147
Wattan, 1874
Watts, Donald J., 3477
Wazhma, 1875, 3038
Waziri, Rafiq, 1876
Weeks, Richard V., 148
Wegner, D., 1531
Wegner, D. H. G., 2604, 2605, 3478
Wei, Jacqueline, 3039
Weiers, M., 1215, 3040, 3479
Weinbaum, M. G., 1877, 2283, 2284, 2285
Weippert, D., 702
Weston, Christine, 1216
Wheeler, Mortimer, 3480
Wheeler, R. E. Mortimer, 3481
Wheeler, Stephen, 1217
Whistler, Hugh, 703
White, Bryan, 1878
Whitehead, Richard Bertram, 3482, 3483
Whitemore, Richard, 704
Whittemore, Richard, 1879
Whitteridge, Gordon, 1880
Wiebe, Dietrich, 705, 706, 1218, 1881, 1882, 2606, 2607, 2608, 2609, 2610, 2611, 2612, 2613, 2614, 2615, 2616, 2617, 2618
Wiegandt, Winifred, 2286
Wilber, Donald N., 149, 150, 1219, 1883, 1884, 2287
Wild, Roland, 1220
Wiles, P., 2288
Willcocks, Sir James, 707
Williams, Maynard Owen, 708, 709, 710
Wilson, Andrew, 711, 2289
Wilson, Horace Hayman, 3484
Wilson, J. Christy, Jr., 3041
Wilson, Michael, 1884
Wirth, E., 2619, 2620
Wittekind, H., 712
Wolanga, 1886
Wolfart, Reinhard and Hanspeter Wittekindt, 713, 3485
Wolfart, R. and M. Kursten, 714
Wolfe, Nancy Hatch, 3486, 3487, 3488
Wolkow, J., 2290
Wolski, K., 1532
Wood, John, 715
Woodd-Walker, R., H. Smith, and V. Clarke, 1533
Wright, John C., 1887
Wright, P. W. M., 3489
Wrong, Dennis H., 2291
Wuelbern, Jan Peter, 2292

Wulbern, J. P., 1888, 2293
Wustenfeld, H. F. and E. Mahler, 3490
Wutt, K., 1221, 3042, 3491, 3492
Wyart, J., P. Bariand, and J. Filippi, 716

Y

Yakoub, M., 2622
Yapp, M. E., 1222, 1223, 1224, 1225
Yaqubi, M. Din, 3043
Yate, Arthur Campbell, 717, 1226
Yate, Charles Edward, 718, 719, 1227, 3493
Yavorskii, I. L., 1228
Yawar, Ali, 1889
Yoder, Richard Allen, 1890, 2622
Yoshitsu, Michael M., 2294
Young, Rodney S., 3494, 3495
Yuldashbayeva, Fatime K., 1229
Yulduz, 1891
Yule, H., 720
Yunus, Parween Etemadi, 1892
Yusufzai, Aziz Ahmad, 1893
Yussuf-zai, Baqi, 1894
Yussufi, Nadjib, 1895
Yusuf, Kaniz Fatima, 2623
Yusufi, Muhammad Akbar, 151
Yusufzai, Saidal, 2295

Z

Zachova, Eliska, 721, 3044
Zadran, Alef-Shah, 1534, 1535
Zahir, Payendeh Muhammad and Sayyid Muhammad Yusuf Elmi, 1896
Zahir-Shah, Mohammed, 1897
Zahma, Ali Muhammad, 1898
Zaidi, Manzur, 1230
Zaki, M. H., 1899
Zalmay, M. Wali, 722
Zaman, Mohammad, 723, 2624
Zambaur, Eduard Karl Marx von, 152
Zamir, Muhammad Hadan, 3045
Zaripov, Sh., 2625
Zarubin, I. I., 1536
Zawak, Muhammad Din, 3046
Zeigler, J. M., 724
Zekrya, Mir-Ahmed Baray, 2626
Zeray, Saleh M., 2296, 2297
Zestovski, P., 3496, 3497, 3498
Zestovski, Paul, 3497

Zhowandai, Saleha, 2627
Zhwandun, 1900
Ziemke, Kurt, 725
Zikria, Nazir Ahmad, 2628
Zipper, Kurt, 3499, 3500
Zirai, 1901
Ziring, Lawrence, 2298
Zudin, P. B., 3047, 3048, 3049
Zulfiqar Ali Khan, 1231
Zur-Mohammed, Hafiz, 1232
Zurmati, Fazl Ahmad, 726
Zurrer, Werner, 2299
Zuyev, U. A., 1537
Zyar, Mojaver Ahmad, 3050